CRUEL WORLD

Alfred A. Knopf   New York   2005

CRUEL WORLD

The Children of Europe in the Nazi Web

Lynn H. Nicholas

THIS IS A BORZOI BOOK
PUBLISHED BY ALFRED A. KNOPF

Copyright © 2005 by Lynn Holman Nicholas
All rights reserved under International and Pan-American Copyright
Conventions. Published in the United States by Alfred A. Knopf,
a division of Random House, Inc., New York, and simultaneously in
Canada by Random House of Canada Limited, Toronto.
Distributed by Random House, Inc., New York.

www.aaknopf.com

Knopf, Borzoi Books, and the colophon are registered trademarks
of Random House, Inc.

Owing to limitations of space, all acknowledgments for permission to reprint
previously published material may be found preceding the index.

Library of Congress Cataloging-in-Publication Data
Nicholas, Lynn H.
Cruel world : the children of Europe in the Nazi web / Lynn H. Nicholas.
p. cm.
Includes bibliographical references and index.
ISBN 0-679-45464-0
1. World War, 1939–1945—Children—Europe. 2. Children and war—Europe—
History—20th century. 3. Children—Europe—History—20th century.
4. Jewish children in the Holocaust. 5. National socialism and youth. I. Title.
D810.C4N53 2005
940.53′083′094—dc22   2004057745

Manufactured in the United States of America
First Edition

For all "La Familia" past, present, and future

And especially
For William, Carter, and Philip

He said that while it was true that time heals bereavement it does so only at the cost of the slow extinction of those loved ones from the heart's memory which is the sole place of their abode then or now. Faces fade, voices dim. Seize them back. . . . Speak with them. Call their names. Do this and do not let sorrow die for it is the sweetening of every gift.

CORMAC MCCARTHY, *The Crossing*

Contents

Acknowledgments

The events of World War II are among my earliest memories, as is the gray atmosphere of postwar Holland, where I lived in the late 1940s. When I was there I did not wonder much about the treeless parks, the odd assortment of nationalities in my school class, the origins of our German housekeeper (undoubtedly a "DP" of some sort), or the fact that ladies of distinguished lineage could be seen filling their large handbags with food at our cocktail parties. As part of the U.S. embassy, we too had to use little blue ration coupons to buy things on the economy, but we could get scarce items such as coffee from the American military depots in Bremerhaven, one of the most heavily bombed cities in Germany, where we occasionally went to pick up supplies. The condition of that place and of the people living among its ruins is a vision I have never forgotten. As life has gone on, I have become more curious about what I saw then and have been struck by the continuing damage done to families by rigid ideologues and by war. It is my aim to give a picture of the overall plans of the Nazis and to show how policies such as theirs simultaneously affect many different communities, which are linked in unexpected ways. The vastness of their operations makes it impossible to describe the fate of every country and group caught in the Nazi web; each story must, therefore, serve as an example of actions that went on in many places.

I am particularly indebted to my mentors in a number of countries, who interrupted their lives to arrange interviews, interpret, find documents and photographs, and otherwise help me. Without them, this book would not have been possible. Here at home, the greatest thanks must go to the late Richard Winslow, who, among many other things, ran one of the first UNRRA teams to go to Germany in 1945, and who spent many hours describing his wartime experiences. To this oral history he added his invaluable archive of documents and correspondence, including the battered briefcase he had used in those dark days. In Greece, Tony Lykiardopoulos opened doors all across that country's complex political spectrum. Christine and Zeno Koenigs took especially good care of us in Holland, while Julia and Christopher Tugendhat did the same in London. In Moscow, thanks to Ekaterina Genieva, director of the All-Russia State

Library for Foreign Literature, I had the privilege of working with Lena Tchnesnokova, who not only acted as guide and interpreter, but taught me much about life in the former USSR and led me to interviewees I would not otherwise have found. There, also, Dr. Patricia Kennedy Grimsted was an invaluable adviser. These are only a few of those who helped. I have listed many others in the Bibliography; for any I may have omitted, my apologies: they are all appreciated.

Particular thanks are due to the late Sybil Milton for her encouragement and for sharing her encyclopedic knowledge; to the staffs of the United Nations Archive; the National Archives; the Manuscript Division of the Library of Congress; the United States Holocaust Memorial Museum, whose photo archivist, Maren Read, is a miracle worker; and the Georgetown University Library. In Europe, archivists at the Imperial War Museum, London; the Benaki Museum in Athens, the Nederlands Instituut voor Oorlogsdocumentatie, Amsterdam; and Memorial, in Moscow, provided invaluable documentation. Paper is not all: the organizers of the sixtieth-anniversary reunion of the Kindertransport children kindly allowed me to attend their meeting, which made history come alive. At Knopf, I am once again tremendously grateful to my editor, Susan Ralston, as well as to designer Anthea Lingeman, Ken Schneider, and especially Ellen Feldman.

More than anything, I owe thanks to all our friends and extended family who have supported us so wonderfully in the last years, which have brought us terrible sadness but also the tremendous joy of a new generation. My gratitude to them, angels all, is beyond words. Special thanks to Daisy, Carter, Philip, Tammy, Sonia, Olivia, William, Robert, and Josephine, who have all tolerated my absences, and most of all to my husband, Robin, who has helped with every aspect of this book, and who has been so very patient.

Washington, D.C.
2004

Germany and Incorporated Austria and Czechoslovakia

LITHUANIA

Memel

DENMARK

Baltic Sea

North Sea

Königsberg

EAST PRUSSIA

Lübeck

Danzig

Hamburg

P O M E R A N I A

Bremen

Ravensbrück ▽

Stettin

Bromberg

Elbe R.

Weser R.

Vistula R.

▽ Bergen-Belsen

Berlin

NETHERLANDS

Hannover

Brandenburg

Frankfurt

Warsaw

G E R M A N Y

Oder R.

P O L A N D

Ruhr R.

Buchenwald

Leipzig

Dresden

Breslau

Cologne

Erfurt ▽ *Weimar*

S I L E S I A

Aachen

Bonn

▽ Ohrdruf

BELGIUM

Hadamar ▽

S U D E T E N L A N D

Cracow

THE RHINELAND

▽ Wildflecken

Rhine R.

Frankfurt

Theresienstadt

Main R.

Lidice

Prague

MORAVIA

Würzburg

BOHEMIA

C Z E C H O S L O V A K I A

LUXEMBOURG

Heidelberg

Nuremberg

Westwall Defenses

BAVARIA

Stuttgart

Strasbourg

Grafeneck ▽

Linz

Danube R.

F R A N C E

Dachau

Steinhöring ▽

Munich ▽

Hartheim ▽

Vienna

H U N G A R Y

Kaufbeuren *Feldafing*

Basel

A U S T R I A

SWITZERLAND

Innsbruck

Klagenfurt

▽ Concentration Camps,
Euthanasia Centers

ITALY

YUGOSLAVIA

— · — Boundaries of 1937

—— Boundary of Germany
August 31, 1939

| 0 | Miles | 200 |

| 0 | Kilometers | 300 |

Western Europe

Detention Camps

Oslo
NORWAY
Stockholm
SWEDEN

SCOTLAND

North Sea

DENMARK
Copenhagen

Baltic Sea

UNITED KINGDOM

EIRE
ISLE OF MAN
Liverpool

Groningen
NETHERLANDS
Berlin

WALES
Harwich
Amsterdam
The Hague
Rotterdam
Utrecht
▽ Westerbork

London

▽ Vught

GERMANY

Atlantic Ocean

Cherbourg

Heerlen
Brussels
Lille
BELGIUM
LUX.

Rhine R.

CZECHOSLOVAKIA

Bayeux
Paris
FRANCE

Drancy
▽ Seine R.

ALSACE
Strasbourg

AUSTRIA

Loire R.

▽ **Detention Camps**

Boundaries in 1937

German boundary
August 31, 1939

Alsace, annexed by
Germany, 1940

Mézières
Vichy
Oradour
Dordogne R.
Le Chambon
Bordeaux

Lyon
Izieu
SWITZERLAND
Evian.
Milan

Venice

UNOCCUPIED ZONE
1940–1942

Rhone R.

Avignon

Florence
Montepulciano
Adriatic Sea

San Sebastián
Bilbao
Guernica
▽ Gurs
Rivesaltes
PYRENEES
▽
Marseilles

CORSICA

ITALY
• Rome

Naples

SPAIN

Barcelona

SARDINIA

PORTUGAL
Madrid

Lisbon

Valencia

MINORCA

Mediterranean Sea

SICILY

Gibraltar

Miles
0   400

Kilometers
0   600

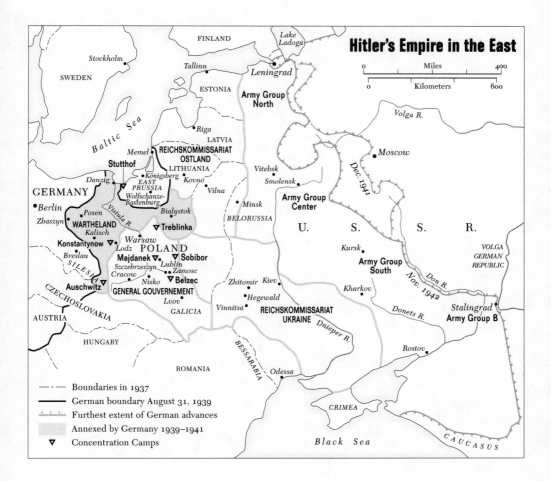

Hitler's Empire in the East

FINLAND

Lake
Ladoga

Stockholm

SWEDEN

Tallinn

Leningrad

ESTONIA

Army Group
North

Miles   400

Kilometers   600

Baltic Sea

Riga

LATVIA

Volga R.

Moscow

Memel

REICHSKOMMISSARIAT
OSTLAND

Stutthof

Vitebsk

LITHUANIA

Dec. 1941

Danzig

•*Königsberg*

EAST
PRUSSIA

•*Kovno*

Smolensk

GERMANY

*Wolfschanze-
Rastenburg*

Vilna

Army Group
Center

•*Berlin*

Minsk

Zbaszyn

•*Posen*

Bialystok

BELORUSSIA

WARTHELAND

Kalisch

▽ *Treblinka*

U.   S.   S.   R.

Konstantynow ▽

Warsaw
Lodz POLAND

Kursk

VOLGA
GERMAN
REPUBLIC

Breslau

Majdanek ▽

▽ Sobibor

Army Group
South

Szczebrzeszyn •*Lublin*
Cracow •*Zamosc*

Nov. 1942

SILESIA

▽ Belzec

Kharkov

Auschwitz ▽

•*Nisko*

Zhitomir •*Kiev*

GENERAL GOUVERNEMENT

Lvov

•*Hegewald*

Donets R.

Stalingrad
Army Group B

CZECHOSLOVAKIA

GALICIA

Vinnitsa•

REICHSKOMMISSARIAT

Rostov

AUSTRIA

UKRAINE

Dnieper R.

HUNGARY

ROMANIA

BESSARABIA

Odessa

Black   Sea

CRIMEA

CAUCASUS

- - - Boundaries in 1937

—— German boundary August 31, 1939

 Furthest extent of German advances

 Annexed by Germany 1939–1941

▽ Concentration Camps

A Note on Nomenclature

The bureaucracies of all the nations involved in the events described in this book were extremely complex. In the approximately thirty-year span described, agencies proliferated, changed their names, and spawned subagencies. This was especially true of the Nazi agencies dealing with race and youth matters and, after the war, the Allied refugee organizations. Added to this complexity is the fact that translators are not consistent in their terminology and use "Service," "Agency," "Bureau," and so on interchangeably to translate the same German word. I have therefore tried to minimize the use of specific agency names in favor of more generic terms. Those who wish to know the details of the permutations and relationships of the Nazi agencies should consult the specialized studies dedicated to them listed in the Bibliography.

BDM	Bund Deutscher Mädel (League of German Girls)
DAF	Deutsche Arbeitsfront (German Labor Front)
DAI	Deutsches Auslands-Institut (German Overseas Institute)
DP	Displaced person
Einsatzgruppe	Special task force
EWZ	Einwandererzentralstelle (Immigration Authority)
Führer	Leader (When used alone, always refers to Adolf Hitler)
Führerprinzip	Leadership principle
Gestapo	Geheime Staatspolizei (Secret State Police)
Heimat	Homeland
HJ	Hitlerjugend (Hitler Youth)
IRO	International Refugee Organization
ITS	International Tracing Service, Arolsen
Jungmädel	Nazi organization for girls aged ten to fourteen
Jungvolk	Nazi organization for boys aged ten to fourteen
Kameradschaft	Group of comrades
KLV	Kinderlandverschickung (Evacuation of Children)
Kripo	Kriminalpolizei (Criminal Police)
Landdienst	Land Service
Lebensborn	SS "Well of Life" Society

Lebensraum	Living space
Luftwaffe	German Air Force
Mädel	Maiden
NAPOLA	National-Politische Lehranstalt (National Political High School)
Nazi	National Socialist
NJS	Nationale Jeugdstorm (National Youth Storm–Dutch Nazi Youth)
NKVD	People's Commissariat of Internal Affairs (USSR)
NSB	Nationaal Socialistische Beweging (Dutch Nazi Pary)
NSDAP	Nationalsozialistische Deutsche Arbeiterpartei (Nazi Party)
NSF	Nationalsozialistischer Frauenschaft (National Socialist Womanhood)
NSV	Nationalsolzialistische Volkswohlfart (National Socialist Welfare Organization)
OPK	Voogdij-commissie voor Oorlogs Pleegkinderen (Custody Commission for War Foster Children–Netherlands)
OSE	Oeuvre de Secours aux Enfants (Children's Welfare Organization)
Ordensjunker	Graduate of an Ordensburg, or Nazi college
Ostarbeiter	Eastern worker, usually from the USSR
Osteinsatz	Eastern Action Mission
RAD	Reichsarbeitsdienst (Reich Labor Service)
RFSS	Reichsführer SS (Heinrich Himmler)
Reich	State or nation
Reichsdeutsche	Full German citizen
RJF	Reichsjugendführung (Reich Youth Directorate)
RKFDV	Reichskommisariat für die Festigung Deutschen Volkstums (Reich Commission for the Strengthening of Germandom)
RSHA	Reichssicherheitshauptamt (Reich Security Head Office)
RuSHA	Rasse-und Siedlungs Hauptamt (Race and Settlement Main Office)
SA	Sturmabteilung (storm troopers)
SD	Sicherheitsdienst (Security Service)
Sopade	Sozialdemokratische Partei Deutschlands–Social Democratic Party of Germany in Exile
SRD	Streifendienst (Hitler Youth Police)
SS	Schutzstaffeln (Protection Squads; a vast elite

	organization headed by Himmler that included racial, security, combat, and many other branches, and that eventually became a state within a state in Nazi Germany)
STO	Service de Travail Obligatoire (Department of Obligatory Labor–France)
Todt Organization	German Public and Military Works Organization
UNRRA	United Nations Relief and Rehabilitation Administration
Untermensch	Subhuman
Volk	Nation-race
Volksdeutsche	Ethnic German
Volksgemeinschaft	National-racial community
VoMi	Volksdeutsche Mittelstelle (Liason Office for Ethnic Germans Abroad)
Waffen-SS	Combat branch of SS
Wartheland/gau	Area in western Poland annexed to Germany in 1939
WEL	Wehrertüchtigungslager (War Preparation Camps)
Wehrmacht	German Army
ZAL	Zwangsarbeitlager für Juden (Forced Labor Camp for Jews)

CRUEL WORLD

Prologue

Just before lunch on May 29, 1945, three weeks after the formal end of the Second World War in Europe, Sister Wörle, head nurse of the children's wards at the Kaufbeuren-Irsee Mental Institution near Munich, approached the bed of four-year-old Richard Jenne and put him to death by lethal injection. She had plenty of experience, having, as she readily stated to her interrogators, previously so injected "at least 211 minors." The time of death was 13:10. Richard, classified as a "feebleminded idiot," had been taken to the hospital some months before and put on a diet carefully calculated to bring him to the brink of starvation. By May 29 he had reached the desired state of weakness and was ripe for Sister Wörle's visit. The death certificate, intended for dispatch to Richard's parents in the town of Ihringen in the German state of Baden, did not mention the injection, but listed the cause of death as typhus.

The American troops who had occupied the picturesque town of Kaufbeuren in the hilly, blossom-laden countryside of Swabia on April 26 were unaware of Richard's demise, and indeed would not discover his body and those of a number of other victims of Sister Wörle and her colleagues for five more weeks. The Americans had arrested the Nazi director of the institution but, put off by a large sign warning of typhus in the hospital, had not ventured inside, where routine continued as usual. On July 2, two medical officers finally entered the premises. What met their eyes was beyond belief: some 1,500 disease-riddled patients confined in the most squalid conditions, among them a ten-year-old boy who weighed twenty-two pounds, and a stifling morgue filled with bodies that had not been buried and that could not be disposed of quickly, as the shiny new crematorium, finished in November 1944, had been closed down.[1]

Richard Jenne was probably the last person to be put to death by the Nazi extermination machine, which in performing this act had come full circle. For it was in this institution, and a network of similar ones, that basic training, using German nationals, had been provided for those who would run the death camps so recently liberated by the Allies. Richard was not alone in his death: millions of other children were deliberately murdered in the Nazi era. Tens of thousands would die of conflict-induced starvation in Leningrad, Athens, the Netherlands, and other war zones. Others did not survive the unprecedented forced transfers of populations engendered by Nazi racial policy and carried out under the most primitive conditions. Thousands of teenaged Hitler Youth died in battle, and children of all involved nations were sterilized, perished during evacuations, died of war-borne diseases, or succumbed as forced laborers. They wasted away in concentration, refugee, and disciplinary camps, and died in the bombings of cities and in the Nazi revenge burnings of hundreds of doomed villages in the USSR, Greece, France, and Czechoslovakia, of which Distomo, Oradour-sur-Glane, and Lidice are merely the best known. A precise figure can never be compiled, but it is vast. The historian Alan Bullock estimates the total number of military and civilian deaths due to World War II in the European nations to be some forty million. Mortality of this magnitude defies comprehension and tends to destroy normal human reactions to the reality of the events, a phenomenon that was highly evident among both perpetrators and victims during the conflict itself. It is therefore necessary to remember, as Bullock puts it, that the statistics are important, "but because they can have the effect of numbing the imagination, which cannot conceive of human suffering on such a scale, it is equally important to underline that every single figure in these millions represents . . . an individual human being like ourselves—a man, a woman, a child, or even a baby."[2]

The discoveries at Kaufbeuren, coming weeks after the more horrendous accounts of conditions in the death camps, and coinciding as they did with the formal entry of Western Allied forces into Berlin, received small mention in the international press. But the Army was sufficiently embarrassed to replace the detachment occupying the town with another. The incident was only a detail in the gigantic mosaic of efforts under way to cope with the tremendous human needs of liberated Europe. The London *Times* of July 6, 1945, reported that the Combined Civil Affairs Committee of the Anglo-American Allies had announced that they had found, thus far, 5.8 million displaced persons in Germany. Of these 3.3 million had already been repatriated, which left 2.5 million to be cared for in camps. Their optimistic assessment was that the problem might "resolve itself" by September 1 into "the care of the residue of stateless persons and those who cannot be sent home." No figures were given for this group, whose fate would then be determined by the so far ineffectual Intergovernmental Committee on Refugees, set up in 1938, which would "have the task of finding places" for them.

The bland Civil Affairs announcement was fine as far as it went. But much is left out of its statistics. Other estimates put the number of the displaced at war's end in Germany alone as high as 12.5 million. The announcement does not mention the 7.8 million expellees from Hungary, Poland, and Czechoslovakia who would arrive in Germany in 1946 or the hundreds of thousands who would continue to move westward from areas controlled by the Soviet Union. It does not include the malnourished populations of newly liberated countries from Greece to Norway, the bombed-out millions of Warsaw, Stalingrad, Berlin, and London, or the exiles and evacuees trying to get home from all over the globe, whose numbers would burgeon after the defeat of Japan. A large percentage of these had, or would, become the responsibility of the Allied armies and help organizations, who were soon faced with situations beyond their most extreme imagining or preparation and challenged in their charitable desires by political policies, racial attitudes, and nationalistic self-interests not in the least moderated by the events of the war.

For large numbers of the children of Europe who had escaped Richard Jenne's fate, life was far removed from the norm. In every liberated nation wild, streetwise groups attached themselves to troop formations and scrounged for food. Parentless children waiting for transfer out of concentration camps played among stacks of corpses, or lay near death in makeshift hospitals. Others, taken to still inadequate refugee camps with their families, fared little better. Evacuated children nervously boarded ships and trains to reunions with parents they no longer knew, while others waited in vain for parents who would never return from concentration camps or battlefields.

Thousands more roamed the countryside alone, moving toward the last homes they had known, along with the masses jamming the roads and trains. Everywhere, children who had been hidden for years, sworn to silence and subterfuge, emerged to deal with a strange world. Many who had been sent from occupied countries at a very young age to foster families in the Reich for "Germanization" would stay hidden until ferreted out, and some would never find out who they really were.

This was Adolf Hitler's legacy. The Nazis' evil utopian dream— a world controlled by a physically perfect people of pure ethnicity in which the racially unacceptable and economically useless would be eliminated— had lasted for only a brief moment in history. But in that time it had grown to monstrous proportions, fertilized by indifference and unwitting support in the nations that had, with enormous human cost, put an end to it.

Hitler's undeviating progress toward the creation of the Aryan super-empire he described in *Mein Kampf* was carefully paced and politically astute. He was only too willing to adjust his ideology as necessary to procure temporary political support or economic advantage, even allying himself for a time with the "Judeo-Bolshevik" rulers of the Soviet Union, the better to devour Poland. Not even his obsession with race was inviolable. Hermann Rauschning, an early colleague, quoted Hitler as stating:

> I know perfectly well . . . that in the scientific sense there is no such thing as race. But you, as a farmer and cattle breeder, cannot get your breeding successfully achieved without the conception of race. And I as a politician need a conception which enables the order which has hitherto existed on historic bases to be abolished and an entirely and new anti-historic order enforced and given an intellectual basis. . . . And for this purpose the conception of race serves me well. . . . With the conception of race, National Socialism will carry the revolution abroad and re-cast the world.[3]

But first, it would be essential to establish total control of German society. New visions must be promoted to replace the bad aftereffects of the First World War, and the economy must be revived by stringent elimination of waste and by full employment. Above all, there must be no more factionalism or variance of point of view, but total obedience to a particular leader, and it must all be achieved without arousing domestic resistance or foreign sanctions.

From the beginning, Hitler recognized the importance of children in his scheme. The state must "declare the child to be the most precious treasure of the people."[4] But not all children. They must be healthy "Aryans," free of "hereditary weakness," and they must also be properly educated. Those not complying with the first criterion would be eliminated. The rest would be removed at a pliable age from the influence of family and religion and be inculcated with Nazi ideology, ranked from high functionary to serflike laborer according to certain rigid mental and physical standards, trained accordingly, and then be used as commodities where most convenient. The children of the conquered lands would be included. In occupied areas populated with unworthy beings such as Slavs, the indigenous would be eliminated or enslaved and the area would be repopulated with individuals "subject to special norms," who would be chosen and resettled by "specially constituted racial commissions." In this way it would be possible to found "colonies whose inhabitants are exclusively bearers of the highest racial purity and hence of the highest racial efficiency."[5] As a result of these theories, expressed in *Mein Kampf* and implemented by gigantic overlapping bureaucracies, thousands of children would have experiences no child should ever have, spend years in wandering and exile, be separated from their families forever, and die. The process would begin at home.

PART I   Producing the Perfect Nazi

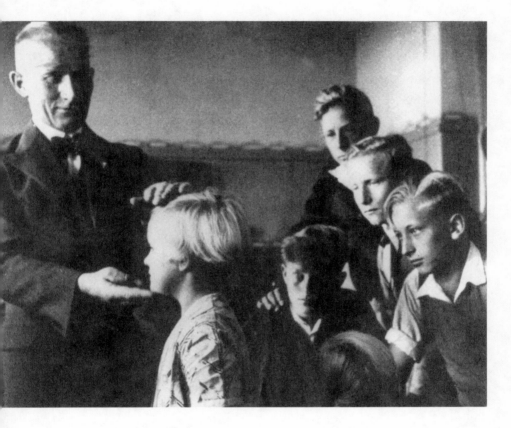

The folkish state must . . . set race in the center of all life. It must take care to keep it pure. It must declare the child to be the most precious treasure of the people. It must see to it that only the healthy beget children. . . .

The folkish state must not adjust its entire educational work primarily to the inoculation of mere knowledge, but to the breeding of absolutely healthy bodies. The training of mental abilities is only secondary. . . .

The crown of the folkish state's entire work of education and training must be to burn the racial sense and racial feeling into the instinct and the intellect, the heart and brain of the youth entrusted to it. No boy and no girl must leave school without having been led to an ultimate realization of the necessity and essence of blood purity . . . this education too, from the racial viewpoint, must find its ultimate completion in military service.

ADOLF HITLER, *Mein Kampf*, Part II

1. Applied Eugenics

Hitler was not very original in his desire to promote the domination of his own "race." This is a desire that has been present since the beginning of time. Even the author of Genesis has God proclaim that he will "make man in our image, in the likeness of our selves." The idea was, and in many instances still is, to keep control of the activities of life in the hands of those who look, think, and act the way you do. Such control, if it is to be total, requires the production of more people like oneself and the subjugation, exclusion, or even the removal of those who are different in race, class, or ideas. By the late nineteenth century biological science had been added to the arsenal of the promoters of such social control and had led to the creation of the field of eugenics, a discipline based on fuzzy definitions and often deliberately skewed research, which would be so perverted by the Nazis that its very name has become unacceptable.

But in the mid-1920s, when Hitler's *Mein Kampf* was published, eugenics was quite the rage. In England and the United States, where it had originated, eugenics was aimed principally at improving the educated white upper and middle classes and controlling the increase of the poor lower classes, whatever their ethnicity. The tendency to poverty and all the negative characteristics associated with it, such as crime and disease, were assumed to be inherited. In the United States this theory was not only applied to those already resident in the country: it was observed that many of the "poor" were recent immigrants, mostly of Southern and Eastern European origin, who also happened to be Catholic and Jewish. This led to the inevitable conclusion that immigration from certain areas should be limited. And indeed, promoters of eugenics were prominent among those who testified in favor of the Immigration Acts of 1921 and 1924, which established quotas based on the percentage of each nationality already in the United States in 1890, that is, before the massive influx of the "alien stream" from Southern and Eastern Europe.[1] Hitler approved highly of this law, noting:

> There is today one state in which at least weak beginnings toward a better conception [of citizenship] are noticeable. Of course it is not our

*An illustration from a German school text on eugenics,
showing various types.*

model German Republic, but the American Union. . . . By refusing
immigration on principle to elements in poor health, by simply exclud-
ing certain races from naturalization, it professes in slow beginnings a
view that is peculiar to the folkish state concept.[2]

Although in the United States there was much advice on proper marriage and the duty of the worthy to reproduce (ideal farm families were,
for example, put on display at state fairs), the main thrust of eugenics was
toward prevention of the increase of those bearing characteristics considered "irremediable" at that time, such as epilepsy, tuberculosis, alcoholism, insanity, and sexual promiscuity. To these, some thinkers would

add the rather less well-defined conditions of "shiftlessness," "asocial activity," and "feeblemindedness." By the outbreak of World War I thirty American states had laws prohibiting marriage for persons suffering from many of these afflictions.

The eugenicists soon concluded that one of the simplest ways to eliminate social degeneracy was through sterilization, a procedure that had been used tacitly since the late nineteenth century on certain criminal and insane inmates in state institutions in the United States. By 1917 sixteen American states had passed laws authorizing sterilizations in public institutions, and more would follow. The practice was eventually extended to include people who were not, in fact, either criminals or hopelessly insane, but who had failed certain intelligence tests, or were considered socially undesirable "trash." The victims of these laws were classified by grossly unscientific standards based on genealogical surveys, visual evaluation, and hearsay. They were viewed not as human beings but as objects that burdened the state.

Finding and classifying such individuals required intensive fieldwork, while extending the laws required heavy lobbying of the local welfare authorities and legislatures. The Eugenics Survey of Vermont,[3] which would result in that state's 1931 sterilization law, is a prime example of the methodology that would later be used by the Nazis. The survey was set up by Henry F. Perkins, a passionate and politically astute zoology professor at the University of Vermont. Perkins himself did not do fieldwork. That job was carried out by a very few dedicated operatives who had no doubt about who was "trash," and in particular, by the zealous Harriet Abbott, who had been trained at the Eugenics Record Office in Cold Spring Harbor, New York, cradle of the U.S. movement. Much information was willingly provided by state welfare and correction agencies that opened their files on individuals in the hope of obtaining better funding from the state legislature. The program required "a census of the feebleminded." All schoolchildren would be tested and "defectives" registered. Recipients of welfare and inmates of institutions would also be tested, and the results would be analyzed according to location, "race" (in this case French Canadians and Native Americans were targeted), and family history. Genealogical analysis would find inbreeding and other degenerate trends, and each family's "expense to the state" would be estimated. From all this information Miss Abbott would create profiles of defective families. Soon 6,000 people had been listed and sixty-two family lines analyzed. Unfortunately, some of these included not a few of Vermont's most respectable citizens, and had to be revised. The hard-line approach of these efforts led to the defeat of Professor Perkins's first attempt to promote a sterilization law in 1927. He and his colleagues did not give up, but they did tone down their rhetoric and put more emphasis on such positive ideas as child welfare, and in 1931, after fierce debate, the Act for Human Betterment by Voluntary Sterilization was passed by the Vermont legislature.[4]

Laws such as this one did not go unchallenged. In England, sterilization, viewed as a violation of the Offenses Against the Person Act of 1861, was never legalized.[5] To many in the United States, the often involuntary sterilizations seemed to violate the constitutional rights of the victims, and laws similar to that of Vermont were suspended or rejected outright by a number of state courts and legislatures. But the eugenics promoters were not easily turned aside. In 1928 they found a case with which to challenge the opposition: that of the "moral imbecile" Carrie Buck. They would take *Buck v. Bell* all the way to the Supreme Court.

Carrie Buck was the daughter of a "feebleminded" woman who had been institutionalized for years. In 1924, the seventeen-year-old Carrie, about to be committed to the same institution on the same grounds, had an illegitimate daughter. If the child could be shown to be feebleminded too, the eugenics partisans reasoned, sterilization of Carrie on hereditary grounds would be justified. The evidence was based on the prevailing eugenics theories. The results of IQ tests administered to Carrie and her mother showed them to be "morons." Harry Laughlin, one of the most active promoters of the science and director of the Eugenics Record Office, served as an expert witness and, on the basis of the family's pedigree, but without actually examining them, pronounced them members of "the shiftless, ignorant, and worthless class of anti-social whites of the South." A Red Cross worker, sent by Laughlin, visited Carrie's seven-month-old baby, Vivian, and said that the child had "a look" that was "not quite normal." A test administered by the Eugenics Record Office concluded that she was "below average." The Supreme Court voted eight to one that the family was afflicted with "hereditary feeblemindedness" and noted that "sterilization on eugenic grounds was within the police power of the state." In his opinion, Justice Oliver Wendell Holmes wrote this much quoted statement:

> We have seen more than once that the public welfare may call upon the best citizens for their lives. It would be strange if it could not call upon those who already sap the strength of the state for these lesser sacrifices . . . in order to prevent our being swamped with incompe-

tence. . . . The principle that sustains compulsory vaccination is broad
enough to cover the cutting of the Fallopian tubes. . . . Three generations of imbeciles are enough.[6]

To make quite sure that this family did not reproduce, Carrie Buck's
younger sister, Doris, who was not in an institution, was sterilized also but
told that the operation had been for a stomach problem. In later years she
and her husband tried in vain to have children. She did not discover the
reason for her inability to do so until 1980, when, she said, "I broke down
and cried. My husband and me wanted children desperately. We were
crazy about them. I never knew what they'd done to me."[7]

It is clear that neither sister would be considered mentally deficient by
today's standards. Little Vivian reportedly did fine at school before her
untimely death in 1932, and, a few years after the sterilization of the sisters, the designers of the intelligence tests would themselves acknowledge
the inaccuracy of the tests administered to the family.[8] Despite this fact,
the policy would continue for decades in a number of states. As recently
as September 29, 2003, the governor of North Carolina made a public
apology and ordered compensation for some 7,600 people who had been
sterilized between 1929 and 1974.[9]

By 1933, when Hitler came to power, nearly 20,000 legal sterilizations had been performed in the United States. Welfare programs
necessitated by the Depression would encourage this effort, bringing the
total to around 36,000 by 1941.[10] But despite Oliver Wendell Holmes and
the eugenics fanatics, science had already begun to demonstrate the fal-
lacies of the statistics and arguments used to promote eugenics theory and
the inherent prejudices it embodied. Thinkers from Bertrand Russell to
Clarence Darrow had also recognized its threat to democracy. Political
opponents, frequently condemned in the heat of debate as lacking in intelligence, might, according to Russell, suddenly find themselves under the
knife; and, stated Darrow in 1926, a group in power, intelligent or not,
"would inevitably direct human breeding in their own interests."[11] Hitler
had absorbed this message only too well. In *Mein Kampf,* he had said:

> A prevention of the faculty and opportunity to procreate on the part of
> the degenerate and mentally sick, over a period of only six hundred
> years, would not only free humanity from an immeasurable misfortune,
> but would lead to a recovery which today seems scarcely conceivable. If
> the fertility of the healthiest bearers of the nationality is thus con-

sciously and systematically promoted, the result will be a race that at
least will have eliminated the germs of our present physical and hence
spiritual decay.[12]

The Nazis got straight to work on these concepts. Despite the examples
of legal sterilization programs in the United States, Denmark, Norway,
and elsewhere,[13] no such legislation had found approval in the Weimar
Republic. Hitler did not hesitate in 1933: the Law for the Prevention of
Hereditarily Diseased Progeny, without any consent clause, was approved
on July 14. Ever the politician, Hitler delayed its publication until July 25
so as not to endanger the July 20 signing of his Concordat with the Vatican,
for which sterilization was, of course, anathema.[14]

Publication of the law was backed by propaganda full of references to
examples from the United States, and indeed by vocal support from some
American eugenicists, who would not change their opinions until such
time as Hitler made shocking verbal attacks on other "Nordic" peoples
and on the United States itself.

Administration of the new regulation was carefully thought out. People
could volunteer for the procedure, or physicians could refer their cases,
without their consent, to hereditary health courts. These consisted of a
panel of three members, one of whom had to be an expert eugenicist, who
was unlikely to be very objective. There was an appeals court, but once an
appeal was denied, sterilization was compulsory. The response was overwhelming: in the first two years after the implementation of the law on
January 1, 1934, 388,400 "denunciations" (ten times the American total
for the century) were filed, mainly by mental institutions. The courts and
operating rooms were pushed to keep up. An American observer, watching from an operating room gallery in Berlin, described the assembly-line
procedure:

> Down below six doctors were hard at work. . . . Hospital beds came and
> went with methodical precision. The doctors made quick, deft incisions
> in white abdomen walls, spread the slit, and applied surgical clamps.
> They probed, delicately lifted a tube which they wrapped and cut. The
> wound was sewed, and the body was wheeled off to be replaced by
> another. . . . For more than an hour I saw women come in with the cra-
> dle of life intact and leave empty shells.[15]

By 1936, 168,989 procedures had been carried out, mostly for the flexible category of "congenital feeblemindedness," but also for epilepsy,
alcoholism, severe malformations, and deafness.[16] There was some con-

sideration of age: all sterilization of children under eleven was prohibited, as was forcible sterilization of juveniles under fifteen. After that, the full force of the law could be imposed.

The number of those eligible for sterilization was extended beyond the obviously handicapped by a clause in the Law Against Habitual Criminals, passed in November 1933, which permitted incarceration of wrongdoers and "asocials" in mental institutions where they could be sterilized for "hereditary criminality." As time went on the definition of "asocial" became ever more elastic. A series of German eugenicists struggled mightily to categorize this group. Various degrees of affliction were identified, and enormous and sometimes contradictory genealogical studies, much like those undertaken in Vermont, were prepared to prove that asociality was hereditary. In the end, the asocial label became a convenient catchall category for anyone who did not fit into the Nazi social scheme. The Nazi criteria were economic and reproductive, and they targeted the traditional welfare categories of the homeless, the chronically unemployed, or "work-shy," who were an expense to the state, as well as homosexuals and prostitutes, who would not have healthy children. In the summer of 1938, Himmler decreed a Reich Campaign Against the Work-Shy and sent some 11,000 of these "asocial" souls to concentration camps.[17]

More victims for the sterilizers would be provided by the Marriage Health Law of 1935, which required medical screening for hereditary weaknesses before a marriage license could be issued. American diplomats reported that the new government's public health offices were not yet in a position to perform this service "except when specifically requested," but that they should be coping efficiently within a year. "Heretofore," they added, "there has been no legal basis for preventing an incompetent suffering from a mental defect, chronic alcoholism, or squandermania from marrying . . . it will no longer be so under the new law."[18] The effects of the law were often devastating. Applicants who were found to have mentally ill relations or a hereditary illness were not only sterilized. They were forbidden to marry a "healthy person," as to do so would prevent that partner from producing the offspring needed for the Thousand Year Reich.

The diplomats were correct about the efficiency of the Nazi government in race matters. Within a few years, an enormous centralized bureaucracy not only had some 12,000 local medical officials working on sterilization and marriage issues, but also had set up a national hereditary index, or *Erbkartei,* where the racial characteristics of every inhabitant would be recorded.[19] All these measures seemed fine to Harry Laughlin, expert witness against Carrie Buck, who, despite the fact that he was himself an epileptic, accepted in 1935 an honorary degree from Heidelberg University (conferred, it must be admitted, in absentia), which he declared to be "evidence of a common understanding of German and American scientists of the nature of eugenics as the practical application of those fundamental biological and social principles which determine the racial endowments and the racial health . . . of future generations."[20]

Although sterilization of criminals, asocials, the mentally deficient, and the physically handicapped could be instituted without too much international criticism, sterilization of healthy, law-abiding individuals on purely racial grounds was not acceptable. This did not lessen Nazi determination to extend the process to those German citizens it defined as belonging to "alien races," who, if allowed to mate with pure Aryans, would defile the nation. Patience and the use of less controversial methods, such as forced emigration, would be also be required in order to rid the nation of these groups. Essential to all the measures was the definition and registration of members of the "alien races," which included, but were not limited to, Jews, Gypsies, and blacks.

Less than three months after Hitler's takeover, Hermann Göring, in his capacity as Minister of the Interior of Prussia, which had jurisdiction over the Rhineland states, ordered a census of the so-called Rhineland Bastards, the illegitimate offspring of "colored" French and American troops sent to occupy that area following World War I. The use of "colored" troops as an occupation force had caused a tremendous controversy in the 1920s.[21] German delegates had gone to the Versailles Treaty talks with instructions to try to prevent such a thing. In this they were supported by American military opinion that use of large numbers of "degraded" troops from the French colonies in Africa would open the French to unnecessary criticism. When questioned on this issue by President Woodrow Wilson, French Premier Georges Clemenceau promised to withdraw the colonial troops, stating, "It would be a grave error to occupy the Left Bank with black troops." For reasons that are unclear, but that certainly included a strong desire to do the opposite of what the Germans wanted, this promise was not kept, and between 30,000 and 40,000 North African, Senegalese, and Malagasy soldiers were deployed, as were a small number of British colonials and even some American blacks. The affair did not become a cause célèbre until April 1920, when, despite contrary advice from both the British and the Americans, a "colored" French contingent was sent to occupy Frankfurt in response to the illegal entry of German troops into the Ruhr. In the ensuing unrest, the French troops fired on a crowd, causing several casualties.

The German and international press went mad. In London's *Daily Herald*, under the headline BLACK SCOURGE IN EUROPE. SEXUAL HORROR LET LOOSE BY FRANCE ON RHINE. DISAPPEARANCE OF YOUNG GERMAN GIRLS, the journalist E. D. Morel wrote that "primitive African barbarians, carriers of syphilis" had been raping German women.[22] Deputies in the German Reichstag spoke of the contamination of German youth, and one correctly noted that in America black men would be lynched for such offenses. The German government was careful not to condemn the black troops per se, instead criticizing the French government for sending an alien race to Europe in order to destroy its civilization. Meanwhile, the drama had elicited a plea from the Pope to remove the troops, and a petition of protest was signed by 50,000 Swedish ladies.

Reports to the U.S. State Department from officers in Germany and later press inquiries told a somewhat less sensational story. In their opinion, French discipline had been good and the few crimes committed—thirteen incidents in eighteen months—had been properly dealt with.[23] Much of the furor was clearly an attempt to gain sympathy for Germany and to put pressure on France to end the occupation. In an attempt to influence the newly elected American President, Warren G. Harding, German propaganda relating to the "Black Horror" was increased in the United States in early 1921 and culminated in a meeting of 12,000 sympathizers in Madison Square Garden. It was not an unqualified success, as anti-German feeling was seemingly still stronger than racial passion in New York, and a counter-meeting by the American Legion garnered 25,000 attendees.[24]

In 1923, a Swedish cleric by the name of Liljeblad, who was trying to start his own movement against the "Black Horror," requested statistics on the number of offspring of black troops in the Rhineland. The German government, not wanting the myth of mass rapine to be discredited, and very limited in its research powers in the occupied zone, had never put together any exact numbers. Liljeblad was forced to do his own calculations, which he based on inaccurate press accounts and hearsay. His conclusions were published in a book he marketed successfully both in the United States and Europe, and in which he declared that in fifteen years there would be 27,000 mixed-race children in the Rhineland, which would be a "curse for all Europe in the future." Indeed, he said that he had himself seen numbers of such children, including one in Mainz with "black and white stripes all over his back." The German government's own statisticians, stimulated by the good preacher's request, had meanwhile done their own research, but could only come up with seventy-eight children, a figure they did not publish, preferring to profit from Dr. Liljeblad's helpful polemics, which had elicited some 67,000 American signatures protesting the presence of the black troops on German soil.[25] Further investigations, also kept quiet, did not appreciably raise the totals, and the issue, overshadowed by more important events and the gradual withdrawal of the offending troops, slowly faded.

But all the publicity had had its effect. In the first part of *Mein Kampf*, published in 1925, Hitler, in one of his diatribes on the willful defilement of German blood by the Jews, noted that "it was and is the Jews who bring the Negroes into the Rhineland, always with the same secret thoughts and clear aim of ruining the hated white race by the necessarily resulting bastardization."[26] This theory was later backed up for the Nazi faithful by their ideologue Alfred Rosenberg, who took France to task for "contributing to the dehumanization of Europe by means of the blacks, just as it had by introducing Jewish emancipation 140 years before."[27] Sporadic articles in the 1920s kept this idea in the public consciousness and passed on to the offspring of the black soldiers the negative characteristics emphasized in the original sensationalism. Fear of blacks soon filtered down to other German children. Six-year-old Melita Maschmann, who would later become a high-ranking Nazi youth leader, was filled with dread at the sight of black soldiers on a train: "We fled into an empty compartment. I cannot remember what my mother said to soothe us; but I remember a feeling of horror, as if all the misery of Germany were incarnate in those black-skinned men."[28]

In 1927 a new consideration brought the Rhineland Bastard question to the fore.[29] Though the oldest ones were only eight years old, it was thought that something should be done to prevent them from reproducing when they reached puberty. One official suggested sterilization via "painless intervention," while another proposed forced deportation under the auspices of a missionary agency. But the time was not yet ripe. The Weimar Health Ministry rejected both proposals on legal and public relations grounds. Such a project would require special legislation of a type still out of the question in 1927.

It was not out of the question after 1933. But the census ordered by Göring found only 145 "bastards." Feeling that this figure could not be right, after all the fuss, the authorities dispatched Dr. Wolfgang Abel, a

Berlin anthropologist, to do further study in Wiesbaden, where 89 of the children had previously been found. After due investigation, which included careful measurement of noses, lips, and head shapes, as well as skin, eye, and hair color, Dr. Abel could only find 33 absolute qualifiers aged five to eleven. Not only were they "black" and, in his opinion, unhealthy, but they also exhibited all sorts of hereditarily undesirable traits such as flat feet and early "psychopathic symptoms" such as crying and nail biting.[30] This was awkward, as, according to the Nazis' own law, they were too young to sterilize.

Once again the low number of "bastards" caused consternation in Berlin. Somewhat weakening its case, the Prussian Interior Ministry suggested that mothers must be hiding the origins of many of the children who could pass as "European" and calculated that there must really be 500 to 600 of them. More thorough physical exams were ordered for students in the Rhineland schools in the hope of finding more "bastards" who would also be hereditarily unfit. But with very few exceptions, the targeted children were not only healthy, but models of achievement at school.

Continued focus on the Rhineland issue eventually led to a number of anxious discussions between officials of the Interior Ministry, the Foreign Office, and Nazi racial officials. The Foreign Office had been besieged by protests from abroad about the radical racial laws being decreed by the new government and about the sometimes violently discriminatory acts being carried out in public against non-Aryans. Important trading partners such as Japan, India, Turkey, and Brazil were concerned about treatment of their citizens who lived and worked in Germany. The Foreign Office worried that retaliatory actions would be taken against Germans resident abroad and that trade would be affected. So far the diplomats had hedged when responding to foreign complaints, saying that the racial decrees were only "emergency acts" against Jews, or anti-miscegenation laws similar to those in many countries, and that non-Aryan foreign nationals were safe. In the opinion of the Foreign Office, a public sterilization campaign aimed at the black offspring of French colonial and possibly American troops would upset other nations even more. In discussions with the racial officials, the German diplomats plaintively wondered if the word "Jewish" could be substituted for "non-Aryan" (apparently feeling that this would not deeply offend any other country), which would relieve them of the difficulty of figuring out which nationalities were or were not "alien" (not acceptable) as opposed to "European-related" (acceptable). But the racial authorities were immovable. Though willing to make concessions for those who were not German citizens, whose problems could be handled case by case, they insisted that no basic difference between Jews and members of other alien races existed, and that it was their objective to rid the German people of all alien blood types.

And so the relentless pursuit of the Rhineland Bastards continued, but in secret. It was clear that the negative public relations effect of a special sterilization law for children would also be too great in Germany itself. Religious leaders would undoubtedly object, and it was felt that the regular health authorities could not be trusted to perform the illegal sterilizations and remain silent. The only recourse was the creation of a special agency within the Nazi Party structure that would not be accountable to the established court system. The procedures would be performed by carefully selected doctors with the "permission" of the parents or guardians of the children. Final approval of the project would, according to the racial hygiene officials, be requested from the Führer.

Whether Hitler authorized this process is not clear. But it is known that, after some delay, the full force of Nazi police and health agencies was focused on the Rhineland Bastards. In the spring of 1937 an office was set up in Gestapo headquarters in Berlin to oversee the project. Three special commissions, much like the hereditary health courts, were appointed in the Rhineland to process cases. Each case was given a number and was reviewed by an anthropological expert. The children, long since registered, were relentlessly hunted down. One seventeen-year-old, newly employed as a cabin boy on a river barge, was pursued through three cities. He had first been examined and measured anthropologically two years previously. On June 16, 1937, he was called to another examination, but, as he was on board a moving barge, he did not appear. This triggered an all-out manhunt involving the Gestapo, various local police departments, and all three Rhineland commissions. Telegrams flew back and forth describing the boy as a possible enemy of the state. The official in charge left orders that he should be called as soon as the child was found, no matter what the hour. At 12:15 a.m. on June 29, commission members were informed that the Gestapo had found the boy near Mainz. Driving through the night, they delivered him to a hospital in Cologne. Here he immediately underwent another physical examination and a hearing before the sterilization panel. His mother and stepfather were not present. Much worse, from the point of view of the commission, sticklers for procedure, was the absence of their anthropologist. Nevertheless, they did have the opinion of another professor who had seen the child's photograph the month before and determined that he was indeed of a "non-European" race and had "negroid" and "malayan" features. The parents had also seemingly "agreed" to the sterilization on a form presented to them earlier. The documents thus being in order, the operation was performed the next day.

The terrible isolation of this boy calls to us across the years. One cannot be immune. No such scruples seem to have bothered the racial hygiene officials in charge of the sterilization program, which would also bring to the operating room a twelve-year-old girl (who at least was accompanied by her stepfather), numbers of fifteen-year-old boys, and at least one daughter of an American soldier, who was sterilized in the Women's Clinic at the University of Bonn the day after the cabin boy. As was done in all these cases, the operation was described in detail in the child's dossier by the surgeon:

> The order for sterilization was given to me. During the operation a section was taken out from both fallopian tubes. . . . The operation and the recovery were without incident. At discharge the belly was soft, not tender, and the incision well healed. After this smooth recovery no future health problems of any kind are to be expected.[31]

But there often were problems, which the Nazi surgeons might not recognize as important, as the 1991 testimony of another sterilization victim shows:

> I still have many complaints as a result of it. There were complications with every operation I had since . . . and the psychological pressure has always remained. When nowadays my neighbors, older ladies, tell me about their grandchildren and great-grandchildren, this hurts bitterly . . . because I am on my own, and I have to cope without anyone's help.[32]

The exact number of Rhineland Bastards sterilized by the commissions is not known, but it was probably far fewer than 300. The execution of this program is especially significant in its circumvention not only of traditional and humane laws, but even of the Nazis' own laws. In the use of secret agencies folded into the police apparatus and the validation of the process by the hard-core eugenics scientists of the time, it provided the model for the vast and horrific programs to come.

By 1945, the total of recorded sterilizations within the Reich had risen to some 400,000, and was probably higher, a figure made especially surreal when one contemplates the extraordinary success, until that year, of the swarthy, clubfooted Nazi Propaganda Minister, Joseph Goebbels, who, despite his hereditary deformity, produced six fine children for the Fatherland.

Dealing with the tiny number of representatives of the "Black Horror" inside Germany, all belonging to a single generation, was not very difficult. The "Gypsy Plague" would be a greater challenge, not on moral but on scientific grounds. For centuries, Gypsies had been regarded with fascination and suspicion in the Western world, and in most places still are. Descendents of nomadic tribes thought to have originated in the Indian subcontinent, their physical characteristics alone were enough to disqualify them from the Nordic pantheon. This was sometimes awkward for Nazi theorists, because, technically speaking, the Gypsies were "Aryans." That unfortunate fact was more than balanced by their itinerant and, to the bourgeois European, unacceptably unsanitary lifestyle, not to mention their frequent lack of formal education, which made it easy to label them as "work-shy," "asocial," and "feebleminded" elements eligible for incarceration in concentration camps and for sterilization.

As was the case with the Rhineland Bastards, registration and classification of Gypsies was seen to be essential to control of the "plague." In this case too, much of the work had long since been done. A Central Bureau for Gypsies had been established in Bavaria in 1899. Its director, Alfred Dillmann, had published a handy *Gypsy Book* for the authorities in 1905, which not only noted that Gypsies were generally criminal in nature, but listed some 3,000 of them by name, complete with genealogy and physical descriptions such as "real Gypsy type" and "apparently epileptic." The most notorious, who had been detained for offenses such as begging, vagabondism, lack of trading licenses, and use of false names, were honored with a photograph.[33] A law passed in Bavaria in 1926, To Combat Gypsies, Vagabonds, and the Work-Shy, which was adopted by the Weimar government in 1929, put in place numerous regulations. Some, dealing with the licensing of animals, control of camping sites, and regulating school attendance of Gypsy children (they could be exempted from attendance if it could be shown that they were receiving "proper instruction" at home) seem reasonable. Less so was mandatory registration with the local police, who could send Gypsies over sixteen to work camps and jail for not having permanent employment and a variety of other flimsy reasons. By this time, the terms "vagabond" and "work-shy" had seemingly become a little unclear, leading the Bavarian Interior Ministry to issue a clarification: "The term Gypsy is well known and does not need further explanation. Racial science gives information as to who should be regarded as a Gypsy." Vagabonds are then defined as persons who are not racial Gypsies, but who, according to their general behavior and conduct, their occupations and their nomadic habits, are comparable to Gypsies. Basic to the vagabond, the regulation continues, is that his occupation serves only as "cover for a dishonest, Gypsy-like lifestyle."[34] By 1933 there were some 150 Gypsy regulations on the books in Germany, including a Prussian law requiring all Gypsies over age six to be fingerprinted and carry a special ID card.

Existing legislation made it easy for Gypsies sent to concentration camps to be sterilized as criminals and asocials, but to the Nazis the "Gypsy Plague" was not a criminal problem; it was a racial one that would require their complete separation from the pure German nation-race, or "Volk." In 1934, therefore, all Gypsies lacking German citizenship were deported. By 1935, more stringent controls on itinerant German Gypsies were in place. With the enthusiastic support of the locals in many municipalities, the traditional encampments of Gypsy caravans were limited to special enclosures, which often were surrounded by fences and put under police guard. In some localities, those in the enclosures were required to observe curfews and could leave only for work, school, or medical care. In order to rid Berlin of Gypsies during the 1936 Olympic Games, an enormous encampment of this type was hastily set up at Marzahn, a swampy area just outside the city next to a cemetery and a garbage dump.

More difficult was the problem of settled Gypsies, who were not covered by the vagabond laws, and who had often intermarried several generations back and could not always be visually distinguished from other Germans. Nazi race officials fretted over the fact that there were no specific laws limiting Gypsy participation in German society. To make do, elements of newly minted anti-Jewish laws were made applicable. While this classification opened the way for the persecution of Gypsies on purely racial grounds, it made life ever so much more complex for the various agencies already dealing with "racial health." Here was another category requiring anthropologic definition and eugenic analysis.

Help was forthcoming in the person of Dr. Robert Ritter, a child psychiatrist trained in Germany, France, and Switzerland, whose specialty was "antisocial" youth and the genealogical tracing of vagabondism and other criminal traits.[35] Ritter, who never joined the Nazi Party, was, despite that fact, a member of his local sterilization board and quite familiar with the racial requirements of the Volk. In 1936, he was offered the directorship of a new branch of the Reich Health Department known as the Race Hygiene and Biological Population Office. Funding would be provided both by the Health Department and SS agencies. The main mission of Ritter's new office was to register all the Gypsies in Germany. Ritter was, at first, reluctant to become involved with the Nazi bureaucracy, but seduced by the possibilities of furthering his life's work, he took the job.

Soon the professor and his assistants, among them the impeccably Nordic Eva Justin (who would later write her doctoral thesis on Gypsy children), using research methods remarkably similar to those of the more extreme Anglo-American eugenicists, were rushing from Gypsy enclosures to concentration camps taking blood samples, making plaster casts of heads, taking photographs, and recording family histories. To make their subjects more relaxed, they sometimes posed as missionaries. By 1937, they were able to produce an extraordinary document "several meters in length on which, in tiny millimeter sized letters and numbers the genealogical tree of all Gypsies living in Germany for the last ten generations had been charted."[36] Ritter was sympathetic to the pure, itinerant Gypsies, whom he felt should be left to pursue their lifestyle. But both he and Miss Justin had concluded in their travels and observations that the hereditary weaknesses of those of mixed German-Gypsy blood absolutely required that they be sterilized. After this had been done, Ritter fantasized, these "bad" Gypsies might be sent to live in remote and strictly supervised reservations where they could, "in keeping with their gifts and talents, practice a satisfying vocation; they could run their own little household, read books at their leisure, go to the cinema, enjoy music or engage in sports."[37]

These idyllic reservations would not long be an expense to the government: Eva Justin had also determined that children with Gypsy blood could not ever become socially well-adjusted adults even if they were removed from their families and sent to special schools, and that they too must be sterilized. Their generations would thus be finite.

The government's own idea of the Gypsy future was rather less romantic than that of Dr. Ritter. In May 1938, SS chief Heinrich Himmler upgraded the small Office of Gypsy Affairs of the Munich criminal police to the Central Reich Agency for Fighting the Gypsy Plague and moved its headquarters to Berlin. On December 8, in a formal decree, all Gypsy affairs were consolidated under control of the Kripo, or criminal police.[38] In early 1939, Himmler, moving right along on the issue, demanded more precise data on each of the 30,000 or so mixed and pure Gypsies in the

Reich. This included names, addresses, and places of employment. Individuals would then be issued identity cards of varying colors indicating their degree of Gypsy blood. An overwhelmed Ritter fussed that he had to "deliver at least three thousand racial diagnoses by April first."[39] The classifications were not easy, given the fact that by Ritter's own estimate some 90 percent of the Gypsies involved had some degree of German blood, thus necessitating five different categories ranging from non-Gypsy to pure Gypsy, with "hybrids" arranged by percentage of German blood in between.[40] The examinations took a lot of time, as the Sinti Gypsy Franz Wirbel later testified.

The Wirbel family had lived in Allenstein, East Prussia, for six years by the time Ritter and Justin arrived on their mission. Franz, seventeen, was apprenticed to a violin maker. In the late summer of 1939, he and his entire family, the youngest being six years old, were ordered to report to the local health department. Refusal to do so, they were informed, would result in incarceration in a concentration camp. At the health office they were greeted by Ritter, Justin, and two assistants. Miss Justin, speaking fluent Sinti, reassured them and told the family that the examination was routine. They were told to undress completely. Questions were asked about previous illnesses. Skull and chin shapes, height of brow, size and shape of nose, color and setting of eyes, and much more were measured and called out to Dr. Ritter, who sat at a long table and filled in forms for each person. Finger- and footprints were also taken, as were samples of blood and hair. At the end, each subject had to sign his form. At no time were they informed of the purpose of the examination. It is not clear if Ritter and Justin knew the exact purpose either.[41] But Himmler did. Only weeks after the examination of the Wirbels, German forces invaded Poland. Here there would be plenty of room for Gypsy "reservations" rather different from those envisioned by Ritter.

In mid-October 1939, all Gypsies were forbidden to change their place of residence. Police were then ordered to take a census and analyze the "social worth" of each family. From this information lists for deportation to the newly formed General Gouvernement area of Poland were to be compiled. The census takers were required to refer to Ritter's data in making their decisions, which were often delayed while the impatient officials waited for the documents to arrive. But numerous apparent Gypsies were, in fact, excused by Ritter's classifications, which were taken as gospel.[42]

The deportations also had to be delayed for some months due to conditions in Poland, which, as we shall see, were chaotic. Not all Nazi officials agreed with these measures. In January 1940, Dr. Leonardo Conti, the

Reich Health Leader, wrote that deportation seemed to him mere expediency that would not achieve "radicalization." In his opinion:

> The final solution of the Gypsy problem can only be achieved through the sterilization of full and part Gypsies. . . . I think that the time for a legal resolution of these problems is over, and that we must immediately try to sterilize the Gypsies and part Gypsies as a special measure. . . . Once sterilization is completed and these people are rendered biologically harmless, it is of no great consequence whether they are expelled or used as labor on the home front.[43]

Despite Conti's objections, some 2,500 Gypsies were sent to Poland in 1940. Everyone over fourteen had to sign a release agreeing to be sterilized if he or she returned to Germany. This first group, after a time in labor camps, was not well supervised, and scores of the exiled families were left to fend for themselves. Many starved or were picked up again and sent to other camps, but, to the disgust of race authorities, a few managed to find their way back to Germany.[44]

Ritter, meanwhile, continued his meticulous classifications of each individual Gypsy in Germany and Austria. Himmler, who was fascinated by all sorts of racial research, and even sponsored SS racial investigations in Tibet, strongly supported Ritter's theories. This admiration led him to exempt certain clans of "pure Gypsies, who were possibly valuable Aryans," from persecution and deportation, a decision much deplored by other Nazi officials but one that saved thousands of lives.

Mixed German Gypsies were not so lucky. On December 16, 1942, Himmler issued his so-called Auschwitz Decree, which ordered their deportation. Mixed individuals could still be exempted for a number of complex reasons, including having important war-related jobs, being married to a German spouse, or being a decorated or wounded veteran, but for many, the exemption required that they agree to sterilization for themselves and their children. As the volume of deportations increased, impatient police officials often made arbitrary decisions without consulting Ritter's lists. But it must be said that more than a few families were saved by delaying tactics on the part of sympathetic local officials and by procrastinations of various kinds.[45]

By March 1943 the deportations of Gypsies, like those of Jews, had become a flood, and included hundreds of unaccompanied children who were removed from foster care and children's homes, including those run by the churches. The thirty-nine children Eva Justin had studied for her

Ph.D. thesis were taken from St. Josephspflege, in Mulfingen (Württemberg), on May 9, 1944. The pursuit of these children was relentless, and appeals to the normal authorities were swept aside with contempt in the name of the Reichsführer SS. The hunters even went so far as to provide a round-trip ticket to a pure Gypsy (and therefore exempt) baby nurse to take a one-year-old "bad" Gypsy orphan to Auschwitz.[46]

The Gypsies were, rather exceptionally, allowed to remain together as families at Auschwitz. Their part of the camp was therefore known as the Gypsy Family Camp. It is not clear to this day what future the Nazis had in mind for them, but true to Ritter's policy, their wives and daughters were used to test new sterilization methods and an estimated 9,432 boys and girls under fourteen became laboratory animals for the much written about Dr. Joseph Mengele, who used them in his eugenics experiments on twins and for research on various diseases.[47] When it suited him, Dr. Mengele hugged the children and fed them candy; he even set up a little kindergarten painted with fairy-tale scenes for some of them. But a child he seemed to dote on one day could be killed with total indifference the next, so that he could examine its organs. The conditions under which the children were used were terrible, as a former prisoner assigned to take care of some of them described:

> The anthropometrical examinations took place as follows: the children were stripped naked and measurements were made for hours (two to five hours). . . . This was a difficult ordeal for the children. Terrified, worn-out, hungry and shivering, they had to get up at six in the morning and walk the one-and-a-half-kilometer road from the block to the outpatient hospital. . . . The room in which the tests were conducted was unheated. The children . . . stood before the x-ray screen from five to fifteen minutes, since the exposure on display was being talked over and discussed. . . . After they returned [to the block] the children had fevers, caught colds, terrible coughs, sinus infections and even pneumonia. . . . Particularly traumatic were the morphological tests. Blood was collected from the children's fingers, then from their veins, sometimes two or three times from the same victims. The children screamed, shielded themselves, would not let themselves be touched. They were very afraid of being pricked.[48]

Far from these distressing scenes, and secure in his racial opinions, Robert Ritter, Mengele's fellow scientist and provider of his guinea pigs, beavered on and finally completed his list of 23,872 German Gypsies in March 1944.[49] By that time thousands had been sterilized and the Family

Camp would soon be liquidated. In the end, more than 11,000 German Gypsies perished in Auschwitz alone, including twenty-three members of violin maker Franz Wirbel's family, whose examinations by Ritter and Justin could, in retrospect, hardly be called "routine."

Forced sterilization and other eugenic procedures, relatively easy to apply to small groups of the racially alien—especially to those of low economic status, who were universally regarded as inferiors in the white world—although useful, would in no way suffice to rid Germany of the half-million overwhelmingly middle-class Jews who held full citizenship. Nor, in the early days of the Nazi regime, was there any way to isolate them. The old ghettos were long gone, and thousands of Jews had not only become completely assimilated, but had served Germany well in war and were major and respected contributors in the economic sector, the professions, and the arts. Extreme anti-Jewish measures would also not help Germany's cause in its byzantine maneuvers to keep Europe appeased while rebuilding its economy and armed forces. Hitler was fully aware of these things, but his determination to be rid of the Jews was beyond reason: it was an all-consuming obsession that he often could not conceal, even in the least suitable circumstances. United States Ambassador William Dodd, in diary entries in the late summer and fall of 1933, noted that one American visitor received by the Führer had reported that Hitler had "talked wildly about destroying all Jews, insisting that no other nation had any right to protest and that Germany was showing the world how to rid itself of its greatest curse." Hitler had spoken in a similar vein to New York bankers Winthrop Aldrich and Henry Mann, who reported, with supreme irony, that Hitler "considers himself a German Messiah."[50]

But Hitler was a consummate politician and, despite these slips of the tongue and intermittent violence by his most fanatic followers, would for five years manage to orchestrate the anti-Jewish campaign with great skill, varying its intensity to fit the mood and needs of the moment, alternating terror with lulls of apparent indifference, which allowed both the German people and the Jews to become accustomed to the latest outrageous regulations and foreign governments to avoid taking concerted action. The process again and again gave false hope to the Jewish population, which was constantly kept off balance by the belief that the worst was over.[51]

The basic idea was to make life so untenable for Jews that they would leave the country. Between 1933 and 1938 a series of laws and decrees would gradually deprive them of most means of employment and virtually every civil right. Along with this went "educational" and propaganda campaigns intended to convey the idea that the Jews, like the other alien races, were biologically dangerous and not quite human. In the new Nazi religious pantheon, they were cast as the foul embodiment of evil. Waxing and waning as events permitted, the Nazi racial poison was fed into Germany's social and psychological fabric, reviving and even surpassing the worst superstitions and intolerances of the past, and validating the vicious urges of those elements of society whose counterparts can be found in any place where prejudice is ingrained and one group is put at the absolute mercy of another.

Indeed, such a process had already reached its ultimate stage in the Soviet Union, only two days' journey from Berlin. Between 1930 and 1938, at exactly the same time as Hitler was setting in motion the process of the elimination of Jews and other alien races from Germany, Soviet leader Joseph Stalin, using the weapons of starvation, deportation, and murder, was ridding himself of millions of mostly Ukrainian kulaks, or land-owning peasants, and their families, who as a nationality and a class rather than a race (the basis for extermination is not important, it seems) had become an obstacle to his collectivization of Soviet agriculture. In the winter and spring of 1932–33, this process reached its zenith in what became known as the Terror-Famine, in which some seven million of the eventual eleven million dead are thought to have succumbed.

This was not the first major famine in twentieth-century Russia. Only ten years before, thousands of tons of emergency rations had been sent there by international relief agencies. But this time no aid was requested, foreign help agencies such as the Quakers were expelled, and no journalists were allowed in the affected areas, whose borders were sealed to prevent both escape and the importation of food. The existence of famine was firmly denied by the Soviet government. But reports smuggled out of the USSR by foreign reporters, who found the countryside strewn with corpses, described scenes of unbelievable horror:

> On a recent visit to the Northern Caucasus and the Ukraine, I saw something of the battle that is going on between the government and the peasants. The battlefield is as desolate as in any war and stretches wider. . . . On the one side, millions of starving peasants, their bodies often swollen from lack of food; on the other, soldier members of the

GPU [secret police] carrying out the instructions of the dictatorship of
the proletariat.[52]

Stalin referred to it as a war too, but one being waged by the peasants
against the government.

The carrying out of instructions was brutal indeed. In order to achieve
the unrealistic wheat production quotas demanded by Moscow, cadres of
dedicated young Communist Party members were sent forth to find any
stores of grain that the peasants might have concealed. Indoctrinated to
believe that the unachieved quotas were due to "sabotage" on the part of
the peasants and armed with long metal drills, they descended on villages
where the corpses already lay in heaps and the hovels were peopled by
whole families near death, to probe every possible place in which the
smallest handful of food could be hidden. The results were catastrophic:

> The peasants ate dogs, horses, rotten potatoes, the bark of trees,
> grass—anything they could find. . . . The people were like wild beasts,
> ready to devour one another. And no matter what they did, they went
> on dying, dying, dying. They died singly and in families. They died
> everywhere—in yards, on streetcars, and on trains. . . . A man is capable
> of forgetting a great deal, but these terrible scenes of starvation will be
> forgotten by no one who saw them.[53]

Many families were driven to cannibalism, which became so widespread that the government had to print a poster forbidding it. A surprised
American reporter saw one in the Moscow office of a Soviet functionary:

> It showed the picture of a mother in distress, with a swollen child at her
> feet, and over the picture was the inscription: EATING OF DEAD CHIL-
> DREN IS BARBARISM. The . . . official explained to me: ". . . We distrib-
> uted such posters in hundreds of villages, especially in the Ukraine. We
> had to."[54]

The surviving populations of whole villages deemed uncooperative
were loaded onto the soon to be ubiquitous cattle cars and sent to lands in
Siberia that often had no infrastructure whatsoever in place for the new
arrivals, and where thousands more would perish.

In an attitude that would have warmed the hearts of the eugenicists, no
quarter was given to the children of the kulaks, who were considered
"Members of the Family of a Traitor to the Fatherland" and whose "kulak-
ism" was assumed to be inherited.[55] As the famine took hold, parents were

forced to let the weakest children die. Some took them to towns and abandoned them, hoping that someone would take them in:

> A peasant woman dressed in something like patched sacks appeared from a side path. She was dragging a child of three or four years old by the collar of a torn coat, the way one drags a heavy bag-load. The woman pulled the child into the main street. Here she dropped it into the mud. . . . The child's little face was bloated and blue. There was foam round the little lips. The hands and tiny body were swollen. Here was a bundle of human parts, all deathly sick, yet still held together by the breath of life. The mother left the child on the road, in the hope that someone might do something to save it.[56]

Boys and girls would arrive home from school to find that everyone in the house had died. Gangs of these children congregated around the train stations catching birds and cats to eat. They begged and stole, and hoped for handouts. The author Arthur Koestler, observing from his train window, thought they looked like "embryos out of alcohol bottles."[57] The small thieves, when caught, were sent to "children's labor colonies," where their future was not bright. In some stations more humane officials put guarded railroad cars on sidings for them and provided minimal rations of ersatz coffee and bread. In one town, it is estimated, some 3,000 children aged seven to twelve died of starvation in the spring and summer of 1933.[58] They were buried in rough holes. A station worker commented, "This procedure became so common at that time that nobody paid the slightest attention to it."[59]

Activists who began to have doubts about what they were ordered to do convinced themselves that for the sake of "the universal triumph of Communism" it was permissible "to destroy hundreds of thousands and even millions of people, all those who were hindering our work . . . everyone who stood in the way. And to hesitate or doubt about all this was to give in to 'intellectual squeamishness' and 'stupid liberalism.' "[60] Those who had too many doubts were deported or executed along with their targets. There are no accurate figures for child mortality, but Robert Conquest, in his devastating history of the famine, estimates that by the end of May 1933 about three million young children had succumbed.[61]

Despite their heredity, some of the children were useful to the Soviet authorities. Healthy children were indoctrinated on the need to guard the interests and property of the state at all costs. They were shown propaganda films of kulaks burying wheat and murdering the young party workers who had come to find it, and were taught to "seek out and recognize the enemy, who was to be removed forcibly, by methods of economic pressure, organizational-political isolation, and methods of physical destruction." Children who turned in their own parents were extravagantly praised in the Soviet press and given prizes ranging from cash to sets of Lenin's *Collected Works*. A thirteen-year-old who had reported his mother for stealing grain from a collective farm was said to have written a poem on his feats that included the lines "Mother, you do harm to the State; I can no longer live with you." The Reuters correspondent who transmitted the incident to the Western press observed that it was not known whether the mother was stealing the grain "in order to supplement the rations of her children."[62]

Nor were deportation and the destruction of family enough. As Stalin continued his paranoid purging of any opposition to his power, the deported kulaks in Siberia and elsewhere were among the first groups targeted for "the supreme penalty," as they were considered "counter-revolutionary insurrectionists." Quotas setting the number to be executed in each region were established centrally. The total came to 72,000 persons, who were to be chosen by local officials, investigated "in a swift and simplified manner," and then sentenced by extralegal, three-man boards. The timing, funding, and organization of the purge were organized down to the rail transport for the condemned. The utilization of the 167,200 souls sentenced not to death but to further exile and the Gulag, was carefully set out. The families of these unfortunates were "not as a rule subject to punitive measures" unless they were "capable of anti-Soviet actions." But they could not live in "border areas," or most big cities, and would be placed under "systematic observation."[63] Wives and children of "enemies of the people" were routinely arrested and "repressed" so that they would not "spread all kinds of complaints . . . and degeneration." As Stalin put it in his toast at a dinner celebrating the anniversary of the October Revolution in 1937: "We will destroy each such enemy . . . we will destroy his kin, his family. . . . Anyone who by his actions and thoughts—yes, his thoughts—encroaches on the unity of the socialist state we will destroy. To the destruction of all enemies to the very end, them and their kin!"[64]

The Soviet actions were not lost on Hitler, but in his early days in power he could not yet, as Stalin had, simply close off vast territories, destroy dwellings, send in indoctrinated party workers to remove all available food, and by massive starvation and deportation to Siberia rid Germany of its half-million Jews. Indeed, as part of its anti-Bolshevist campaign, the Nazi press had been printing highly critical reports of the situation in Russia.[65] The capability to act as Stalin had would only come later. As the fate of the Gypsies demonstrates, the secret reaches of the soon to be conquered areas to the east of Germany, which would provide the German Volk with the vital *Lebensraum,* or living space, Hitler believed it deserved, would have many uses.

       In the winter of 1933, the possibility of serious danger seemed remote to German Jews, who, like most of the diplomats reporting from Berlin, could not imagine that the extreme acts of the Nazis were much more than "measures which have taken place in the heat of the moment of victory."[66] George Messersmith, the American consul in Berlin, sure that "moderate" elements in Germany would soon prevail, reported on March 25: "There is much reason to believe that the Chancellor, Mr. Hitler, does not approve of the indiscriminate and general action which has been taken against Jews in the Government, in the professions and in business. . . . The Chancellor is said to be aware of the fact that the program of discrimination against Jews, if allowed to continue, may wreck the National Socialist [Nazi] party itself and the present government." Noting that the anti-Jewish acts were detrimental to the "extraordinary good-will enjoyed by Germany in the United States and Britain," he said that "prominent Germans of moderate opinion" believed that the Chancellor "must make a definite statement which will make the Jewish situation known in a sane and clear way to the outside world."[67]

The Chancellor was indeed about to make some "clear" statements, but they would not be "sane" in the view of the rest of the world. On March 29, the *Völkischer Beobachter,* the leading Nazi newspaper, issued instructions for a boycott of Jewish businesses on April 1.[68] This action was blamed in another Nazi journal, *Der Angriff,* on a supposed "campaign of atrocity propaganda inaugurated against Germany" in foreign newspapers, where "lies regarding the alleged sanguinary persecutions of Jews were spread." These lies, it alleged, had led to threats of boycotts of German goods. The German people, they declared, would now "switch from an attitude of defense, and are going to attack. They will hew off the heads swollen with poison of the Pan-Jewish hydra of lies." This rather florid threat was followed in a later paragraph by a more practical one: "If the attempt is made to boycott German goods abroad, the German people will be in a position to see to it that no Jew will find any occupation, that no one will buy anymore from Jews."[69]

The day after the boycott announcement, using the special powers granted him in a suicidal Enabling Act passed on March 24 by the Reichstag, Hitler dissolved the legislatures of the individual German states, thus centralizing power even more in his own hands. Consul Messersmith, though apparently still convinced of Hitler's personal moderation, began to see what was to come:

> The developments have been so rapid and of so momentous a character that as from yesterday a state of crisis exists and it is not possible for anyone . . . not even those who are supposed to be leading . . . the National Socialist movement, to state definitely what will happen tomorrow. . . . It is now evident that the (anti-Jewish) movement has reached an intensity and a diffusion of action which was not contemplated even by its most fanatic proponents, and there is real reason to believe now that the movement is beyond control and may have a bloody climax.[70]

It was one thing to fulminate against the Jews but quite another to define just who they were. That remains a problem to this day, given the human propensity to marry those in proximity, no matter what their religion or race, and to create variants of religions that suit new circumstances. The Nazi definition of Jewry, though always spoken of in racial terms, was not only determined by the anthropological examinations, no matter how pseudo, used for other alien races, but by the declared affiliation of the individual, his spouse, if any, his parents, and his grandparents. This combination of seven or more people led to extremely complex situations and caused much grief to the courts and the burgeoning phalanxes of bureaucrats assigned to deal with Jewish matters. With the passage of the Nuremberg Laws in September 1935, which codified existing anti-Jewish regulations and added many more affecting normal activities, clearer definition of who was a Jew became essential.[71] The problem for the Nazi racial agencies was how to protect the German part of a mixed person's heritage, which might be useful to the state in the form of military service or labor. People with three or four "Jewish" grandparents were no problem. Those with one or two, who were therefore a quarter or half German and were known as *Mischlinge*, were more difficult. To make things worse, many in these categories had married pure Germans or Jews, thus putting their children in still other categories. The basic definition, stated in the First Regulation of the Reich Citizenship Law of November 14, 1935, and continually refined, was as follows:

Jew: A person descended from two Jewish grandparents who belongs to
the Jewish religion or is married to a Jewish person on September 15,
1935, and a person descended from three or four Jewish grandparents.

    Mischlinge of the second degree: Persons descended from one Jew-
ish grandparent.

    Mischlinge of the first degree: Persons descended from two Jewish
grandparents but not belonging to the Jewish religion or married to a
Jewish person on September 15, 1935.[72]

"Belonging" to the Jewish religion did not simply mean membership in
a synagogue, but was based on whether the person had ever regarded himself as a Jew. The *Mischlinge,* though given considerable protection, were
still subject to serious restrictions. Needless to say, even this clarified version of the definition of a Jew did not cover every case, and all sorts of petitions and lawsuits to escape final classification continued to go through the
courts with varying degrees of success.

For those categorized as Jews, an inexorable series of decrees continued to be promulgated. Taking lessons from the segregation laws of the
United States and the colonial powers and harking back to the myriad regulations used over the ages to isolate and exclude Jews, the laws limited
employment, transportation, and shopping. They restricted housing, forbade the use of telephones, denied entrance to public toilets and baths,
and even prohibited the keeping of pets. There was a new rule almost
every day, which put the newly defined victims in ever more miserable situations. The aim was to separate them totally from the pure Aryans. It was
hard to cheat. Every Jew had to carry an identification card indicating his
status, and all other documents, from ration cards to passports, would
eventually include racial classification. The ultimate identifying mark, the
yellow star, of which Hitler originally disapproved, would not be used in
Germany itself until 1941. But this badge was, by then, hardly necessary,
as the Nazi security police had had full control of the central Jewish communal organizations since 1939 and, through them, knew exactly where
most Jews were to be found come the day when any still in Germany
would have to be removed involuntarily.

2. Purging the Unfit

In the cold of mid-February 1941, a scene that might have been taken from the darkest Brueghel painting but for the modern machinery involved, unfolded in the main square of Absberg, a small farming town in Bavaria. As most of the population watched, over 100 "feebleminded" inmates of the Ottilienheim Convent, located right on the square, were loaded into two huge, dark gray buses. The patients, many of whom worked in the local agricultural industries, did not go willingly but were dragged out of the convent one by one. Some of the gathered townspeople wept openly while others made "irresponsible" remarks about their government. The Nazi official reporting this "unrest" noted with disgust that "even some Party members" were among those who cried. He blamed the chaplain of the convent for "arranging" the negative mood in the very Catholic town by having those who were about to be transported take Communion before leaving. The official assured his superiors that the incident would be carefully investigated, but suggested rather curtly that "somehow more tact should be used in the removal of such people, who are to be done away with in the course of the Reich defense."[1] The fact that those who departed on the gray buses would not return was by now common knowledge in this town and many others. The plea for more "tact" would soon be satisfied. But the removal process, begun in 1939, would continue until the end of the war.

By the middle of 1938, great progress had been made in the cleansing of the Reich. Racial examination and classification was well advanced and organized. The Gypsies had been herded into reservations and criminals and political dissidents filled the concentration camps. Thousands of Jews had emigrated, and thousands more from all these groups had been sterilized. But this was not nearly enough. The handicapped, sterilized or not, especially if maintained in state institutions, were a burden on the economy and would be more so in the event of war, which only a few in the Nazi leadership knew was coming very soon. The

Hier trägst Du mit

Ein Erbkranker koftet bis zur Erreichung des
60. Lebensjahres im
Durchfchnitt 50.000 RM.

*A propaganda illustration showing the cost to
healthy citizens of maintaining those with a
"hereditary illness."*

process of purification would therefore have to be speeded up. The most efficient method for ridding the state of the useless handicapped was, of course, death, or more acceptably, "euthanasia."

Consideration of this option was not a bolt from the blue for the Nazis. Prior to World War I, the concept had been studied in many places, but discussion was usually limited to the need to relieve the sufferings of the terminally ill. In Germany, however, the forced triage imposed on mental institutions by the starvation conditions of World War I had led some thinkers to extend the parameters of euthanasia beyond those who were terminally ill to those considered "unworthy" of life.

There was little question of who the victims would be. Thirty percent of the most severely mentally ill patients held in state institutions in World War I had died as a result of drastic reductions of their rations in favor of those who were more useful to society. In 1920, two scientists, Drs. Karl Binding and Alfred Hoche, published a work entitled *Permission for the Destruction of Life Unworthy of Life,* which proposed giving the government the right to kill the comatose and beings "of manifest negative value," a category that was not very clearly defined. The authors argued that mistakes that might be made in these killings should not be considered too serious, as "humanity loses so many of its members on account of error that one more or less hardly counts in the balance."[2] The "balance" was not humanitarian but economic. The learned doctors had carefully analyzed the cost to the nation of each mental patient, and could see no reason to maintain the lives of those who were merely "ballast" in the ship of state.

The idea of legalized euthanasia met with strong opposition in the 1920s. Numbers of German physicians and psychiatrists pointed out the dangers of such a policy, which many felt would open the way to indiscriminate condemnations. They correctly predicted that, if such measures were implemented, anyone sent to an asylum would go in terror, and that the nurses in a place where euthanasia was commonplace would soon become brutalized. The intellectual debate would continue into the 1930s, with the balance tilting ever more toward death as the Depression took hold, but even Hitler did not dare implement large-scale extermination of these useless and "degenerate" citizens until he had the cover of war.[3] It is clear, however, that the issue was on his mind: at the 1929 Nazi Party rally in Nuremberg, Hitler mused out loud that "if a million children a year are born in Germany and 700–800,000 of the weakest people are eliminated the end result might be an increase in strength."[4]

In the postwar trials of those who would eventually run the euthanasia programs, testimony is repeatedly given that shows Hitler's interest in the subject. Hans Heinrich Lammers, chief of the Reichschancellery, who was in daily contact with Hitler, testified in 1961 that Hitler had discussed the euthanization of mental patients in 1933 during planning conferences on the heredity laws.[5]

Karl Brandt, a physician on Hitler's staff, also testified that Hitler had planned as early as 1935 to implement euthanasia measures as soon as war broke out, "since the public resistance which one could expect from the churches would not play such a prominent role amidst the events of wartime." He noted that Hitler had said soon after the invasion of Poland that he wanted to bring about "a definite solution to the euthanasia question" and "gave me general directives on how he imagined it."[6]

There were other, more macabre indicators of preparations. In July 1934, U.S. consulates reported that a law had been passed in May of that year to reduce the red tape involved in cremation and make it "the equal of burial," noting that the legislation had been promoted by an Aryan religious group and that it would "upset the orthodox churches."[7] To prepare public opinion, Nazi speakers were sent forth to lecture professional groups about "the heavy burden upon the nation of those with hereditary diseases," while the SS magazine *Das Schwarze Korps* ran articles reassuring its readers, "A child that is born an idiot has no personality. It would hardly last a year if it were not kept alive artificially. It is even less conscious of its existence than an animal. One does not remove anything from it if one snuffs it out."[8]

By 1938 tours of insane asylums, during which patients were displayed in a sort of freak show, were being given to military personnel and high school students. The students of one school were required to write up their observations for racial hygiene class. They had been well prepared. Few of them omitted to mention the financial burdens to the state caused by the care of the inmates, or their animal-like aspect. Those students who said the patients were not nearly as disgusting or repellent as they had been led to believe, or who wondered if relatively healthy people might not be made worse by being locked up, or who objected to the display of the sick as "exhibition objects," had their papers corrected in red ink and were instructed to reread their racial hygiene texts.[9]

The "general directives" for the "solution to the euthanasia question" that Hitler had mentioned were formulated in yet another secret expert committee, much like the one that had dealt with the Rhineland Bastards. This one would eventually settle on the typically excessive title of Reich Committee for the Scientific Registering of Serious Hereditary and Congenital Illnesses, or Reich Committee for short. Hitler's personal doctor, Theo Morell, was also set to work to study the history of euthanasia back to the nineteenth century. His research included a long-suppressed 1920 report by a Dr. Ewald Meltzer, director of a home for feebleminded children, who had sent a questionnaire to the parents of his patients asking them how, in theory, they would feel about "the painless shortening" of their child's life. To his surprise, a majority of those responding implied that they would not object to such a death for their child, as long as they did not have to make the decision themselves or be told the exact circumstances, because, as one respondent put it, "it is difficult to confirm a death sentence for one's own flesh and blood."[10] Morell's report advised killing the handicapped because their lives were not really lives but terrible animal existences that inspired disgust in others and were expensive for the state. Advocating a more businesslike approach, he noted that "5000 idiots costing only 2000 RM [reichsmarks] each per annum equals 100 million a year. With interest at 5%, that corresponds to a capital reserve of 200 million."[11]

Hitler and his staff were also encouraged to begin a child euthanasia program by petitions from parents requesting permission for euthanasia for critically ill or handicapped newborns. Dr. Brandt testified that just such a letter, received in early 1939, had been the catalyst for the activation of the program. He was sent by Hitler to examine the child, who apparently was blind, lacked parts of limbs, and "seemed to be an idiot." After seeing the child Brandt assured its doctors, who agreed that it would be merciful to end its life, that they would not be prosecuted if they did so. The child was then given a lethal injection.

For Hitler this incident was an indication that the medical community would not be greatly opposed to his long-cherished plan. This would not be true of the churches or the judiciary, for whom euthanasia was still murder. The killing operations in Germany must, therefore, circumvent the judicial system. This time the secret agency involved, which would keep the name Reich Committee, would be concealed within Hitler's personal chancellery, the Kanzlei des Führers, or KdF, and would be run by Karl Brandt and the head of the KdF, Philipp Bouhler. But the information upon which they would proceed and the personnel who performed the acts of euthanasia would be provided by mainstream social agencies.

On August 18, 1939, Interior Ministry health professionals were ordered to register all newborns and children under age three who had specified handicaps. To encourage thoroughness the grassroots reporters were paid 2RM per report. The registration forms were gathered by local officials, who mailed them not to a government agency, but to an anonymous post office box in Berlin, thereby giving the impression that the information was for some private scientific or statistical research project. Once the reports were in Berlin, nonmedical bureaucrats made a first selection. The forms were then sent on to three pro-euthanasia experts, who without seeing the children marked the forms "+" (kill) or "−" (let live). The follow-up on the registrations was very thorough.

One institution, in early 1942, received a letter asking if twelve-year-old Hans K., "who has been in your institution since 25 April, 1941, for hereditary feeblemindedness," could "ever become a useful member of the Volk." The negative reply was a death sentence.[12] Once a child was chosen, the parents would have to be convinced by their local health organizations to release it from home or institution. Special children's wards were set up to receive the condemned children, usually within existing institutions and usually far from cities, which made it difficult for parents to visit. The little ones were not transported in the gray buses. They generally went by train.

Eventually there would be some thirty children's euthanasia wards scattered all over the country. The first one opened in 1939 at Görden, a large hospital complex just outside Brandenburg that became the training ground for doctors sent to handle the euthanasia cases in other centers.

Not everyone was cut out for this work. One asylum doctor, named Hoelzel, when asked to take on euthanasia duties wrote to his superior, Dr. Hermann Pfannmuller, one of the most vicious of the killers, and declined the post. Hoelzel acknowledged that although the "new measures" were "convincing," it was "another thing to carry them out *oneself*, in their final consequence. I am reminded of the difference which exists between judge and executioner," adding that

> as vivid as my desire is in many cases to improve upon the natural course of events, as repugnant it is to me to carry this out as a systematic job after cold blooded deliberation. . . . I yet feel myself somehow tied emotionally to the children as their medical guardian, and I think that this emotional contact is not necessarily a weakness from the point of view of a National Socialist physician. However it hinders me from combining this new duty with the ones I have hitherto carried out.[13]

By October 1939, with the killings moving apace, those running the program had stopped worrying about emotions and had begun to worry about the possibility of being prosecuted for murder. They therefore prevailed upon Hitler to provide some sort of formal authorization. The Führer, aware that such a document would be political dynamite, wrote the following extremely convoluted statement (no two historians translate it the same way) on his personal stationery:

> Reichsleiter Bouhler and Dr. Brandt are charged with responsibility to extend the powers of specific doctors in such a way that patients suffering from illnesses considered to be incurable, may, in the best human judgment and after careful assessment of their condition, be granted a mercy death.

The document was carefully backdated to September 1, 1939, apparently in an effort to associate the killings with the war effort.[14]

On the basis of this vague note, which was also used by Hitler's minions as justification for adult euthanasia, some 100,000 lives would be terminated. Planning was well under way for the adults in yet another secret office, known as T4 after the confiscated villa at 4 Tiergartenstrasse in

Charlottenburg in which it was located. Here, under the direction of SS Sturmbahnführer Victor Brack, also of the KdF, another massive registration system was set in motion and technical problems confronted. The preferred method for killing the relatively small number of handicapped children was with drugs. This was not practical for the tens of thousands of adult patients targeted for elimination. The planners, using nonsensical economic statistics, had set themselves a quota of one patient per thousand of the German population, or about 70,000 handicapped souls, for "disinfection." After considerable discussion, carbon monoxide gas was chosen as the most efficient method. In the fall of 1939, as the German Army poured across Poland, construction and testing (with human beings) of gas chambers and crematoria were begun at the Brandenburg asylum, just down the road from the children's center at Görden, and at the remote Frankenstein-like castle of Graefeneck in Württemberg. Four other centers would be used at various times during the war.

Victor Brack, worried about exposure of the agency, realized that a number of local functionaries would have to be prepared for a sudden jump in death rates and cremations in their jurisdictions. In April 1940, therefore, the German Conference of Mayors was briefed in a secret meeting. After the usual line emphasizing the uselessness, expense, and lack of humanity of those deemed "unworthy" of life, Brack explained that it was necessary to eliminate them for the sake of more curable patients and the war wounded. To do so, the incurables "must be packed into primitive special asylums," where "everything must be done in order to have them die as quickly as possible." It would be necessary to act very cautiously, "for the public must not learn of it. It is difficult above all because of the church, which is absolutely opposed to cremating the dead; a dispute now with the Pope is completely undesirable. It is also dangerous because of the Americans, who could enter the war against us for such a reason." But, he quite mistakenly added, "one can keep the entire problem secret from the population; that is not such a big problem."[15]

As Hitler had foreseen, the fact that the state would take over care of a severely handicapped child was a godsend for some parents. Such was the case for the pregnant mother of Klara E., who, in the absence of her soldier husband, felt unable to cope with the blind, paralyzed Klara plus her four other, healthy children and the family farm. Some parents even asked for euthanasia. But the majority had to be persuaded to relinquish their children, and some actively resisted, often with the collusion of their doctors. This became very irritating to the authorities in Berlin, who, in Sep-

tember 1941, issued a chilling directive in order to stiffen the resolve of
the local health professionals.[16] In no uncertain terms they were told that
it was in the best interest of the *Volksgemeinschaft,* or community of the
people, that children with severe mental problems be given "promising
treatment or be institutionalized." The necessity of treatment could not be
questioned, and had been spelled out in previous directives. Institutionalization, it continued, would free the parents from economic worries and
stress and allow them to take better care of their healthy children. It
would also "clarify" the hereditary characteristics of the child's problem
and "where appropriate" dissuade parents from further procreation. Caretakers, the directive warned, are sometimes not prepared to send a child
away, as they often think they see improvement when, in fact, they are
really only "adapting" to its condition. This, they note, is especially true of
"mongoloid" children, "whose affection, friendliness and love of music
often inspire unrealistic hope in their relatives." Such parents should be
told that "timely" institutionalization was the best for them and the child.

At least one local bureaucrat was not impressed by this loveless broad-
side. The unnamed director of the state health office in Tuttlingen was
ordered to send ten-year-old Gunther F. to the killing ward at Kaufbeuren,
where "the best treatment" and "modern therapies" could be given to him
with "the equipment installed by the Reich Committee." He was told that
"if the parents or guardians make unexpected difficulties, they should be
informed about the respective circulars of the Reich Ministry of the Interior [used as a front organization for communications from the Reich
Committee] in a proper manner." The Tuttlingen director would have
none of this and replied: "As a matter of principle I will not admit children
into the Reich Committee institutions against the will of the parents or the
guardians. For the time being you will consider the case closed."[17]

It is clear that most parents were not suspicious at first. The files of the
institutions are full of letters from mothers wanting to visit, send laundry,
and asking for news. The institutions themselves soon developed public
relations techniques aimed at calming anxiety. In many cases they simply
lied. Letters full of sweet euphemisms such as "your little son" or "your
dear Annemarie" and phrases subtly preparing parents for the coming
decline in the child's condition were sent in reply to inquiries:

> Children who suffer from disturbed development of the kind affecting
> your child always remain mentally retarded. . . . Experience shows that
> 90% of these children fail to grow older because of their susceptibility

to infectious diseases. . . . Should your child become ill we will notify
you immediately. You do not need to worry. We have recently com-
menced a course of medication.[18]

The "course of medication" was, in fact, a big worry. A series of doses of
Luminal was the preferred method of killing children. Luminal depresses
the respiratory system, and the victims, after a couple of days, usually
developed pneumonia, especially if they had been weakened by starvation
rations in the preceding weeks. To speed things up a dose or so of morphine mixed with scopolamine was given at the end. There is considerable
evidence that the children's deaths were not always painless. The Luminal
process and its accompanying suffocating pneumonia often took days.
Some of the more sadistic doctors preferred other methods, such as starvation or electric shock. There is also evidence that the children realized
in their innocent way what was going on: in one institution nurses were
surprised to find them playing something called "the coffin game."

Efforts to remove a child from the custody of the Nazi health authorities once it had been declared "incurable" were seldom successful, but did
occasionally occur. One doctor sniffily noted that "against medical advice"
he had had to give a child back to the "unreasonable father."[19]

The case of Elly O. is more typical. Elly was a cheerful four-and-a-half-
year-old spastic child, described as "euphoric" and "a chatterbox," who
talked to everyone and only cried when faced with "extraordinary situational changes." She was able to repeat long sentences and name most
ordinary articles. She had been taken into a Bonn clinic after her family's
house in Aachen had been bombed and her mother and two siblings had
been evacuated. Two weeks after the bombing Elly's mother wrote to say
that she would like to pick up the child in a week's time, since she was now
able to take care of her again. The clinic doctor, trying to arrange Elly's
release, informed the local authorities that although the child's condition
could not be cured, there was no reason she should not be allowed to
return home. But the authorities refused to release Elly on the grounds
that insufficient care could be provided by her "bombed out and homeless
mother." They recommended, therefore, that the child be sent to another
institution. No effort seems to have been made to check the parents'
accommodations. Elly was kept at the Bonn clinic for two more months
and on March 24, 1944, was sent with nineteen other small patients to the
euthanasia ward at Kalmenhof Hospital in Idstein, near Wiesbaden,
where she died thirteen days later of "pneumonia." The report does not

tell us if cheerful Elly cried much in the course of this "extraordinary situational change."

Elly's father did not believe that the reported cause of her death was correct. Despite the difficulties of wartime travel, he went to Idstein to find the truth:

> I arrived at Kalmenhof and saw first of all a group of children, who I asked about my daughter. The children answered that they knew her, but that she had been fetched and had not come back. . . . I went to the home and looked for a doctor or anyone who could give me precise information on the whereabouts of my child. I found a doctor who told me that she had died on April 7 of pneumonia. Since this explanation did not satisfy me, I demanded exact details. I said that I did not believe my child had died a natural death. They told me that I had better be careful or I would be taken away. When I asked to see the grave of my child I was taken to a cemetery where I saw a number of mounded graves. I was told that one of them was that of my child. When I asked if I could buy some flowers to put on the grave they refused. . . . I was not allowed to speak to the head doctor. I am still convinced that my child did not die a natural death at Kalmenhof.[20]

Parents were, of course, never allowed to be at such children's bedsides when death came. Notification of the final illness usually arrived after the child was dead. Indeed, the mailing of the letters was carefully planned to do just that. Most were also deprived of the comfort of a funeral. Those parents who did manage to arrive before the children were buried were appalled by what they found. One mother found a note in the pocket of her son's clothes that clearly indicated his misery: "Dear Mommy, I will not stay here with these people. . . . I will go my own way. I will not stay here. Come and get me." The boy, not mentally ill at all, but an "asocial" juvenile who had been transferred to the euthanasia ward from a juvenile training camp, had tried three times to escape before he was beaten to death. The death certificate indicated that he had died of "poor blood circulation."[21] Another suspicious father, who was allowed to view his son's emaciated and bruised body, confronted the head doctor and asked to be told the real cause of death. The man pointed to the gold Nazi Party badge in his lapel and said, "What they all die of."[22]

Especially distressing to families was the lack of information. The euthanasia committees, for both adults and children, often did not notify families when patients were moved. Relations would arrive to visit and

find the person gone, with no information as to his whereabouts. The files
are full of desperate letters from searching relatives. The stories all have
tragic endings, none more so than that of a Jewish woman who had stayed
behind in Berlin to be near her institutionalized daughter while the rest of
her family managed to get out of the country. On the advice of the sympathetic director of a local center, she wrote four times to the "asylum"—in
fact an extermination camp—at Chelmno, near Lublin in Poland, to which
the girl had been moved, but her efforts were useless. "Where can I look
further?" she wrote the director again in January 1941. "Perhaps you are a
father, dear Director, and can well understand, that I have spent agonizing
months of sleepless nights worrying about my dear child."[23]

By the fall of 1940 not only the children's relations were upset. On
October 16 a curious dispatch entitled "Mysterious Deaths of Mental
Patients from Leipzig Consular District and the Connection Therewith of
the Black Guard (SS)" went from the American consulate in Leipzig to the
embassy in Berlin. Earlier in the month a vice consul had been asked by
an acquaintance if he had noticed anything odd about a group of death
notices that were appearing in the local papers. The informant told him
that the mother of someone he knew had been institutionalized and had
then been moved with no notice. After weeks of writing letters and
searching, the daughter discovered that her mother was in an asylum at
Hartheim, near Linz. Shortly thereafter, she was told that her mother had
died and been cremated. The ashes would be sent to the cemetery in
Leipzig. When she went to the cemetery to make arrangements, the gar-
dener there exclaimed, "My God, what in heaven's name is going on here:
this is the fifth urn of this nature I have received from Linz today!" The
consul also reported that in the first two weeks of October, twenty-two
very similar death notices indicating sudden death and cremation "near
Linz on the Danube" had appeared in the papers and that the inhabitants
of Leipzig were "stricken with a fear of the far-reaching consequence of
this horrible affair. A feeling of horror and complete insecurity of life has
begun to set in." But, the consul added, "the notices . . . have become so
obvious in wording, containing almost direct accusations, and have
aroused so much attention, that it is felt they will soon be suppressed."[24]
Other American consulates reported similar rumors.

Victor Brack's declaration that it would be easy to hide the killings from
the public had run into reality. The stream of gray buses going to the
killing centers, which were heavily guarded by the SS, and the evil-
smelling smoke emanating from their chimneys was the talk of the surrounding towns. Village children playing games threatened one another

with incarceration in the creepy castles. Rumors that the inmates were being used as guinea pigs for some secret lethal gas spread rapidly and were reported to Berlin. There was more solid evidence too. In March 1941 a nurse who worked in one of the killing centers sent an anonymous letter to the American consulate in Berlin in which she said:

> Unfortunately I am obliged to be the bearer of sad information; our Government is murdering masses of the spiritually ill and other sick persons in experimental stations with poison gas. . . . I assure you that recently not hundreds but thousands have been murdered.

She included addresses of victims' families for verification and ended her passionate appeal with "the expectation that you will do what lies in your power to bring the murderers to justice."[25]

A steady stream of complaints flowed into the Ministry of Justice. Shocked local officials revealed that a Nazi welfare organization was trying to claim public funds released by the demise of large numbers of mental patients.[26] A high-level bureaucrat who had a schizophrenic son wrote, again anonymously, to say that what was going on was "plain murder, just as in the concentration camps," and defiantly continued, "This measure uniformly emanates from the SS in Berlin. . . . For seven years now this gang of murderers defiles the German name. If my son is murdered, woe! I shall take care that these crimes will be published in all foreign newspapers. . . . I shall demand prosecution by the public prosecutor." Obviously believing that the Führer was unaware of the process, as many others did, he added in a postscript, "at the same time I write to Hitler."[27]

The Chief Prosecutor of Stuttgart reported that the city's Guardianship and Probate Court had received some seventy "stereotyped" death notices issued by the killing centers and had become suspicious,[28] while a courageous judge in Brandenburg, Dr. Lothar Kreyssig, unimpressed by the informal note Hitler had written to authorize the euthanasia process, which was shown to him by the Minister of Justice, tried to institute murder proceedings against officials of the program.[29] All this led the Minister, Hans Gürtner, to suggest to the Reichschancellery that since Hitler had refused to publish a law legalizing the killings, despite the fact that one had been drafted by worried officials from a number of agencies, he should "discontinue immediately the secret extermination of insane persons. The recent procedure became publicized so rapidly and widely and not least by the attempted camouflage. . . . It is impossible for our authorities to pretend that the Reich Justice Administration knows nothing of the matter."[30]

Himmler too was getting letters about the goings-on at Graefeneck. One, from a highborn schloss dweller, Frau von Loewis, arrived with a flowery cover letter from a male Nazi friend describing her as a "Nordic goddess descended from heaven" and "an ardent follower of the movement." After saying that his "unlimited trust in my Reichsführer SS" had assured him that Frau von Loewis would not suffer any "unpleasantness" because of her letter, the writer of the cover letter smarmily suggests that "there are certainly things which a man can stand but access to which should not be allowed to a woman. . . . Therefore if we must to-day undertake certain things because we want to fight for the eternal life of our people, things before which a woman would shudder, they must be handled in such a way as to keep them really concealed." In her own letter Frau von Loewis not only expressed her dismay at the open-ended nature of the euthanasia process, but also confirmed that the most awful thing "is the public secret which creates a terrible feeling of unsafety." The matter, she declared, "must be brought to the Führer's ears before it is too late and there *must* be a way by which the voice of the German people can reach the ear of its Führer!"[31] We do not know if Hitler got these messages, but Himmler, noting that "the population recognizes the gray automobile of the SS and think they know what is going on at the constantly smoking crematory. What happens there is a secret and yet no longer one," ordered his men to discontinue operations at Graefeneck.[32]

The gassings and cremations at Graefeneck and Brandenburg stopped, but the killings did not; they were simply slowed down and transferred to other institutions less visible to the public. Nevertheless, resistance continued to build. By the summer of 1940 the churches, whose institutions were responsible for nearly half the disabled in Germany, had become fully aware of the deaths. Pastor Gerhard Braune of the Protestant welfare organization known as the Innere Mission, horrified at an order to transfer twenty-five "feebleminded" girls to one of the killing wards, began an investigation. He succeeded in finding the disguised offices of the Reich Committee and confronted officials there with his evidence. All was denied, causing Braune to send a detailed memo to Hitler, who replied that he could not cancel the program but would make sure that the process would be carried out "more carefully."[33] A few days later Braune was arrested on vague charges by the Gestapo.

Shortly after this effort, another pastoral protest was issued by the Protestant Bishop Theophil Wurm of Württemberg, who wrote an eloquent letter to Minister of the Interior Wilhelm Frick, stating, "The decision as to the time when the life of a suffering human being should end rests with the Almighty God." He emphasized: "It is certainly a source of much grief to parents if one of their children is not mentally intact, but as long as God permits this child to live, they will let it feel all their love." Wurm too blamed the rejection of Christianity on the SS and not on Hitler, who, he felt, had embraced "positive Christianity." And, he continued, "If young people begin to realize that life is no longer sacred to the State, what conclusions will they draw therefrom for private life? Cannot every violation of the rights of another person be justified by saying that the elimination of that person was useful to the person committing the crime? On this sloping plane there is no stopping."[34]

On August 11, 1940, the Catholic bishops also protested, and in December the Vatican decreed that it was not "permissible on the basis of an order by the state authority directly to kill those who, although they have not committed a crime worthy of death, nevertheless cannot be of any further use to the nation and are rather a burden for the nation and a hindrance to its energy and strength."[35]

The only trouble was that most of these protests were not made public, but were politely contained within high government and church circles by officials afraid to rock the boat. Public protest would not take place for eight more months, until the Catholic bishop of Münster, August Count von Galen, angered at the lack of response to the protests lodged via the bureaucracy and by reports of the imminent removal of a large number of "unproductive national comrades" from his own diocese to the killing centers, spoke out in a thunderous sermon on August 3, 1941. After exposing the methodology of the killings, he revealed that he had formally accused the agencies involved of murder.[36] The sermon was read in all the churches of the diocese and soon reached the Allies, who printed thousands of copies that were dropped over Germany by the RAF. Three weeks later Hitler, aware that all cover was blown, ordered that the adult euthanasia program be ended. The publicity was embarrassing, but in fact the program had already eliminated well over the targeted number of 70,000 "lives unworthy of life" at an estimated cost savings of 885 million reichsmarks. The T4 office that ran the program continued to exist under different designations. Its well-trained personnel and state-of-the-art facilities, as we shall see, would soon be expanded and used to "disinfect" a new category of "unproductive" victims, both within the Reich and in the greater privacy of the newly conquered lands to the east. And adult euthanasia, in conditions that can only be described as medieval, would soon begin again, using the more subtle measures of starvation and drugs already employed for the children.

For the young there was no amnesty: the Reich Committee, on specific orders from Hitler, not only continued its operations, but raised its age limit to include teenagers.[37] By March 1943 its parameters would be expanded to take in the perfectly healthy offspring of foreign forced laborers and half-Jewish children from reform schools. The handling of these children was no more gentle than it had been for those who had gone before. Four siblings, Klara, Alfred, Edeltraud, and Amanda Gotthelf, who were sent to the Hadamar Institution, all died within three weeks of "enteritis." The official who had been asked to send them could not believe it:

> These strange casualties disconcerted me so that my scruples could not be put aside even by the official statement of the Hadamar Institution. On the other hand I had to consider the fact that the official statements . . . could not be discussed as unworthy of belief. I would never have succeeded in obtaining a rectification or clarification of the procedures. Nothing else remained to me than to avoid a repetition of such events . . . therefore I personally instructed the heads of our institutions . . . by word of mouth to send no more children to Hadamar under any circumstances.[38]

We do not know if he succeeded in this effort.

It is known that nearly 100,000 children were registered with the Reich Committee, of whom an estimated 5,200 were killed outright. Many more were retained in the institutions for other reasons and died in a less direct manner. Incentives to continue the children's program were high for the professionals involved. The nurses and other technicians received bonuses for each death. Not all the motives were financial. The operatives were sworn to secrecy on pain of death. After the war many would testify that they had felt terrible about what they were required to do, though they clearly agreed that many of the pathetic children in their care were better off dead, but that they had been powerless and feared the doctors who were in charge. The detached sadism of Nurse Wörle, who killed Richard Jenne after the defeat of her Nazi superiors, casts doubt on these often repeated excuses.

For many in the medical profession, the institutionalized children, like Dr. Mengele's twins, were an all too tempting pool of experimental objects useful for research. Proposals were submitted for research on polio, Down's syndrome, and spina bifida. In 1942 one of the doctors on the Reich Committee proudly pointed out that "the Reich Committee children are serving science in two other areas: they make it possible to test the scarlet fever vaccine ... and are available for the extraordinarily important area of immunization against TB."[39]

In a Heidelburg research institute thirty retarded children aged three to thirteen were used in endocrinological experiments for a doctoral dissertation, aptly entitled "Metabolic Endurance Tests in Feebleminded Children," which would be published in 1946. The experiments involved the precise measurement of fluid intake and excretion, necessitating force-feeding of the fluids, which the doctoral candidate, Monika Schneider, admitted, "made the experiment more difficult." Other measurements were procured by drawing blood at frequent intervals, after the injection of large doses of adrenaline and insulin. Alas, the experiments were inconclusive, as the author felt she would need several hundred more "idiots" to be absolutely sure of her results, and noted that one could tell only so much from the living child. All was not lost, however: when the children were shipped off to their assigned killing centers, Dr. Schneider, clearly aware of their fate, followed up with a request that "the entire glandular system" of patient Ditmar K. be returned to her "along with the brain."[40]

Documents show that all of the killing centers were linked to research institutes of some kind, thus nothing went to waste. Brains were especially in demand. Indeed, researchers could order brains from whichever type of handicapped child they wanted. Dr. Carl Schneider, father-in-law of the studious Monika and director of the Racial Political Office of Baden, would peruse the children's dossiers and then have suitable organs sent to him by courier.[41]

Görden, the original child euthanasia institution, was closely linked to the Kaiser Wilhelm Institute for Brain Research in Berlin-Buch. Here Dr. Julius Hallervorden would accumulate a collection of some 600 brains. "If you are going to kill all these people," he is said to have remarked to an American investigator after the war, "at least take the brains out so that the material can be utilized."[42] And they were in fact utilized until 1990 at the Max Planck Institute in Frankfurt. At least thirty-three of the brains were from children aged seven to seventeen from Görden who all died on the same day in October 1940. A witness at a postwar trial testified that these children, plus about sixty-five more, had been sent there "for the express purpose of killing them."[43] The autopsies were done immediately following the executions, which seem to have taken place, en masse, in the adult gas chambers at Brandenburg, just down the road.[44]

Any parent who has taken a child to a routine physical with its usual blood tests knows how frightened even a child held in its mother's arms can be during the ordeal. At least one of the Nazi doctors withdrew from the programs when his own child was born with a birth defect, perhaps having found that one could love an imperfect being. But this sort of humanity seems to have been rare in the eugenically inclined, and acceptance of the concept of the promotion of a pure and superior Aryan race was not much questioned, even when the methodology was felt to be extreme. Hitler, orphaned at the age of nineteen, who admitted his unfitness for marriage and remained childless, did not have to deal with the reality of the emotions of parental love and loss.

3. Increasing the Master Race

Parallel to the Nazis' obsession with purification of the population was their determination to increase its numbers. The loss of millions of young men in World War I and the economic disasters and depression of the 1920s and 1930s had led to a precipitous drop in the German birthrate. The Weimar government had been perfectly aware of this problem, which was common to all of Europe, and had instituted public programs to promote child health and welfare. All sorts of groups campaigned for a renewal of the large family of the nineteenth century. There was the eternal concern that the "best" people were having the fewest children and that the nation was threatened by the supposedly higher birthrate of the Slavic peoples and the godless example of the Communists, who were not fussy about free love or divorce. But the need for lower-class mothers to work in order to support the children they already had, plus the dawn of women's liberation, kept families small. In addition, very large families had become associated in the public mind with the poor and uneducated trash deplored by the eugenicists.[1]

The Nazis were not interested in the traditional moral aspects of producing children. They were only interested in purity and numbers. A large reservoir of racially pure individuals was vital to support their expansionist plans. To this end they issued a series of decrees, welfare directives, and propaganda statements that appeared to promote the return to the large, cozy, old-fashioned family, but in fact aimed to transform it into a hatchery for future Nazi cadres. Their program was doomed from the beginning, for it not only violated every human need and desire and flew in the face of the civil and religious traditions of centuries, but was also economically impossible.

German families of "alien" or "mixed" race were, naturally, excluded from the new programs. Marriage between those of alien race and Aryans had been forbidden by the Law for the Protection of German Blood and Honor one month before the Marriage Health Law was passed in 1935. Those who tried to compromise with the Nazi authorities in order to follow their hearts, even when helped along by sympathetic local officials, rarely succeeded, as the case of Liselotte W., twenty-one, daughter of a completely assimilated family with some forgotten Gypsy ancestors, demonstrates. This technically ideal family, consisting as it did of five boys and one girl, was not informed of its unacceptable genealogy until 1942. The father was a decorated World War I veteran, and one of the sons had by then been killed in the invasion of France. The four other sons belonged to the Hitler Youth. Despite recommendations by the local police that the family be considered "German," the father and sons were threatened with loss of their jobs and sterilization. Liselotte, five months pregnant by an Aryan soldier, went so far as to volunteer for sterilization if she could be allowed to marry her beloved. This request was ignored and the girl was instead jailed for being "asocial." Due to her condition, the prison doctor declared her unfit for work or incarceration in a concentration camp, "as she was within a few months of delivering a child." This opinion, no doubt well meant, was instead a death sentence. Liselotte was deported to Auschwitz, where she died of dysentery shortly before her child would have been born. Her death had one positive effect: her father and brothers were only sterilized and not deported or killed.[2]

Drastic anti-Gypsy measures were one thing, but even membership in the highest social classes of the Reich was no protection from the marriage laws. Wehrmacht Captain Melchior Kuno von Schlippenbach, a graduate of the prestigious Salem boarding school, wanted to marry Ilonka Dudkova, a Czech national. In order to get permission, the young man had to undergo an intense racial examination himself and submit scores of documents, which included "four photos of [his] bride in the nude, one view each side . . . perfectly nude for racial examination." After a "vivid complaint" on his part, the girl was allowed to wear a two-piece bathing suit in the photographs. She was then declared "racially suitable," and in 1942 the couple was duly married and soon had a daughter. While Melchior was off at the wars, Ilonka, again pregnant, moved in with her parents. This violated a special regulation of the Führer forbidding Germans to live with Czechs and was reported to the SS. Ilonka, forced to leave her family home, unwisely moved into the house of the Czech widow of a full-blooded Jew, who also had two children. This, of course, was much worse in the eyes of the racial authorities, who advised Captain von Schlippenbach by letter that they assumed that he himself would disapprove of "your child being reared in the same household with half-Jewish children," and demanded that he move his family elsewhere. The captain rushed to Prague to deal with the situation and was told by the racial authorities that if his wife did not move to Germany and he was killed in action, his children would be taken away from their mother, be given new names, and be put up for adoption by a childless married couple in Germany, as there was otherwise no guarantee that they "would be brought up in the German sense." When von Schlippenbach objected to these remarks, the Nazi official said that he "should have thought these things over before marrying a foreigner; after all, there were enough nice and decent German girls."[3]

The population promotion programs for acceptable couples began innocuously enough in 1933 with a Marriage Loan Plan, which provided low-cost loans to help newlyweds set up housekeeping. For each child the debt was reduced by 25 percent, and was eliminated after the fourth child was born. The drawback was that the mother could not work if she accepted the loan. This was fine with the Nazis, who saw the program not only as useful for promoting childbirth, but also as a solution for the high male unemployment of the time. Because of the no-work rule, use of the loans, especially in rural areas where women traditionally took part in farmwork, was at first slow. By the late 1930s as both the German armed forces and war industries burgeoned, unemployment had turned into a labor shortage and the no-work rule had to be relaxed. By 1939, 42 percent of newly married families were taking advantage of the loans, despite which they continued to average only one child per family.[4]

The loans were only the beginning. Every possible avenue was used to promote having children. Birth control clinics, viewed as Communist strongholds, were closed and penalties for abortion were toughened. Abortions could only be performed to protect the hereditary health of the race, in which case they were mandatory. After 1935, doctors were required to notify race authorities of every suspicious miscarriage, which was then investigated by the police.[5] By 1941 only those of "alien" race could have an abortion with impunity and indeed were encouraged to do so. Enforcement of these laws would become ever more draconian: by 1941 all sales of contraceptives were banned for the pure German. The grounds for divorce were also expanded in favor of reproduction.[6] Infertility, reluctance to have children, or "irretrievable collapse of a marriage" became valid grounds for "no blame" divorces, the idea being that those locked into unhappy marriages were less likely to produce offspring. Child support requirements were made less stringent so that divorced men could better support a new family. These measures led to a divorce boom in 1939, but once again produced no appreciable increase in births.[7]

Everyone felt the pressure. When Albert Speer, then Hitler's favorite architect, first introduced his wife of six years to Hitler in 1934, the Führer, not knowing she was five months pregnant, said, "Six years married and no children? Why?" Speer later recalled that he would have liked "the floor to open so that I could disappear."[8] He did not further disappoint his Führer: by 1943 the Speers would have six children. Martin Bormann, Hitler's closest assistant, outdid them with nine. Goebbels also had six, and Hitler Youth leader Baldur von Schirach, four. But Göring and Himmler, the great promoters of the Nordic race, only had one legitimate child apiece, while Hitler, of course, had none.

The state gave every possible sort of help to acceptable mothers. Poorer women were provided with everything from layettes to baby cereal. Existing welfare organizations were hugely increased and consolidated under the banner of the National Socialist Welfare Organization (NSV). By 1941, a special division called Aid to Mother and Child had set up some 29,000 counseling centers for pregnant mothers and dispatched droves of midwives, home aides, and visiting nurses to help them. Thousands of pregnant women were sent off to special spalike maternity homes for month-long stays to have their babies and recuperate.[9] In addition the National Socialist Womanhood, aided by a myriad of subagencies, sponsored practical courses in mothering and home economics and also urged its six million members to have large families.[10] None of this was altruistic. At the counseling centers the women and children were carefully observed for flaws and educated in Nazi family policy. In the maternity homes, often installed in villas confiscated from Jews, indoctrination classes filled a good part of the day. Before meals grace was said to the Führer. With hands raised in the Nazi salute, the mothers thanked him for their food and intoned, "To thee we devote all our powers, to thee we dedicate our lives and those of our children."

After meals there were folksy songfests and dramatic performances punctuated by warlike singing ("Hurrah, Hurrah to the battle front march we, with weapons, with tents, with helmets and lance, to kill the enemy"). Further procreation was encouraged by lectures on sex, and a volume of "stimulating" literature was given to the girls when they left the homes.[11]

NSV follow-up of the children was extremely careful. As one matron told an American observer, "We keep the children safe for Hitler until the schools take them over at the age of six." Platoons of uniformed nurses made regular visits to the homes of small children, whom they expected to give the Nazi salute and encouraged to play war games so that they could grow up to be "fighters for the Führer." Mothers who discouraged this were reprimanded, and all were under constant pressure to have more children.[12] Special preschool day-care centers were set up across the country for working mothers. These facilities were manned by teachers specially trained by the NSV. The 1936 guidelines published for the centers listed not only obvious activities for the children, but required that they be educated "in National Socialism and service to the *Volksgemeinschaft.*"[13] The premises were, accordingly, festooned with Nazi flags and pictures of Hitler. Furnishings and architecture, whenever possible, were strictly Germanic in style, and uniforms were provided even for six-month-old babies. Here too the children were taught warlike songs with much emphasis on dying for the Führer, whom they must obey in all things. Girls were encouraged to play with dolls and engage in other maternal activities. The tiny boys in one such center in the country near Nuremberg, when asked what they wanted to do for Hitler, declared that they "would eat a lot" and "get strong" so that they could become soldiers and "shoot Frenchmen."[14] The health of the children was carefully monitored as well. Teeth were brushed daily, medical exams were frequent, and both food and exercise were plentiful.

Despite such strenuous efforts, the birthrate rose far too slowly for Hitler's liking and the abortion rate did not decline. To boost the family the Party initiated a series of promotions, some sillier than others. At the 1935 Nuremberg Nazi Party rally Hitler proclaimed that the effort to increase the population was "the woman's battlefield." "Child-rich" families in some localities were given rent reductions and free movie passes. Honor Cards, showing a mother surrounded with small children and emblazoned with the motto "The most beautiful name in the world is Mother," were handed out to all mothers with three or more children under ten. These documents were supposed to get them preferential treatment by certain agencies and discounts at shops. This seems to have been a flop, as neither the local bureaucrats nor shopkeepers seemed to think having a lot of children was a good reason for the unfunded perks suggested by the Nazi leadership. After 1936 various types of bonuses were handed out by the central government. Mother's Day became a national holiday, and in 1938 the Honor Cross of the German Mother was instituted for those who had produced at least four children. Presentation ceremonies for the three million crosses were elaborate, and all members of the Hitler Youth were henceforth required to salute those wearing the medal. By 1940, probably because of the economy and not because of the Honor Cross, the abysmal birthrate of 1933 had nearly doubled, but it still was far below the mythic numbers of the late nineteenth century so passionately desired by the Nazis.[15]

While help for married mothers, no matter how much ideology was included, was generally well accepted, Nazi efforts to protect and encourage single mothers and remove the stigma of illegitimate birth were less successful. The NSV homes did not discriminate against hereditarily correct unwed mothers or their so-called state children, and ran an adoption and foster home service for them. But they did suggest that a single mother should be sterilized after her second child. Hitler, Himmler, and a number of other Nazi theorists privately regarded monogamy and marriage as unnecessary restraints imposed on the increase of population by hypocritical bourgeois morality. This view was, however, not shared by all the Party faithful, most of whom clung to their traditional religious roots. The Nazi theories themselves were confusing. Unwed mothers did not fit in very well with the concept of the *Kinderreich* family nurtured by its Honor Cross mother. Everyone was also aware that the archenemy Communists had sanctioned illegitimacy. Loyalty to the Führer was all very well and good, but changing the ancient view of the unwed mother as immoral or "asocial" and therefore unworthy of being a "German" was another matter. Even respected Nazi race specialists were opposed to illegitimacy on the logical grounds that one could not be sure of a child's purity if its father was unknown. Such children were also popularly thought to be less healthy as well as mentally unstable. Mainstream agencies, for the time being, did little more than give single mothers the polite title of "Frau," tax relief, and equal access to welfare. Still more discouraging was the fact that fathering an illegitimate child remained a court-martial offense in the regular German Army. Even hard-core Nazi formations, especially those limited to women (such as the National Socialist Womanhood, whose leader, Gertrud Schotz-Klinck, patriotically produced eleven children), continued to fire unwed pregnant employees. It was within the secretive bosom of the SS that a more radical experiment would be instituted.[16]

From its inception, racial requirements for membership in the SS had been far more stringent than those for the rest of the population. Aryan ancestry, in some cases, had to be proven back to 1800, and longevity of one's forebears, loyalty, physical vigor, and numerous other characteristics were considered. Such paragons of Aryanism were not supposed to marry just anybody. Even before the Nazis came to power, future SS wives were subjected to the same criteria as their husbands. As of January 1, 1932, on threat of dismissal, no SS wedding could take place without the required certificate.[17] All who were approved were solemnly entered in the Clan Book of the SS. By 1934, SS members were routinely encouraged to marry young and produce at least four children, or, if this was not possible, to adopt hereditarily "worthy" children and raise them "in the spirit of National Socialism." In 1935, with the ostensible aim of promoting this policy, Himmler set up a small organization within the SS Race and Settlement Main Office (RuSHA). Known as the Lebensborn Society, its declared objective was to support SS families that "have many children and are racially and biologically sound." But it also promised to place and take care of unwed expectant mothers who were racially and biologically sound if examinations of the families of both parents showed that their child would be "equally valuable," and to take care of the illegitimate child once born.[18] Himmler knew what he was talking about: despite his fulminations about bourgeois morality, his own two illegitimate children were carefully concealed from the public and his own wife.[19]

Real financing for Lebensborn would come from other SS and Nazi Party funds, but certain categories of senior SS officers were required to join the society and fees were deducted from their paychecks. Membership for the lower echelons was voluntary. In 1939 it remained at a disappointing 8,000 out of a possible 238,000,[20] and only 110 SS *familles nombreuses* were receiving aid from the organization, for the very good reason that despite their leader's urgings, 61 percent of the SS remained unmarried, while the 93,000 who were married had produced only 1.1 children per family. The statistics were not improved by the fact that the background tests required so much investigation that by 1937 there was a backlog of 20,000 marriage applications, or by the totally contradictory regulation stating that selected officers could not marry before age twenty-five.[21] Such minor problems were not of great concern to the SS chief, whose real motivation in founding Lebensborn was to prevent the abortion of Aryan children. Himmler calculated that at least 100,000 "worthy" children, who would otherwise be aborted, could be saved each year if the mothers were provided for. This, he mused, would, in thirty years, be enough to supply an army of 400,000 men and add 832 million reichsmarks to the GNP.[22]

The first Lebensborn home opened in August 1936 at Steinhoring, near Munich. By 1939 there were five more in Germany and Austria. The homes, like the NSV ones, were usually discreetly located in former institutions or villas in suburban or country settings. Basic organization was much like the NSV homes, but the interiors were better appointed and indoctrination far more important. A veil of secrecy hung over the inmates, who were addressed by their first names plus the honorable prefix "Frau" even if they were unwed, which was the situation of approximately 50 percent of the residents. SS doctors responsible for admissions were "bound by secrecy not only by their professional code but beyond that by special oath to the Reichsführer SS," and were expected to "stand up for the honor of expectant mothers" and protect them "from social ostracism."[23] Admission was, theoretically, not easy. In addition to the already complex SS requirements, the candidates had to produce hand-written biographies, photographs, and a sworn statement that the listed father was the real one. The father's identity had to be revealed and acceptable racial data supplied for him. If this was impossible, the mother was rejected.[24] Himmler himself had the final word on admissions. "With the pedantry of a poultry breeder"[25] he pored over the dossiers, and often scolded his confused operatives, who were not always clear about who was "Dinaric" or "Eastern Baltic" (both undesirable racial categories) and whether or not their "racial souls" were as they should be.

Clearly totally ignorant of feminine inclinations, Himmler envisioned that each home would become "a community of mothers" where all would be equal and happily learn Nazi ideology. It was hoped that after indoctri-nation classes on such stirring subjects as race theory, the mothers would sit around and discuss the ideas in *Klatsches*. This was, alas, seldom the case. Nor did the community idea work well. The married mothers did not wish to associate with the unmarried ones, and wives of higher SS officers wanted perks such as single rooms and exemption from kitchen duty. Men were allowed only in public areas and bedtimes were early. The general atmosphere was more that of a very strict boarding school or even a reform school than a cozy club. Food was plentiful, stodgy, and the source of many complaints from the mothers. The menus were personally vetted by Himmler, who was big on potatoes and sunflower seeds and even sent around a recipe for oatmeal, which he ordered served every day at break-fast, having heard that it was good for the nerves.[26]

Schedules were inflexible and the women under constant observation for physical and attitudinal weakness, both grounds for expulsion, despite which some of the ladies boldly declared that they were not "birth machines" and should not be treated as if they were "in Dachau." Emo-tional outbursts were not taken lightly. One mother, who had worked for the SS in Russia and horrified the other women by telling them of the mass killings of Jews and their babies that had taken place there, was immediately thrown out.[27] Secret dossiers, filled out by home officials, were kept on each mother and child and, stamped top secret, sent on to Himmler himself, which earned them the name Reichsführer Question-naires. The SS leader divided the families into four categories: the women in Group I, the most desirable category, were often employed by Lebens-born or other SS agencies, while those in Group IV were expelled. The criteria for retention in the program at this stage were even less scientific than those used for admission. "Worldview" and "character" were given the same weight as race and health. Frau Else W. was described in her file as "quiet, restrained and smart" but lacking in "leadership qualities" and "energy." She was criticized for complaining a lot during her pregnancy and delivery, and it was noted that her happiness at having a child was overshadowed by various "groundless" complaints over "alleged" physical problems. Luckily for Else, a thirty-six-year-old first-time mother who very well might have had a tough pregnancy, her subsequent report cards improved and she was kept in the program.[28] But many another mother and child were ejected on the basis of such observations.

Babies born in Lebensborn homes were not registered with the local civil authorities and therefore had no recognizable "place of birth." Those who were accepted became wards of the SS, which set up a special guardianship office for their support.[29] This led to dreadful complications with the mainstream children's agencies, and many normal routes to medical care, education, or welfare were closed to Lebensborn children, as they were not listed in any known jurisdiction. The problem was remedied in part by the establishment of official birth registers within the homes and the use of false cover addresses. The SS even went so far as to establish false identities, and actively supported elaborate deceptions. The headmistress of a German school in occupied Holland became pregnant. She was transferred to Germany under a false name. At term she had the baby at a Lebensborn home, where it remained while she returned to Holland. After a time she "adopted" the child and it was sent to her but retained the false surname.[30] Rejected mothers and children, whose birth certificates were equally baffling to lower-level bureaucrats, did not have the dubious support of this system and faced terrible difficulties in the real world.

Despite all the promotion of motherliness, it was the child that was important to Himmler. The babies were kept in nurseries separate from their mothers under the watchful eyes of teams of nurses, who proudly reported that diapers were changed six times a day. This was not just a matter of efficiency. Under the close supervision of the nurses, an "unworthy" child could be immediately identified. If the defect was not too serious, mother and child were simply expelled. Otherwise both parents were liable to sterilization and the child was sent to an institution and an uncertain future.[31] The children were taken to the mothers for breast-feeding, which was compulsory but was often resisted by mothers wanting to pre-

Babies taking the air on the terrace of a Lebensborn home.

serve the contours of their bosoms. SS pediatric theory held that children did not remember anything up to the age of two and could be kept in "collective" situations without detriment until then. After two, family life was considered essential, and if the mother could not support her child when it reached that age, the child was sent to a foster home.

Accepted children were made true members of the greater SS community in a naming ceremony that was essentially a bad parody of the traditional baptismal rite. The ceremony was performed with high drama. In one home, the room in which the event took place not only boasted flowers, laurel branches, Nazi flags, and a bust of Hitler, but also included a portrait of the Führer's mother. All the staff, residents, and often a few relatives of the child were invited. SS officers chosen as "godfathers" (Himmler himself if the child was born on his birthday) accompanied the mother and child. The celebrant, usually the director of the home, gave a little homily, making clear that the concept of original sin, as well as the teaching of the Church that unwed motherhood besmirched a woman, should be rejected as "un-German." After a musical interlude, the celebrant asked the "German Mother" if she promised to bring up her child "in the spirit of the National Socialist worldview" and the "godfather" if he would supervise the child's education in the ideas of the "SS-Clan." Once these assurances were given, the director held an unsheathed SS ceremonial dagger over the child and said: "I take you into the protection of our clan and give you the name so-and-so. Carry this name with honor!" The names suggested were archaic Nordic ones such as Freya, Gerhild, or Sigurd, and were not popular. Many mothers quietly chose to skip the naming ceremony and secretly baptized their children later on.[32]

All Himmler's strenuous efforts were, in the end, insufficient to make illegitimacy acceptable to German society or even to the majority of the SS, who were not enthusiastic about adopting or taking Lebensborn children into foster care. Locals employed at the homes, though glad of the abundant food and adequate pay, did not much respect the unwed mothers, an attitude exacerbated by the rule that employees could be fired if they found themselves in a similar situation, though they were often allowed to go to a different home to give birth. Even SS doctors and nurses took posts at the homes only as a last resort and felt stressed by the constant need for deception. Rumors of "stud farm" activity and other sinister goings-on were rife but untrue. Such implications appalled the essentially prudish Himmler, who also quailed at the thought of artificial insemination, which he feared would water down Aryan strength. Still, the homes with their assurance of secrecy were true havens for many desperate women, and, in the end, a large percentage of the mothers managed to keep their children. Enrollment remained low until the war was well under way, when the homes, in most cases located far from the constant bombing and well provided with food, had great appeal. It is estimated that about 5,000 illegitimate babies were born at Lebensborn homes in Germany between 1935 and 1945—rather fewer than the hundreds of thousands Himmler had envisioned.[33]

The advent of war led to an upsurge in procreationist propaganda quite separate from Lebensborn. But as soldiers went off to battle and possible death, their wives and lovers became less enthusiastic about having children who might be orphaned. To counter this trend, Rudolf Hess, the Nazi Party's deputy leader, went public and let it be known that the Party was prepared to assume guardianship of war orphans, legitimate or not, noting in a highly publicized Christmas letter to the pregnant unwed fiancée of a soldier who had been killed that "the highest service a woman can render to the country is the gift of racially healthy children for the survival of the nation."

This declaration was taken up by SS publications, which not only agreed, but also promoted the idea that soldiers heading for the front should leave an "heir" behind. A public furor ensued, with strong negative reaction from both the Catholic Church and the Wehrmacht.[34] Even Himmler had to backpedal, and in a long and defensive new proclamation said that his earlier statements had been "misunderstood." He had not meant that SS men should try to seduce ladies whose husbands were off at war. This indeed was an insult to German womanhood. But, he hedged,

> even should one man out of a population of 82 million have the baseness or the human weakness to approach a married woman, there are still two prerequisites necessary for seduction: the one who does the seducing and the other who lets herself be seduced. We do not believe it is unethical to approach the wife of a comrade but that the German woman herself is probably the best guardian of her marriage.[35]

And, of course, her offspring would be taken care of should the father, legal or otherwise, succumb. Despite the protests, the genie was out of the bottle, and the number of illegitimate births rose immediately. The SS, having launched its campaign, was not deterred by controversy. Quite the opposite. As the war expanded into the vast reaches of the Soviet Union and tens of thousands died, its exhortations only increased:

> After the victory over Soviet Russia, German soldiers will have to protect the whole of Europe against any invading armies. . . . In the end, it will be the German mothers, who, as equal victors, will stand alongside the generals . . . German mothers, who presented their people with sons in sufficient numbers to make victory possible.[36]

Indeed, the Nazi press declared, "A girl who shirks her highest duty is a traitor, just as much as the soldier who abandons his post." American diplomats monitoring the German press from Switzerland reported numerous ads such as the following in the *Süd-deutscher Sonntagspost*:

I am a soldier, 22 years old, tall, blond, blue-eyed; before offering my life for the Führer and the Fatherland, I should like to associate with a German woman, to whom I would leave behind a child as heir to German fame.[37]

By January 1944 the German mothers did indeed stand beside the generals, not in victory, but in the horror of loss. Despite all the incentives, total war had caused the birthrate to plunge once again to its 1933 low. But Hitler was not deterred in his population planning. In thoughts recorded previously by Martin Bormann at the Führer's Eastern Front headquarters in a remote area of East Prussia, as some 73,000 of his troops, which by now included thousands of teenaged German boys, faced imminent death in the Ukraine, the beleaguered Nazi leader had said that although he was sure that the war would still be won on the battlefield, it was clear that it would be lost on the population front. Estimating that three to four million women would have been widowed or remain unmarried after the war, Hitler proposed that, despite this, they be persuaded to have as many children as possible. Convincing them would require a great deal of "education," as women often became "fanatical in their virtue" once they were married. The "education" would have to await victory, since "not every soldier forthwith would desire that in the event of his death his wife or his betrothed should beget children by another man." But once the war was over, and the husbands and lovers safely dead, the negative-sounding word "illegitimate" would have to be eliminated from the German language. The fact that many famous men had been illegitimate should be emphasized. Monogamous marriages based on love and compatibility should, of course, be encouraged, and children should bear their father's names, but the state should also encourage "marriage-like relationships" and provide shelter and food for illegitimate children. The number of boarding schools run by the NSV should be greatly increased to "help" the mothers of such children, especially as "the best and ablest ones" were for the most part "wild boys and cannot be controlled by their mothers alone." It was not until paragraph 28 of this document that Hitler went completely beyond anything previously proposed by declaring that "by special application a man should be able to enter a marriage relationship not only with one woman but also with a second, the second woman as well as her children also taking his name." This arrangement too would be supported by the state, if necessary: the funds would come in part from an extra tax on bachelors.[38] All this, declared the man who had decimated his nation, must be done so that the lives of the dead would not have been given in vain.

4. Education for the New World Order

In Nazi ideology, as in all extremist thought, indoctrination of the rising generation was crucial. The hours spent at school were captive hours that, ideally, would be controlled by the state. Here the child could be weaned from his family and fed National Socialist principles. The Nazification of the German schools did not happen overnight, and would, in fact, never succeed entirely, because the process was not limited to racial purification, but aimed at a complete reorganization of the school system and a transformation of the intellectual standards of the nation, efforts that were tacitly resisted by a considerable number of educators.

Purging the schools of racially and physically undesirable students and teachers and instilling racial awareness was only one part of the Nazi plan for education. Once convinced of the superiority of his race, the young German must be prepared not only to increase and defend it, but to provide it with new territories by conquest. It would not be enough to hate domestic enemies. The countries that had punished Germany in World War I must in turn be punished. Enclaves of Germans all over the world must be made aware of their racial origins and rescued by their brethren in the Reich. Hitler had discussed such a struggle at great length in his aptly named *Mein Kampf,* which is a call to battle for German youth. In Hitler's view, education must, above all, provide a physically strong citizenry able to respond to a "really great spirit" (which, one presumes, refers to Hitler himself) as opposed to "physical degenerates," too weak in will to "follow the lofty flight of such an eagle." The development of mental abilities and scientific schooling was secondary to the "promotion of will power and determination, combined with the training of joy in responsibility." Further, the proper formation of children was "not an affair of the individual, and not even a matter which primarily regards the parents," but "a requirement for the self-preservation of the nationality, represented and protected by the state." The German people, which in Hitler's view lay "broken and defenseless, exposed to the kicks of all the world," needed to imbue its "young national comrades" with the conviction that they were "absolutely superior" to others.

Nazi education would not end with secondary school, but would continue in the "post-school period" and be "a preparation for future military service," which, when successfully fulfilled, would allow the child to receive two documents: "his citizen's diploma, a legal document which admits him to public activity, and his health certificate, confirming his physical health for marriage."[1] What the exact fate of Aryans unable or unwilling to complete this process might be was not yet explained.

In practical terms, Hitler's proposals were a clear blueprint for the creation of a self-renewing reservoir of youth pre-indoctrinated and physically trained for military service. Intellectual pursuits and long-term study, especially in the humanities, did not fit into this program. In order to get the young into government-controlled service as soon as possible, it would be desirable to shorten the time spent in secondary school and severely limit the number of students admitted to universities. Such a program would also benefit the German economy, devastated like so many others in the Depression, by reducing the number of "unemployable" university graduates, who represented a "dangerous intellectual proletariat." Students would be forced to enter the workforce and become wage earners at a younger age, and, it was thought, would marry earlier and begin producing more little Aryans for the Fatherland.[2]

Implementing these reforms would be an enormous undertaking. Although admiration of the military and resentment at the nation's treatment after World War I was strong in Germany, and its teacher force was conservatively inclined, the complete transformation of educational standards in Germany's traditionally rigorous schools was a delicate subject. Even the most ardent Nazis were often also alumni of proud institutions and were dedicated, as alumni always are, to preserving their traditions.

The German school system, like that of most European countries, was made up of a complex array of class-based and denominational schools controlled in 1933 by private interests, local governments, and religious entities. Religion was taught in all schools, whether they were run by churches or not. In the secular schools, each denomination, including Judaism, had its own religion class. In 1926, a law had been passed requiring students of all backgrounds to be grouped together for the first four years of school. There the standardization ended. From then on the children were divided into two tracks: those who would leave school for the workforce at age fourteen, having completed eight years of school, and those who would continue on for five more years to finish secondary schools. These were in no way uniform, and parents could send their children to more than sixteen types of schools, from Catholic to Jewish to vocational to highly intellectual and classical. Such diversity did not please the Nazis, who particularly disliked the denominational schools, which would become one of the first elements to succumb in the Party's slow but relentless drive to eliminate the churches altogether.

Hitler was well aware of the power of the churches and of their hold on the populace. Like the Jewish community, the Christian church hierarchies could not at first comprehend that their destruction was the Nazi aim, and they not only cooperated with the new regime but, in the early years, supported it strongly, often rivaling their new government in their fervid patriotism, anti-Communism, and anti-Semitism. Yet it soon became apparent that there was to be only one religion in the future Reich and that it would not be Christian. Belated and courageous resistance in the fatally divided Protestant denominations was ruthlessly suppressed. Hitler's 1933 Concordat with the Vatican was soon violated, and in March 1937, the repressions in Germany led Pope Pius XI to issue a cryptic encyclical entitled *With Burning Sorrow,* which warned of "destructive religious wars . . . which have no other aim than . . . extermination."

Hitler could not with impunity take all the churches away from the millions of committed worshippers, especially in heavily Catholic Bavaria, but he could begin to take their children away from the churches by gradually closing the parochial schools and phasing out the traditionally required religion courses and activities in the secular schools. Teaching staff was reduced and religion grades were put at the bottom, instead of the top, of report cards before being deleted altogether. School prayer was made optional in 1935. Soon crucifixes were banned from classrooms, and in 1938 even that old standby the Christmas Pageant was forbidden.[3] After strong protests in some jurisdictions, the crucifixes were put back, but by 1941 religious instruction for children over fourteen had vanished from all but the Jewish schools. In the same year the Catholic kindergartens, the last remnant of the parochial system, were closed.

There were belated protests from the German pulpits. Catholic bishops, gathered at a meeting in Fulda in 1941, exhorted parents to become the religious teachers of their children for "the home of any Christian family must become a small house of God." And Bishop Clemens, Graf von Galen of Münster, warned parents of the possible subversion of their children at school:

> What do they hear in the schools to which nowadays all children are forced to go without regard to the wishes of their parents? What do they read in the new schoolbooks? Have them show you, Christian parents,

the books, especially the history books of the higher schools. You will be horrified at the lack of regard for historical truth with which the attempt is made to fill the inexperienced children with distrust of Christianity and Church, yes, with hatred of a belief in Christ! . . . Let your parental household, let your parental love and loyalty, let your model Christian life be the strong, tough, unshakably firm anvil which receives the fury of the enemies' blows, which strengthens the still weak powers of the children again and again.[4]

The bishops' fears were well founded. In the fall of 1941, the American representative to the Holy See noted that the Vatican Secretary of State, referring to Poland and Russia, where the Church had virtually ceased to exist, had "drawn a very gloomy picture of the present situation of the Church in occupied territory and felt that it would only grow worse in future."[5] That the same fate awaited the German Church was made clear in almost simultaneous cables to Washington from Berlin and Zurich. The Berlin embassy reported that the Papal Nuncio had received copies of a manuscript by Nazi theorist Alfred Rosenberg entitled "Culture and Religion in the Third Reich," which proposed that all priests be athletic Nazi officials. They would be required to marry, as celibacy "robs the population of new blood." The document also advocated "the complete abolition of Papal power in domestic politics" and indicated that the new "Reich Church" would be headed by the Führer.[6] These ideas were augmented in the Zurich cable, which reported on a radical thirty-point program for the "National Reich Church." The new entity would have only one doctrine, "race and nation," and was determined to "exterminate irrevocably . . . the strange and foreign Christian faiths imported into Germany in the ill-omened year of 800." All church property would be taken over by the state, and the present clergy, "who only lie . . . to the German nation, goaded by their love of the position they hold and the sweet bread they eat," should be removed. The Bible would be burned and replaced by *Mein Kampf,* and every German should "live and complete his life according to this book," which would also be the only adornment on the altars. The altars, oddly enough, would be retained in the old churches. God could be acknowledged, but there was not to be any "unworthy" kneeling or Communion. The new religion would not be forgiving: "The National Reich church does not acknowledge the forgiveness of sins. . . . A sin once committed will be ruthlessly punished by the honorable and indestructible laws of nature and punishment will follow during the sinner's lifetime." Last but not least,

Point 30 required that on the day of foundation of the new church, "the Christian cross must be removed from all churches, cathedrals and chapels within the Reich and its colonies" and must be "superseded by the only unconquerable symbol of Germany," the swastika.[7]

These fantastic changes lay in the future, and the Catholic Church, survivor of centuries of similar assaults, bulwarked by tradition, was never in serious danger. Though some of the highest Nazi officials substituted the new "naming ceremonies" for traditional christenings, others did not: even Hitler counted Göring's daughter among his many old-style "godchildren." And to the end, many an altar boy covered his Hitler Youth uniform with a surplice during Communion. But basic curriculum requirements and the appointment of personnel in the denominational schools were already in the purview of the state, and it was in these areas that Nazi control would immediately be felt.

Even before 1933, there had been incidents that gave a preview of the coming purge of the teacher corps. In May 1932, Nazi youths in Party uniforms (which were forbidden by Weimar dress codes), elated by the success of their Party in a by-election, hung a swastika flag over their Berlin school in expectation that Hitler would be called to power. After requests by faculty members to remove the flag were ignored by the pro-Nazi janitor, one of the teachers, a Jewish war veteran who had lost an arm in battle in 1917, climbed across the roof and, applauded by all, pulled the flag down. His glory was short-lived. After hearing complaints from the Nazi youths, the school's director, to the outrage of the great majority of his students, decreed an investigation and suspended the teacher.[8]

A year later such an investigation would no longer be necessary. In early April 1933, the Law for the Restoration of the Professional Civil Service was promulgated. The first of hundreds of anti-Jewish laws that would be enacted during the twelve years of the Third Reich, this one required that all "non-Aryan" employees of the government, which included teachers, "retire." In many jurisdictions the existing educational bureaucracy was replaced with Party loyalists, and committees of three teachers (a favorite Nazi format), which were soon dubbed "Murder Committees," were set up to investigate the racial background and political leanings of their peers.[9] Enforcement was frequently applied without warning. A teacher arriving at school one day would simply be notified that he could no longer go to his classroom. These abrupt dismissals were often a shock to students and victim alike. As one teacher recalled:

There was nobody to say goodbye to, because everybody else had gone to the classroom.... In the afternoon ... colleagues, pupils, their mothers came, some in a sad mood, others angry with their country, lovely bouquets of flowers, large and small in their arms. In the evening, the little house was full of fragrance and colors, like ... a funeral, I thought; and indeed, this was the funeral of my time teaching at a German public school.[10]

Jewish teachers such as this one were not the only ones purged. Anyone suspected of leftist or overly religious leanings could be fired, sometimes in humiliating conditions. Those who managed to stay on had to sign a declaration that "neither by written nor spoken word had they said anything publicly against National Socialism and its Führer."[11] In one top Berlin school it was reported that "an old teacher was chased from the school with a mob of children hooting behind him."[12] In the elite Grosse Schule Gymnasium in Wolfenbuttel, a popular Protestant religion teacher was removed for persisting in teaching Luther's catechism and the Scriptures instead of the doctrines of the Nazi "German Christian" Church. His replacement's "religion" class, which dwelt heavily on *Volkisch* ideology, was declared an elective and was so thoroughly boycotted that it had to be canceled. Furious Nazi authorities ordered an investigation, expelled some of the dissenting students, and availed themselves of the opportunity to fire the school's revered headmaster (who had managed for some time to circumvent their sillier directives) on charges of "failing to prevent a church instigated conspiracy."[13]

Even for patriotic and politically correct teachers, who were in the great majority, the first years of Nazism were confusing indeed. Basic curriculum requirements had always been set by the state in order to guarantee equal preparation for the diploma, but the various schools and localities had had great leeway in their choices of subjects, textbooks, and religious instruction. Individual teachers tried to deal as best they could with the extremely fragmentary and illogical instructions and prohibitions emanating from both Berlin and their local Nazi governments, which might suddenly issue a directive condemning the German icon Goethe for being too international and liberal, or in an arbitrary fit of rather impractical chauvinism eliminate the teaching of French in Karlsruhe, which lies right on the French border.[14] Other pronouncements, such as the following guidelines for history teachers, were simply too ridiculous to swallow, and were even condemned by Propaganda Minister Goebbels:

> The superior Egyptian culture was the result of the influx of Nordic
> Hittites. The Nordic Indians, Medes and Persians created the history
> and culture of Asia. . . . The ancient Greeks with their superior civiliza-
> tion originated from Germanic Central Europe, and Grecian civiliza-
> tion deteriorated when democracy was introduced into the country.
> This was due to the fact that the inferior southern races intermingled
> with the Nordic master race. . . . The Nordic blood injected into
> decayed Italy created the High Renaissance. . . . International influ-
> ences and the influx of foreign elements have retarded German
> progress, contaminating German blood.[15]

Coordinated directives for the schools were slow in coming, due, in
great part, to a struggle within the Nazi leadership over who would control
the educational system. As in every field, the teachers were required to
join a central, government-controlled organization, the German Teacher's
League. Alongside this umbrella organization existed more extreme Party
groups, including the National Socialist Teacher's Union, while certain
preexisting organizations, such as the upscale Congress of German Philologists, continued to function.

The confusion was resolved on May 1, 1934, with the creation of the
federal Ministry of Education under the direction of Bernhard Rust, Education Minister for the state of Prussia, a former teacher who in pre-Hitler
days had been fired for political activity and rumored mental instability.
During the summer and fall of 1934 a barrage of directives began a more
coordinated transformation of the schools. More Nazi texts became
required reading. Elected parents councils and faculty advisory groups
were abolished in favor of the Führerprinzip, or "leadership principle,"
which would soon rule all government organization and which put complete control of school affairs in the hands of the headmasters, who were
naturally appointed from among the Party faithful. Saturday classes
were to be given over to Nazi Party and Hitler Youth activities. Proposals
were floated for an extension of the summer vacation, which would, as we
shall see, allow the young even more time for such programs. Speakers
were sent forth to the teachers organizations to promote the new ideas.
On October 28, 1934, the secondary school teachers belonging to the
Congress of German Philologists were informed that

> it will no longer be tolerated that anyone speak against Germany.
> Within the scope of that which is national, and in the name of that
> which is social, we shall clearly and unequivocally permit every source
> of energy, every genius, particularly in the field of science, to develop

itself completely and freely. . . . Nevertheless, the people and State are in complete control, and we cannot deviate from this even if objective science should be the theme of discussion.[16]

In another meeting one speaker repudiated purely objective science that "did not adopt a definite attitude," while another stated outright that the "aim of higher institutions of learning" was to train the "political fighter for Adolf Hitler's Germany."[17]

To back up these theories, the Minister of Education showered the schools with helpful pamphlets and teaching instructions. Grammar teachers were given lists of suggested essay titles, such as "Adolf Hitler, the Savior of the Fatherland" or "The Renewal of the German Racial Soul." These measures were not at first taken very seriously by many teachers, who often ignored the new academic offerings and continued to use the classics or taught the new matter with obvious sarcasm. Even those who were willing to go along with the new ideology were unsure just how to introduce the "Nazi spirit" into math class or whether to present Charlemagne as a hero or a traitor to Germanism. In Catholic areas crucifixes were left on the wall next to the obligatory portraits of the Führer, and many instructors did not give a quite proper Nazi salute. One popular teacher greeted his students daily as follows:

> He entered our classroom, walked to the wooden map holder that stood in the front corner by the window, raised one of its arms until it pointed toward the ceiling, saluted it silently with his own raised arm, then turned to us, smiled and said: "Good Morning, boys, sit down." There was no German salute for us, no "Heil Hitler," in his classroom and we knew exactly what risks he took.[18]

Education Minister Rust could not, at this early date, simply fire every recalcitrant teacher and still keep the schools going. It was clear that a new cadre of uniformly trained Nazi teachers would have to be provided. This was fiercely resisted by the more elite teachers, but Rust plowed ahead. In late 1934 he ordered education authorities in the various states to move teacher training colleges away from the established university centers, deemed "too intellectual," to more bucolic locations, where the students could be indoctrinated without interference and would presumably benefit from contact with the pure German peasantry. In addition, special vacation camps were to be established, where present and future teachers would be given courses on the principles of National Socialism and be forced to participate in programs emphasizing "military sports" and "a sense of community." This, of course, had little appeal to old-line teachers, and observers of the German scene reported in the spring of 1935 that neither idea had been generally implemented in the provinces.[19]

But while individual teachers could run their classes as they liked, they could not stop the predominance of "approved" texts. The racially oriented history themes advocated by Minister Rust were backed up by "geopolitical atlases" of Germany showing the various expansions and contractions of its tribes and principalities, the "encirclement" policy that forced Germany into World War I, the resulting loss of colonies, and the nation's "enslavement and mutilations," all illustrated with cartoonlike graphs showing the economic hardships caused by Germany's postwar reparations payments. Even more lurid maps, festooned with warlike symbols, showed the Reich's military weakness vis-à-vis its neighbors. All this was followed by detailed charts showing the enclaves of German settlement in Eastern Europe and by graphs that revealed Germany's declining birthrate in relation to other races and predicted that by 1960, Slavs would outnumber Germans by nearly two to one. Despite this imbalance, another graph titled "Overpopulation in Germany—Lack of Inhabitants in the East" somewhat confusingly informed the student that Germany's population density was fifteen times that of the Soviet Union.[20] Articles in the amusement sections of newspapers backed up these ideas. In the NS Kurier for Württemberg and Hohenzollern, a jolly picture urged boys and girls to clip out and collect maps and pictures of monuments in areas "previously controlled by Germany." These included the cathedral of Strasbourg in France and buildings in Upper Silesia, which "with approximately 1 million inhabitants went to the Poles and with it a flourishing coal and iron industry."[21]

The American diplomat who transmitted this information noted that the idea seemed to be to "kindle the feeling of revenge in the German people." Part of the revenge was aimed at the United States, characterized as a "leaderless and democratic" mongrel society made up of "European rejects" mixed with Negroes and Jews, which was now the richest nation in the world but which would soon succumb to labor troubles and racial strife.[22] The prediction was backed up by heavy coverage in the Nazi press of the spate of vicious lynchings of American blacks.[23] In case the kids didn't read the papers, leaflets on population issues appeared regularly in people's mailboxes. Writing thirty years later, Melita Maschmann still remembered what the colorful pamphlets looked like:

> I must have been still at primary school the day I pulled a map out of our letter box which pleased me because of its gaiety. The countries of

Europe stood out from one another in bright colors and on each country sat, crawled, or stood a naked baby. I showed the map to my
father . . . he explained to me that each of these children was a symbol
of the birthrate of the country. The German families had on average far
less children than, say, Polish families. That was why only a frightened
little girl sat on the patch of blue that meant Germany. On the yellow
patch, just next door to the right, a sturdy little boy was crawling on all
fours aggressively in the direction of the German frontier. "Look at the
boy," said my father. "He is bursting with health and strength. One day
he will overrun the little girl."[24]

The indoctrination was not limited to history and geography. Familiar
math books were replaced with such titles as *Aerial Defense in Numbers*
and *National Political Application of Algebra*. Even the dreaded word problem was adapted to the new ideology:

An airplane flies at the rate of 240 km per hour to a place at a distance of
210 km in order to drop bombs. . . . When may it be expected to return
if the dropping of bombs takes seven and one-half minutes?[25]

Physics and chemistry classes dwelt on aeronautics, calculating missile
trajectories, and toxic gases. Grammar books no longer asked pupils to
parse sentences or pluralize innocuous phrases full of grandmothers and
dogs, but used examples filled with innuendo, like this one on the prefix
"in": "Example 53: If the German people remain unified they will be
invincible, incomparable, inimitable, indomitable. . . ."[26]
The most elementary reading texts had a military air. One, entitled
Rhineland Children, ended its chapter on vowels with these stirring verses:

> Listen to the drums, boom, boom, boom—
> Listen to the trumpets, tateratata!
> Come on, clear the camp![27]

Even the fairy tale was put to work as a "preparation for the struggle for
existence." Teachers, who might not have thought of this themselves, were
instructed, in a volume entitled *Volk und Führer,* to select tales "in which
combative contrasts emerge most clearly" and in which "the boy must
be strong; a German child must be faithful and true . . . faithfulness is
stronger than death." The fairy tales, of course, had to be Aryan and not
the narratives of "primitive exotic peoples." One helpful text even provided the proper interpretation of *Cinderella,* giving a new slant to the

Wir wol len un ſer Haus ſchön ma chen.

O ja, Ma mi, ru ſen al le.

Ich ho le un ſe re 🚩

E rich + Fi ne ſu chen Ro ſen.

Min chen + Len chen ma chen ei nen 🏵

Ju li us, ma le ein ſchö nes ⚡

Nun al le ans Haus.

Ho le ei ner un ſe re ⎯⎯

Ich, Ma ma, ich. – Ja, E rich auch.

An elementary school reading text laced with Nazi symbols.

ugly sister theme. The tale symbolizes the conflict between a racially pure maiden and an alien stepmother: "Cinderella is rescued by a prince whose unspoiled instinct helps him to find the genuine Cinderella. The voice of the blood within him guides him along the right way."[28]

Young teenaged boys, in the so-called Viking years, were required to read the ancient Nordic sagas, not so much as illustrations of Germany's heroic ancient days, but as examples of the Führerprinzip. Here were noble leaders followed unto death through terrible adventures by a totally devoted band of heroes filled with "blind confidence" in their own physical prowess. Bringing this theme into the modern day led to the glorification of other German heroes from Frederick the Great to Bismarck. Crime and mystery were out, while the military exploits of the Red Baron were in. Adventure in general was thought to be a good thing, "because a fair shot of adventure runs through the blood of every German" and "forms a preliminary step toward the heroes." Unfortunately, some of the most popular adventure stories involved non-Aryans and had to be brought into line. *Uncle Tom's Cabin* was banned, as "counter to the ideas of the National Socialist political education" and "literary counterpropaganda to the colonial idea." *Robinson Crusoe,* clearly a "Nordic hero capable of surviving the most adverse conditions," was fine, but Man Friday was not. Hardest of all to reconcile with the new ideology were the immensely popular "Red Indian" tales of Chiefs Winnetou and Tecumseh, written by German authors Karl May and Fritz Steuben, which even Hitler had read in his youth. Warnings that Germans "should meet the colored danger with all . . . necessary sharpness" were waived for the noble savage Winnetou with the argument that "the lack of racial consciousness and the failure to grasp the importance of establishing racial bonds among themselves" had led to the downfall of the Red Indians, who were therefore a good object lesson. The Red Indians not only survived the onslaughts of racial science, but the Winnetou books were even used as prizes for the Hitler Youth and, perhaps thought to be relevant, would later be sent to troops fighting partisans and protecting German settlers on the eastern frontiers of the extended Reich.

Deciding on the role of girls in this warlike scene was difficult. The Nazis believed not only that the sexes should be educated separately, but also that girls should study completely different subjects in order to prepare themselves for the future. Separate schools were already the norm in the Catholic parts of the country, but in some areas coeducation had been instituted as a means of saving education funds. Special home economics schools for girls had existed for years, but were generally looked down upon. These were immediately upgraded, but fitting domestic science into the already crowded curricula of the academic high schools was a problem. Education Minister Rust at first feebly suggested that the girls' mothers could take care of that sort of thing and ordained the inclusion of a few needlework courses. It was not until 1938 that a general decree regulating all the schools, while timidly leaving in place a "language" track with reduced science and mathematics, instituted a home economics track at the academic high schools. This was loaded with racial theory and practice sessions in the Nazi welfare agencies. These regulations, and others forbidding coeducation, were never well enforced. Academically inclined students and their parents found all sorts of loopholes, and, in the end, the enormous demands of the German workforce, depleted by the induction of men into the armed forces, would require reversal of the policies, complete with propaganda urging girls to prepare themselves to serve their country.[29] It would be in the extracurricular area that the Nazis would assert their greatest control over women.

Despite the success of Winnetou in gaining Hitler's approval, there was clearly no place for real non-Aryan children in the new educational scene. But all German children who were citizens were entitled to an education. The Nazis' first emphasis was, therefore, on rearrangement rather than direct expulsion of students. A special decree, the Law Against the Overcrowding of German Schools, ordained that non-Aryan students must never be in the majority and limited the number of such pupils in any school above the elementary level to 5 percent of the total enrollment. Certain children, those whose fathers were World War I veterans or who were of mixed parentage, were exempted. This law was augmented in March 1935 by an executive order instituting measures to select those students who would be allowed to go on to and remain in secondary schools after fourth grade. The criteria were not very academic. No child with "serious infirmities resulting in a decrease of their vitality" or "afflicted with hereditary diseases" could enter secondary school. Those "showing no realization of the necessity of physical hygiene and cleanliness" would be dismissed if they did not improve, as would those committing "serious breaches of the rules of public decency and morals" or "persistent offenses against the spirit of comradeship and a disregard of the general welfare of the community." And "pupils devoid of a sense of order . . . as well as those not having an 'open character' " were not to be allowed to continue either. Once accepted, it was not only important to have passing grades, but also "high character . . . on the athletic field" and "special aptitude for leadership." Last but not least was the "requirement for National Fitness," which noted that no non-Aryan was to be given preferential treatment, that Jews could not have scholarships, and that "students harming the state in any way or violating the principle of national fellowship of all Germans are to be excluded from secondary schools."[30] These rules were particularly good for getting rid of Gypsy children, described not only as "afflicted with lice, neglected and entirely incapable of being educated," but also as constituting "a moral threat to their classmates of German blood," which was construed, with strong support of the local citizens in some jurisdictions, as grounds for eliminating education for them altogether.[31]

The measures, however, like many other Nazi rules to come, were terribly difficult to translate into concrete action where cleanly scrubbed, bright, middle- and upper-class Jewish children were concerned. It was all very well to require their segregation, but it put school districts to a lot of trouble. Some jurisdictions put them in separate classrooms or separate buildings. Proposals were floated to build separate elementary schools, financed in part by the Jewish community, wherever twenty or more Jewish children were available. There were, of course, existing Jewish schools, but their capacity was limited, and many assimilated Jews and "Christian non-Aryans" did not wish to attend them. On top of all this, different rules applied to the different degrees of *Mischlinge*, or children with varying numbers of Jewish parents and grandparents. Such children, many of whom had been baptized as Catholics or Protestants, often fell between two stools. As one school principal said: "There are Jews and there are Christians, but worst of all are the half-breeds."[32]

While the Catholic Church continued to help its converts, most of the German Protestant denominations quickly abandoned theirs. Expelled from their "Aryan" groups, these children were, at first, not eligible for Jewish ones. A doctor who had converted to Protestantism just after World War I wrote, bitterly, in 1933:

> [My children] have lost the protection that Jewry had always and everywhere provided to its members. They have [received] no protection from the Christian church, and I imagine, cannot expect any. They are outlaws as Christians, they are outlawed as Germans. Can one imagine a more cruel fate visited upon the innocent?[33]

A tiny number of such youngsters were taken in by the Quakers, who also helped the children of Social Democrats and other banned political groups. The Quakers were regarded with mixed feelings by the Nazis, who kept them under careful surveillance. Hapless Gestapo agents assigned to this duty were often lulled to sleep in Quaker meetings and were reluctant to send in negative reports, since many of them had, as children themselves, been fed in the Quaker soup kitchens that had provided meals for hundreds of thousands of impoverished Germans after World War I.

As time went on, school became an increasingly lonely battlefield for Jewish students. The mortification of children forced to endure the most vicious references to themselves, in the presence of their peers, day after day, is hard to imagine. Their isolation was compounded by the fact that the children often tried to hide their misery from their still patriotic families, as well as by the fact that some parents, for a long time, simply did not believe that such things were possible.

Parental attempts to help often made things worse. The mother of Marianne Regensburger, who had already been denounced for playing the Vir-
gin Mary in her school play (an eminently suitable role, one would think),
dyed the girl's hair blond in an apparent effort to make her look Aryan.
This was to no avail: Marianne's teacher told her that "even with blonde
hair you'll never be an Aryan."[34]

European children in the 1930s did not usually ride on school buses.
They walked, bicycled, or used public transportation. For non-Aryans this
usually most carefree and fun part of the school day soon became a physical and psychological gauntlet. The streets were frequently filled with the
uniformed marching groups so beloved by Northern Europeans, the Nazi
ones sporting ritual daggers and other accoutrements. As they marched,
they sang patriotic and political songs that often contained racist lyrics. It
was impossible to avoid the ubiquitous propaganda. Kiosks were plastered
with posters exhorting the German Volk to defend itself from Jews. Some
candy stores and even some shops where required schoolbooks were sold
began to display signs suggesting that Jews go elsewhere, and special vi-
trines set up in public areas displayed pages from the semi-pornographic
magazine *Die Stürmer*, which specialized in cartoons of hideous Jews
molesting innocent Aryan maidens. Most Jewish teenagers could not resist
the desire to look at this filth; others were sometimes forced to do so by
gangs of Hitler Youth bullies, who made their lives generally miserable:

> I had to run and escape the mob of boys who found it fun to wait for me
> on my way home to pounce on me like a pack of dogs on a rabbit. I
> didn't keep count of the torn trousers and shirts, the black eyes, the
> bruises, bloody knees, elbows, the tears and my father's reproaches. "A
> Jewish boy doesn't brawl in the streets, just run away," he said. In a
> short time I became a good runner. By 1936—I was eleven years old—
> I even became fairly good at boxing and wrestling.[35]

Long before 1941, when wearing the yellow star would definitively
identify them, older Jewish children were made conspicuous by their very
lack of badges. Before the Nazi takeover, the wearing of badges denoting
Party preference or membership in a myriad of organizations, much like
the T-shirts of today, was extremely popular. After 1933, Jews were not
allowed to wear the swastika or other Party emblems and uniforms,
though many longed to do so. Half-Jewish Verena Groth, the only "non-
Aryan" in her school, had no problems with her classmates, and even participated in Nazi parades when the whole school was sent. "You simply
went along," she later told her interviewer. "To place yourself apart would

have been superhuman." But it was impossible for her to blend in without the right clothes: "The others ran around in their uniforms. . . . And as I was the only one of seven hundred girls . . . not to be part of it . . . when you're twelve or thirteen years old, that was very hard."[36] Another little girl, in her longing to be included, had a dream in which classmates and teachers teased her and tried to take away a swastika armband that she was wearing on grounds that Jews were not allowed to wear the Nazi emblem. In the dream, she triumphantly announced that Hitler himself had met her, had said she was a good child, and had given her the armband. After that, in her fantasy, the teacher and children were kind to her.[37]

Any ceremonial occasion could be a trap. It was hard to know what to do. In most schools, Jewish children, despite the fact that they were not considered part of the Volk, were required to give the Nazi salute at the outdoor morning assemblies. Even though their parents had often told them not to, most, not being "superhuman," saluted anyway. Those who did not risked punishments such as having the offending hand whipped with a bamboo rod.[38] Berlin pupil Klaus Scheurenberg, however, had quite a different experience when he did salute along with his classmates:

> The physical education teacher saw me do this. In front of everybody he came over and gave me a murderous beating. "You Jew boy," he screamed, "you are not allowed to give the German salute." I started to cry. I was only eight years old. "I'm German too!" I cried back. He screamed even louder, "What, you're a German? You're a *Sau-jude!*" . . . That's why I went to my religion teacher and asked her what a *Saujude* was. What was a Jew?

The teacher explained that being a Jew meant lighting the candles on Friday night and keeping the Sabbath day holy. Klaus, who had assumed that everyone did that, was amazed to hear that only the Jews did.[39]

Once inside the doors of the school, traditionally a refuge from the streets, things were no better. At one elementary school Aryan children were sent with sponges and soap to scrub seats where Jewish children had sat.[40] Jewish boys, no matter how good, could not represent their schools in sports and school trips, and were usually excluded from excursions. Even if they were allowed to go along, there were tortures:

> We had a tough hardcore Nazi as a physical education and swimming teacher. The first day we had to put on our bathing trunks and stand alongside the pool. When we were all lined up, he said, "Herz, step forward. And you stay there. We won't go into the pool with a half Jew."

From then on I spent swimming class, two hours every week, standing
at the edge of the pool in my trunks.[41]

Some merciful teachers warned parents to keep their children at home
on such occasions, but others could be devastatingly cruel, even when the
celebration was Mother's Day. "You have to be present for the festival," a
teacher told two little girls, "but since you are Jewish, you are not allowed
to join in the songs." When one of the children protested that she too
wanted to sing for her mother, the teacher answered, "I know you have a
mother . . . but she is only a Jewish mother."[42] It is terrible to imagine
what it must have been like to stand silently in the midst of the singing
children.

Not even the most innocent childish friendships were allowed to survive, a fact that the humiliated children often tried to conceal from their
parents.

> [The children] tried with all their willpower not to let us know about
> their suffering, but the signs of pain in the girl's childlike face were too
> evident to escape our eyes . . . it was the younger one who had to tell it,
> since the child's resistance was now broken and, with the wild sobbing
> which followed, there was not one word we could understand. . . .
> "Daddy," she said, "until now, sister was sitting beside her best friend,
> though they had not been allowed to be together on the way home, nor
> during the recreation hour. But now the teacher said, in the presence of
> all the girls, that it was no longer possible to have an Aryan girl sitting
> beside a Jewish girl. This would be a disgrace for an Aryan. And the
> teacher ordered her to take her seat in the last bench against the wall,
> and no Aryan girl could take a seat in this row. Now she is sitting alone
> in the rear of the classroom."[43]

There was no refuge in the intellectual sphere either, where every
opportunity was taken to drive home the Nordic and Germanic message.
All disciplines emphasized the conspiracy of "International Jewry" and the
inferiority and biological unattractiveness of the "non-Aryan" races. This
was not particularly aimed at the non-Aryan students, but was part of the
indoctrination of their German peers. It was as if the "alien blood" students did not exist as sentient beings.

The themes introduced in geography and history were developed much
further in biology. The teaching of racial studies and eugenics soon was
required in designated classes. This order was a bonanza for the extremists
whose eugenics texts had gone unread for years. Hundreds of books and

pamphlets were published for all levels of instruction. Written in turgid and propagandistic prose, they are guaranteed to put all but the most ardent fanatic to sleep. Ostensibly biology texts, the books, after providing minimal introductions to genetics and prehistory, were dedicated almost entirely to a totally unscientific definition of races and their supposed characteristics.

In one such volume, published in 1934 and typical of the genre, Europe was divided into five main racial types: Nordic, Dinaric, Alpine, Mediterranean, and Eastern/Baltic.[44] Photographs and charts illustrated and compared physical characteristics. Needless to say, the best-looking and best-groomed were the Nordics. Eyes were compared, as were lips, chins, noses (Nordic—thin; Mediterranean—curved; Dinaric—quite fleshy; Eastern—thick, not curved; and so on), faces, heads, and body shapes. To this were added spiritual and intellectual qualities that read like bad horoscopes and that, naturally, demonstrated the superiority of the Nordic race.

Outside Europe things got more complicated: the Indians (from India, not Winnetou), originally "Indo-Germans," had, alas, gone downhill due to mixing with lesser races, but the fact that an Indian, Dr. Chandrasekhara Raman, had won the Nobel Prize for physics in 1930 made clear that the Nordic element in India had not yet been completely eradicated. In Africa, the Negro had "triumphed biologically" over the white settlers and would soon do the same in the hopelessly heterogeneous United States. What's more, the French, in throwing out the Huguenots in 1685 and the aristocrats in 1789, and in carrying on the Napoleonic Wars and World War I, had severely diminished their Nordic population, which accounted for their "intellectual decline." A separate section was reserved for the Jews, who were worse than anybody, as they were not a "pure" race, but a complicated mixture of Oriental and Middle Eastern peoples who had also mixed with Dinarics, but who could easily be distinguished from the latter by their even fleshier noses.

The books also included a detailed explanation of the Nuremberg Laws, which, the authors claimed, would keep Germany pure while allowing Jews to lead their own lives. Miscegenation of any kind was condemned. Along with the Jews, Negroes and the yellow races were specifically mentioned, and the reader was cautioned that mixing with "Middle Eastern" and "Oriental elements" to "the east of our Reich" was also to be avoided, thus introducing the Slavs, who would be the next ethnic group to be designated subhumans, or *Untermenschen*.

To keep these undesirable races from prevailing, the schoolchildren were taught, it was the duty of all Germans to trace their own purity. For this, one textbook noted (rather contradictorily, after all the noses and chins), visual analysis was insufficient. Nordic appearance, it was forced to admit, did not always indicate Nordic race. Indeed, a small dark type (like Propaganda Minister Goebbels) might well be impeccably Nordic. True race could only be determined by genealogical analysis. In one pamphlet, designed for twelve-year-olds, a highly decorative and rather heraldic fold-out chart was provided and full instructions given. Students were advised to create a family archive, complete with handwriting samples, photographs of ancestors, and other documentation, as a complete family history would make it easier to tell the race of a person.[45] The students were also required to note any "special susceptibilities, talents, psychopathic dispositions or important illnesses" in their families, "as much can be done with this information," which would lead to better "selection" and improvement of the "hereditary mass." Thus children became unwitting informants for the various racial agencies.

The courses on racial hygiene were of the greatest importance, for on the outcome of the pretty little genealogical charts, as we have seen, whole lives depended. They would determine whom one could marry, where one could travel and work, how much food one was allotted, and, eventually, whether one would be put to death. It was bad enough to deal with one's classification as an *Untermensch* even if one was prepared. For some, the shock of discovering this status in the course of a routine homework assignment could be devastating. Half- or quarter-Jewish children, many of whom had been baptized and whose protective parents had kept knowledge of their ancestry from them, sometimes became suicidal or physically ill at the revelation of a heritage that overnight closed to them most educational and career options and simultaneously turned them into social outcasts. Hatred for the "guilty" parents was not uncommon.[46]

The situation was not always without black humor. In the bosoms of families there were even jokes: "What does the ideal Aryan look like? As tall as Goebbels, as slim as Göring, as blond as Hitler."[47]

And memoirs and oral histories are full of examples of blond, blue-eyed Jewish children being not only mistaken for "Aryans" but also held up as perfect examples of the race:

> Most of the classes had been gathered that morning in the big hall, since an officer of the new *Rasseamt,* the office of races, had come to give a talk about the differences of races. . . . He said that there are two

Jewish children are humiliated in class.

groups of races, a high group and a low one. The high and upper race that was destined to rule the world was the Teutonic, the German race, while one of the lowest races was the Jewish race. And then . . . he looked around and asked one of the girls to come to him. . . . "Look here, the small head of this girl, her long forehead, her very blue eyes, and blond hair," and he was lifting one of her long blond braids. "And look," he said, "at her tall and slender figure. These are the unequivocal marks of a pure and unmixed Teutonic race." You should have heard how at this moment all the girls burst into laughter. Then from all sides of the hall there was shouting, "She is a Jewess!" You should have seen the officer's face! . . . The principal got up . . . quickly and . . . dismissed the man, thanking him for his interesting and very enlightening talk. . . . At that we began again to laugh.[48]

Some mixed families tried to fight the system by requesting an "Aryanization" proceeding. One Aryan grandmother of immaculate propriety signed an affidavit saying that her son was not the issue of her Jewish husband but of a traveling "manufacturer from the Black Forest." Her son and his blond children, accompanied by an Aryan uncle, then went off to a special race institute in Tübingen for a hearing. The daughter remembered:

> My father . . . was very stately [while] . . . this Aryan uncle . . . looked incredibly Jewish. We went up there, indeed to a castle in Tübingen, and the professor walked over purposefully to this uncle and said, "Good day, Herr Dr. Goldmann," and my uncle said, "You have erred, Herr Professor. I'm the Aryan part of the family." . . . And you could not *laugh* . . . we just about exploded. The scientists got very red faces. . . . My father . . . looked more like Kaiser Wilhelm. . . . Anyway, their whole theory was overturned within a quarter of a minute.[49]

The experiences of Jewish children varied widely from school to school. Worst off were children in country schools, where they often had few fellow sufferers. In the big high schools of cities like Berlin, some students continued without serious harassment, and almost all had certain teachers and loyal fellow students who protected them for a time. But the pressure on both the Jewish students and their sympathizers was unrelenting, and protective actions soon became dangerous. By 1936 nearly two-thirds of an estimated 60,000 Jewish children between five and sixteen had left the mainstream German schools to attend purely Jewish ones. Even here they were not entirely free from government supervision. The German Ministry of Education still controlled many aspects of the curriculum, and diplomas embossed with both swastika and Star of David were sometimes given to secondary school graduates. For many from assimilated families, the Jewish studies given at these schools were their first contact with both culture and religion. But there was no question that for the children, no matter how assimilated they had once been, the segregated schools were a refuge.[50] One boy, sent to a Jewish boarding school in Potsdam, recalled that after months of humiliation by his history teacher at the local *Realgymnasium*, where he was the only Jewish student, and had, therefore, had to bear the "full measure of the [teacher's] venom," he at last "felt free and happy and in a loving atmosphere, conducive to learning."[51] And American Ambassador William Dodd, himself an educator, noted that the separation might be "beneficial in removing Jewish children from the ordinary schools where they occupy a definitely humiliating position."[52] On November 15, 1938, in the aftermath of Kristallnacht, when Jewish businesses all over Germany were looted, synagogues burned, and thousands of Jews beaten and sent to concentration camps, the Nazi government finally found its excuse to expel all the remaining Jewish students from the schools on the grounds that it was now "self-evident that German students find it unbearable to share classrooms with Jews."[53]

The Nazis had even more draconian plans for the universities than for the schools. In April 1933, the Reich Ministry of the Interior, ostensibly in order to reduce the number of unemployed graduates in the country, limited the enrollment in the fall of 1934 to 15,000, of whom only 10 percent could be women. This drastic downsizing cut the size of the incoming student body by more than half. The 20,000 rejected applicants were helpfully directed to their district labor offices for help with job searches or placement in vocational training programs.

The reductions, combined with an already declining number of applicants due to the Depression and the fact that admission was limited to medically vetted "nationally reliable" students, who in any case were increasingly seduced by Nazi action propaganda to do less studious things, led to such small enrollments that several universities were faced with financial crises and the policy had to be reconsidered.[54] The universities, traditional bastions of independent thinking, would, in addition to losing new scholars, also no longer provide any refuge to nonconforming academics of long standing. Despite their intellectual independence, university professors too were civil servants, and the Civil Service Law of April 1933 also applied to them. To the astonishment of the entire world, this led to the dismissal of hundreds of Germany's most famous scholars, among them numerous Nobel Prize winners, including Albert Einstein.

Within days of the publication of the law, the pro-Nazi German Students' Union, one of the major student organizations, had sent around a secret memorandum to its local leaders soliciting lists of "undesirable" professors. In addition to Jews, they included those with leftist political views, pacifists, those who had made critical remarks about the Nazi Party, or anyone a disgruntled student might not like. This document was leaked to the international press and reported in London's *Daily Telegraph* under the headline HITLERITE WAR ON PROFESSORS. STUDENTS' BLACK LIST. ABILITY A MINOR CONSIDERATION.[55] The government did not, at first, dare dismiss Aryan full professors, whose positions were traditionally inviolable, but instead passed a law that made retirement mandatory at sixty-five and allowed the federal Education Minister to transfer academics from one institution to another at will or to abolish the chair they held, thereby forcing their retirement. Lower-level instructors, like the schoolteachers, were required to go to four-week courses at Nazi indoctrination camps more suitable for ten-year-olds, where they "slept six to a room, wore uniforms, did digging and sports, were given educative lectures."[56]

The purge was not limited to personnel, but included whole subjects that the Nazis felt were frivolous, unpatriotic, or racially unacceptable. One result of the new policy was the nationwide ceremonial burning of books. But this was only a superficial indicator of what was to come. In his remarkable diaries of the war years, the Dresden professor of Romance languages Victor Klemperer, who was Jewish, gives a vivid account of both his and his department's slow and torturous exclusion. Some professors were briefly protected by secret maneuvers of the university faculty committees, but the process was inexorable, if not always convenient for the students. In April 1933, for example, Jewish professors at Dresden were forbidden to conduct examinations. Just how their students were supposed to finish their courses, which still went on, was not clear. The problem for students of Romance languages at Dresden was solved in July 1936, when the department was closed down altogether except for one course in Italian, presumably useful for dealing with representatives of Axis ally Benito Mussolini.[57] Romance languages and other unacceptable subjects were replaced by courses such as "Studies of Culture and Volk" or biased lectures such as "The Political and Economic Problems of Asia" (i.e., of the contemptible Slavic nations), which were made compulsory at certain institutions.

Faculty resistance to the Nazi decrees was cautious. Germany's professorate had traditionally been conservative and nationalist and included a considerable percentage of non-Party members who supported Hitler's election. But even academics who agreed with the Nazis on matters of foreign policy and anti-Semitism were appalled at the reduction of their powers both in university committees, where the Führerprinzip was instituted, and vis-à-vis the students. As Klemperer put it: "No letter, no telephone conversation, no word in the street is safe anymore. Everyone fears the next person may be an informer."[58]

This was not mere paranoia. American Ambassador William Dodd noted in his diary the case of Hermann Oncken, the distinguished (and Aryan) head of the History Department at Berlin, who had been violently attacked by one of his own students for his less than flattering description of the Oliver Cromwell Interregnum in seventeenth-century England, which, the students claimed, was really a criticism of the Hitler government. After much publicity, Party guru Alfred Rosenberg ordered the

Ministry of Education to "retire" the professor. The protests of other students saved Oncken for the duration of the semester, but by the summer he had been dismissed.[59]

Protests of this nature by faculty were rare, however, as professors sought to ingratiate themselves with the new regime in order to get funding for their pet programs, or lay low in hopes of taking over the suddenly vacated positions, research files, and other perks of the purged. The cynicism of these maneuvers was not lost on the students: years after the war, a distinguished professor of medieval French at Oxford, sent to Germany for a graduate semester in the 1930s, recounted with outrage that when she had inquired about the dismissal of a well-known Jewish professor she was told by the man's colleagues that "he had never really been very competent."[60] Even the Nazis were sometimes amused by the unseemly eagerness of those professors who could not wait to jump on the bandwagon and flaunt their insignia-laden Party uniforms at academic functions.

The violence of the pro-Nazi student demonstrations that had disrupted the universities for years before Hitler's chancellorship, combined with the denunciations and the very real threat that the institutions might be closed down entirely, led academic authorities to seek compromises with the various militant organizations and to resort to underground machinations to preserve their turf. The fear of closure was not unfounded. One had only to skim through *Mein Kampf* to understand the truly vicious anti-intellectual bent of the Führer, an attitude that he frequently restated, perhaps most eloquently in a 1938 speech in which he declared that intellectuals, on whom he, as usual, blamed the German defeat in 1918, were

> not bearers of faith, not unshakable, and above all, they do not stand fast in moments of crisis and danger. For while the broad, healthy mass of people does not hesitate to forge itself together into a *Volksgemeinschaft*, [the intellectuals] scatter like hens in a chicken run. And therefore one cannot make history with them, they are useless as supporting elements of a society.[61]

These sentiments were frequently echoed by others in the Nazi leadership. Julius Streicher, editor of the vicious magazine *Die Stürmer*, is said to have told one group of professors to their faces that they were "old men with beards and gold-rimmed glasses and scientific faces" who were "worth next to nothing" and separated from the people by "so-called higher education."[62]

It must not have been easy to be a university student and rationalize support for a regime that felt one was useless. Indeed, the Reich Student Leadership, spinning Hitler's remarks, said he must have been referring not to real academics, but to people "with long hair and broadly padded shoulders."[63] The student leaders, just as fearful as their professors of university closure, which would have made them superfluous, saw cooperation with faculty as necessary to the success of their appointed mission to achieve total enrollment of the student body in their political education courses. This was difficult, as German students traditionally attended lectures only in their own disciplines; nor were there distribution requirements that could be transformed into ideological instruction sessions. It was thus necessary to work with the university authorities in order to introduce extra courses, make them compulsory, and keep track of attendance and grades. The interest in success was more than idealistic. In March 1935, the National Socialist German Students' Association had been recognized as a major Party formation, equal in status to the Hitler Youth and the SS, and its officials, frequently ambitious "students" of a certain age, relished their power. Their uneasy cooperation with the university administrations was marred by frequent dramatic flare-ups, byzantine intrigues, and ferocious competition with other Nazi student groups, like the German Students' Union, for the total commitment of those who had formerly belonged to non-Nazi organizations such as the Catholic Students' Union, all of which had been successfully absorbed or abolished by the late 1930s.[64]

The student leaders were often so busy with their recruiting, propaganda, and paramilitary activities that they had little time to prepare for their own courses, much less to write lectures for political seminars that could be taken seriously at the university level, or to monitor the "Nazi scholarship" of the faculty. Even when ideological study groups were set up, it was hard for the untrained instructors to think of much to say except to repeat the platitudes the students had been hearing for years at school and in Hitler Youth meetings, or to assign readings from the excessively boring writings of the Nazi leaders and those who had inspired them, none of which stood up well to analytic scholarship. Courses in the scientific disciplines that were taught with a Nazi slant were even less successful, but the student leaders were not daunted. When it was pointed out that the requirement that Einstein's "Jewish" theory of relativity be eliminated from physics courses made study of that subject pointless, the ideologues in the Hamburg University student union solemnly set about doing research to isolate "Aryan elements in the theory." As a result of these excesses, absenteeism and apathy became the order of the day as students went off to study for their real exams in the little free time left to them after the endless extracurricular activities imposed by the authorities. By the fall of 1937, the effects of the Nazification of academe were beginning to be felt outside the universities. Officials of the Air Force, economic planners, and the president of the Reich Research Council had all complained that there were not enough qualified engineers, and even Nazi ideologue Alfred Rosenberg declared that the Party should not be too dogmatic when it came to science. A Hamburg professor pointed out that Nazification of scientific knowledge might be detrimental to the national interest, particularly when it came to the development of new weapons.[65] Industry was less circumspect: a chemical industry journal stated flatly in 1939 that "the leadership in chemical research has passed to foreign countries."[66]

It was, in fact, a miracle that students got any studying done at all. Required duties ran the gamut from military to agricultural. Students tried all sorts of ploys to avoid these requirements, among them the trick of transferring frequently from one university to another (a practice long condoned in Germany), so that the Nazi bureaucrats never quite caught up with them.[67] Sports were made compulsory for all students in the spring of 1933. In September the Nazi storm troopers (SA) set up a special University Office to organize "physical and mental [training] in the spirit of the vanguards of German revolution." Irritated faculties were forced to rearrange their entire academic schedules to accommodate the new program, whose organizers, even more irritatingly, thought nothing of changing the schedule again whenever they felt like it. Three semesters of heavily military training were required. Students who did not complete the program would not be allowed to register for the next year. The training was so strenuous and time-consuming that professors at Hamburg soon noticed a dramatic rise in absences, a "certain lassitude" in seminars, and a catastrophic drop in grades so severe that the program was dropped after only one year.

The withdrawal of the SA from the campus took some pressure off students during the academic term, but did not make their vacations any more fun. These were consumed by a number of obligatory programs. First came a Student Labor Service, quickly set up in the spring of 1933, which demanded four months of work and political indoctrination in special camps, plus six weeks of paramilitary training prior to matriculation at a university. Jewish students, of course, were not accepted, and other undesirables, such as those intending to study Catholic theology, were exempted in the hope that they would stay away and thus be marginalized.[68]

The pre-freshman labor camps were only the beginning. Eager student leaders had similar proposals for later vacations, but these were often a flop, as many students needed to earn money in the summer to pay their tuition. A plan to replace factory workers with students so that the former could have paid time off had a pathetic response. More successful was the Land Service (Landdienst), which involved, for the most part, working in farm areas bordering Poland.

While the Land Service was moderately popular, its companion activity, the so-called Harvest Help, decidedly was not. In 1939, students at Munich and Heidelberg reportedly demonstrated openly against this activity. They whistled at its Nazi promoter in one assembly and threw eggs at another. Twelve students were whisked off to Dachau, despite which, in the night, graffiti reading DOWN WITH HITLER appeared in the corridors.[69] Other students were found to be volunteering for summer training in the Army in order to make themselves ineligible for Harvest Help. This was not good for the Reich Student Leadership, which had been ordered to guarantee enough student help to get the harvest in as early as possible, "in light of frontier policing measures which have become necessary on the German Polish border." The drain to the Army was stopped and some 45,000 students were found to cut the grain just in time for the motorized elements of the blitzkrieg to roll over the newly shorn fields into Poland.[70] The students who had wanted to opt for the Army would soon not have any other choice.

The social side of university life was not ignored. The Nazis did not at all like the idea of their youth, fresh from night-and-day indoctrination in the Hitler Youth and other organizations, suddenly being released into the traditionally free and wild student life. Now, being in loco parentis, the Nazis were faced with all the problems that this entailed. From the earliest days of the regime efforts had been made to unify all university social organizations into a single Nazi federation. This meant dealing with a myriad of student clubs, denominational associations, fraternities, and the famous Student Corps, regarded as elite organizations out of keeping with the *Volksgemeinschaft*. But this process had to be handled carefully, as many of Germany's leading citizens were alumni of such groups, among them State Secretary of the Reichschancellery Lammers, one of Hitler's closest aides, who in 1934 was given the nearly impossible task of trying to bring them all into line with Nazi requirements. Students being students, the Nazi measures were not always accepted as quickly as Reich officials might have liked by the traditionally secretive and independent groups, even when they were pro-Nazi. Some Corps refused to certify the racial purity of their members and to expel non-Aryan members and alumni. In one celebrated incident, Corps Palaiomachia of Halle threw out its Nazi members instead and its leader declared, "Whosoever wears the colors of my Corps is my Corps brother. . . . I do not sacrifice my brother for my own sake or for that of my race."[71] The confessional fraternities balked at removing religious requirements. All deeply resented giving up the colorful banners, caps, and uniforms their members had worn for centuries. These were to be replaced by a universal, dull, black and red cap. Even harder to suppress were the ancient fencing fraternities, whose members were willing to go to jail rather than give up their duels, which they carried on in remote wooded areas after the ban went into effect.

There was no humor in the handling of the students. In May 1935, students of the ancient and exclusive Saxo-Borussia fraternity at Heidelberg were severely punished for "grave injury to the obligations to People, State and the University which are incumbent upon all students." Two crimes had brought forth this verdict. On May 21, the students, dressed in dinner jackets, had left their house in the midst of a broadcast of a foreign policy speech by Hitler and proceeded "to an inn in Heidelberg where they entered with much noise, one of them blowing a tune on a champagne bottle." A few days later, in another inn, "the members of the Corps loudly discussed the question as to how one should eat asparagus, and in particular how the Führer ate it." The case was reported in the *Völkischer Beobachter* under the headline "TREASONABLE CONDUCT OF THE STUDENT FEUDAL REACTION." Somewhat later, Baldur von Schirach, the Reich Youth Leader, issued a decree calling upon all Hitler Youth members to resign from the Student Corps or face expulsion from the Hitler Youth, which would greatly lessen their chances of advancement in many fields. Von Schirach had not been amused by the asparagus; referring to the incident in his decree, he thundered that it had furnished "a frightful picture of brutishness and lack of discipline, indeed abysmal vulgarity, of a small clique of Corporation students who swagger and carouse while Germany works. When such elements in their depravity do not stop with the, to us, holy personage of the Führer, they let themselves be judged."[72] Von Schirach's rules for the Hitler Youth were universalized by a decree of

May 1936 declaring that no Nazi Party member could belong to an existing student fraternity.

The Nazis did not want to destroy the Student Corps entirely; they
wanted to transform them into useful units of their youth structure. They
envisioned groups of thirty or so students organized into *Kameradschaften*
who would live together in one house and there receive group indoctrination and participate in suitable activities. The houses they had in mind
were the former Corps houses, and indeed a number of banned Corps
happily rented their buildings to the Nazis and continued their meetings
elsewhere in secret, while others wanting to go along with the new regime
did convert themselves into *Kameradschaften*. These, alas, were not enthusiastic enough for the Nazis and were soon dissolved. It is easy to see why
the *Kameradschaften* were not popular with the young, as their schedule of
required activities started at 6:30 a.m. with "defense sports exercises" and
included "tidying and housework," a required afternoon nap, and ideological training and "special functions" run by the Nazi Party well into the
evening, leaving the students only one hour of free time all day.[73]

The rather monastic life of the *Kameradschaften* did not entirely reflect
Hitler's preferences. The Führer apparently felt that men living together
too long would become homosexuals. In at least one Nazi institution,
rooms with two men were forbidden—triples and singles were fine. To
avoid this corruption, he urged more contact with women. This did not
mean the drunken semi-orgies often encountered in American fraternities, but decorous events that were described as "exercises in etiquette
with ladies."[74]

Although the authorities tried to encourage the *Kameradschaften* later
in the 1930s by lifting the ban on fencing and other modifications, they
never did become the perfect cells of Nazi ideology that the leadership
had envisaged. Once the war began, the houses reverted, with caution and
a certain complicity on the part of local authorities, to their old ways. The
facade of conformity was necessarily maintained, as the Nazis were apt to
make surprise inspections. One house, after a frantic search through its
own closets, managed to borrow a picture of the Führer from the *Kameradschaft* next door just in time to avoid being closed down. The Nazi fear
of the universities and the Student Corps was not entirely unfounded: the
members of the famous White Rose resistance group all came from this
milieu, and almost all those involved in the failed July 20, 1944, plot to
assassinate Hitler were Corps alumni who had used reunion meetings to
exchange information.[75]

5. Hitler's Children

While its gradual transformations of the traditional education system were in progress, the Nazi government had been busily constructing a parallel structure that would not be burdened with the irritating traditions of the past. In the new world of Nazi youth, children would spend as little time as possible in the still private confines of home, where old ideas and books might lurk, and where loyalty to church or local custom could vie with the New Order, whose leaders now set out to fulfill its slogan: "He who possesses the youth, possesses the future." The "youth" referred to was, of course, limited to totally healthy children of documented pure Aryan descent.

By 1938, Hitler was able to sum up the schedule as follows:

> These young people learn nothing else but to think as Germans and to act as Germans; these boys join our organization at the age of ten and get a breath of fresh air for the first time, then, four years later, they move from the Jungvolk to the Hitler Youth and there we keep them for another four years. And then we are even less prepared to give them back into the hands of those who create our class and status barriers, rather we take them immediately into the Party, into the Labor Front, into the SA or into the SS . . . and so on. And if they are there for eighteen months or two years and have still not become real National Socialists, then they go into the Labor Service and are polished there for six or seven months. . . . And if, after six or seven months there are still remnants of class consciousness or pride in status, then the Wehrmacht will take over the further treatment for two years and when they return after two years or four years then, to prevent them from slipping back into old habits, once again we take them immediately back into the SA, SS, etc., and they will not be free again for the rest of their lives. And, if someone says to me—there will still be some left out; I reply: National Socialism is not at the end of its days but only at the beginning.[1]

This degree of control, whose success was greatly exaggerated in the Führer's peroration, had not been achieved overnight. For years before Hitler became Chancellor of Germany, the Hitler Youth (HJ) had dedi-

Three German children wearing Hitler Youth uniforms are taught how to salute.

cated itself to the elimination or absorption of other long-established youth organizations. These ran the gamut from the revolutionary Communists to the romantic *Bündische* movement, which sought to renew German life through communal outdoor activity featuring camping and fireside singing, to right-wing groups, including monarchists, some of which were trained in paramilitary exercises by the Weimar Army. Adding to the mix were both Protestant and Catholic church-run organizations. In the last year of the Weimar Republic, violent demonstrations by paramilitary elements of the Hitler Youth had led to their being outlawed in many jurisdictions. Parades and the wearing of uniforms were forbidden in April 1932. This had little effect: the Nazis merely took off their uniforms and renamed themselves the National Socialist Youth Movement. A few months later, hoping to appease Hitler, the weak Chancellor Franz von Papen revoked the ban, and the Hitler Youth was once again able to parade in its full glory. At Hitler's accession the struggle became moot. All youth organizations were immediately "coordinated" under the leadership of the half-American Baldur von Schirach, who was appointed Youth Leader of the Entire German Reich in June 1933. Suppression of rivals to the Hitler Youth was now only a matter of time.

Resistance to the early Hitler Youth was serious. Middle-class parents deplored its lower-class makeup, its lack of supervision of coed activities, and its penchant for street violence. Opposition to membership was particularly strong in the Catholic Church, which had its own well-organized youth movement. The issue was not support of Hitler, which was often wildly enthusiastic, but control of the young. In August 1933, after their bishops had thanked Hitler for signing the Concordat with the Vatican and had declared that the new Chancellor had been "appointed by God," thousands of Catholic Youths pledged allegiance to Hitler in a ceremony at Berlin's Neukolln Stadium.[2] Many of the other beleaguered youth organizations made strenuous efforts to emulate the Hitler Youth. The Catholics allowed rifle practice on their camp outings and Protestants advocated "militant Christianity." A Jewish group in Berlin dressed its distinctly noncombative boys in gray shirts and black-edged gray scarves, which looked quite like the Hitler Youth uniform.[3] Another Jewish organization, in Breslau, had full-fledged paramilitary training complete with war games pitting the "Germans" (themselves) against an unknown foe, after which they sat around the campfire singing a mixture of "idealistic Cossack and Nordic songs."[4] Some older Jewish students, full of patriotism, tried to convince Hitler that they should be allowed to participate in the Hitler Youth and, for a time, a few were cynically granted a kind of associate membership as propagandists.[5]

But the newly powerful Hitler Youth had no intention of sharing. Under the leadership of von Schirach, the competition was gradually gobbled up. Using a full panoply of political dirty tricks combined with the placement of representatives on school councils, heavy propaganda, and, especially, the brilliant cultivation of peer pressure among the children themselves, the Nazis had, by late 1936, gained some five million "voluntary" members, up from approximately 120,000 in January 1933.[6] Confident that opposition was no longer a problem, Hitler now promulgated a Law Concerning the Hitler Youth, which declared that "all German young people, apart from being educated at home and at school, will be educated in the Hitler Youth physically, intellectually and morally in the spirit of National Socialism to serve the nation and the community." Membership was, however, still not compulsory; that requirement would not be instituted until December 1936.[7] Meanwhile, those who did not want to cooperate were easily kept in line by such measures as being refused entrance to examinations for the *Abitur*, Germany's elite high school diploma, if they were not HJ members.

The appeal of the ceremonial activities of the Hitler Youth formations was so seductive that compulsion was hardly necessary. The desire to belong to something glorious was especially strong in depressed and defeated Germany, whose citizens longed for pride in their country. Melita Maschmann, by now a teenager, never forgot her feelings on the night of Hitler's accession:

> Some of the uncanny feel of that night remains with me even today. The crashing tread of the feet, the somber pomp of the red and black flags, the flickering light of the torches on the faces and the songs with melodies that were at once aggressive and sentimental. . . . For hours the columns marched by. Again and again amongst them we saw groups of boys and girls scarcely older than ourselves. . . . I longed to hurl myself into this current, to be submerged and borne along by it.[8]

At age ten, boys—called cubs, or *Pimpfs*—became candidates for the Jungvolk, the lowest level of the Nazi youth movement. Girls went into the Jungmädel. The boys wore spiffy uniforms with brown shirts and black shorts, swastika armbands, and military-style caps. The girls' plumage was limited to a more conservative blue skirt and white shirt, but no less adorned with badges. Clothes were not all. Each child was given a fat training manual that emphasized military activities, and a report book, in which his achievements, or lack thereof, would be carefully noted throughout his youth. Activities were strenuous and time-consuming.

Wednesday night, nationwide, was reserved for indoctrination sessions known as Home Evenings, even though they were held in Hitler Youth facilities. The younger children were sometimes treated to exciting light shows in rooms draped in red and black. Other offerings included a sixteen-week German history course that was "calculated to strengthen . . . national faith." For the convenience of German youth groups abroad, the course was repeated in special broadcasts aimed at Africa, Asia, and the Americas. An excerpt published in the German press gives an idea of what the children heard:

> Now there commences a short radio play, "Henry I and His Son Otto." The thirteen-year-old son is indignant that his father has concluded a truce of nine years with the Huns and that he will even pay tribute to them. This shame no Saxon could bear. The father explains to him what he needs the nine years of peace for. He wants to create a cavalry army with which he can beat the Huns definitely and not only temporarily. The short play closes with an address by Henry to his army leaders.[9]

Despite such stimulating dramas, the Home Evenings frequently degenerated into somnolence. More sophisticated teenagers were soon bored by silly propaganda pamphlets and worse movies. The endless and often repeated speeches soon lost their interest, discussions of *Mein Kampf* tended to "fizzle out," and in general the meetings were "fatally lacking in interest," which led some leaders to allow the time to be spent on games and songfests.[10]

Saturdays, set aside as State Youth Day, were different. On these days, spent outdoors, even the youngest children routinely marched ten to twelve miles in training exercises. Weekends were filled with exciting, if grueling, terrain games, generally beloved by boys of any nationality, which involved map reading, espionage, and team competitions for "victory." These field exercises would become more and more military and chauvinist in nature as the child progressed through the system. The Jungmädel, whose Home Evenings were more oriented toward domestic science, had equally strenuous and practical Saturday outings. In one "espionage" exercise an entire troop was sent to track down two "spies," one German and the other foreign, in a crowded department store and prevent them from exchanging secret documents. This had to be done without attracting the attention of the store personnel or the customers. The game, which was successfully carried out, was considered good practice for the "time when they might have to catch real spies."[11] Such activities were even more serious at the innumerable summer camps and Outward Bound–type excursions that took the young people away from home for weeks on end with the object of building up their group loyalty and suppressing individualism.

Transitions were fraught with anxiety. Induction ceremonies for the Jungvolk were scheduled each year on Hitler's birthday, April 20. All through the preceding night the boys were, typically, marched to a dramatic site, preferably a medieval castle lit with flickering torches. There, in the breaking dawn, they would be exhorted to become soldiers "hard as iron" who would "make Germany what she should always have been" and to join "our great community of loyalty."[12] There were fanfares of trumpets and the singing of "Deutschland über Alles," after which the boys would surround a Nazi banner and each take an oath to "devote all my energies, all my strength to the savior of our country, Adolf Hitler. I am willing to give up my life for him, so help me God. One People, one Nation, one Führer!"

Final acceptance was not automatic. Six months later the boys were required to pass the *Pimpfenprobe*, an extremely tough series of tests, both on the contents of their fat training manual and of their physical prowess, which culminated in the dreaded *Mutprobe*, or test of courage, in which they were asked to perform such daunting feats as jumping from second-story windows in full battle gear. Only then were they given their special daggers, embossed with Hitler Youth symbols; these were objects that every German boy, Aryan or not, deeply coveted.[13]

The dagger was worn on a leather Sam Browne belt. The basic Jungvolk uniform was thus embellished with the badge of full membership. Those who rose to leadership positions got more badges and caps with gold eagles.

Uniforms were of extreme importance in all of Nazi life, permitting easy identification by superiors, pride on the part of the wearer, and humiliation for the excluded, who were condemned to drab civilian clothes. The new Nazi-wear also compensated some children for the loss of traditional uniform elements such as the elegant visored caps, a different color for each grade, formerly worn by students of the elite schools. These had been banned and burned in ceremonial bonfires by the new government in an attempt to erase class differences. Uniforms of other youth organizations, such as the very fancy ones of the monarchist German National Bismarck Youth, were actually collected and destroyed by the Nazis in order to ensure the complete obliteration of the organization. The Nazi uniforms were on constant display as the Jungvolk, led by their own fabulously accoutred drum and bugle corps, marched through town and country and participated in every traditional holiday parade and in the innumerable new ceremonies invented by the Party to honor often bogus youthful martyrs and heroes.

All this was much more fun than school and going to church. Neither parental disapproval nor the most dreadful racial discrimination could quench the desire of most small children to belong to the glorious scene. The pressure became especially strong in 1936, dubbed the Year of the Jungvolk, when the Hitler Youth went all out on recruiting. Elementary school teachers were ordered to encourage their pupils to join. The aim was universal membership of ten- to fourteen-year-olds in time for Hitler's forty-seventh birthday. The schools were bombarded with emotional movies and other visual aids. Each Nazi Party district was divided into small units in which strenuous recruiting activities took place. One Hamburg school offered a prize to the first homeroom to achieve 100 percent Jungvolk membership. The teacher put a large chart on the blackboard with a space for each child, which was filled in if he joined. Those who said they did not have parental permission were asked to bring their parents to see the teacher. Day by day, by twos and threes, the empty squares were filled. Nobody wanted to be the cause of the class losing the prize. But this class happened to include Hans-Jürgen Massaquoi, son of a German mother and an African father. He too wanted to fill in his square, and was stunned to hear that he was ineligible for the Jungvolk. Unable to believe this, he forced his mother to take him to the local Jungvolk meeting place. Looking in the door he could see the lucky members:

> Most of them, I noticed with envy, wore the small black *Dolch* (dagger) with the rhombus shaped swastika emblem of the HJ. Ever since seeing it displayed in the window of a neighborhood uniform store, I had secretly coveted this largely ceremonial weapon. Even the words *Blut und Ehre* (blood and honor) engraved on its shiny blade, and whose symbolic meaning had totally eluded me, stirred my soul.

But mother and son were unceremoniously thrown out of the building, and at school the teacher simply erased Massaquoi's empty space from the chart—and class membership was complete. The prize, a Monday off from school, was won; but not for Massaquoi, who was required to come to school anyway and sit in another classroom.[14]

Even small Aryans with high qualifications could be denied membership if their parents were not politically correct. So great was the shame of this that suicide attempts by ten-year-olds were not unheard of, and hatred or rejection of the "guilty" parents was common. Such rejection of family was exactly what the Nazis had in mind. For children and teenagers, one of the biggest attractions of the Hitler Youth was independence of parental control. Responsibility and pride came early. Jungvolk leaders could be in command of a troop of thirty or more by the time they were fourteen, and the majority of all leaders were in their twenties. Hitler Youth "duties" were perfect for adolescents, who could use them as an excuse for not doing homework or chores. Grades often plummeted as HJ "officials" on duty skipped classes without consequences from teachers who feared Party retribution. Parents who complained could be intimidated by the authorities. The pressure to conform was tremendous, and often led to more serious choices than whether or not to do the dishes.

Sixteen-year-old Jürgen Herbst was scheduled to participate in a long-planned Jungvolk night exercise, reminiscent of present-day paint-ball competitions, which consisted of an ambush and mock battle in which the "object of each group was to tear off the colored strings we and the boys of the opposing group had tied around their wrists." This important event coincided with his father's last night on leave from the Eastern Front. Herbst "felt torn as I never had experienced before. . . . I did not want to disappoint my father and tell him, through my actions, that I valued him less than the excitement that awaited me in the woods." But "duty" proved stronger, and the boy, "feeling terrible," went to the exercise. His father, who was not a Nazi and who disapproved of the influence of the Hitler Youth, was killed one month later. Years later, still full of anguish, Herbst wrote:

> More persuasive in my reactions than the supposed career benefits were the emotional rewards and immediate gratification I reaped from being acclaimed and followed as a leader of boys . . . [and] my fear that, had I not joined my comrades that night, they would have accused me of cowardice. . . . I was afraid that they would exclude me in the future from sharing in their most treasured memories.[15]

Choosing between parents and Nazi laws was no easier for girls. One *Mädel* who had just enlisted and was fearful that the authorities would see her going into a Jewish-owned store with her mother, said:

> "Mutti, I cannot go inside with you. . . . You know this schism. . . . I am in the Army and then I shall go into a Jewish store?" And then Mutti said "Why not then . . . ?" Can you picture this being torn back and forth of a young person? I would *like* to. I have nothing against the human beings, but I *may* not. Well, I still see this schism in me, I see the store in front of me, and then my mother did go inside. . . . And I stood there outside, but had a very, very bad feeling. . . . For the first time I knew that the humane stood to the rear of the Party-political. And I can never forgive myself.[16]

Another boy, eleven years old, having been told by his "big and strong" Jungvolk teacher to discourage his parents from doing business with Jews, was appalled when, the day after Kristallnacht, he discovered a Jewish business acquaintance of his father's sitting in the kitchen. That night his father helped the man escape into France. "When he came back, my mother asked him, 'Are you sure no one saw you?' 'You can rest assured,' my father told her, and at that moment I saw a smile light up my mother's face. And for the first time in my life I wished I wasn't my parents' son."[17]

Above all, it was exciting to be working for a cause. Melita Maschmann, then seventeen, noted that it was not important that she be happy, but that it was important that she "should work for Germany." Life in the Bund Deutscher Mädel, or BDM, the girls' version of the Hitler Youth, now had "a meaning independent of self," and she "discovered the ability to look

Bund Deutscher Mädel girls at a Nazi Party ceremony.

away from myself, to cease contemplating my own happiness and to serve the people of my nation" and "took refuge in a fanaticism for work which kept its hold on me . . . until the end of the Third Reich." In this case, as the Communist youths had done in the Ukraine, the fanaticism not only led her to "look away," but also to be persuaded to try to infiltrate an allegedly Communist youth group run by the brothers of a Jewish school-mate. In this she failed dismally, as the Jewish family had not been convinced of her sudden political transformation and had canceled the meeting that Gestapo agents, hiding outside as Maschmann went to the designated house, had intended to raid.

Action was indeed the thing, but it is clear that the slogans and ceremony also had their effect. Maschmann later wrote that in low moments she would be invigorated by a "glance at the . . . flag" or by calling to mind "one of the texts which expressed what we considered the purpose of our lives."[18] Above all it was music that inspired sacrifice. These emotional responses are true in most societies; it was the Nazi objectives that were so chilling. The American journalist Dorothy Thompson, driving through southern Germany in 1934, stumbled upon a Hitler Youth summer camp near Murnau and was shaken by what she saw:

> They were beautiful children. . . . They sang together, and no people sing in unison as the Germans do, thousands of them, in the open

air, young voices, still soprano, and the hills echoing! It made one feel sentimental.

An enormous banner stretched across the hillside [and] dominated the camp. It was so huge that you could see it from the farthest point. It was so prominent that every child could see it many times a day. It was white, and there was a swastika painted on it, and besides that only seven words, seven immense black words: YOU WERE BORN TO DIE FOR GERMANY!

There's lots of time to think when one drives a car. From Murnau to Munich thoughts kept racing through my head. "Little child, why were you born?" My father, who was a minister, would have said, "To serve God and your fellow man." My teachers would have said, "To become the most you can. To develop the best that is in you." Times change.

When I looked at my speedometer I was driving sixty-five miles an hour. I wanted to get away from there.[19]

Nowhere was this upsetting message driven home more effectively than at the most important ceremonies of all for the Hitler Youth, and indeed for any Nazi: the Nuremberg Party Days. These weeklong propaganda extravaganzas were given international press, newsreel, and radio coverage, and were the occasion for major Nazi policy announcements and showcasing of their military might. In the cast of some 700,000, Nazi youth formations held star billing and each region and organization sent only its best. Planning and training went on all over Germany for months before the event. In 1938, hundreds of trains brought more than 80,000 Hitler Youth and BDM girls to the convocation. They were lodged in an enormous tent city at Langwasser, just outside town. The two-mile march to this encampment through the "narrow inner city, which was a sea of flags," was already euphoric for ten-year-old Alfons Heck:

> The sidewalks were packed with people and occasionally young women would rush up and plant a kiss on the cheeks of the marchers. Add to that the sound of dozens of bands placed at strategic locations, and you have an inkling of the overwhelming atmosphere of belonging to something majestic, which was called *Deutschland*.

On the Day of the Hitler Youth, the boys and girls, carrying hundreds of flags, marched into the stadium and, after performing complex marching maneuvers, lined up to hear Hitler. Alfons, one of the youngest and smallest participants, who was given a place in the front row, would never forget the emotional impact of the speech:

Here was our mighty leader, telling us quite humbly how hard his own adolescence had been, how little hope it had held . . . especially after the bitter defeat of World War I. . . . And then his voice rose, took on power and became rasping with a strangely appealing intensity. It touched us physically because all of its emotions were reflected on our faces. We simply became an instrument in the hands of an unsurpassed master. . . . "You, my youth," he shouted, with his eyes seemingly fixed only on me, "are our nation's most precious guarantee for a great future. . . . You, my youth," he screamed hoarsely, "never forget that one day you will rule the world!" . . . We erupted into a frenzy of nationalistic pride that bordered on hysteria. For minutes on end, we shouted at the top of our lungs, with tears streaming down our faces: "*Sieg Heil, Sieg Heil, Sieg Heil!*" From that moment on, I belonged to Adolf Hitler body and soul.[20]

Hitler had good reason to encourage his youth. As he spoke that day at Nuremberg, Germany teetered on the brink of war over control of the Sudetenland, a large slice of Czechoslovakia bordering on Germany where the majority of the population were ethnic Germans. Indeed, his final Nuremberg speech, two days later, was so threatening that American correspondents listening in Prague expected to see German bombers overhead the next day, and the Czech government proclaimed martial law in its German districts.[21] But the excited Hitler children were oblivious to these realities. After the speeches, everyone gathered around a huge bonfire, which "lent an air of mysticism reminiscent of ancient Teutonic festivals," and sang Hitler Youth songs while Baldur von Schirach handed out medals—including one to the astonished Alfons Heck. This, like everything else, was not spontaneous or personal: for propaganda reasons, the troop leaders had been ordered to find two of the newest Jungvolk boys to present to the Reich Youth Leader.

At age fourteen there was another major transition, when the Jungvolk and Jungmädel became Hitler Youth and BDM members, respectively. Only the Jungvolk's own leaders stayed behind to bring along the new recruits. Things immediately became more serious. While the outings and indoctrination sessions continued, the HJ and BDM teenagers were now used for any number of community services, political activities, and military construction projects by mainstream Nazi agencies that competed ferociously for control of their services. The prewar HJ/BDM bureaucracy was enormous. Thirteen different departments made films, printed books, published newspapers and propaganda, and organized local formations.

They ran a medical service; had a foreign department; organized a plethora of military, industrial, and agricultural training programs; and set up elite schools and leadership training programs. The Hitler Youth even had its own junior Gestapo, which would eventually emulate its big brother in every way.

The young people required to enter the HJ/BDM ranks were not usually aware of the octopus-like aspects of the organization. The majority simply joined a local *Kameradschaft* of fifteen members. Three *Kameradschaften* made a *Schar,* and three *Scharen* made a *Gefolgschaft.* The latter units had their own flags and team spirit, and their carefully chosen leaders, following the Führerprinzip, had absolute power over their subordinates. The groupings, ever larger, continued until the *Obergebiet* of some 375,000, of which there were six in the whole country. The BDM structure was the same; only the names were different.

There is no question that, throughout its existence, the HJ/BDM performed important community service, especially in poor areas. But there was enormous variance in the enthusiasm levels and organizational efficiency of the units, due in large part to the lack of well-trained leaders who could deal with the Hitler Youth's explosive growth. Exciting ceremonies did not happen every day, and inexperienced unit chiefs, "for lack of knowing anything better to do, let us stand in formation for hours, saluted each other, and marched us around the block," noted one bored participant.[22] By 1937, the compulsory HJ activities had begun to seem dangerously routine to some members and many of the exercises pointless.[23] Teachers in many schools, irritated by constant press attacks from the HJ leadership, began to reassert their power. A Nazi official complained, "They have even begun giving the pupils homework on the days when they have activities, with the result that they stay away."[24]

Administration and financial accountancy left much to be desired among the paperwork-shy youth leaders, and morality was far from perfect. Youth was supposed to lead youth, but the resulting discipline was often lax. There were cases of homosexuality, teenage pregnancy, and other promiscuity. A twelve-year-old Jungmädel in Aachen got in trouble for passing a dirty song around her unit. Recruiters for the SS were shocked at the situation in the inner city of Frankfurt, where they found "signs of degeneration" and all sorts of physically and racially unacceptable boys in the HJ ranks. They were particularly upset by the "feminine elements" in some units, lads who not only had "broad pelvises, narrow shoulders, secondary female sexual characteristics" and "feminine movements," but also sported longish hair, were "heavily perfumed," and were fit only for "aesthetic functions" such as leading discussion groups.[25] No one mentioned that this description fit not only the plump Youth Leader, Baldur von Schirach, but even more so the rotund and jewel-bedecked Luftwaffe chief, Hermann Göring.

To counter these trends more interesting volunteer options were promoted. Boys could apply for Motorized, Naval, Aviation, and even Mounted Hitler Youth units. These were immensely popular and, of course, provided even greater premilitary training. To make sure that all boys would have such training, Hitler authorized the creation of a massive network of HJ War Preparation Camps (WEL). Those still in school went during their vacations, and employers of young workers were required to give them leave.[26] Once the war began, those sent to the WEL camps and recruited for paramilitary units were younger and younger. In 1942, Alfons Heck, aged fourteen, four years after his epiphany at Nuremberg, was taken into an Aviation unit, and to his immense satisfaction, had completed thirty solo glider flights by the end of his Easter vacation. From that time on his only ambition was to fly fighter planes.[27] Boys in these units were sometimes excused from duty with the other agricultural and labor services that were otherwise routinely required of all young people.

Thousands of other children were kept busy by the Hitler Youth's endless competitions in everything from sports to carpentry. The National Vocational Competition had 3.5 million entrants by 1939. The contestants competed first at the local level and then moved up to the national championship. The winners of each branch contest, which included coppersmiths, electricians, and so forth, were taken to Berlin to be feted and to meet Hitler.[28] This did not always turn out as the Nazis had planned. The 1944 Reich Electrician winner was Herman Rosenau, a half-Jew who had been sent off like everyone else to a WEL camp by recruiters who, by that late date, were more interested in cannon fodder than racial profiles. Herman, previously excluded from Hitler Youth membership, did well at the camp and won badges for firefighting and other talents. Later he remarked:

> I must say I enjoyed the time I spent and the duties I had. . . . It was the first time I wasn't excluded from taking part. No one treated me like some kind of an exotic crippled insect. I was a normal person like everyone else. Being an outcast even during school days, when my good friends . . . had become leaders in the HJ was naturally depressing.

Rosenau did not get to see Hitler, who by April 1944 no longer ventured out much into bomb-shattered Berlin, but received his prize from

Dr. Robert Ley, head of the German Labor Front, and was interviewed on the radio before dining with a group of the highest Nazi officials. Herman was delighted: "For me personally this was a triumphant situation. There I sat, a 'sub-human' with all the big men, and not one of them knew who I really was." The Hitler Youth leadership, once enlightened, canceled the award and asked for the medal back. Herman did not return it: "I had my pride. . . . After all, I had been declared winner of a national competition."[29]

Physical fitness was one of the unathletic Führer's healthier obsessions. Fit bodies would prepare children for battle and hard labor. Competition and team spirit, as any sports fan knows, can easily be manipulated into the most fanatic dedication and mutual sacrifice. On the more practical side was the fact, clear to any boarding school headmaster, that athletic competition was an excellent outlet for adolescent energy and aggression. Soon an enormous program, once again totally centralized under the Hitler Youth, was under way. Athletic achievement medals were awarded at every level of youth organization. The National Sport Competition, begun in 1935, involved some 80 percent of all teenagers by 1939. The choice of sports was not like that of most countries, however. Nothing could have been further from the vaunted playing fields of England. Emphasis was not on soccer, hockey, or rugby, but was oriented toward gymnastics, running, swimming, and shooting, which were useful in the ubiquitous "terrain" competitions.

By 1936, a separate office had been set up by Baldur von Schirach to deal with "military sports" as distinct from the others. Its shooting instructors were kindly provided by the SS, and later, at the behest of the famous future Desert Fox, General Erwin Rommel, by the regular Army. The program was a big success, and by 1939, 51,500 boys had qualified for the exclusive Hitler Youth Marksmanship Medal.[30]

The more bucolic aspects of life were not left out of the HJ/BDM equation. For girls and boys who had finished their schooling, a period of work on the land or in other worthy pursuits run by the government was obligatory before they could enter regular employment or continue their studies. From the beginning, the "Blood and Soil" theories of the Nazis had glorified rural life and the peasant as the purest element of the Volk. It was felt that young people should be brought back from the cities, whence industry had lured them, and should be encouraged to remain in the country. In 1934, the Prussian state government had mandated a compulsory Land Year for children aged fourteen to eighteen who had completed their schooling. The estimated 25,000 youngsters were to live in rural

homes controlled by the Ministry of Education. "The people," declared
the law, "must be brought back to nature"; doing so would lead "to the
selection of the racially valuable" and create "political-soldierly characters
as against weak intellectuals." An American diplomat reporting on the law
also noted that the program would "relieve unemployment" and that it
appeared to be "another attempt to indoctrinate the children of Germany
with National Socialist ideas."[31]

Not to be outdone, von Schirach's Reich Youth Directorate (RJF),
heavily supported by Himmler and the SS,[32] soon instituted its own competing Land Service. From the leadership levels of the HJ/BDM, youth
wardens were appointed to organize rural children and promote child welfare especially in southern and eastern Germany, where conditions were
often very primitive. Their activities included improving schools, health
care, and nutrition as well as prevention of excessive child labor and promotion of "genetically healthy" marriages. Melita Maschmann noted:

> All the rural programs had mixed receptions. Urban parents were often
> not happy that their children were being sent to remote places, and did
> not feel that careers on the farm offered a great future. While the young
> people certainly were a help in some tasks, such as the harvest and
> childcare, many conservative farmers felt that the program was "some-
> thing newfangled and unwelcome." They did not credit city girls with
> the ability to work and they were afraid that we would be critical or
> poke our noses into their affairs.[33]

Less prosperous farmers treated both boys and girls like the forced
labor that would soon replace them. During her Land Service stint,
Maschmann was required to wash a sick man's filthy underwear, do heavy
fieldwork, and deal with an alcoholic widow and her feebleminded son,
both of whom tended to pass out by afternoon. But in the end she was
inspired: "The physical exhaustion . . . changed suddenly into an un-
quenchable joy in creation." She endured because she believed she was
needed, and she loved life in the camp where the workers were lodged, as
its homogeneous makeup seemed to her to exemplify the "National Community."[34] Maschmann, who would rise relatively high in the BDM hierarchy, did not stay "on the land," but it is estimated that more than 20
percent of participants, mostly drawn from poorer families, would have
done so had the war not prevented them from doing so.

Not everyone did farmwork. Girls could do a Home Economics Year as
nannies and housekeepers. Both boys and girls could also be called into
the Reich Labor Service (RAD). This organization, originally created by

the Weimar government to combat unemployment and used for big government projects such as canal building, was soon taken over by the Nazis.
Its brown-uniformed members marched at the Nuremberg rallies, carrying gleaming shovels on their shoulders. Its ideological aim was to
acquaint young men with manual labor and, as was true in all Nazi formations, eliminate class differences: Hitler in 1934 referred to the RAD and
other such formations as "social smelting-furnaces in which gradually a
new German man will be formed."[35] The Nazi addition of military drills
and indoctrination on top of the physically demanding work indeed had a
"smelting" effect, as a 1938 report from exiled German Social Democrats
shows:

> 4:45 AM get up. 4:50 gymnastics. 5:15 wash make beds. 5:30 coffee
> break. 5:50 parade. 6:00 march to building site. Work until 14:30 with
> 30 minute break for breakfast. 15:00 Lunch. 15:30–18:00 drill.
> 18:10–18:45 instruction. 18:45–19:15 cleaning and mending. 19:15
> parade. 19:30 announcements. 19:45 supper. 20:00–21:30 singsong or
> other leisure activities. 22:00 lights out. . . . The day is thus filled with
> duties. The young people, who have been deadened by excessive physi-
> cal exertion, have neither the strength nor the time for the slightest
> flicker of independent intellectual life.[36]

That, of course, was the whole idea.

        Needless to say, many young people tried to escape these activi-
ties altogether. The Hitler Youth police force, known as the Streifendienst,
or SRD, was, therefore, constantly expanded.[37] The SRD had been set up
in 1935, before Hitler Youth membership became compulsory. In an
attempt to improve the organization's reputation, SRD patrols were sent
out to control members indulging in "wild wandering and idle tramping."
This they achieved by secret surveillance of HJ and BDM groups in youth
hostels and camping areas or on the streets. In addition, they enforced
curfews, pursued expelled HJ members who still wore the uniform, and
tried to identify and infiltrate youth groups carrying on anti-Nazi activity.
Reports on the latter were sent back to headquarters and on to the grown-
up police, who then took action.
        In 1936 the Law Concerning German Youth was expanded to make
Hitler Youth membership obligatory, and was bolstered by a stricter Disciplinary Code. Enforcement of its measures now also became the duty of
the SRD. Working along with the Gestapo and the Kripo, the SRD spied

on their own leaders, opened mail, and patrolled movies and bars (much to the irritation of the proprietors) for underage colleagues. By 1938, they could also detain fellow juveniles for anything that violated the race and sex laws. The SRD was especially zealous in spying on the churches and could denounce pastors who made inflammatory sermons. Outdoors, they tracked down groups meeting in the country and watched highways and forest trails for suspicious activity.

Violators of the Disciplinary Code could, on SRD authority, be brought before special Hitler Youth courts completely independent of the mainstream legal system. These trials were hardly objective. All court officials were in the HJ leadership corps. There were no defense representatives and the accused were not allowed to see evidence relating to their political evaluation. The Hitler Youth generally avoided total expulsion, which would lower its available manpower pool, and, at this stage, tended to use public humiliation and fines instead.

All this police action was needed, for despite vicious suppression and exile of their leaders, the old youth organizations such as the Boy Scouts had not disappeared entirely. A number simply continued their activities and sang their old songs under the guise of Hitler Youth meetings held in secret forest hideouts or mountain retreats, and even, in one ingenious case, in boats floating down a stream.[38] Catholic groups were particularly defiant, and for a time maintained dual membership. Attempts to stop this practice were, for a time, successfully challenged in the courts, enabling 2,000 Catholic boys to go on a pilgrimage to Rome and be received by the Pope in 1935, and several thousand others to attend Catholic summer camps abroad as late as 1937.[39]

More difficult to control were the "wild" gangs whose main objective was rebellion against any kind of compulsory service. These increased when the war began and led the authorities to impose curfews for the young "due to the changed conditions of life wrought by the war." Teenagers under eighteen were not allowed to "loiter" after dark and could not be in a café without an adult after 9:00 p.m. They could not drink spirits, smoke cigarettes, or chew tobacco in public. Dancing without an older "guardian" present was forbidden, and no dancing at all was allowed after 11:00 p.m.[40] This was waving the red flag. The defiant "wild" groups then, as now, dressed in far-out clothes, drank a lot, and indulged in jam sessions where they listened to forbidden American songs and "Negro Jazz." The famous "swingboys" of Hamburg, who numbered into the thousands, had wild parties, many of which were held in middle-class houses when parents were out of town. For this crowd, appearance as far removed from the Hitler Youth uniform as possible was the thing. Hitler Youth reject Hans-Jürgen Massaquoi, who had gravitated to this milieu, sported long hair and sideburns, which were worn along with "knee length double-breasted jackets, wide-bottom pants that nearly covered our shoes, starched shirt collars, waist fitting navy blue overcoats, matching homburg hats and—as a touch of elegance—white silk scarves."[41] Provoking the SRD was half the fun:

> Part of the excitement of being a swingboy was the harassment of the HJ. . . . Rarely did a week go by without a HJ patrol showing up at our popular hangout. They would quietly block the exits, then fan out and systematically go from table to table in order to check—of all things—the length of the male patron's hair. Swingboys with the longest hair were . . . marched under guard to a facility where . . . barbers stood ready to give them the clipping of their lives. . . . Those who had their locks forcibly sheared "wore" their baldness like a badge of courage.[42]

In Duisburg, the less elegant Kittelsbach Pirates, made up of boys of many persuasions, specialized in ambushes of HJ boys in the streets and anti-Nazi graffiti. The SRD did not always prevail in such confrontations. In Kiel, a patrol trying to break up a secret jazz session was routed when the musicians beat them with their drumsticks and wooden flutes.[43]

There were many other such groups all over Germany, most with colorful names such as Bush Wolves, Dreadful Stones, Navajos, and Municipal Bath Broth, few of which ever had any real political effect, but which, all through the war, remained objects of strange fascination and doubt to their more dutiful peers who glimpsed them only infrequently. Jürgen Herbst, now seventeen and proudly on his way to join the famous Grossdeutschland Regiment of the Wehrmacht, was caught in a bomb shelter with a group of Edelweiss Pirates:

> All of us stared mesmerized at the small group of youngsters, boys mainly, who sat on the floor at the center of the gray concrete hall. . . . I had considered them a nuisance who, in their dress and behavior, contrasted unfavorably with us boys in the Jungvolk and were best ignored by us. . . . Now as I watched them strumming their guitars and listened to them singing their sorrowful tune I could not help but be strangely moved. . . . Long-haired, gypsy neckerchiefs over their collars, their pants slit at the sides, the boys ostentatiously mocked the soldierly look that German youths were to show. The girls in their sweaters and skirts billowing over gray corduroy pants looked as if they had just crept out from under the bombed out ruins outside. Their message was of death

and sorrow, not of final victory, which was then the main theme of Nazi propaganda. . . . I did not think the scene augured well for my going to war.[44]

The rules for teenagers were made even stricter in 1939 and 1940 by two Youth Service laws, which equated duty in youth programs with military service and made public service compulsory for sixteen- to eighteen-year-olds.[45] This was beefed up by an SS Police Order for the Protection of Youth, which implemented short-term "youth service arrests" for evaders. Under this measure offenders aged fourteen to eighteen, after a quick hearing, could be given weekend detentions on bread and water or be incarcerated in a variety of punishment camps.[46]

Such was the fate of Karma Rauhut, who, with the help of sympathetic teachers, had been able to evade BDM membership for years, first by going to a private school outside her home district and later through family influence. One classmate who had wanted to denounce Karma early on had hesitated to do so because of these possibly powerful connections. Rauhut later noted that "if one had no connections one was done for. . . . One could create a certain free space for oneself . . . if one had enough connections and maybe also a little bit of money. . . . You did not want to stand out. You only wanted to carry on with your style of life without selling yourself." Despite her efforts, Karma, in the end, could not avoid her Duty Year. Disqualified by her record of evasion from the nicer jobs, she was sent to a windswept, barbed-wire-enclosed "work duty" camp peopled mostly by reform school girls and prostitutes, who cheered her up no end. She needed support, for, in this place,

> everything was done to destroy a personality. And it happened very fast. Astonishingly fast . . . withholding of food, withholding of sleep, away from everything, and always living under a threat. One becomes kaput very fast. . . . The more intelligent and sensitive a human being is, the faster he goes kaput. . . . Takes only days.

When Karma became too ill to write home, her parents asked a young Luftwaffe doctor to check on her. With his aid she escaped, married her rescuer, and, with the help of his commanding officer, spent the rest of the war in hiding in Austria.[47]

For the truly incorrigible, Himmler set up a special "youth protective custody camp" for boys at Moringen in 1940, and another for girls at Uckermarck in 1942. Eventually, juveniles could be sent to these camps without reference to parents, legal guardians, or the courts. The inmates were given the now standard physical, racial, and psychological examinations, and the "unfit" were often sterilized before being sent on to other institutions. Those who remained were treated as concentration camp inmates and used as forced labor. The camps were not large, but knowledge of their existence had great deterrent effect.[48]

As time went on, the SRD came more and more under SS control and eventually would be the main feeder organization for its racial and police agencies. From its ranks also came those destined for concentration and death camp administration. For these special forces the SS height limitation was generously lowered from five foot ten to five foot six. After 1939, it was not unusual for SRD boys to be taken out of school for special operations and "auxiliary police work." Training camps proliferated, and a full-time school for teenaged spies was set up at Pretzsch-on-the-Elbe. Boys destined for the spy school were extracted from their local schools or apprenticeships, often over the protests of parents and teachers. The SRD boys were zealous as only fanatic teenagers can be, especially when it came to sex crimes, and sometimes had to be restrained by their elders, many of them sinners themselves, who suggested that they "not take their jobs too seriously where girls of 17 and 18 were concerned" and that they not treat "sober tasks" as "romantic adventures."[49]

In the end the SRD and its adult allies prevailed. The majority of HJ and BDM members conformed, as there was very little way to resist. Even the swingboys would eventually be swept up in the draft. The safe thing to do was not to rock the boat. Fear of punishment and humiliation were very strong, but often not clearly recognized, as Jürgen Herbst relates:

> I had realized . . . that there were reasons why people were afraid to speak, although these reasons were not entirely clear to me in all their details. I was afraid myself, afraid what I might do to my mother . . . [and others] if I spoke to anyone about the things I knew about them. . . . I wondered whether it was the same with my friends, but it was exactly that fear that kept me from asking them. . . . I assumed that they shared it, yet I didn't know for sure.

The smallest slip or unconsidered remark could cause agonies of fear of denunciation. Sitting around one night during a bombing raid with school-mates who were repeating German victory propaganda such as "Göring said no British bomber will ever fly over our country," Herbst inadvertently exclaimed, "This is how they lie!":

There was abrupt, absolute stillness. My eyes fell on one of my class-mates, who happened to be the son of our local SS chief. As I stared in his face, an ice-cold hand seemed to brush down my back. . . . "What did I say? What have I done?" was all I could think.[50]

Nothing came of the incident, but Herbst was afraid for a long time.

The easiest way to deal with such doubts was action, which the war provided in plenty. Few will decline to fight for their country once war is under way, and German youth, like that of all other countries, obeyed the call. How this could have been true after the all too recent slaughter of World War I, in which, day after day, the cream of Europe's youth leaped out of trenches only to be mowed down by the thousands within an instant, is impossible to explain, except by the fact that it was a new generation, heavily indoctrinated, and that the physical ghastliness of war cannot be communicated by word or image, but must be experienced to be understood.

The training of future Nazi leaders was not limited to extracurricular activities: a many-faceted school system was also created for them. Within a year of the takeover of the government there were forty-nine Hitler Youth leadership training academies, foremost among them the Reichsführer school at Potsdam, and entrance into the higher levels of the HJ was greatly expanded.[51] But these short-term programs were not considered to be enough. The real need was for a complete Nazi education that would not be contaminated by other influences. Two secondary school systems, the so-called NAPOLAs and the Adolf Hitler Schools, were set up to provide such instruction. For high school graduates there were the Ordensburgen, with three-year courses, and a graduate-level Hohe Schule, personally authorized by Hitler in January 1940, which was supposed to become the center for Nazi ideological and educational research after the conclusion of the war.[52]

The Nazi Party was not united on the format or control of these institutions. The Hitler Youth, the Army, the SS, and other agencies competed to use the schools as recruiting grounds. Time also militated against them. The Hohe Schule, which planned an Institute for Research into the Jewish Question with a library made up of items confiscated from synagogues and Jewish collectors, would never open. The fantastic Ordensburgen,[53] set up by Labor Front leader Robert Ley, were also limited by the war. The students, known as "Junkers," a title taken from the Prussian nobility, were to be housed in very fancy new "castles" that began to be built at the expense of the Labor Front in 1934. In these luxurious palaces, strong, blond young men would receive much indoctrination and sport and little academic training. Indeed, it was discovered that more than one hour a day of academics at the castles was rare and that only one lecture every two or three days was not unusual. Some Party leaders noted that "many Junkers cannot digest a lecture delivered with spirit and intellectual content. They do their best to understand and retain it, but even then what has been learnt is isolated and a relationship to other preceding lectures does not exist."[54] Remedial tutorials did not seem to improve things, and some of the disillusioned students tried to get out of the program altogether, despite the fact that Ordensjunkers got big allowances, were to be allowed to travel abroad, and, if married, could have their wives come for long visits.

The secondary schools, controlled by various Nazi interests, were far more serious. The NAPOLAs, or National Political High Schools, were started in 1933, and the Adolf Hitler Schools in 1937. The Adolf Hitler Schools, entirely controlled by the Nazi Party, were, like the Ordensburgen, academically weak and little more than controlled sources for SS recruiting.[55]

The NAPOLAs and the similar Oberschule at Feldafing, near Munich, founded by the SA, were a different story. These were traditional, military-style boarding schools, whose classes were called "platoons." They were not a Nazi invention, but were related to the cadet schools of imperial Germany and Prussia, which had been closed by the Allies at the end of World War I. Revived in 1933, their director and most of their faculty came from the prewar German youth movement and not from the Hitler Youth, and they reported to the Minister of Education and not to the Nazi Party. These schools succumbed only gradually to the control of Himmler, who greatly expanded the Nazi secondary school system during the war and even set up similar Reichsschule, aimed at the Nazification of racially acceptable boys and girls, in the occupied lands.[56]

By 1942 there were forty-two NAPOLAs, two of which were for girls. Each school had its own orientation toward a certain discipline, but the basic curriculum was that of mainstream German secondary schools. Their mission was to provide a well-educated supply of dedicated Nazi youth who would become functionaries for all sectors of public service at home and abroad. Students from all social classes were to be put into a highly structured setting theoretically reminiscent of the famous British public schools, where "removed from the spoiling influence of the parental home" the "need to survive wakens," and the boy is toughened and provided with "security and firmness of will." For all of this "the authoritarian principle" was considered "indispensable."[57]

The NAPOLAs, which became very popular, were ferociously selective. Ten-year-old children were nominated by their local elementary schools and interviewed by NAPOLA representatives. Only 20 percent normally made the first cut. This triage was followed by an eight-day examination at the nearest NAPOLA. During the ordeal, academic exams were given in the mornings and athletic tests in the afternoon. Physical capacity and character were closely observed. This was not always fun: nonswimmers, for example, might be thrown into the deep end of a pool (with lifeguards ready) to see how they would cope; others were dropped miles from the school at night and ordered to find their way home through unknown terrain. Of those taking the exam, only 30 percent were admitted, and even then they had a six-month probation period. In glaring contrast to England and the United States, where mothers and fathers normally schemed and plotted for their children's admission to the top schools, parental desire was not even considered. One widow who had lost a son in the war, and who wanted to keep her remaining child at home, was told:

> My dear lady, you had better adjust your ideas. Your son is not your personal property, solely at your disposal. He is on loan to you but he is the property of the German Volk. To object to his name being put forward for an elite school is tantamount to insulting the Führer and the Reich.[58]

Once in, these children received a very solid, if completely Nazified, basic education. Hours were spent listening to the speeches of Goebbels and Hitler, and every Nazi ceremonial occasion was celebrated. Reading lists, while including the German classics, were heavily laden with military and Nazi texts. But there was an excellent pupil-teacher ratio, and the teachers were not mere Party hacks. Community service was required, as were reports on such work and suggestions for the improvement of society. One boy who had worked with miners thought they needed more pay. Another felt juvenile delinquency was due to the absence of religion. They were also prepared to be an elite. A "colonial" attitude with "an air of superiority and aloofness, impeccable manners and style" was encouraged. Even the sports were rather gentlemanly; they included horseback riding, sailing, and golf.[59]

Cultural activities were not neglected. At the SA Oberschule in Feldafing, a short bus ride from Munich, the boys, chosen from families whose financial means would not normally have included such frills, were treated to an enormous variety of Munich attractions, which included its museums, concerts, theaters, and even a marionette show. They also went to Nazi propaganda extravaganzas such as the Degenerate Art exhibition, at which modern works unacceptable to Hitler were displayed in a negative light, and the Eternal Jew show, in which Jews and their culture received similar treatment. There were longer trips too. They saw *Siegfried* at Bayreuth, cruised on the Rhine, and went to air bases, military memorials, and the 1936 Olympics in Berlin.

All of this was aimed at producing "a new human type needed by the future National Socialist Reich." If the yearbook comments of the graduating class of 1938 of Oberschule Feldafing are any indicator, the experiment was a success. The graduates said that they had arrived at the school with many differing views and desires, but that within days they and their teachers had become a "firm community" and from then on had "lived National Socialism." They were leaving the school with "a single goal in their hearts: to serve the whole of Germany and its people" and "act as young German National Socialists."[60]

So confident were the directors of these schools in their boys that, up to 1938, they ran exchange programs with elite British and American schools such as Rugby, St. Paul's (London), Choate, and Phillips Andover. The Feldafing school even had plans for an international summer school where German and foreign boys would form comradeships and build "bridges from people to people."

It is not clear just how the International Schoolboy Fellowship, which sponsored the exchanges in the United States, decided to send a selection of American prep school boys to these Nazi elite schools, but in the fall of 1937 a dozen or so recent graduates, who had little knowledge of Germany or Europe, arrived in Germany and, overnight, found themselves dressed in lederhosen or fatigues, marching to and from their classes. On formal occasions and in public, the uniforms were expanded to full Nazi panoply, complete with swastika armbands.

The Americans were not required to take the full course load and did not have to worry much about grades. Choate graduate Walter Filley, sent to Feldafing, concentrated on German language and history. He was particularly struck by the dominance of the theme of the "reawakening" of Germany. School plays and readings, written by the students themselves, ran heavily to skits on the heroism of soldiers and sailors dying at the lost battles of Langemarck and "Scapa Flow" (Jutland) and strident dramatizations of the "German Spirit" in dialogues between such patriotic icons and reformers as Martin Luther, Baron von Stein, and Count Gerhard von Scharnhorst.[61] Equally striking was the constant emphasis on the decadence of the "East." Distinguished professors lectured on Germany's "destiny in the East" and implied that since France and England had taken away all of its colonies elsewhere, Germany now would be justified in seeking others in that direction. Anti-Polish sentiment ran high, and Filley saw maps on which the borders with Poland, which had gained large chunks of German territory in 1918, were depicted as dripping with blood. When he innocently suggested that a classmate named Komorowski must be of Polish descent, the boy attacked him and had to be restrained by other students. Anti-Jewish comments were frequent, but when Filley objected to a particularly nasty cartoon in *Die Stürmer* that was posted in the local village, the other students told him that that sort of thing was "not for us, but for the people."

The German students were allowed to read newspapers and listen to the radio, but their knowledge of the world was as limited as was that of the Americans. Filley found that the oldest boys were the most open to discussion, up to a point. The American students were allowed to receive the Sunday *New York Times,* which upset their hosts when it ran anti-Hitler cartoons and articles. The German boys all believed that the Jews, which included President Franklin D. Roosevelt, ran the United States. Filley and his fellow American students defended their country and its ideas, but were determined to "learn and observe" and tried to avoid serious confrontations. This was more difficult the following fall for Frank Lee, another exchange student from Choate. He too was well received, but late in the fall he was called before the headmaster for having said to a chambermaid, who had reported him, that he considered Julius Streicher, editor of *Die Stürmer,* "an animal." The headmaster suggested that in the future he "keep quiet." Lee's mother did not like this story, and the boy simply did not return after Christmas vacation.[62]

The Americans participated fully in the off-campus excursions. So it was that, within days of his arrival in September 1937, Filley found himself dressed in full regalia, in the midst of a formation sent to take part in the ceremonies welcoming Italian dictator Mussolini to Munich. A few months later, holding a flaming torch in each hand, he formed part of the protective cordons on the streets as Hitler returned in triumph after his takeover of Austria. As Hitler passed, the crowd surged forward, and Filley was only a few feet away from the Führer's open car. Later he mused that he could have changed history had he assassinated the German leader with his flaming torch at that moment, but the idea had not occurred to him then. Filley, like so many others at the time, including most of the Austrians, was not unsympathetic to the idea of the Germans "regaining" Austrian territory. The feeling was different a year later. Frank Lee had also seen Hitler close up during ceremonies surrounding the Munich Conference and the annual celebration of the Beer Hall Putsch. But any positive feelings he had about the achievements of the Nazi government were "really turned around" by the "sight of kids laughing at burning stores and broken windows" after Kristallnacht.

Despite all the Nazi activity, the Americans made friends with their classmates and had as much fun as anybody on the many ski trips and camping excursions. Filley felt that his fellow students were a decent bunch and that few were fanatics, but that all were being conditioned by a "steady drumbeat of propaganda" to defend their country and restore its pride.[63] Another Choate boy wrote in the school newspaper that students sent to Germany had made "many startling discoveries, such as that all Germans are not necessarily born criminals, and that Hitler is not Beelzebub, Machiavelli, and Judas Iscariot combined and re-incarnated,"[64] an opinion they undoubtedly would later revise.

For the German boys who came to the United States there were also revelations. They were instructed to guard against exaggeration, and respect the institutions of other countries, but to know their facts and be able to provide convincing evidence of the worth of National Socialism lest they and Germany be put down. One boy horrified the Connecticut family he stayed with before the opening of school by immediately putting a photograph of Hitler on his bureau, and amazed his peers by declaring that he had "let his Führer down" when he lost a tennis match to a girl. But, like the American students, the Germans soon learned to blend in. They were warmly welcomed and some were quite taken with "this rather strange but lovely type of American girl" they met at school parties. They found that the Americans were "interested in Germany and made comparisons between Roosevelt and Germany, between the New Deal and the German labor service." But, concerning Kristallnacht, "even Americans who were very friendly toward Germany said, 'Not this. This we can't understand.' "[65] In England, where they were also well received, they found "a lack of toughness" on the sports field and were surprised that "anti-German propaganda" was so widespread and that people were "misinformed" about Hitler's programs.

No one's beliefs were changed by the exchanges. Rolf Stoves, a German student at Choate, though full of praise for American hospitality, noted that although he was constantly assured that America was a free and democratic country where he could do as he pleased, everyone "tried to convince me how bad it was in Germany and that I had better change my belief." With time, he continued, he had "learned to understand the reasons why our form of government looks so terrible to democratic observers," but he hoped that the Americans would "understand that we Germans like the form of government we chose for our country as well as you like your political ideas."[66]

On one thing the boys from all countries agreed: the idea of confronting their new classmates on the battlefield filled them with dismay. Rolf Stoves hoped "with all my heart that someday the United States and Germany will come to a peaceful understanding . . . and safer peace for all nations."[67] This hope was not to be fulfilled for a long time: more than half of his class from Feldafing would perish in the coming war.

The war would open a plethora of new opportunities for Nazi control of children, and they took advantage of every one. For years the Nazi Party had run camps in the country to improve the health of city children. Once the bombing of cities began, tens of thousands of children were evacuated to the countryside under this program, the Kinderlandverschickung, or KLV. Children aged six to ten were sent to families, and ten- to fourteen-year-olds to communal camps. In addition, a plan was made to place mothers with very small children in rural homes. This plan was not obligatory, and some parents were reluctant to send their children far away. But the fact that schools were often moved in toto often persuaded them otherwise. Estimates of the total number of children who did eventually participate in this program range from three to five million. The exact number of camps is also unclear, probably due to the fact that a "camp" could have anywhere from twenty children in a house to a thousand children in a large establishment, but they surely numbered in the thousands, many of which would be set up in newly conquered Poland.

Specially trained cooks and housekeepers, plus medical staff, were provided, but these adults were not entirely in control. Yet another special training school was set up to prepare teenaged HJ and BDM members for duty as "camp squad leaders" who, in addition to carrying on HJ activities, would supervise the children during the time they would normally have spent with their families. Once separated from parents and the mainline school authorities, these children too were available for full-time indoctrination and premilitary training.[68]

By all accounts, conditions in the KLV camps varied tremendously. In his memoir, *A Hitler Youth in Poland,* Jost Hermand describes five different camps to which he was sent in the course of the war. The contrasts are staggering. One was a brick schoolhouse with no running water or electricity, in a tiny and remote Polish village, without stores or post office, where "when it rained the main street dissolved in an impassable field of mud"; another was a large and luxurious villa, given to Hitler by Mussolini, in San Remo on the Italian Riviera, where the boys were waited on hand and foot; and there was an exciting ski camp, where they received training suitable for mountain troops.

The routine in the Polish village camp was standard. In the morning classes were conducted by teachers, some of whom lapsed into apathy in this remote location. When they went home in the afternoon, the boys came under the control of their usually seventeen-year-old HJ camp leaders, who supervised competitive games, marching, and "physical hardening." There were the usual songfests and indoctrination sessions. The leaders (one of whom carried a club and gave his orders with whistle blasts) had absolute authority, and sadistic punishments and "mindless harassment" were not rare.

In this totalitarian world of children, one's place in the pecking order became all important: "We ourselves were part of a pyramidal social hierarchy in which the individual had to assert himself, often quite cruelly, in order to be accepted." No one helped anyone else. At the top were the boys who excelled in the sometimes vicious games and roughhousing. Being tagged a "sissy" was anathema; one of the worst things that could happen was to have one's mother visit. Many mothers did try to move near their children, but this practice was publicly condemned as "disruptive" by Hitler Youth chief Artur Axmann, who succeeded Baldur von Schirach in July 1940. The boys, therefore, aware that their outgoing mail was censored, never complained in their letters home, lest a parent appear, and they concealed the true situation in their camp from their family when they went home. In the absence of parents, gaining the approval of one's peers governed behavior, as Jost Hermand vividly describes: "Even when the local Party leader, with whom we normally had little to do, ordered us to chop the heads off chickens, twist the heads off pigeons with our hands or clobber little rabbits behind the ears with a stick and then cut their throats, we did it without blinking an eye. After all, none of us wanted to be called a 'sissy.' "[69] This must have been especially hard for thirteen-year-old Jost, an unathletic boy with a stutter, who loved animals. But status was all, and he even stabbed himself in the thigh with his HJ dagger one evening in order to impress his colleagues.[70]

Supervision, drill-sergeant-like during physical activities, was markedly lax in the little leisure time the boys had, and virtually nonexistent at night; dormitory life was rife with hazing, mass masturbation, and sexual sadism. There was no contact at all with the outside world by radio or otherwise. This group of fifty boys did not leave the isolated camp once between June 1943 and February 1944 and knew little of what was going on in occupied Poland, but occasionally they had a glimpse:

> One afternoon . . . we saw an SS man on a bicycle . . . his dog running alongside. Because there was so little variety in our bleak schedules, some of us decided to run after him. We saw him suddenly stop and order his German shepherd to jump at a very pregnant Polish woman. . . . The dog obeyed. The woman, probably a maid who worked for some of the German farmers, was very large and already somewhat awkward; with a scream she fell on her back and stared up at the growling dog in great fear. The SS man got off his bicycle and stomped on the woman's belly with his boots until she died from internal injuries.

The horrified boys did not try to protect the woman. Jost's reactions were very confused; he

> knew only that the woman was unmarried and so she had committed a sin. . . . We perceived this scene—which is among the most horrible memories of my early life—not as something political, but rather as vaguely oppressive, and we accepted it fatalistically. . . . Afterward we felt extremely embarrassed . . . we never talked about the incident again for fear of coming under suspicion of having been accomplices . . . we all knew that something dreadful had happened. Yet we weren't able to fit what we had just experienced into our very limited view of life.[71]

It was not until the summer of 1944, when appalling sanitary conditions and poor food led to outbreaks of hepatitis and a nasty plague of boils, that Jost, whose arm was infected, defied the communications taboo and smuggled a letter describing his plight to his mother via a Polish nurse. Frau Hermand did not just reply; she traveled to Poland and appeared in the offices of the feared Gauleiter who ruled the area in which the camp was located. This led to an investigation by Party authorities and the replacement of the camp leader, who had not reported the illnesses so as not to appear to be a "worrywart." Conditions became more humane after this crisis; the boys were even allowed to keep pets.[72] At the last camp Jost attended, in a small town with modern conveniences, good teachers and normal contact with people soon brought the boys back from savagery. They were allowed to wear civilian clothes, and grow their hair longer. Here, in late 1944, they at last learned the true state of the war. Fear of the HJ leaders receded, and the boys began to question their authority. In January 1945, Jost's group fled before the Red Army. When at last they arrived in Berlin, waiting HJ officials told them they were to be sent to a new camp in Pomerania:

> But we just sneaked away from them, mingling with the other refugees, and then we ran as fast as we could through the gate. I don't know how long it took me that evening to walk from the Silesia station to Rüdesheimer Platz. It was after midnight when I rang the bell. After a little while, my sleepy-eyed mother . . . opened the door. At first she didn't realize that the half frozen, dirty young man standing in the doorway was her son. But when she recognized me, she took me in her arms. I was home again at last.[73]

PART II   Seeking Refuge

Hatred of foreigners . . . seems to be the oldest collective feeling of mankind back to the tribal age and Anti-Semitism only one of its specified forms; the Old Testament laws, racial and economic, against the Stranger in Israel could have served as a model for the Nuremberg Code; the Greek word "barbarian" simply means "foreigner," and for the Frenchman, more conservative in his habits than the Greek, the foreigner has never ceased to be a barbarian— whether he was an Italian navvy, a Polish miner, or a German refugee.

ARTHUR KOESTLER, *Scum of the Earth*, 1941

6. The Floodgates Close

Hitler's determination to purge the German people of "alien" elements and force hundreds of thousands of unwanted German citizens to seek refuge in other countries could not have come at a worse time. Since the beginning of the twentieth century, huge waves of migrants, seeking refuge from revolutions, war, poverty, and depression had swept into the more peaceful and prosperous areas. The High Commission for Refugees of the League of Nations, set up in 1921, was still dealing with the problems of several million Russians displaced by World War I and the Bolshevik Revolution. Everyone had thought that the Bolsheviks would not last and that the Russians would soon go home. They were wrong. In their places of exile the Russians formed a "social group *sui generis*, least favored in the fight for existence."[1] Soon they would be joined by Greek refugees expelled from Turkey, plus countless others uprooted in both international and internal conflicts. The problem of what to do with the resulting hordes of stateless human beings had been partly solved by the issuance of so-called Nansen passports, which gave certain refugees a modicum of civil status in the countries in which they now found themselves.

These enormous demographic movements, combined with shaky economic conditions and fears of Communism, had led to feelings of unease and the imposition of immigration controls and quotas in a number of countries. In 1924 the United States Congress, in an effort to "protect" the country from the mostly Eastern European and Mediterranean influx of the late nineteenth and early twentieth centuries, passed the Johnson-Reed Act, which limited total immigration to some 150,000 a year and granted lopsided percentages of the quota to England (66,000) and Germany (26,000). No special concessions were provided for refugees. Interestingly enough, Mexico, the source of much cheap agricultural labor, did not have such a quota.

In this period, as today, starvation and displacement were worldwide phenomena. Every American child was told not to waste food because of the starving Armenians or Chinese. Years after the end of World War I, feeding programs set up by Herbert Hoover's American Relief Commis-

Refugees arriving in New York.

sion, often in conjunction with the Quakers, were still funneling food to families in Belgium, Germany, and Austria,[2] as well as to millions in the famine-stricken Soviet Union.

The 1929 stock market crash in the United States was only one element of a worldwide spiral into depression and unemployment that would last throughout the 1930s. By early 1932 Germany had six million unemployed. In the United States, by early 1933, an estimated 4.7 million families needed relief, a demand that soon would exceed the capacities of local agencies and charities.[3] An Episcopal bishop noted that "vast multitudes . . . have lost financial security forever. In bewilderment and bitterness they will seek a sign of hope and no sign will be given." Millions could not pay rent: small children in jammed day-care centers were observed playing "eviction" and moving their classroom furniture from one corner of the room to another. Others stood in line to eat in soup kitchens, and by 1932 an estimated 250,000 teenagers, some as young as thirteen, had left home and taken to the roads and trains in search of work and sustenance.[4] Nature did not help. Years of unprecedented drought in the American heartland would culminate by 1936 in the Dust Bowl and the desperate migration of tens of thousands of families. And in England, George Orwell, exploring the depressed mining areas of the Midlands, where long-term unemployment combined with a severe shortage of housing had created unparalleled squalor, described a family unable to find a house and driven to living in a trailer:

> Most of the people I talked to had given up the idea of ever getting a decent habitation again. They were all out of work, and a job and a house seemed to them about equally remote and impossible. Some hardly seemed to care; others realized quite clearly in what misery they were living. One woman's face stays by me, a worn skull-like face on which was a look of intolerable misery and degradation. I gathered that in that dreadful pigsty, struggling to keep her large brood of children clean, she felt as I should feel if I were coated all over with dung.[5]

It was not a moment conducive to the reception of refugees anywhere.

The United States normally granted immigration visas only to persons who fulfilled a number of complex health, social, and economic criteria. Most important among these was the "likely to become a public charge" (LPC) clause, which denied entry to those unable to support themselves. This could be overcome by an affidavit from an individual in the United States who would guarantee support, but organizations could not sponsor immigrants, a regulation that would cause great problems as the number of refugees increased. American consuls processed the applications according to guidelines emanating from Washington, but the final decision was left to their judgment. Those accepted were given a quota number and told to wait for it to be "called." This could take a long time, since the total number permitted to enter in a given month was carefully controlled. Conversely, if the visa was not collected or used by a certain date, it became invalid.

In September 1930, two and a half years before Hitler's accession, President Herbert Hoover, responding to the crash of 1929 and the resulting gigantic rise in American unemployment, had ordered the consulates to enforce the LPC clause strictly and to reduce the number of immigration visas granted by 75 to 80 percent. The drop in admissions was dramatic. The United States' total, worldwide immigration figure for February 1931 was 3,147, the lowest for any month since 1820. A little earlier the Secretary of Labor had begun to hunt down and deport illegal aliens. In addition, some 100,000 legal Chicano workers were persuaded to return to Mexico after a vicious anti-Mexican scare campaign in the press. The theme of this exercise was exemplified by the testimony of Vanderbilt genetics professor Roy I. Garis, who told the House Committee on Immigration and Naturalization, which was pondering the imposition of a Mexican quota, that even legal Mexican-Americans were "human swine" whose minds "run to nothing higher than animal functions—eat, sleep, and sexual debauchery." To speed things up, the American authorities provided trains to take these citizens back to Mexico.[6]

America was not alone in its anti-foreign campaigns. France, whose depression had started a bit later than that of the United States, imposed nationality quotas on certain professions in 1932, and some three million resident aliens, mostly Poles and Italians, who had been welcomed in earlier years to solve labor shortages, were now not very graciously encouraged to leave. By 1936, 450,000 of them had done so. In France, the aliens, like the Mexicans in the United States, were often refused unemployment relief and vilified by nativist polemicists, who accused them of being Fascists or Communists (which of course some of them were) and questioned their morality: "This crowd of immigrants, many of them uprooted and ill-adapted, work to increase criminality . . . and unarguably contribute to demoralization and disorder. No less pernicious is the moral delinquency of certain Levantines, Armenians, Greeks, Jews and other 'metic' tradesmen and traffickers."[7]

In England, where unemployment had reached well over two million by the early 1930s, the government was equally reluctant to take in anyone who was not self-supporting. The British had no specific quotas, but their Aliens Acts of 1914, aimed at the same groups targeted by the United States, had been reinforced in 1919 and 1920 and the British government also did not allow special consideration for refugees. The Home Office, given enforcement power, granted entry on a case-by-case basis, and up to 1933 kept the numbers very low.[8]

Franklin Roosevelt, elected in 1932 and inaugurated in March 1933, only weeks after Hitler's accession, was, like the German leader, faced with enormous social and economic problems. Both would create nationwide projects to relieve unemployment and revive the economy, the difference being that Hitler had conveniently rid himself of the checks and balances that controlled what Roosevelt could and could not do. The American President's social programs, unprecedented in scope and expense, were utterly dependent on a Congress in which nativism, sheltered by the sacred cow of immigration quotas, reigned supreme. Any attempt to increase the quotas was not only politically dangerous, but inspired the more extreme opponents of immigration, without success, to propose legislation to reduce or abolish the quotas altogether. Nativism was not limited to the Congress. It lived in organizations that ran the gamut from the

Daughters of the American Revolution to Father Coughlin's Social Justice Movement, and thrived in the Washington corridors of the State Department and other agencies that were also dependent on the Congress for their appropriations. Along with nativism, the defense of bureaucratic fiefdoms, endemic genteel anti-Semitism, and varying degrees of fear of immigrants as fifth columnists, Communists, and spies—all reputed to be entering the country in secret droves—made any large exceptional admission of German refugees out of the question. Even Einstein would be temporarily refused a visa on the basis that he was too left-wing.

This inflexible attitude was not necessarily shared in the embassies and legations abroad where individual consuls were frequently sympathetic to applicants, but could not risk major defiance of policy without peril to their careers. Despite all the opposition, a combination of pressure by interested groups and behind-the-scenes action by various agencies allowed the number of visas granted to German applicants, who were thought to be almost entirely Jewish, to rise from 1,300 in 1933–34 to 20,301 in 1937–38. This annual figure involved no change in the official limit, and in late 1937 it was felt by many in Washington that if continued for a few more years its maintenance would suffice to take care of most of the Jews remaining in Germany, who, it was now clear, would eventually be forced to leave.[9]

The European nations and Great Britain, despite their anti-immigration stances, did not refuse entry to the early waves of refugees from Nazism, who were regarded as temporary political exiles. France, particularly, true to its long tradition as a nation of asylum and transit, allowed an estimated 50,000 to 60,000 to enter, over half of whom soon moved on to other countries. Of these, it is thought, some 17,000 to 20,000 were German Jews.[10] In England numerous charitable organizations came forward to help the 4,000 to 5,000 early arrivals.[11] There was considerable sympathy for the victims of Nazi extremism and calls for expanding aid to them resounded in Parliament. As is always the case, the rich and well connected soon found refuge and positions. Furthermore, the German government, at this stage, still permitted many of those fleeing to take enough assets with them to assure entry into various countries and make survival possible once they had arrived.

To those who made it to Paris, London, or Amsterdam the relief of a civilized reception and of freedom were overwhelming. German author Hermann Kesten, newly arrived in Paris, wrote, "What a dream exile is. You cross the border and immediately the terror becomes 'foreign.' In the same instant you begin to doubt the reality of the horror in Germany."[12]

The euphoria did not always last. Freedom was fine, but the prohibitions on employment or expiration of residence permits soon led the less well heeled to resort to lives of nomadic and ill-fed illegality, moving themselves and their children from one house or room to another. Meanwhile, those hoping to leave the Continent entirely once again joined the lines of applicants at foreign consulates. Here, as time went on, despair was palpable: " 'We still have the ocean,' a man with two little children and a young wife said. . . . 'Maybe I escaped only that we might die together in Holland.' "¹³

Behind the scenes, each of the "receiving" governments worried about how many refugees there were to come and how long the pressure would last. The situation was delicate. No one wanted to "upset" Germany by strong censure of its Jewish policies, as that would violate the diplomatic taboo of interfering with the internal affairs of other nations. Quite apart from their own immigration rules, many governments reasoned that elaborate plans to take care of German exiles would be a sign of acceptance of Hitler's policy and only encourage the expulsion of more. An ineffectual branch office of the League of Nations High Commission for Refugees, carefully detached from the main body in order not to offend the Germans, who were still members of the League, was set up in mid-October 1933, in order to "formulate plans for an international solution to the German refugee problem."¹⁴ Its chief, James G. McDonald, an American purposely chosen to put pressure on the United States, which was not a member of the League, wanted to propose to Hitler a ten-year plan for the "removal of Jews and the transfer of German property for their support." But many prominent German Jews, such as the bankers Georg Solmssen and Max Warburg, despite their now "troubled" lives, felt that Jews everywhere should keep a low profile and seemed determined to wait things out in Germany.¹⁵ McDonald was equally stymied from the opposite direction, confiding to the American ambassador in Berlin, William Dodd, that "he had raised 500,000 pounds sterling from English Jews but that the givers were not enthusiastic and did not wish many German Jews to enter England" and that in the United States "there is much interest in limited circles but no enthusiasm for taking persecuted Jews into the country."¹⁶

This fear of overt action extended even to the possible rescue of children. A 1934 program to send 250 German Jewish children to the United States, which waived many of the immigration rules and which had been negotiated with great difficulty in Washington, had to be suspended for two years when not enough Jewish families (gentiles were not permitted to take the small refugees) could be found to take the children, one problem being that the organizing agency, the German-Jewish Children's Aid, was unable to come up with the $500 per annum funding provided to the foster families for each child. Appeals to the American Jewish Joint Distribution Committee to support the program were rejected because the JDC "considered it more cost effective to either care for the children in Germany or finance their passage to Palestine."[17] Things were not helped when an inaccurate statement by the American Jewish Congress claiming that 20,000 more children would be coming led to ferocious attacks on the program by nativist organizations. The chairman of the American Coalition of Patriotic Societies even went so far as to demand a congressional investigation of the program, suggesting that the children were from "communist families."[18] Nevertheless, the U.S. government did continue to authorize a tiny trickle of entrants, and by March 1938, 351 had arrived under this program.[19]

But the flow out of Germany did not cease. In January 1935, a plebiscite held in the Saar Territory, an enclave administered by the League of Nations since World War I, overwhelmingly favored its reunion with Germany and caused 7,000 Saar residents who felt differently to flee to France. This group, considered "international refugees," was more or less successfully resettled there and in Paraguay with funding from the League of Nations.[20] A 1934 law severely restricting the assets that could be taken out of Germany without permission, and the passage of the Nuremberg Laws in September 1935, made the position of the Jews infinitely more precarious. Applications at the consulates increased, but there was as yet no real panic. Some who had fled in the first wave, mistakenly convinced that the Nuremberg Laws were the final word, even returned to Germany, and many both there and abroad were further lulled in 1936 as anti-Jewish propaganda was toned down in preparation for its nationalist extravaganza at the summer Olympic Games in Berlin. From 1935 to 1937, despite the promulgation of the Nuremberg Laws, the total Jewish emigration from Germany remained at a steady 20,000 to 24,000 per year.[21]

What little public focus there may have been outside Germany on its discriminatory policies toward Jews and their need for refuge was blown away in the summer of 1936 by the outbreak of the Spanish Civil War. Idealistic supporters of the leftist Spanish Republic came from all over the world to defend democracy as the military insurrection led by Army officer Francisco Franco gathered momentum with the support of Spain's upper classes and Catholic hierarchy. Governments were less enthusiastic. The democracies, afraid of a Communist takeover in Spain, soon agreed to a nonintervention pact and arms embargo, which prevented the elected Spanish government from acquiring arms from its neighbors. The French Popular Front, though sympathetic to the leftists, went along under pressure. Meanwhile, Germany, Italy, and the Soviet Union, all seeing an opportunity to bring Spain into their orbit, sent massive military support to the respective sides and promoted their radicalization. The world read with fearful fascination the press reports, written by such luminaries as Ernest Hemingway and George Orwell, of yet another confrontation between left and right, which became ever more extreme and in which the innocent would die by the tens of thousands.

At the beginning of the war, much of the fighting was concentrated in Spain's Basque region. Hundreds of vacationing children from all over the country were stranded in the coastal resorts. For most there would be no school for a very long time, and some would not get home for twenty years. By August 1936, intense battles had pushed more than 40,000 Basque citizens over the frontier into France. The American Ambassador to Spain, summering in San Sebastian, where the Spanish government traditionally moves in July, witnessed the exodus:

> I saw pitiful scenes. Hundreds, thousands of women and children and old men poured across the border from their ruined homes. . . . Penniless, friendless, they staggered into an alien land, bringing as much of their pathetically meager belongings with them as they could carry. . . . And all their faces were marked by tragedy and horror. . . . The men lifted toddling babies in their arms for a last kiss and then returned to the fighting. . . . A small boy with a harassed desperate expression sat on a coping, his arms around a loved dog.[22]

As international sympathy grew, committees from a number of countries sent in shipments of food and clothes. Representatives of established refugee organizations, such as the Quakers and the Save the Children Fund, were soon on the scene. In November 1936, under sponsorship of the French Popular Front, the Committee to Aid the Children of Spain was created to provide shelter for the young and get them out of the war zones. The French labor unions enlisted more than 5,000 working-class families as eventual foster homes, and twenty "colonies" were established for groups.[23] They would all be needed. Even before the final defeat of the Spanish Republicans in early 1939, France would spend some eighty-eight million francs on relief.

Basque authorities, who had taken advantage of the war to declare their long-sought autonomy, were soon feeding 40,000 refugees a day in soup kitchens. A hundred thousand homeless were billeted in requisitioned apartments and houses in Bilbao, and the flow only increased as the fighting resumed after a brief lull. These efforts were well organized, but lack of food would soon overshadow all else. Save the Children representatives inspecting a home for 200 babies saw "bottles . . . being prepared with water and a little flour." Older children lived on tasteless black bread, lentils, and fifty million pounds of chickpeas shipped in by the Mexican government, and spent a great deal of time wandering the streets to find more food. Every crumb was precious: forty-three years after the fact, a woman remembered with anguish the day she had, as an eight-year-old, broken a bottle containing her family's ten-day ration of olive oil.[24]

Quaker help organizations soon reported appalling conditions in other regions of Spain. More than 4,000 people, forced to flee the fighting in Málaga, were housed in a camp near Murcia, where they were given one meal a day. At this early date the Quakers had little more to offer than condensed milk and cocoa. The future looked daunting: 137,000 more refugees were scattered in the vicinity and in Málaga itself. One woman had lost her two smallest children in the chaotic flight. Everywhere there were sick and dying babies and overwhelmed services. Soup kitchens in Barcelona were feeding 2,000 children daily, and even the men of the International Brigades were sharing their food with thousands of children in eastern Spain.[25] By June 1937, Franco's Auxilio Social, which was modeled on the Nazi NSV welfare organization, was also feeding 30,000 children, including many from Republican families, and desperately needed funding to feed thousands more. At this early stage, Quaker worker Wilfred Jones found the care being given exemplary and full of "genuineness, of helpfulness, cheer and brotherhood . . . regardless of the sympathies of the parents of the children."[26]

To this misery was soon added a new element: the bombing of civilian targets. By November 1936, Italian and German air squadrons supporting the Franco rebels and Russian planes supporting the Republicans were raiding defenseless villages and cities daily. The Spanish government had few antiaircraft guns, and none would be supplied by the determinedly noninterventionist democracies. In the north, valiant resistance by the ten-plane Basque Air Force, led by one nineteen-year-old ace who shot down nine German fighters before being killed himself, was of no avail.[27] Children found themselves in a surreal new world:

I was only nine then. Our days were lived around the air raid sirens, the race to the shelters. Our first shelter . . . burned after a direct hit. We took to the train tunnels. . . . The hours and days we spent in the refuges were endless, and we never knew what we would find when the raid was over.

They would find terrible things, as the experience of one twelve-year-old demonstrated: "I volunteered to help clear away rubble from a few houses in my barrio, which had been hit. Till I die, I'll never forget the horror of finding pieces of the children who lived there among the bricks and debris."[28]

On March 31, 1937, German planes bombed the Basque town of Durango, blowing into small fragments some 400 civilians, most of whom were at church.[29] This was followed by the now legendary attack on Guernica, where the German Condor Legion had the opportunity to experiment with the new incendiary bombs that would be so useful later over London. The Nazis had chosen their moment well. It was market day, and at four-thirty in the afternoon the center of town was full of people and livestock.

The people were terrified. They fled, abandoning their livestock in the marketplace. The bombardment lasted until seven forty-five. During that time, five minutes did not elapse without the sky's being black with German planes. . . . The planes descended very low, the machine gun fire tearing up the woods and roads, in whose gutters, huddled together, lay old men, women and children. . . . Fire enveloped the whole city.[30]

Göring, welcoming the triumphant Condor Legion home from this exploit, noted happily that the Luftwaffe had gone to Spain because it had "burned to show what it could do."[31] The Italian Air Force, not to be outdone, later bombed Barcelona continuously for forty-eight hours with its experimental "super bombs," which could destroy whole blocks at a time.[32]

By now children in all of Spain were faced not only with the normal horrors of civilians in a combat zone, but also with the terrible scenes unique to civil war. In the "insane hatred, the mad-dog spirit of the rank and file on both sides,"[33] all restraints had gone; personal and class hatreds surfaced and executions and counterexecutions initiated on the slightest pretext decimated entire towns. All over Spain women and children were held hostage for their husbands and fathers, and many perished. There were public executions. In some places so many spectators came to watch these events that soldiers had to be called in to hold back the crowds and send away the staring children.[34] Troops and militiamen from the various factions killed on sight whoever they thought might be an enemy. They were often mistaken.

Carlos C., a thirteen-year-old boy from a nonactivist monarchist family in San Roque, near Gibraltar, lost three uncles and a cousin in one day as a battle raged for control of his town. Anarchist militia took the uncles from the house and shot them. When the family was told, Carlos rushed out to find one of them who was said to still be alive. The boy found him on the floor of a hospital corridor, where the uncle soon succumbed to the twenty-one bullet wounds he had sustained. On the way to the hospital, Carlos had seen another uncle's body being carried away; on his way back, he found the bodies of his other two relatives in the street. Later, Carlos remembered with surprise that when he got home he had felt no emotion:

> I didn't feel what had happened as a great personal tragedy. Rather, as I related what I had seen, I felt something of a hero. No one at home dreamt of eating anything, but I was hungry and slipped away to the kitchen. All I could find was a tin of condensed milk which I gulped down.[35]

Carlos was not unusual. Most of Europe's children would, in the next years, develop a self-protective shell of voyeurism and casualness toward the monstrous events around them. Observers noted that, after a time, children in Madrid, which was under artillery fire for months, did not even stop playing when the shells began to fall, and that collecting hot shrapnel fragments, often from streets strewn with corpses, was all the rage. In Barcelona, when leftist elements dug up the remains of nuns and priests and displayed them in the streets, groups of thirteen-year-olds made fun of the grotesque exhibitions: "When we got bored looking at the same ones in my neighborhood, we'd go to another barrio to see the ones they'd dug up there. . . . We kids would make comments about the different corpses—how this one was well-preserved, and that one decomposed, this one older."

The children's coolness was not always as real as it seemed. Five-year-old José Antonio Pérez, who, with his little brother and mother, spent an agonizing last night in jail with his father, who was to be executed by a firing squad the next morning, believed for many years that he had not actually been there but had only heard the events vividly described by his mother. It was not until he happened to visit the prison much later in his life that he recognized the room where they had all been together and knew that he had actually "lived through that night."[36]

By the time of the attack on Guernica, the Spanish Republican government had already begun to encourage the evacuation of children from its besieged cities and towns. This project, though worthy, was also quite partisan. Eligibility for evacuation was determined not only by loyalty to the government, but also by the political affiliation of each family. The Spanish Republican government was a coalition of parties, which included Communists, socialists, anarchists, and, to make things especially complicated in the Basque region, Catholic separatists. Places in the groups to be evacuated were, therefore, allotted according to the percentages each faction had garnered in the last election. The process began in the Basque areas. Parents were required to go to a central office to request evacuation for their children. The first groups, aged five to twelve, were carefully screened and given medical examinations. There was considerable publicity, and even a reception at which the candidates were shown a movie of the French workers resort that would later house them.[37] After the bombings began, Basque government officials, desperate to save their own families, were not above a little blackmail: foreign diplomats noticed that permission to evacuate their own nationals included pressure to take refugees. The American consul in Bilbao, when reprimanded by the State Department for even discussing the admission of 500 Spanish children to the United States, indignantly cabled back: "I made suggestion concerning Basque children to be able to evacuate our nationals. . . . Less tactful cultivation of officials in power probably would have resulted in disaster rather than the excellent success achieved entirely within our policy."[38]

For the young Spanish refugees, access to the United States, "within our policy," was far less possible than for the German ones: the Spanish yearly quota was 252.[39] The Basque attempt to send 500 children to the United States was, therefore, no more successful than the earlier Jewish program. Sympathy for the children was strong in many quarters, and the Roosevelt administration had authorized the consul in Bilbao to waive visa restrictions if the children could be certified by the Department of Labor as "bona fide temporary visitors." Yet, despite offers by many members of the Basque community in the United States (and by some 2,700 other families) to take in the children, the plan, once again, was torpedoed by the fierce combined opposition of a few powerful congressmen, the Sons of the American Revolution, and, most importantly, a number of major Catholic organizations, notably the Knights of Columbus, whose leader indignantly wrote that "the attempt . . . to bring Basque children to the

United States is an unholy exploitation of children for Communist propaganda purposes."[40] There would not be direct financial aid for the children from the U.S. government either. All funds had to be funneled through private organizations, which were carefully tracked to make sure that there were no violations of American neutrality. It was not until two years into the war that U.S. authorities, having been informed by the Spanish government that more than three million people, of which one million were children, had been driven away from their homes and that the food situation for them was "desperate," gave permission to the Federal Surplus Commodities Corporation to supply 250,000 bushels of wheat to Spain. Even then, arrangements for the handling and distribution of the food had to be made through private charities. Finally getting into the spirit of things, the United States prodded the Brazilians to send surplus coffee to Spain, and in December 1938 upped the available wheat shipments to 500,000 bushels a month.[41]

The more liberal Popular Front government in France was kinder. By the middle of June 1937, when Bilbao fell, unleashing a further flood of unprocessed refugees into France, some 15,000 children, accompanied by priests and teachers, had left their families and been evacuated in a stream of vessels escorted by British warships. Edith Pye, a Quaker social worker, was deeply moved at the sight of the first groups to arrive in France, "crowded like ants into the landing barge, waving and singing and shouting 'Viva la France.' " Though they were thin and undernourished, "they were all beautifully clean and tidy, hair combed and neatly clothed."[42]

Soon other countries, sometimes grudgingly, joined in the rescue effort. In Britain the private National Joint Committee for Spanish Relief had been proposing the transfer of children to England for months. Despite the strong urging of the British consul in Bilbao, the idea did not take root until public outrage over Guernica convinced the Cabinet to authorize the entrance of children of the "noncombatant" ages of five to twelve, with the stipulation that no state funding would be provided. Pressure from social workers would soon convince the British authorities to raise the age limit to fifteen in order to protect young girls from rape. In the heat of the moment fund-raising was no problem. A British team in besieged Bilbao, working fifteen hours a day and constantly interrupted by air raids, had by mid-May processed some 4,000 children, who left for England on two ships.[43] Belgium, Denmark, Mexico, and other countries either took more children or subsidized the colonies in France, and enthusiastic Communist parents would sign up for 4,000 to 5,000 children to go to the USSR.

Getting there was not half the fun; the well-meaning rescue workers had much to learn about small evacuees. The voyages, especially by sea, are repeatedly described as disastrous. The ships were jammed. Children slept everywhere, two or three to every available bunk, and even in the empty swimming pool on one vessel. One group going to Russia, on a ship manned by an inscrutable Indo-Chinese crew, was housed on old mattresses in a hold full of coal dust. In scenes that would be repeated again and again in such evacuations, fear and homesickness were rife and seasickness almost universal. Older children who had promised their parents that they would take care of younger siblings were often overwhelmed by their lonely duties:

> My mother told me I was responsible for my two sisters: I can never forget her exact words: "My son, promise me one thing, that you now accept the responsibility of the family; stay together." After that I only cried in private. I was myself just nine, but I carried my five-year-old sister on board ship, and came back to help my crippled older sister up the gangplank. I lined up to get food for them both.

These nightmares were dispelled for a time by the spectacular welcoming ceremonies put on in every country for the first arrivals. In France, white bread and milk were waiting on the dock for those disembarking: "They gave us hot milk . . . so hot it burned my tongue. I drank four glasses anyway. What a sensation of joy and satisfaction came over me."

A group sent to Belgium by train was, despite cold and rain, met at midnight by a large, emotional crowd, "many crying for joy," who showered them with hugs and candies. Those arriving in the British port of Southampton were amazed at the sight of enormous decorations covering the waterfront, which were left from the recent coronation of George VI but which the children assumed were in their honor.

The Soviet Union eclipsed all the rest with a three-day welcoming extravaganza that was exhaustively covered in *Pravda*. A crowd of thousands, here too waving handkerchiefs, greeted the ship as it docked in Leningrad. The 1,745 children, by now well coated with coal dust, were "bathed carefully by jolly nurses in such clean big white aprons" and allowed to choose new clothes from a roomful laid out for them. Once spruced up, they were housed at the posh Astoria Hotel, still one of St. Petersburg's best. Here, serenaded by an orchestra much given to somewhat inappropriate repetitions of "La Cucaracha," they were fed gargantuan meals. Eleven-year-old Juan Rodríguez Ania, who had made the trip with his brother and two sisters, thought he had "reached Paradise after being in Hell." The high-powered treatment went on and on. There were banquets and speeches put on in Leningrad and Moscow by Soviet youth organizations before the children, who all expected to be home for Christmas 1937, were distributed to well-appointed summer colonies in the south of the USSR. In time, two or three thousand more Spanish children would join this initial group. The Soviets, clearly hoping for a Communist takeover in Spain in which the Russian-trained children would eventually play an important role, continued to treat their young guests exceptionally well. In the fall, they were placed in special boarding schools. Supervision and structure in these institutions were both caring and strict. The elite treatment continued in extracurricular activities that were frequently conducted by Bolshoi Ballet dancers and top soccer players.[44]

To make the children feel more at home, teachers were brought in from Spain. For these adults, often fervently enthusiastic about Communist ideas, the realities of the USSR, from which the children were carefully shielded, soon made clear that there were problems in "paradise." They were appalled by the abject poverty of most of the people, by the severe shortages of food, and by the "harsh political conditions." Rosa Vega, expecting advanced and innovative teaching methods in Russia, was surprised to discover rigid and slow-paced classes evidently "designed for children with a slower learning rate" than the "more lively" Spanish children, who were expected to do much of their work on their own: "It was evident that there was considerable fear of individual initiative. In each of the older children's classes one of the pupils was appointed as invigilator to walk up and down to ensure that the children were studying—a sort of policeman."

The children were not the only ones who were watched. Spanish-speaking Russian supervisors monitored the classes and subjected the visiting instructors to "self-criticism" sessions on weekends. The monitors' job was not to be helpful but to ensure that no one made remarks hostile to Communist orthodoxy. "There was a lot of terror, a lot of fear; it was the height of Stalin's show trials."[45] Luckily for her, Rosa Vega fell ill and returned to Spain, for, at the triumph of the Fascist Franco regime in 1939, most of her Spanish colleagues would either be imprisoned or sent to work in factories, thus leaving the children entirely in the often brutal hands of the Soviet authorities.[46]

In the West, despite the demonstrations of affection upon arrival, subsequent events were also not always so cheery. In France and Belgium most of the children were placed in foster families. In order to expedite matters, the boys and girls were taken in groups to a location such as a schoolroom, where the families who had volunteered to take "a child" would choose which one they wanted. This was standard procedure world-wide when dealing with orphans and homeless children. Although some families were touched by the little groups of siblings and took two or three, most could take only one. Few experiences seem to have been more traumatic for children than this. "Families would take one child only. My brother was taken by a rich-looking family. I clutched my little sister's hand to await our luck. My father was dead, my mother in France. I was her sole protection in the world. But she was led away sobbing." Even worse for self-esteem was not being chosen at all; but this at least sometimes allowed siblings to stay together. "We were divided by num-bers, like pieces of meat. Everyone was claimed but us. My sister was crip-pled and no one wanted us three, so the Red Cross had to put us in an orphanage."[47]

In England the Spanish children were given physical exams immedi-ately upon arrival, after which red, white, or blue ribbons were tied to their wrists indicating that they were either "verminous," "clean," or "infectious." The poor reds had all their clothes destroyed and were given hand-me-down English outfits, which, of course, marked them for good as having been louse-ridden. Red, white, and blue siblings were separated from one another, thereby destroying the comfort given by what remained of family life. From festive Southampton the 4,000 children were taken to a huge tent city set up and furnished by a host of generous volunteers and corporate donors. There they would be gradually sorted out and distrib-uted, not to families, but to some ninety smaller colonies. The British, thinking in Boy Scout terms, were not well prepared for children who had been politicized and made streetwise by their life in a war zone. Nor did the caretakers have any idea of Spanish language or food. From the begin-ning, there were problems. The first meal of beans and "whole boiled Spanish onions," which bore no resemblance to anything ever consumed by the children, was a disaster. The refugees also had never tasted mar-garine, ubiquitous in England, and were puzzled by the constant cups of tea, used at home only for illness.

Once again, the lack of a structured program led to mischief and van-dalism, and resulted in the imposition of reform-school-like measures in some institutions and the expulsion of some older boys to Spanish refugee colonies in France. Within the tent camp Catholics and differing socialist factions soon got into fights and had to be segregated. The Catholic Church agreed to take 1,200 children into various homes and orphanages, but only after careful screening of the children for their religious beliefs. The Catholic homes were not cozy either: pro-Franco nuns and priests were frequently suspicious of the "left-wing" Spanish children, and the little families of siblings who had sailed away together were further diminished by Catholic insistence on separate-sex facilities. All these problems were reported with much drama in the press and soon led to lobbying for repatriation of the children and a falloff in funding, which shrank even more as it became clear to business donors that the Franco regime was winning and would soon control Spanish commerce.[48]

As Franco's position became stronger and his regime was recognized by other nations, pressure to repatriate the children continued to grow. The Spanish Fascists regarded the presence of tens of thousands of children in camps abroad as a public embarrassment and a source of future opposition. With the exception of the USSR, from which most of the young refugees who survived their stay would not return for twenty years, the governments of the countries of refuge were anxious to be rid of the children. But the civilian committees sponsoring them were rightly suspicious of the promises and documentation produced by the representatives of Franco and the Spanish Church, which, recent research has revealed, were often falsified by the government. Before allowing repatriation, the caretakers demanded that proof be given that the children's families had requested their return and could care for them, but verification was often impossible. By the end of the Civil War, more than half of the young evacuees had gone back to Spain. Of these, it is certain that many whose parents were political prisoners went into children's homes run by Franco's Auxilio Social, where they were subjected to Nationalist indoctrination. But hundreds of children, their civil status unclear, would remain alone in their various nations of refuge, dependent on the rescue committees, forced to lead precarious and nomadic lives in and out of institutions and foster homes, seizing whatever educational and employment opportunities came their way, and destined never to return to Spain.

The victory of Franco's forces in Spain would add exponentially to the number of refugees of all ages. By early January 1939, in terrible winter conditions, some half-million Spaniards and their foreign supporters were in flight toward France, but this time the French, already burdened with tens of thousands of German and Spanish refugees, were less welcoming and closed the border. In late January, with several hundred thousand men, women, and children hovering at the frontier, dying of starvation and exposure, the French relented and opened their borders to the wounded and civilians. Noel Field, an American member of the International Military Commission of the League of Nations, reported:

> At the time of crossing the border, the refugees were already in a pitiable condition, having eaten for the last time from two to three days beforehand, wandered sometimes for many days under frequent bombings and machine-gunnings from the air, carried their belongings up the mountains as far as their strength lasted and then thrown all excess baggage away, their shoes worn out, their feet often bound in rags, with festering wounds, frequently falling by the wayside, or else dragging themselves to the camps driven on by the hope of better conditions in France.[49]

The camps to which Field referred, hastily improvised by the French, could, at first, hardly be dignified with the name. An American embassy official transmitting a report to Washington wrote that "the conditions portrayed are shocking almost beyond belief." Already routine in the USSR, such scenes, and worse, would become all too familiar to millions in the next five years:

> The so-called camps of St. Cyprien and Argeles consisted of nothing but two enormous sand beaches . . . about twenty-four to thirty hours walking distance from the border. They had been . . . enclosed with barbed wire . . . but no shelter whatsoever or any other facilities had been provided within the enclosures. . . . On arrival . . . [the refugees] were driven through barbed wire fences, guarded by Senegalese with bayonets fixed, and left to their own devices without food or any other supplies. . . . Despite the bitter cold, they were even lacking the firewood which up to then they had found in the forests.[50]

The conditions were bad enough for soldiers, but for the thousands of women and children among the refugees survival was not easy. Freezing winds swept the beaches and drove sand and refuse into eyes, clothing, and food. Torrential rains in late February drenched everything, creating "by this added nightmare, indescribable misery." No tools, building materials, bedding, or even straw was provided for weeks. People dug holes in the sand, but these soon filled with water. A few managed to make reed huts. For some days there was no food at all, "then truckloads of bread were brought . . . and thrown across the barbed wire fences as if in a zoo." Sanitary provisions were completely lacking:

In the beginning the refugees made efforts to dig latrines with their bare hands . . . but they soon had to abandon this since the wind quickly filled in the pits which they had dug. The refugees had to perform their bodily functions wherever they happened to be . . . and the whole beach on which they live is gradually becoming foul with human excrement.[51]

Conditions in the camps improved slowly in the next few months and thousands of Spaniards acceptable to the Franco government were sent home. Special trains were provided for pregnant women, and a number of camps were set up for mothers and children. By mid-July 1939 half of the Spanish refugees had been repatriated and a few thousand taken in by Mexico, Venezuela, Russia, and other countries. But many rejects remained in the awful enclosures. The American naval attaché to France, on a visit to the camp at Gurs, near Bayonne, felt that it would take fifteen more months to "dispose" of the camps and their blacklisted occupants. Meanwhile, maintenance of the remaining refugees was costing the French government four to six million francs a day,[52] and six months after the end of the Civil War, the consortium of organizations known as the International Commission for the Assistance of Spanish Child Refugees was still helping and soliciting funds for women and children in 2,000 different locations in France, as well as for 800,000 people, mostly children, that Franco's Auxilio Social could not adequately care for in many of the devastated areas of Spain. These victims were about to be joined by millions of others.[53]

If Guernica had aroused sufficient humanitarian outrage in the nations of refuge to inspire any number of groups to work for the evacuation of Spanish children, the Nazis' brutal takeover of Austria and, six months later, their attack on the German Jewish community on Kristallnacht would be the catalyst for similar actions to save the threatened children of Germany and Austria. But the rescue efforts would come very late and only after it had become obvious that the nations of the world, for myriad reasons, were not prepared to take in the massive numbers of families who were in danger of expulsion, not only from the Reich, but from a number of other countries. Governments can deal with the idea of a few hundred thousand refugees on a temporary, humanitarian basis, but the prospect of caring permanently for many millions had become, by 1938, more of a threat than a duty to most politicians.

Jews scrub Vienna streets under the supervision of Hitler Youth boys.

Until March 12, 1938, when Hitler's forces marched into Austria, the truly desperate situation of Jews in the Reich had not been taken seriously in the outer world, or even in the German Jewish community. Emigration had proceeded calmly, at a manageable pace, and many thousands of German Jews had found havens of a sort. Most of those who had departed, and even more so those who still hesitated to leave, had persisted, along with the rest of the world, in the belief that reason would prevail, and that Herr Hitler would not survive very long in office.

The scenes in Austria, in the full glare of public scrutiny, were appalling. The Austrian Nazis, who had been hoping for this takeover for years, were in the streets within minutes of the resignation of Chancellor Kurt von Schuschnigg, who had been betrayed by his own Nazi ministers. British journalist G. E. R. Gedye reported with amazement "the pathological anti-Semitism of the Nazis":

> It was an indescribable witches Sabbath—storm troopers, lots of them barely out of the schoolroom, with cartridge belts and carbines . . . marching side by side . . . with men and women shrieking or crying hysterically the name of their leader, embracing the police and dragging them along in the swirling stream of humanity . . . motor lorries filled with storm troopers . . . hooting furiously . . . men and women leaping, shouting and dancing in the light of the smoking torches . . . the air filled with a pandemonium of sound in which inter-

mingled screams of "Down with the Jews! *Heil Hitler! Heil Hitler! Sieg Heil!* Perish the Jews. . . . Down with the Catholics! *Ein Volk, Ein Reich, Ein Führer.*"[54]

Until the early hours of the morning this "howling mob, comprising perhaps 80,000 to 100,000 of Vienna's population of 2,000,000," marched through the Jewish quarter of Leopoldstadt, looting houses as it went. The next day, American journalist William Shirer described the public humiliation of Jews forced to scrub the streets and clean public lavatories with their bare hands, while storm troopers jeered and urinated on them in "an orgy of sadism." Jews were beaten and arrested on the streets for no reason; they were fired from their jobs, and thousands were taken to concentration camps. Even small children soon learned the Nazi attitude. A kindergarten teacher walking in the park overheard the following exchange by two five-year-olds who, until that day, had gotten along perfectly well:

> "Why have you not got a badge [swastika]?"
> "Because Mother has not bought me one."
> "I know why you have not got one—because you are a Jew!"
> The little boy nodded.
> "Well, if you are a Jew, you must give me money!"
> And the small boy . . . produced two coppers out of his pocket.[55]

Now fear was predominant in the Jewish community. To the delight of the storm troopers, there were hundreds of suicides. Carts removing the bodies, sometimes of whole families, were labeled "Neighbors, Please Copy."[56] For those not previously so inclined, there could now be no doubt that emigration was the only thing to do. Within hours the roads to the frontier were jammed. Thousands took to the woods and mountain passes. The airports and train stations were mobbed. At the stations and on the departing trains storm troopers robbed and arrested hundreds. The Czechs gave no political asylum this day, and after waiting for hours in the stations, carload after carload was sent back into Austria from the Czech frontier and soon from all the others, which were also sealed.

In case anyone still had doubts, the Nazis, under the aegis of Adolf Eichmann, immediately set up a special agency dedicated to the expulsion of Jews and soon were requiring that 300 persons be processed for departure each day. Those who were released from prison had to promise to leave Austria within six weeks. Making it more difficult for the émigrés to find a place of refuge, they were not only stripped of most of their assets, but were required to sign a document pledging that they would never return to Austria.

The calm, if often quietly desperate, negotiations for visas that had gone on for years at the consulates of the United States, Great Britain, and other nations of refuge were transformed, overnight, into scenes of hysteria. Some, who acted fast and got to the American consulate in the first hours after the takeover to get a quota number, were, in fact, rewarded with success, and, if they could gather all the proper documentation, and especially the essential affidavit of support, could get out within a few months. But within a few days the consulate was dealing with 6,000 people a day, of whom no more than 500 could be interviewed in the eleven hours the office stayed open. Soon the quota for Austria of 1,413 per annum was booked for years ahead.

Public and press opinion had also been galvanized in the United States. Only days after the takeover in Austria, President Roosevelt expressed a desire to offer the Austrian émigrés a place of refuge as had been done "for so many fine Germans in the period of 1848," and asked his Cabinet if they thought an increase in the German quota would be approved by the Congress. The response was negative. Vice President John Nance Garner told him that "if it were left to a secret vote of Congress, *all* immigration would be stopped."[57] Instead of attempting this perilous change, Roosevelt and his advisers somewhat ameliorated the situation by ordering the amalgamation of the German and Austrian quotas and use of all of its 27,370 annual slots. They also set up a Presidential Advisory Committee on Political Refugees to coordinate refugee matters at home and called for an international committee to consider the problem. By March 23 invitations to a meeting at Évian-les-Bains, a resort town in France, to set up a committee "for the purpose of facilitating the emigration from Austria and presumably from Germany of political refugees" were presented by U.S. envoys in all the major nations of Western Europe and the Americas except Spain, which was obviously not qualified. The original proposal reassured the invitees that they would not be responsible for funding the émigrés and that "no country would be expected or asked to receive a greater number of emigrants than is permitted by its existing legislation."[58]

The existing legislation, had it been left intact, would, if spread over ten years, probably have provided adequate refuge for the remaining Austrian and German refugees. But by the time the Évian Conference took place, many nations had changed their immigration laws. It was increasingly clear to all that the earlier anti-Semitic noises made by other countries were serious and that things would not stop with Germany and Austria. In May 1937 a Polish mission had, with the consent of French Prime Minister Léon Blum, himself a Jew, gone to the French colony of Madagascar to see if it would be a suitable place to send large numbers of Polish Jews.[59] In December of the same year, the Romanian government had passed anti-Semitic laws and stated that it wished to expel most of its 800,000 Jews, and neighboring Hungary, under pressure from its powerful Nazi Party, also instituted anti-Jewish measures.

Now, as preparations for the conference proceeded, the Romanian government suggested that not only Romania, but Czechoslovakia, Hungary, and Poland be added to the list of nations whose political refugees would be received abroad, intimating that "Romania would like to dispose annually of a number corresponding to the Jewish birth rate."[60] Undersecretary of State Sumner Welles replied with some feeling that it would be "unfortunate" if the "mere existence" of a refugee committee "should anywhere be construed as an encouragement of legislation or acts that would create a new refugee problem."[61] Thirty-two nations agreed to come to the Évian Conference, which did not take place until July 6, by which time many drawbridges had been raised.

On March 21, the Dutch government increased its border guards and tightened its admission rules. This move had been contemplated for some weeks. Since 1933, thousands of German refugees had entered the Netherlands legally, but many more were suspected of being there. Town officials in the border areas had noticed that if one or two refugees were given permission to stay, they soon would be joined by others, who used the addresses of the original entrants to get past the border controls. The change in policy was not limited to new arrivals: on May 7, all foreigners were required to register with the police. These measures met with considerable public protest and accusations that the government was inhumane, though one Jewish newspaper noted that a greater influx of refugees would destabilize the economy and lead to "a surfeit of foreigners." By now, some 25,000 Jews and 7,000 German political refugees were known to have entered Holland, of whom 25,000 remained. Despite the new measures, 1,800 more refugees were admitted and registered by Jewish organizations in Rotterdam and Amsterdam. There was, in fact, no real way to know how many were in the country, as many foreign Jews never registered with the Dutch Jewish Council at all.[62]

On April 21, the British too, who before had had no visa requirement, fearing an uncontrollable flood of penniless arrivals off Channel steamers and convinced that those emigrants who arrived would probably not be able or willing to return to the Reich, informed the German government that visas would in future be required for all of its nationals who desired to land in Great Britain. On the same day, the British Consul General in Vienna, still unaware of the centralized nature of the expulsions, reported that

> the distress and despair amongst the Jews are appalling. This consulate-general is literally besieged every day by hundreds of Jews who have been told to leave the country and who come vainly searching for a visa to go anywhere. Every consulate in Vienna is in a similar position. . . . Unless pressure from international quarters can be brought to bear upon the Reich Government to force them to intervene in Austria and regulate the Jewish problem along the lines obtaining in the rest of Germany, it is impossible to predict the horrors which may come about.[63]

Arab resistance against Jewish emigration to Palestine, a British mandate since 1920, where more Jews had gone than anywhere else, particularly from Poland, had led the British to reduce immigration there sharply as well. By the early spring of 1938, a stage of intermittent warfare existed there that would become particularly fierce at the time of the Évian Conference.

Despite the scenes of horror before the eyes of the world, the meeting at Évian had no concrete results. Most delegations spent their time explaining why they could not take more refugees. Only the Dominican Republic, apparently desiring to increase its white population, offered to take a substantial number. The Jewish agencies in attendance did not help matters with their endless squabbling and rivalry among themselves. In the end it was decided to set up the Intergovernmental Committee on Refugees, which would "explore" further solutions.

While these deliberations were going on, the job of the British consular officials had become more and more difficult. According to guidelines issued in May, only "bona fide" visitors and businessmen were to be given visas without delay. The problem was deciding who was "bona fide." Consuls were instructed by the Home Office to "discreetly question" visitors "who appear to be of Jewish or partly Jewish origin . . . as to their family circumstances, and how their business or employment has been affected by recent events, and if it is suspected that emigration is intended the applicant should be invited to say so frankly" so that his application could be dealt with on its merits. All visitors would have to sign a document noting that violation of the visa would lead to forcible deportation back to Germany or Austria. The temptation to cheat was enormous, as the criteria for acceptance eliminated all but a few. Leading scientists, artists, industrialists who wished to transfer their businesses, "distinguished persons of international repute," schoolboys, and students enrolled in long-term programs all had little problem. "Prima Facie unsuitable" were, however, small shopkeepers, retail traders, artisans, agents and middlemen dependent on commissions, minor musicians, and the "rank and file" of professional men—lawyers, doctors, dentists—that is, most people.[64]

By midsummer, the situation at the British consulate in Vienna had reached the boiling point. Day after day the sixteen consular officials had to enforce the guidelines and decide which of the 600 to 700 persons who appeared each morning would be granted salvation. The desperate applicants, by now forbidden to work in Austria and many with departure ultimata, were not always polite. Extra ushers were brought in to keep order in the waiting areas. Soon there were charges of bribery and favoritism as "bona fide" applicants with appointment cards, who, the consular officer reporting on events felt, "cannot be left to be jostled about by hundreds of low class Jewish emigrants," went to the head of the line.

> The ushers are pushed about and occasionally struck and often insulted and it is little short of remarkable that the good order which generally obtains can be maintained. . . . I have twice recently, with the utmost reluctance, had to appeal for police help when the crowd has got out of hand and a policeman is now permanently stationed outside the main door.

Articles appeared in the *Spectator* accusing the government of adding to the persecution of the Jews by not increasing the consulate staff. The head of the Vienna passport office, in a letter sounding as if he himself were on the verge of tears, vehemently defended his employees, noting,

> It is not possible for anybody who is not directly concerned with the work to form an idea of the difficulties involved and of the responsibilities connected with it. . . . The staff are so overwrought that they will burst into tears at the slightest provocation and every means must be found of easing their burden.

Pressure was not confined to working hours: "Almost everyone has a 'pet' Jew, my consular Colleagues here, personal friends . . . both here and at home, Members of Parliament . . . our own Diplomatic Services." From all of these the passport officers received a "stream of letters" and often felt "bound to see their protégés." Even out of the office "life becomes a misery," for at every lunch or dinner there was "always a fellow guest who has a 'friend' who he is sure I will help. . . . As often as not it is the host or hostess who asks this and to refuse point blank when full of their food and drink is not always easy. In this way arises the charge of favoritism."[65]

This sort of dilemma was not limited to the diplomats. The daily processing of people, all of whom had problems that defied solution, after a time turned the most sympathetic workers into hard-nosed bureaucrats, for in the end choices had to be made. Henri Eitje, an Orthodox Jew who worked with the Amsterdam Refugee Committee, remarked that those who merely gave money to the rescue organizations did not have to worry about the terrible decisions that faced him. Some refugees he found to be "poor material" to work with; many were not satisfied with arrangements that were made. Eitje noted that if he had provided help to everyone who threatened suicide, which happened several times a week, soon all the refugees would declare this intent. There were other problems too. It was harder to find support for Eastern and stateless Jews. In addition, the Dutch Jews felt that the German Jews made little effort to adapt to Dutch customs, and indeed the German refugees had attempted to set up their own help organization, independent of the Dutch Jewish Council, but were prevented from doing so by the Dutch government.[66]

Meanwhile, George Rublee, an American international lawyer, appointed director of the Intergovernmental Committee established at the Évian Conference, had come to London to try to negotiate an "orderly emigration plan" with Germany, but both bureaucratic delays in the summer of 1938 and the Munich crisis in September, which was followed by a series of dramatic events, delayed the beginning of any serious negotiations. As officialdom plodded along, the potential number of refugees grew steadily: shortly after the Munich meetings, Italy passed racial legislation that threatened the 15,000 or so Reich Jews who had fled there.[67] The German takeover of the Sudetenland produced another multifaceted mass of 127,000 refugees, including Jews, exiled German political dissidents, and anti-Nazi Czech Sudetens. Now they too tried to flee to England, France, Poland, and anywhere else they could. More would be added in March 1939, when Hitler took over another large piece of Czechoslovakia.[68]

The possibility that tens of thousands of Jews resident in the expanded Reich might also seek refuge in Poland had not been lost on officials of that doomed nation either. On March 31, 1938, the government quietly revised its citizenship laws and required all of its nationals living abroad to register by October 6 at Polish consulates in order to have their passports renewed. Those who had been out of Poland for more than five years would not get new passports unless approved by the consuls. The decree was directly aimed at the 40,000 Polish Jews who had lived for many years in Germany and who, it was now all too clear, might soon have to come "home," where they were equally unwelcome.[69] A few months later, preparing the ground for Poland's coming abandonment of its citizens, Foreign Minister Jozef Beck told American Ambassador Anthony Biddle that the Évian Conference had been "an excellent beginning for further study and search for a solution of the Jewish problem as a whole and not limited merely to the refugee aspect." The minister had apparently detected "distinct evidences" that the Polish "Jewish issue" might also turn into a "refugee problem." Beck had concluded that before the problem could be solved "as a whole" the Palestine question had to be settled "definitely," and indicated that he felt that Jewish leaders would "retard other settlements in hopes of bettering their position vis-à-vis Palestine." Once the issue of Palestine was solved, other areas of settlement could be explored, an effort that "might serve to instill the Jews with hope and thus replace the potentially dangerous effect of . . . increasing despondency over their dismal outlook." Ambassador Biddle, apparently deeply persuaded by this diatribe that the outlook for the Polish Jews was indeed "grim," now also urged their inclusion in the groups to be rescued.[70]

The German government, which had not been fooled by the Polish maneuver, on October 28 peremptorily ordered all Polish Jews in Germany to leave. Six thousand left voluntarily. Some 15,000 of those who resisted were immediately loaded onto trains and, having been refused entry by the Poles, were left stranded in a no-man's-land between the two frontiers near the tiny town of Zbaszyn (pop. 7,000). Here, in conditions remarkably similar to those the Spanish refugees would soon endure, hundreds perished and thousands more would spend months in misery. Among them were the parents of a seventeen-year-old student in Paris, Herschel Grynszpan, who was so upset by their treatment that he assassinated an official at the German embassy, thereby triggering the events of Kristallnacht.

Only days after this expulsion, the Polish ambassador in Washington rushed to the State Department to request, once again, that his country be "included" in the considerations of the Intergovernmental Committee, as he feared that "unless some gesture were made to Poland to show that its problems were being dealt with on a parity with Germany there might be anti-Semitic outbursts in Poland." When this request was rebuffed, the ambassador, knowing that there were still some 25,000 Polish Jews in Germany who would soon follow the rest to no-man's-land, reiterated that "it was a frightfully urgent matter." The American official retorted that the "acute" situation in Germany and Austria must be dealt with before "a more chronic situation."[71] In a simultaneous and equally unsuccessful approach to the British Foreign Office, the Polish Ambassador in London declared that for Poland "the question of finding an outlet for her Jews was one of vital necessity."[72]

But the Polish government still had a card to play: it now threatened to expel equal numbers of German nationals. For the Nazis, deep in secret plans for the conquest and resettlement of Poland, this was not a good thing. A compromise was negotiated: Poland agreed to take back its nationals and their dependents, but only if they could bring their household goods, tools, and assets with them. The Nazis, about to take over Poland, assets and all, happily agreed. A number of the Jews were thus allowed to return to Germany to liquidate their assets and put the funds into a special account, from which an undetermined amount would be transferred to Poland. This was no humanitarian decision: the Polish government expected to make some hundred million marks on the arrangement. The Jewish community in Poland, fearful of having to support its brethren, was pleased as well. Alas, they were the more deceived. The American embassy later reported that groups of Jews, carefully escorted by German police, had begun to arrive in Poland with only the ten marks in cash allowed to all Jews exiting Germany. To the dismay of both the Polish government and the Jewish community, the expellees, fully aware of the anti-Semitic attitude of the Poles, and hoping they would not be in Poland for long, had not brought their household goods and professional tools with them, but had shipped them to German ports, hoping to export them to other countries. Even worse, many, still hoping for "better treatment in the future," had not even liquidated their German assets. Thus, an American diplomat commented, "the precautions taken with the German Government by Poland to avoid taking back Polish Jews without resources have been defeated largely by the action of the repatriates themselves."[73]

The treatment of the expellees by the Germans at the frontier, even after they had complied with all the regulations, was horrendous, as one Quaker team observed:

> The German Police take the deportees from the trains after dark in groups of about twenty. Dogs are set upon them, and they are chased into the woods and swamps. One woman we saw had been bitten in the leg. A woman came with 2 children, one she could carry, the other fell

behind. She was not allowed to go back for it, and the little thing perished in the swamp. . . . Most of them are able to find their way into Poland in a day, but others are sent back and forth, wandering for a fortnight.[74]

At this stage many testified to the humane attitude of numbers of individual Polish guards and people in the frontier region who, against regulations, fed and sheltered the wanderers. The police in cities such as Katowice were less sympathetic. The Quakers observed raids to round up refugees who, even if they had visas for England and other countries, were loaded into trucks and returned to the limbo of no-man's-land. In Warsaw, as in Vienna, the U.S. consulate was overwhelmed with applicants, and the Polish quota of 6,000 per annum was booked for years.

Although open violence and dispossession of Jews in Germany had grown slowly since the riots accompanying the takeover in Austria, public persecution there did not become fully fledged until after Kristallnacht. Despite all the publicity given to the Austrian situation, the carefully orchestrated German actions, which included giving schoolboys and Hitler Youth groups a holiday so they could participate in the "demonstrations,"[75] came as a shock. Reading about horrors did not prepare people for witnessing the real thing. The American consul in Stuttgart, writing in the formal style required in diplomatic cables, which did not disguise his distress, said:

> I have the honor to report that the Jews of Southwest Germany have suffered vicissitudes during the last three days which would seem unreal to one living in an enlightened country during the twentieth century if one had not actually been a witness of their dreadful experiences, or if one had not had them corroborated by more than one person of undoubted integrity.

The "vicissitudes" included "the wailing of wives and children suddenly left behind, the imprisonment in cells and the panic of fellow prisoners . . . as well as the forcible eviction of children from the Jewish State Orphan's Asylum in Esslingen, just outside Stuttgart, where the children were chased into the streets."[76]

Now it was the turn of the consulates in Germany to receive the onslaught. The Dutch reported 40,000 to 50,000 requests for entry in a few weeks. By this time, there were already so many refugees in Holland that the government, like those of France and Switzerland, had begun the construction of special camps to contain them. Among these was one at

Westerbork, another dismal, flat, and windy place, which would receive its first inhabitants in October 1939. Meanwhile, there were terrible scenes at the Dutch frontiers as desperate families, many with small children, who had been pushed toward the border by German police, were sent back into the Reich.[77] Similar incidents took place in Luxembourg, which, after some weeks of turning a blind eye to the hundreds of forced illegal entrants, on December 1, 1938, "with the utmost reluctance," deployed its entire police force in an attempt to halt the crossings.[78] The American consulate in Stuttgart now further reported that

> so great had become the panic . . . that when the Consulate opened after Armistice Day, Jews from all sections of Germany thronged into the office until it was overflowing with humanity, begging for an imme-diate visa or some kind of letter in regard to immigration which might influence the police not to arrest them. . . . Jewish fathers and mothers with children in their arms were afraid to return to their homes without some document denoting their intention to immigrate at an early date.

By November 15 at this consulate alone, several thousand people a day, who "had been handled with the greatest possible consideration and sym-pathy as the enormous crowd would permit," were "filling all the rooms and overflowing into the corridors of a building six stories high."[79]

With the pretexts fabricated on Kristallnacht, expulsion of Jews from Germany proper would soon reach the same pitch as it had in Austria. On November 12 a decree titled On Eliminating the Jews from German Eco-nomic Life denied them most remaining forms of employment. On top of this, the Jewish community was to pay a fine of one billion marks for Gryn-szpan's passionate act. All Jewish children were now banned from the schools and curfews were imposed. And, in late January 1939, a Reich Central Office for Jewish Emigration, similar to Eichmann's organization in Vienna, was set up in Berlin under the command of SS Police Chief Reinhard Heydrich. This agency stopped at nothing in its promotion of emigration. German shipping lines, eager to make money, were encour-aged to sell passage to emigrants without visas and leave them in foreign ports without reference to the receiving country's laws. This practice would soon backfire. Even Shanghai, where no visas were required, would limit entry in late 1939 after it had received more than 16,000 refugees.[80] U.S. and South American authorities mercilessly turned away many such ships, the most famous of which was the ill-fated St. Louis, whose courageous captain, disobeying orders from the Reich (where the vessel's wanderings had become a public relations disaster) to bring his passengers straight back to Hamburg, radioed home that he had to put into Southampton due to "storms" in the North Sea, thus allowing his cargo to find refuge, albeit temporary for some, in England and Western Europe.[81]

The Nazis, working closely with the Jewish community in Palestine, also facilitated illegal emigration to that area. The clandestine traffic was promoted as well by the Poles and Romanians, whose citizens were not technically refugees, and was a bonanza for every kind of profiteer and con artist. Switzerland, France, and Italy knowingly helped the illegal travelers get to the decrepit ships, mostly of Greek ownership, which would take the refugees, among whom were many unaccompanied children, to Palestine. British consuls in the eastern Mediterranean described "shocking conditions reminiscent of the slave trade," but British interception of the ships roused enormous public protest. This was hardly surprising, as some of the vessels sent back to their ports of origin broke down and sank en route, while those that made it were often not allowed to dock, leaving the passengers in ghastly conditions.[82]

By late 1938, one small wedge of hope remained. Certain elements in the German government—most particularly Göring, who was in charge of economic development—while eager to expel the Jews and take their assets, had not approved of the violent Kristallnacht activities. This group now seemed open to suggestions from abroad on how to facilitate emigration. George Rublee, who, despite lack of support from British and American diplomats, had courageously persisted in his attempts to speak with the highest Nazi leaders, now managed to negotiate a complicated five-year plan with Göring. This agreement would allow emigrating Jews to take a certain percentage of their tangible goods with them, and set up a fund in Germany that would use 25 percent of confiscated Jewish assets for their resettlement. A private international corporation would raise more funds and handle matters outside Germany. Rublee did not "believe that [Göring] was actuated by humane feelings" but that "he felt that the persecution was damaging Germany and that if the rest of the world was willing to take the Jews out it was foolish not to permit this to be done."[83]

The rest of the world was not very willing. Not only did the simultaneous spectacle of the half-million Spanish refugees streaming into France give everyone pause, but the controversial rescue plan was rightly viewed by many groups outside Germany as pure blackmail. Some Jewish entities felt that the international corporation would confirm the existence of

Hitler's favorite bugaboo of "International Jewry." Others, however, saw acceptance as a means to save thousands of lives. As the redoubtable Dorothy Thompson put it: "It is easy to tell people inside a fortress to die for a principle rather than accept compromise."[84] After much further fussing, the corporation, known as the Coordinating Foundation, did come into being, but not for six long months, and by then it was of no use, as the German invasion of Poland, and the entrapment of millions in the Nazi web, was only weeks away.

7. Saving the Children

As the doors of refuge inexorably closed, it had become clear to many that it might at least be possible to save the children of Jews and other groups deemed unacceptable by the Nazis from the narrowing vortex of violence, national self-interest, and bureaucracy that threatened their families. The Spanish experience had set a certain precedent. The individuals caught up in events were not concerned with the diplomatic ramifications of their flight. Having overnight lost all status and means of livelihood, facing incarceration if they did not leave the Reich by a certain date, they sought a safe haven, and often the only way to get there was illegal. For such fugitives, children were a dangerous impediment; thus long-lost relatives and all sorts of help organizations were deluged with appeals to take people's offspring.

Organizations suitable for handling such transfers already existed in the Western nations. Indeed, they had been receiving more appeals for rescue than they could handle ever since 1933 and had already taken action. A Kindercomité of upper-crust ladies in Holland, having heard rumors that unaccompanied refugee children were wandering in the woods along the frontier with Germany, set out along forest tracks in their cars and were "speechless with emotion" when they saw small figures, "shy as deer," running away among the trees. Reassuring the children, the women bundled them into their cars and smuggled them past the border patrols, which were not about to stop ladies of such standing.[1] American organizations, as we have seen, could offer little help, but Britain, closer to the scene, had done better. Under the auspices of the well-funded Central British Fund for German Jewry,[2] it had already allowed in small groups of children. In 1936, after the enactment of the Nuremberg Laws, the Central British Fund was joined by the Save the Children Fund and the Quakers in the Inter-Aid Committee for Children from Germany, which had quietly aided 471 threatened children of various categories to emigrate by 1938.[3] But, like everyone else, the British Jewish community was still not completely convinced of the danger facing those in Germany and was inclined to limit itself to funding programs in the Reich that would help their German brethren "adjust" to the situation. The community proposed to fund a four-year plan to send German Jews aged seventeen to thirty-five, plus 2,000 orphans and poor children, to Palestine. The problem, once again, was how to save the children from Germany and still avoid the "dumping" of Jews by Romania and Poland. This attitude did not help British attempts to raise funds for the project from Jews in the United States, as the American Jewish Joint Distribution Committee had always resented its British cousin's lack of support for "Eastern" Jews.[4] The Joint was not the only fussy mainstream Jewish organization: even in the face of the mounting danger, bureaucrats of the long established Youth Aliyah program in Palestine and of the Jewish Agency for Palestine refused to lower their screening standards or to speed up their processing, noting huffily that they were "not a rescue organization." Although this stance did eventually change, for many children who had applied, it would be too late.[5]

Kristallnacht not only increased exponentially the number of children needing immediate help, but also swept all these subtleties away. One British social worker felt that the violent events in Germany had activated a passionate desire to save threatened children that resonated even in the remotest areas of her country.[6] And indeed, within days, a new entity, the Movement for the Care of Children from Germany, was put together from members of existing British help organizations. For this group, as for the National Joint Committee for Spanish Relief, speed was of the essence. Negotiations with different groups of Jews and consultations with child welfare groups were set aside. Using all possible pull, the committee, within a week of its formation, had managed to arrange a meeting with Prime Minister Neville Chamberlain and Home Office officials, who approved the unrestricted entry of unaccompanied children up to age seventeen. No passports would be necessary. A special pass would be issued for each of the children, who would be chosen by the central Jewish organizations in Germany and Austria. The idea was to get as many children as possible to England immediately and then worry about their placement. Soon Holland, Belgium, France, Sweden, and Switzerland joined in and offered to take some 4,650 more.[7] Once in Britain, the German children, like the Spanish ones, would be housed in one large group, this time at a summer camp at Dovercourt on the North Sea coast. Transportation would be by train across Holland to ferries, which would go to Harwich.

To achieve this exodus, complex arrangements had to be made with German railroads, British ferries, and Dutch child care agencies. For once, all were agreed. Preference was given to orphans who had been thrown out of their institutions, young boys in concentration camps, and homeless children whose parents had been arrested. On December 1, less than three weeks after Kristallnacht, the first group of 320 children left Berlin and another was being made ready for Saturday, December 10. Their departure was delayed until Monday, December 12, when the Chief Rabbi of England, apparently not fully aware of the urgency of the situation, fussed that the children should not travel on the Jewish Sabbath.

Meanwhile, the various agencies had persuaded a remarkable Dutchwoman, Gertruud Wijsmuller-Meijer, one of the heroines of the rescue of children, to go to Vienna and try to convince Adolf Eichmann himself to release children from that city. Mrs. Wijsmuller was the childless wife of a well-to-do banker and had been working with the Dutch Kindercomité for some time. To this snappily dressed woman, known to the children as "the lady in the hat," bureaucratic rules were meaningless. She was chosen because she was not Jewish, which, it was thought, would make access to Eichmann easier. She not only accepted the task: she took a plane, not so usual in those days. Once in Vienna she stayed at the fashionable Hotel Excelsior in order to impress the Gestapo. Getting to the Grand Executioner was not easy, but after much harassment by the Gestapo, she was rudely received on December 5 by Eichmann, who was seated at a desk on a raised platform with a large and vicious-looking dog at his side. Mrs. Wijsmuller was not impressed; nor was she humiliated when Eichmann required her to remove her gloves and shoes and raise her skirt above her knees so that he could check to see if she had any of the sixty-five or so physical characteristics that, according to the Nazi race agencies, would indicate she was a Jew.[8] Apparently she passed, as Eichmann later described her as "a very pure Aryan, but quite mad."[9] The Nazi emigration chief was only too delighted to be rid of hundreds of Jews and, just as aware of the Jewish Sabbath as the British rabbi, authorized that first departure for Saturday, December 10. Mrs. Wijsmuller, delighted at this result, politely invited Eichmann to have coffee with her the next time he was in Amsterdam. Such cultivation of the Nazis would stand Mrs. Wijsmuller, and many other rescue workers, in good stead and enable them to bend many a rule and get many an additional child out.

Mrs. Wijsmuller now had four days to choose the children, give them physicals, and arrange trains, food, and escorts plus transit arrangements through Holland. She and her team did it. This would be only the first of her extraordinary performances. Once the Kindertransports got going, she went to Germany four times a week to escort the groups, now limited to 150 at a time, and to facilitate their handling. Soon she was such a fixture on the German railroads that the Gestapo did not bother with her too much and she was able to cheat more and more. Indeed, things got so

folksy that on the occasion of her fiftieth trip, the Gestapo insisted on giving her a party at the main transfer station, complete with band and wine.
Feeling that a refusal to accept this bizarre celebration would have
"ruined everything," she limited her disapproval to dressing entirely in
black.[10] And on it went: from Prague she brought out a group of half-
starved Sudeten-German children whose parents had been jailed for
being anti-Nazi. The children had been put in a camp: "It was the first
time that we saw truly malnourished children," Mrs. Wijsmuller later
recalled. "The Jewish children were still well fed." In Holland Dutch railway workers and Kindercomité ladies plied them with food. At the ferry
dock, porters tenderly carried the children on board.[11]

A few months later she chartered seven airplanes and provided fuel for
them in order to bring over several hundred Baltic refugee children
stranded in Sweden. Sixty more were loaded into ferries at the Hook of
Holland on the day Germany invaded Poland, despite protests from the
authorities. And in May 1940, at the fall of the Netherlands, as thousands
jammed the port town of Ijmuiden, Mrs. Wijsmuller got seventy-five Jewish children out of an Amsterdam orphanage and onto several buses, and,
well after most people had been ordered to disperse, arrived at the locked
gates leading onto the dock and a ship about to sail to England. Just as all
seemed lost, she ran into a director of the steamship company and persuaded him to open the gates. Two hours later the seventy-five children
were on their way to safety.[12] Mrs. Wijsmuller continued her daring efforts
throughout the war, and is said to have been personally involved in the saving of some 10,000 children.

There were many other heroes. Refugee workers plucked 185 children
out of limbo in Poland's no-man's-land; 124 more were brought from
Danzig. Two young Englishmen, Nicholas Winton and Trevor Chadwick,
did similar work in Czechoslovakia, which had lost the Sudetenland in
1938 and then most of the rest of the nation to Hitler in March 1939.
Thousands of Czechs, Jewish and otherwise, were forced from their
homes. Here there was no central Jewish organization to assemble and
process the children, who would have to be found one by one. Chadwick,
on a private first visit, "got a clear impression of the enormity of the task.
We so often saw halls full of confused refugees and batches of lost children, mostly Jewish, and we saw only the fringe of it all."[13]

Soon Chadwick was in the thick of things. His first rescue was of twenty
children, who flew back to England on a small plane: "They were all
cheerfully sick, enticed by the little paper bags . . . except a baby of one

who slept peacefully in my lap the whole time." He and Winton returned again and again, trying to find the "most urgent, helpless" cases and match them to families in England. Between them they brought out 664. It was never routine. At one point, blocked by the entrance of German troops into Czechoslovakia, Chadwick tried to get in to see Goebbels for authorization to pass. The little propaganda chief was not available, but Chadwick managed to persuade lower-echelon officials to let him through, noting that Nazi officials reacted well to "groveling." He too found that adherence to bureaucratic niceties could be fatal, and at one juncture · printed up false British passes for the children when the real ones did not arrive in time.[14]

As the children's rescue trains started rolling toward England, there were many in the United States who wished to join the effort. Secretary of Labor Frances Perkins had already been considering legislation to that effect. In New York a group that would eventually evolve into the nonsectarian Committee for German Refugees met to plan and promote the rescue. The response was immediate. By early February, 5,000 people had offered homes, and support was expressed by the AFL-CIO, an array of church and welfare groups, and a number of lawmakers.[15]

Members of Congress had, for years, been receiving letters from constituents pleading for help in bringing in endangered relatives and friends. Senator Robert Wagner of New York was no exception. His "Alien Files" for 1938 and 1939 alone fill ten archival boxes. The applicants run the gamut of nationalities. There are Czechs stuck in Warsaw; people in Canada; Poles, Germans, and desperate families in what has suddenly become "Vienna, Germany." Wagner's office did indeed write to the consulates on behalf of many of these constituents. The detailed replies describe a myriad of problems, deceptions, lost documents, and, above all, the huge backlog of applications. Over and over again Wagner is forced to reply that "he cannot advance people on the lists." The senator was no more willing than anyone else to attempt to change the basic immigration quotas for adults, but by 1938 he did feel that an exception could be made for children.[16]

In February 1939, Wagner and Congresswoman Edith Nourse Rogers (R.-Mass.) introduced bills that would, in the following two years only, allow the entrance of 20,000 refugee children under fourteen outside the quotas. There would be no cost to the taxpayer. Transportation and support were to be privately funded. Although Jewish support was hesitant, there was overwhelming enthusiasm in many other quarters for this project. Protestant and Catholic clergymen, Governor Herbert Lehman of New York, presidents of colleges, Chicago department-store mogul Marshall Field, Helen Hayes, and Henry Fonda backed the idea. The Federal Children's Bureau approved, as did the YWCA, Herbert Hoover, Fiorello La Guardia, and Mrs. Calvin Coolidge, who said she would personally take twenty-five children.[17]

This sort of across-the-board endorsement would seem to be enough to pass most any legislation, but it would not withstand the dedicated fanaticism of the anti-immigration and nativist groups. These included, as before, the American Legion, various coalitions of "patriotic" societies, the DAR, and the obscure but numerous Junior Order of United American Mechanics. To these groups the 20,000 children constituted a "foreign invasion," a flood of aliens who would take support from the millions "of neglected boys and girls, descendants of pioneers, undernourished and ill," who also needed help. The facts that the available number of adoptable children in the United States was far below the demand and that the 20,000 would not get state support were ignored by the "charity begins at home" faction. The old argument against separation of families was rehashed. At joint hearings in April 1939, both sides were heard, with the restrictionists dwelling ominously on the fact that admission of the 20,000 children would soon lead to the total closure of quotas. Anti-Semitism was ever in the background, and the specters of a foreign conspiracy to dump refugees and "Communistic and internationalistic plots" were evoked.

Despite all the invective, the bills were reported favorably but were immediately subjected to a second round of hearings before the far less sympathetic House Committee on Immigration and Naturalization, whose members were apparently unswayed by the pathetic presence off the Atlantic coast of the refugee-laden SS *St. Louis,* which was getting major press coverage. In the end, two unacceptable bills were proposed. One would have used available quota numbers for the children and deprived 20,000 adults already in the pipeline of their chance to escape. The other, far more cynical, would have allowed the children in, but would have banned all other quota immigration for five years. Wagner, seeing that the cause was hopeless, withdrew the bill in July 1939.[18]

The threatened children and their parents were not privy to all the machinations of officialdom, and thought only of finding help. By the time of the Kindertransports to England, hundreds and perhaps thousands of children no longer had parents who could confront the bureau-cracies for them. In the very early morning of June 13, 1938, in Berlin, Gideon Behrendt's father was taken away by the Gestapo. His mother had died some years before. Not knowing what to do, Gideon and his brother went off to school. Four weeks later he received a postcard from his father, who had been taken to Buchenwald. The brothers, now without funds or food, managed to get themselves into a Jewish orphanage, and from there were chosen for a Kindertransport.[19] When two other boys were thrown out of a Vienna orphanage, the elder, aged fourteen, put his little brother, nine, into another institution and went to live with a relation. Soon he was arrested, but released due to a bureaucratic error. After that he wandered the streets, sleeping in the hallway of a sympathetic lady. The boy did know enough to go to the U.S. consulate and the Austrian Jewish Commu-nity offices. On one such visit he happened to see someone who had been in his orphanage who was in touch with the Kindertransport organizers:

> I told him of my arrest and my fears, and pleaded with him to be one of the children to leave since I had no one who could help me. After a time he agreed to put me on the list of children. I then told him that I could not possibly leave without my nine-year-old brother for whom at the age of fourteen I was responsible. He finally agreed.[20]

By such small coincidences did children survive.

For those whose families were intact, the preparations and departures were often more difficult. Only a few beloved toys or pictures could be included in the single small suitcase allowed: "I remember my main worry being that I might not be allowed to take my love tokens—a collection of small cloth animals. My mother, with the insight of selfless love, knew that these objects must be packed at all costs. . . . I was twelve years old."[21]

Parents—or more often mothers in the absence of arrested fathers—agonized over which of their children to send. As had been the case with the Spanish children, older siblings were entrusted with little sisters and brothers. The lucky ones had a relative waiting for them in England. Hardest for the parents was sending a very small child into the unknown, but many were sustained by the hope that the separation might only be temporary, and that at least the children would meanwhile be housed and safe from violence and starvation. From small towns and cities they con-verged on the stations. Sometimes parents were not allowed on the plat-forms. There were devastating scenes in the waiting rooms. Boys and girls who had never seen their parents cry were astounded. Small children were bewildered and scared. Teenagers, looking forward to the adventure of it all, were sometimes ashamed of the overly demonstrative farewells. A few parents with cars chased the trains from station to station waving to their children until they could no more.

Though the Nazis were happy to release children, their escorts had to pledge that they would return, and only a few were allowed to accompany the small refugees. Adult supervision and comfort were therefore meager on the trains as they crossed Germany. At the Dutch frontier Nazi border guards searched each car. One eleven-year-old remembered that there was "one Nazi per compartment . . . the one in our compartment pulled down the blind, made us stand in the gangway, pulled down all the suitcases from the racks, opening them and throwing everything on the floor." He stole things from the bags, and took money from the children's pockets. "Fear was in all of us until the moment the whistle blew, the Nazis left and the train passed over the frontier. At this moment we opened the windows, shouting abuse and spitting at them. . . . It was terrible that we children should have learned such hatred."[22]

The change in atmosphere, once out of Germany, was total. As had been done for the Spanish children, the rescue committees had gathered at the Dutch stations groups of people who cheered and waved as the trains came in, and lavished drinks and treats on the new arrivals.

> We were momentarily stunned and returned the cheers and waved frantically. We were not only free . . . we were welcomed back to humanity by humanity. . . . This touching reception intoxicated us. . . . Up to then we had been subdued children. . . . But from this point onwards we were a noisy, boisterous bunch of boys and girls.

Later, on the Channel ferry, a roomful of fifteen- and sixteen-year-old boys stayed awake all night telling forbidden political jokes about Hitler, Goebbels, and Göring: "The jokes . . . were not memorable, but the occasion was. We did not need to look over our shoulders or lower our voices and the realization that we could say what we liked with impunity engendered an atmosphere of enormous gaiety."[23]

The euphoria, as before, was short-lived. Charitable organizations, no matter how well meaning, are no substitute for family life. In the movement of hundreds of people, the personal touch is soon lost. In a sense, those who deplored the separation of families were right. The children felt the difference right away. Siblings were often separated from the beginning, as the social workers liked to put particular age groups together for ease of handling:

> My brother, who was only two, was allowed to come to England with me. When we were going from the train to the boat he was far ahead of me leading the long line of children. He looked like a drummer, with his chamber pot strapped on his back. I was ten years old and had promised my mother to look after him. But as soon as we had said good-bye to our parents we were separated and we have never lived together again at all.[24]

The children's first impressions of England were of dark and cold and confusion. They could understand nothing of what the kind porters and English helpers were saying. The groups who went to London went first to a large hall in the Liverpool Street station to be matched with their new families. Most were taken away immediately, but there were, of course, mix-ups and failed meetings. At Dovercourt, the camp where the unplaced were taken, the improvised nature of the evacuations was immediately evident. Food was plentiful and the children were happy being with one another. But the camp consisted of unheated summer cabins and a huge "central hall something like a hangar at an aerodrome" with loudspeakers broadcasting incomprehensible messages in English. Here "the many children wandered about or crowded around the stoves. . . . The beds were awfully cold and there were not enough of them." Children used to feather beds struggled with inadequate blankets and went to bed fully dressed. While this spartan regime was good training for the incomprehensible British lack of central heating in private houses, it was very uncomfortable. It snowed and water froze in the jugs. There was no running water in the huts, and the counselors had to devise all sorts of strenuous exercises to keep the children warm during the day. To make things worse, a terrible winter storm flooded much of the camp—a blessing in disguise for the children, who were evacuated to institutions with heating, and who later had blissful memories of these warm interludes. Horrified local observers soon took groups of children to better quarters while they awaited placement.[25]

The organizations did their best, but, despite a successful nationwide funding campaign, their money and personnel were not adequate. As the numbers arriving at the reception centers increased, the social workers charged with finding and vetting suitable foster families could not keep up. In the matching process, once again, children were often subjected to the "cattle market" method: they were lined up so that foster parents could choose. One cross-eyed girl, after months of being passed over, finally refused to come to the choosing area. Such agonies prompted social workers to stop the lineups in favor of other methods.[26]

It was particularly hard to find Orthodox Jewish families willing to take children, and many of these were eventually placed in Christian homes; at one point the Central Jewish Organization in Germany, which was responsible for making up the transports, was told to hold back Orthodox children. Teenaged boys were a problem too. By midsummer of 1939, the Movement for the Care of Children from Germany was so overextended that it had to inform the Home Office that it could not take in any more children for the time being. Despite this, the continental organizers continued to work, and several more groups, including one from the Jewish School for Deaf and Dumb Children in Berlin-Weisensee, got out before the declaration of war. The total number of children brought to England in nine months by the Movement was 9,354.[27] In December 1939, when the organizations were almost completely out of money, the British government, having little choice, finally authorized a subsidy of eight shillings a week for each refugee, a sum that still had to be matched by the Movement.[28]

In the end, far more children were sheltered in group homes and hostels than the Movement had foreseen. These ran the gamut from impersonal group shelters to austere and Dickensian vicarages, and, more happily, included cozy converted town houses lovingly supervised by rich families, which many of the children, to this day, remember with happiness.[29] They also included agricultural training centers for future kibbutz dwellers at the barely habitable Gwrych Castle in North Wales and, rather suitably, on the far better appointed Scottish estate of Lord Balfour, whose declaration had created the Jewish homeland in Palestine.

The responsibilities of those who worked in the hostels were awesome, but sometimes also a godsend to adult refugees who could otherwise only legally work as domestic servants unless they had special dispensation. Needless to say, both the experience and dedication of the overseers varied wildly. At age twenty-eight, Marianne Wolman, aided by a cook and a cleaning lady, was put in charge of a house sheltering twenty-five boys aged five to thirteen. All had lost their parents to prison or execution. Like the Spanish Civil War refugees, these boys were at first "violently aggressive." For almost two months they fought incessantly and trusted no one. Marianne had to hide in a remote part of the house from time to time in order to get away from "the yelling." At the local school, where they at first understood nothing, they behaved "unacceptably." They calmed down gradually, but Marianne found that she never had time to give "total attention to an individual child." This changed when one of the boys got appendicitis and she visited him daily in the hospital. When he got home he clung to her, wanting the attention to continue. Soon another boy had stomach pains and went to the hospital. It was not until the third case that Marianne realized that a desperate need for individual affection was the true cause. For four months she had no days off. Finally, she went to spend a day with her future husband and was gone until evening. When she returned she found that all the boys, thinking she had abandoned them, had, despite fervent reassurances from the staff, packed up their "little bundles" of possessions and prepared to go away. "So I could see that they didn't really trust me. How could they? Their parents were taken away from them and killed, so why would they trust that I would not also disappear?"[30]

The foster families came in all varieties too. Some children found themselves in upper-class and even stately homes and were sent to the best schools. Both in the hostels and in the families there were overlaps with the Spanish children. The Attenborough family, of movie fame, had set up a hostel for sixteen Basque children and now took two Jewish girls into their house.[31] These were the lucky ones. Others were sent to versions of Harry Potter's Muggle family and went to work at age fourteen. There were cases of child molestation and other problems that required moving children from one foster home to another, sometimes more than once. These cases were more than balanced by the kind, but often uncomprehending, generosity of most foster parents, who in some cases had never heard of Vienna or met a Jew before.

For everyone, the adjustments were complicated. Everything from food to lifestyle was utterly different. The boys and girls had the wrong clothes, and they had no knowledge of local lore and customs. Twelve-year-olds were humiliated by being put in classes with six-year-olds until they could speak more English, a wholly unnecessary measure, as any child placed in total immersion will learn a language within months. For these children, learning the language was paramount, not only for the basics of life, but above all to rid themselves of the stigma of being German. For, although few in Britain were very clear about what was happening to Jews in the Reich, they were all quite clear about who was Britain's primary enemy.

Once placed in their communities, the children did not forget those who had been left behind. The effort of even very small children to try to have their families come too was remarkable:

There was a boy of three or four in our transport who continually repeated a name and an address. After we had left Germany he asked to write it down. They were people in England who might help his parents.[32]

History does not record if he succeeded in making contact, but others certainly did. The older children who came early on were often successful in finding sponsors for their parents. For the later arrivals, the failure to achieve this goal left lifelong feelings of grief. Egon Guttmann, only eleven when he arrived on August 2, 1939, immediately began asking ladies in his new neighborhood if they could sponsor his mother as a domestic servant and take in his little sister, who was three and a half. Miraculously, he succeeded, and the process was set in motion. But August 1939 was too late, and, despite all his loving efforts, they both would perish.[33]

When parents did arrive, things were not always better. The instant loss of status, home, and income was a shock, no matter the country in which one landed, and in England there were few remedies. Men were not allowed to work, and women, like Marianne Wolman, were limited to menial or domestic jobs. Overnight, proud families became dependent on loans, gifts, and the tiny stipend the Jewish organizations could provide. They were forced to live in squalid rooms and often could not afford to have their children with them. In such circumstances it did not take long for some family structures to fall apart. In their efforts to adapt to new homes, new schools, and a new nation, the children, desperate to belong, were ashamed of their parents' recent poverty and their "foreign" ways. One child of six

> found it impossible to love two people as my mother. At first, my mother's visits, and especially her departures, were an agony. Gradually as my foster mother took over my affection—and I welcomed this—my own mother's visits were still an agony, but now because of the guilt feelings they aroused in me.[34]

Children sent to hostels and boarding schools that, trying to be kind, also employed their mothers were often miserable as well, all too aware that being children of the help lowered their standing in the eyes of their peers. This sort of thing might have been remedied by more sensitive organizers, but by September 1939 there was little time for such niceties, as it had now become important not only to evacuate endangered child refugees from the Continent, but also to save all the children in the countries threatened by war with the Reich.

The governments of Germany's western neighbors had been preparing civil defense and evacuation plans for their citizens with varying degrees of seriousness for some time. The Netherlands, though counting heavily on its neutrality, by March 1935 had made contingency plans that included its traditional defense of flooding strategic areas, and holding out in a central "Fortress Holland." The plan would, of course, require the evacuation of large numbers of people to predetermined communities. But as war clouds gathered in the summer of 1939, it appeared that little had actually been done to implement these plans. This led to the hasty creation of a Bureau of Civil Evacuation, which went to work only after the outbreak of war, and only days before the first orders for flooding were issued. Soon arrangements were made to evacuate some 300,000 people from flood areas, 2,000 of whom had left by November 1939. Hundreds of other residents, feeling nervous, moved on their own. For town and city dwellers, plus 440,000 others in border areas, an elaborate scenario, based on presumed German military moves, was prepared. Three days after the threat of an invasion was confirmed people would be moved to the Fortress in carefully prepared groups.

Towns and cities were divided into sections with a hierarchy of leaders. The signal to leave would be the continuous blowing of police car horns or the beating of drums (sirens and church bells being reserved for aerial attacks). Families should pack up no more than thirty kilograms of possessions per person, lock up their houses, turn the keys in to a central authority, and proceed to a designated meeting place. Pets were allowed, and 130,000 cows were to be rounded up and driven cowboy-style to safety. The human groups would be taken by boat and train to large buildings in staging areas (200,000 beds were ordered) and from there would be placed with local families. Special trains were planned for the German Jewish refugees at the Westerbork camp, so near the Reich border: they were to be moved clear across Holland to Terneuzen, a small town in the southwest near the Belgian border. But in their haste, the Dutch authorities never precisely solved the problems of what to do with such special cases as tuberculosis patients, prisoners, and the mentally disturbed.[35]

In France, householders had long since been advised to build air-raid shelters in their gardens or take refuge in the Paris Métro. Wardens were appointed, and gas masks, taken everywhere, became the subject of many cartoons and fashion satires. They were supposed to be donned when repeated single blasts of police car horns were heard—a measure that led to frequent false alarms in traffic-ridden Paris. Evacuation planning, started well before 1938, was briefly put to the test at the time of the Munich crisis, making clear that much more had to be done. As was the case in Holland, the idea was to send the "useless" population of the twenty-five *départements* closest to Germany and the major cities such as Paris, Lyon, and Marseilles to areas away from presumed military operations. This would be done almost entirely by rail, with three to four times the normal number of trains laid on.

On August 31, 1939, with war clearly inevitable, 16,313 Parisian schoolchildren were evacuated in twenty-seven trains. This first operation was not entirely smooth: the children of eighteen school districts ended up in Chartres, where two had been expected, causing a wild scramble to take care of them.[36] For the rest of the populace, the evacuation plan was initiated on the morning of September 1. Notices were posted in affected towns informing the French that they too could take only thirty kilos per person, which had to include bedding, a cooking pot, and food for three days. Children under seven were to have labels with identifying information sewn onto their clothes. Some owners of food stores simply gave everything away before going to their assembly points. Many people from small villages had to walk to these meeting places carrying all their impedimenta and children, who were in varying stages of excitement and exhaustion. Along with them went others on peasant carts pulled by oxen, tractors, and bicycles. There were endless waits at stations for the packed trains, which, when the finally departed, left behind station squares full of carts, excess baggage, and bicycles. They were haunted by abandoned French cats and dogs, less fortunate than their Dutch cousins, as they were absolutely forbidden on the evacuation trains.

Most of the 250,000 residents of Strasbourg were evacuated in this manner to the Dordogne, just east of Bordeaux, since become a tourist mecca, but then a very primitive area. Things were immediately difficult as multiple batches of 10,000 or so Strasbourgeois, speaking their Germanic Alsatian dialect, descended on Perigueux and the charming but utility-free villages of the region. Local children rudely referred to their new neighbors as *boches*. What lodgings there were not only lacked electricity and plumbing, but often had no beds or stoves. The evacuees were expected to cook, as the locals did, on tripods over open fires and to use hanging stew pots, both of which had been thoughtfully provided by provincial officials who were appalled at the thought that they would have to supply real stoves with ovens. Food was a problem too: distribution was spotty and, this not being an area blessed with cows on the Dutch scale, both butter and milk were hard to come by. While all these hardships could be tolerated while war threatened, the fact that no invasion was forthcoming led to discontent, as did the absence of job opportunities, a situation not appreciated by the permanent residents, who resented the fact that the government-subsidized Alsatians spent their days sitting around in cafés. It was not all bad. Children soon grew to love the freedom of the country, and at Christmas a volunteer group set up 500 Christmas trees and distributed some 58,000 presents to local and evacuee children alike.

Farther north the Parisian evacuees were not much better off in their bucolic refuges. But for them it was easy to go home when sleeping in a damp barn and hauling firewood palled. Nevertheless, some 520,000, once moved out of town, did not go back. In the city itself, despite sporadic air-raid scares, the war spirit soon evaporated. The blackout was spotty, and restaurants began to serve chic "safe" suppers in their *caves*. Schools reopened. Rationing, tentatively instituted, was rather a joke: one Cabinet minister, on a "meatless" day, made do with oysters and grilled sole. By November, although large stadium events were forbidden for fear of air attacks, horse racing and dancing were once more permitted, ski resorts were opening, and Riviera hotels were hoping for the usual influx of British tourists in the spring.

To the British, who had lost some 1,400 souls to bombing raids in World War I, the now far greater danger of air attack was the first concern, especially in London and the industrial cities of the North. Since 1924 civil defense planning had been going on sporadically and secretly under the auspices of the Committee of Imperial Defense. By 1935, an Air Raid Precaution Department was at work, which began testing gas masks and tried to interest local governments in preparing evacuation plans. Reaction to this was mixed. Lack of funding from the central government did not help. Some pacifist local officials did not want to create a "war psychology," and one mayor even suggested unilateral disarmament. By May 1938 it was clear that the complexities of transporting, billeting, and feeding thousands of people were far too difficult for any local authority, and planning was taken over by a Special Committee in London. Priority was to be given to mothers with children up to five years of age, unaccompanied older children, and the infirm. Other children would be moved in school groups with their teachers, and once in the safety of the countryside would

British infants sport special antigas suits.

be placed in foster families. Evacuation was voluntary for the needy and arrangements did not extend to middle- and upper-class families and schools, which were thought to have both the intellectual and the financial resources to take care of themselves.

Working day and night, the planners had a program ready for government approval by late July 1938. But by late September, as Europe teetered on the brink of war, there had been no response from the Cabinet. Despite this, the terrified planners managed to see to it that children were issued gas masks and sent to school with packed suitcases. Chamberlain's concession of the Sudetenland to the Führer postponed the crisis, but it was now clear that serious civil defense measures were crucial. Work continued, and by the early summer of 1939 things seemed to be ready. All that was needed was the transmission of the very suitable code words "Pied Piper" to set the evacuation process in motion.[37]

By late August 1939, the moment was close. Teachers were called back and schools opened early. On August 28, Edward R. Murrow of CBS, reporting back to the United States, described "pictures in today's papers . . . of school children carrying out a test evacuation. . . . We saw pictures of them tying on each other's identification tags, and they trooped out of the school buildings as though they were going to a picnic." Their older siblings, meanwhile, were reporting for induction into the Army. Three days later, as ultimata flew back and forth between the diplomats, Murrow reported that "all schools in evacuation and reception areas are to be closed for instruction tomorrow . . . until further notice." Children were to go to school with their gas masks, bags, and food for one day and would be taken to "safer districts." Parents would be told later where they were.[38] By September 4, 600,000 mothers, teachers, and children had been evacuated from London and another 900,000 from other endangered areas. It was an amazing performance. The London evacuees, seen off by frightened and tearful parents who expected bombs to start falling at any moment, left from 168 prearranged stations. Four thousand special trains were laid on and the whole railway system schedule rearranged to facilitate the exodus. At the reception areas all across the country crowds of volunteers, Boy Scouts, and medical personnel awaited the arrival of the trains.

Once the destinations had been reached, things got complicated right away. Some people had taken the wrong train. Overeager volunteers mixed up people's luggage. Children had to be sent to preliminary centers where they would be given medical examinations before being billeted in areas with school facilities suitable to their age groups. At one center "receiving 500 children, one or two minor operations were performed, one child was found to have scarlet fever and sent to hospital, several were incipient cases."[39] The ideal of keeping whole schools together immediately fell apart in rural areas, where children had to be billeted in several small villages, making it difficult for the accompanying teachers to keep track of them. The number of children needing shelter all at one time was so great that "compulsory measures" had to be used on foster parents in some areas, and the exhausting placement process went on late into the night. The university town of Cambridge had planned on processing 8,000 evacuees a day for three days. In the end a total of 6,700 came, but even that was a challenge to the program.

Some children going to more remote areas, such as Wales, had to be accommodated overnight en route. By the time they got to this first stop, the picnic atmosphere had often worn off and confidence was waning. Terence Nunn was in one such group, which was lodged in a spooky, deserted hospital that, with its barred windows and jagged fire escapes, looked much like a prison. The interior was no more comforting. There was no dining room, and the children were randomly served an unappetizing supper. Bathrooms were overwhelmed, and lodging was in a vast, gloomy ward, where Terence spent a restless night in a hospital bed shared with another boy.

From this dreadful place groups of thirty or so were extracted the next day by roll calls. Nunn was not chosen until late afternoon, by which time he was sure that he had been forgotten. From the hospital his subdued group was taken on another train to a dark valley dotted with slag heaps and mining machinery. Terence was placed with a grim mining family that might have been from another world.[40] He was not alone in this culture shock. Dorothy Brand, who would be put in seven different billets during the war, some a delight and some truly awful, began by being left alone in the pitch dark outside her first foster home. Once admitted, she was kindly welcomed, given hot chocolate, and shown to a sofa bed in the living room. But, close to tears throughout, she could not bring herself to ask where the bathroom was, and spent a few agonizing hours before discovering that it was in an outhouse, a new experience for her.[41]

Mismatching was not only a downward phenomenon. Far more often middle- and upper-class country dwellers were appalled at the verminous and ragged inner city children or slovenly mothers and babies brought to their doors, whose appearance and emotional condition had not been improved by the long trip and processing. The feeling was frequently mutual. Poor children faced with maids and butlers or ultra-proper bourgeois households were just as miserable as Terence Nunn was in Wales, and sometimes had to be rebilleted. As one organizer put it:

> We saw so much anger and distress in the early days. . . . Human life when uprooted is even more complex than it is normally. Problems that would have been taken in one's stride at home became greatly magnified and needed all the patience and skill of a large number of people working long hours . . . being indeed at the beck and call of everyone.[42]

Problems in Britain were also exacerbated by the fact that after the outbreak of war in September 1939, the expected bombings did not take place. The lack of a crisis atmosphere led both to a decline in altruistic feelings on the part of foster families and of fear on the part of the evacuees. Mothers with small children went back home in large numbers and many parents, for whom the obligatory charge of about ten dollars a week for each evacuated child was a hardship, brought their offspring back.[43]

But for every mismatch and each upset foster family there were a hundred success stories. The generosity of the foster families cannot be exaggerated. Some took in six or eight children. Whole houses were converted to suit the evacuees. Many children quickly became attached to their new "Aunties" and "Uncles" and maintain contact to this day. The evacuation agencies learned fast. Outings and communal teas were arranged, and special "cheap days" were instituted by the railroads so that parents could visit their children. Above all, when the bombing began in earnest, British determination to survive soon swept away worrying about petty problems.

Those dealing with evacuation did not only have to cope with British social differences. They also had to move the recently settled Kindertransport children and other foreigners to safer areas. For some, this displacement would be nasty.

In November 1939, the British authorities ordered all Axis citizens sixteen and over to register with the police and present themselves to Aliens Tribunals, set up all over England, which would decide if they would be put in detention, remain at liberty in a restricted area, or be freed as "refugees from Nazi oppression." To young people recently rescued from similar scenes on the Continent, this was a frightening process. No lawyers were allowed at the tribunals, but the aliens could bring one person with them, often a representative of the refugee organizations. By March 1940, 73,800 persons had been examined and the overwhelming majority allowed to go about their business. Some 6,109 were helped financially so that they could complete ongoing emigration, mostly to the United States. Things would change dramatically in May 1940, when Hitler's forces swept across Northern Europe to the shores of the English Channel. At this time, all Axis nationals over the age of sixteen, male and female, were taken into custody and put into various kinds of camps.[44] Among them were hundreds of the recently rescued Kindertransport children. Whole hostels were removed at one time, while individual teenagers were picked up at their new homes: "It was a pretty awful moment for me when I, a girl of 17, was fetched by two (kind) policemen and shipped off to an unknown destination."[45]

The "unknown destination" for most was the Isle of Man, safely located in the middle of the Irish Sea. Once there, many internees were relegated to empty houses in a cordoned-off section of the very charming seaside town of Ramsey. Here they were provided with mattresses and food and little else, but were not uncomfortable. The route to the Isle of Man, however, could be harrowing. Though the arresting officers were usually pleasant, the internees, often separated from friends and family, were not given any information about what was happening, and the constant presence of much less pleasant armed guards and barbed wire in the processing camps, where real Nazis and Jewish refugees were mixed, was terrifying. Luggage was searched and much stolen by camp personnel. In the detention areas there was the by now familiar overcrowding and lack of sanitation. Letters to the outside world were censored and restricted in number.[46] Many boys, eager to get out of the camps, asked to be included in the transports of aliens being sent to Canada and Australia, for many a tragic choice. One ship was torpedoed off the coast of Ireland and half its passengers lost. Another, the hideously overcrowded *Dunera,* made it to Australia despite submarine attacks, but en route the internees, who were treated like criminals and had to sleep on tables or the floor for the eight-week journey, were terrorized by a sadistic guard force made up of ex-convicts. The plight of the interned refugees soon caused objections in Parliament, and the *Dunera* crew was duly punished.[47] By 1942, most of the young internees had been released and were taken into the wartime workforce and the armed services. Here they were appreciated, but nothing could quite erase their loneliness or their aching desire for home.

On the European continent, the troubles of children would soon be far worse. In the early dawn of May 10, 1940, German forces invaded neutral Holland, Belgium, and Luxembourg, heading for France. The long-planned offensive took place not at the heavily defended Maginot Line, pride of the French high command, but on a front reaching from the north of Holland down to the hilly and theoretically impassible Ardennes in southeast Belgium. Here three massive columns of Panzer forces extended "back for a hundred miles far behind the Rhine,"[48] waiting to roll across Belgium and the north of France. In glorious summer weather thousands of the bronzed young men so carefully nurtured by the Nazis poured into Western Europe, their glowing health and conditioning contrasting markedly with the pale, unathletic draftees of the Allies.[49] Despite repeated warnings of impending attack and the blitzkrieg tactics demonstrated in Poland, the neutral countries and France had done little to prepare for a confrontation with the Germans' brilliant new style of warfare, a fact that would render the carefully drawn evacuation plans of several countries useless.

In Holland the appropriate signals were now given, and in towns across the eastern part of the country families began to make the dreadful preparations necessary for total abandonment of their lives. In Wageningen, a small town on the Rhine that was to be evacuated by boat, a little stream of people was observed carrying pets to be euthanized by the veterinarian. By the time families were assembled on the dock, the sounds of battle were quite distinct. The loading not only of 12,000 people, but also of archives, hospital equipment, and various provisions took hours. It was late afternoon before the convoy left, heading down the Rhine toward Fortress Holland. They were too late. The Germans, using newfangled airborne troops, had simply bypassed Holland's flooded fields and other Dutch defenses and taken many of the Rhine bridges before they could be blown up. The Wageningen convoy was forced to stop with several others totaling fifty boats and 20,000 people. After thirty-six very uncomfortable hours on the vessels they were put ashore and dispersed to villages along the river. Those who tried to escape by foot and train did rather better, including the 130,000 cows, which were driven into the Fortress area and were undoubtedly requisitioned by the German Army. On the fourth day after the invasion, Holland, impelled by the gratuitous bombing of Rotterdam, surrendered and the evacuees slowly made their way home. There they often found sections of their towns in ruins and their houses looted. It was all quite surreal: ducks, rabbits, and chickens, released from their coops before their owners departed, wandered the neighborhoods, and the trees were made colorful by uncaged parrots and canaries.[50]

By the time the good burghers of Wageningen were assessing the damage to their dwellings, the vanguards of the Wehrmacht were well across Belgium. Before them some two million of Belgium's citizens, using every known kind of conveyance, headed toward France. Among them were tens of thousands of young men between sixteen and thirty-five, who had been asked by Belgium's fleeing political leaders to cross into France and regroup in Toulouse, where, theoretically, they would be of use to the Allied cause. Once arrived, they spent some weeks languishing in a stadium before being moved, like the Spanish refugees before them, into a number of primitive camps where living conditions were filthy and food inadequate.[51] There was, in fact, little else the French authorities could do at this fateful moment, for their scenario of carefully staged evacuation of towns by train had evaporated before the Nazi onslaught, despite the heroic efforts of French railwaymen. People fleeing the bombing of towns in the north of France did indeed get on trains heading away from artillery barrages and the rapidly advancing tank divisions. But the mixing of civilian and military activity on the rail lines would prove fatal. Troops and ammunition trains on tracks next to those jammed with families were relentlessly dive-bombed by the Germans. Stations, usually in town centers, became the sites of terrible carnage. On May 19, an officer traveling to Arras from Rambouillet reported seeing bodies everywhere. Hundreds and hundreds. Men, women, children, old people. Against a wall, a mortally wounded woman, holding in her arms a child of about two, its head split completely open. At her side, two children of about three and five who are crying. The scene is horrible. The station is in ruins. A train of refugees has been savagely bombed and machine gunned. . . . Dead, everywhere dead.[52]

The trains did not stop running, but much of the fleeing populace, which could not, in any case, be accommodated in the jammed cars, took to the roads. Mainly on foot, but also in elegant cars and peasant carts, on bicycles, and even in baby carriages, all loaded with grotesque mounds of possessions ranging from chandeliers, fur coats, and mattresses to sugar beets, they went in a human flood some six million strong across the center of France. Antoine de Saint-Exupéry, looking down from his plane, likened the processions to ants leaving a destroyed anthill. The exodus built on itself; as towns were eaten empty and sucked dry of gasoline, their inhabitants too, exhausted by aiding those who had already passed, joined the stream. Not everyone gave in easily to the need to leave. In Metz, school authorities refused to cancel the hallowed Baccalauréat exams until the last moment. In nearby Nancy the examinations went ahead and were not called off until frantic parents came to the examination hall en route to the station to extract their children.[53]

The roads were not safe either. German planes strafed them frequently, scattering families, who leapt into roadside ditches, or ran for whatever other cover was available. But many never had a chance. A Belgian family, driving past the scene of such an attack saw "near one car . . . a small girl, eyes wide with fright, beside the bodies of her parents." Not knowing what else to do, they took the child with them, soon discovering that she spoke only Russian and that her name was Masha. For three days she traveled with them, occasionally calling for her mother at night. Completely by chance they found the representative of a colony for Russian émigré children and took Masha there. When the matron spoke in Russian "the little girl ran into her arms, and looked around only long enough to say goodbye to her rescuers. She never saw them again."[54]

Children died too, and sometimes it was too much to bear. One exhausted mother lost her reason when her ten-year-old son, whom she had protected from twenty previous attacks, was killed in a roadside ditch.[55] Tens of thousands of children were separated from their parents in the chaos of stations or air raids. Lost-and-found reports poured into the authorities and filled long columns in newspapers:

Jean Leroy, born 29 June 1939 and Jean Olivier, born 17 July, 1939: found in the same packing case. Near them a name: Mme Hareng of Cotenoy.[56]

Three-year-old boy, giving the name Jean Tavares, was found alone in a wheat field at Ides, morning of June 18. His parents please communicate.[57]

History does not record if the three little boys got home as 90,000 others eventually did, but many thousands did not.

The French too had immediately begun massive internment of foreigners, especially those of Axis and Eastern European nationality and suspect political background, such as Social Democrats and Communists. This was nothing new; like the Dutch, the French had, since early 1938, begun to keep track of where foreigners who might be a problem were living and by November of that year had decided to lodge some in "special assembly centers,"[58] just as the wave of Spanish Civil War refugees exploded into the south of France. By September 1939, some 15,000 male aliens, of whom half would be released by the end of the year, were in such camps. In May 1940, many of the aliens were detained all over again. This time women and an estimated 5,000 children were included.[59] In these roundups, simultaneous with the general chaos of fleeing millions, distinctions of status and any protests, no matter how valid, were obliterated. Thousands were held for days in the huge stadiums at Roland Garros, now site of the French Open tennis tournament, and the Vélodrome d'Hiver in the outskirts of Paris. Families were split up and groups, constantly augmented by other refugees coming from Belgium and Holland, were moved about arbitrarily, unable to communicate their plight or whereabouts to anyone. The squalid camps set up for the Spaniards, by now half-empty, were filled up again.

By September 1940, a German commission searching the holding pens for political dissidents to take back to prisons in the Reich listed forty-six such camps in France.[60] The number held is unclear, but certainly amounted to nearly 250,000 persons, of whom 60 to 70 percent are estimated to have been foreign Jews, a figure that was increased by the dumping of further thousands from the German provinces of Baden, the Palatinate, and the Saar. Conditions in the camps, according to many with firsthand experience, were worse than in those run by the Nazis, such as Dachau. Hundreds of internees, guilty of nothing more than being in a state of exile, would die in these places of dysentery, hunger, and exhaustion before any welfare agencies could get to them.

There was no dearth of agencies. In addition to the numerous and very humanitarian French ones, numbers of such groups had been sent in by other countries. These, which included the Oeuvre de Secours aux Enfants (OSE), the Russian Student Christian Movement, the American Friends Service Committee, Czech Aid, the American Jewish Joint Distribution Committee, Swiss Aid, and the Red Crosses and YM/YWCAs of several nations, had been dealing with various waves of refugees for years and even decades.[61] Most would first be deeply involved in helping the refugees fleeing Nazi forces: the Unitarian Service Committee found several carloads of canned milk in Portugal and, with the help of many other groups, was able to distribute it in the south of France soon after an armistice with the Germans was signed. The Catholic Church and French health agencies set up homes for abandoned babies and orphans.

As the native refugees gradually returned home, the foreign agencies focused their attention on the foreigners in the camps. It was soon clear to all involved in this work that more coordination would improve efficiency, not only in the field, but also in dealings with both the Nazis and the Vichy government. In early November 1940, therefore, about two dozen agencies of all denominations banded together into the Coordinating Committee for Relief Work in Internment Camps, commonly known as the Nîmes Committee, whose extraordinary board included an abbé of Jewish origins, an exiled Russian princess, several rabbis, and an array of Quakers, Swiss, and Swedes. Funds came from a plethora of sources, many illegal, and entered France in strange ways. No bank accounts were maintained; most of the money was kept in suitcases under the beds of the workers. Involvement in politics was strictly avoided. The focus was on improving food and the physical condition of the detained; on keeping up morale by setting up libraries, schools, cottage industries, and entertainments; and on facilitating emigration out of France.

The plight of children in the huge camps was particularly grim. In the survival-of-the-fittest atmosphere that prevailed in these places, where finding the minimum amount of food necessary for survival involved constant intrigue, the terrible pressure on mothers with children is not hard to imagine. Odds of survival for orphans were not good. An OSE official, who took 100 children to a home in Limoges from the camp at Gurs, where clothes were so scarce that mothers were reduced to wrapping their babies in old newspapers,[62] wrote that he had "seen hundreds of children in Russia, Hungary and Poland after pogroms or famine, but none like these. . . . Passengers in the train that brought them were moved to tears by the sight of the starved youngsters. At Toulouse doctors forbade us to move them further, as the children were too weak to stand more travel."[63]

Delivery of services to these victims within the large camps was logistically difficult, and although colonies like the one at Limoges, sponsored by many organizations and subsidized by the French government, were slowly being set up, thousands of children were still in the camps in early 1941. Concerned Nîmes Committee representatives were, with much effort, eventually able to convince the French government to create a special "family camp" at Rivesaltes, a former army base near Perpignan. It was not much of an improvement. Set once again on a dusty, treeless plain buffeted by either freezing or torrid winds, it lacked sufficient water and, as a horrified International Red Cross inspection team reported, the barracks, which lacked the most primitive amenities, were infested with fleas and rats, mortality was high, and most residents were clothed only in rags.[64] Males over the age of fourteen were separated from the women, hardly a "family" situation. Assigned food rations and care packages were plundered by corrupt administrators, and women took to cooking greens gathered from the rocky landscape on little open fires. Children raided garbage cans for scraps, with resulting outbreaks of cholera. No plates or cups were supplied to the residents, so that children wanting to partake of the milk sent in irregularly by the American Red Cross presented a bizarre collection of usually filthy cans, pots, and basins to the distributors. They needed the milk desperately:

> The children looked as though they could hold two quarts of milk instead of the pint given them; a boy who said he was twelve looked like a nine-year-old. . . . These were Spanish children, now in their third year in internment camps. Some had been born there . . . some had been orphaned when typhoid swept the camp at Argeles. . . . The Jewish children, interned less than a year before, were in notably better condition.[65]

This happy distinction would not last long. Despite reports in the American press about conditions in the camps and recognition of that fact by the pro-German French regime established in 1940 at Vichy, nothing changed. Indeed, things only got worse. In early October 1940, the Vichy government had given provincial prefects the right to intern foreign Jews at will, and their percentages in the camps rose steadily. Jews at Rivesaltes were mixed in with everyone else at the beginning; but in April 1941, under the pretext of letting families celebrate Passover together, they were all placed in a separate part of the camp. Gypsies were thrown in too. Seemingly by chance, this sector had the most dilapidated barracks. There was no electricity, and the buildings were crawling with vermin. Food rations were smaller than those in the main camp, even for children, who soon were stricken with intestinal infections. Malnutrition of the little ones was magnified by the fact that the Jewish barracks were the farthest away from the milk distribution center, so that those who were sick could not make it there. A Swiss nurse, Friedel Bohny-Reiter, wrote in her journal that she was "frequently filled with immense rage at the sight of the way in which people are treated here. By what right?? . . . It angers me that people are deprived of their right to liberty, that they are treated like . . . no, worse than animals."[66]

It soon became clear to the foreign welfare agencies that the main way they could help the camp inhabitants was to get them out of the camps and, if possible, out of France. This was encouraged by the Vichy government in order to lower the cost of refugee care. German citizens were a problem. Each one had to be approved for release by Nazi agencies. It was also necessary to travel to the various consulates and agencies in order to secure visas and exit permits, a requirement made virtually impossible by the fact that internees could not leave the camps without the most elaborate arrangements. In all these matters the welfare agencies could be of assistance.

Release was far easier to achieve for children than for adults, since the Vichy government took a benign view when it came to the young. By mid-1941, dozens of farm schools, baby homes, and schools had been established, among them a school for 100 Czech boys and girls at Vence on the Riviera, and a Jewish trade school (ORT) for 150 boys. Not all the activity was aboveboard. CIMADE (Comité d'Inter-Mouvement Auprès des Evacués), a French Protestant youth organization, set up, among other things, a secret network that smuggled internees into Switzerland.[67]

In June 1940, the violence of war reached Great Britain as Göring's Luftwaffe, possessed of bases nearer the Channel, began to soften up England in preparation for an eventual landing by German forces. The defeat of the Allied armies in France and the dramatic evacuation of many of their units from Dunkirk made an invasion seem plausible indeed. A new series of evacuations were now set in motion in Britain. But the scenes taking place on the Continent led the British government to also consider sending their children overseas in order to protect them from both battle and occupation.

In Dover, closest to France, where bombing had been frequent, groups of children heading for evacuation trains moved through crowds of exhausted troops and shell-shocked civilians just rescued from the beaches of Dunkirk.[68] By August, when coastal cities such as Southampton and Portsmouth were being hit with regularity, it became clear that the original evacuation plans were inadequate. Soon the bombing would reach London. After a certain numbers of days and nights of overwhelming noise and fear, people in Britain, like their continental counterparts, began spontaneous flight to anywhere else:

> The sirens began to wail . . . then after that, all I can say is, all hell was let loose. The next half-hour was the noisiest I have ever known in my life. All the heavy guns were firing; the planes were screaming down because it was a dive-bombing attack, and the pompoms on the warships in harbor opened up. . . . I do remember hearing the bombs whistle down. My first reaction was: "Oh—they do whistle after all."[69]

The cumulative effect of many nights of such violence led to what one government observer described as "listening tension." Listening for the planes, listening for the bombs, which would eventually produce a "resistance break" and an overwhelming desire to flee. Now it would be the turn of the British authorities to struggle to set up soup kitchens and makeshift accommodations in such uncomfortable milieux as movie theaters and empty school buildings.[70]

Vivid reporting of the plight of civilians in Britain and on the Continent once again led to an outpouring of American proposals for aid to the stricken countries. At the end of June, President Roosevelt requested, and Congress approved, $50 million to provide supplies for the refugees. Supplies were fine, but suggestions, such as one made by Francis Biddle, the Solicitor General, to send ships to Bordeaux to evacuate endangered continental children from the battle zone, once again fell into the morass of immigration rules.[71] Seven different bills were introduced in Congress to save not only the children of and in France, but also other groups, such as several thousand Polish children who had managed to get to France, Spain, and Portugal. Congressman William Schulte (D.-Ind.) proposed the issuance of a special visitor's visa for any European child under the age of sixteen "who sought asylum from the dangers or the effects of war" but tribalism again prevailed, and the bills were defeated. Chauvinism was not limited to the Americans. Fifty needy French children who were threatened with malnutrition, and for whom the Nîmes Committees finally managed to get visas by devious means, were refused exit visas at the last moment by the Vichy government, which found it unacceptable that they should be separated from their families and be exposed to foreign ideas. In the end, the committee managed, with extraordinary effort, to extract only some 300 children from France before the Germans took over that country entirely in 1942.[72] One of the last groups of children to get out left on a train for Lisbon that was to pass near the Gurs camp, where their parents were still interned. In a fit of humanity, the French allowed the parents to go to the station to say good-bye, a scene so sad that even the police are said to have wept.[73]

British children were a different story when it came to immigration into the United States. Here there were no ethnic or quota problems. The British quota was 65,000, and its children were perceived by certain elements as being from the same crowd as the Founding Fathers and other "real" Americans. Hundreds of families who could afford to do so had already sent children over to stay with friends and relatives for the duration, and many in the British government wished to extend this possibility to everyone. Despite the disapproval of Prime Minister Winston Churchill, who felt that overseas evacuation of the young people might be construed as "defeatist," Parliament authorized funding for the evacuation plan on June 18, 1940. The process was to be organized by the Children's Overseas Reception Board (CORB). Only English-speaking countries were considered (offers from South America were politely refused), and the boys and girls were to be lodged with families. Parents were expected to contribute six shillings—about $7.50 a week—to their upkeep, a pittance that eventually led to some resentment on the part of American foster families as the war years passed and support of the children became burdensome.[74]

But in 1940 all was euphoric support. There was enormous press coverage of the British program. Under the aegis of such luminaries as Eleanor Roosevelt and Marshall Field, the United States Committee for the Care of European Children was established on June 20, 1940. Fifteen thousand offers to take children were received in the first three weeks. Liaison was soon established with CORB and the U.S. government's Children's Bureau, and some 15,000 children, by now dubbed "Seavacs," were scheduled to arrive in Canada and the United States by the end of August,[75] while other large groups were prepared to go to Australia.

There were still problems: a few basic changes would have to be made in the daunting American immigration procedures before the British children could enter. Although quota numbers were no problem, it was necessary to remove the restrictions on the number that could be admitted each month. The rules requiring that a child must be entering to join a parent and the prohibition of sponsorship by an organization were waived. In addition, a system of group affidavits for financial support was permitted, as was the use of visitors' visas for an indefinite time period. The latter privilege applied only to British children, who still had a country that was perceived as being able to take them back at some point in the future.[76]

Cutting such red tape was one thing, finding a way to get the children across the sea quite another. British vessels were vulnerable to German submarine attack, and under the U.S. Neutrality Act, the only American ships that could enter the European war zone were those carrying Red Cross supplies. This rule was immediately attacked by the very determined American Women's Committee for the Release of Mercy Ships for Children, which soon had hundreds of other ladies' groups backing it, not to mention a very influential men's committee. Under this onslaught Congress quickly amended the Neutrality Act to allow unarmed U.S. vessels to transport the children if the ships were given a safe conduct by the Germans.

The way now seemed clear for the entry of thousands of British boys and girls, but even this seemingly desirable influx was a threat to the true nativists, who once again viewed the measure as a wedge that would eventually allow entry to millions of unwanted aliens. One congressman wanted to limit the rescue to 75,000 children. Another insisted that all escorts be American citizens, warning that otherwise "one or more adults could come in for every child." Others felt that the project was merely a propaganda ploy by Roosevelt to get the United States into the war. Despite all, the bill passed on August 27, 1940. But the Mercy ships were not to be: vessels could not be found for the project, and, more importantly, the Germans refused safe conduct.[77]

The British government, which had received some 200,000 requests for evacuation overseas, now decided it would risk the use both of its own vessels, with identifying markings painted over, and those of the Polish and Dutch governments in exile. By the time the first groups left, the bombing of London and other cities had become so intense that the dangers of the sea seemed minimal by comparision. The farewells for parents were no less difficult than those of any of the groups that had already sent their children off into the unknown, while they themselves stayed in a danger zone:

> The morning long dreaded has come. Last night I delayed as long as I could over drying Hilary's slim, fairy-like body and brushing Richard's thick nut-brown hair. Sleepless, I looked at their sleeping faces. . . . At the docks we are ushered into a large covered shed, to wait for what seem indefinite hours. . . . Beyond the enclosure we see now the gray-painted hull of the anonymous liner, waiting to carry away from us the dearest possessions that are ours on earth. . . . At the entrance to the gangway, they turn and wave cheerfully. Then the tarpaulin flaps behind them, and they are gone.[78]

The dangers were real, even before the ships sailed. One group arrived at the embarkation port in the midst of an air raid and had to seek shelter in the musty basement of the train station. During a lull in the bombing, they were moved to a cleaner school building. The raids continued for hours, destroying the school kitchens, and the hungrey children could not board their ship until after dark the following day.[79]

Once aboard, the most important thing was the lifeboat drill. Lumpy life jackets were issued immediately, and the passengers had to wear them at all times until it was felt the ships were beyond the reach of submarines. Drills were repeated daily at random moments to make the children, as well as the escorts, familiar with the procedure, not always an easy task with bunches of excited and obstreperous five-year-olds.

Most of the ships traveled in convoys that formed up outside the ports, and seaplanes accompanied them for the first hours. During the day the presence of the surrounding naval escorts and the towering warships was unforgettable and comforting. Some were so close that their crews were plainly visible and every command could be heard.[80] But the day was not the problem. Submarine attacks came at night, preferably in rough weather, when the attackers were less visible. On August 30, 1940, the *Volendam*, carrying 335 Seavacs plus some 300 other passengers and crew, was torpedoed and sank. Miraculously, the lifeboat drills having been well learned, all but two crew members survived and were taken back to Scotland. This was considered a setback, but did not lead to cancellation of the CORB program or a falloff in private passengers.

On September 12, therefore, the liner *City of Benares*, with 90 children, some of whom had been rescued from the *Volendam*, and 200 other passengers, left Liverpool as planned in a convoy headed for Canada. Five days out into the Atlantic the weather turned stormy and German spotter planes were seen. According to one witness, the British escorts had by then turned back and the Canadian ones that were supposed to replace them had not yet appeared. Late that night the ship was shaken by multiple explosions. Cadet Officer D. Haffner, only seventeen himself, rushed to the damaged area of the ship to search for children. It was a dreadful scene: many of the cabins had been transformed into a mass of jagged metal, and the children inside had been killed or wounded. Water was pouring in as Haffner took all the children he could find to their lifeboat stations.[81]

Elsewhere in the darkness, older children and escorts struggled to get themselves and the littlest ones into life jackets and to their boat stations. Bess Walder, a teenaged Seavac dressed in nightgown, dressing gown, and raincoat, got three smaller children on deck and returned for a fourth. To her horror she found the cabin door blocked by a fallen wardrobe. Walder managed to force her way in and saw that the child was near death. Wrapping the girl in a coat, she struggled out of the cabin, by now half full of water. Collapsing staircases blocked access to the decks, and when Bess finally found her way to the lifeboat the injured child was dead. Saying a prayer, one of the escorts gently lowered her body into the water. As Bess, feeling herself at the limit of her endurance, moved off from the doomed ship in her lifeboat, she felt that the worst was now over. She was wrong.

Walder's overcrowded lifeboat soon began to take on water and capsized. She and eight others managed to cling to the keel. In the night the wind rose and huge waves repeatedly lifted the boat out of the water and smashed it down again. By dawn, so numb that all feeling was gone in their faces and fingers, Bess and one other girl were the only ones left on the boat; they were totally alone on a sea where only large fish and ice floes could be seen.[82] Cadet Officer Haffner, pulled by a miracle into another boat, had been put in command because of his uniform. He managed to shelter everyone under the canvas boat cover so that they would be protected from the sleet, snow, and freezing salt spray. Here the sea was not empty, but strewn with debris and bodies, many those of children.[83]

Exposure was the worst enemy. One man held the stiffened bodies of two dead children in his arms and sang to them so their dying mother wouldn't know they had succumbed to the cold. "I didn't know women and children could die so easily," he said after his rescue. The children who survived had been no less heroic: one ten-year-old also held a dying nurse in his arms and vainly tried to encourage her by saying over and over, "I see the boats, nurse. It won't be long now."[84]

The final toll was high: 206 adults and 87 children died. One recently bombed-out London family alone lost 5. Public outrage at this sinking was enormous. For the CORB program the loss was disastrous: two weeks after the sinking, it was canceled. Although small private groups of children continued to be sent, the mass removal abroad of British children did not take place. In the end, only about 16,000 children, the vast majority privately sponsored, would go the United States and the Dominions.[85]

PART III Out for Blood:
The Nazis Go Global

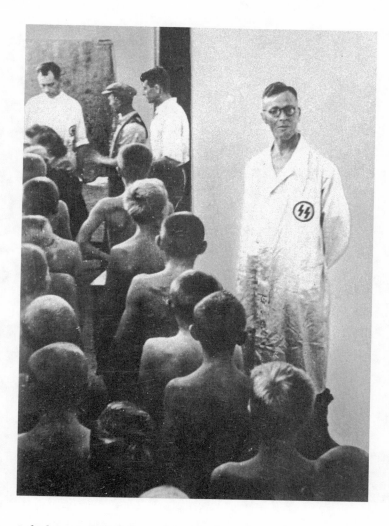

I think to identify Nazism exclusively with anti-Semitism is very short-sighted. Our plans for the world were so wide-reaching, and so terrible, that we can only thank God we lost the war.

MARTIN BORMANN, JR., quoted by Gitta Sereny in
"Children of the Reich," *Vanity Fair*, July 1990

8. Good Blood

In their zeal to purify and mold the citizens of Germany itself and expel all those of alien race, the Nazis had not forgotten those of German blood scattered all over the world. Hitler aimed to make full use of the members of the "German Diaspora." His original impulse was to recover or conquer the areas bordering Germany, leave all resident ethnic Germans in place, expel the non-Germans, and replace them with people of proper racial descent, who would presumably be available as a result of his efforts to increase the German population. In addition, he intended to locate ethnic Germans living beyond the contiguous areas and lure them back to help repopulate the new Reich, soon to be extended well beyond the border areas at the expense of his neighbors. Hitler was indeed interested in a world empire. Recovery of Germany's remote ex-colonies, lost after World War I, was desirable, but the ideal Reich would be a contiguous one peopled by a pure race. The gathering in of the world's ethnic Germans was a vast undertaking that would require that they all be found, listed, and vetted for suitability as German citizens.

The first signs of this policy were noted, with some concern, by U.S. diplomats in the summer of 1933. On July 14, the Nazi government passed a law declaring that German citizenship "might be withdrawn from all Germans who refuse to return to Germany when summoned to do so by the Minister of the Interior," and also from those "the Government considers to have acted in a hostile or disloyal manner toward Germany." In addition, citizenship could be arbitrarily withdrawn from anyone who had gained it between November 9, 1918, and January 30, 1933. People denied nationality under these rules would lose any property they owned in Germany, and their children, even if still in Germany, would also lose their citizenship. This action would take care of political refugees. But it was not enough. Present German citizens would be divided into three main categories: those of pure blood who were "worthy" of full citizenship, those of pure blood who were not, and those of "alien blood."

The classification was reported with considerable disgust by American Ambassador William Dodd, who, happily ignoring the existence of segregation in the United States, noted vehemently in his cable to Washington that "the sacred American principle that all men are created equal, that they are endowed by the Creator with certain inalienable rights has no room in Hitler's Third Reich." And he added that it was especially strange, given the fact that Hitler himself had only become a German citizen in 1932, and then only by a bureaucratic ruse. In a more practical mode, the Ambassador also pointed out that the new law might result in visiting Germans being stranded in the United States, and cause "a collision with our immigration laws."

While the first and third categories of citizens were easy to identify, being loyal Nazis or Jews and members of other unacceptable races, category two was less obvious. A naturalization document published by the state of Baden made things clearer. Naturalization must be "especially justified." Dissenters, freethinkers, and atheists should be suspected of being Communists, and "representatives of liberalism may also fall under this category." Foreign nationals could not be naturalized in principle until they had performed "special services" for Germany. If the petitioner descended from an alien and a German parent, the competent district physician had to decide which line of descent was predominant. Hereditary defects were, of course, unacceptable, and political adherence since 1918 was investigated. Nazi Party membership and military service in the correct World War I formations would help. But in the end, full citizenship could only be granted to those "who support the national government without reserve" and are willing to "hold their opinion abroad." It was abundantly clear that millions of ethnic Germans, no matter how pure their blood, would not find a place in the new Valhalla.[1]

As we have seen, keeping track of the varieties of citizens within the Reich proper was an immense, but possible, task, in which the new powers accorded to Nazi governmental agencies could be employed to investigate both public and private sources of human demography such as church registers, census archives, tax returns, and medical records. Tracking Germans worldwide would be much harder, but by 1934 the process was well in hand.

There was no need to set up a new agency for this foreign project. The Nazis simply took over a number of existing organizations founded to promote German cultural and business activities abroad and maintain links with émigrés. Principal among these were the League for Germans Abroad (VDA) and the German Overseas Institute (DAI). The new official status of these organizations was not made public so that they could continue to operate "where the government and the Party are not able and may not do this on account of political reasons.[2] By December 1933, Rudolf Hess, deputy leader of the Nazi Party, had let it be known that all nongovernmental organizations concerned with ethnic German questions would be controlled from the Reich by a "Volksdeutsch Council." This was necessary because "abroad tension had developed between a generation striving toward leadership and the old leadership which could be fatal. . . . Therefore, discipline had to be ruthlessly established within the German national groups." Indeed some of the tensions had already had a negative effect. It was reported that some ethnic German parents in Brazil had not sent their children to the local German school because of "the interference with these schools of the . . . National Socialist Party."[3] Hess was not alone in this project: virtually every Nazi agency from the Propaganda Ministry to the Tourist Office would soon have programs to compete for the souls of ethnic Germans abroad.

By 1934 the DAI had become the premier covert organization, though the fact that its letterhead featured a Hansa ship with a swastika on its sail might have made some people suspicious. For years the DAI had been receiving information on Germans abroad and had kept a file of their addresses. The United States, with its large population of German background, was of particular interest. The pre-Hitler efforts had been somewhat haphazard. An unknown correspondent from New York City had covered reams of paper with spidery notes on the names of German and other immigrants of interest, including the upper-crust denizens of the Hudson Valley. Sometimes these files were enlivened by lurid, if seemingly irrelevant, *New York World* clippings about scandals such as the Brewster murder case of 1926.[4]

In 1935, recent immigrants to the United States from Germany were surprised to receive a series of folksy *Heimatbriefe,* or "letters from the homeland." Their responses, often containing information on other relatives and their current addresses, were carefully filed. The replies range from wildly pro-Hitler to wildly pro-California. One correspondent even sent back information on the Flower Festival in his new hometown.[5] As the 1930s went on, the flow of information increased. There were lists of prominent Americans with German names, of German seamen living in port cities, of loyal people in Central America and Cuba. There were bibliographies on Mennonite and Moravian settlements. Students in the German city of Bremen were put to work checking shipping manifests back to the eighteenth century for emigrants. German consulates were requested to inform the DAI of every German who handed in his passport and to provide statistics on former German citizens in their jurisdictions.

The more traditional officials of the German Foreign Office did not take kindly to such busywork and told the DAI that they might find the information through the U.S. Department of Labor.[6] This agency, clearly suspicious of such inquiries, sent them on to the State Department, which asked the German embassy for an explanation. The embassy replied, somewhat revealingly, that the information was needed to update German military rolls and "to benefit individuals so that they would not incur the possibility of molestation if they should enter German territory."[7]

And on it went. Names and addresses on form letters that began with "The following person is particularly important to us in our work . . ." poured in. The subject's profession was noted, and the sender was asked to check one of two comments asking whether the subject was "a convinced supporter of a volkish, National Socialist worldview," or, if his worldview was not known, whether he had shown readiness to undertake "independent Volksdeutsch activity."[8] All this information was carefully entered in personal dossiers in a central file in Stuttgart. Each dossier also included the subject's reasons for emigration, hobbies, language proficiency, religion, and the names and ages of all children under eighteen.[9]

The reports on American society received back in the Fatherland did not always give a recognizable view of the United States. One intrepid operative toured Connecticut by car in the late 1930s. His vision of the Nutmeg State, written in a Baedeker-like style, is quite startling. He was shocked to note that the "fertile soil of the valleys and less fertile soil of the highlands" was tilled not by real Yankee farmers, but by former inhabitants of Russia, Poland, and Italy and their children. This fact could only be ascertained, however, by actually talking to the individuals, who not only looked like Yankees, but, deceptively, lived in colonial-style houses. Indeed, two-thirds of the population seemed to be "foreign-born" or the children of the foreign-born. The tobacco industry he found to be controlled by Jews and Russians. The magnificent dairy and poultry farms did have some German owners and workers, but many more were run by Poles, Italians, Swiss, or "other foreign ethnic groups." The factories, banks, and financial institutions were still owned by "old Americans," but they did not do much of the actual work. Personal service, he correctly noted, was performed mostly by people of "foreign origin or alien race." He was impressed by the "multiplicity of churches and synagogues" where members "pray to their God in language and manner brought from their lands of birth." The Connecticut Germans, sad to say, seemed not to be particularly unified, and had "adapted themselves remarkably well to American life."[10] Missing entirely the miracle of the United States, he never seemed to realize that, despite their ethnic and social differences, all the groups he described considered themselves real Americans.

By February 1938 another DAI official, Heinz Kloss, felt he had enough material on the United States to propose an ambitious educational program. To start, the DAI should publish a German-American "*Heimat* Atlas." This tome would list the number of ethnic Germans in each town and its principal German organizations, thereby making it possible to approach "separate German splinter groups." The atlas would be bilingual for those who were no longer fluent in their "native" tongue. He also proposed the publication of textbooks for German-American schoolchildren, which would point out similarities between Germany and the United States, such as the Reich Labor Service and the Civilian Conservation Corps and the "German Jewish question and the American Negro question." The books would include the poems of a "little known Texas-German Homeland poet" and pioneer tales from "the North-Dakota Russo-German communities," which only a truly dedicated researcher could ever have found. The DAI official, apparently ignorant of the subject matter of Bible studies, also suggested supplying church schools with maps of the Reich, as he had observed that many of them had maps of Palestine, but not of Germany. Most importantly, "young German-Americans," especially ones born "over there," should be sent for at least six months a year to towns in Germany so that they could bond with the inhabitants.[11]

It is not clear which, if any, of these secret projects actually bore fruit, but at least one reaction survives. Carefully saved in the DAI files is an article from an unknown Pennsylvania newspaper that accurately notes that "a certain Heinz Kloss," who had visited Allentown from Germany in order to "study" the local culture and traditions, was suspected of being a "Hitler agent" and of having "a lot to do" with unsolicited mail being received by local citizens:

> Names and addresses of Pennsylvania-Germans in Allentown and Lehigh county have been placed on mailing lists in Germany to provide an outlet for Nazi propaganda in this country, it was learned today.
>
> For several months now . . . Lehigh-countians of German stock have been receiving letters, magazines and pamphlets. . . . One of the more prominent issues is "*Die Heimat*," a cultural magazine printed in Germany. An Allentonian said today that on several occasions his name has been included in items appearing in the publication, though he had never submitted any information to the publisher. . . .
>
> The publications are not well received locally, and as one Pennsylvania-German put it: ". . . As far as we are concerned our home-

land is America, and the less we hear of and from Germany, the better
we feel."[12]

By the late 1930s the activities of certain overt pro-Nazi groups established by Americans, such as the publicity-seeking Amerikadeutscher
Volksbund (known as the Bund), were the source of such public outrage
that, in 1938, German Ambassador Hans Heinrich Dieckhoff, brother-in-
law of German Foreign Minister Joachim von Ribbentrop, aware that the
often absurd displays of the Bund were making German-American relations worse by the day, advised the German government to sever official
relations with them and forbid Reich citizens to be members. Among
other things, the Bund, perhaps also influenced by Winnetou, had unsuccessfully tried to enlist the "pure ethnic" Native Americans as "natural
partners," and had flirted with the Ku Klux Klan. Even worse, the federal
government had outlawed the Bund Youth camps.[13] The Ambassador also
tried to point out that very few ethnic Germans in America had any interest in National Socialism and that the "conspiratorial child's play"[14] being
carried on by the DAI would only have disastrous results. This was soon
borne out by a plethora of congressional hearings and investigations aimed
at subversive German activities, which exposed spying by exchange students, the fact that several German nationals had been jailed for trying to
obtain military secrets, and the sleazier activities of the Bund leadership.

But the final blow to any mass movement of German-Americans to the
Reich was struck in early November 1938, by the violent events of Kristallnacht. In a series of telegrams, Ambassador Dieckhoff noted that "large
and powerful sections of the American people" who up to then had
regarded Germany as a "stronghold of order and a bulwark against riots
and against unlawful encroachment upon private property" had changed
their views. Public opinion, he reported,

> is without exception incensed against Germany and hostile toward
> her. . . . The outcry comes not only from Jews but in equal strength
> from all camps and classes, including the German-American camp.
> What particularly strikes one is that, with few exceptions, the
> respectable patriotic circles, which are thoroughly anti-Communist
> and, for the greater part, anti-Semitic in their outlook, also begin to
> turn away from us. . . . That men like Dewey, Hoover, Hearst and many
> others who have hitherto maintained a comparative reserve and had
> even, to some extent, expressed sympathy toward Germany, are now
> publicly adopting so violent and bitter an attitude against her is a seri-
> ous matter.

Indeed, the Ambassador continued a few days later, "the good prospects for a gradual spread of anti-Semitism have suffered a serious setback," as "even the most bitter anti-Semites are anxious to disassociate themselves from methods of this kind," a trend that Dieckhoff felt had been demonstrated by the fact that "in an old Protestant church in Massachusetts they went so far as to have a rabbi preach for the first time, departing from a 300-year-old tradition, in order to show that in a situation like the present they stand by the Jews."[15]

A few days after these telegrams were sent, the Roosevelt administration firmly demonstrated its displeasure with Germany by sending the German Ambassador back to Berlin for good. The Nazi leaders did not give up on their efforts to retrieve ethnic Germans, however. On December 16, Göring, desperate for skilled labor for his Four Year Plan, claiming to have heard rumors that German workers were being fired by U.S. firms and being replaced by Jews, ordered the Foreign Office to come up with a "bold scheme" (within three or four days) to "attract people of German origin here from America (even those who are already American citizens)." Göring had Hitler's approval for this plan and even speculated that "it would be possible to organize an exchange of people of German origin returning home for Jews to be sent there." The workers were to be lured by subsidized travel in the lower classes of German shipping lines, free temporary housing in Germany, plus numerous other perks. Dieckhoff, newly back from Washington, wearily pointed out to his untraveled superiors that "in the case of German Americans we must never forget that they are not compelled to live under foreign dominion . . . but that they went to America of their own free will in order to live there as Americans."[16]

The outbreak of war would prevent further efforts to retrieve German blood from the United States, but the more fanatic Nazis were ever hopeful. In an April 1942 memorandum to Hitler's chief of staff, Martin Bormann, SS chief Heinrich Himmler, not the least convinced by Dieckhoff's observations, still advocated a postwar continuation of the sub rosa efforts in America in order to "call back each single man of German blood who has any value whatsoever to the German Reich, for the settlement of conquered soil." Recognizing that these former Germans would be "undoubtedly politically poisoned," he advised solving that problem "by means of personal propaganda. . . . Each individual family must be called back by employing their personal ties."[17]

Efforts similar to those in the United States went on in every country where ethnic Germans could be found. South America was the target of

great activity. The Nazis considered its German populations to be much
more open to National Socialist thinking than those in the United States,
since they had arrived in the New World far later and tended to maintain
closer contact with one another. Among many other things, German agencies subsidized German schools there and encouraged pen pals, scholarships to the Fatherland, and faculty exchanges.[18]

Few countries on earth were left unlisted. Agents were active in South
Africa, Spain, Romania, the Baltic states, Denmark, Slovenia, Slovakia,
and even Papua New Guinea, a former German colony that had become a
British protectorate. A secret memo from that remote outpost reported
442 ethnic Germans still in residence. The agent was pleased to report
that the Lutheran mission had decorated the train station with swastika
flags for his arrival and that he had been serenaded by a black oompah
band playing Nazi songs (perhaps not exactly what Hitler had in mind). A
list of local loyalists was appended, which informed officials back home
that one colonist was "an energetic Führer type," that another had a
signed picture of Hitler in his house, and that several others would be suitable administrators should the colony revert to Germany.[19]

If the overseas Germans were a long shot for use as workers or
settlers, there were other candidates closer to hand. For the vast regions
that would be taken from Poland and the Soviet Union, Himmler, with
Hitler's blessing, had conceived one of the greatest projected displace-
ments of human beings in history. The plan was to eventually push the
great mass of the Slavic population east beyond the Ural Mountains, and
to create an "Eastern Wall" of resettled Germans, who would provide a
buffer zone between Aryan and Slav. In this zone, magnificent autobahns
would soon take the new blond, blue-eyed inhabitants to sunny beaches in
the Crimea. The settlers, in theory exemplary Germanic farmers, would
be protected by fortress garrisons reminiscent of the Wild West novels so
beloved by Hitler, and would, temporarily, use Slavic serf-type labor
to help till the land. German ethnic groups long established in these
somewhat exotic regions, which included, among others, Transnistria,
the Volga, Bukovinia, Bessarabia, and the Baltic countries, would be
rearranged within the new areas and united with others brought from
around the world. It was a glorious dream, which from the beginning
would have to be altered to fit the byzantine realities of power politics in
the late 1930s and early 1940s.

Indeed, in 1938 Hitler had grudgingly had to concede the "Germanic"

Forced migration.

territory of the South Tyrol, with its 200,000 ethnic Germans, to Mussolini in return for the latter's acquiescence in the Nazi takeover of Austria. The following year, after the German entry into the Sudetenland on the pretense of further consolidating Germandom, and Hitler's subsequent subjugation of the supposedly independent remains of Czechoslovakia in Bohemia and Moravia, Mussolini, quite rightly fearing that the South Tyrol might soon suffer the same fate, insisted that all ethnic Germans be evacuated from there forthwith. Hitler, whose secret plans for the invasion of Poland were well under way, could not afford to alienate Mussolini, and was forced to consent. This was extremely awkward, as the Germanic organizations, which for years had been stirring up the South Tyroleans, as well as the Sudeten Germans, to push for minority rights *sur place,* now had to persuade the former to settle elsewhere in order to give control of Czech territory to the latter.[20] Even more awkward was the fact that, for the moment, Hitler did not yet have any place to move 200,000 people.

Before this problem could be dealt with, the German invasion and dismemberment of Poland had begun. To the astonishment of the world, Hitler's accomplice in this effort was the Soviet Union, with which he had signed a Treaty of Nonaggression on August 23, 1939, a little more than a week before his long-planned invasion.

Joseph Stalin, certainly the Führer's equal when it came to the cynical use and elimination of human beings, had territorial plans as well. He was far more interested in gaining control of the Baltic states, with their vital seaports, and the areas bordering on Romania, than he was in central Poland. He too envisioned a buffer zone—to protect himself from Germany. Hitler, with the declarations of war of France and Great Britain after his attack on Poland, was again forced to concede territory occupied by a large number of ethnic Germans, this time to Stalin. Since his future plans also included the betrayal of the USSR, it was clear that any Germans living deep in its bosom would be in grave danger when the moment of invasion arrived, and would have to be moved. Stalin, suspicious of a group that would undoubtedly be loyal to the Nazis, was only too glad to get rid of the ethnic Germans. The final agreements with the Soviet Union, therefore, included a secret protocol that gave the Germans permission to relocate Reich citizens and others of "German descent" from the Baltic states to German-controlled areas.[21] This would add some 86,000 souls of good blood to Hitler's new empire from Estonia and Latvia alone, and more would follow from Lithuania. A few days later Hitler was also able to advise Mussolini that "a climatically and topographically suitable area" would soon be set aside in Poland for the South Tyrolese.[22]

Only days after these diplomatic agreements were reached, responsibility for all the resettlement was eagerly taken over, after considerable Machiavellian maneuvering, by Himmler, who was given a nest egg of ten million reichsmarks to get things going. The resettlement of so many hundreds of thousands of *Volksdeutsche*, would require an entirely new organization. In a decree dated October 7, 1939, Hitler created the Reich Commission for the Strengthening of Germandom (RKFDV). Stating that "the consequences which Versailles had on Europe have been removed," Hitler declared that the Greater German Reich could now "accept and settle within its space German people who up to the present had to live in foreign lands." Himmler was given a threefold commission:

1. To bring back those German citizens and ethnic Germans abroad who are eligible for permanent return to the Reich;
2. To eliminate the harmful influence of such alien parts of the population as constitute a danger to the Reich and the German community;
3. To create new German colonies by resettlement, and especially by the resettlement of German citizens and ethnic Germans coming back from abroad.[23]

Himmler was authorized to use the services of a whole list of established agencies for this project, which had to gather, move, and resettle millions of ethnic Germans to as yet undesignated areas from which equivalent thousands of undesirables would have to be ejected. Nor could the gathering of ethnic Germans be done in a slapdash manner. Every single one, as the citizenship laws required, would have to be racially, medically, and politically screened to make sure he or she was truly German and truly "worthy."

The territory part was easy. Within a week of the creation of the RKFDV, most of the west of Poland, including the areas around Posen and Lodz, was annexed to Germany. These areas, which included the new Gaus of Danzig–West Prussia, Zichenau, Katowice, and the Wartheland, were to be reserved for ethnic Germans. The names of towns, rivers, streets, and so on were Germanized and Polish culture was to be suppressed. Henceforth Poznan would be called Posen, and Lodz became Litzmanstadt. The central and southern part of Poland, which contained the cities of Warsaw, Lublin, and Cracow, the so-called General Gouvernement, was to retain a majority Polish population under German rule and would be used as a dumping ground for all those not welcome in the annexed zones. For the time being, the east of Poland, taken over by the Soviet Union in mid-September, lay beyond Nazi control and was not available for settlement, but that would soon change.

Organizing the processing of the new settlers was equally swift. The Liaison Office for Ethnic Germans Abroad (VoMi), set up by Himmler in 1937 to dominate all the previously established organizations in the ethnics-abroad field, was to evacuate the German groups. Another agency, the Immigration Authority (EWZ), would vet them for suitability, after which the RKFDV would place them in new settlements. To make sure the new arrivals would not "contaminate" any pure Germans, the EWZ brought in officials from the police, the Ministry of Health, the Reichsbank, and the SS Race and Settlement Main Office (RuSHA), plus statisticians and nutritionists.[24] One could not, after all, be too careful. Finding trained personnel was not a problem—the agencies involved had been doing this sort of work at home for years—and by October 12, 1939, the first of many processing stations was open for business in the Baltic port city of Gdynia.

The resettlement and eviction plans were all very fine on paper, presupposing as they did that ethnic Germans, wherever they were, would happily divest themselves of property, liquidate businesses, abandon homes they had lived in for generations, and become enthusiastic pioneers in unknown locations. The policy also assumed that Germans already in the areas in which their racial brothers would appear would support the policies and welcome the new arrivals with open arms. It was, alas, not so simple.

In Estonia and Latvia, where the first resettlements would take place, the German authorities had to tread a fine line. They had to persuade the ethnic Germans to leave voluntarily without betraying to the world that Hitler had essentially abandoned the Baltic states to the USSR. The resettlement must, above all, not be seen as a rescue of Germans from a Soviet takeover, or as the evacuation of a potential war zone. The evacuees, described in one German document as a "feisty group bound by strong tradition" who would be perfect for "border placement," should, therefore, never be referred to as refugees by the German agencies, but as people who were "answering the call of the Führer."[25]

Hitler made the resettlement public knowledge in a speech to the Reichstag on Friday, October 6, 1939. In his oration he rather vaguely referred to "the creation of a Reich frontier which . . . shall be in accordance with existing historical, ethnographical and economic conditions" and to "the disposition of the living space according to the various nationalities" as well as to "an attempt to reach a solution and settlement of the Jewish problem." Ethnic German Jews, if one could use such a phrase, would not be included in the evacuations. Russia and Germany, he said, would transform Poland and its surrounding areas from a hotbed of intrigue against both of them to "a zone of peaceful development."[26]

The human objects of this exercise in the Baltic states would not hear any official details of the evacuations for two more days. By then the American chargé d'affaires in Tallinn, the capital of Estonia, startled at this dramatic reversal of Germany's traditional policy of encouraging "these ancient eastern bastions of Germanism,"[27] had already reported the presence of German transport vessels in the harbor.[28] The arrival of other ships was soon noted in Riga and other Baltic ports. Rumors and questions streamed back and forth between the ethnic German organizations and Berlin. Those about to be moved were not the only group surprised by the massive and hasty nature of the evacuation.

Despite Hitler's efforts at deception, it was clear to the non-Germans in the Baltic governments that their doom was sealed: the loss of the German minority meant that the Soviet Union would soon have total control. The Estonian Minister President burst into tears at the news, declaring that it was "the end of Estonia." The Soviets, for their part, were upset by the speed of the German actions and told the German Ambassador that they were "astonished" at the "panicky" promotion of emigration, which would expose their own nefarious motives to take over the Baltics and "compromise the action of the Soviet Government."[29] Soviet Foreign Minister Vyacheslav Molotov also feared that the clearing of ethnic Germans from these states could be the prelude to a Nazi attack on the Soviet Union. Hitler soothed Molotov by saying rumors to this effect were American and English "propaganda," and that the removal of the ethnic Germans would make clear Germany's "political disinterestedness" in the Baltic countries.[30]

It is not hard to imagine the complex emotions that now faced the ethnic Germans in the Baltic states. The *Times* of London reported, "Almost every German family in Latvia appears to be divided and tormented." There was little time for hesitation: the Baltic Germans were expected to leave within the week. "Groups to-day show deep distress, not knowing what to decide—not wishing to go to Germany, but afraid to remain . . . believing that Hitler has made some agreement whereby they may soon be abandoned." Some were defiant. One perceptive young man stated that he did not wish to leave and become "Hitler's cannon fodder." On the Sunday after the announcement the churches were crowded and "during the service great numbers of worshippers were in tears."[31]

The Nazi organizers had no such torments. Now the years of meticulous list making and planning were justified. Ethnic German leaders had secretly been summoned to Germany to confer with Himmler and other officials more than ten days before the announcement.[32] Twelve thousand new ID cards had already been printed up, as had flyers with details of the evacuation. On October 9, notices appeared in the local Baltic German press announcing to potential evacuees that they could "look with pride upon their centuries-old work in this country" but that a new task had now been set for them: "Together we will resettle and rebuild the German Eastern areas won back by the Reich."[33] Meanwhile, behind the scenes Nazi operatives spread rumors of coming Bolshevik horrors. Processing offices opened the same day and produced reams of detailed instructions, interspersed with admonitions to remain calm, covering everything from hand baggage to the shipment of furniture and tools.

The scare propaganda worked only too well in some quarters. Within days, as banks and government agencies were overwhelmed with people closing accounts and trying to sell property, it was necessary to publish reassurances and warn people against wild rumors. Officials pled with evacuees to refrain from unannounced visits to the various agencies and discouraged panic selling of real estate, urging people instead to convey title to a German Trustee Agency, which would liquidate it in consultation with the Baltic governments in order to spare the individual or the "entire folk economy" unnecessary losses.[34]

In Latvia individuals were directed to special "Option" offices, where before representatives of the Latvian and German governments they could simultaneously renounce their Latvian citizenship and receive one of the already printed "returnee" cards on which a departure date and ship would be specified. In Estonia, evacuees were instructed to leave the keys to their houses at the German legation before embarking. Everyone labored over endless inventories of their bonds, furniture, silver, and jewelry. Those who had doubts about this somewhat casual relinquishing of their entire net worth were scornfully asked if they doubted "the word of the Führer."[35] Notices went out that all archives and documents should be delivered to a central office. Trustees of foundations were ordered to fill out other forms, and all valuable art objects were to be reported to a central office. And not least, every applicant was exhorted not to forget the genealogical documents that would prove that he or she was an Aryan.[36]

Speed was of the essence in this operation. The longer people had to think about what they were doing, the more likely they were to change their minds about leaving or try to go to destinations other than Germany. Of course, there was resistance to the precipitate evacuation, which essentially required the complete surrender of self to the Reich government and transfer to a totally unknown destination. Hesitancy was countered by ever more strident and threatening notices in the German papers. At frequent intervals *Volksdeutsche* were urged to be part of the first groups to "undertake the new tasks on the borders of the Folkdom of the Greater German Reich," and to think only of the future and not look back. It was pointed out that their children would have greater opportunities and that Hitler cared for them. As time went on, irritation with the laggards began to show. *Volksdeutsche* unwilling to leave their houses were described as "utterly stupid" and deserving of the "self-inflicted punishment" staying behind would cause.[37] When this sort of pressure failed, Realpolitik came to the fore, and ethnic Germans who had been openly anti-Communist were visited at home and threatened with exposure to the future Soviet authorities.

Enthusiasm for resettlement generally followed generational lines. *Volksdeutsche* youth, having been indoctrinated for years in local Hitler Youth–type organizations, were more enthusiastic than their parents, and numbers of young people are believed to have left on their own. Despite all the glowing German reports, the exodus was terrible for many. Non-

German wives refused to leave; there were divorces and suicides. But so great was fear of the coming Soviet takeover and so strong the pressure of the Nazi agencies that within a week of the initial notice of evacuation the first groups set sail into the unknown. The captains of the vessels were only told where to head once they had cleared the harbors. Embarkation procedures were efficient, even military in feeling. The travelers were first gathered into temporary quarters near the port, where they were welcomed with handouts containing strict instructions: no smoking, no drinking, no eating except in designated areas. Bunks were assigned. Each family had to bring its own bedding, crockery, and food. Lights out at 10:00 p.m., reveille at 7:00 a.m. Doctors and nurses would make rounds, and baby baths were available on application. Children under the age of seven slept in the women's section. The need for discipline was emphasized. Only in the last paragraph was any human feeling revealed. The travelers were wished a "good night, a smooth transition, a good crossing and a happy reunion in your new home in the Third Reich."[38]

The ships sent from Germany made multiple voyages, and by the end of the year had removed more than 10,000 Estonians and some 47,000 Latvians. By the spring of 1940 thousands more would follow. But to the chagrin of the Nazis, a good number of *Volksdeutsche*, especially those whose affairs had required complex arrangements to settle and who thus had time to reconsider, did not leave. Settlement of affairs was not the only reason. Before the last transport had left, coded letters were being received in the Baltic states indicating that conditions in the Glorious Reich were somewhat less than perfect. One early evacuee wrote home that his compatriots should not leave until "after Jan's wedding." A reasonable thought, except that the Jan in question was only two years old.[39] The "bad Germans" who held back were excoriated in the local German press, which predicted that they would be "despised by their fellow citizens . . . there will be joy if they perish. Let them ponder the fate of their children who will have to be brought up among strangers in an alien atmosphere, who will be shunned by their school mates and who will never be able to find a place for themselves."[40] Prophetic words, which, in fact, would apply not to those who stayed, but to many of those who left, for the moment they set foot on the transports they became stateless persons and would remain so for the rest of their lives.

Those who stayed behind did immediately lose their former status of a protected minority. On December 21, 1939, the Latvian Ministry of the Interior declared that "Germanism in Latvia is dead forever." German schools and churches were closed, German-language newspapers were no longer published, and people were encouraged to "Latvianize" their names.[41] After the predicted Soviet takeover of Latvia and Estonia in 1940, such measures and more would persuade 16,000 more of the remaining "Germans" to leave for Reich territory.

The Estonians and Latvians were only the first of the groups that would be moved to satisfy the arrangements agreed to by Hitler and Stalin. Even as their transports gingerly crossed the Baltic through the minefields laid down by the German Navy, an exchange of White Russians and Ukrainians in the German zones of Poland was being negotiated for ethnic Germans in the Soviet sectors. In the summer and fall of 1940 it would be the turn of Bessarabians, Bukovinians, Lithuanians, the leftover Estonians, and Latvians, plus the ethnic Germans in the Polish General Gouvernement, a total of some half million souls. In each case the methodology of persuasion and evacuation was essentially the same, even if the modes of transport—which included trains, Danube steamers, and long wagon trains accompanied by cattle—were often more colorful than the steamers coming from Riga and Tallinn.

By the spring of 1940 some 1,500 camps and holding centers had been set up to deal with this forced migration. There were reception camps where arrivees were deloused, washed, and quarantined before going on to "observation" camps. Along with food and lodging in these staging areas there were German lessons and political indoctrination classes for those who were a bit vague about National Socialism. Floating schools and Hitler Youth units were set up for children under the age of fourteen, and particular care was supposed to be given to health matters. This was not altruistic. Ahead of the unsuspecting resettlers lay the racial and political exams that would determine their fate, and Himmler wanted as many healthy new Germans as he could get.

Despite his quick action in the Baltic states, Himmler had been a bit late when it came to finding suitable places to settle the evacuees. His organization had to compete with other occupation administrators, opportunistic German businessmen who swarmed in to take over confiscated Eastern industries, Göring's Four Year Plan operatives, and the Ministry of Agriculture, to name only a few. The situation was made even more difficult by the opposition of each newly installed local Nazi governor to settlers not of his own choosing.

Albert Forster, Gauleiter of Danzig and a friend of Hitler's, considered the Balts troublesome foreigners who would need all sorts of services. He did not want to deal with this mostly white-collar group, which included many useless old people and children. Forster thought it would be much easier to accommodate himself with the Poles and create a thriving industrial enclave with himself and his cronies in control. Faced with the fanatic land grabbing going on and Forster's refusal to take more than a few thousand Balts in Gdynia, Himmler was forced to send some of their ships on to Stettin and other ports.

It is not clear what the passengers from the Baltic countries expected to find when they arrived. For young children the boat trip was exciting. Their older siblings were happy to be going to fabled Germany, where all the neighbors would speak German, where they wouldn't have to take Latvian at school, and where they would be able to get the latest cool toys—the object of the moment being a sort of go-cart called a Hollander.[42] Some adults were optimistic too: one former inmate of an Estonian mental hospital, blissfully unaware of the Nazi hereditary health laws, expressed the modest hope that he would be taken to an equally good institution in the Reich.[43] But if the voyagers had imagined that they would immediately progress to Berlin or to the idyllic flower-covered villages full of dirndl-clad lasses so often shown in German propaganda magazines, they were disappointed. Andreas Meyer-Landruth, seven years old at the time, remembered that "upon disembarking we realized we had been tricked since we were not in Germany itself." His mother, who had come ahead of her husband with the children, "cried from morning to night and we had absolutely no idea what would become of us."[44] Still, arrival ceremonies in Gdynia and other ports were quite colorful. Flags were flying and loudspeakers played cheery German songs. But many passengers were immediately repelled by the sheer numbers of arrogant and impersonal uniformed representatives of the Nazi youth, police, and welfare organizations who waited on the docks to conduct them to quarters in or around the ports or to trains that took them to temporary "quarantine" lodgings in Posen or in towns and villages scattered all over northeastern Germany and the newly annexed area of Poland.

Evacuees found many of the lodgings provided in the seaports full of bedbugs and other vermin; luckier ones ended up in shuttered resort hotels and former Polish mental and old age institutions on the coast. The latter, unbeknownst to the settlers, had been made available by the SS, who had taken several thousand former patients to a remote site near Danzig and executed them. Those who went to Posen were housed in a former Polish school, where the food was plentiful and medical care adequate, but sleeping facilities were limited to straw on the floor.

Country life was not idyllic either. Hundreds of Baltic families, isolated from one another, were billeted for months with sometimes disagreeable German peasant families and battled cold, sickness, and depression. One family with three children aged six months, two, and five, rejected by all the peasant families in the village of Selchow in a remote area of Pomerania, was finally given an unheated laborer's house near the horse barn. The mother, by helping with the chores, managed to get enough milk for her children. There were almost no vegetables, and the baby had to stay in bed most of the time because the floor was too cold to sit on. Winter came early and water froze in the kitchen. They had no news at all from their parents or friends. So passed their first Christmas in the Fatherland. Finally, in early spring, this family too went to the straw-bedding building in Posen, where the malnourished baby nearly died.[45]

By now the straw, according to another evacuee, who arrived in March, was not exactly clean. The group in the camp was very mixed: upper- and middle-class families were often terrified by the drunken fights of some of their less cultured countrymen. Order was supposed to be maintained by students from the elite Nazi Ordensburgen schools. One evacuee described his youthful camp commandant as "in fact, as handsome as the young Siegfried of the Sagas." But most in the camp found the Ordensjunkers "uneducated and untrained." In one of the women's sections was a "typical example of this type, very young, excessively superior and remote. When he wanted us to do something he whistled instead of calling us. We Baltic women soon came into conflict with him."[46]

From this and a hundred similar camps the new settlers were called to their final racial examination. This typically took place in a large hall where an array of officials clad in the myriad showy uniforms of the Nazi agencies, ministries, police, and youth organizations waited. Families were kept together while the birth certificates and genealogies of each member were examined. Assets were inventoried and arrangements made for compensation for items that had been left behind. Political affiliations and participation in ethnic German activities were considered. Everyone over six years old was photographed in the nude and given a medical exam by SS physicians in which the by now well established criteria for Aryan noses, head shape, and coloring were closely analyzed. There was no room for levity here. One young man who was told after his physical that the only good thing about him was his teeth retorted that his brains were good too, but that the doctor couldn't tell that from the examination. This was noted as insolence, and the youth was told that he was, accordingly, disqualified from service in the SS, a reprimand he only later realized was a blessing.

It was in this daunting arena that anyone of "alien race" who had managed to hide among the other resettlers would be detected. At each stage of the examination spaces on a large file card for each subject were filled in with grades, and at the end a racial classification was awarded that determined the subject's permanent place in the pecking order of his fellow Germans.

The classification formula set up by the racial agencies was highly complex and varied according to the status of the subject. In general, the analysis was distilled to a group of numbers and letters, each of which was fraught with meaning to any official who saw them. Thus "Iag/I" meant that the subject was a very desirable population addition, pure Nordic, perfect physique, and good family, while "IV F," so familiar to American GIs, here too was the category of the reject, indicating that the subject was totally unacceptable and of alien blood.[47] Once this classification was established the candidate was either given naturalization documents or told that action on his status would be "delayed." The racial indicators, combined with the subject's experience, would determine where he would be placed for settlement. This factor too was shown by symbols. "A," or *Altreich*, oddly enough, was for the less desirable settlers and meant that the subject would be sent to a strictly supervised life in Germany itself and would not be trusted with his own farm or business. "O" (*Ost-Falle*) indicated that the family was particularly worthy to be part of the Eastern Wall of German Blood and would be placed in the new eastern territories in a relatively independent situation as close to his old one as possible. "S" stood for *Sonderfall*, or "special case," and was used for those of doubtful loyalty or race who were destined for eventual deportation or forced labor.[48] After this processing, from which there was essentially no appeal, the settlers who were selected to stay in Poland went back to their camps to wait for allocation of permanent lodgings.

The assignment of housing and farms was only slightly less arbitrary. In the towns, a few lucky settlers were shown several choices by SS real estate agents. The word soon got around that one should not take the first places offered, as these were generally quite squalid. During this process it became abundantly clear to the new arrivals that, contrary to the propaganda they had heard, the houses they had been seeing had been vacated under duress. Some wondered at first why those who had been forced to leave had not, like themselves, packed up more things. The truth did not take long to dawn on them. In some houses half-eaten meals still were on the dining room table, desks were full of personal papers, and unmade children's beds told of small bodies lifted up in the night. Settlers who could find lodgings on a different basis, for example, by renting them from Polish *Volksdeutsche*, felt less guilty, but for most there was no choice, and they moved in only to be haunted by the thought of former residents, often cultured middle-class Poles, some of whom had even served in the German Army in World War I and won the Iron Cross, which was duly displayed.

The ghosts who haunted the houses were not always immaterial. In the chaotic deportations of Jews and Poles that had taken place, many had escaped the Nazi net or had made their way back home. It was not unusual to find the former owners at the door politely asking if they could collect a few of their things. One settler, a small boy at the time, to this day remembers the image of the former Polish owners of his new home disappearing into the snow, pulling a sled loaded with a small pile of their family papers, photographs, and paintings.[49]

In Lodz, a more energetic Polish materfamilias made six trips to her old house and each time removed an enormous bundle of possessions. The visits were dangerous for everyone, as contact with the former inhabitants was strictly forbidden. The nervous Baltic family, perhaps not aware of the fate of many Poles, was relieved when the elderly woman "finally disappeared for good, thanking us heartily and shedding a few tears."[50]

In the country the housing authorities seem to have made some effort to put people at their accustomed social levels. Titled Baltic Germans often ended up in decrepit small manor houses once owned by minor Polish gentry, which they worked hard to restore, while peasants from Volhynia were given simple farms. But none of the settlers were given clear title to their new property. Ownership remained in the hands of the various Nazi agencies, which meant that the families could be evicted at any moment.

Nevertheless, by the summer of 1940 many of the relatively small group of Baltic settlers in western Poland were more or less comfortably established and only prayed that they would not have to move again. True to their word, the Nazi agencies had sent on their cattle and household belongings. For the time being food was abundant and staff even more so, as Poles were protected from deportation if they worked for Germans. But living in the midst of the resentful indigenous population, which still outnumbered them by a vast percentage, was far from comfortable. If Himmler had wanted a frontier situation, he certainly had it now. The children of these families, in the way of all children, were not unhappy: many still remember the arrival of wild geese, the excitement of parades, or the fun of hunting expeditions in the country. But they remember other things too:

> A Pole who had supposedly profiteered in grain was hanged in the market place, and we children were assembled to watch the scene. Another time seven Jews were executed there. It was ghastly, and a woman behind me, who couldn't stand the spectacle, fled, crying hysterically. But we were young kids of 12, 13 and 14 . . . and we stood there with wide open eyes and looked upon it all as a game.[51]

In many cases the resettled Baltic Germans, entirely defeating the purpose of the exercise, quickly learned Polish and in the end got along better with the Poles than they did with some of the Reich Germans, whose arrogance and corruption they found unattractive. And indeed, many Nazis considered the Balts overeducated, old-fashioned, and too religious.

At the opposite extreme from the relatively well-to-do Baltic Germans were the settlers who came into the annexed provinces of Poland from the border areas of the USSR and eastern Poland. This group consisted in large part of very primitive peasants and farmers, most of whom spoke little German and were illiterate. During the winter of 1939–40 tens of thousands, enduring terrible seasonal conditions, had come to the reception camps in long wagon-train treks to await processing. To help the overwhelmed resettlement agencies, in the spring of 1940, the Nazis mobilized the youth and student organizations that had been preparing for so long to take part in the *Osteinsatz,* or Eastern Action-Mission. They would be busy: by mid-November there would be nearly half a million resettlers of all categories.[52]

Leadership elements of the Hitler Youth and the Bund Deutscher Mädel had, along with representatives of all the other German civilian agencies, come into Poland just after its surrender. Their job was to organize the ethnic German youth already there and to prepare for young resettlers. For many students and young people, whether they were true Nazis or not, the opportunity to work in the newly conquered areas was an adventure and, above all, a way to contribute to the war effort. Patriotic fervor, fueled by the incredible success of the German forces and the disinformation that blamed Poland for starting the war, was high. After all the boring afternoons at Hitler Youth meetings, here was action at last and the chance to help and serve. But the help and service was not to be given to all who were in need: it was for ethnic Germans alone and not for the defeated Slavic *Untermenschen.*

A Hitler Youth "Germanizing" a resettled child.

From the reminiscences of many young occupiers, it is clear that they had not given much thought to the feelings of the Polish enemy and viewed them as beings from another world. Arriving in Posen on a dreary November night, BDM leader Melita Maschmann got her "first intimation of the hostility of the land in which I now wanted to work" when a young woman she asked for directions "gave me a hostile look and turned her back in silence." Her billet was the parlor of a lower-middle-class Polish household much like those she knew in Germany: "There were plush armchairs and lace mats and *art nouveau* twirls on the furniture." Here she spent three uncomfortable weeks sleeping on the sofa. The room was unheated. She could hear muffled conversation and children crying and sometimes she heard shots. One night, "the feeling crept over me that I was shut away in a tower with my escape barred by enemies," and she pushed a chair against the lockless door. Fraternization was forbidden, and she did not try to speak to the other unseen inhabitants of the house, whom she assumed were Polish refugees. The minimal contact she did have with her landlady made her uncomfortable:

> I found these conversations distasteful. I did not know how to treat the woman. When I moved out she begged me with tears in her eyes to stay.

She was clearly afraid of the next compulsory lodger. The thought then occurred to me that the refugees whom I had never seen, but whom I had heard all the more clearly, must be hiding in the house.

Maschmann's feelings of superiority toward the locals was bolstered by the fact that she seldom saw educated-looking Poles in Posen, which confirmed the Nazi propaganda that they were a primitive people incapable of decent self-government. She did not know then that most of the intelligentsia and professional classes had already been imprisoned or deported. Oppressed by the dreary poverty in the town, with its "particular smell of saturated clothes, stale bread, unwashed children and cheap scent," she still was upset for a time by the "visibly starving" children who begged for food. From her room she often watched Polish children stealing coal from the piles in the street that were meant for the soldiers. At one point she was overcome by her feelings:

> At first my sympathies were entirely on the side of the children. I gave them to understand by signs that they need not be afraid of me, but they mistrusted my uniform. They scuttled back silently into the darkness on their rag-bound feet. One afternoon I wrested a girl of perhaps eight from the hands of a sentry. In her fear of being beaten she had to let fall her bucket [of coal] and held both arms folded over her head. . . . The soldier glared furiously at my silver-trimmed uniform coat. He could not make head or tail of my intervention.

But, as had been the case with the Communist Party workers in the Ukraine during the famine, she soon was describing as "politically naïve the 'uncontrolled way' I had reacted to this encounter with human misery." The Poles, she reminded herself, "even if militarily defeated—remained dangerous enemies: their strength lay in their biological superiority; it was a kind of suicide for us to try to save their children from starvation." The endless barrage of propaganda on the Slavic population menace published at home had had its effect. Her mind from then on would be entirely focused on helping the *Volksdeutsche* population.

It was not hard to feel sympathy for the ethnic Germans in Poland. Thousands of indigenous *Volksdeutsche* had been killed by Poles during the fighting; vengeance and atrocities had taken place on both sides. And some ethnic Germans, isolated in the countryside, rightly lived in fear. But many others, who had lived in Poland for generations, of course had Polish friends, especially if they were children. These would have to be reeducated. Maschmann's job was to establish hostels and schools for the *Volks-*

deutsche. This she did by driving around the countryside in a decrepit car that was constantly mired in snow and mud. In each little village she would find a "pathetic handful" of ethnic German boys and girls waiting for her visit. Since they had never lived under Nazi rule, the children and their leaders were not at all clear about ideology: "One of these groups, when I came into the room, was even listening piously to the life story of a Polish national hero."[53]

The youth effort was major indeed. Along with the Ordensjunkers sent to deal with the Baltic arrivees now came thousands of Hitler Youth, BDM *Mädels,* and students of many varieties performing their various work requirements. BDM officials, in one report on the project, noted that the newly arrived settlers were "in low spirits." This was understandable, the report continued, as they had left their villages behind and were now spread out over the countryside. Besides, the confiscated farms were often filthy and run-down, so that adjustment was difficult. It was a terrible contrast to what they would have found in the clean villages of Germany proper. The BDM and Hitler Youth, therefore, would send teams to help out and to lighten things up with songfests, games, and "village evenings which would ease the way of the settlers into the German folk-community" and, at the same time, set up BDM and HJ cells.[54]

Many of the students were used to "Eastern Duty," having done previous stints on farms in the east of Germany proper. In the summer of 1940, packed trainloads of students, burdened with bicycles and backpacks, left Berlin for the East.[55] The atmosphere was festive. As students are wont to do, they stayed up all night singing and talking. After all the blackout precautions at home, some were amazed to find the Polish cities brightly lighted. Once in Poland they were taken to an orientation camp that combined doctors, teachers, construction technicians, and welfare workers. Housing was in villas that had "formerly belonged to Jews and Poles." One girl found the digs ugly and garishly painted, noting that they also had flat roofs, a feature considered unacceptable by volkish Nazi architects. During orientation they were given lectures on the genealogy of the Volhynian and Galician Germans and told of their recent hardships. Nazi plans for the development of the annexed areas were revealed, and the squalid conditions of Poland were vividly described, making the students realize "how big the problems needing to be solved really were."

After a few days of such orientation they were taken to their work stations, and in many cases left quite alone. On the way, some local occupation officials had the foresight to teach the students a few words of Polish "in case they couldn't understand the villagers," who, despite their German blood, frequently did not understand a word of the language. Those assigned to be teachers usually lived right in the schoolhouses, which had been confiscated from the Poles. Having been prepared by their orientation to be teaching in primitive barns and sheds, they were sometimes surprised to find that, as a result of recent efforts by the Polish government to upgrade education, many of the school buildings were new and full of light, and that the only serious cleaning they had to do was to get rid of the Polish books and flags and replace them with portraits of the Führer and other suitable emblems.

Supplies were hard to come by: one ingenious teacher glued a wall map of Germany to the back of one of Poland, and used pebbles and toothpicks for arithmetic instruction. Furniture for the volunteers was also scarce. One girl, having found her assigned room totally empty, was given lodging for some weeks by the local butcher, the only native ethnic German in the town. She was well cared for, but there were drawbacks: the only radio in the village was in her room, the roof leaked in three places, and the room shared a wall with the local pub, run by the butcher, where local Germans and Poles, happily ignoring anti-fraternization rules, together indulged nightly in considerable quantities of schnapps.

The children were a challenge: few spoke German and some had never been to school. One teacher was faced with a class of thirty-two mostly illiterate ethnic Germans resettled from Russia who spoke a mixture of German and Russian and six local ethnic German children who spoke only Polish. Their ages ranged from six to fourteen. In the six weeks of her tour of duty, she could do little more for this disparate group than teach them a few basic words of German, a lot of Nazi songs, and some "Homeland" studies, since "the children knew nothing or very little about Germany and the Führer." Another teacher, at the end of her stay, admitted that she was in no wise trained for her job, but felt that she had at least given the children some self-confidence and, most importantly, the ability to hold their own in the face of the "still more numerous Poles," something of an understatement, as the Poles, despite continuing deportations, continued to outnumber the Germans nine to one.

In general, the new settlers and local ethnic Germans were indeed glad to see the volunteers, who, as the Ordensjunkers had been for the Baltic settlers, were often their only day-to-day contact with the German authorities, and whom they immediately besieged with requests to intervene for them with the occupation authorities for any number of problems from first aid to funerals. In addition to the teachers there were other groups of German students, who lived in small "camps" or "lagers" of ten or twelve around the countryside and who concerned themselves with farm, welfare, and construction problems. These camps were not luxurious. The first job was to set up the camp itself—all that was provided in the confiscated houses and buildings the students were given were the straw mattresses on the floor. The schedule was rigorous and military in style. Reveille was at 6:00 a.m. Workdays were ten hours long, not counting housekeeping, which was laid out in remarkable drill-sergeant-like detail (perhaps necessary, given the universal antipathy of teenagers for these activities):

> 1. Bedroom: bedding must be ready (uniformly) by open windows by 6:45 (shake out straw bags). Beat blankets weekly. Put away laundry and clothes neatly in lockers! Shoes should not be in lockers or under beds! . . . Damp-mop floor daily!

In the same tone the students were exhorted to wash out their basins, hang up their towels, disinfect the toilets daily, and scrub everything in the kitchen to the nth degree. On top of all this, in the girls' camps at least, they were supposed to "always look for fresh flowers" and plant a kitchen garden. Permission to spend a night away had to be obtained from the local administrator, and the whereabouts of each girl at all times was required to be posted on a notice board.

From these camps the girls, imbued with ideas of the Thousand Year Reich, and particularly eager to increase the number of Germans, went forth to help the new "colonizing" families. The work was hard and the German maidens were frequently confronted with appalling social situations. Some of the villages were in ruins from the war, and the new families might arrive at any time of the day or night.

One group, whose official escort had not appeared, had found its way through the strange and hostile countryside by bravely asking directions to their new village. They arrived hours late, in rain and pitch darkness, with no one to greet them. BDM leader Melita Maschmann, who came to check, was "already in the village when I saw the German settlers' carts. Their hurricane lanterns gave off a feeble circle of light." She could hear women weeping. Everyone was terrified of revenge by the expelled Poles, and it took hours to persuade the new arrivals to go into the dark houses. Inside was little better than out. The BDM leader reported that "one woman with eight children, whose husband was at the front . . . was in a particularly bad way because the house which had been allotted to her was completely empty." A huge straw bed was made for her and the children. There was one candle for light. The young woman was so afraid of Polish thieves, and undoubtedly so hungry for company, that she insisted that her mare and its little foal stay in the house too.[56]

Enormous families were, of course, just what the Nazis wanted, but they were not easy to raise. An official report proudly noted that one student, sent to take care of a Volhynian family with six children whose mother was in the hospital, and whose house had become "very neglected," had soon "put the house back in order and run it perfectly." This brief remark does not give any idea of the challenge that must have faced that girl. Melita Maschmann, put in a similar situation, this time with seven children, gave a more graphic description.

The house given her resettled Volhynian *famille nombreuse* had two rooms. A third room was being built. The mother, once again, had been in a hospital for months. The desperate father, in a masterpiece of understatement, apologized to Maschmann for the mess: "You must not be alarmed, Fraulein. There has been no woman here for four months and seven children make the place untidy." In the two rooms were three beds that the whole family shared. The farmer also had a feebleminded brother, who slept in the barn and who, among other things, when given chicken to eat, swallowed it bones and all. Maschmann was afraid of him. Of the seven children, only one was a girl, "thirteen, but she has the body of an eight-year-old and the face of an old woman." This was because she had been running the household alone during her mother's illness. The family had been living on potatoes and thin soup. Bread was too expensive and available only on Sundays. Maschmann plunged in and cooked, sewed, and scrubbed, all the while trying to gain the trust of the children and teach them crafts and more German. When not engaged in these activities, she hoed potatoes with the feebleminded brother. Such energetic measures worked well with this family, but they were not well received at Maschmann's next stop.

This time she was dealing with an ethnic German Polish family, who took a dim view of her interference. They were much better off than the first group. The wife used "two Polish maids in the kitchen" and "did not do much work herself." The unfortunate parents had had five children of whom four had died, and the fifth was sickly. Maschmann's main objective was to save this Germanic mite for the Fatherland. The wife resisted her at every step, which made Maschmann more and more officious: "I scrubbed out the living room and kitchen, although I was rather cramped by the two Polish maids, who were busy sewing and peeling potatoes. I only wanted to show the woman that I [had] come to work." The wife drove Maschmann mad by talking to her husband and the maids in Polish.

The BDM girl, trying to force the family to speak German, retaliated by asking "after every sentence" what the wife had said. The two women clashed over what to feed the dying child and how to dress it. Carrot juice prepared for the baby was surreptitiously poured out. When Maschmann told the wife, "emphatically, that she was responsible for the life of her child and therefore must not simply ignore well-meant advice, the mother retorted that she would treat it 'the way my mother treated me.'" The father, when told he should speak German in his own house, replied, "'German or Polish, it's all the same to me.'" Finally, one day, Maschmann got the baby away from the mother and "fled behind the barn" with it. She then undressed it, "coated it lightly with cream," and "let it kick naked in the sun for three minutes," taking care to "keep its little head in the shade all the time." Before she could wrap the baby up again, the mother "appeared and made a great scene," and from then on would not allow Maschmann to touch the child at all. Defeated, the German left, undoubtedly much to the relief of everyone. The child, clearly suffering from some ailment that could not be remedied by either Nazi or Polish superstitions, died soon afterward.

Again and again the students ran head-on into primitive superstition. The settlers clung to their faith healers and folk remedies and were suspicious of doctors. A simple layette and crib made by one of the German girls for a baby about to be born were destroyed by a couple who believed that such preparations were bad luck and would make the child die.[57] The absence of religion was also difficult for the new settlers, especially when it came to funerals, for nothing in Nazi ideology, though it constantly demanded the ultimate sacrifice for the Fatherland, could ever take the place of the comforting assurances established religion gave about the afterlife. When faced with death, even the Hitler Youth sometimes turned to prayer.[58]

The students did go on excursions to other places in the newly conquered land. In Warsaw, for many, "the sight of the destroyed city and the ruins of the Castle made clear to us for the first time the destructive power of War." On such outings they also had their first glimpses into the Jewish ghettos. To these visions they reacted, at least in their official reports on their trips, as they had been taught to react: as people looking at creatures of another species living in another dimension. In the reports there is, of course, no indication that they realized that the shocking condition of the people and dwellings might be the result of the Jews having been forced into the overcrowded ghettos and denied adequate sustenance by the Reich leaders the students admired so much. But in later accounts it is clear that some were disturbed by what they saw. In Kutno passersby like Maschmann could look through holes in the walls of one temporary holding area for Jews set up in an old factory, "right into the inmost rooms":

> Everywhere a roof offered shelter from the rain the families were huddled together. . . . Many men, women and children lay on the bare earth. Some had managed to bring straw with them; a few, feather beds. All were enveloped in an oppressive lethargy. . . . The only exception was offered by a few ragged children who stood close by the fence. . . . The wretchedness of the children brought a lump to my throat. But I clenched my teeth. Gradually I learned to switch off my "private feelings." . . . This is terrible, I said to myself, but the driving out of the Jews is one of the unfortunate things we must bargain for if the "Warthegau" is to become a German country.[59]

Both Poles and Germans stopped to stare at the Jews. Occasionally someone would throw in some food. One German official was overheard saying, "I have to show this to all my friends who pass through. They all want to see it. Just a few hundred Jews on a dump, a nasty bunch—filthy and no respect. Dozens of them often stand up here begging by the fence." A little later, student Ilse P. of Hamburg, viewing the more organized Lodz Ghetto, wrote that it "made a big impression on us. Here we saw the real greasy Eastern Jews walking around among their run-down and dilapidated houses." In Warsaw, a tour of several hours through the ghetto gave her "a real view of the life and activities of the Warsaw Jews" and of propaganda fulfilled.[60]

But many of the German youths in Poland were good observers and not easily deceived. They had been told that the new "German" settlers had idealistically given up everything to "answer the call of the Führer" and reclaim land from the unworthy Poles. But one group of boys was "surprised" to discover how unhappy a group of *Volksdeutsche* farmers brought from the rich, wine-growing areas of the Black Sea region were in Poland. These farmers not only complained bitterly about their forced resettlement and the "worthless sandy Polish soil" they had been given, but even spoke "longingly" of "Papa Stalin" and proudly displayed their Soviet hero medals.[61] That this was a serious problem is confirmed by a personal request to Himmler from the Nazi governor of the Warthegau (the most important province in the area of Poland annexed to Germany) to send such settlers, who had "years-long Bolshevik political indoctrination," not to him, but to the Reich proper, where they could be properly "monitored" for their "asocial attitudes."[62]

Doubts about what they were doing and seeing crept into the dutiful reports that the students were required to file at the end of their time in the East. One boy noticed that the native ethnic Germans were deeply resentful when the incoming settlers sometimes got better farms than theirs. The new settlers, unclear about racial policy, let their children play with Polish ones and were too nice to the Poles, who often cheated them. It was clear to him that Germanic community spirit was slow to come in many villages and that the indigenous Germans would often rather help their Polish neighbors than the "strange" German resettlers. The young envoy, clearly having gotten deep into village jealousies, advised the establishment of more community centers and cottage industries, and noted that "more can be achieved by speaking firmly to the settlers than by listening to them too sympathetically."[63]

The young people were often sent to villages from which Poles had recently been evicted, in order to get the emptied houses ready for arriving *Volksdeutsche* settlers. The official line was that the Poles were being given houses somewhere else. The empty houses were generally a mess. The Poles, having suspected for some time that they might be thrown out, had hidden and sold as much furniture as they could, knowing by now that it would otherwise be confiscated for the new settlers. The squalid conditions only confirmed the students' negative view of the absent Poles. But sometimes, due to a lack of SS manpower, they were forced to take part in the actual expulsion of Polish families. On these occasions their job was to watch as the families departed and make sure that the Poles left behind enough furniture for the new arrivals. It is not hard to imagine the hatred this engendered. Melita Maschmann, by then leader of her own BDM camp, admitted later that this sort of action must have been harmful to her charges:

> In the task they had been given they had to force themselves to play military roles more suited to men. It required a different temperament from ours to watch unmoved as whole families were driven from their ancestral farms. And now, in addition, to have to intervene if these people, whose future was bleak, secretly tried to take their cherished possessions with them under the eyes of the people driving them out.[64]

Those who worked in the *Volksdeutsche* processing camps also had eye-opening experiences. Josef N., a medical student, spent the spring of 1940 with an SS Labor Agency team classifying potential *Volksdeutsche* from Poland. The team consisted of a doctor, a racial analyst, two medical students, and a clerk. The procedure was much the same as that used for the Baltic settlers, but the social level of the candidates was very different. After the medical and racial examinations, the team determined the "fitness for work" of each family. Josef was appalled by the condition of these supposed members of the Master Race: "One can have no idea of the filthy and unkempt condition of those who come to the examinations," he reported. Many had fleas and lice and were covered with sores and scratches. Few had clean underwear, and most "had no idea that one should not come to the doctor in such a filthy state."

The young student soon realized that few of these *Volksdeutsche* had ever been to a doctor. He saw badly healed fractures, homemade prostheses, festering wounds, rickets, malnourished babies, and all sorts of diseases. This was blamed on the high cost of medicine during the "Polish period" and on discriminatory practices toward ethnic Germans. On one day only 11 of 136 examinees owned a toothbrush and many did not know what one was.

Decisions on classification were difficult, and the guidelines unclear. What, for example, should one do if the father of a family was ill but everyone else healthy? Josef felt that it was wrong to put the minor children of such a family at a "disadvantage" by classifying them as "unfit." He also could not help noticing that the racial examiner's judgments were based on the most superficial evidence and were essentially "unfounded." A woman he observed had been given the low grade of Class III while the man with her was Class I. The racial examiner expressed outrage that a superior German type would marry such a low-grade woman. As it turned out, the lady was the man's mother. Josef felt that this example reflected the bizarre nature of the racial analysis procedures. Must not half of the man's chromosomes be from his mother? The student was also critical of quick rejections based on height alone ("I think immediately of Richard Wagner, Frederick the Great, and Napoleon"), as well as others resulting from wrong answers to questions such as "What is the capital of Germany?" With youthful fervor the medical student concluded his report with the observation that anyone with knowledge of human nature could tell a competent person from an unworthy one, but that a doctor could do so better than a labor official and thereby avoid a lot of "nonsense disguised as science."[65] Josef's criticisms were clearly taken by his superiors as suggestions for improving the methodology for finding good German blood, but to us they reveal much more about the cynical interagency rivalries that made the whole *Volksdeutsche* program so schizophrenic. The rejects Josef was worried about would not be wasted: they would simply be used as lower-level forced labor where their chances of survival were at least equal to those of the tall, Nordic-looking young people who passed the racial tests and who were generally slated for the Waffen-SS and an uncertain future on the battlefield.

Some of the Hitler Youth boys sent to Eastern Duty were very young indeed. In the summer of 1943 Jürgen Herbst and eight other Jungvolk leaders, by now aged about fourteen or fifteen, proudly set out for their *Osteinsatz*. This vacation duty would finally make them part of the real war effort. Before they left they were allowed to sew an Assignment East merit badge on their uniforms. After a stopover in Berlin, where they saw all the sights, they boarded a troop train headed for Katowice. On the platform were hundreds of soldiers returning to the Eastern Front, many of them drunk. The boys spent a miserable night in the corridor of the jammed, blacked-out train, "trying as best we could to keep our uniforms from getting soiled on the dirty floor." At dawn they "entered the Silesian industrial area with its coke ovens and gas flames shooting up into the air all along the track. A penetrating smell of gas and coal pervaded and painted everything outside a water-streaked dark gray." Dour Hitler Youth officials in Katowice gave them their assignment, which was in one of the many camps set up for the *Volksdeutsche* youth.

When the boys arrived at the camp, they were surprised to see that it was surrounded by barbed wire and guarded by an armed sentry, not the norm for Jungvolk camps in Germany. A senior Hitler Youth official soon made clear to them that they would not be teaching the boys in the camp patriotic songs and arranging scavenger hunts, but that they would be guarding the camp perimeter so that no one could escape. In secret conversations with the inmates it became clear that the boys they were guarding were teenaged Polish *Volksdeutsche* being used as apprentice miners, who were on "vacation." This consisted of two weeks in the camp under the supervision of sadistic Hitler Youth leaders who were supposed to be "Germanizing" their charges, but whose exercises looked more like hazing or torture. The older HJ members coveted duty at the camp, as it exempted them from military service. On the side, they ran a black market operation, which provided them with all the luxuries of life. The newly arrived Jungvolk boys, invited to attend a late night "leaders' banquet," were staggered to find a huge spread that featured meats, fruits, and real coffee—all unobtainable in Germany itself. Alas, the secret conversations they had had with the "campers" did not remain secret for long, and the boys from the Reich were accused of treason and threatened with expulsion from the Jungvolk by the gun-toting camp commander. For the duration of their Eastern Duty they were separated and transferred to small towns, where they were supposed to "contact" and work with the local Hitler Youth groups.

Herbst, the son of genteel middle-class intellectuals, bravely sallied forth, dressed in his Jungvolk leader's uniform, to find his assigned group, said to be gathered at a local country fair some two miles away. He found them: "By the looks of their clothes they worked on farms and in the coal mines. Many of them wore shirts with their sleeves cut off, showing arms that were the size of my thighs." This crowd was clearly not interested in songfests. After some awkward conversation Herbst managed to impress them by his prowess at the fair's shooting gallery and left as fast as he could:

> When I was on my way, I couldn't help but look back frequently, making sure I was not being followed. Something told me I had better get home before darkness set in. It was not a good idea, I thought to myself, in the summer of 1943 when dusk fell to be a lone boy in a Jungvolk uniform in the midst of a Polish rye field.

He did not try to make contact again, and from then on his Eastern assignment consisted of excursions with the kindly *Volksdeutsche* family with which he was billeted. It was all very educational. He went down into a coal mine and visited the hellish interior of a steel mill. As they left the mill, Herbst also had a brief glimpse of a group of Jews:

> A vista opened over an immense open pit mine. We looked down into a vast hole, dug into the ground, a hole in which dozens of gray-clad men and women, each wearing strips of yellow cloth on their backs, were pushing small carts loaded with black coal up the winding rails that led from the pit to the plant.

His guide told him that they were "Jews from the concentration camp" who were "helping to keep the plant productive." These prisoners, who looked for all the world like insects on an anthill to the horrified Herbst, were the luckier ones. By 1943 hundreds of thousands of their brethren had already died in the extermination camps.

Once home, Herbst, full of doubts after what he had seen but afraid of retribution, did not reveal his experiences to anyone. As he later wrote:

> If I had learned a lesson from my Polish experience it was how to turn people's attention away from scenes I did not want them to see and to keep them from asking questions I did not want to answer. I had

learned how to keep silent on issues such as corruption, cruelty, and
steel mills with concentration camp labor, which I knew no one wanted
to hear about.[66]

   Not all the *Osteinsatz* students were enthusiastic volunteers. Some participated as part of their required national labor service and were not
happy campers. This was particularly true of urban working-class girls who
often had to leave well-paying jobs and a lively social life behind. Bored by
Germanic folk dances, patriotic songs, and other such instruction, they
preferred to talk about sex and longed to listen to forbidden American pop
songs. The noble aspects of farm labor, so beloved of the Nazis, had zero
appeal, and they found it hard to take the racial theory lectures they were
forced to listen to seriously. They crept out at night to find German soldiers, got pregnant, were lazy at work, had fights in their dormitories, and
generally drove the hard-line BDM leaders to distraction.[67]

   By 1942 the *Osteinsatz* program was very large. A report on the BDM
alone indicated that 449 camps were operating by then and that some
7,000 maidens had been involved in that year. This did not include administrators and leaders.[68] The Hitler Youth numbers were even greater, and
their activities were coordinated by a special HJ Action Staff headquar-
tered in Lodz. By the spring of 1944 some 47,000 HJ and BDM members
had participated along with at least 16,000 members of other youth organizations such as the Landdienst. Their task was vital: nearly 730,000 children of resettlers and Poles thought to have German blood would
eventually be available for the Nazi armed forces and further colonization
of the *Lebensraum,* if they could be properly Germanized by their peers
from the Reich.[69]

9. Bad Blood

While the complex resetting of the incoming *Volksdeutsche* was going on, yet another array of organizations had been planning the equally complex operations necessary to get rid of the indigenous population of Poland. This process did not involve just the evictions so upsetting to the BDM maidens, but would include the massive killing, imprisonment, or deportation of hundreds of thousands of people.

From the beginning of the invasion of Poland, the long years of indoctrination and propaganda that had depicted the Slavs as prolific *Untermenschen,* no better than the subhuman Jews, were immediately evident in the merciless comportment of members of the hard-core Nazi military formations, who swept away all efforts by more moderate elements in the German Army to observe the traditional rules of warfare. Only a week before the invasion Hitler had exhorted all his forces to show no mercy toward the Poles. They were told to "close their hearts to pity," to "act brutally," and to pursue the Poles "until complete annihilation" had occurred.[1] And indeed, foreign observers in Poland during the fighting noticed much gratuitous action, such as the targeting of small rural villages of no strategic value, often full of people seeking refuge from the fighting, with resulting loss of whole families.[2]

For children in the war zone, the flight from the larger towns, where bombardments were expected, was often exciting at first. But what seemed an adventure soon turned into horror. One ten-year-old boy recalled the exodus from the towns as being "like a national holiday . . . it was like going on a day's outing in the country. . . . The one lane dirt road was packed with people, wagons and horses." Another boy remembered people in the village where he took refuge "walking around in the warm sunlight. . . . I started playing with the local boys. Within minutes I had new friends. A lovely, lovely day." The idyll did not last. In the late afternoon the boys heard the sound of planes. "I was standing and looking at the planes as they dived out of the sky throwing explosives and incendiary bombs. . . . The houses around me collapsed." The planes returned, "streaking down with their machine guns blazing, shooting the people down . . . They were all running in different directions, some with their clothes on fire. Blindly running. Cats, dogs, horses, cows, all of them aflame, too all running. Madly, pointlessly, agonizingly." One boy's mother threw him on the ground and covered him "with her own body. . . . Some time later I stood up and was completely alone. Mother had gone off and all I saw around me was total chaos and destruction with dead bodies everywhere."[3]

But such random brutality was not all that Hitler had in mind. The references to "annihilation" were made more precise two days after his first pronouncement with the organization of seven special SS mobile units known as Einsatzgruppen, whose mission it was to "combat all anti-Reich and anti-German elements." That this meant the immediate elimination of as many members of the Polish "leadership class" as possible, which included most professionals, the nobility, and the clergy, was made clear in comments to subordinates in the next few weeks by Hitler and SS police chief Reinhard Heydrich. The same criteria applied to Jews and to the "primitive, inferior classes" of Poles not immediately needed to keep industry and agriculture going in the new territories. The Einsatzgruppen, aided by the notorious, black-uniformed Selbstschutz, a local militia made up of long-resident ethnic Germans who were only too happy to settle long-festering scores with their Polish neighbors and point out Jews to the Nazis, would execute some 60,000 souls of all ages and ethnicities in their three months of activity in Poland.[4]

Everywhere men were dragged from their houses in front of their families and were taken to be executed or beaten. Children were not exempt: witnesses in the town of Bydgoszcz watched with horror as a troop of Boy Scouts, aged twelve to sixteen, were lined up against a wall and shot in retaliation for the killing of ethnic Germans by Poles.[5]

But this was still not enough for Hitler, who did not just wish to avenge the Polish atrocities but planned to eradicate Poland both as a people and as a nation. The project would be greatly facilitated by keeping the population in a state of "splintered" uncertainty, and nothing makes people more helpless and "splintered" than moving them about at random with no warning.

Thousands of both Jewish and gentile Poles had already fled eastward before the armies during the fighting. Nazi units soon began to deport tens of thousands more to the General Gouvernement to make room in the newly annexed areas both for administrators and opportunists from the Reich and for the *Volksdeutsche* settlers. The following account is typical. And in fact the conditions under which this family from Gdynia was moved were positively luxurious compared to those of later victims who would be deported in the dead of winter on a few minutes' notice.

> On October 17, 1939, at 8:00 a.m., I heard someone knocking at the door of my flat. As my maid was afraid to open it, I went to the door myself. I found there two German gendarmes, who roughly told me that in a few hours I had to be ready to travel with my children and everybody in the house. When I said that I had small children, that my husband was a prisoner of war, and that I could not get ready to travel in so short a time, the gendarmes answered that not only must I be ready, but that the flat must be swept, the plates and dishes washed, and the keys left in the cupboards, so that the Germans who were to live in my house should have no trouble.

The family was allowed to take along one suitcase and one bag of food. At noon the police came back to collect them and all their neighbors. Amid shouts and blows the Poles were loaded on trucks and then put in filthy cattle cars, which were locked. In this family's car were forty people, including six children under ten. There were no sanitary facilities and no food. After three days they arrived in the General Gouvernement and were unloaded in Czestochowa, site of one of Poland's holiest shrines, where the totally unprepared local population gave them immediate help, while the German soldiers who opened the car shouted, "What! Are these Polish swine still alive?"[6]

Different measures were used for the 2.2 million Polish Jews in the annexed areas. An SS plan, instituted on September 21, even before Poland had surrendered, decreed that all communities of Jews numbering 500 or fewer be removed from the villages and countryside and be concentrated in ghettos in larger towns and cities situated on main railway lines. From these holding areas the Jews could easily be moved to a projected "Reich Ghetto" near Lublin in the General Gouvernement or elsewhere. The process was to begin in early November 1939 and continue over the course of the following year. Meanwhile, Nuremberg-type laws were imposed, and the Polish Jews would have the distinction of being the first to be required to wear identifying badges: in the General Gouvernement a white armband with a blue Star of David, and in the annexed areas, a yellow star.[7]

The idea of sending Jews "to the East," first suggested in September 1939, had the support of Hitler and seemed to be sanctioned in the same speech that had set off the resettlement of the *Volksdeutsche*. Once the lines of demarcation between the Russian and German zones of Poland were established, Berlin authorized the immediate expulsion to the Lublin district of some 80,000 Jews already gathered in the newly annexed areas around Katowice, and gave orders for those of Mährisch-Ostrau in Czechoslovakia to be prepared to follow.

Rumors of the deportation plan and of this newly available disposal zone in Poland reserved specifically for Jews soon spread among the SS upper echelons in other German-controlled areas where the outbreak of war had now closed off most remaining routes to refuge.

In Austria, Adolf Eichmann saw a golden opportunity to speed up Jewish emigration. Without consulting his superiors, he decided to add the Jews of Vienna to the expellees and thereby win accolades for making the Austrian capital the first city to be completely "cleansed" of Jews, or *Judenrein.* Facilities in Poland were to be built by advance transports of poor Jewish men who were a drain on the Jewish communities that had to support them. Families would follow later. By October 13, 1939, everything from lists of deportees to train schedules had been organized; the only trouble was that, as had been the case with the Balts, no exact destination for the trains had been determined. In a hasty trip to the Lublin region Eichmann found a desolate, swampy area near the small town of Nisko that he decided was ideal.

Meanwhile, competition for dumping grounds had become fierce, and Eichmann was determined to get rid of his undesirables first.[8] The first transport left Mährisch-Ostrau on October 17, the same day as that of the Polish residents of Gdynia. More followed from Vienna. Conditions on the trains were about the same as those for the Poles, but the Jews, when they arrived, had no local population to take care of them. There was not even a camp. The exhausted deportees were expected to build one themselves with materials that had been shipped along with them. The trains kept coming, and thousands of people, who by now included women and children, were driven away from the inadequate facilities and shot when they tried to come back after wandering about the surrounding countryside. It was reported in the American media that Polish peasants had been forbidden by the Gestapo to take Jews into their houses and that the object of the exercise was "not to settle the Jews, but to expose them to the peril of painful death from cold and famine."[9] Some of the more fortunate deportees managed to escape to the Russian-controlled zone. The publicity aroused panic among the Jews of Vienna, who even appealed to the Pope to stop the deportations.[10] Himmler, under pressure from both the Wehrmacht and the civil authorities to maintain order and irritated by

Eichmann's challenge to his control of the region, which he wished to use for his own deportations, quickly ordered a stop to the chaotic operation, and some of the unfortunates were actually sent back to Austria.[11]

Soon after this debacle Hitler removed the SS units in charge of deportations and police actions from the control of the disapproving Wehrmacht and replaced the military government in Poland with civilian administrations answerable only to their local Nazi governors, whose commitment to the programs of the Führer was unquestioned. The sidelining of the Wehrmacht suited Himmler very well. It was his dream to rid not only the newly annexed Reich territories, but also eventually all of Poland, of its twenty million Jews and Slavs. Himmler and his advisers recognized that this task would take a few years, and that while it was in progress, the greatest possible use should be made of the human assets now at the disposal of the Nazis. The magnitude of the operation would require enormous administrative and material resources, which immediately began to be organized. The madness of the chess game involving millions of people that the Nazis now proposed is staggering. Millions of Poles, useful as forced labor, would be moved into Germany proper, while millions of Reich Germans would be moved out of Germany to fight and to administer the newly conquered Eastern territories where the ejected Poles and sequestered Jews would be replaced by other millions of resettled ethnic Germans. And this project was to be set in motion even as the conquest of Western Europe and the attack on the Soviet Union were being planned. Hans Frank, appointed governor of the General Gouvernement, writing in his diary in the fall of 1939, gives some idea of just what Himmler had in mind:

> By Spring 1,000,000 Poles and Jews . . . must be received by the General Gouvernement. The resettlement of the ethnic Germans and the taking on of Poles and Jews (10,000 daily) must be accomplished according to plan. Especially urgent is the instituting of forced labor for Jews. . . . The critical questions of housing and feeding are still to be cleared up. . . . The families of good racial extraction in the occupied Polish territory (approximately 4,000,000 people) should be transferred into the Reich and individually housed and thereby uprooted as a people. . . . SS General Krueger explained that, starting 15 November, the entire railroad net of the General Gouvernement will be at the disposal of the resettlement transports.[12]

Himmler's own planned deportations of Jews to their projected enclave in the General Gouvernement began soon after the redistribution of authority. But the operations were still not well organized and were far too public. The ghastly conditions prompted negative reports from Nazi welfare authorities and even from the SS. Deportees arrived in the dead of winter, once again without money or supplies of any kind. From the cattle cars in which they were moved they frequently had to walk miles through snow to remote villages that had no facilities for them. Many died of exposure. Children were especially vulnerable:

> The half-frozen body of a five-year-old girl was found wearing around her neck a cardboard sign with the words "Renate Alexander, from Hammerstein, Pomerania." This child was visiting relatives in Stettin and was included in the deportation; her mother and father stayed in Germany. Her hands and feet had to be amputated at the Lublin hospital. The bodies of the deportees who had died of exposure were piled on sleds and buried in the Jewish cemeteries at Piask and Lublin. . . . The General Gouvernement has declined all responsibility for these occurrences.[13]

Nor did protests from the Wehrmacht cease. In February 1940, General Johannes Blaskowitz, commander of the Ober-Ost military region, wrote a courageous memorandum to his superiors saying that the "slaughter" of tens of thousands of Jews and Poles was bad not only from the propaganda point of view, but that "in view of the huge population neither the concept of a Polish State nor the Jews" could be eliminated in this manner. The public violence against the Jews, he felt, would soon change Polish hostility toward them into pity, and cause both groups to "combine against Germany." But, he added, "the worst damage which will accrue to the German nation . . . is the brutalization and moral debasement which, in a very short time, will spread like a plague among valuable German manpower. . . . People . . . with warped characters will very soon come together so that, as is now the case in Poland, they can give full expression to their animal and pathological instincts." Other officers wrote that the honor of the whole German nation had been besmirched and that the units that had committed atrocities should be replaced by "sound, honorable" ones.[14]

The protesters were too late. The people with "warped characters" were now in full control. But even they did not like chaotic situations, and once again, due to objections by Governor Frank, who refused to accept such disorganized and unlimited dumping of Jews in his bailiwick, and to fears on the part of economic czar Göring that the unrest caused by the deportations would affect Polish industrial production, the deportation of

Jews from the annexed areas to the East was temporarily halted in favor of continued confinement in ghettos.

The formation of the ghettos was uneven and often chaotic. Sizes ranged from small sections of minor towns to the vast enclaves in Lodz (200,000 plus) and Warsaw (450,000). Lublin was not closed off until April 1941, and others, including the "model" transit camp–ghetto at Theresienstadt, in the former Czechoslovakia, continued to be set up until 1942. But by the summer of 1941 some two million Jews were jammed into these proto-prisons and tens of thousands more would later be similarly confined in Lvov, Bialystok, Vilna, Kovno, and many other locations after the Ukraine and the Baltic states were taken from the USSR.

In the beginning, both the Nazis and the Jews regarded the ghettos as temporary, but for very different reasons. For the Germans they were holding pens from which the waiting millions, whose numbers would meanwhile conveniently be diminished by lack of sustenance, could eventually be transported east of the Urals, or even to Madagascar. To the Jews, they seemed to be refuges in which, if they were cooperative and productive, they could appease the Nazis and survive. In this way of thinking, they, like the rest of the world, completely misunderstood the inflexibility of the ideologues at the top of the Nazi racial agencies. That they did so was not totally naive, for within the Nazi regime and economy itself, as we have seen and will continue to see, there were many whose pragmatism modified, but never eliminated, the tenets of the fanatics.

From the beginning, the Nazi authorities, as they had done in Germany, vested administrative power in each ghetto in a Jewish-run council, or Judenrat. In Poland and the Eastern territories there would be no official, central Jewish organization. Thus each ghetto was isolated and had its own rules, which also varied according to the policies of the local Nazi authorities. The social structure of the large ghettos was as complex as those of any city. There were rich and poor families. There were businesses, banks, taxes, complex politics, and social welfare agencies. There were even foreign relations of a sort: under the auspices of organizations such as the Red Cross, the American Committee for Polish Relief, and the Joint Distribution Committee (JDC) in New York, which had long supported impoverished Polish Jews, both funds and food shipments continued to trickle through for a time. Survival parcels from relatives in Russia and elsewhere were also allowed to come into the Jewish enclaves.[15] The JDC also sponsored the National Society for the Care of Orphans (CENTOS) in Poland, which by the summer of 1941 had 88 children's homes and "corners" in 143 locations helping some 12,000 children. In addition, CENTOS, in a tremendous effort that still reached only 30 percent of the needy, had set up 122 food kitchens catering to over 47,000 mainly poor and "refugee" children, that is, those whose families had come into the larger ghettos from small communities and were, therefore, at a disadvantage.[16]

For a time, things were not too bad. Parents tried to keep life as normal as possible, Schools, permitted by the German authorities in Lodz but forbidden in Warsaw and Theresienstadt, and often operated by political organizations such as the Bundists and the Zionists, flourished, secretly when necessary, in all the ghettos. Most famous among them was the combined school and orphanage run in Warsaw by pediatrician and teacher Janusz Korczak, who, refusing all proposals to save himself and let the children go to their fates alone, marched along with his pupils to the deportation train, holding two of them in his arms.[17] There were also youth clubs, choruses, and even makeshift summer camps, sometimes set up in cemeteries. In Warsaw, the Nazis at first even let Jewish children go swimming at a segregated beach on the Vistula River.

Educational and cultural programs were particularly strong at Theresienstadt, the ghetto to which the Nazis took foreign watchdog groups such as the International Red Cross.[18] The camp was installed in an outwardly attractive former fortress town built in the reign of the Hapsburg Emperor Joseph II. The regular residents were gradually moved out, and by 1945 some 130,000 people, of whom approximately 12,000 were children, would pass through the camp. Established as a transit camp for Czech Jews, it was also used for upper-class German Jews who were war veterans or who still had assets and art collections that they might be induced to sign over "legally" to the Reich. Theresienstadt was fancy indeed compared to all the other camps, boasting a library of 130,000 books, an outdoor café, manicured gardens, and other apparent amenities. The Nazis even made a film about it, entitled *Theresienstadt: Hitler's Gift to the Jews*, which was shown back home.

Early on, in a kibbutzlike arrangement, the Jewish council in Theresienstadt separated the children from their parents, whom they were allowed to see once a week, and lodged them in a number of dormitory-style group "homes." Babies, some of whom were born in the camp, were housed in a special nursery where their mothers were allowed to come to feed them once a day. In the "homes" illegal schooling went on full tilt. If disturbed, the children were trained to pretend they were cleaning their rooms or doing one of the other light tasks expected of them. Here, an extraordinary subculture flourished that produced plays, a children's opera, and a literary magazine.

The magazine, *Vedem*, is much like any other school publication, full of childish landscapes and saucy caricatures, until you notice that the poems are all about prison and the interviews are with workers at the delousing station, the central mortuary, and the crematorium, a busy place where by April 1945 most of the 33,430 who died in the camp would be burned.

Trade and industry continued in a truncated fashion in all ghettos. Items manufactured for Polish firms could, for a time, still be sent out. Those who had lived within the walls before the ghettos were set up still had their possessions, and those coming in were allowed to bring things with them. Many would live off the sales of these items.

While supplies lasted, shopping in the Warsaw Ghetto was a popular pastime for the wives of Nazi officials, including the wife of Governor Frank, who ordered, of all things, picnic baskets and a Turkish coffee machine from the incarcerated Jews and who even took her three-year-old son, Niklas, along in her heavily escorted limousine as she shopped for lingerie and furs.[19] Cottage industries and bartering were ubiquitous: whole families worked at remaking clothes or the required star armbands. The Judenrats actively solicited German contracts in order to keep their economies going, and more work was provided by the creation of a special Jewish police force, labor gangs requisitioned by the Nazis, and eventually, in some ghettos, large workshops and factories connected to war industries.

The semblance of normalcy did not last. The ghettos were, after all, prisons, in which control of vital elements such as fuel, food, and water remained with the Germans. None of these were provided in quantities adequate to maintain life for long. Rations for Jews were set at 15 percent of those for Germans, and existence could be sustained only by resort to the illegal black market, bribery, and smuggling, all of which flourished, though participation was punishable by death.

The JDC and other international organizations tried to help by sending in food. The Germans, not uncooperative, decreed that 17 percent of all incoming foreign aid be allocated to the Jews. As a special favor, 1,000 tons of food were allowed into the ghettos for Passover in 1940. By February 1941, six other shipments would come in via Switzerland. More could have been sent by the JDC, but influential leaders of the organization in New York objected to the project because it would violate the British blockade of German-held territory, which was based on the theory that sending food to any occupied country indirectly helped the Nazis. Unable to conceive of the realities of the situation, the JDC objectors argued further that "feeding civilian populations in the war area was a responsibility of the German government, and any food shipments would free Germany from its obligation to provide food."[20] The American War Refugee Board, belatedly established in January 1944, also tried to improve food supplies to the few Jews still surviving by then in the ghettos by having them declared internees, which would have made them eligible for food packages. The International Red Cross, asked to approach the German government on this issue, refused, as it was unwilling to endanger its tenuous privileges in the Reich, noting in its refusal that in any case the proposal "had no prospect of success." The British relaxed their blockade in August 1944, but by the time the resulting small-parcel program got organized, as the British must have been aware, it was far too late.[21]

In the ever-growing quest for food, ghetto children became vital to their family's survival:

> We can observe scores of Jewish children from the age of ten to 12 or 13 stealing over to the Aryan side to buy a few potatoes there. . . . These they hide in their little coats, with hems swollen so that the children look like balloons. . . . Emaciated three- or four-year-old children crawl through the culverts to fetch merchandise. . . . Imagine what a mother must go through when her child is in momentary danger of death.[22]

The dangers were real. The small smugglers had to get past the guards posted all around the ghetto barriers, and all sorts of subterfuges were used to get through the principal entrances. Getting caught was bad, but hunger was a powerful incentive. Thirteen-year-old Sabina Wylot had a close call:

> Extreme poverty, shortages of everything, exhaustion, the indigent state of my family. . . . Daily sights of listless dying people, those who had died of hunger being gathered up from the streets. It was like this day after day. Corpses, corpses, corpses. . . . Father died of starvation. . . . Provisions were being stolen. . . . With collected, begged-for money I would pass under the wall . . . for flour, kasha, onions, and potatoes. . . . With little bundles and bags, I would return. . . . Mama became ill with typhus. . . . Taken to the hospital, she returned . . . the shadow of a person but still alive. . . . Going under rubble and walls to the Aryan side, I set out again. . . . This was the last time I saw my mother and sister. While returning with my purchases, I was caught, along with a few other children. . . . Military policemen ordered all the children to pour out their purchased possessions and stand against the wall. . . . I was

rescued, thanks to a blue-uniformed policeman who convinced the military police that I was not a Jewish girl.... He gave me a kick in the behind saying, "Get lost little girl." ... In a few moments shots were heard, and probably not a single child survived. This one cannot forget.[23]

Despite these heroic efforts there was never enough to eat. Soon starvation, starting with the poorest families, was pervasive in many ghettos. In the overcrowded lodgings, where six or seven people often lived in one room, disease also took hold. In the summer of 1941 there were outbreaks of typhus, which, along with tuberculosis and other diseases, would increase steadily during the following winter as fuel supplies dropped, pipes burst, and sanitation facilities, already limited, were further diminished. The number of orphans soared. In Warsaw people soon became inured to the sight of emaciated little beggars, often too weak to eat bread even when it was given to them, and to small, newspaper-covered bodies in the street.[24] In most areas no "Aryan" doctors were allowed to enter the Jewish areas in order to treat them, and Jews were not allowed in Aryan hospitals. Nor were Jewish doctors and hospitals supplied with sufficient medicines or food. In one town, which had no Jewish doctors, the Aryan director of the hospital persuaded the Germans, always terrified of disease, to relent a little:

> The Germans agreed that the hospital can give medical attention to Jews only one hour a day and only when no other patients were present ... we still have no right to admit Jews into the hospital except in case of infectious diseases such as typhoid fever. So I was forced to release ... a few Jews I was treating for other reasons.[25]

With hindsight we know that no sensible suggestions mattered to the Nazis: one way or another the Jews were to be removed completely from Nazi-controlled areas. Just how had not been quite defined by the late spring of 1941, but it soon would be.

While the ghettos were thus being consolidated and left to their inexorable decline, the rearrangement and suppression of the Polish gentiles, next on the Nazi elimination list, continued apace. By December 1940, Himmler had summarized his policies and guidelines in a rather elegantly printed booklet entitled *Der Menscheneinsatz*, a hard-to-translate word meaning roughly "population utilization."[26] The human realities of the plan are made plain in a remarkable diary of the war years kept by a doctor in the small town of Szczebrzeszyn, in the General Gouvernement near Zamosc, who reported the arrival of over 5,000 Poles to his locality, mostly in trainloads of a thousand, between December 1939 and March 1941. The transports ran heavily to older men, women, and children. Many had been beaten and all were exhausted, filthy, and hungry. As had been the case with the nearly simultaneous Jewish transports, no warning of their arrival was usually given to town authorities, who had to care for the masses of people until they were redistributed to surrounding villages, a process that often took weeks:

> October 14, 1940: Tonight a new group of evacuees. . . . This was a large group of over 1,000 people. Around sixty people requested medical attention. Eight were admitted to the hospital, including two women in labor. The evacuees were temporarily housed in warehouses filled with straw. In the hospital kitchen, from 2:00 a.m., we prepared food. . . . Around noon the mayor requested the help of all citizens. The city administration was not prepared for an emergency like this and help was not sufficient. Seeing this fills you with the urge for revenge.[27]

A thousand more came on both November 4 and on January 18, 1941. By now it was very cold:

> Winter is here in full force, with freezing temperatures and blizzards. In these conditions the poor evacuees are dying by the hundreds, especially the young children. The last transport was held up for seven weeks in . . . unheated barracks with little food. Many children were sick with measles.[28]

The idea was not only to "splinter" the Poles and to put them in a "minority" role, but to physically reduce their numbers as surely, if more gradually, as was being done with the Jews. As the brutal evacuation process shows, the methods of attrition were manifold. Executions for a myriad of violations were a daily event. But there were far less obvious methods, beginning with the most basic one of lowering the birthrate and allowing an increase in infant mortality—just the reverse of the population laws instituted in the Reich.

The legal age for marriage was gradually raised to twenty-eight for men and twenty-five for women, well above the norms for that era, and consideration was given to banning marriage for Poles altogether. The result of this ruling was an increase in so-called illegitimate births, but it is clear that many Poles simply kept their marriages secret.[29] This development inevitably raised the question of abortion. A German doctor working in Poland told one of the *Osteinsatz* maidens that he would willingly perform abortions on Polish women, noting that "it is in fact murder, but it is finally the same if I shoot the enemy on the battlefield or if I kill his children while they are in their mother's body." The doctor, however, had not yet performed any such procedures, as they were still against both Polish and German law.[30] His dilemma would soon be solved. On March 9, 1942, the Reich Health Leader, Dr. Leonardo Conti, wrote to Himmler and declared that punishment for performing abortions on Poles was "not in the interest of Germany, it rather is desirable from our point of view that as many Polish women as possible have abortions carried out or carry them out themselves." Conti suggested that the right to punish abortions "be removed from the Polish courts." Himmler agreed.[31]

Subsistence for "illegitimate" Polish children was made entirely the responsibility of the father. No German welfare funds were to be expended, as "it must be the primary principle not to spend one German penny for Polish welfare. This method of putting the racially undesirable Polish child at a definite disadvantage, even though it will not, in general, reduce the number of illegitimate children, will at least not encourage a rise in the number." The fathers, if known, would be required to "make especially large payments" into a general fund from which all surplus would be "turned over to the *German* youth fund," and subsistence claims were removed from the court system and handed over to the racial agencies.[32]

Welfare for pregnant Polish women and newborns was minimal indeed. Prenatal care and access to pediatric clinics were denied. Tuberculosis and rickets were left untreated. Food rations for Poles were in general lower than those for Germans, and pregnant or nursing mothers could only get an extra fat allowance with a doctor's prescription. Children under the age of six were allowed a pint of milk a day and those up to fourteen, half that.

Not surprisingly, the death rate rose and the birthrate fell—but not enough to satisfy the Nazis. By 1942 it was clear that the only way to be rid of twenty million Poles (three or four million were to be kept as laborers) was mass deportation. One proposal calculated that if 700,000 to 800,000 Poles per year, using 100 to 120 trains, could be deported to Siberia, the "problem" would be solved in thirty years. The writer recognized the fact that the Polish problem could not be solved by liquidating the Poles like the Jews, as doing so "would burden the German people with guilt for years to come and lose us the sympathies of people everywhere, particularly as our neighbors would be bound to reckon that they would be treated in the same way when the time came." He also pointed out that he had suggested earlier that the problem might also be solved by "more or less voluntary emigration overseas," perhaps to Brazil, which, "with its capacity for 1,200 million people," urgently needed additional population.[33]

Getting rid of the Poles was important to the racial agencies, but they were determined to make quite sure that not a drop of possible German blood be wasted in the process of ethnic cleansing. The theory was that a great deal of German blood had flowed into Poland "through the mistakes of German history"[34] and must be recovered for the Reich, especially when it came to malleable children. On October 23, 1939, Himmler ruled that certain small, well-defined ethnic groups in Upper Silesia, such as the obscure Slonzacs and Gorals, were to have "special racial examinations." Their children were "to be screened in the schools for the purpose of a rough pre-selection." If the children proved to be "of a low standard," it would be considered "proof of the negative qualities of the parents" and the whole family would be "evacuated." If the children were of a high standard and the parents were not, the parents would be evacuated without them.[35]

This was only the beginning. By November 1939, preliminary guidelines for the racial analysis and handling of the entire Polish population were forwarded to Himmler from Nazi Party offices in Berlin,[36] ordering that, before deportation, all Poles, like the incoming *Volksdeutsche,* were to be given racial examinations, and those "suitable for Germanization" or "ethnic transformation" were to be kept segregated from those who were not. "Ethnic transformation" was again based on the proper racial qualifications. Officials were warned to be on guard against "pseudo–ethnic transformation" (wrong race, right language and politics), which even if "unconscious" would lead to "dangerous adulteration of the intellectual-psychical structure" of Germandom, as the inherited "slavonic" mind could never be "transformed into a Teutonic one." While adults might be beyond salvation for Germandom, racially valuable children of untransformable parents should not be sent into limbo with their families, but were to be taken from them and educated in suitable institutions or be put in a German foster family. These children should not be older than eight or ten, as "ethnic transformation" was not usually successful after that age. Most importantly, such children were to be isolated completely from their Polish relatives. Other Poles could not adopt them, and Polish church institutions would not be permitted to keep "biologically healthy chil-

Blond children with "Germanizing" potential are taken by force from their "bad blood" parents.

dren." However, Poles with a "neutral attitude" who were willing to send their children to German institutions could, in this wise, avoid immediate deportation themselves.

The Nazis were determined, after they eliminated the existing Polish intelligentsia, to prevent the training of replacements. Only a "primitive agricultural class" would be allowed to remain. Their children would go to school only up to the age of ten, and the admittedly "outstanding native female teachers," who were "representatives of Polish chauvinism" with "a far greater influence on the political education of the child than the male teacher," would be replaced by retired policemen.

In "Reflections" written some months later, Himmler refined these policies. Pure Polish children, he mused, need not learn to count higher than 500 (one wonders how they could be prevented from doing so) or be required to read, but should only be taught to write their names. Other than that, it would suffice for them to know that it was "a divine law to obey the Germans." But Himmler did have some doubts: apparently inspired by the sight of numerous "Nordic"-looking families in the depor- tee holding camps, he reiterated that all Polish children between six and ten must be "sifted" in order to find those with "valuable blood." Their parents, he wrote,

> will be given the choice of giving up their child . . . and so remove the danger that this sub-human people of the east might acquire a leader class from such people of good blood, which would be dangerous for us

because they would be our equals, or they would have to agree to go to
Germany. . . . One has a strong weapon against them in their love of
their child.[37]

Once in Germany the chosen children, whose names would be Germanized and who would be kept under careful surveillance, should be made comfortable and not be "treated as lepers" or called "Polacks." This oddly human touch contrasted sharply with recent instructions to the German press requiring that "articles dealing with Poland must express the instinctive revulsion of the German people against everything which is Polish" and "must be composed in such a way as to transform this instinctive revulsion into a lasting revulsion. . . . It must be suggested that Gypsies, Jews and Poles ought to be treated on the same level."[38] Himmler's order referred, of course, only to Poles with signs of "good blood," but the distinction was too difficult for the average German to fathom, particularly as the chosen children, in fact, usually had no German "blood" whatsoever.

Himmler, very good at grandiose theories and romantic visions, would leave the details of implementation of this massive "sifting" to others, though the documents show he frequently intervened in decisions at the lowest levels. Racial officials now scrambled to implement the guidelines. Luckily, the bureaucratic rules for racial processing, already set up to deal with the resettlers and ethnic Germans of Polish citizenship, were easily extended to the rest of their countrymen.

Among the first groups to be analyzed were the defenseless children who were residents of Polish orphanages and children's homes. The Nazis had immediately begun searching for ethnic German children in these institutions, as it was widely believed that the Poles had systematically and deliberately been Polonizing such children. Now, all children in public institutions or in foster care "whose appearance indicates Nordic parents" were to be brought in for racial and psychological testing by the Nazi Youth Department. Acceptable ones aged two to six would be sent to German foster families while those aged six to twelve would go to German boarding schools.[39]

Teams of SS doctors toured the institutions. When they arrived the children were lined up and looked over. Possible candidates were then sent off for physical exams. Only perfect bodies were acceptable: a crooked ear or flat feet were disqualifiers. If a child was chosen, the fact that it was already in foster care, or even was occasionally taken care of by blood relatives, was not grounds for exemption. The absence of any rights on the part of parents or guardians soon became cruelly evident. If the child was in a home, visiting rights were ended: parents could only look at their children "through the grate of the enclosure."[40] If the child was with foster parents they were ordered to bring it in for racial testing; should the child not appear, it would be forcibly retrieved by workers from the Youth Department.[41] Foster mothers who unsuspectingly responded to the summons of the authorities had devastating experiences:

> I received the summons to report together with my child to the German Youth Department in Lodz. . . . When I called I was told that I had to leave the child there and that I myself had to go to work [i.e., forced labor]; thereupon the official immediately called a German woman, who, disregarding my screams, snatched the child from my arms and walked out.

This woman found out where her daughter was and persuaded an official to let her take the child out for one day so that she could be baptized. The two fled to a friend's house and hid there for six months, but were eventually denounced by an ethnic German woman who had once been their neighbor. The child was taken away and the mother was beaten. When the war ended four years later, she heard that her daughter had been sent to a family in Hamburg. The record does not indicate if the girl ever came back.[42]

The Youth Department did not accept excuses. One guardian who appeared at the office without her niece, to explain that the child's parents had died from lung disease and left the girl in her care, was thrown out and threatened with prison if she did not come back with the child and her three sisters. More formal appeals, no matter how polite, were equally useless. Multiple letters written by both the aunt and grandmother of nine-year-old Halina Bukowiecka, in which the relatives went so far as to pledge not to request further welfare from the state, were brusquely rejected. An office memo indicated that little Halina had long since been sent to Munich.[43]

Equally stringent measures were applied to children of families that, in the opinion of the racial agencies, were ethnically valuable, but who wished to remain Polish. These families were given several chances to convert; when they did not, they and their children were taken away. The Youth Department in Lodz was informed two days before Christmas that

> the couple Zajdel and their son Stefan (14) have been sent to a concentration camp, because they refused to be registered in the German Peo-

ple's List. The husband and son are in the concentration camp Gross-
Rosen, the wife in Ravensbrück. Their release is not to be expected in
the near future.

Their two younger children, aged twelve and nine, were, over the objection of at least one German social worker, taken from their grandmother's
care and put in a children's home.[44]

In another case, thirteen of the forty-four families in the village of
Orlowo, near Mielec, who had "pure" Polish names were sent away without further ado as the town was being evacuated for incoming ethnic Germans. Frightened by this, many of the rest, whose names were Germanic,
quickly registered as ethnic Germans. Those who refused the offer to register were given three months to reconsider. When they still refused, their
property was confiscated and their children taken from them. The day the
race officials arrived in the village to carry out their orders, Josef
Schwakopf, who despite his name had refused to register as an ethnic German (which made one liable to be drafted into the Wehrmacht), jumped
out of the back window of his house, taking his two-year-old son with him.
He went to hide with friends:

> After about half an hour my wife, Zosia, followed me, took our son with
> her and returned home and told me to run away as they were looking
> for me, but she did not know what was in store for our son. . . . When
> she returned home . . . the German woman teacher Schneigardt came
> and inquired after our daughter . . . who was at that time with her
> grandfather in Mielec. My wife, not suspecting anything, indicated the
> place where our daughter was staying . . . from there our daughter was
> taken away. . . . Our son was taken from my wife by force and with a
> trick, tempting the child with sweets, and when my wife tried to defend
> the child they threatened to use arms.

In a particularly cruel action, some of the children were given to local
ethnic German families, known to the parents, who shuttled them about
the occupied East before fleeing with them to Germany as the tide of war
turned.[45]

The Orlowo case was not racially complicated. But sometimes the race
officials had a terrible time deciding what to do, especially when faced
with more upscale victims. In February 1943, a confused SS officer sent
his superior, General Odilo Globocnik, the notorious SS police leader in
the Lublin district of Poland, a memo on five different cases. All these
individuals, though proven to have at least 50 percent German blood, had

refused ethnic German status. All were well educated, middle- or upper-class, married to Poles, and very defiant. Johanna A., 50 percent German, was a doctor who refused to learn German. Maria L., 100 percent German, married to a Polish prisoner of war, was not only hostile herself. Her teenaged sons were too, and the eldest had declared that "he would feel like a deserter" if he committed himself to Germandom. Stanislas K., a gentleman farmer, 75 percent German, married to a Pole (which made the whole family 62.5 percent German), "had caused considerable trouble to the registration clerk," and his daughters had also refused registration. The exasperated official was particularly irritated by the attitudes of two sisters, Brunhilde and Ingeborg von W., daughters of a Baron who held full German citizenship. Both ladies had married Poles. Brunhilde, whose husband had been killed in action, he described as "a renegade of the worst type" who "gives a very bad example to the population owing to her position and mental capacities"; and he noted that she only admitted to being of German blood "after having been reminded by her father." Ingeborg, also interviewed in the presence of her father, "showed such an obduracy that it is not possible to recognize her as a German woman."

The cases were apparently so difficult that, classified as Secret, they went to Himmler himself. The SS chief suggested that Johanna A. be sent to a non-German area of Poland and that Maria L. go to the concentration camp at Ravensbrück, while her sons, "who were of very good race," should "with the assistance of the police" be separated, sent to "two specially well-managed boarding schools," and forbidden to correspond with their mother until "the mother has become conscious of the treason committed." Stanislas K. and his family were to be separated and sent via concentration camp to "armaments camps," that is, forced labor. Brunhilde and Ingeborg were to go to concentration camps too, and their children handled like the others. Himmler closed his letter with a request for a complete dossier on each case, noting that he himself would make the final decisions. The investigations went on for more than a year. By then Maria L. had given in and accepted her German status, and her sons, by now too old for boarding school, had become good draft material. Stanislas K., it was felt, had considerable useful expertise, and should be sent to Germany to farm. Things were not so good for Brunhilde and Ingeborg. It seemed that their father, the Baron, who had had to "remind" them of their German blood, was, in fact, of Jewish origin. On the memorandum containing these findings Himmler personally indicated his judgments. Maria and Stanislas were not to be taken into "protective custody," as their "reclamation for Germandom was of interest." Brunhilde and Ingeborg were to be arrested. Next to the investigating officer's comment that he "would be grateful for a further decision as to what is to happen" to the small children of the two sisters, "who cannot be admitted to a German Folk School as they are of Jewish origin," Himmler wrote: "sterilization . . . somewhere as foster children,"[46] an astonishingly lenient decision for such children in 1944.

Once the young children who were orphans or who had been taken from their families had been gathered up, they were sent to an institution in Lodz for a full-fledged racial examination. Those who were accepted by the SS went on to special children's homes still in Poland, at Brockau, Kalisch, and Pushkau, for further observation and preliminary indoctrination. In these homes they were given German language instruction. Discipline was strict and physical punishment frequent, and the children were frequently returned to Lodz for more blood tests and physical examinations.[47] After a few months of careful observation, race officials decided which children were suitable for further Germanization, and responsibility for them was transferred to the Lebensborn organization, which took them to Germany. Children from two to six were taken to Lebensborn nursery schools and many of the older ones, from six to twelve, went to boarding schools.

Himmler took a personal interest in these "Germanizable" children. One girl long remembered being carefully scrutinized by the Reichsführer SS when he visited her children's home. The quest was not limited to Poland. Himmler and his top aides spotted Nordic-looking children in all sorts of holding camps in Czechoslovakia, Romania, Yugoslavia, and numerous other places, and had them checked out by Lebensborn physicians. Despite their dedication to scientifically determined pure race, those who worked with the children had few illusions in this regard. A woman who worked in the legal department of Lebensborn testified later:

> The selection of Polish children intended for Germanization was determined by outward racial appearance. Nobody cared about any possible German origin of these children. . . . This can be deducted especially from the fact that . . . a half-Jewish Polish boy was sent to Germany for Germanization, despite the fact that his origin was plainly shown in his Polish papers.[48]

At the boarding schools in Germany, the children's Polishness was supposed to disappear. Guidelines for the handling of the Polish children noted that "special attention is to be given that the expression 'Polish children suitable for Germanization' may not reach the public to the detriment of the children. The children are rather to be designated as German orphans from the regained Eastern Territories."[49]

At one of the boy's schools, the new arrivals, dressed in spiffy dark blue suits piped in light blue, were mixed in with their German peers and referred to only as *Ostlandkinder,* or Eastern children, never as Poles. Along the way their Polish names were changed to German ones with similar initials or sounds. Alina Antczak, for example, would become Hilga Antzinger, and Josef Milozarek became Josef Mueller. Despite the prohibition on their native language and the severe punishments incurred for using it, the Polish children spoke it whenever they were together, a fact that could not be concealed, so that it soon was common knowledge in the local villages that there were Polish children in the schools.

Far worse for the children was the prohibition on contact with parents and relatives. At one point the Minister of the Interior noted that "it has been shown in the course of time that it must be expected that . . . Polish relatives and friends will attempt to find the location of the children." This could easily be done by making inquiries at local police registries, where all residents were required to be listed. To prevent this, special registries were created for the children so that their names did not appear in the public record.[50] Outgoing communications from the homes and boarding schools were also strictly forbidden. One girl reported later that "we were punished for every postcard we wrote to our parents. Letters addressed to us were torn and burnt. I know that from the girl who cleaned the room of the headmistress."[51]

Despite such draconian orders from on high, some staff members at the schools, moved by the terrible homesickness of the Polish children and by their concern for the well-being of their families, ignored the considerable secret postal activity. Older children easily found Polish forced laborers or sympathetic townspeople who sent their letters on. One teacher even claimed to have helped his charges write letters home in German so that they would get past the censors. And despite all, some parents did manage to make their way to the schools and demand the return of their children, at what risk and hardship it is hard to imagine. Sometimes they were successful. One teacher agreed with a parent to certify his son as a chronic bed wetter, sufficient grounds for the child's expulsion from the school and return to Poland.[52] According to another Lebensborn employee, a number of children whose relatives managed to find them were returned to them, even if the children had already been placed with German foster parents. In these cases the German foster parents, much as one would replace a defective piece of merchandise, "received Norwegian children as substitutes from the Lebensborn society."[53]

After a time, either Dr. Gregor Ebner, chief of Lebensborn, or one of his assistants personally evaluated the children in the boarding schools for adoption by German families. Even after having been through many previous analyses, not all of them made the cut. Children who remained too "fully aware of their Polish race" or who could not or would not learn German were sent back to youth camps in Poland.[54] Some who reached the age of fourteen, the age limit for education of the less worthy, were sent as apprentices to industries such as Siemens-Schukert in Berlin. Others went to work on farms, where little parental affection could be expected.

Dr. Ebner did not limit his evaluations to the Polish boarding school children. In August 1941 he voyaged to a resettlement camp at Schloss Langenzell, near Heidelberg, to inspect a group of twenty-five ethnic German orphans from the Banat region of Romania. It is clear that the visit was inspired by the fact that a high Nazi official had seen two of the children, a sister and brother, on a previous visit to the camp and wished to adopt them. Dr. Ebner did not think much of the group of children, noting in his long report on the visit that "only a few children can be designated as a gain to our folkdom." The young people, ranging from three and a half to twenty-one, were divided into three groups: group I was "very good and useful for our folkdom," II "average," and III "inadequate." The small sister and brother desired by the Nazi official were the only ones designated as group I, despite the facts that the boy, six and a half, was hospitalized with diphtheria and their mother (neé Aron, which Ebner hastened to add was a common Romanian surname and not Jewish) had died of tuberculosis. It helped that they were "fair and blue-eyed . . . good-natured, well-behaved" and that three-and-a-half-year-old "Little Maria" was the "favorite of the whole camp." Ebner strongly recommended that they be kept together in their adoptive family. Eighteen children were put in group II. Considered "too old" for full adoption, they were to be sent to work or put in foster homes—even though three of them were only seven years old. The standards were tough indeed. Two brothers, aged seven and ten, were described as follows:

> They are both fair and blue-eyed, but round-headed, very intelligent and bright boys, speaking German very well. In the camp they work as clever interpreters. Both are well mannered and well liked in the camp for their friendly disposition and intelligence. Only for reasons of their

Alpine cranial formation I rate them with mark II, otherwise the boys would deserve mark I.

In general Dr. Ebner was quite benign in his judgments of the mark II group. He was not so kind about the five "mark III" children, all of whom, having defects such as TB, "degenerate formation of the skull," or "Gypsy characteristics," were destined for sterilization or worse. But the trip was not a total waste: at the end of his report Ebner added that he had seen "six other good-looking and well built young men 17–19 years old . . . whom I consider fit for the Waffen-SS."[55]

Things were not ideal for either the children or the parents once adoption or placement in foster homes in Germany did take place. The changes of name, sometimes done more than once, and the spurious birth certificates provided by Lebensborn immediately caused concern and suspicion on the part of the new parents. Many of them nervously demanded official certificates of adoption from Lebensborn, which were duly fabricated and provided. The children were often clearly not the age indicated in their documents; the files are full of requests from foster parents for medical verification of a child's age. Most of these involve small children who seemed several years younger than their official ages. SS health officers attributed this to the fact that "almost all children coming from the East are found backward in their development." Elaborate X-rays and much mumbo-jumbo about average weights and heights were provided to the parents, but it is clear that the obliteration of the children's origins, whose records started only "with the time of the seizure of those children by the German authorities,"[56] had in many cases been all too successful.

German parents who grew to love their adopted children were often in for experiences just as devastating as those of the biological parents. Nazi race theory did not provide for love or permanent relationships. The children taken away by the state were farmed out to German families to be raised, but never belonged to them unequivocally, and were always subject to surveillance. A distressed SS *Untersturmführer* wrote to his superior to say that he had discovered that an already adopted child not only had a mother who was alive, but that the mother was an epileptic. The foster parents, with whom the six-year-old girl, Rosalia K., had been for "quite some time," did not want to give her up. The officer now asked if it was "justifiable" to leave the child with her foster parents or whether she should be sent back to Poland. His superior had no qualms. The epileptic mother had been afflicted since the age of fourteen and not only had her fits "increased considerably" in the last year, but she was "addicted to excessive use of alcohol." The child, therefore, "undoubtedly was suffering from hereditary affliction," although she had not shown any epileptic symptoms up to now, and would surely "act as a further hereditary transmitter of the disease." Germanization or education or adoption by German families could, therefore, "not be justified."[57]

Relations with older children, who had clear memories of home, were even more difficult for the adoptive families. Some, like eleven-year-old Jan Sulisz, tried to run away:

> I was sent together with other children to F. where we were boarded among farmers in the neighborhood. The German woman U. . . . had all our documents and handed us over to the farmers. I was handed over to a German woman in R. . . . where I ran away after a week. She reported me to the police and I was caught and beaten. I stayed with the guardian up to 8 May 1945 and went to the German school all the time and worked on the farm.[58]

Far worse was the situation of Alina Antczak, also eleven when she was "handed over" to her foster family. Alina was not an orphan. She had been temporarily placed in a Polish children's home when her parents fell on hard times. Efforts by her mother to get her back after the German invasion were unsuccessful. Alina later reported that her foster mother, who apparently had no illusions about the girl's origins, "constantly shouted and beat me for slight mistakes and said very often 'you Polish swine.' " In the summer of 1944 Alina was informed that her father was dead. When she secretly read the letter from Lebensborn containing this news, she found that the authorities had advised her foster family to tell her that "my mother was dead too so that I would not think of my parents any longer and it would be easier for me to get used to the foster parents." Alina, with nowhere else to go, stayed put. She was not allowed to go to the Catholic church or to write to her family, whose true fate remained unknown to her until a neighbor, who went to Poland in 1944, smuggled a letter out for her and brought back news of her parents, who were both very much alive.[59]

Foster parents also sometimes inadvertently became involved in the worst horrors committed by their government. The revelations were gradual and presented impossible choices. A Frau Dr. Weiss in Baden, who wished to adopt a child through Lebensborn, was sent by an official of that agency to the Polish children's home at Pushkau, where she picked out a boy of eight and a girl of about four. At the time she was told only that they were not Polish, but were from Czechoslovakia. Sometime later, feeling some doubt about their "German" origins, she requested more information on their background. The official sent to investigate later testified that he had discovered that they were the children of a professor from Prague, who had been shot, but that the mother of the children, who had been incarcerated in a concentration camp, was still alive. This distressing information was revealed to Frau Dr. Weiss, who realized that she probably would not be able to keep the children, but who decided, in "agreement" with Lebensborn officials, that the children should remain with her until the end of the war, which, it being by now late 1944, was undeniably near.[60] It is not clear if Frau Dr. Weiss was also told that she had become the guardian of two of the handful of children who survived the reprisal actions against hundreds of Czech families that followed the assassination of Reinhard Heydrich, who, in addition to his SS duties, had been appointed Deputy Protector of Bohemia and Moravia, but she must have suspected the truth.

Vengeance for Heydrich's death had reached its height on June 10, 1942, with the massacre at the village of Lidice and its subsequent obliteration. On that occasion, the Nazis had systematically murdered all the males over sixteen in the town. The women and children had been gathered beforehand in the town's schoolhouse and then moved to a gymnasium in the nearby town of Kladno, so that they were not immediately aware of the slaughter. After a time, policemen came to the gymnasium and began calling out the names of individual children, who, in many cases, had to be forcibly taken from their mothers:

> We had to walk upstairs to a room between two rows of [policemen], where some forms were made out. Then we were chased out into the courtyard where we had to board waiting trucks; our mothers and girls over sixteen remained in the building and we were told that the mothers would follow us. The smaller children cried and the older ones had to take care of them and quiet them. We were accompanied by several SS men and several young German women.[61]

The ninety or so children thus chosen were sent by train to Lodz and dumped into a bare room without even straw on the floor. Toilets were in a small hut across a courtyard. Food consisted of a breakfast and supper of black coffee and bread and a lunch of soup with potatoes and barley. After a time, a team of racial examiners chose seven children from this group for Germanization. The candidates were then processed through a series of camps, where they remember a few kind nurses among the many strange people surrounding them, and were finally taken to the children's home at Pushkau, where they were put in with Polish children. Here the routine consisted of school attendance in a nearby town in the mornings, all lessons being in German, and work in the kitchens of the home in the afternoons. They were frequently punished: one favorite penalty was to make a child stand barefoot in his nightshirt in a cold hallway until midnight. More serious failure to obey the rules could lead to solitary confinement in a windowless basement for a week.[62]

A few more Lidice children were later added to the group at Pushkau. The rest, clearly bad-blood children "not desired for Germanization," were to be "further sent through the Polish camps," and the SS was informed that "special care will not be imperative."[63]

News of the massacre, which the Nazis had proudly announced on Radio Berlin in order to intimidate the Czechs, instantly became a worldwide cause célèbre. The timing was not auspicious: the broadcast came at the same time as publication of the agreement between Molotov and Roosevelt to create a second front in Europe, and certainly was instrumental in engendering enthusiasm for that policy. Secretary of State Cordell Hull condemned the action at Lidice as "unworthy even of savages,"[64] and the poet Edna St. Vincent Millay composed a passionate, if somewhat melodramatic, narrative poem that was read on NBC and shortwaved to England, referring to Hitler as "the butcher of human-kind."[65]

This furor caused the Lodz SS to hesitate briefly about precisely what to do with the "un-Germanizable children" of Lidice and other Czech hostage groups. Ten days after the slaughter, they were still urgently requesting orders from on high for the "further disposition of the children." It is not clear what their ultimate fate was, but various documents indicate that more than 100 Czech children from this category perished in the maze of Nazi punishment and concentration camps.[66]

A few days after the Lidice children had been taken away, their mothers were condemned to life imprisonment in the women's concentration camp at Ravensbrück. Those who were pregnant were allowed to give birth, after which the babies were taken from them and killed by strangulation or lethal injection, if they were lucky. For other babies death came more slowly: two mothers were taken to a hospital in Prague with their infants, but were not allowed to nurse them. Instead, under the supervision of a German nurse, they were forced to feed the newborns mush or badly cooked gruel. After six months they were taken for interrogation, which they were told would take only an hour. Instead they went to Ravensbrück, and never saw their malnourished children again.[67]

As time went on and the needs of the Nazis for workers and soldiers became more urgent, "Germanization" became ever more flexible. Children of partisans and resisters from certain areas whose parents had been executed or sent to concentration camps became of greater and greater interest. Himmler suggested that although "bad" Czech children were to be taken to "certain children's camps," those of "good racial stock who, unless subjected to proper care and education, are of course likely to become the most dangerous avengers of their parents," were to be sent "on probation" to Lebensborn homes.

Later in the war, all sweetness and light, he wrote of the children of Balkan partisans, "We are Germans and we cannot look on while innocent children of a people which in itself is decent and good become depraved and broken through the unpropitiousness of circumstances." He ordered that "all orphaned youth in the whole Balkan area be gathered by our Division Commanders" and sent to special schools in the Reich on "scholarships." Somewhat revealing his hand, he then noted that these children, "who can move in two directions, either to the communists, if we do not care for them, or to us, if we do something for them," were to be returned home "as decent men and women . . . when order and stability are re-established."[68]

No endeavor was seemingly too remote for the promotion of Germanization. In the summer of 1941 Himmler received letters indicating a need for female household help in Germany proper. He demanded that suitable workers be found. Choosing girls for this work was most difficult, not only because they would be living in close proximity to German children, but also because it was foreseen that their employers might invoke the *droit du seigneur*, or, as Himmler's chief for such matters, Ulrich Greifelt, put it, "girls unsuitable for Germanization may not be employed for folkdom reasons." Extremely meticulous racial analysis of the entire family of the domestic candidate was, therefore, essential. The result of these stringent rules had led to a shortfall of domestics, who up to the summer of 1941 were recruited only in the annexed areas. It was therefore decreed that racial analysts be dispatched to look for maids and nannies not only in the General Gouvernement dumping ground for Poles, but even in the sectors of the USSR that by then had been conquered by Hitler.[69] Himmler himself justified the plan in a flowery ordinance issued from Hitler's Eastern Front headquarters on October 1, 1941, one day after the Führer's final assault on Moscow had begun. As the German armies struggled forward in the autumn mud, Himmler wrote that "one of the greatest calamities is at present the shortage of female domestic help." National biology "was dangerously at risk," he continued, as the "doubtlessly existing desire of many women to have children, and many children at that—is frustrated by bitter reality." This reality was not that several million of their husbands would soon die in the Russian winter, but the fact that there were not enough nannies. Therefore, more girls, aged sixteen to twenty, must be brought in, who

> are unobjectionable with regard to race and whose assimilation with the German folkdom is desirable. Thus, simultaneously, blood of the same kind lost to an alien nation is won back and again added to the German nation. . . . For these future mothers of good blood it means, in addition, a social rise when they are given the chance of working in Germany as domestic help and of later marrying here. I therefore order that girls of Polish and Ukrainian descent who meet the requirements of the racial evaluation groups I and II shall be selected by the racial examiners. Assignments may only be made to households of families with many children who are firm in their ideology and fit for training such girls.[70]

By December only 521 girls had been allocated. An apologetic official noted that he was facing competition from many local labor offices and administrations that wanted the girls for "defense industries and agriculture." But the real reason for the low number was that only 3 to 5 percent of those examined could be declared eligible for Germanization; most came from agricultural backgrounds and were unsuitable. Moreover, there had been problems with the girls who had already been sent. It was "hardly possible to prevent correspondence with their families," the official wrote. Homesickness was a "big factor," and "many of the allocated girl-servants have been obstinate and had to be punished. Several suicides occurred."[71] One such girl, Zofia Pieskarska, sixteen when she was sent to Germany, later revealed why:

> I was to be sent away for work and . . . was photographed and medically examined; for instance, my head was examined in great detail. Finally I was sent away with a group of other girls; they were sent to factories. . . . I was directed to one of the German houses, a doctor's. I worked with him as a maid, but I was treated there like a social equal: I used to eat with them, go visiting with them, and went with them to the movies and

theaters. However I was under special supervision . . . a German civilian came to the house of my employers who talked to my mistress and afterwards to me. He asked how I felt, where I go, who I keep company with, whether I write letters home; he told me also that things in Lodz were quite different now. . . . I also know that my mistress was periodically asked about me by telephone by the Gestapo.[72]

Luckily for this girl, her mistress was not a Party member and told her all about the surveillance. She also did not allow her to go to the carefully controlled social events laid on by the Nazi Servants' Association, and warned her to stay away from nearby Polish forced labor camps and German soldiers. Three years after Zofia arrived, she was told that she now had official permission to go out with German soldiers, and that if she married one she would receive German citizenship after the war; but the Gestapo inquiries did not cease, and Zofia resisted this kind offer.

Zofia was fortunate in her placement; many of the other domestics had major problems. And it is clear that, after a time, even quite loyal Nazis did not want rebellious, miserable help who spoke no German, and that the problem was not so much finding "racially suitable" girls, but households that would take them.

On November 9, 1944, apparently unimpressed by the fact that the Russians were in East Prussia and the American Third Army was crossing the Moselle at that very moment, one of Himmler's aides wrote to a Baron in Westphalia, who was also a high-ranking member of the SS, to ask if he would be willing "to employ Polish women of German stock." The girls in question, two sisters, had not only refused to register for screening, but had insisted they were Polish and, on order of Himmler, had been sent to Ravensbrück. The official noted that "the Camp Commandant was instructed to take care personally of the sisters and to influence them humanely in order to win them over to Germanism." There is no explanation of how this was done, but after six months in the camp the sisters decided to apply for German citizenship after all. The officer confessed, "Admittedly, it cannot yet be said whether the personal attitude of the sisters is solidified." But Himmler had apparently decided that "in order to further influence the sisters in the German way of life, it has been proposed to grant them greater liberty and to employ them in households where there are many children." "In this connection," the aide continued rather lamely in his letter to the Baron, "the Reichsfuehrer-SS has thought of you."[73] The Baron's reply is a masterpiece of evasion, which also gives us a telling glimpse of the "bitter reality" of German life in 1944:

According to your statements . . . both sisters are not yet strong in their inner feeling for Germanism. I must point out, that I have 25 male and female Poles on the farm that is near the house; part of them emphasize their Polish nationality even though they work willingly. . . . However, a fanatic reaction would immediately result from this side. Considering this, neither my wife nor the Mamselle, who is over 65 years old, is in the position to supervise sufficiently. . . . In addition to that, the Labor Office wants to take my last two trained maids in exchange. With the sisters, my wife and the Mamselle could not do the work that is necessary with all the people in the house. . . . At the moment the household runs smoothly, because my wife . . . took over the entire care of the children in addition to the housework in the bedrooms. The constant moving in the house and in the farm because of the evacuees needs much concentration on the part of the lady of the house, especially as we anticipate taking in my parents-in-law as soon as Hildesheim is going to be attacked and more relatives as soon as it is Bad Oeynhausen's turn.[74]

The exact number of "Germanizable" young people who were actually placed in foster families, schools, or jobs requiring racial purity is not known. Recovered German documents indicate that the numbers of acceptable children were not vast, while postwar claims from the affected countries indicate that hundreds of thousands of children were taken to Germany. The fact is that Germanization involved only a small, physically "perfect" group; many thousands of other Polish young people would not be so pampered, but would be used very differently by the Nazis.

Despite their pathological insistence on racial purity within Reich borders, the Nazis, well before they streamed into Poland in September 1939, had cast their gaze upon the huge potential labor pool that conquest of Poland would make available to them. Absorption of the Austrian and Sudeten industrial labor forces had done wonders for the German economy, but shortages of manpower were still enormous. First consideration was given to the utilization of Polish prisoners of war in agricultural areas, as had been done in World War I.[75] Once on Polish territory, German labor officials wasted no time bringing in employment functionaries; within a month some 115 labor offices had been set up. Meanwhile, 300,000 newly captured Polish POWs were being rushed into the Reich to help bring in the 1939 harvest. But this was not nearly

Auschwitz mug shots of a young Polish prisoner destined for forced labor.

enough. In November, Göring, chief of Hitler's ambitious economic Four Year Plan, and Agriculture Minister Walter Darré requested the massive conscription of 1.5 to 2 million more workers. By January 1940, even as all the other ethnic rearrangements were going on, Hans Frank was ordered to recruit and transfer 750,000 Poles into the Reich, of whom 50 percent were supposed to be women. Obligatory quotas of workers were to be provided by each town and village in the General Gouvernement.[76]

This hasty process, which would introduce hordes of foreigners of alien blood into the Reich, did not fit in at all with Nazi racial theory. But economic necessity ruled. Himmler, who was just getting his racial classification system under way in Poland, huffed that he could not "screen a million individuals in four weeks," but conceded that the labor was needed. The Polish workers, unlike the "Germanizable" children, would have to be transferred unanalyzed and upon arrival be "treated en bloc as Poles." Just what this entailed was made clear in a body of regulations approved by Hitler, Himmler, and Göring known as the Polenerlasse, or Decrees for Poles.[77]

The rules were drastic indeed. The Poles were to be totally segregated from the German population and would be required to wear, at all times, a badge identifying their social status: a purple-and-yellow square emblazoned with the letter P. Poles could not patronize German restaurants or barbers, ride on public transportation, or go to movies. Their church services must be completely separate, and they were subject to a curfew at night. To prevent fraternization with the natives, they were to be housed separately in camps containing balanced numbers of men and women. If there were not enough women, Polish brothels should be provided, for, above all, sexual contact between the Slavic Poles and the Nordic Master Race had to be prevented. Indeed, intercourse with a German was punishable by death.

Segregation was not all. It was also necessary to establish the fact that Poles were lesser beings. Their wages and food rations were set lower than those of their German coworkers, they had no access to the normal legal system, and a vicious propaganda campaign, complete with nasty posters, proclaimed that "the Pole can never be your comrade," and advised German citizens who had been working with Poles for years that "there is no such thing as a decent Pole—just as there is no such thing as a decent Jew."

News of these conditions soon got back to Poland. At first the idea of working in Germany had appealed to many in Poland, where unemployment had been high for years and was now exacerbated by the war. Within three months recruitment had fallen off so badly that German authorities in the General Gouvernement made registration for labor in Germany compulsory for everyone aged fifteen to twenty-five. Coercive measures, which included taking people off the streets, or surrounding whole villages and raiding each house, were begun to fill the local quotas. This caused panic in many a town:

> The volunteering for Germany has completely stopped. . . . Fewer and fewer young people can be seen walking on the streets. Some are hiding in small villages or in the forest. We are particularly worried about the future of the young girls . . . we have learned that some young women have been placed in Germany's public houses. . . . Most young boys are not sleeping in their homes anymore. . . . The Germans are trying to destroy our most valuable asset, our youth.[78]

Governor Frank, worried about potential unrest, stopped short of "excessive measures" and massive roundups, and by June 1940, only about a third of the targeted 750,000 had been sent to Germany.[79]

The process did not stop, however, and by mid-1944 over a million "pure Polish" laborers had been sent to Germany from the General Gouvernement. The methods of recruitment became more and more "excessive," especially for the young. During the massive continuing deportations of Poles from the German annexed areas to the General Gouvernement in 1940, thousands of young people were removed from the transports and sent to unknown places in Germany.

In the towns the most vulnerable to forced recruitment were teenagers who were not yet employed. At the age of fourteen they were required to register with the Labor Office. If they did not, they were easy to find: in many areas, despite Himmler's theories, the Germans had restarted the schools as a way of keeping tabs on children. As the war wore on, "recruiting" would include loading a whole class onto trucks direct from the classroom, and the registration of children as young as thirteen. To protect their offspring, parents tried to find them jobs, but this often did no good.

The day fourteen-year-old Julian Nowak of Posen[80] went to register, proof of employment in hand, all present were locked into a dark hallway at the Labor Office until everyone had been "certified" for departure to the Reich. To prevent defection before their train left, the Nazis kept everyone's ID cards. Julian and ninety-seven other boys from Posen were sent to a textile factory in Bremen. There they were lodged at first in a barracks with no bathing facilities. Soon they were covered with lice, which they would keep until their liberation in 1945; even when they were moved into better housing, they had very few changes of clothing. In the first days, indoctrination sessions made clear to the young boys the drastic punishments that would result from not wearing one's badge, or from having sexual relations with German or even Polish girls. The former were of a superior race; the latter, if they became pregnant, would be a loss to German industry. To make the gravity of this clear, the boys were later taken to witness the double hanging of a fellow worker and a German girl who had broken the rules.[81]

In the factory the boys were mixed in with adult workers from many countries, whose barracks were segregated by nationality. There were a few ways out of their situation. One boy's parents declared themselves to be *Volksdeutsche,* and he was released; another was sent home when he lost several fingers. At eighteen, no longer considered children, boys were moved to a different camp, not necessarily an improvement. There was nothing childish about the work. The factory ran day and night in eight- and twelve-hour shifts. Much of the work was far too heavy for fourteen-year-olds, and some was deadly. In one area the air was so full of lint and dust that noses and mouths became clogged within minutes. The boys noticed that no Germans worked in that room.

Julian Nowak was at first put in a room with ten carding machines. Fortunately for him, his supervisor was an elderly German woman who spoke Polish and who patiently trained him. She was friendly and told him "that she felt sorry that such a small boy had to work so hard, so young and so far away from his family." Sometimes she let him sit down or sleep a few hours on the night shift. This kindness made the boy relax a bit too much, and at one point, when he did not respond quickly enough to an order given in German, which he did not yet understand, the foreman kicked him and hit him in the head.

There were other disciplinarians too. The camp commander had a punishment room in one of the basements. Here the boys were whipped for such infractions as not saying good morning in German loudly enough. The number of lashes depended on the crime. When the commandant was in a jolly mood, he let the boys choose which whip would be used from the extensive collection hung on the wall.[82] For more serious offenses, such as getting into fights with Hitler Youth in town, stealing food, or trying to run away, the boys were sent to a special punishment camp, where for six weeks they would shovel sand out of dump trucks or do other hard labor for ten hours a day until their hands swelled up and they were so weak they could not climb stairs. In this place, shaved bald and dressed in shirts with a fluorescent stripe visible in the dark, they dreamt only of escape. But at night guard dogs and armed SS, who did not hesitate to shoot, patrolled the camp, and the boys knew there was no way to flee.[83]

Death was a frequent occurrence both at the factories and in the punishment camps. The dead were buried in shallow graves within the confines of the camp. The boys tried to decorate the graves of their friends with crudely carved markers and flowers plucked from the roadside. At night the guard dogs often dug up the corpses, which the children duly reburied the next day.

Moments of fun and leaves were few and far between, and homesickness was palpable. There were escapes, but survival outside the camps was almost impossible. Within, such pastimes as card playing were forbidden, and singing a Polish song at the wrong moment was grounds for being sent to prison. Treatment of young women was only marginally better than that of the boys. Celina Drozdek was just nineteen when she and thirty-nine other girls were sent to a jute factory in Bremen in 1940. The group was housed in a former children's home that was at first positively luxurious compared to the boys' barracks, but by 1942, when Celina escaped, it was crammed with more than 1,000 women. Life in the building was strictly controlled. Curfew was at 8:00 p.m., and uniformed officers made frequent inspections during which the women had to stand for hours in the halls. Celina was lucky to be assigned to kitchen duty. Here she was warm and was at least assured of her proper rations.

Even the distribution of food in these camps was carefully regulated according to racial rules. The midday meal for everyone consisted of soup, but there were separate pots for each nationality of forced laborers in the huge factory, and still another for the German staff. Their pot contained "thick and tasty" soup with meat and vegetables; they also got rice pudding with vanilla sauce for dessert. Czech, Belgian, French, and Hungarian laborers, being of Aryan origin, got less meat in their soup and no pudding. The Polish pot had no meat at all, and its potatoes were sometimes transferred to the French pot when that one needed thickening. Later, when Russian workers began to arrive, there would be a Russian pot containing a thin gruel with a few potatoes, beets, and oats. All the soups were carefully inspected, and if the chief cook felt the Russian soup was too thick, she ordered it to be diluted with water. For reasons that are unclear, the spoon used to stir the Russian pot absolutely could not be used in any other one. Not only were the Russians lowest in the soup pecking order, but their dormitory consisted of a windowless room with no beds and their sole recreation of one half hour a week took place on a balcony.[84]

This complex classification was not limited to soups, but in theory governed every aspect of the forced laborer's life. By the end of 1942 each nationality had its own classification: "A" were the Italian allies, soon to be demoted. "B" were "Germanic" peoples such as the Dutch and Norwegians. "C" was for "non-Germanic" peoples with whom the Nazis were allied or linked, such as the Hungarians and the French, through their pro-German Vichy regime. "D" denoted Slavs: Poles, Croats, Serbs, Czechs, Slovenians, and, lowest among these, Russians. Though satisfying to the racial agencies, these classifications and their accompanying sets of rules and privileges were too much trouble to enforce for factory supervisors and were reduced to a simplistic "East is bad and West is acceptable" classification by the average German.[85]

The subtleties were even more lost on the young workers, whose main thoughts were of food and home leave, which was sporadically available. The temptation not to return from such furloughs was often overwhelming, but every worker knew that relatives would be punished and no further leaves would be given to his campmates until he had returned. Family crises were not grounds for release. Henryk Grygiel was not allowed to go home when his mother was dying. Permission was given for him to attend her funeral, but camp officials took so long over the paperwork that he arrived too late even for that.[86]

In the early days of the war things were not all bad. The boys amused themselves by pretending not to understand German, and other minor irritating acts that drove their bosses crazy. There were walks and some dancing during the free time allotted on Sundays, and great efforts were made by each barrack to make secret decorations for Easter and erect some sort of a Christmas tree. The young workers were allowed to send home group photographs, in which they look quite presentable, but all other letters sent and received were censored. At every opportunity the kids went into the towns to spend their tiny stipends on more food or, having removed their badges, to sneak into a movie. Along the way there were kindly people both in the camps and the towns who tried to give these children a small amount of affection. But as the war went on, both living and working conditions deteriorated steadily. To many of these young slaves, it seemed that they had lost forever the possibility of a real life, which was, of course, what the Nazis intended.

On September 17, 1939, the Soviet Union invaded Poland, as had been secretly arranged beforehand with the Nazis. The USSR was just as eager as its ally to begin cleansing the buffer zone between East and West. The criteria were different, being based not on race, but on class and economic status; nonetheless, the required purging and rearrangement of the residents of the area would be no less ferocious than that carried out by the Nazis.

In the Soviet-controlled territories the ideologies and enmities were also long established. Poland had been the object of Russian desire since tsarist times. In 1920, the Red Army had attempted to take Warsaw and had been humiliatingly defeated by Poland, where the nobility, the Catholic Church, and an independent peasantry—all anathema to the Communists—were still firmly in place. After this conflict, millions of Poles were forcibly repatriated from the Soviet-controlled areas of Belorussia and the Ukraine, but over a million had remained in the USSR and had been the targets of continuing Soviet repression, totaling nearly 40 percent of those purged as national minorities in the 1930s.[87] The feeling was mutual: in the areas of the Ukraine that the Poles administered, they were also given to brutal measures against the Ukrainian majority, who deeply resented the Polish "military colonists" who had been sent in to Polonize the region after World War I.

The genetic card was played by the Soviets in Poland too. Their invasion was explained as a mission to rescue Soviet "blood brothers," that is, the Belorussians and the Ukrainians (whose numbers Stalin had so recently decimated in the USSR proper), and as an effort to impose order in the now disintegrated Polish state while assisting its population to "reconstruct its statehood."

As they moved into their new territory, the Russians, like the Germans, took every advantage of the existing ethnic hatreds. Poles who thought the

Soviets were now turning on the Germans were, at first, not disabused of this opinion, while the Ukrainians and Belorussians were encouraged to attack the minority Polish landowners and administrators.[88] In the vacuum left by the removal of the Polish administration, makeshift governments and militias of locals sprang up, but these independent entities would not last long. On October 1, 1939, the Soviet Politburo issued to officials five pages of detailed instructions for the "Sovietization" of the area.[89] The effects began to be felt within days.

That "liberation" had been a myth soon became clear. Total economic exploitation, collectivization, and other Soviet policies were to be introduced. Anything of value, including whole factories and buildings, was shipped east. And, as had been the case in the Ukraine, private food supplies were forbidden to the peasants. Businesses were expropriated, Polish symbols and language were prohibited, and, in order to provide quarters for Soviet administrators, arbitrary evictions were instituted. Families were thrown out on a moment's notice and forced to find new lodgings in towns and villages already overwhelmed with refugees from the German-occupied areas. The threat of Sovietization and the dreadful living conditions led thousands of Ukrainians and Jews (who of course were rejected) to apply for repatriation to German-occupied Poland under the auspices of a German Repatriation Commission.

Meanwhile, the Soviets too had plans for demographic rearrangements, which would also require classification and census of the entire population. It was an effort just as massive as that of the Nazis. Wasting no time, the Soviet authorities sent in hundreds of Party officials and Komsomol members, the Communist equivalent of the Hitler Youth, to do the paperwork.[90] In the process of this registration, most of those who had served in the Polish armed forces would be discovered and slated for eventual execution. Refugees were identified, and everyone's ethnic origin was recorded. Workers were required to join unions and fill out forms giving personal information.

On October 11, while Hitler was organizing the transfer of the Balts, the Soviets announced that there would be a plebiscite on October 22. Preparations for the election gave the new overlords further opportunity for the gathering of personal information under the guise of voter registration. During the political campaign, mandatory and infinitely boring propaganda meetings, usually conducted in Russian, created opportunities for surveillance and intimidation. Voting was obligatory: those who did not appear at the polling place were fetched by militiamen. Ballot boxes were taken to hospitals and even synagogues, and every corrupt practice ever heard of in an election was used to assure a massive turnout.[91] Needless to say, the election returned assemblies in the Ukraine and Belorussia that voted for full incorporation into the USSR, and cleared the way for a "legal" restructuring of society that would differ from the Nazi model only in the categories of groups to be eliminated or incarcerated.

Some 65,000 Polish prisoners of war went immediately to concentration or labor camps. On November 10, 1939, a commission on refugees was formed to decide the fate of the hundreds of thousands of civilian Poles who had fled east before the Germans. A few weeks later, the Politburo ordained that 33,000 of them, plus 21,000 families of "military colonists" who had lived in the region since the end of World War I, would be sent to Siberia as forced labor. Any property they left behind would revert to the state. Simultaneously, the Soviet government instructed the various commissariats involved, and especially the Commissariat of Forestry, to prepare for the arrival of these "resettlers." Transportation would be arranged by the NKVD. Far more generous than the Nazis, the Soviets allowed their resettlers to take along 500 kilograms per family of the necessities of life, such as clothes, bedding, utensils, and tools. What they chose would later often determine their survival.

Accommodations for the voyage were, in theory, not so bad. Convoys were to consist of fifty-five railroad cars, four for freight and the rest designed to hold twenty-five persons each. The settlers were "guaranteed" one hot meal and 800 grams of bread per day during the trip. In order to avoid resistance, the actual deportations were to be carried out without notice, on a single day. The planning was incredibly elaborate. Special teams carefully charted train routes to the settlement areas, how each targeted house was to be approached, and how the families were to be moved to the heavily guarded train stations. Reality, except for the element of surprise, would bear little resemblance to the written plan.[92]

The first deportation took place on February 10, 1940. Before dawn, in the winter darkness, small detachments of Russian troops arrived at thousands of sleeping houses. Twelve-year-old Kazimierz F. remembered that the soldiers

> surrounded the house all around so that no one escapes . . . and started knocking on the door until they knock it down and bust inside. We all sprang from our beds and were standing there as if grown into the ground. . . . Three come in and scream . . . hands up. Dad put his hands up, and they started towards him and led him to the other room at gunpoint. The others started searching for weapons. Mama started crying and we all did too. And they started talking. . . . "We give you two hours

to pack up and are leaving in two hours." . . . When Mama heard these words she fainted immediately and me and sister started packing. . . . After two hours they loaded us by force into the sleighs. We were all bidding good-bye to our family house. When we were riding we were watching our house until it disappeared from view.[93]

This scene was repeated with little variation for some 28,000 families totaling 139,590 people.[94] At some point during the chaotic hours of packing, a sentence was read to the deportees to inform them that they were now Soviet citizens being "resettled" to another country.[95] The Russian troops looted freely; attempts to deceive them by plying them with vodka were to little avail. Sometimes the soldiers could be kind. Clearly having witnessed such scenes before, they often gave the deportees good advice: at one house a soldier found a saw and an axe in the attic and advised his prisoners to take them along.[96]

The transfers to the trains stayed long in the children's memories. They recalled the mournful howls of their abandoned dogs as they moved away from their houses. The overburdened sledges in which they rode often turned over, throwing everyone into the snow. "The frozen children cried, the NKVD man shouts to stop crying." Sometimes the sleds stopped for hours in the freezing cold. At the stations, groups waited in locked enclosures to board the trains, and those who tried to escape through the windows were shot. Loading the trains was dreadful. Families were often separated, luggage was lost, and the directive to put only twenty-five people in each car was nowhere observed. One child saw a woman who moved too slowly be decapitated as the freight car doors were slammed shut.[97]

> They put 70 of us into one small freight car . . . and they locked it with a key and in a moment we felt a violent jerking of the train so that all of us fell down. In the car one could hear the weeping of mothers and little children. It was very cold in the car, those who stood close to the door froze to the door and someone else who could not get up from the floor ended his life there.

This group had no food for two days. "On the third day they opened the car and half of the people were dead already, lying on the floors, frozen and starved from hunger and lack of air." The dead were piled in heaps and covered with snow "so that it would not be seen that so many had died."[98]

Other large deportations took place in April and June 1940. The April group consisted mainly of 66,000 family members of the 21,857 Polish officers, policemen, and intelligentsia who had been executed at Katyn and other sites that spring. In June, whole families of Polish "refugees" who had fled the Nazis were sent off again to the remotest reaches of the USSR, which are remote indeed.

Deportations continued even as the Germans invaded the USSR in June 1941. By late summer the total number of deported Poles reached an estimated 400,000, among them many Jews who had been refused repatriation to the German-occupied areas.[99] The deportations were not limited to Poland: all along the western Soviet borders "undesirables" such as landowners and small-time capitalists were sent to Siberia. The hardest hit were families in which the men were taken off to hard labor while the women, children, and elderly went elsewhere.

The conditions on the journeys, which often lasted for more than a month, varied greatly, being affected by weather, individual train commanders, and the ingenuity of the deportees. In the hours before their departure from Lvov in the summer of 1940, the "refugee" father of ten-year-old Janka Goldberger, who had fled east from Cracow when the Germans invaded, somehow managed to get himself appointed chief of his cattle car, and scrounged enough lumber to build platforms, which doubled the space available to its fifty-six passengers. He also installed a wide pipe in the floor for a latrine. The families were able to spread their bedding about on the platforms and Janka "thought it fun" when she first climbed into the car. Her "berth" was on the top tier, where it was hot and the air was bad, "but there were tiny barred windows which were sometimes un-shuttered."[100]

On all the deportee trains, the Polish children, who had already noticed the extraordinary shabbiness of the Red Army when it had invaded Poland, were amazed at the conditions in the USSR: "Poverty peered out from people's houses and faces. The people were poorly dressed. The houses were old and dirty . . . we saw very few cattle. The forests were devastated."[101]

As Janka's convoy rolled across the vastness of the USSR, boredom and lethargy set in. The deportees were let out briefly from time to time, but at stops far from stations, where the trains often spent the day so that they would not attract the attention of local populations. The guards were bored too, but normally kind to the children, whom they did allow to slip out at stations to buy food and get water. In less populated areas the deportees frequently went for days without stopping. On Janka's train bread and soup were distributed once a day, but on many others the "Russians didn't find provisions because they didn't have any themselves."

There was often no water, and the temperature ranged from raging heat to hideous cold. Cars with hole-in-the-floor facilities were luxurious. Janka and her peers were highly amused at the sight of people in other cars who were held by two strong men as they "stuck the relevant part of anatomy out of the door." From time to time the train was stopped, and everyone was forced into log cabins for communal baths while their clothes were deloused. The adults were less amused. All feared death or torture at their destination. The guards, when asked what things would be like, said only, "You will get used to it. But if you can't, you will die like a dog."

As they moved east across the Volga and past the great cities toward Lake Baikal, things became more relaxed and even the adults were allowed to disembark at stations to buy or barter for food.[102] This was not mere kindness. In a memo highly critical of the deportation operation, the Main Administration of Escort Troops in Moscow noted that "the convoy troops were obliged to feed themselves by forced requisitions at the railway station canteens," as "food supplies were irregular."[103]

After thirty-two days, the Goldberger family arrived at a "classical" concentration camp in Tynda. From here, jammed so tightly into trucks that they could not move, they were conveyed hundreds of miles farther into Yakutskaya Oblast, deep in the Siberian taiga, nearly 5,000 miles from Cracow and home.

From hundreds of railheads, other groups slowly moved toward similar destinations. The vast majority were women, children, and the old. Eleven-year-old Harold Olin, deported from Romania with his mother and grandmother, did the last stage of the trip to his new home via barge. For two weeks, the leaky, lice-infested vessel was pulled by a tugboat from Novosibirsk to Pudino, a small town "surrounded by quicksand bogs, which were impenetrable for most of the year . . . it was impossible to walk out of there, because there were no solid roads connecting to the mainland." During the winter access to the area was by a single road across the frozen wasteland. From Pudino the families went on foot to villages with collective farms, the closest of which was some ten miles away.

Arrival at one's destination, as was true in all such forced travel, brought no relief. Who does not dream of a bath, food, and warm shelter after a grueling journey? Memos to the Commissariat of Forestry notwithstanding, here, as in the German dumping area of Nisko, virtually nothing had been done to prepare for the "resettlers." Harold Olin's group of thirty was "forcibly quartered" in the few existing two-room log cabins of the collective workers who had been sent out a few years before. The latter, many of whom were exiles from the Ukraine, deeply resented this measure, as they had had to build the cabins from scratch when they arrived.[104] The Olins' cotenants were another fatherless family of four. There was no plumbing, and in the winter the inside temperature seldom rose above 40 or 45 degrees. In another place, the deportees were simply "let off and ordered . . . to look for housing, so the people lived under open sky for a few days," and in yet another "they stuck us in stables and Cossack mud huts, taking no interest in us and not even asking us about food."[105]

Compared to these settlements, that of Janka Goldberger's family was unusually good. Here latrines had already been prepared, water was plentiful, and a canteen was in operation. The new arrivals were required to finish building the huts they lived in and collect wood for the winter, but at least everything was new and clean. All ages participated in this work. The children gathered small branches and mud to insulate the walls. They needed no urging: the camp commander had made clear that if these tasks were not completed before the snows came, they would freeze to death.

Tasks such as building one's own shelter had to be done in one's free time, of which there was precious little. The "resettlers" had been brought all this way to work, and their duties often began within hours of their arrival. It was hard manual labor in sawmills and munitions factories, and on collective farms. Children as young as ten worked alongside their elders in order to earn enough to buy food. But there was not always enough work for the number of deportees, nor were most women and teenagers capable of performing much of it:

> Because Mama was a burly, strong woman . . . there were many occasions, especially in fall and winter, when she was given tasks normally performed by men. One of the most physically demanding . . . was to dig up the tree roots, after first chopping down the tree. The uprooting was done by alternately chopping in the ground with an axe and digging with a shovel. She would come home completely wasted, absolutely spent.[106]

Illness, injury, or exhaustion meant lost work hours and less food. It was a vicious circle. Children picked berries in the forests and helped cultivate vegetable gardens in summer. Still, there was never enough to eat. Mothers in most camps, when not working, walked for miles to find locals with whom they could exchange their few possessions for food. But the inhabitants themselves were frequently so impoverished that they could provide little. In winter, the shopping trips could be fatal. One child later wrote this account:

Mama with brother went on monday said goodbye and went one day passed and another its cold outside and had to stand on line for bread third and fourth day passed we worry why Mama isn't coming back on five day. . . . This . . . woman comes over and says that one woman with a boy froze to death. . . . Dad went to the commander . . . to give us a horse and wagon to bring frozen mama. . . . Commander says no horses they went to work.[107]

The woman was found by farmers two kilometers from the village. Frozen in her sledge, she still held her small son in her arms.

Despite the ghastly conditions, many of the exiled children, like their counterparts everywhere, had happy moments. Some of the camps had schools for the younger ones with teachers who were kind, if frequently insistent on the rejection of religion and on other tenets of Soviet ideology. The children explored the forests, made makeshift skis and sleds, and fashioned fishing poles. Parents did their best to protect them from full knowledge of the high death rate. But as malnutrition and exhaustion, exacerbated by terrible hygiene conditions, set in, this became more and more difficult, and when the food ran out, death surrounded them all:

My grandmother . . . was getting more and more sickly. Medical help was not really available unless you could take a patient to the hospital, and we had no means of transportation. She became bedridden in the second year and with the traveling nurses only able to offer an aspirin and some generic drug but once a month, she didn't survive very long. By the time she died, her bedding was crawling with lice and bed-bugs. . . . The infestation was so profound that, despite its value, the bedding had to be burned. . . . She was kind and gentle, and deserved a better end.[108]

The death of a grandmother was one thing, the loss of brothers and sisters or the sole support of the family quite another. When the adults died or could no longer work, even very young children were forced to earn what they could by begging, shoveling snow, or working in the fields and forests.

Eleven-year-old Stanislaw K. lost his mother and a sister in the first winter. He and two other sisters were sent to a Russian orphanage, where he was brutally punished for praying by being "locked in an old toilet for two days," during which time he was given no food. He escaped from the orphanage and managed to rejoin his older brother at his former camp, where he survived by stacking large pieces of lumber.[109] He was lucky.

One source estimates that 20 percent of the children taken to Russia died.[110]

The deported Poles were saved from this slow annihilation by the German attack on the Soviet Union in 1941. A few days after the invasion, the USSR signed a pact of mutual assistance with the Polish government in exile and more than 300,000 Poles were suddenly set free. Release was all very well, but there was now no possibility of returning home.

Thousands of men managed to join Polish Army units being formed in the USSR and, along with several thousand children, were eventually evacuated to Allied-controlled areas in the Middle East. But many others remained in exile in the remoter areas of the USSR for three more years, in conditions little better than those they had endured in the deportee camps. Janka Goldberger, her family miraculously intact after four years in exile and another thirty-day train journey, finally arrived back in Cracow, itself also miraculously undamaged, in the summer of 1945. Here, for the first time, she would learn the details of the extermination of the Jews and realize that she owed her life to her exile in Siberia.[111]

10. Germanizing the West

By the summer of 1940 Western Europe, like Poland, had fallen to the Nazi war machine and tens of millions more human beings were under varying degrees of German sway. In Hitler's grand vision of the New Europe, the former "Nordic" nations such as Holland, Denmark, and Norway would become integral parts of the Reich. The Germanic regions of Belgium and France were to be lumped together with these, while the rest would be carved up into new provinces (Himmler fantasized about a reincarnation of the ancient Duchy of Burgundy as an SS fiefdom) in which, once again, those of German blood were to be identified and, where necessary, extracted. The status of the rest of the French population was never precisely delineated by the racial agencies, but it seems to have fallen somewhere in between the "Nordic," which must be preserved at all costs, and the "Slavic," which was to be gradually eliminated.

These plans were not immediately revealed. Control of the vast conquered area was no easy task and would require local cooperation. In addition, Germany desperately needed the economic resources of the Western occupied lands and had to keep its workers contented enough to ensure maximum production and encourage them to volunteer for work in the Reich. The desirable elements in the Western populations, and especially their children, would, therefore, have to be won over gradually and then be integrated into the German mainstream. How this was done would depend on the racial makeup of each country, its political structure after surrender, and the inclinations of the German administrations, some military and some civilian, that would rule each subjugated nation.

Himmler could hardly wait to start work in the Nordic West. A high-ranking SS deputy was in place in Norway within weeks of its invasion.[1] Himmler himself secretly toured Holland and Belgium as soon as they had surrendered, noting happily that "the people would clearly be a [racial] benefit to Germany."[2] By the summer of 1941, an SS genealogical office was busily digging up records and making lists of Huguenot refugees, the Walloon Reform community, and other subgroups of Netherlandish culture.[3]

Here, in contrast to the East, German forces were expected to behave correctly at all times and discipline was strict. Occupation troops were encouraged to have friendly relations with the peoples of the Nordic lands, so similar in language and blood. In this they would often be bitterly disappointed, not only because nobody likes being conquered, but also because it soon became clear in the West, as it had to the Baltic *Volks-deutsche,* that being Nordic or even Nazi was not quite enough for equal treatment: one must also be German and renounce national loyalties.

The reasons for this were not entirely ideological. Citizens of foreign nations, no matter how racially desirable, were not technically liable for induction into the German armed forces, and Hitler desperately needed more manpower. In 1943, SS officials estimated that there were some 600,000 "Germanic" draft-age boys in the "Nordic" countries alone.[4] The young must therefore, as in the Reich, be prepared through youth activities and indoctrination to volunteer for German formations and, even better, become Reich citizens. In Holland, anyone already holding legal rights to German citizenship, such as German women who had married Dutchmen or businessmen who had become naturalized citizens, were now offered dual citizenship. The response was not great: few were willing to undergo the stringent racial testing required and the dual citizens had little to gain. They risked social ostracism if they stayed in their country of residence, their food rations were not increased to equal those of true Reich Germans until March 1944, and the young men were immediately liable for the German draft.[5] The methods used to lure potential new citizens were not always nice. In both Holland and Norway, underage girls, by applying to the Nazi authorities, could marry German men without the parental permission required by their national laws, and thus immediately gain Reich German citizenship.[6]

The Nazis were no less determined to save and promote the birth of babies of good blood in the new territories than they had been everywhere else. Belgian prisoners of war of Flemish origin were sent home quickly in the hope that they might increase the Germanic populace while their French-speaking countrymen were kept on in Germany as forced labor.[7]

For the racial fanatics there was no purer reservoir of Nordic blood than Norway. Three weeks before the final surrender of that country, Nazi health officials had already suggested to the Lebensborn Society that each Norwegian woman "who presumes that the father of her expected child will be a German soldier should be found out as quickly as possible, perhaps by confidential report to the troop physician." After the usual careful selection she would not only be taken care of during pregnancy and childbirth, but, preferably, be taken to Germany for the birth of the child.

Lebensborn officals were very taken with this idea, noting that it offered "a unique opportunity to transplant Nordic women in large numbers into the Reich," which, astonishingly, was desirable, as "women of purely Nordic appearance are rather rare in the Reich, and since southern Germany is especially poor in Nordic blood, a transfer of purely Nordic women to southern Germany is particularly desirable."

Taking such women to the Reich was necessary because otherwise their children "would be lost to Germany." Once there, the mothers, who, "experience teaches, always want to be near their children," would be likely to stay on. If they didn't, their children would be offered up for adoption.[8]

Himmler and his representative in Norway, Wilhelm Rediess, received this idea enthusiastically. Rediess foresaw a large illegitimate production, which, he thought, would not be a bad thing. Indeed, in an internal memo, he urged that German soldiers be encouraged to have as many children as possible by Norwegian women, in or out of wedlock. This, he mused, might produce "20 or 30 divisions more to defend the space our comrades conquered."[9] Recognizing that some of the ladies in question might not be lucky enough to marry their soldier lovers and thereby "enter the sphere of influence of the German Reich," he suggested that the Norwegian legal code be revised so that these children would not automatically have Norwegian citizenship, but would be made available for adoption in the Reich. This abrogation of Norwegian law was eventually achieved (after much fussing) with the help of the collaborationist government of Vidkun Quisling.[10]

The mothers, who were apt to be unpopular at home due to their relations with the soldiers, were strongly encouraged to go to Germany. They were offered free passage, health insurance, care at Lebensborn homes, and employment. Somewhere between 400 and 2,000 women are said to have taken advantage of this offer. When they did go, their experiences were often not quite as advertised. Many a lover turned out to have lost interest or to already have a wife at home,[11] and the girls had to fall back on the support of Lebensborn. For the far greater number who stayed in Norway, Lebensborn set up nine homes there. The first opened in April 1942. Here, in often overcrowded and unhygienic conditions, more than 6,000 children, of whom some 4,000 were illegitimate, are said to have been born. Of these, fewer than 250 can be documented as having been transferred to the Reich.[12]

The children's journeys, undertaken late in the war, could be harrowing. In the midst of constant Allied bombing, groups of twenty or so tiny children were flown to Leipzig and other German cities. A ship taking others across the Baltic hit a mine and was plunged into darkness. One of the escort nurses, herself a Lebensborn mother who had brought her own son along, "snatched him up and held him in her lap." Later she recounted that the damage to the ship had been slight and "nothing happened to the children." The bunk beds in which they were sleeping had collapsed, but the "children in between were fine." Still, one cannot help thinking they too might have needed laps to sit on.[13]

The precise fate of the other 3,750 or so children is unclear, but some were undoubtedly given to German officials in Norway for eventual return to the Fatherland. As it became known that the children could not be adopted by Norwegian families, the mothers warned one another not to put their babies up for foster care, a resistance that could have dire results. The SS commander of Trondheim threatened to send police to seize one such child, whose mother wished to have it adopted locally, as it "was the child of a German soldier and therefore, according to regulations, could be given only to German foster parents, not Norwegians." This action was stopped only by the concerted intervention of other occupation officials, who employed the mother and were sympathetic to her plight. After this scare, the mother decided to keep her child.[14]

Norway was the only country with such an extensive Lebensborn program. In Holland, governed by Reichskommissar Arthur Seyss-Inquart, who did not want to kowtow to Himmler, such war babies were taken care of by the Nazi Welfare Organization, Himmler's main competitor, and a planned Lebensborn home was never opened.[15] Homes established in Belgium and Denmark also never amounted to much.

There were plenty of babies needing care; the SS itself acknowledged that occupation soldiers had fathered some 85,000 in France alone. The German military authorities felt early on that, as a good occupation practice, they should make it possible for support cases involving German personnel to be dealt with in each conquered country, and not by courts in Germany proper. Hitler thought this a fine idea, but not for everyone. To him it was a racial question: such measures should apply only in Norway and the Netherlands. As for Belgium and France, the Führer declared that "we wish to protect and care for illegitimate *Germanic* children; we have no racial interest in French ones." To regularize this, he issued a decree in July 1942 providing full care for "racially worthy" offspring of Norwegian and Dutch women.[16] The order did contain provisions for extension to other areas, which, after endless debate between the Wehrmacht and the SS, were belatedly applied to a small group of war babies fathered by German forces occupying the remote Channel Islands, inhabited by people of mixed English and French descent and language—but not to the 85,000 in France.[17]

Meanwhile, the Nazis had been busy with their racial rearranging in dismembered France. The borders of the *département* of the Ardennes were closed to returning refugees, who were replaced with *Volksdeutsche* from the East.[18] Within weeks of the fall of France, Alsace-Lorraine was annexed and thousands of its citizens deemed too loyal to France, not to mention all its "alien-race" Jews and North African residents, were unceremoniously deported to Vichy France, the southeastern section of the country still under French control. This was done in the now all too familiar manner: the deportees were given half an hour to pack and were deprived of most of their assets. By the end of July 1940, Alsace and Lorraine had become Reich provinces. The French administration was replaced and the French language totally prohibited in the schools. By 1941, the wearing of berets had been forbidden, children had to sing "Deutschland über Alles" instead of "La Marseillaise" at school, and racial screening was in full swing. German-speaking Alsatians and Lorrainers who were not enthusiastic about their new rulers were, like their Polish brethren, shipped to camps for vetting as "re-Germanizables." German Alsatians resident in other parts of France and South Tyroleans were, meanwhile, moved into the newly annexed area. But so little did Hitler trust the "Germanic" inhabitants of these new provinces that full Reich citizenship was granted only in exceptional cases. Volunteers for the Army and the SS were not accepted until just before the Nazi invasion of Russia, and conscription, instituted in early 1942, was limited to boys who had, by then, some indoctrination at school and in the Labor Service. Even then the Nazis were careful not to have too many Alsatians or Lorrainers in one unit.[19]

In the rest of France, the racial collectors had to be more patient. It was not until late 1943, having assumed control of Vichy France, that Nazi security police, "in the course of a large action . . . against the students of the former Alsatian University of Strasbourg," which had relocated to Clermont-Ferrand at the beginning of the war, were able to examine "107 male and female students along racial lines," as it was "well-known that among the students there are many persons of German descent." Despite the fact that their political opinions were distinctly anti-German, "37 percent of the students were classified as having biologically valuable characteristics" and were slated for "transfer to the Reich."[20] The rest were sent by cattle car to Auschwitz and Buchenwald.[21]

Earlier in 1943 the SS racial agencies had also established a branch in northern France and Belgium and had begun registering possible recruits there. This was a small operation, which targeted mostly Polish-Silesian miners of ethnic German origin who had worked at German mines in the Ruhr and had moved to France during its occupation of the Ruhr after World War I. But no group of ethnic Germans was seemingly too small to ignore, and in March 1943 complex guidelines for vetting went forth to a branch office in Douai.[22] In early March 1944 this office received an order from the chief of the Race and Settlement Main Office in Prague to investigate the family of "the Pole" Johan Nendza, now resident near Lille, for its "fitness for re-Germanization." The inquiry was to be "completed as speedily as possible since the results are urgently needed . . . for the purpose of forming the genealogical decision." Three weeks later M. Nendza was astonished to receive a curt order to present himself, with his whole family, at the offices of the racial examiners in Paris. Four train tickets were enclosed. Nendza wrote back, very politely, to say that he did not understand the request. He had not applied for a job or requested any change of nationality. He felt that there was some mistake, and therefore, he was returning the train tickets, which, he declared firmly, "he had no intention of using." Undeterred, the racial examiners wrote again, this time more politely, to say that the Nendzas must come, but that it was all a formality and their return fare would also be paid. They all went except for Johan's wife, who was "ailing." For each member of this simple family, like so many others, a file card and photograph were made and sent back to the race agency. Along with the cards went a cover letter that rated the parents as rejects. Mme Nendza's evaluation was based on her photograph. Johan was unflatteringly described as "an unharmonious specimen of a person of mixed blood" and "subnormal height." Their children, as was often the case, did better. Both were classified as eligible for "naturalization," as they were "harmonious," the son being "a person of mixed blood of the dinaric-Nordic-east-baltic race" and the daughter "falic-east-baltic."[23]

No one in the northern France group was actually resettled, but everyone over the age of fourteen was carded, graded, and had his identity card stamped with suitable symbols for future exploitation. The long final report on this project is full of complex social statistics and ridiculous commentary. It appears that more than 5,000 persons, among them some 1,000 children, were registered and categorized. Of these only 6.7 percent were worthy of "unrestricted citizenship." Even fewer expressed a desire to be resettled in the East or to go to Germany. But, the report stated

hopefully, these reluctant souls (who had deteriorated under French influence—but not to the level of the Poles in the East) should be considered
as "falling within the conception of a pending folkdom" that could be
brought to an "ethno-politically clear position" through German schooling
and other measures. The agency noted candidly, however, "We are concerned with a group who could not be judged uniformly," adding that "the
people of German stock of Northern France . . . cannot reap for the time
being any advantages . . . since they are rejected by the majority of their
environment and since the general mood of the population of Northern
France, during the months of the processing, was neither pro-German nor
revealed a belief . . . in the final victory on the part of Germany."[24]

While these measures were fine for retrieving those who had a link, no
matter how tenuous, with the Reich proper, the Reichskommissars of each
of the "Nordic" occupied lands had their own ideas about how to win over
the other millions of young people in their power. Things did not start out
well for them in Norway or Holland. The day the Germans had taken
Oslo, Vidkun Quisling, leader of the 4,000 members of the Nasjonal Sam-
ling, the tiny Norwegian Nazi Party, had declared himself Prime Minister.
This was astonishing to all, not only because the King and government
were still in the country and had not surrendered, but also because Quisling, who had spent considerable time ingratiating himself in Berlin, had
never managed to get himself or any member of his party elected to the
Norwegian Parliament. His lack of support immediately became clear to
the Germans, and after six days he was removed from office. To make
things even worse, resistance to the Germans continued for two more
months, during which time Quisling's efforts and person were ridiculed
in what remained of the Norwegian press and future resistance to him
guaranteed.

At the fall of Norway the King and government fled to England and
Hitler appointed Joseph Terboven, the tough former Gauleiter of Essen,
as Reichskommissar. Terboven moved quickly to get control. By the end of
the summer of 1940 the only legal political party was the Nasjonal Sam-
ling, whose members were appointed to fill most high government posts.
The unpopular Quisling was not yet one of them. His role for the time
being would be to build up his party behind the scenes. In this he had
some success: by 1942 there were 40,000 members, and on February 1,
Quisling was allowed to form a government.[25]

By this time the Quisling government's Minister for Education was
deeply involved in trying to bring the universities and schools into line.

Portraits of Quisling were hung in the classrooms, German replaced English as the second language, and teachers were ordered to teach Nazi theory and give the Nazi salute upon entering their classrooms.[26] This they blatantly ignored. Their students joined in the fun. When all the schoolchildren of Oslo were ordered to go to a Hitler Youth exhibition, they obeyed, but kept their eyes on the ground as they ran through.[27] Pro-Norwegian graffiti were everywhere. Children cheered when British planes flew over, and adorned themselves with a series of provocative badges and symbols that, as soon as one was forbidden, they replaced with another. First came flags, then paper clips symbolizing solidarity. Red pixie hats combined with other white and blue garments were popular. When the red hats began to be confiscated from the children's heads, 75 percent of the children switched to blue ones. Less obvious defiance came in the form of a red-tipped match worn on one's hat, which stood for "flaming hatred."[28]

Outraged by the situation in the schools, Quisling ordered obligatory membership for teachers in a "Teachers' Front," described by a pro-Quisling newspaper as "a strait jacket for all those who are unwilling to do their duty to the State and to Norwegian Youth," which did nothing to encourage participation. Quisling's effort was, at any rate, far too late. The teachers, like many other professions, had long since set up an underground communication system. Following instructions sent through this grapevine, 12,000 of Norway's teachers refused in writing to put on the "strait jacket." A hundred thousand parents supported them. Thirteen hundred teachers were arrested, and nearly half were sent through a series of brutal camps to the Arctic. The final camp at Kirkenes was reached after a ghastly boat journey in freezing conditions. There, considerably better treated by the Wehrmacht, the teachers would spend six months. Meanwhile, their colleagues not only did not surrender, but also wrote messages to their pupils praising them for their courage and exhorting them to believe in liberation and to work hard, as "laziness is desertion."[29] After two months of this, Quisling relented and the schools reopened, unchanged.

Efforts to centralize sports and youth activities were no more successful. The young simply boycotted the Nazi competitions. A Norwegian version of the Hitler Youth, theoretically obligatory for every child between ten and eighteen, seems not to have gotten very far either, due to widespread resistance and a blasting by the Church hierarchy, who declared unacceptable "the forced mobilization of all children from the age of nine or ten upwards and their subjection to influences which innumerable par-

Reichskommissar Arthur Seyss-Inquart of the conquered Netherlands sees off Dutch children being sent to summer camps and indoctrination in Germany.

ents must regard as intolerable in regard to the obligations laid on them by their conscience."[30]

Farther south, in the Netherlands, similar events were taking place, but at a different pace. Reichskommissar Seyss-Inquart was equally interested in control, but wary of the Dutch Nazi Party, or NSB, which was far more established than that of Norway. Like Quisling, its leader, A. A. Mussert, dreamt of having his own Nazi nation independent of German control. This was not at all what the Reich Nazis had in mind. They envisioned a completely restructured Netherlands, which, like Austria, would be annexed to Germany.[31] Seyss-Inquart realized that such a drastic change would not be popular so soon after the defeat of the Dutch, while surrender discussions were still in progress. His policy, therefore, would be one of gradual Nazification and circumvention of Mussert and his cronies.

To the citizens of Holland, whose Queen and government had also fled to England, it seemed important to try to maintain their usual lives. Four days after the invasion, before the surrender was firm, school authorities in the northern province of Groningen had ordered their schools to keep functioning as "normally as possible." No one was excused from attendance. They appealed to both students and teachers to stay off the streets, avoid contact with the military, and "speak as little as possible" about "the circumstances in which we find ourselves." They were also asked to remain calm and support one another in the realization of "the responsibility that everyone has for a loyal attitude in the face of the occupying power."[32]

As usual, things did not seem too bad at the beginning. The schools soon reopened, and in a grand gesture, whose purpose, he declared, was to thank the Dutch for taking care of Austrian children after World War I, Seyss-Inquart arranged for 6,000 Dutch children to go to summer camps in Austria.[33] This was done with much fanfare and photo opportunities of the Reichskommissar seeing off trainloads of smiling children waving swastika flags.

Reality soon set in. One teacher noticed that most of the eight-year-olds in her class, when assigned compositions, wrote quite despairingly about the invasion. On the playground the little ones played war games and took "prisoners." Things were worse in the fall, when several high schools had to be closed for anti-German demonstrations; in a parochial school in The Hague the following song was heard:

> *Saint Nicholas cannot come*
> *And he will bring us nothing this year*
> *Because the Krauts have come*
> *And are the bosses here*
> *And they take everything away:*
> *Coffee, chocolate, and tea.*[34]

It also now appeared that education was not an area in which Seyss-Inquart wanted to go all that slowly. School libraries had been purged in the summer of 1940 and anti-German passages had to be excised immediately from textbooks while new editions were awaited; these would emphasize only *Volkisch* aspects of Dutch history such as the migration of Germanic tribes into Holland. Questions on Dutch national history were forbidden on examinations. The teaching of English and French were subordinated to German. Students were also warned not to show any outward signs of loyalty to the Dutch royal house.

Patriotic teachers took full advantage of the page- and paragraph-excising sessions, during which the banished passages became more memorable by their very exclusion. The absurdity of some of the cuts was happily emphasized: in one popular book a scene in which the hero tries to jump over a stream, but falls in instead, had to be excised because it was considered to be a negative view of Hitler's plan to invade England. Children drew cartoons in the margins to remind them of what had once been there. One class, ordered to get rid of its first-year Greek text, written by a

Jewish classicist, simply cut out or blacked out the author's name—a girl who covered hers up with a strip of orange paper, a reference to the Dutch royal House of Orange, was not criticized by the teacher. Fifty years later it was the only author's name the girl still remembered.[35]

To counter all this, a pro-German, but not NSB, official had been put in charge of education and was required to report to a German supervisor who was a member of the SS. This gentleman was itching to eliminate the denominational school systems in Holland, but was restrained by Seyss-Inquart, who was all too aware of the very strong Catholic and Protestant allegiances in the Netherlands. There were other methods of control, however. In September 1940, the Germans declared that they had the right to approve the appointment or firing of teachers in all types of schools. The measure was gradually tightened so that the Nazis could, when necessary, dissolve recalcitrant school boards and replace them with more cooperative ones. The Dutch teacher corps, traditionally divided between Protestant, Catholic, and state schools, did not defy the Nazis as openly or with as much unity as the Norwegians had, but their resistance was strong. In this many of the officials of the Ministry of Education were tacitly complicit.

In early 1942, little progress having been made, strict Nazi guidelines were promulgated to "put an end to irregularities." Any "attitude other than decisively positive cooperation in the formation of our youth" was not permissible. All school inspectors were required to confirm in writing that they did not have any problem supporting the guidelines. One brave soul replied that he saw no reason for such a confirmation, since the guidelines "left no freedom of choice: they are an order," and that he was perfectly aware of the consequences of not obeying them. This inspector was fired a few months later.[36]

By the summer of 1943, teachers and school administrators were "resigning" and being arrested with increasing frequency.[37] The circumstances under which they were forced to leave were often not pretty, depending as they did on denunciations, the corrupt enlistment of children, and the lowest aspects of human pride and ambition, as the following unedifying case, which could have come from any Nazi-controlled country, demonstrates.

On July 9, 1943, a school inspector from Heerlen, in the southern province of Limburg, reported on an ongoing investigation into the actions of two teachers, Mssrs Vleugels and Vermeulen, at a Catholic boys school that provided two years of continuing instruction for working-class children after the six elementary years. The inspector complained that the board of the school seemed not to want to talk to him, though both it and the teachers knew perfectly well what the problem was. On July 7 the inspector had visited the school and found that both teachers in question were doing nothing to make clear to the students, aged twelve to fourteen, what the great problems being dealt with in Europe were, and were not promoting better relations between the Dutch and Germans. Indeed, opined the inspector, that was exactly why Vleugels and Vermeulen seemed to have been appointed in the first place. The inspector had then taken the trouble to give a little history lesson to the classes of the teachers in question, during which he had emphasized the fact that the Netherlands had had continuing wars with the British in the seventeenth and eighteenth centuries, while their relations with Germany had always been good. In the course of the lessons, it had become clear that the children not only knew nothing of these things, but that they were also very anti-German. The boys were also unable to name all the Germanic peoples and had no knowledge of economic relations between Germany and Holland, nor of the fact that what was good for Germany was good for the Netherlands. The inspector was sure that the suspect teachers had never taught history this way and that they never would. He felt that they were unfit to teach in the school and that their unfitness sprang from their anti-German and anti–National Socialist mentality, which also led him to question their loyalty.

But these ideological problems were not the whole story. The inspector also had a written declaration on the subject from "the only National Socialist student in the class," and a fellow teacher, Mr. Ramecker, had said that both of them had often made anti-German remarks to school personnel. Indeed, Ramecker had helpfully written down all such remarks in a little notebook, which had now disappeared. Ramecker suspected the two teachers of stealing it. This was confirmed by the fact that some of the students had noticed Vermeulen searching Ramecker's desk, and had seen the notebook in his hands. Now, the suspect two were avoiding Ramecker, "who is pro-German." Getting personal, the inspector then went on to say that "characteristic of the mentality of Mr. Vermeulen, in addition to the things that you already know about him, is the fact that, last year, when I already was an inspector, he turned his back on me when we met at the station." In a pompous conclusion, he continued that he did not wish to force the appointment of a particular teacher, but only to do his duty to see that the children were entrusted to teachers who would educate them in "a positive way."[38] The accused teachers had good reason to be afraid: dismissal could mean deportation to a concentration or forced labor camp and loss of all support for their families.

The Nazis' gradual but relentless pressure on schools in the Germanic countries was not limited to the intellectual sphere any more than it was at home. Here too categorizations and listings were introduced that would help locate the undesirables when the moment came to be rid of them. Despite the application of many of the Nuremberg Laws, Jewish children were not immediately excluded from the schools. But by the spring of 1941, German security forces in Holland had noticed signs of resistance: entire school outings to swimming pools had been canceled because Jewish pupils were not allowed to enter such places. Teachers were said to be giving Jewish students better grades in order to show their anti-Nazi feelings, and schools known to be "pro-Jewish" were very popular, even with non-Jews.[39] At the end of the term in July 1941, therefore, all Jewish schoolchildren were given special registration forms that they were required to fill out then and there, and a few days after the new term began in September, they were informed that they must withdraw and go to separate schools.[40] Both the Catholic and Protestant schools strongly protested the removal of baptized children of Jewish origin from their institutions. The churches were not punished for this defiance. Seyss-Inquart, in order to "spare them the martyrdom" that he felt was their real objective, did not reply to the church protests, but instead, through the Dutch Jewish Council, threatened the parents of the Jewish pupils if they refused to take part in the segregation. Protest in the public schools was silenced in the same manner.[41] School authorities quickly organized the necessary reshuffling of facilities, as non-Jews were removed from buildings taken over for the 10,000 children who were affected, and vice versa. For some Jewish students this now meant a very long trek to school, as they were not allowed to use public transportation. In the countryside, where many schools had only one or two Jewish students, special arrangements had to be made. This latter problem was solved in January 1942 when all Jews living in small towns were required to leave their homes and move to Amsterdam.[42]

In August 1943, school inspectors were also instructed to list all children who had "speech defects" so that they could be "helped." Categories included children in special schools, such as the seriously hearing-impaired and those "who spoke poorly or not at all." In these doomed institutions the Jewish pupils had kindly been allowed to remain.[43]

Children in primary and secondary schools were generally not greatly affected by Nazi measures; but to this day they remember the expulsion of their Jewish classmates. One girl defiantly drew a portrait of an expelled friend on the blackboard. For days, no one could bring themselves to erase it. But it was dangerous to leave the drawing there, and the deed was finally done, with some emotion, by one of the teachers.[44]

It was soon clear that complete control of the Dutch schools would, as was the case in the Reich proper, take a long time. A chain of entirely German schools was, therefore, created to promote Germanization. Before the war eight German schools had already been established; it was now only necessary to be sure that they were staffed by Nazis. Forty-two more such schools were soon set up in buildings requisitioned from resentful town fathers. But their capacity of 10,000 was only slowly filled. Catholic Reich Germans avoided them, and 30 percent of the places were therefore opened to Dutch children, who were expected to come from Dutch Nazi (NSB) families.

From the beginning the NSB children had had a hard time at school. Within weeks of the German takeover, it was clear to everyone who was "right" or "wrong," and nowhere more so than at school. The NSB children were relentlessly teased and even beaten up. These incidents were often not punished by "right" teachers. Things were not improved when NSB students denounced popular teachers, as they had in Heerlen. The transfer of Dutch children to German schools was at first forbidden by the nationalistic Dutch Nazi leader Mussert, but hundreds of protective NSB parents sent their children anyway, and Mussert was soon forced to relent.[45]

An attempt to set up a Dutch version of the Nazi boarding schools (NAPOLAs), known as NIVOs (Netherlands Institutes for Folkish Education), was a flop, due to NSB-Nazi competition for control. The German Nazis considered the NSB insufficiently interested in purity of race and excessively attached to their religions. Priority of language became a major issue. An SS officer involved in the school explained, with almost mystical passion, why the Dutch boys could not get the right message from the frequent Nazi ceremonies at the school unless they were fluent in German:

> Not only music shapes the ceremonies, but even more essentially the word. And the word that is spoken and professed, that word is in the Führer's *Mein Kampf* and in his speeches. That is the foundation for everything. . . . In order to understand the word of the Führer, one must know and especially, experience, his language. One must absorb it into oneself as a possession.[46]

The NIVOs were soon closed and replaced by two "Reichsschule," one for boys and one for girls, which were completely under German control.

Things did not go too well at these boarding schools either. The boys' school, which opened in September 1942, was set up in a former Jesuit monastery in Valkenburg, in the east of Holland. The local population was immediately outraged when the school demolished the monastery church in order to make space for a projected gymnasium. The students were equally unhappy with the drill-sergeant-like methods of some of the teachers, who often hit and kicked them. Not surprisingly, the ten- to twelve-year-olds cried a lot and wanted to go home. No one had told them or their parents that classes would be conducted entirely in German, and many had great difficulties with their lessons. There was also fussing about the lack of religion and the fact that Protestants and Catholics were mixed together, not normally the case in Holland. Students were to be brought in from Germany to maintain the two-thirds German majority and to inspire the others, but homogenization was difficult, as the Reich boys, resplendent in full regalia, were required to spend a great deal of time at Hitler Youth meetings, which were closed to the "foreign" Dutch boys. Eventually this rule was modified and other mellowing improvements were instituted: housemothers were hired for the unhappy little boys, a parents committee was set up, which raised funds for a nice tapestry for the school, and a serious PR effort was made to attract more Dutch children and counteract the continuing opposition of Mussert.

To attract more students, a fancy brochure was published full of the universal boarding-school-type photos of immaculately groomed and uniformed boys earnestly reading in the library. The headmaster even went so far as to make a film about school life, which was shown at theaters all over Holland. This was generally well received by Dutch Nazis, though some critics took exception to the scenes showing boys throwing grenades, which, they felt, might put off the average Dutchman, and said that there had been too much emphasis on sports and not enough on the very nice bedrooms and washing facilities in the schools.

Despite all, the headmaster trusted some of the boys in the first graduating class enough to send them off to indoctrinate Polish *Volksdeutsche* for their Land Year, and by February 1944, things were going so swimmingly that Himmler himself came to visit. Alas, all was brought to an abrupt end by the Allied invasion of Normandy, when the entire school was evacuated to the NAPOLA at Bensburg, just across the border, and eventually, by war's end, on to Schleswig-Holstein.[47]

The girls' school was far less successful, if considerably more colorful. Its headmistress was the Baroness Juul Op Ten Noort, who had met, and clearly charmed, Himmler at a prewar Moral Rearmament meeting. The

Baroness was very pro-German and for that reason had been thrown out of the NSB by Mussert, but she was consoled by Himmler with her job as headmistress. The school curriculum followed the Nazi Party line for women. Mme Op Ten Noort taught the racial studies class and served as a living example of Nazi procreationist policy when she became pregnant and disappeared for a time to "study in the East," only to return with an "adopted" child named Heinrich, who was generally thought to be the son of the Reichsführer SS himself. This did not go over too well with the parents of the girls or enhance their reputation at the boys' school, whose faculty found the girls to be snotty "little goddesses" who lived in a slovenly manner and did not even use proper tablecloths on Sunday.[48]

Mussert was more successful in keeping control of the Dutch equivalent of the Hitler Youth. The National Youth Storm (NJS), as it was called, banned in 1933, was revived at the German takeover. The Youth Storm had a long way to go. In 1940 its membership was only 1,500, way behind the Boy Scouts (46,000) or the Catholic Youth (32,000). By war's end there were still only some 12,000 "stormers" and "stormsters." The Hitler Youth, immediately after the fall of Holland, sent in representatives who invited NJS children and leaders to come to Germany. Mussert, fearful that his youth would be lost to Holland, reluctantly authorized a few short summer visits to HJ training camps. He need not have worried. Though many of the Dutch children were favorably impressed with the camp activities, the feelings were not mutual. The visitors were criticized for giving the Dutch Nazi greeting of "Hou zee" and not "Heil Hitler." Some German children refused to speak to them, as "an enemy stays an enemy." The Dutch youth leaders, new to the whole concept, could not understand much of the racial and folkdom lectures; they were outraged when one history teacher declared that the only Dutch person he had ever heard of was Rembrandt, who was really German. On top of this they were told that Holland's heroic, eighty-year-long fight for independence from Hapsburg Spain in the sixteenth and seventeenth centuries, which holds the same status in Holland as the American Revolution does in the United States, was a "mistake of history" that had separated them from their German Motherland. These statements led one Dutch boy to declare vehemently that acceptance of such imperial German teachings would be a "betrayal of our Fatherland." At the end of the sessions the Dutch were evaluated by their German mentors. The report cards were not flattering. Few were thought to have "leadership" potential: one girl was criticized for talking about her English boyfriend, others for talking back, crying, being "colorless," or too religious. None of the girls who applied for membership in the Bund

Deutscher Mädel was accepted, and the visits were not repeated in subsequent years.[49]

Pressures on the elementary and secondary school systems of Francophone Belgium and France were superficially much the same as those in Holland. But in these non-Nordic areas the Germans promoted fragmentation and not a unified system. In Belgium, the Germans, as always taking advantage of local problems, joined in the eternal competition for control between Flemish and Francophone culture, but they did not yet attempt to challenge the control of the Catholic Church over most of the Belgian school system.

In France, schools opened as usual in September 1940, and early acts of defiance were soon suppressed. Flowers put on British military graves by children on All Saints' Day were removed. In Paris, an entire section of the new military government, the Kultur und Schule division, devoted itself to the revision of textbooks and other scholarly pursuits. As there had been little time for proper vetting before school opened, here, too, many texts were purified by simply tearing out offensive pages, such as descriptions of the German defeat in World War I and maps showing Alsace as part of France. For after-school the Germans promoted a French-language comic book that featured nasty caricatures of Jews and a hero named Marc le Téméraire, who eventually volunteered to fight on the Eastern Front.[50] French education regulations and appointments were closely supervised, buildings were arbitrarily requisitioned, and German officials were apt to drop in to classrooms without warning to see if the propaganda posters they sent out were properly hung. German language study was made obligatory and German Institutes were set up in provincial cities in the Occupied Zone.

None of this could stop the innumerable adolescent pranks and manifestations of nationalism aimed at making the Germans look ridiculous, many of which were encouraged by teachers. The "Marseillaise" and the British national anthem were defiantly sung as German soldiers went by, "V" graffiti were everywhere, and until the Nazis figured it out, the bizarre sight of students carrying two fishing poles, or *"deux gaules,"* was seen in many a city street.

The Germans were not the only ones who wished to make changes in the French educational system. Marshal Henri-Philippe Pétain, head of the new French government, which, to his surprise, had not been allowed to return to Paris but had been relegated to the provincial spa town of

Vichy, also had visions of a New Order for youth and family that were remarkably similar to those of Adolf Hitler. The major difference was that Vichy favored a prominent role for the Catholic Church. For generations, French education had been riven by a debate over the secular versus the clerical in the schools. With Pétain and his "Révolution Nationale," the pendulum swung back to the latter.[51] In addition, many high-ranking Army officers blamed the ignominious fall of France not on their own ineptitude and their outdated reliance on the Maginot Line, but on the teachers of the secular primary system, who had "failed to instill in young Frenchmen the spirit of sacrifice." Pétain even told American Ambassador William Bullitt that "schoolmasters" had brought France to her knees. This obviously called for drastic reform of the system:

> The era of least effort is over. We no longer desire to see hanging about our city streets young men sloppy in their bearing, slack and slovenly in their behavior, sadly vulgar in their talk. We can no longer suffer those young fops whose sole ambition was to rise late, install themselves in a café, allow free rein to their confused desires and take themselves off to bed late, content with their empty day. A novelist of immorality [André Gide], who, we hope, will no longer have any readers, set them on the road to defeat by teaching them that "every pleasure was good to be taken." Our country, to be saved, needs bold men capable of achieving something.[52]

The Vichy reforms began right away. By July 1940, only weeks after the armistice, teachers deemed "too independent" began to be dismissed, among them men who had fled during the fighting, political activists, and foreigners. In October, Jews were forced to resign and Freemasons had to sign a declaration renouncing their membership. All teachers were eventually required to sign a loyalty oath to the Pétain government. The new French regime had its own ideas about books and began a campaign to get rid of works that were deemed too "republican" or anti-clerical. When combined with the German efforts, this process, left to a variety of local officials with a variety of ideologies, caused chaos and confusion as to which were the "right" books, and had little real effect.[53]

It soon became clear that Vichy France was no less fragmented than the Third Republic, which had preceded it. Everyone had his own ideas about how to transform youth and their education, a situation the Germans did nothing to relieve, as a unified French youth was the last thing they desired. Some Vichyites urged more sports and Nazi-like indoctrination. Others harked back to the days of chivalry and Joan of Arc. The Maid of

Orléans was, in fact, useful all across the French spectrum, both for having been anti-English and for having rid France of an invader. All factions called for more service and obedience, discipline, honesty, and morality, with everyone in his place. "Liberté, Fraternité, Egalité" was, significantly, replaced by Pétain's "Travail, Famille, Patrie."

None of it was much fun. Church and state inveighed against coed activities of any kind, and dancing was discouraged. That was not all. In an effort to reconnect Frenchmen with their native soil and break down what was viewed as the overcentralization of the Third Republic, regionalism was heavily promoted. In the provinces children were taken on field trips to local historical sites and given courses in regional dialects such as Breton and Flemish. This was fine with the Germans, who had already carved considerable chunks off the borders of France and planned to reduce it to a small rump state in the future.[54]

In the short history of Vichy a series of ministers of education culminating in the very pro-German Abel Bonnard decreed and revoked a dizzying array of initiatives for the schools. God was put in and taken out of the secular schools several times. The stately Marshal Pétain, who, like Hitler, had no children, but who loved to visit schools, floated above it all, and graciously received the pupils' flowers, songs, and obligatory letters.

Despite all the ferment, little actually changed in the French school system. The separate primary and elite secondary tracks continued despite innumerable suggestions, many not new, for their reform, and nothing from battles to hunger ever caused the sacred Baccalauréat exam to be canceled. Efforts to introduce more physical education, to this day not a strong tradition in France, were not a success, as many parents could not see any reason for it and such luminaries as the archbishop of Bourges declared that "the natural method used, in which young males display themselves almost naked, offends decorum and shocks our Christian souls." Even worse, the athletes might be seen by girls, "and we know the inmost mind of adolescents." His fellow bishop at Viviers noted that exercises were "unbecoming to females and should be avoided."[55]

If the Germans in France were determined to stamp out any anti-German manifestations in the schools, they were even more determined to prevent the establishment of a strong national youth movement by Vichy. The Scouts and Catholic Youth continued on as ever. But, inspired by their desire to reform France and raise it from prewar decadence, a plethora of French organizers would eventually set up new groups. Two of these, officially sanctioned by the Vichy government, were considered too nationalistic by the Germans and were not allowed to operate in the Occupied Zone. The Compagnons de France, organized immediately after the armistice to take care of teenagers who had been scattered about by the invasion and those who were unemployed, was operating a camp by August 1940. Its regulations and ceremonies, with much flag raising, saluting, and an elegant dark blue uniform adorned with the *coq gaulois*, were much like the Hitler Youth, but its activities were not militaristic and its orientation was decidedly French. Boys were sent out to harvest crops, build roads, and, it being France, run restaurants. There was even a music and theater section.

The heavily funded Compagnons were criticized variously for being dropouts, sheltering Jewish and Gaullist members (which was true), and, by the Church, as being too totalitarian. German suspicions were not misplaced: by 1942 many of the Compagnon leaders, disillusioned with Vichy, were deeply involved in Resistance activities.

For boys of draft age, some of whom had already been inducted but had not completed training by the time of France's surrender, Vichy set up the Chantiers de la Jeunesse. This group, which was made obligatory for all French boys reaching draft age in subsequent years, was somewhat Boy Scout–like in atmosphere and was headed by the former French Army General Paul de la Porte du Theil. Small camps were scattered in remote areas all over Vichy France, and there was also a Naval Section. Emphasis was on "manly" training combined with uplifting group sessions around campfires. The by now familiar themes of godliness, cleanliness, community, moral education, exercise, and discipline were combined with supposedly inspiring manual labor of various kinds. Indoctrination sessions and ceremonies in which the troops sang songs with lyrics such as "Venerable one, I would that I were able to kneel, simply, as one does before the Holy Image at your feet"[56] glorified Pétain and earlier suitable historic heroes (Charlemagne, Napoleon, Louis XIV) and vilified the recently defeated Third Republic. The Germans suspected that the Chantiers were an army in waiting and kept them under careful surveillance. This seems not to have been the case, although the Chantiers and their large alumni organization could, according to General de la Porte, have enabled the French to field forty divisions in a short time. As the threat of an Allied invasion of France increased, the General was arrested and, as we shall see, the Chantier youths were used to supply manpower for quite a different purpose.[57]

The universities of the Western occupied nations of course did not escape the German desire for total control either. In the Nordic lands, unlike the Slavic ones, the various Nazi governors and commanders were determined to keep the universities going not only as training institutions for vital professions but also as centers for Germanization. The idea was to have these universities conform in every way to those of the Reich, a process that would require the by now usual purges of faculty, appointment of professors of Nazi ideology, and the introduction of racial studies. Once again the Nazis would be surprised at the resistance to the suppression of religions and national loyalties even by those sympathetic to their ideas. The university faculties and students were determined to continue in their traditional manner, and were particularly resistant to the appointment of their collaborationist countrymen to professorial chairs.

The earliest student reactions were fragmented, nationalistic, and passionate, consisting in the main of graffiti insulting to the Reich, rudeness to German soldiers, defiant bouts of singing, and a proliferation of anti-German leaflets and information sheets. In the summer of 1940 no one was sure how long the occupation would last or how extensive German control would be. The Sorbonne in Paris reopened within weeks of the French surrender. Officially this was done so that students could take the exams they had missed during the invasion, but secretly because keeping the classrooms filled would discourage requisition of the buildings by German agencies.[58]

As the summer wore on, the inability of the Germans to reduce Great Britain to surrender sustained the defiant student mood across the Continent. At the beginning of the academic year in Oslo, 800 members of the Student Union, who previously had protested the brutal arrests by the Nazis of more than 1,000 Czech students, rose as one to support the declaration of their honored speaker, seventy-year-old writer Dr. Johan Scharffenberg, that their exiled King Haakon was "the living expression of the will of the Norwegian people to regain their freedom and independence." This was not at all what the Nazis had in mind, and both the speaker and the president of the Student Union were immediately arrested, but, for the time being, the school remained open.[59]

In late October students in Paris, already outraged by Pétain's friendly meeting with Hitler at Montoire, demonstrated peacefully, but firmly, to protest the arrest by the Germans, condoned by Vichy, of famed physicist Paul Langevin, a longtime anti-Fascist whose daughter also had made the mistake of marrying a Jew. The large crowd was contained by a combined Franco-German police force impressively armed with machine guns.[60] This incident inspired both the Germans and the university authorities to issue dire warnings against any further demonstrations, especially on the

fast-approaching Armistice Day, November 11, when the French traditionally celebrated the German defeat in World War I and memorialized
their war dead. The red flag had now been raised. Plans for a demonstra-
tion at the Arc de Triomphe spread like wildfire—by word of mouth and
leaflets—through the lycées and universities of Paris.

On the morning of the eleventh all went to class as usual. It was not
until the afternoon that ever growing groups of students began to be seen
wandering aimlessly up and down the Champs-Elysées below the Arc de
Triomphe. All was well until a German staff car pushed its way into one of
the groups. This provoked shouts of "Vive la France" and rude comments
about the Germans. At the same moment a phalanx of a thousand high
school students from the famous Lycée Janson entered the Etoile, followed by others from the Lycée Carnot and many more. The idea was to
keep moving at all times and walk under the Arc de Triomphe in groups of
three or four, which, the students theorized, would give the police no
grounds for action.

Unfortunately, Hitler salutes given by uniformed boys from a French
Fascist youth group that had its headquarters on the Champs-Elysées led
some of the passive demonstrators to lose their cool. Stones were thrown
and windows broken. The French police at first did nothing. The Germans, not so shy, arrested five students. Now the French police began to
charge into the amoeba-like crowd, which had continued to grow. By
6:00 p.m. the Germans had had enough. Heavily armed, motorized Wehrmacht units appeared at both ends of the Champs-Elysées and began
zigzagging on the sidewalks in their vehicles. These maneuvers, plus the
use of machine guns, dispersed the demonstrators in less than an hour.[61]

Five days later all the universities in Paris were closed on the grounds
that the demonstrations had been "incompatible with the dignity of the
German Army."[62] The lycées remained open, but under guard. Wild
rumors, later disproved, of many deaths and injuries circulated. In fact,
only a few participants were injured or arrested, but the incident, with its
blatant use of force, made clear to all the realities of open resistance to the
Nazis. The masks of "correctness" had fallen; a time of fear and waiting
had arrived.

Ten days after the closure of the universities in Paris and Dijon, students
in Holland at the University of Leiden and the Delft Technical University
also went on strike, to protest an order expelling all Jewish professors and
instructors from Dutch institutions of higher learning. At Leiden, which
stood to lose ten faculty members, the students, led by a popular professor,
defiantly sang the national anthem in their assembly before dispersing.

Both schools were closed down. Delft reopened in April 1941, but Leiden, Holland's premier university of liberal arts, whose motto was *"Presidium Libertatis,"* or "Bulwark of Liberty," and where resistance to the appointment of Nazi professors and the teaching of courses in racial science persisted, would remain closed until the war was over. Its students, after being allowed to take certain examinations, were dispersed to other institutions.

Some of these were run by pro-Nazis, but in most the *rector magnificus,* as the president of a university was known, was all too aware of events in Czechoslovakia and Poland, where thousands of students and faculty had been sent to concentration camps, and agonized over what to do. Closure of the universities would leave the students in a state of limbo that would immediately be exploited by the Nazis. Some rectors therefore urged students to keep politics off campus and continue their studies.[63]

Despite these warnings, continued purging of the faculties and the increase of Nazi-skewed lectures led to sporadic protests by both faculty and students, which were harshly punished. But Seyss-Inquart was loath to give up on his idea of converting the Dutch elite through the university system, so most universities stayed open. In June 1941 the students again protested the imposition of quotas for Jewish students, who by October would no longer be allowed to graduate. This led to abolition of all student organizations. The measure did not stop students from becoming involved in resistance activities. But it was not until 1942 and the introduction of extreme measures in two areas—Jewish persecution and forced labor—that resistance would become the central activity of many students' lives.

PART IV Radicalization and Resistance

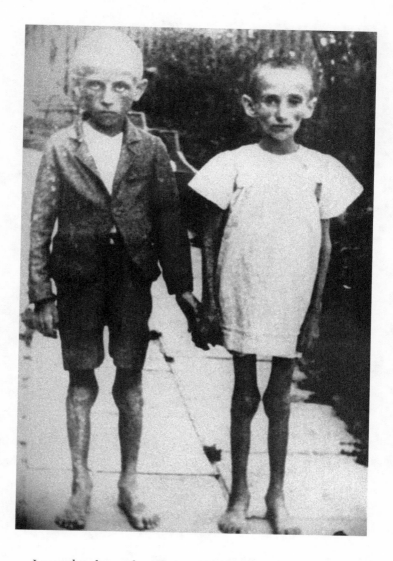

I wanted to discuss the suffering of humanity in general, but perhaps we'd better confine ourselves to the sufferings of children.

FYODOR DOSTOYEVSKY, *The Brothers Karamazov*

11. Nightmares in Utopia: Russia and Greece

In late June 1941, Hitler could finally turn to the conquest of the territory that from the beginning had been the real object of his desire: the vast stretches united under the aegis of the Soviet Union. The Nordic nations of the West were mostly in his control, and Britain, almost everyone thought, would not last long. France, of no interest to Hitler except as an economic asset, posed no further threat, and the Balkans, including Greece, had also been somewhat shakily secured.

In retrospect it seems incredible that the Soviet government, always suspicious of its unlikely ally, despite warnings from many sources, was so surprised when German forces crossed its frontiers in the early hours of June 22, 129 years to the day after Napoleon, whom Hitler particularly hated, had done the same. The Germans were more than a month behind their planned schedule, but Hitler was confident of another rapid blitzkrieg victory, mistakenly believing, as invaders often do, that the supposedly primitive and downtrodden peoples of the Soviet Union would quickly abandon their regime. And indeed, many of them were at first so inclined, but the racial and economic policies of the Nazis, which were applied with the greatest possible brutality, instead inspired the majority of Russians to ferocious resistance in this conflict, which to this day is referred to in the former Soviet Union as the "Great Patriotic War" and not as World War II.

Hitler's dogma concerning the Jews and Slavs was by now well established and, as we have seen, underlay the ethnic cleansing and resettlement of populations already in progress in Poland. To these were now added the "Asiatics" and "Mongols" of Russia, in fact all one and the same. In Hitler's view, Russia, the "colossal empire in the East," was now "ripe for dissolution," which would occur as soon as "Bolshevik" and "Jewish" domination, virtually synonymous to him, were eliminated.[1] After that, much of the Soviet territory could also be colonized by settlers of German blood.

Some were already there: the Nazis planned to embrace the 1.5 million ethnic Germans, long resident in the USSR, who were expected to play an important role in the new scene. But these were only a tiny fraction of the

A German soldier prepares to execute a Jewish mother and child in the USSR.

projected Germanic populace. To make room for the future thousands who would be brought in from the Reich and its newly occupied lands, Himmler mused at a gathering of SS officers, the "Slavic" population would have to be "reduced" by 30 million,[2] an estimate later raised by Nazi racial analysts to 46 to 51 million.[3]

Nazi resettlement experience in Poland had been instructive. Its chaotic nature had not discouraged the ideologues, but better organization and tougher guidelines were clearly needed. For Russia, therefore, precise directives dealing with political and racial policy were debated and negotiated long before the invasion. Hitler soon discarded all thoughts of local rule in favor of the total destruction of indigenous leadership and bureaucracy. In the months before their forces were to go into action, the Army High Command and that of the SS were repeatedly instructed on Nazi population policy for the East, and turf divisions for the carrying out of various activities were carefully drawn. In March 1941, military leaders were reminded by Hitler that they must "rid themselves of obsolete ideologies" and that the coming war could not be fought in "a knightly fashion," but was "a struggle . . . of ideologies and racial differences" that would "have to be conducted with unprecedented, unmerciful and unrelenting harshness."[4] It would, in short, continue the "war of annihilation."

The "harshness" would encourage actions not usually permitted to the military. The great cities of Russia, and particularly Leningrad, viewed as the seat of Communism, would not be allowed to surrender, but were to be "wiped off the face of the earth"[5] without concern for their populations, which, indeed, were to be shot down as they attempted to flee. All "commissars," who were "bearers of ideologies directly opposed to National Socialism," a vague group that included anyone who could be remotely associated with the Soviet government, were to be liquidated, even though this was forbidden by the rules of war.

That was just the beginning. On May 13, in the so-called Jurisdictional Order, German forces were authorized to punish "offenses committed by enemy civilians" by shooting them on the spot instead of wasting time with courts-martial and the like. Although soldiers were supposed to consult with their officers before carrying out executions, it was ordered that they not be prosecuted for these executions if they failed to do so, "even where the deed is at the same time a military crime or offense."[6] This opened the way for the wanton killing of entire communities, particularly those suspected of giving aid to refugees and partisans. Those to be exterminated included Russia's five million Jews, who were continually described as vermin and linked to banditry and Bolshevism in the reams of Nazi propaganda aimed at the troops.[7]

To get this dogma across to the average soldier, a special booklet, titled *Der Untermensch*, was issued. This remarkable document, replete with photographs of starving and brutalized Eastern children juxtaposed with happy Germans doing folk dances, and written in the purplest of prose, must rank among the most outrageous propaganda documents ever published:

> The *Untermensch*—which seems biologically similar to humans with its hands, feet, eyes, mouth and a sort of brain, is, in fact, a totally different, terrible creature . . . mentally and morally lower than any animal. Within this creature is a cruel chaos of unsuppressed fury, inexpressible will to destruction, the most primitive greed and unconcealed obscenity. Subhuman and nothing else. . . .
>
> For self-preservation he needed the swamp, hell, but not the Sun. And this underworld of Subhumans found their leader: the wandering Jew! He understood them . . . he fanned their lowest lusts and greeds, he let horror come over humanity. . . .
>
> Endless stretch the steppes of the Russian area. . . . Rough and steep is the cultural drop between Central Europe and this gigantic area. . . . Poorly utilized, fruitful womb of black earth which could be a paradise, a California of Europe[!] . . . in actuality uncared for and wantonly neglected . . . it is an eternal indictment of the Subhuman and his system of sovereignty.[8]

Although the Wehrmacht was thus exhorted and authorized to carry out these draconian directives as part of the battle plan, the Nazis were not sure, after its timid performance in Poland, that it would do so with sufficient vigor. Taking no chances this time, four mobile special units, the infamous Einsatzgruppen, bigger and more sophisticated than the units used in Poland, were created to clear the newly conquered areas of as many Jews and "Bolsheviks" as possible during the fighting phase of the invasion, that is, before the complications of a law-ridden civil administration and greater public scrutiny were in place.

More positively, they were also supposed to seek out and register Russians of German origin wherever they found them, and, after eliminating those who had succumbed to Bolshevism, put the rest into positions of authority across the countryside. A Lebensborn operative was put in charge of this program and ordered to "immediately take care of the Ethnic-German children which are still of good and unmixed blood."[9] The units, controlled by the SS, would, by special agreement between SS agencies and the military High Command, be allowed to operate on the front lines within Wehrmacht combat areas.[10] By early June the Einsatzgruppen had been briefed, trained, and positioned with the Army groups poised to enter the USSR.

The invasion force was gigantic. Some 3.2 million German troops (whose experienced officers by now had triumphed in Western Europe and Poland), aided by strong Romanian and Finnish forces, swept across the frontiers and, within days, with brilliant success, had advanced more than 100 miles into the USSR. By July 11 they had taken 328,878 Red Army prisoners of war. Reeling from the shock, the Soviets struggled to cope. Stalin, fearful of a coup due to his failure to foresee events, and depressed at being outsmarted by Hitler, retired to his dacha in a state of near collapse.[11]

But these conditions of panic were soon overcome. On July 7 a revived Stalin, making the war personal, called on his "comrades, citizens, brothers and sisters, fighters of our Army and Navy" and "friends" to "selflessly fight our patriotic war of liberation against the Fascist enslavers." In the same speech he ordered the Red Army and the civilian population to evacuate all valuable property and food stocks that might be captured by the enemy and destroy what could not be moved. He also instructed the people to form partisan groups and to create, in the occupied areas, "intolerable conditions . . . for the enemy and his accomplices, who must be persecuted and destroyed at every step."[12] But to make sure that those of his "friends" who might be inclined to choose "liberation" by the Germans from the Stalin regime would not do so, political commissars, removed from all Red Army units in 1940, were once again placed in its formations, and a number of officers were executed as scapegoats for the initial military debacle. This was bolstered by an NKVD order on August 16 (by which time the number of Soviet POWs had risen to 432,000) declaring that officers and political operatives taken prisoner were "malicious deserters" whose families could be arrested, and indeed that "everyone who has been captured is a traitor to the motherland."[13] The stage was now set for a fight to the death between two dictators to whom the rules of conventional warfare and the sufferings of individual citizens were irrelevant.

On the civilian front, the Soviet response to the invasion was massive. The arbitrary movement of groups of people is far easier in a totalitarian society than it is in a democracy, and within days the Soviet measures, many of which would rend families asunder forever, would surpass anything undertaken in the West. In the first week of July a plan was set in motion to move as much heavy industry as possible out of the western USSR. Hundreds of thousands of workers, often without their families, accompanied the machines. Throughout the summer and fall, thousands of trains ran night and day under heavy bombing. By November, a million and a half freight cars full of machinery for 1,523 plants, some of them huge, had been moved to the Urals, Siberia, and the Volga region, where local populations, working in terrible weather and without adequate food, constructed new buildings to house the arriving equipment, often completing them within fourteen days.[14]

Fearful of bombings like those being visited on London, both parents and the authorities immediately began the evacuation of children from the cities. In Leningrad, thousands were at first sent to the countryside west of the city and thus directly into the teeth of the blitzkrieg. Here too the Nazis indulged in strafing of passenger trains, killing hundreds of children in the process. Soon children were being reevacuated back to the city, but many would be stranded in the areas taken by the Germans. The luckier ones went east, to Siberia and the Volga region, but there were simply not enough trains to hold all of Leningrad's children, whose hopeful parents jammed the railroad stations and the streets leading to them in their efforts to send them away.

Once again politics would influence evacuation policy to the detriment of the mainstream population: the NKVD sent out criminals, deserters, ethnic Finns and Germans, and politically suspect groups such as former nobility and kulaks before everyone else.[15] Other children never had a chance: farther south, near Kaunas, in Lithuania, Red Army men in units out on training exercises learned with despair that their sons and daughters, some in a vacation camp, had been overtaken by the German lines.[16] For those able to escape, the evacuation voyages, like all others in this war, were horrendous. Trains often languished on sidings for days without food or water and took months to get to Siberia, where the children, clad in summer clothes, suffered terribly in the cold.[17]

The young people who stayed home were immediately swept up in the defense efforts. Regular Army units were rapidly mobilized. Student nurses were sent to field hospitals at the front. All male citizens aged sixteen to sixty and females aged eighteen to fifty were required to make themselves available for civil defense in towns and villages. A People's Volunteer Corps was formed. Young Communists, university students, and some 90,000 teenagers were recruited as fire watchers, air-raid wardens, and auxiliary police. Thousands from these sometimes chaotic formations, including schoolchildren, went out along with their elders to prepare fortifications along a 200-mile line south and west of Leningrad.

For the older students it was, at first, all a lark, and they flocked with their friends to the recruiting centers and went out to the construction sites taking little with them, thinking they would be back within a day. In town, during the idyllic white nights, they sat on roofs with their buckets, shovels, and axes, reciting poetry and watching the surreal scenes around them. "It was so quiet . . . hardly any cars on the street. Strange. I felt as though I were flying over the city—a silvery city, each roof and each spire engraved against the sky. And the blimps! . . . At night, in the air, they swam like white whales under the clouds."[18] The realities of war came soon. German fighters continually strafed the streams of refugees heading toward the city and those working on the outer defenses of Leningrad.

> Over the roads the shells fell. Methodically. Precise. The Germans had an artillery spotter . . . who through his binoculars could see the road as well as the palm of his hand. Soldiers dashed from their dugouts, grabbing youngsters and women, pulling them from the road, out of the line of fire. A herd of cattle, stirring up a cloud of dust, frightened by the flaming asphalt of the road (set afire by a shell), dashed out into a mined field.[19]

Despite the efforts of the soldiers, thousands of young people were killed and hastily buried nearby. There was little food and no facilities for the workers, who, after weeks away, would straggle back into the city in pitiful condition. By the end of June, the young volunteers were not just being recruited for construction work, but also were being sent into the front lines, where their total lack of training led to enormous losses. The Germans and their allies gave no quarter to the teenage fighters. Most of the boys in one defiant detachment, wounded and captured near Vyborg, were shot, and one was dragged by the neck behind a car and left for dead.

By July 10, as rumors of airborne attacks on Leningrad multiplied, plans were being made to train children as young as eight in hand-to-hand combat. Other groups of young boys were sent to paint over road signs so that the Germans would lose their way if they penetrated the city. The paratroopers did not come, but on September 9 the Germans cut the last rail line out of Leningrad, and no further escape was possible. The killing on the outer defenses would continue and, once German artillery was within range, death would prevail in the city.[20]

Similar efforts would later be made in Moscow as the German vanguard advanced to a line less than fifty miles from the capital:

> Those were dreadful days. . . . I was ordered, like most of the girls at the factory, to join the Labor Front. We were taken some kilometers out of Moscow. There was a large crowd of us, and we were told to dig trenches. We were all very calm, but dazed, and couldn't take it in. On the very first day we were machine-gunned by a Fritz who swooped right down. Eleven of the girls were killed and four wounded.[21]

Some two million other Muscovites fled or were evacuated eastward in enormous rail convoys, which went in sporadic stages to various cities in Siberia. Once again, the Germans would be stopped just short of the city.

In all the chaos of the first triumphant weeks of the invasion, the implementation of the Nazi extermination policies was easily shrouded in deception. In the Baltic nations, and in eastern Poland and the bordering areas of the Ukraine, considerable use was made of local dissident groups and ancient hatreds in the carrying out of the program. Pro-German and nationalistic militias in the Baltic states were recruited as auxiliary police forces to help root out Communists, partisans, and Jews. The commander of the Einsatzgruppe operating in that area later testified:

> It was desirable . . . that the Jewish question not be raised immediately, as the unusually tough measures would also have created shock in Ger-

man circles. It had to appear to the outside that the indigenous population itself reacted naturally against the decades of oppression by the
Jews and against the terror created by the Communists in recent history, and that the indigenous population carried out these first measures of its own accord. . . . It was the duty of the Security Police to
initiate these self purging actions and to guide them into the proper
channels.[22]

In areas where pogroms and massacres could not easily be fomented,
the killings of Jews were said to be reprisals for looting or partisan activity.
In the early days the targets were mostly men. Large groups were also still
taken away for forced labor. As the Einsatzgruppen themselves became
more accustomed to these executions, the killing would be extended to
women and children. The numbers being shot rose exponentially, and less
and less care was taken to hide the murders from the inhabitants or from
regular German troops. Indeed, Romanian troops participating in the
murders in the southern USSR did so with such gusto that even the SS was
"disturbed" and felt that more discipline should be introduced into their
operations.[23]

Whether the target group was large or small, the Nazi killing methodology was, with a few variations, the same. Troops would enter a village or
town and order Jews to assemble for "resettlement." Sometimes the soldiers went from house to house, forcing Jews before them. Those too old
or young or too sick to walk were often shot in situ. The rest were taken to
a planned killing ground, where huge burial pits had usually been dug,
sometimes by the victims themselves. In the first five months of their
activities, the Einsatzgruppen would kill some half-million people, of
whom the vast majority were Jews. These unbelievable events have been
described many times; but almost every historian returns to the account of
a Nuremberg witness, the German engineer Hermann Graebe, simply
because his words convey, better than any other, the horror that results
when one group of humans has been indoctrinated to regard another
group as so alien that it must be exterminated:

> I accompanied M. to the . . . site and near it saw large mounds of
> earth. . . . A few trucks were parked in front of the mounds from which
> people were being driven by armed Ukrainian militia under the super-
> vision of an SS man. . . . I could now hear a series of rifle shots from
> behind the mounds. The people who had got off the trucks—men,
> women and children of all ages—had to undress . . . they had to place
> their clothing on separate piles for shoes, clothing and underwear. . . .

Without weeping or crying these people undressed and stood together in family groups, embracing each other and saying good-bye. . . . I did not hear a single complaint or plea for mercy. . . . I watched a family of about eight, a man and a woman . . . with their children of about one, eight and ten, as well as two grown up daughters of about twenty and twenty-four. An old woman with snow-white hair held the one-year-old child in her arms, singing to it and tickling it. . . . The child squealed with delight. The married couple looked on with tears in their eyes. The father held the ten-year-old boy by the hand speaking softly to him. The boy was struggling to hold back his tears. The father pointed . . . to the sky, stroked his head and seemed to explain something to him. At this moment, the SS man near the ditch called out something to his comrade. The latter counted off about twenty people and ordered them behind the mound. The family of which I have just spoken was among them. . . .

I walked around the mound and stood in front of the huge grave. The bodies were lying so tightly packed . . . that only their heads showed, from almost all of which blood ran down over their shoulders. Some were still moving. Others raised their hands and turned their heads to show they were still alive. . . . I estimate that [the ditch] already held about a thousand bodies. . . . The people, completely naked, climbed down steps which had been cut into the clay wall of the ditch, stumbled over the heads of those lying there and stopped at the spot indicated by the SS man. They lay down on top of the dead or wounded; some stroked those still living and spoke quietly to them. Then I heard a series of rifle shots. I . . . saw the bodies contorting or, the heads already inert, sinking on the corpses beneath. . . . I was surprised not to be ordered away, but I noticed three postmen in uniform standing nearby. Then the next batch came up.[24]

A slower methodology was used to eliminate the Soviet prisoners of war, among whom were thousands of the teenagers so hastily recruited to defend the nation. By late September 1941, their numbers would reach more than 1.8 million, and by war's end, more than 5 million. Of these, more than 4 million died.[25] The Germans would later admit to killing 3.7 million, but the policies of Stalin were also responsible in great part for this slaughter. The prisoners' chances of survival were, unbeknownst to them, marginal from the beginning. Though tsarist Russia had adhered to the Hague Convention of 1907, the Soviet regime had refused to sign the 1929 Geneva Convention, and, despite strong efforts by the International Red Cross, the United States, and other nations to persuade them to do so once the war began, continued to reject it and to refuse all help.[26] As had been true during the famines Stalin had inflicted on the Ukraine, he did not wish any scrutiny of his operations by foreign observers and was willing to sacrifice millions of his own citizens to maintain his secrets.

Hitler was delighted at this attitude, which released him from any requirement to allow inspections of the POW camps and enabled him to make whatever feeding and shelter arrangements he desired. These were precious few. Even before the invasion, orders had been issued not to waste food on the Russians. At the sites where they surrendered, the Germans had made no provision to care for the hundreds of thousands of prisoners, some of whom were as young as fifteen. Rationing quotas promulgated by the Nazis in August 1941 were far below the Geneva Convention standard, and even these were seldom fulfilled.[27] Early plans to take the POWs back to camps that had been prepared for some 790,000 of them in the Reich and Poland were canceled when the sheer numbers of captured "Bolsheviks" became too threatening to Nazi officials. Instead, in ghastly forced marches, during which hundreds of men, so weakened by hunger that they could not go on, were shot in full view of the local population, the prisoners were sent away from the combat zones and confined in excrement-covered transit enclosures with virtually no food and no sanitary facilities whatsoever. The wounded were put to death by lethal injection. Tens of thousands more prisoners died of typhus. But most of the POWs, in some places as many as 2,500 a day, died of pure starvation.

But two could play at this game. In the spring of 1943 the Germans would find a mass grave at Katyn, near Smolensk, containing the remains of 4,000 of the Polish officers who had been murdered by the Russians. German prisoners of war taken by Soviet forces, most notably after Stalingrad, would also receive brutal treatment.[28] One German soldier remembered that the Russians had forced some captives "to stand naked in the cold with hands raised and poured water over them until they died from exposure."[29]

The USSR's ethnic German population would also suffer. Soon after Hitler's rise to power, Stalin had taken certain precautions in regard to those living west of the Urals. In late 1934, the Central Committee of the Communist Party, under the guise of recording the original nationalities of all Soviet workers, had, like the Nazis, managed to create secret files on all the ethnic Germans in the nation, including their occupations and the size of their families.[30] Within a few weeks, as one official involved in the list project later testified:

> Every German born in Russia or brought there temporarily or permanently as a worker in the wide field of Soviet industry . . . was individu-

ally registered to the fullest extent . . . and this [was done] in each and every National Commissariat, and also all personnel data were listed. . . . Thus there was no longer a single corner in the whole Soviet Union that was not completely covered by the registration, nor were there any longer Germans whose official employment and family size were not known.[31]

In January 1935, all Germans living in a sixty-mile-wide strip along the western borders of the USSR were rounded up and sent to remote Murmansk. In other areas, they were carefully removed from jobs in strategic industries and services, and many were put under surveillance. Once the Nazis invaded, ethnic German men aged sixteen to sixty in the western battle zones were evacuated east in the very first convoys, along with the livestock and industrial matériel. Their wives, teenaged daughters, and young children stayed behind to work on fortifications and then were also sent east, not necessarily to the same places as their male relatives.

Rounding up ethnic Germans in the combat zones was necessarily haphazard, and many were left behind, but in the case of the Autonomous Volga Republic, farther to the east, where two-thirds of the population was of German descent, many of their families having lived in the region since the days of Catherine the Great, the deportation was highly organized and complete. In early July 1941, NKVD units moved into the capital and major towns and isolated them. Communications and transportation were closed down. German community leaders were shot, and commando units took control of houses and farms. Incidents were fabricated to imply that the German residents were saboteurs and spies. The first transports left in late July, and by the end of September the area had been completely cleared of its 500,000 or so German settlers and the Autonomous Volga Republic dissolved.[32] Within days of the departure of each relay, refugees and evacuees from the war zones, including a large group of Spanish Civil War children, were brought in and placed in the abandoned houses and institutions of the Volga Germans. Here too, half-eaten meals on tables, miserable unmilked cattle in the barns, and other evidence of the rapid departure of the former owners shocked the new residents.

More deportations in the usual cattle cars would take place from every German enclave, and as the summer passed and the cold set in, death stalked these groups as it did all others. In one train sent from the Caucasus in November 1941, 400 children died. And, like the Poles before them, the deportees who survived were billeted in the mud huts of long-exiled kulaks and found little to sustain life at their remote destinations.[33]

This apparently precautionary deportation of ethnic Germans was only the beginning of Stalin's campaigns against minority groups of which he was suspicious and whose cultures he was determined to obliterate. Later on, in even more brutal circumstances, the Crimean Tatars, the Chechens, the Kalmyks, and many other groups would suffer the same fate.

It did not take long for the early euphoria of the young German soldiers involved in the rapid conquest of the USSR to dissipate. Even though their progress was extraordinary, there was little feeling of glory. This was not France. The impoverished and filthy conditions to which much of the Russian populace had been reduced in many places confirmed the *Untermensch* propaganda with which German soldiers had been indoctrinated, but many were also shocked by the sight of the starved POWs, hanging bodies of "partisans," and piles of Jewish corpses. This unease was not limited to the naive. Even Himmler, in charge of the whole program, was visibly undone by the one mass execution he is known to have witnessed in Russia. Afterward he tried to reassure the death squad by telling them that the responsibility was his alone, and that in nature man was permitted to defend himself against "vermin." The Reichsführer SS was not upset enough to cancel the program, however: that same day he asked an assistant to look into "more humane" methods for the executions, a request that would lead eventually to the development of the mass gas chambers.[34]

Added to the horrors of atrocities, for younger recruits, was the shock of the first battlefield deaths of their friends and other realities of war. Within weeks of the invasion, less experienced replacement troops, far more than had been foreseen, were being sent to Russia, not in glorious tank formations but in the ubiquitous cattle cars to remote stations from which they marched, sometimes for weeks, to join their units. Along the way they had little rest or water, and could not keep clean. Once they were with their formations, after every tough engagement more unconquered Russia stretched before them.[35] The desolation of the country was daunting, and it was increased by the loss of population, which, in vast areas near the front lines, had been killed, conscripted into labor gangs, or expelled, leaving mainly children and old people behind. In these zones, any "refugee" found "wandering" about was suspected of being an "agent." Soldiers were told to be especially careful of children aged eleven to fourteen, who were likely to be partisan couriers, and of women, who were probably not only spies but provocateurs who would lure soldiers into racial pollution.[36] All these dangerous individuals could be, and were, shot without any interrogation.

In September, the journalist Alexander Werth, visiting such an area near Smolensk, which had temporarily been retaken by the Red Army, was struck by the "tragic pathos of the whole scene . . . where every village and every town had been destroyed, and the few surviving civilians were now living in cellars or dugouts." The town of Dorogubuzh had been bombed for hours in broad daylight, though no military formations were present, and its population reduced from 10,000 to 100 women and children, who were being fed by the Russian soldiers. At one headquarters a colonel had "adopted as 'son of the regiment' " a pathetic little fourteen-year-old boy, whose father and mother had both been killed in the bombing of a nearby village. Another officer, desperately worried about his own wife and daughter in German-occupied Kharkov, told Werth that he "could not imagine the hatred the Germans have stirred up among our people."[37]

It was not always easy, however, to tell exactly who had been responsible for such scenes. An anonymous Baltic doctor, working on epidemic prevention for the Germans in Russia, wrote a secret and revealing letter to the International Red Cross in Geneva.[38] In it he begged the organization to do everything in its power "so that this great cry of distress—one of the greatest that there has ever been—will be heard." The situation, he wrote, was "infinitely worse" than "what you saw in Poland." Soviet troops were destroying everything in their retreat, "without bothering about what happens to the civilians who remain . . . in most cases more than ¾ of them . . . composed of women, children and old people," already undernourished due to shortages caused by the Russo-Finnish War and Stalin's induced famines. Food supplies were diminishing rapidly. The terrible conditions, he predicted, would inevitably lead to epidemics, which the Germans, when they captured such areas, terrified lest their armies be contaminated, would "take the necessary steps to prevent": "The orders which we have been given in this matter are really frightful: if infected persons cannot be cared for, or isolated, they are to be destroyed. Which means that, as there are neither sufficient medical supplies, nor the means of intervening in time when necessary, thousands and thousands of human beings will be annihilated." In closing he wrote:

I hope that I shall not be sending this letter in vain, and that those who have been spared by Providence the most terrible misery will make it their humanitarian duty to bring aid to those who are enduring the most

terrible sufferings existing in this world, without worrying about ideological questions and without letting themselves be frightened by the
difficulties to be overcome.

There was nothing the Red Cross could do. Instructed to live off the
land, the German troops, like locusts, devoured cattle and requisitioned
crops so voraciously that the predicted problem of hunger exploded
almost immediately among the remaining population. This was of little
concern to the Nazi leaders, who had all made clear in public statements
at one time or another that the starvation of Slavs was not their concern,
and, indeed, was desirable. In early September 1941, the German government had publicly announced that under the Hague Convention it not
only was not responsible for feeding the Russians, but was "entitled to lay
claim to the resources and stocks of the occupied country for the use of its
own forces." Blame for the "consequences" was attributed to the USSR's
own scorched-earth policy and the British blockade, and the Nazis at the
same time piously stated that they would not block Allied aid shipments to
civilians.[39]

Within the German command there had been little planning for the
future—the war was supposed to be over within weeks and most of the
German troops expected to be home for Christmas. But by November
there was no end in sight. Along the overextended front many units were
receiving only sporadic deliveries of rations that often had to be retrieved
from food kitchens miles away. By now, precious little was left on the land.
There were other problems too. Cold weather had set in, but no winter
uniforms had been distributed, leading the troops to strip warm clothes
from Russian corpses and requisition them from civilians and the hapless
Soviet POWs. One Luftwaffe pilot complained that, from the air, he could
not tell his own forces from the enemy.[40] By December 1941, a full year
before Stalingrad, much of the German Army was already living as the
Russians were, and, like eighteen-year-old Ernst Kern, his unit of mountain troops reduced to nine from its original hundred, surviving on what
the *Untermenschen* could provide in a remote and frozen village in the
Ukraine, a hundred miles north of Rostov:

> A thorough pessimism began to paralyze us. We no longer lived but just
> existed . . . the decreasing rations made it clear that the supply line
> largely failed. During the days of rest at Dimitrewka, we were lying apa-
> thetically all day before the stove, with limbs hurting, the lice itching
> and tormenting, and hunger and the Ukrainian disease eating our bow-
> els. The only thing we found to eat in the houses was sunflower kernels.

They saved us from starving. So we chewed them like the Russians, who were spitting the shells in a monotonous rhythm while dozing behind the stove. This we had accomplished, we the predestined world conquerors.[41]

There would be no Christmas at home this year, and certainly not next, for Kern or the thousands of others fighting in the East.

Far to the north, in besieged Leningrad, cut off since early September from the outer world, and under constant bombardment, for 3.5 million citizens and soldiers, among them some 400,000 children, hunger was by now the greatest enemy. By mid-September the German lines were so close that the defenders, who were of all ages, could take trolleys to the front, in the process passing by "familiar streets that each remembered like a dream—here was the fence around our childhood home, here stood the great rustling maple. . . . I went to the front through the days of my childhood, along the streets where I ran to school."[42]

Unbelievably, the hastily dug defenses held. On September 17, major German units had been withdrawn in order to augment the forces struggling toward Moscow, while the remaining Germans dug in to wear down Leningrad. During the coming winter, they calculated, "ceaseless bombardment" along with "terror and hunger would do their work." In the spring all who remained alive would be taken prisoner or "sent to the depths of Russia." The city itself, including the port area much desired by the German Navy, would be razed and the sections north of the Neva would be given to Finland.

By October 1, the total rations of meat, fat, pasta, and pastry for all children sixteen and under had been reduced to a total of about five and one-half pounds a month, plus a daily bread ration of one-third of a loaf. Even this meager amount could not always be provided, and would be cut several more times before the end of the year. By late October, people were beginning to die of starvation. To make things worse, winter came early, and by November the city was covered with snow. Few had fuel for more than the most minimal heat, and the aerial bombardment was virtually continuous. By the end of December, more than 133,000 bombs and shells had rained down on the city, the shells fired from six gigantic German artillery emplacements.[43]

In November the death rate began a rapid rise. People ate glue, lipstick, pets, even paper. Diarrhea and scurvy flourished. In a phenomenon that would be observed in many war areas, men and teenagers died fastest and newborns were especially vulnerable. Fighting water and electricity cutoffs, lack of fuel, and the decimation of their staff, the Leningrad Pediatric Institute struggled to invent new baby formulas from available foods and, increasing its patient load sixteen-fold, fed 7,000 to 8,000 children a day, many of whom weighed only one-third their normal weight. In the process they also observed a "catastrophic drop" in the length and weight of newborns. The Institute was bombed again and again; during one attack, doctors "calmly performed the delivery" of a boy suitably named Viktor. In the spring of 1942 the undaunted staff planted every inch of the Institute's gardens with vegetables and fruit. The director, Dr. Yulia Mendeleva, using her Communist Party connections to the utmost, later claimed that she had even persuaded high-ranking friends in Moscow to send 1,000 milk cows to Leningrad. How they got there, and if they survived the siege, is not explained.[44]

Not everyone was so high-minded. The situation brought out the lowest as well as the highest aspects of human nature. Corruption, theft, and black market activity were common. Party members ate better, as did workers in the food industry. Two thousand people were arrested for cannibalism.[45] Conversely, soldiers at the front often generously shared their larger rations with civilians, and many parents doomed themselves by giving portions of their food to their children. Teachers at a day-care center noticed children saving portions of their tiny food rations in jars, not to eat later as they first supposed, but to take home to their parents.[46] But soon many inhabitants were in terrible condition. A submarine captain, granted leave to see his family, found this dreadful scene:

> his wife, her body badly swollen, her eyes sunken in their sockets, hardly able to move. His daughter with puffy eyes—the first sign of dystrophy—sat on the bed muffled in bedclothes, eating soup made of library paste. His mother-in-law wandered about the dark, cold room mumbling, laughing and crying—she had lost her reason. The windows had been broken by bomb blasts and replaced by plywood. The walls were black with smoke. . . . There was a flickering kerosene lamp. Outside, shells could be heard bursting.[47]

By November 9, only a week's worth of food remained in the city and the rations were cut again. The day before, the Nazis had captured a vital rail line that had carried a thin stream of food to Lake Ladoga, from where it was taken to the city by boats. In Munich Hitler exulted: "No one can free it. No one can break the ring. Leningrad is doomed to die of famine."[48]

He was wrong. Extra food was parachuted in by the Red Army. The railroad was retaken within the month, and by late November, Lake Ladoga had frozen solidly enough to allow the establishment of the famous "Road of Life" across its icy expanse. Via this precarious route over half a million more Leningraders, many of them children, would be evacuated, and food would begin to arrive in tiny increments, not enough to save many, but at least enough to allow the authorities, on Christmas Day, to increase the tiny bread ration for children from 125 to 200 grams, or from five to about seven ounces.[49]

But before that time and despite the Christmas distribution, in family after family, starvation took one person after another. Six-year-old Mikhail Ostrovsky began the siege with two grandparents, both parents, and four beloved, childless aunts. By late January only Mikhail and the aunts were still alive. Unable to feed him, they put him in a kindergarten that received food from the authorities. To augment the minimal rations, the headmistress, Nina Ivanova, would load her charges and a big can on sleds and pull them to the front, where she begged the soldiers to give her vodka. This she diluted and fed to her children three times a day to give them a few more calories.

Mikhail did survive, and in early 1943 was evacuated to Novosibirsk, in Siberia, along with his aunts. They departed Leningrad on a ship that was bombed during the journey. Once ashore they continued for four weeks in a packed, two-level cattle car. One aunt, stricken with dysentery, was removed from the train at Tyumen, where she died. Once in Novosibirsk, the skeletal Mikhail spent two months in a hospital gradually bringing his food intake back to normal.[50]

Mikhail's experience was far from unique, but at least he had his aunt; thousands of other children were left totally alone. Teams of Young Communist workers and many others went out to help those who could no longer leave their apartments. What they found was terrible beyond words:

> The door to the apartment was open. . . . My eyes met a frightful sight. A half-dark room. Frost on the walls. On the floor a frozen puddle. On a chair the corpse of a fourteen-year-old boy. In a child's cradle the second corpse of a tiny child. On the bed the dead mistress of the flat . . . beside her, rubbing the dead woman's breast with a towel, stood her oldest daughter. . . . But life had gone, and it could not be brought back.

Another worker, who saved more than a hundred children, recorded in her diary in January 1942:

> To the 17th Line, House 38, Apartment No. 2. . . . Yuri S., 9 years old. His mother was dead. The youngster slept day and night with his dead mother. ("How cold I got from mama," he said.) Yuri didn't want to come with me. He cried and shouted. A touching farewell with his mother ("Mama, what will happen to you without me?"). . . . Prospekt Musorgsky 68, Apartment 30. Took a girl, Shura S., born 1931. Father at the front. Mother dead. . . . Little girl dirty, scabs on her hands. Found her in a pile of dirty linen under the mattress.[51]

To Russians, the most famous such case is perhaps that of Tanya Savicheva, who, between December 28, 1941, and May 13, 1942, recorded the names of seven family members who had died on the appropriate pages of her alphabetized notebook, ending her entries with the comment "All die. Only Tanya remains." Like Mikhail, Tanya was eventually evacuated, but for her it was too late; she died of chronic dysentery in the summer of 1943.[52] Watching the demise of relatives was devastating to young children, who witnessed their hallucinations and often dreadful death throes and who sometimes lived for weeks surrounded by frozen corpses that could only be taken to the icy cemeteries with great difficulty. During the spring and summer of 1942, the large number of deaths, continued evacuations, and ever improving imports of food, plus a huge gardening program on every square inch of open ground, would finally ease the situation. But by then, the U.S. mission in Moscow reported, some 650,000 people were said to have died of starvation in Leningrad and its suburbs.[53] By the time the siege ended, the total deaths are estimated to have been nearly twice that number: more than in any other city ever devastated by war.

Little Tanya and Mikhail and the thousands of others starving in the Soviet Union did not know it, but they were not alone in their suffering. In his preparations for the invasion of the USSR, Hitler had, since the fall of 1940, been trying to forge partnerships in the Balkans, which would protect his southern flank. Alliances with Bulgaria and Yugoslavia were to be negotiated, and a takeover of the northern provinces of Greece was planned. As is usual in the Balkans, things did not go smoothly. Mussolini, who had unwisely attacked Greece in October 1940, had not been able to prevail against combined Greek and British forces, and Serbian elements in Yugoslavia had staged an anti-German coup.

Outraged and impatient with all this, Hitler ordered yet another invasion, which after only ten days of preparation was to conquer Yugoslavia and Greece with minimal losses. German forces crossed into Yugoslavia on April 6, and by April 27 were in Athens.[54] There, in an act of extraordinary arrogance, the Germans raised the swastika flag over the Parthenon. Tony Lykiardopoulos remembers that his mother cried when they looked up and saw the banner "against the blue, blue Athenian sky."[55] Eleven-year-old Athena Lagoudaki, staying with friends in Salonika, peeked through shuttered windows as the ominous German tanks rolled by. On the radio she heard an archbishop wish the people luck and warn of hard times to come. The national anthem then began to play, but was suddenly cut off when the Germans captured the radio station. Little did Athena know how hard the times would soon be. She and her family were lucky. Taken in by relatives who owned wheat fields in Larissa, one of the most productive agricultural areas of the country, they would survive by bartering their surplus grain, soon to be as precious as gold, for such nourishing items as beans and honey.[56] This was not the case elsewhere. On November 17, 1941, an official of the Agricultural Bank of Greece pointed out that the total disruption of maritime communication and land transportation had made the normal distribution of olive oil in the country impossible. That fact, combined with the requisitioning of commodities by Italy and Germany plus the consumption of reserves in many locations since Greece had been invaded in April, had eliminated the only source of fat for most of the people and would, he declared, "have sad, if not fatal results." Indeed, if the situation was not remedied before the winter, "mass catastrophe" would be the result.[57]

Olive oil was not the only thing lacking. The foreign food imports on which Greece depended had ceased when the invasion began. Here too German forces, for the most part billeted with Greek families, lived off the local economy. Soldiers were also given the right to send weekly packages weighing five kilos each to their relatives back home, a practice that encouraged all sorts of pilfering. Warehouses were sealed up and their contents seized. The German Army paid some entrepreneurs well for supplies, thus helping food prices, already rising due to shortages, to skyrocket, and undermining the chaotic efforts of the Greek puppet government and the Italians, who were occupying most of the country outside the big cities, to stockpile and ration supplies. Greedy farmers even sold their seed stocks; corruption and profiteering were rife. Mean-while, Thessaly and Macedonia, the major grain-producing areas of Greece, had been taken over by the Bulgarians, who were doing their own exploit-ing. In the fall of 1941, at the urgent request of their own envoys to Greece, the Germans and Italians sent sporadic shipments of grain to Salonika, but the distribution was left to the German authorities, who con-trolled the fuel supplies, the railroads, and most major shipping, and it is not clear just what happened to these provisions.[58]

It did not take long for the predicted effects of the disruption of the normal food production and distribution system, fragile at the best of times, to appear. A chain reaction began. Lack of fuel led not only to lack of food distribution, but also to unemployment as industries closed. By May, in Athens-Piraeus, most people's reserves were gone. The more affluent, of whom there were fewer and fewer, for a time lived off the booming black market, but by the autumn, prices were fifty to sixty times what they had been before the invasion, and only the very rich or well con-nected could buy what little there was for sale. The legal bread ration in Athens was below that of Leningrad, hovering, after July 1941, between 100 and 160 grams a day, or between four and six ounces. There was essentially no meat at all: butchers sold dog and cat until these too van-ished, and by late October, as one International Red Cross official put it, starvation had "appeared in all its horror."[59]

In December, the wife of the Swiss consul in Salonika, back in Switzer-land for Christmas, reported: "Starvation stalks the streets of Salonica. Famished men and women collapse on the pavements and their bodies are later on trundled away on open carts drawn by gaunt horses staggering in their traces from the effects of hunger."

She also noted that the Greeks were now convinced that the Germans (whom she refers to as "anti-Semitic military bag men") were using hunger for the purpose of "deliberate extermination." This idea, she wrote, should be "viewed as the logical appraisal of German behavior in Greece since the invasion of Russia." News of the horrible conditions in the Soviet Union had begun to get around, and everyone wondered who would be next. The consul's wife observed that "Salonica is full of wounded and frost-bitten Germans from the Russian front. . . . The ter-rors of the winter war in Russia for the Germans are so great that officers and men frequently break into fits of violent weeping when ordered to return to the Eastern front."[60]

German behavior in Greece, and indeed in all the other non-Slavic

A soup kitchen in Athens, 1941.

countries, was ruled by indifference rather than racial principle; neverthe-less, the result was much the same. Some months later, Göring would bluntly define Nazi policy toward the conquered peoples, at a meeting of the Nazi heads of government of the countries occupied by the Reich, all of whom faced eventual problems similar to those of fragile Greece, and from whom he was demanding ever larger quotas of food:

> In all the occupied territories I see the people living there stuffed full of food, while our own people are starving. For God's sake, you haven't been sent there to work for the well-being of the peoples entrusted to you, but to get hold of as much as you can so that the German people can live. . . . This continual concern for the aliens must come to an end once and for all. . . . I have the reports of what you are planning to deliver in front of me. When I contemplate your countries it seems like nothing at all. I could not care less if you tell me that your people are collapsing from hunger. They can do that by all means so long as no German collapses from hunger. . . . I am only interested in the people in the occupied territories who work producing armaments and food. They must get just sufficient so that they can do their work. . . . It does

not matter what happens to the French.... Belgium is a poor country.... They won't need to deliver bread grains, but they won't get
any.... Norway: They've got fish.... You must give me some meat....
I haven't time to read letters and memos in which you tell me that you
can't do what I ask of you.[61]

The food situation continued to deteriorate in the large urban setting
of Athens. A few days after the Swiss report, a British informant reported
from there that he had "seen complete starvation ... in one single day
there were 1,200 corpses for burial," most of them children whose bodies
were taken to the cemetery in batches of ten to twenty at a time in "small
hand carts."[62] By Christmas the number of corpses had so far outstripped
the burial facilities that the Medical Society of Athens asked the Orthodox Patriarch to waive his church's prohibition of cremation.[63] Under the
auspices of the International Red Cross, soup kitchens and a few shipments were allowed in from Turkey on the small steamer SS *Kurtulus*,
which came to be a symbol of survival to Athenians; but these supplies
could save only a few. Milk sent from the Vatican kept some babies alive,
but none of this was enough. To the despair of all, after five trips the gal-
lant *Kurtulus* sank, but in any case, there were as yet no more supplies for
it to bring.

In December 1941, International Red Cross official Alexander Junod
saw firsthand the "hell in which the Greek people are now living." He
described scenes in Athens that might have been taken from the note-
books of the Leningrad workers. The winter was unusually cold in Athens
too; it even snowed. No less passionate than the Baltic doctor who had
reported from Russia, Junod, the proper bureaucrat, wrote:

This country which nature has endowed with such beauty ... this country blessed by the Gods ... which has illuminated and kindled the
greatest minds in its incomparable expression of art and wisdom, is
today a true country of hell, a valley of the worst suffering and the
blackest misery in which death mercilessly reaps innocent lives. It is
impossible, even for the most daring imagination, to conceive of the
extent of this suffering, all the horror of famine, all the savagery of the
martyrdom of this population. One has to see the people falling dead of
hunger on the sidewalks, one has to see the garbage trucks taking
masses of cadavers to the cemeteries, one has to visit the neighborhoods where those near death sleep next to the dead that the carts and
trucks have not yet taken away. When one sees all these things, one will
be able to have a small idea of the whole tragic situation.[64]

And Junod did visit the neighborhoods. The train station was full of gaunt people selling and bartering every possible object for food. Outside, "ragged beggars of all ages" held out their hands. He saw "little children, very thin, very pale, glassy-eyed, crying and asking for food." Others crowded around restaurants hoping for leftovers and pawed through garbage piles. Women and children sat and slept in doorways; they died there in the freezing nights. In middle-class neighborhoods people wasted away slowly and died with dignity in their empty houses, having sold everything possible and not wanting to beg.

Things were, naturally, worst in the slums and shantytowns of the Greek capital, still populated in large part by World War I refugees. The soup kitchens, including those especially set up for children by the Greek Church, could not feed their unappetizing but life-saving "mess of pulse or bligouri (a dish made of boiled wheat)"[65] to their estimated 800,000 clients more than two or three times a week, and the amounts distributed were too small to sustain life for long. Exhausted parents trekked into the country to cut grass for stews that provided no nourishment. As in Leningrad, hungry children awoke to find dead parents:

> In the Dourgouti quarter . . . Androniki P., 40 years old, at her door wrapped in a filthy coverlet. She has sold what little furniture she had in order to buy food. A few boards have been torn out of the floor to be used for heating. In a corner lie her three sick and crying children. The mother watches the agony of the children with a wild and somber gaze; they will soon follow the same fate as their father, who died a few days ago in the same room. No one could get up to report the death, the neighbors did not discover it for a while, and the body stayed there for three days with the living members of the family. It is not surprising that, after this three-day tragedy, the poor woman has gone mad.
>
> . . . Jannitsa 9. Irene O. has watched her husband and one of her children die of hunger; with agony she is now awaiting the fate of her remaining child. . . . At Epano-Petralona . . . a widow . . . has six sick little ones, swollen by hunger disease. Once she was given a little olive oil and the swellings got better, but the children cannot stand up because they are so weak. . . . In Kaissariani . . . the widow Marie M., dying on her bed, holds her baby in her arms. Her husband died two months ago; who knows who will die first, the mother or the child.[66]

By late January, Alexander Junod estimated, there had been 40,000 deaths in Athens alone, eight times the normal mortality, and the winter was far from over. By the spring the situation was equally desperate on many of the Greek islands and in the remote mountain regions, where, due to transportation difficulties, even what little food was available could not be delivered. So tenuous was life that the Red Cross reported that even a delay of one day in shipping would cause the death of hundreds.[67]

There was no dearth of organizations desirous of helping the innocent victims of the war in the USSR and Greece, or indeed in the nations previously attacked. But well before the streets of the Polish ghettos, Leningrad, and Athens had become strewn with emaciated bodies, the issue of humanitarian aid to the occupied countries would fall into the same political and bureaucratic morass as that of immigration. The issue was control of the flow and distribution of the donations.

The British, desperately alone by the spring of 1941, clung adamantly to their shipping blockade of Axis-controlled areas, which had been put into effect two days after the German attack on Poland in 1939. Their objective was to prevent anything that might aid the German war effort from reaching Nazi-controlled territory. (The *Kurtulus* shipments to Greece were allowed, as they came from *within* the blockaded zone.)[68] The British determination was not surprising, as voracious Nazi consumption of the production of the conquered lands was obvious long before Göring's little pep talk. Help to one country would bring appeals from all the others, the British rightly argued. The blockade, as well as all types of asset transfers, were monitored by the newly instituted Ministry of Economic Warfare and enforced by the Royal Navy. All neutral shipping leaving from or going to German-controlled areas was required to declare its cargo and be certified by British consuls. Ships entering certain territorial waters could be boarded and searched, and, if necessary, their cargoes confiscated. In the British view, any food, clothing, or medicines sent into the Reich would help the enemy.

The United States government was limited in deliveries of aid by its own Neutrality Act, a law carefully watched by isolationists, and it was only with the greatest difficulty and intrigue that Roosevelt was able to send vital supplies through the Lend-Lease program first to Great Britain and later to the Soviet Union. The American government, no more eager than Britain to have uncontrolled shipping crisscrossing the Atlantic, also had to restrain private organizations, such as Greek War Relief, which, with great enthusiasm, was putting pressure on Congress to allow its donations to be shipped to the Mediterranean.[69]

All these complications made getting any help to the innocent in the war zones difficult, but once again, it could generally be facilitated if the aid was for children and the pressure of public opinion was strong. In early 1941 the British had reluctantly allowed a few shipments of dried milk for children to go from the United States to Vichy France, technically still independent. Permission was given on the grounds that the American Red Cross would control all distribution and that nothing would go to the Occupied Zone. The United States, in particular, hoped to inspire independence and anti-German feelings in Vichy with these donations.[70] News of barter arrangements for food between the two parts of France soon put the milk shipments in a bad light in England, and further ones were only approved by the British, who considered the U.S. policy extremely naive, after a personal appeal by Roosevelt.[71]

There is no question that the blockade was effective. Hitler's ever-growing need for raw materials and food would force him, early on, to make deals with Stalin that were not always to Germany's advantage, in exchange for millions of tons of wheat and access to Russia's Arctic, Black Sea, and Pacific ports. Later, at the height of his successes in the East, Hitler would refer to the conquered areas of the USSR as his "blockade proof lebensraum."[72] The Nazis, of course, had their own blockade carried out by U-boats operating to prevent the provisioning of Allied-controlled territories, which, in 1941, mostly meant Britain.

The delivery and control of aid, humanitarian and otherwise, after 1941 to the Soviet Union, overnight transformed from enemy to ally, was fraught with problems. The blockade was not the issue here: within hours of the Nazi invasion, while Stalin was still in a daze, Churchill, who had immediately seen the weaknesses of Hitler's war plan, was on the air, promoting an alliance with Russia, which, only moments before, would have been unthinkable. It was a brilliant speech. After noting that the Nazi regime was "indistinguishable from the worst features of Communism," of which he had been a "consistent opponent for the last twenty-five years," he said that "all that fades away before the spectacle which is now unfolding." Making the attack personal, as Stalin would do some days later, Churchill conjured up a vision of the destruction "in hideous onslaught" of "the ten thousand villages of Russia, where the means of existence was wrung so harshly from the soil, but where there are still primordial human joys, where maidens laugh and children play." Now, he declared, "we are resolved to destroy Hitler and every vestige of the Nazi regime . . . we shall give . . . help to Russia and to the Russian people. We shall appeal to all our friends and Allies in every part of the world to take the same course." Noting that the invasion of the USSR was "no more than a prelude to an attempted invasion of the British Isles," which Hitler had hoped to accomplish "before the winter comes" and "before the fleets and air power of the United States will intervene," he concluded, "the Russian danger is . . . our danger and the danger of the United States just as the cause of any Russian fighting for his hearth and home is the cause of free men . . . in every quarter of the globe."[73]

The trouble was that Britain had little food or arms to spare. Churchill's speech was a clear challenge to the United States to expand its Lend-Lease program, already controversial, to a regime regarded in many American quarters as far more dangerous to U.S. interests than the Nazis. In mid-May, polls had shown that 70 percent of Americans felt that the aid going to Britain was sufficient or even excessive.[74] Sending arms to Russia, which many thought had no chance against Hitler's war machine, seemed like a bad idea to the War Department; but on June 25, Roosevelt publicly committed the United States to providing aid to the Soviet Union.[75]

As would be the case in all future aid efforts, months would elapse before anything actually was transferred. In the meantime, yet another array of hastily organized, nationality-oriented private organizations, each with its own agenda, clamored to be allowed to send humanitarian aid to the new war zone. The Soviets were not at all reluctant to take such capitalist donations: soon after the invasion, a Russian official in Washington asked the State Department if fund-raising would be permitted in the United States. The State Department, wary of Communist machinations, reluctantly noted that such efforts could not legally be prevented.[76]

By the fall of 1941, people with relatives in the far reaches of Russia were writing to Eleanor Roosevelt to ask for help in sending food parcels to them. Polish groups demanded aid for the tens of thousands of Polish prisoners deported to Siberia in 1939, who had now been released by the Soviets and were, in terrible conditions, attempting to make their way to Allied refugee centers in the Middle East. The Mennonites wanted to help the Volga Germans; the Rockefeller Foundation wanted to send typhus vaccine. An organization called Russian War Relief, with an impressive array of names on its masthead, splashily advertised a major fund-raising rally in Madison Square Garden in the New York Times. To all these, the State Department had to reply that no representatives could go to Moscow, as, in the past, the Russians, ever fearful of spies, had "consistently refused to grant permission to foreign relief organizations to operate in Soviet territory."[77] The suspicions were mutual: Russian War Relief was later infiltrated by FBI informants, and J. Edgar Hoover notified the State Department that informants at a meeting of the Mosholu branch of the organization in the Bronx had reported that "most of the faces were familiar as being those of members of the Communist Party, International Worker's Groups and other pro-Communist groups."[78]

In mid-September, the State Department finally permitted the American Red Cross to send a special team to the Soviet Union to try to coordinate the distribution of humanitarian aid, some of which had already been shipped with no specific destination. At a three-power conference with the British Red Cross and the Russian Red Crescent organizations, an alliance was set up to deal with such incoming materials. American diplomats were not optimistic about the chances of the American Red Cross being allowed to supervise any of the aid distribution, a measure upon which they normally insisted. Ambassador Laurence Steinhardt suggested that only one person stay on, to live and work from the embassy for a short time and then go home. This advice was inspired by the fact that German forces were rapidly approaching Moscow, causing the embassy to be evacuated to Kuybyshev, a town on the Volga some 600 miles to the east. There the necessities of life were already in such short supply that the ambassador appended a plaintive appeal to the Red Cross for canned goods, blankets, soap, and toilet paper for the diplomatic staff.[79]

The Red Cross, not to be denied, went to Kuybyshev too. A few weeks later, Russian Vice Foreign Minister Andrei Vyshinsky questioned both their presence there and their requests for "special privileges." Perhaps having been briefed on the magnitude of the aid already en route, he soon relented, "apologizing with dignity and cleverness" for not having "completely understood our original proposals." Delighted Red Cross officials made Vyshinsky an honorary member of their organization and presented him with a lapel pin. But the Soviets still refused to allow "Amcross" workers to travel freely in the country or even to supervise distribution of the incoming materials, stating huffily that such demands were "an attack on [our] integrity." After a few more attempts to change this, it became clear to the Red Cross that they must either concede their most cherished principle of control or leave. They conceded, noting that "the important thing is to meet the need and not be too exacting with reference to conditions."[80]

Red Cross business and communications, plus those of a representative of Russian War Relief, which also represented several other organizations, would henceforth be conducted from the diplomatic safety of the American embassy, and their humanitarian shipments would be mixed in with military ones in the convoys struggling to Soviet ports. Russian secrecy on the true conditions across the country, most of which were hidden from the Russian public, allowed only glimpses of the truth, and priorities had to be deduced from shipping requests. The little that could be learned was daunting enough. In January 1942, informants reported that the only people getting eggs and milk in Moscow were children under the age of two. Unlike most countries, Russia had little food available outside the rationing system, even on the black market, and then only for barter. In March, the Soviets requested that extra food be shipped "at expense of trucks," a drastic admission. By April, the Red Cross knew that the only food issued per person in Moscow for the month of March had been salt, eight ounces of herring, and a pound of pickles. Children got an additional four ounces of red caviar and eight ounces of flour. Of the situation in Leningrad they heard only rumors. Everyone knew there were typhus epidemics, but not exactly where or how bad. That they were ongoing was made clear by the steady demand for Lend-Lease soft green soap, "which is needed as base for certain preparations and because efficacious against vermin."[81]

Unaware of these complications, private Allied organizations poured in help. Among many others, Lady Churchill announced in November 1942 that two million pounds sterling worth of aid had been sent from Britain, including 50,000 children's coats and the equivalent of three years' worth of all the novocaine normally used in Britain. The American Jewish Council for Russian War Relief had also pledged $1 million to rebuild destroyed Jewish areas in the areas liberated by the Red Army. By August 1943, the American Red Cross would calculate that goods valued at $19,897,608 had already been sent or were on the way to the USSR.[82]

The children's clothes were desperately needed. In September 1943, Amcross reported that there were 350,000 war orphans in Soviet-controlled areas who needed "sets" of clothing: "Two suits warm underwear, two pair wool mixed stockings, two flannel pajamas, one pair shoes, skirt or trousers, heavy sweater, overcoat, overshoes, woolen cap, scarf, mittens, also two each blankets sheets cases towels."[83] Red Cross workers were never quite sure where everything went; it is certain, however, that the Red Army and party officials got priority. But children seem to have been high on the list. One Moscow family, living happily but hungrily in exile in Siberia, vividly remembers eating Spam and a "big fat omelet" made with powdered eggs "from the USA."[84] The beneficial effects of the aid were described with emotion, tangible even in his staccato cable, by an Amcross worker named Hubbell, who, in December 1943, almost a year after its liberation, was, exceptionally, allowed to visit Stalingrad.

Here virtually all hospitals, nurseries, and clinics for children had been destroyed. Forty-five thousand children had been orphaned in the city alone, and almost double that number in the surrounding area. In the sub-urb of Beketovka, the 80,000 remaining inhabitants were almost entirely women and children. Child health facilities had been constructed in base-ments, the remnants of apartment buildings, mud huts, and tents. There was still no electricity or running water; Hubbell observed "women and children, every one seemingly carrying yoke 2 pails including small tots." The water, taken from the Volga, was boiled and chlorinated. Old tin cans served as cups and dishes. There were no ambulances, practically no sur-gical equipment, and only one X-ray machine for the entire province. Nor were there sufficient supplies of soap, towels, or sterilizers.

In this chaos, the local Red Cross chairman, Zenia Kozintseva, who was "badly crippled all her life" and who had "lost everything," had wrought miracles "beyond belief." Thirty war orphans' homes had been set up in peasant huts, which also served as schools. Three thousand pairs of shoes and 65,000 articles of clothing had been distributed, allowing children "to leave their abodes" and attend classes. Red Cross nurse's aides had been sent to the train station to pick up "all unattached children on trains": so far they had reunited 3,500 mothers and children separated during the siege. Hubbell saw a seventy-eight-bed nursery facility for "tots under four" that had been set up in the basement of a destroyed hospital, "where reconstruction plastering building stoves all done by nurses themselves clean warm meager equipment but all comfortable equipped with Amcross layettes whose baby blue flannel blankets each bed contrast white walls impressive heartening sight." In another "restored" three-by-ten-foot base-ment that lodged a mother, a two-month-old, a five-year-old, and their grandmother, Hubbell was touched by the enormous gratitude he found for shoes and other warm clothing donated by "the Sheridan, Wyoming County Chapter of the American Red Cross," a world away both literally and figuratively.[85]

In mid-February 1942, the British relented on the issue of food for Greece. They were encouraged not a little in their decision by confidential reports from Italian diplomats who said that over a million people were endangered. The Axis powers were only too happy to let the Allies feed the Greeks, who were not on the racial extermination list, and promised that the incoming supplies, to be distributed by an International Red Cross commission, would go to the population. Meanwhile, the Germans, who had been using the British blockade as a "chief propaganda argument in Greece,"[86] did not cut down on their requisitioning. The British had also been correct in thinking that the Greek shipments would give other occupied countries ideas. In the hothouse atmosphere of London, where the various governments in exile jockeyed for attention on many issues, the plan to aid Greece could not be kept secret for long. On January 22, 1942, the Belgians also appealed for relief for their children and young mothers. By now the British, feeling that "the entry of the United States into the war had removed the danger of any really large scale food relief to enemy Europe being forced upon us," were more amenable to such a request. In February, trying not to show favoritism, the British Ministry of Economic Warfare approved the idea of exploring "an Anglo-American scheme of providing milk concentrates (but not vitamins) for children in the worst affected areas of Europe," their concern that the program would help the Nazis having been assuaged by evidence that the supply of milk products in the United States and the shipping available to move them was not very great.[87] But providing clothing, also desperately needed in this region, was not allowed, on grounds that "quite small quantities of good quality wool are very useful for stretching supplies of synthetic material," and that it would be hard to prevent people from "selling or exchanging clothes for other goods or for money, especially in a country where the purchasing power is all in the power of the occupying forces."[88]

Finalizing the details of the shipments to Greece, which necessitated negotiations with Germany, Italy, and Sweden, took until June 1942. An attempt by the Axis Red Cross organizations to get control of distribution was defeated, and in early August three ships supplied by neutral Sweden, with the wonderfully unwarlike names of *Camellia, Eros,* and *Formosa,* finally left Canada for Greece. By 1944 there would be fourteen vessels, paid for in large part by the United States Lend-Lease program, steaming back and forth with all sorts of vital items.[89]

Getting to the ports was the easy part. It was far more difficult to transport things within Greece and to make sure they went to those who were neediest. Internal documents of the central International Red Cross Commission reveal much agonizing, familiar to all welfare organizations, as to just who should be eligible for the food distributions. Refugees, war victims, children, and "the poor" would be included, while the very rich and farmers would be excluded. It was, however, no longer easy to say who was rich and who was poor. Money was often not accepted in exchange for food, if there was any; this pitched many salaried families into the "poor" category. As the British had feared, there were more serious problems: the Axis promise not to requisition the food was not always observed. Local Red Cross distribution subcommissions and roving representatives reported constant threats and interference from occupation authorities and collaborators. Lack of transportation controlled by the Red Cross made it extremely difficult to get food to the remote mountain areas and to many of the islands. In one town, commission functions were completely taken over by the mayor and officers of the occupation force. The Italian commandant of Coropi, in Attica, demanded that a shipment of hazelnuts meant for the children of the town be given to him instead, which, after protest, was done. And in Piraeus, flour earmarked for the Greek islands was taken by the Germans and "distributed by other entities."[90] Despite all, as had occurred in Leningrad, the incoming food, limited and misdirected though it was, raised the rations for many from nearly zero to about a quarter of the normal minimum, which might be just enough to sustain life, especially for children, until more help could be procured.

The Nazis, after their own fashion, had also begun an aid program in the Soviet Union. Despite the military setbacks that had foiled Hitler's plan to defeat the Red Army within weeks, by the fall of 1941, the Nazis did control large sections of the USSR, which were well enough secured that they could be placed under civilian occupation. A Reich Ministry for the Occupied Eastern Areas, or Ostministerium, under longtime Nazi Party leader Alfred Rosenberg, had been set up to coordinate policy for these regions, which were subdivided into Reichskommissariats ruled by Nazi appointees of varying degrees of fanaticism and independence.[91] Within these territories, both the Wehrmacht and the SS carried on their respective duties and projects, as did other mainstream Nazi organizations such as the Nazi Welfare Agency, the Labor Front, and the Hitler Youth. Competition for scarce resources, which included labor and food, was ferocious among these agencies, and the opportunities for corruption were endless.

Opinion was also sharply divided on how to treat those elements of the Soviet population who were useful and sometimes sympathetic to the German war effort. Many high officials had found the *Untermenschen* attractive, and despite the strong prohibitions on fraternization, some German soldiers had even found romance. One recruit fell in love with a Ukrainian girl and soon became part of the family scene:

> I was head over heels in love, and I never would have let her go if fate had allowed it to be different. . . . My Russian got pretty good. . . . I saw, for instance, that the young people there read good books and were very interested in music. . . . I also learned to do some Russian dances.

Even though I was a young soldier I still felt the need to be part of a
family. The Ukrainians gave me the opportunity to do that. . . . These
people were later terribly disappointed by . . . certain German administrators . . . they were deported and shunted west . . . many died a miserable death, starving in labor camps.[92]

Even Himmler was so impressed at the sight of bouncing blond Ukrainian children that he ordered an experimental integrated kindergarten set
up for those who were said to be orphans to see if they could be Germanized.[93] Hitler was even more taken with the bouncing blond young ladies
of the region, who were soon included in the nanny recruitment program
that had been launched in Poland.

Despite this enthusiasm, Hitler, as well as the Reichskommissar of the
Ukraine, Erich Koch, basically opined that the populace should be treated
"like Negroes," a policy not always shared by Minister for the East Rosenberg and the governors of the various other subdivisions of the territory.
To add to the confusion, in the war zones the military would soon be
employing over a million Russians, known as "Hiwis," or *Hilfswillige* (willing helpers), in the very bosom of their armies, much of the Hiwis' willingness being generated by a desire for food. What once again became clear
was that it would be absolutely necessary to make use of the locals, no
matter how bad their "blood," for every kind of activity from agriculture to
fighting, because there simply were not enough Germans to keep things
going in these vast regions, a reality that would lead to the same ever-
mutating policies already being seen in Poland.

It was in the midst of this confusingly fluid situation that Himmler
decided to activate the first of his thirty-six long-planned utopian areas of
Germanic colonization in the USSR. The SS-controlled areas of the
Lebensraum, after being cleansed of undesirable elements, were to be settled by networks of pure German villages arranged around support bases,
or *Stützpunkte*, reminiscent of American Wild West forts. Preference for
land grants would go to SS veterans and other carefully chosen racially
pure ethnic Germans.

So popular was this program that, by the fall of 1943, Himmler himself
had to curb unseemly land grabbing by the SS.[94] But in 1942 the SS
troops, still busy fighting and exterminating, were not much use on their
new farms. Colonists would therefore have to be drawn from the *Volksdeutsche* population of the USSR and elsewhere. Himmler also had high
hopes that settlers from the arch-Nordic countries of Denmark, Norway,
and Holland could be tempted to emigrate to the new territories. An

agency was even set up in the Netherlands that hoped to recruit some five million Dutch citizens, not only to help populate the *Lebensraum* but to "relieve overpopulation at home."[95] This program was not a success, and Himmler was thrown back on the "colonists" available locally, who, in the Soviet areas, having been thinned out by the Russian deportations, were not an impressive group, and ran heavily to women and children. Nevertheless, in the late summer of 1942, the SS chief ordered the first project on Soviet soil to proceed. The settlement area, centered on a village to be called Hegewald, was to be established some eighty miles west of Kiev along the main rail line running from Zhitomir to Vinnitsa, where Himmler's eastern headquarters were located. A special task force, or *Sonderstab*, commanded by SS Standartenführer Henschel, a protégé of Himmler, went right to work.

The times were hardly propitious. An attempt to set up an SS *Volkschule* just to the north of Hegewald had been delayed indefinitely due to "increased activities of partisans." The officer in charge, requesting more arms for his men, reported in late July that all traffic had to move in armed convoys, which were frequently fired upon, and that the roads, often mined, were closed between 6:00 p.m. and 8:00 a.m.[96] Food was also in desperately short supply across the area, but news of this sort did not dampen the colonizing spirit. Back home, 500 students were being recruited to come help out in the fall.[97] A complex staff of carpenters, nurses, social workers, and administrators was set up. Elaborate guidelines were issued for the preparation of the villages for some 43,000 settlers. These would be made up of both indigenous *Volksdeutsche*, who would be suitably rearranged, and new arrivals. All would be given farms of 35 to 40 hectares (90 to 100 acres). Windmills were to be repaired, houses made ready for winter; floors, windowpanes, and stoves were to be installed or repaired. "Beautification," however, would have to wait. The dwellings, as usual, would be those of evicted and liquidated Ukrainians, whose abandoned furniture, food, and livestock would be distributed to the *Volksdeutsche*. The new arrivals would have to get right to work on their new farms; to facilitate this, kindergartens for children aged two to six were required. The settlers moving in were to bring their teachers with them, and entire schools for the older children would be moved intact to the new locations.[98]

Before all this could happen, thousands of Soviet Ukrainians would have to be moved out to other villages 300 miles to the south. Internal documents from the offices of those who organized the operation reveal a distinct lack of enthusiasm for a project that promised to be very difficult.

In the course of the fall and winter, fifteen villages were to be resettled, with only enough people left behind to run the sawmills and the state collective farms, which the Nazis had inherited from Stalin and found quite convenient. There was no question of any "voluntary" resettlement. The population, estimated to be a mix of 10 percent Poles and 90 percent Ukrainians, would, the German officials noted, "resist being moved to large farms in the South." Furthermore, since moving the Ukrainians by truck would consume 100,000 liters of valuable gasoline, they would have to go by train. And since these were, as usual, in short supply, one official proposed that the women and children go on one train and that the men and livestock "trek" on foot to the new locations. During the evictions, they gloomily noted, large numbers of police would be needed both to prevent people from "fleeing to the woods" and to guard the empty houses from bandits.[99]

None of these thoughts were revealed in the overly jolly notice posted in the targeted villages on October 10:

> Farmers! The insuperable German army has finally freed you from the Bolshevik Plague. Never again will the hatred of the Jewish exploiters flow over the fertile earth of the Ukraine. Be grateful to the brave German soldiers who have made it possible for you to live a worthwhile human life again. Despite the war there is . . . renewal across the land which only aims at your welfare. German will and German love of order will guarantee the rights of every family.
>
> Now the time has come to give you back your own lands. By doing so we will fulfill your most ardent wish to get back what the Bolsheviks swindled from you. But this wish cannot be fulfilled in this village at the present time, as the population is too dense. In the blessed regions of the Dnieper, of which your poets sing, we will give each family one hectare of its own to settle on. In addition, you will later have the possibility of sharing the common wealth. You will till better soil in the south of the Ukraine than in your old village. Later, when winter still reigns here . . . spring will come there and you can go to your fields earlier, which will give a greater harvest.
>
> Transport will be by train. You can take your important possessions with you. In addition each family can take one cow or bull, and two families can take one horse. . . .
>
> Think that by moving you are giving your children a new and happy Fatherland. Off to the Dnieper! Off to the sunny South![100]

This lyrical document fooled no one. By the eleventh of November, 10,623 people, 1,230 horses, 2,133 cows, and 614 carts had been sent away on fourteen trains, which were found despite the needs of the gigantic German offensive, which had just taken all of Stalingrad except a small strip along the Volga. An understated report on the deportation notes that problems of the first few days caused by "the flight of whole families" were solved by having Ukrainian security escorts describe the destinations in positive terms over loudspeakers at the train stations and by further "reassurances" from settlers who "returned temporarily" for various reasons. The report does not say so, but many of the evacuees clearly believed that the trains were going not to the Sunny South, but to forced labor or concentration camps.[101]

Such fears were well justified. Not far to the west, in the Polish provinces bordering on the USSR, Himmler had also ordered Odilo Globocnik, the SS and Police Leader of Lublin, to make plans for another SS colony near Zamosc. To the SS leaders, national distinctions in the Polish-Soviet border areas were irrelevant: their aim was to rid the entire region of Slavs, be they Polish or Soviet citizens. Zamosc, once a Hanseatic city, could now be completely re-Germanized. The planned string of villages and support bases would stretch from Galicia to Bialystok and include the city of Lublin, whose population of Reich Germans was to be increased, on Himmler's orders, from 4,000 to 10,000. The Reichsführer SS had authorized Globocnik to bring in 27,300 top-class ethnic Germans, many of whom were still in holding camps, from a mind-boggling array of locations, which included Bessarabia, Bukovina, Romania, the Baltics, Leningrad, Serbia, and Bulgaria. Forty thousand more carefully vetted "borderline class A" *Volksdeutsche* from Croatia, Slovenia, Flanders, and Bulgaria would follow a few months later. Excited VoMi officials said they could take care of 98,300 settlers in Lodz en route.[102] A research memo indicated that "space will be created by pushing out the Poles; the Jews will vanish from the city."[103] It was all to be done by the end of September 1942. The methodology for this ambitious project, known as Program Heinrich,[104] was virtually the same as that for Hegewald, but, in this case, action on evicting the Poles was delayed by the fact that Himmler and Heydrich had simultaneously ordered the "resettlement" of the whole Jewish population of the General Gouvernement, not to mention that of Western Europe, which would mean that the area's rail system would be fully booked.

Both Poles and Jews in the Zamosc region were by now used to sporadic arrests, disappearances, killings, and the evacuation of villages, but the rapidly increasing public violence aimed at the Jews in the spring of 1942, undoubtedly related to the actions that had been going on for

months in the USSR, soon created an atmosphere of terror. By early
August it was rumored across Poland that 5,000 Jews a day were being
killed in Warsaw. On August 8, in the small town of Szczebrzeszyn, all Jews
were told to gather the next morning for deportation. Throughout the
night, houses were searched and people were brought to the town square
before being sent away. But thousands more still remained in hiding. In
this town, and many like it, the hunting would go on and on, well into
December, in a frenzy of killing that took place in full view of everyone.
Volksdeutsche, Polish, and even Jewish police hoping to save themselves
participated. By late October, the Germans had turned the pursuit over
entirely to these local enforcers. On October 24, Jews were marched by
the hundreds to the cemetery and killed. More came from surrounding
towns. All Polish men over the age of fifteen were ordered to take shovels
there to bury them. The process went on for nearly a week. Dr. Zygmunt
Klukowski noted in his diary that most of the victims in the cemetery were
women and children, as many of the Jewish men had managed to flee to
the forests. He also observed that "people walking on the street are so
used to seeing corpses on the sidewalks that they pass by without any emotion." It did not matter anymore who the dead were: "The body of a Polish
boy, killed for robbery, lay on the street for more than twenty-four hours"
and was equally ignored.[105]

If the Poles believed the German purification urge would be satisfied
by this orgy, they were wrong. Even as the last Jews were being killed or
deported, Nazi attention and manpower had turned to the Poles. In one
town the church was surrounded during Mass and all the young people
were taken away. Dr. Klukowski wrote in his diary, "People were sure that
the Germans were only interested in the complete liquidation of the Jews,
so the new wave of arrests . . . came as a real surprise."[106]

The height of the deportations of the Polish population came at the end
of November. An elaborate instruction memo, containing minute details
on feeding, escorts, and procedures, once again went to the relevant
authorities. The Poles were to be brought in trucks to a transit camp in
Zamosc. There they would be divided into the usual categories. Groups I
and II would go to Lodz for re-Germanizing and then on to the Reich.
"Good" working families would return to farming. Group III ("unworthy"
for work) individuals, children under fourteen from Groups III and IV, as
well as Group IIIs over sixty were to go in "special trains" to "retirement
villages." All Group IVs except children were to go to Auschwitz-Birkenau
as laborers, probably in the huge I. G. Farben plant conveniently located
next to the concentration camp. Careful records, described at some

length, must be kept of the classifications and assignments. It is in the course of reading these paperwork instructions that one notes that one of the designated groups is "unaccompanied children." Indeed, with the exception of infants under six months, the children of all categories were to be taken from their parents. Even in this dry Nazi document it is clear that those involved knew that the separation, which would involve some 30,000 children, might cause terrible scenes, and require special measures at the railroad stations.[107]

As usual, reality bore little resemblance to the impeccable Nazi memo. In the winter cold, hundreds died in the transit camps even before they were loaded onto trains. There was little food. Arrangements at the receiving end were not efficient, and many more died on the trains. The exact fate of all the children is not known. A few were rescued. According to one witness, some small children from Group III were handed over to the Polish Central Welfare Organization.[108] As word came that trainloads of children would be passing through their towns, inhabitants of Warsaw and Kutno, sometimes fired upon by SS security police, rushed to the stations, where they succeeded in "buying" or extracting some of the small, often dying, bodies.[109] A few children were selected for Germanization from the thousands sent to a special new children's camp at Lodz, where most would be used for forced labor. It is known that 119 went to Auschwitz, where all the boys were killed by lethal injection and most of the girls died of typhus and other causes.[110] The evacuations continued for almost a year. In the end, 110,000 Poles were removed from some 350 villages in the Zamosc area, to be added to the thousands already displaced from other Polish regions.[111] So terrible were the events of these evacuations that even SS General Globocnik confided to his assistant, Hermann Höfle, that he could not look at his own little niece without "thinking about the others." And when Höfle's own twin babies died of diphtheria a short time later, he is said to have broken down at their interment, screaming that their deaths were "the punishment of heaven for all my misdeeds."[112]

There was no dearth of elaborate planning for bringing the incoming *Volksdeutsche* to the new Zamosc and Hegewald settlement regions; indeed, an eager young SS staff had been working on proposals for these colonies for many months. Their first setback came in Zamosc, for which, by October, only 3,900 families, some unsuitable, were even available. Everything had been held up by the lack of trains, the fact that the settlers were to come from hundreds of small camps all over Europe, and the shortage of racial examiners. To make things harder, those employing the settlers where they were currently living often did not want them to leave.

By December, some 17,000 Croatians had arrived but were stuck in the Lodz transit camps. Himmler was outraged and demanded that the situation be resolved by the spring of 1943.[113] But the Reichsführer's anger was of little comfort to the hapless *Volksdeutsche* being brought into the evacuated villages who were rightly terrified by the threat of partisan raids. Dr. Klukowski reported that settlers coming "from Bessarabia . . . are so afraid of staying that shortly after receiving their new houses they escape to the towns, particularly Zamosc," since "many times the evacuees come back to burn down their own houses or kill the newcomers."[114]

The transfers to Hegewald were less geographically challenging. Most came from Polish and Ukrainian areas and once again were moved there in treks with cattle and mattresses piled high. Renovation of the houses, left in particularly bad shape by the departing Ukrainians, was behind schedule due to the shortage of lumber, but it was felt that most could be made livable "before snowfall." The SS economic office and RKFDV folkdom officials pledged stipends and household equipment to help the families set up. Clothes and shoes were more difficult to procure, but Hegewald officials were excited to get a telex on November 4 reassuring them that clothing, shoes, and stockings for "10,000 Volksdeutsch," which had been put "at our disposal by the Reichsführer SS," was on its way from the "train station Auschwitz-East."[115]

Even Christmas was to be adapted for the new SS world. Early in December a memo was issued on "Organizing Volks Christmas Eve Ceremonies in the Villages of the Hegewald Settlement." In no uncertain terms it stated that the SS and VoMi, with the aid of numerous other agencies, must divide up responsibilities and organize the festivities, which were set for very specific days and hours between December 23 and December 26 to allow for the presence of "important" guests. VoMi must procure two trees for each village. One would be in the room where the party would take place and the other in the village square. The indoor tree must be "especially beautifully decorated with apples, cookies, candles, homemade ornaments of straw, garlands, runes, and pine cones." The apples and cookies would be supplied by the local SS garrison. Tree stands must be made in the villages in the shape of a cross or "sunbeams." Every family would get presents of flour, sugar, or baked goods. For the children there would be candy (to be procured by the Hegewald supply office). Children under ten would get toys (supplied by Waffen-SS construction units). These must be nicely arranged about the room and would not be handed out until the end of the party.

A proposal for the ceremony itself, to be put on by the children and teachers with the help of BDM maidens, was also helpfully appended. The theme was to be the idea of a Volks Christmas, as "is usual at home"— where that might be for the uprooted new settlers not being specified. The memo writer stated that "we do not want a religious ceremony"; instead, participants should think of the winter solstice, the return of light, and life freeing itself from frozen winter. The struggle of "our people surrounded by the dark powers" should be emphasized and the soldiers and, especially, the Führer remembered. After these instructions come two long pages of suggested poems, carols, and pageant text. A few old standbys such as "O Tannenbaum" and "Silent Night" were allowed. The poems, for the most part, evoke rather beautifully the universal longing for spring and the end of cold and darkness, and provide reassurances that the eternal order of nature will continue and the warm sun will return, most of which was probably wasted on listeners whose German was often marginal. It is in the lines to be spoken by the children lighting the candles on the Christmas tree that war propaganda takes over, as indeed it had, by now, in every belligerent country:

> Child 1: I bring a light for all the soldiers who bravely perform their
> duty for Germany.
> Child 2: My wish candle is for the Führer who always thinks of us and
> Germany.
> Child 3: My light will burn for all Germans who cannot have Christmas
> Eve ceremonies tonight.
> Child 4: I bring my light for our Mothers who take care of us all year
> long.
> Child 5: Secret silent wings are spread over you, my German land. A
> thousand flames reach out to turn the darkness from you.
> Child 6: Every people decides its own fate—either freedom or slavery.
> And even if the darkness is so great a way to the Light is always free.
> Child 7: Flame shoot up! Light us, for our Volk, to safety.[116]

The children surely did not know it, but by the time of their pageants nearly three-quarters of a million men had been killed, wounded, or taken prisoner in the campaign to take Stalingrad, and thousands more, trapped in the besieged city, in no way able to "decide" their fate and in awful cold and squalor, were celebrating, with the pathetic supplies available to them, their last Christmas. The Hegewald children's young Nazi mentors, earnest and dutiful though they might be, were undoubtedly ecstatic to be on duty there and not in Stalingrad.

Alas, things never did go quite right in Settlement Hegewald. Even during the preparation stages other agencies, clearly dubious about Hege-wald's importance, kept stealing craftsmen working on the project. Food was an eternal problem. Two days after the last Christmas party a delega-tion of *Volksdeutsche* ladies from one of the more remote settlements arrived at SS headquarters to complain that they had not received promised livestock or been given any bread for two months. The *Volks-deutsche*, they said, were constantly being cheated by the remaining Ukrainians and also could not keep up with the work required to produce their milk quotas and care for big families, many of which were run by sin-gle mothers.

It also appeared that the shipments of clothes promised from Auschwitz-East had not arrived. There was a big demand for them: the Hitler Youth, for example, wanted tons of articles for the KLV children evacuated from the Reich.[117] Hegewald chief Henschel and Himmler, who both had demanded further shipments in time for Christmas, com-plained. A reply from Oswald Pohl, head of the SS concentration camp system, informed Himmler that the demand for clothing "from the Jewish resettlement" could not be satisfied to the full because "the delivery of rags is very high." In addition, although some 570 carloads had gone to the Ministry of Economics, "the transportation holdup to the Ukraine" had been "especially noticeable . . . and prevented the delivery of old clothing intended for the racial Germans there." Things would be sent once the transportation situation improved, but, meanwhile, some 211 carloads were in storage in Lodz. A careful categorized list, innocent unless one knows the fate of the former owners of the stored items, was appended. The last category reads as follows:

CHILDREN'S CLOTHING
Overcoats 15,000
Boys' jackets 11,000
Boys' pants 3,000
Shirts 3,000
Scarves 4,000
Pullovers 1,000
Drawers 1,000
Girls' dresses 9,000
Girls' chemises 5,000
Aprons 2,000
Drawers 5,000
Stockings 10,000 pairs
Shoes 22,000 pairs[118]

There were more difficult problems. The SS projects were constantly undermined by the urgent needs of other agencies. The population of the entire region bordering the war zones was in constant flux, making arrangements difficult. In the spring of 1943 it became clear that many of the Ukrainians who had been evicted were filtering back to Hegewald and hiding with unevicted relatives. The "Sunny South" to which they had been sent had not been idyllic. What houses there were had to be shared with two or three other families, and there was neither food nor furnishings. Threats that the infiltrators would be arrested and sent as forced labor to the Reich had little effect, according to one Ukrainian official, as things in the south were so bad that "it was all the same to them."[119] Since February, more *Volksdeutsche* had also been brought in from areas about to be retaken by the Red Army and were living in the usual squalid camps while they awaited housing. One desperate camp official even applied for two "bath cars" known to be on a siding in far-off Posen.

Despite all, during a lull in the Red Army's relentless advance in the spring and summer of 1943, the SS bureaucrats, keeping up a nondefeatist front, continued their planning fantasies. In July, a hundred HJ and BDM boys and girls were scheduled to be sent to Russia for youth theater projects.[120] Arrangements were made for student interns from the Reich to work in the area as far ahead as the spring of 1944 in order to save the *Volksdeutsche* population, which had been "biologically weakened" by twenty-four years of Bolshevik influence and marriage with foreigners.[121] The nervous young SS leaders in some villages, who continued to report in regional meetings the "terrible unhappiness" and need of the *Volksdeutsche*, reduced in some places by July 1943 to picking greens in the fields to eat, were sent back to their posts with renewed exhortations to continue precise implementation of Himmler's utopian plans. But now their work was dangerous: teenaged BDM maidens heading out to their welfare posts had to be escorted by soldiers in "full battle kit" who were reminded "not to forget their gas masks."[122] By late August 1943, major partisan violence had reached well into Himmler's little paradise, and by November, the inhabitants of the Hegewald utopia, such as it was, were in flight before the vanguards of the Red Army.

Late 1943 saw the burgeoning of partisan violence in the East, which was supported by the Soviets and various competing interest groups such as the Ukrainian nationalists and encouraged by the clear perception that the Germans were losing. There were many causes. Contemptuous and cruel treatment, unrestrained murder, and hunger were major among them, but nothing was more likely to generate resistance than the brutal programs to "recruit" labor for German industry.

The idea of bringing *Untermenschen* from the USSR to work in the Fatherland was, at first, anathema for hard-core Nazis and, indeed, for most Germans, who had heard nothing but propaganda on the bestiality of the Slavs for years. It was this attitude that at first limited the use of Soviet POWs to the most menial labor and such projects as testing the efficacy of Zyklon B in the gas chambers being readied for the Jews at Auschwitz. There, on September 3, 1941, the gas was used on the Russians for the first time for the purpose of exterminating human beings instead of lice. It did not work very well. The following morning some of the 600 prisoners used for the experiment were still alive. The amount of gas used was then doubled, this time with satisfactory results. After this initial experiment, hundreds more Soviet POWs were executed in this way. Once the gassing system was working, more than 10,000 Russians were brought in during October 1941 to speed up construction of Birkenau, the extension of Auschwitz, and its crematoria. Most of these also perished. Some were not very old. Records at Auschwitz show that Soviet children as young as eleven were classified as prisoners of war.[123]

Soviet civilians, though employed by the Germans in low-grade jobs all over the occupied USSR, were not supposed to be sent anywhere near the pure-blooded citizens of the Reich. As we have seen, in the early stages of planning for the invasion of the Soviet Union it had been assumed that the millions of German soldiers involved would be home in a few months and that they would resume their old jobs. They would bring with them huge amounts of food for the homeland and massive amounts of raw materials for German industry. Meanwhile, the carefully controlled Polish forced labor, French POWs, and volunteer Western workers would fill in at home, and bringing labor from the USSR was not contemplated.

But even as the German forces entered the USSR, the need for more labor had become so acute in some industries in Germany that many economic leaders had begun to gaze eastward. By October 1941, Hitler, over Himmler's vehement objections, had authorized the deployment of Russians, both POWs and civilians, in war factories within Germany.[124] There was not much distinction between the two categories. All the regulations created for the Poles plus many worse ones were applied to the Soviet workers. They were to be kept in work gangs carefully segregated from both the German people and other forced laborers. Police supervision would be constant. They could not be used as individual workers, and were to have the hardest and dirtiest jobs and be kept on starvation rations. As Göring put it at a meeting of labor administrators:

> Shoveling dirt and quarrying stones are not [the job of German skilled workers]—that is what the Russian is there for. No contact with German population, in particular no solidarity. . . . Russians to arrange own food (cats, horses, etc.). Clothing, housing, maintenance a bit better than what they had back home, where some still live in caves. . . . Range of punishment: from cutting food rations to execution by firing squad; generally nothing in between.[125]

The "housing" would be in unheated barracks within barbed-wire enclosures, and the civilians' clothing, such as it was, must clearly display a badge reading "OST" for *Ostarbeiter,* or Eastern worker. At this early stage the planners did not feel that there would be too many civilians, as the 1.6 million POWs available seemed sufficient. But by early December 1941, the situation of the Soviet prisoners of war was so terrible that only a few thousand were fit enough to be sent. Nazi officials reported that 2,000 a day were dying, and that ten of the fifteen POW camps were quarantined due to typhus epidemics. Of those transported, 25 to 70 percent died en route and the rest were too weak to work when they arrived. Attempts were made to remedy this situation by setting up rehabilitation camps, sending the POWs to work on farms to be fattened up, and urging industries to run their own recovery centers. But, on grounds that *Untermenschen* should not ever be treated as well as Germans, the hard-core Nazis would never relent on the matter of sufficient rations, even when it was clear that their policy was hurting production. One directive, acknowledging that cat might not be a good enough kind of meat, upgraded the allowable types to "horse meat and meat stamped by inspectors as unfit for human consumption." Not surprisingly, 400,000 more POWs died between November 1941 and January 1942, and only slightly more than 160,000 of the 3.5 million prisoners taken by March had been sent to work in Germany, far fewer than were needed.[126]

Attention now necessarily was focused on Soviet civilians. This should have been fertile ground for recruiting, especially in the Ukraine, where Soviet suppression had been ferocious and many were attracted by the possibilities of a better life in the capitalist world. Once again, the German authorities put up posters and made promises to lure workers, and a certain number did respond, but from the beginning voluntary recruitment was a farce. In many towns and villages local officials, given worker quotas that had to be filled by the week or the day, resorted to brutal roundups and raids in which anyone over the age of fifteen could be taken from bed or off the street. Often, a town that did not meet its quotas was burned to the ground in reprisal. Not that there was any reward for volunteering. The workers, the great majority of whom were women and teenagers, were treated like POWs or concentration camp inmates.

Protests from German industry and the various labor administrations had no effect on the Nazi police and racial formations responsible for gathering and transporting the workers. The gatherers were fanatically determined that the Slavs should be treated like beasts. Werner Mansfeld, appointed by Göring to coordinate the recruiting from the USSR, complained that it was "absurd to transport these workers in open or unheated freight cars, only to unload dead bodies at their final destination." He was also aghast at what happened once they got there: well-fed and clothed laborers who were "diligent and careful, and work at a pace that some German workers find hard to maintain," were reduced within weeks by lack of rations to states of such weakness and collapse that they could hardly stand, much less work, and were also made vulnerable to typhus and tuberculosis.[127]

Efforts to keep this situation secret by prohibiting letters home from the *Ostarbeiter* were not a success. Word filtered back, and was made manifest by the Nazis' own policy of sending "unfit" workers, which included the ill and the pregnant, back in transports that were even more gruesome than those going out and were plainly visible to anyone at a railroad station:

> There were dead passengers on the returning train. Women . . . gave birth to children who were tossed from the open window during the journey . . . people sick with tuberculosis and venereal disease rode in the same coach. The dying lay in freight cars without straw, and one of the dead was ultimately thrown onto the embankment.[128]

In early April 1942, with labor shortages ever more desperate and draft calls ever higher, labor "recruitment" for the entire Nazi Reich was centralized under Fritz Sauckel, a technocrat who cared only about producing the bodies required. He was soon joined in this slave trade by Himmler, whose SS had by now set up a string of armaments factories linked to his concentration camps. More and more force would be used to procure the workers, whose minimum age was ever younger. Despite the terrible conditions, the operation was a statistical success: eventually there would be some 2.8 million *Ostarbeiter* and Soviet POW laborers working in Germany proper. The variety of experience among those conscripted was enormous, depending greatly on the attitudes of the procurers, who ranged from benign to corrupt and whose own lives and careers often depended on achieving their quotas. It is clear that illicit profits also could be made on this human trade and that hundreds of young workers were sold outside the official work projects.

On the more benign side was Wilhelm Kube, Generalkommissar of White Ruthenia, the Nazi name for Belorussia, who ordered Hitler Youth emissaries to set up a youth organization to recruit and prepare indigenous children aged fourteen to eighteen for work in Germany. The organization, which is said to have sent thousands of boys and girls to the Reich, was inaugurated in June 1943 with a rather surprising ceremony in which orchestral performances of music by local composers and patriotic songs ("I Love My Fatherland") were combined with speeches by Kube and other Nazi officials, and which closed with the "White Ruthenian national anthem," whatever that might have been at the time.[129] Kube's project did him no good: he was assassinated by an indigenous chambermaid who planted a bomb in his bed.

Efforts like Kube's were the exception. One of the easiest places to find "recruits" was among the people who had been under German control since the first days of the invasion, many of whom had already suffered considerably at the hands of the Soviets. The experience of the Abramov family, who lived near Smolensk, is typical. The father, executed by the Soviets in 1938 for being a Trotsky sympathizer, had left a wife and six children. When the Germans arrived in 1941 the Abramovs' home was taken as a billet for soldiers and the family was moved into a neighboring house with four other families, totaling twenty-five people. This house was burned in a Soviet aerial attack, and their cow, "which served as our wet-nurse," was also killed. In return for food, Mrs. Abramov and the older children were required to clean and cook for the Germans. Their dreary but relatively safe existence changed dramatically one day, when all the families of the village, who do not seem to have been involved at all in partisan activity, were selected to go to Germany:

> In the early morning of February 3, 1943, the . . . families were herded like animals. . . . There were only three sleds tethered to cows. The sleds carried only the very young and a few scant belongings. We walked from 15 to 30 km every day; as we went along we cleared the road of snow. . . . The Germans added more people from nearby villages on the way. Premeditated or unintentional attempts to lag behind were punished brutally. . . . One young girl stayed too long in a dug-out

where we were staying for a short break. The escort found her there, took her out and, for our education in front of everybody, hit her head with the butt of a machine gun. They left her in the snow . . . all covered in blood.

The group was taken first to an internment camp in Mogilev, on the Dnieper, and, after a time, loaded onto trains and taken to another typhus-ridden camp in Latvia. Here the many dead were put in coffins and taken outside the gates, where their bodies were dumped in a ditch so the coffins could be recycled. When Mrs. Abramov became ill, her children, fearing she would be sent to the infirmary, from which no one ever returned, "covered her with our emaciated bodies, so she wouldn't be noticed" until she had recovered.

The Russians were "lined up by family to be sold . . . as indentured servants . . . we were chosen like the slaves in ancient times." The five older Abramov children were sent to different farms and only the youngest boy, aged seven, stayed with his mother, who was sold to a farmer whose son was serving in the German Army. Her job was to keep house and maintain the barnyard while her son took "two horses, three cows, two calves, seven sheep, and five pigs out to pasture." By August 1944, the farm was in the midst of the battle lines, and everyone made frantic efforts to save themselves and the livestock. An explosion severed Mrs. Abramov's leg at the knee and knocked out her son. After the battle, Mrs. Abramov was nowhere to be found. The farm owner claimed that she had been taken to a hospital, but the reunited children, after a long search, found her body hidden under a pile of branches in a bomb crater. Red Army medics who examined the body told them that their mother had died, not from the leg injury, but from a "dagger or bayonet thrust under her left shoulder blade." The farmer was arrested, but was soon released when the Red Army moved on, and the children, now orphans, survived for some months by working on other farms until they were returned to Russia.[130]

Vladimir Kuts, fourteen, would not have any family to comfort him. He was arrested in the Ukraine when Nazi police found propaganda leaflets dropped by Soviet planes in his mother's house. Left to fend for herself when the Soviets sent her husband to Siberia, she was not interested in the propaganda but was drying out the papers in order to use them as fuel. Vladimir was sent alone to a railroad repair facility in Germany. Too small to do the heavy railroad work required, he was moved on to a camp near Stuttgart, where he was given the task of filling bags with lime. This was little better: the filled bags were still too heavy, the fumes and dust in the works made it hard for him to breathe, and the lack of food inexorably weakened him. He was saved by the intervention of some adults who told the foreman that the boy's father was in a Stalinist prison, and persuaded the plant authorities to send him off with a group of workers being made available to farmers. He was in such bad shape that at first no one chose him, and he was about to return to the lime factory when a farmer, who had been delayed, rushed in and took him away. To this day he feels that the farmer, a kindly man who nursed him back to health, was sent by God.[131]

Russian orphanages were another fertile source of recruits. Tatyana Bessonova, fourteen, an orphan from Orel who had been sent for upbringing to a collective farm at age six, was now forcibly taken from there and sent, with two other girls, to work at a small sawmill in Hanover, where she was treated "fairly."[132] Aldona Valinskaya was not so lucky. Before the war, the Soviets had executed her father and arrested her mother in Moscow, and Aldona had been sent to an orphanage in the southern Ukraine that contained some 400 inmates classified as "children of enemies of the people." When the war began, most of the staff fled, leaving the children and a few teachers behind. The children, some very small, survived at first on field greens, fruit, and sunflower seeds. After a time they were briefly caught up in the front lines. As the Germans moved in, the remaining caretakers disappeared and the children were left alone, but found some work and food at a nearby collective farm. Eight of them were chosen for Germanization. The Jews among them were told that they were being taken to "the ghetto." But their fellow orphans, who had given them little souvenirs before they were driven away, learned the next day that all the Jewish children had, in fact, been executed in the night.

Later, some of the older Russian children were sent to Germany. Aldona, sixteen, and eleven others were supposed to go to Cologne. But just across the Polish-German border they were approached by a *Volksdeutsche* woman who told them to get off the train, took them to a café, and sold them to German women who "examined their teeth and hands like cattle" and took them off to various employments. Aldona went to a farm where she was expected to do hard manual labor. Her boss was tough: the Russian girl later noted that "German women whose husbands were at the Eastern Front were more cruel." Aldona managed to escape with two other workers, but they were caught and would spend the next year living on prison trains so awful that the real prisons in which they occasionally stopped seemed luxurious in comparison. At one such stop, a subcamp of Buchenwald, Aldona, who had clearly been classified as a criminal type as well as an *Untermensch*, was sterilized. The interrogations

and transfers continued until 1944, when a relatively merciful camp commander let her work in the kitchen of an air base where no German would
stay, as it was constantly being bombed. There she survived and was liberated by three Americans she has never forgotten, named Michael, Lester,
and Fred.[133]

As the partisan warfare intensified and their parents were killed, imprisoned, or sent to forced labor, more and more children related to the
resistance fighters were left alone without any shelter at all. In many
places the easiest thing for the SS to do was just shoot them, as had been
authorized from the beginning in the efforts to reduce the Soviet population. But many felt the children could be useful. The notorious SS partisan
hunter Oskar Dirlewanger, a released convict, employed them as human
mine detectors: women and children were sent across suspected minefields to clear them for Nazi troops.[134] By the fall of 1942, Hitler, Bormann, and Himmler, encouraged by labor recruiter Sauckel, had also
persuaded themselves that the unaccompanied children and young people
in the Ukraine and Belorussia might be utilized. In January 1943, Himmler, whose Jewish slave labor forces by now were being depleted by mass
exterminations, ordered that partisan children and juveniles were to be
collected in special camps and that those "of racial value" were to be
assigned as apprentices "to the plants of the concentration camps." This
was not the same "racial" evaluation that sought out children for Germanization, but seems to have been limited to weeding out Jews and hard-core
Bolsheviks. Those who passed were to be educated, giving "special consideration to ideas concerning obedience, diligence, unconditional subordination and honesty towards the German Masters." They must be able to
count up to a hundred and read traffic signs, and would be trained to be
"farmers, blacksmiths, masons, spinners, knitters, etc."

Implementation of this order seems to have been somewhat trying to
SS underlings. It was ignored or even resisted in some Nazi quarters
where more moderate treatment of the indigenous population was beginning to seem like a good idea. Nevertheless, SS General Erich von dem
Bach-Zelewski, in charge of anti-partisan activities, who would later win
eternal notoriety for his vicious suppression of the Polish Resistance in
Warsaw, was reported to be "establishing camps for children between 1 to
10," while, from Berlin, SS economic czar Oswald Pohl ordered a camp
for Russian "children of partisans" between ten and sixteen to be set up in
Poland as a branch of the adult concentration camp at Majdanek.

By the summer of 1943 many were having second thoughts about
deporting children. One SS police unit in Latvia, either for lack of facilities

or of desire to deal with the problem, reported that they had "been forced" to return the approximately 1,000 children in their custody to Russian families, even though, regrettably, "this would lead to a strengthening of the Russian ethnic group in Latvia and in due course to an education of the children according to Russian principles." Later they explained defensively that the children were from "harmless Russian people." By July even the SS leader in the Ukraine had clearly begun to think that the removal of small children of partisans was bad propaganda. He proposed that "the . . . public . . . be shown clearly that we even conduct . . . antipartisan warfare with all the humane spirit compatible with our interests of self-preservation. The Ukrainian public shall know that innocent children will be spared." From now on, he suggested, the seized children should be put in local camps supervised by security forces, where care, upkeep, feeding, and "handicraft education" would be carried out by "indigenous personnel." The age limit for entrance to these "humane" camps would be limited, however. In his view, "only children between 2 and 6 years of age can be taken into consideration, since with more grown-up children the idea of hatred and vengeance cannot be eradicated."[135]

Even this small "humane" idea was blown away a week later by a Himmler order declaring that the Führer had decided to clear the entire population out of the partisan areas of the northern Ukraine and central Russia. The men were to be handed over to the labor authorities "with the status of prisoners of war," the women sent to forced labor in the Reich, and "a part of the female population and all children without parents" would go "to our reception camps." From these camps, Himmler mused, the children could, among other things, be sent to work on farms or plantations of kok-saghyz, a plant used in the manufacture of synthetic rubber in factories being developed by I. G. Farben, whose labor force would consist in large part of the children's parents and older siblings.[136]

The proposed plantations and much else would fall by the wayside once it had become clear that the Germans' huge offensive at Kursk, in which they had hoped to regain territory lost after Stalingrad, had failed. There would be no rubber plantations. Instead, the Nazis would soon issue scorched-earth orders and begin a massive, yearlong retreat that would gradually move the *Volksdeutsche* settlers and the occupation administrations back to Poland and Germany. Along with them would go as much of the local population as possible for use as forced labor.

The Nazis were aided during their exodus from the USSR by collaborators who knew that they would be killed by the Soviets if they did not retreat along with the German forces. Among them was Mieczyslaw

Kaminski, half Polish and half German, brought up as a Russian, who had established himself as a pro-Nazi, anti-Soviet warlord near Briansk, just to the west of the Kursk battle area, where he set up a nice economic empire for himself and helped the Nazis hunt down partisans.[137] When the Germans began to withdraw, Kaminski offered his services and that of his "army," a motley collection of outlaws of various descriptions. One of his services was to organize human shields of women and children for the retreating Nazis. Olga Pavlovskaia, five years old at the time, was put on the leading edge of such a formation and remembers picking flowers in the woods during a rest stop. She and her mother managed to escape further along by hiding in the bushes.[138] Things did not work out so well for six-year-old Nikolai Mahutov, his ten-year-old brother, and hundreds of other children who were forced to drag logs with long ropes along the roads ahead of the Germans, in order to detonate any mines. His mother and three-year-old sister were also in the human screen.

By November 1943, Kaminski and his prisoners had progressed some 300 miles west into Belorussia, where, for the winter, the captives were put into a snowy barbed-wire enclosure with no permanent shelters and little food. A partisan raid enabled Nikolai and many other children to escape. Not all survived in the wintry forests, but Nikolai, with his mother and siblings, managed to find his way to a well-established partisan group. Here the little boy attached himself to one of the leaders and went with him on raids to steal salt from German Army supply depots. At the end of the winter Kaminski's brigade attacked the partisans again, and Nikolai, recaptured, continued to serve as a human shield until, still not quite eight years old, he was liberated by Soviet troops near the Polish border.[139]

For children who were sent across that border and farther into Poland the war would last much longer. Anti-partisan operations had been particularly intense in the region around Vitebsk in northern Belorussia. A large number of children were processed through a filth-ridden transit camp in Vitebsk known as the "Fifth Regiment" after the former military installation in which it was located. From there, trainloads of Russians were sent principally to Auschwitz and Majdanek, where men and older boys were separated from the women and children.[140]

At Majdanek an estimated 5,000 children, some with their mothers, were put in Feld V, the new section that had been built for them. Groups from particular villages were kept together, which made things marginally more bearable. During the day, the mothers were sent out to work in the fields. Some little children went with them and pulled weeds near the electrified fences. Very small ones huddled together trying to keep warm.

Sick children were taken to the "hospital," which was often a death sentence. The morning after her three-year-old sister had gone to the infirmary, nine-year-old Elena Putilina and her mother, working in the fields as usual, heard the little girl call their names. Looking up, they saw her in a wagon full of children being taken to the crematorium. Elena remembered that her mother started to scream but "immediately began to be beaten by an overseer with a whip." They never saw the child again. For healthier little ones, at both Auschwitz and Majdanek one good use was found: they were an excellent source of blood, which if not pure enough to allow them to live in the Reich, was apparently acceptable to save the lives of German soldiers.

It soon became clear to the Nazis that the mothers would work more efficiently if the children were not with them, and a separation was decreed. By the fall of 1943, in response to Himmler's orders, the Polish children's camp at Lodz-Konstantynow, to which the Zamosc children had been sent, had been enlarged to take the Russians, and another facility had been prepared in a castle at Potulice, near Bydgoszcz (Bromberg).

The scenes of separation were horrendous. The Jewish children who had been swept along with the rest in the partisan operations were taken away first, but, as their compatriots once again witnessed, they did not go to Lodz: "They put us in the barracks so we wouldn't see, but we could observe that all the [Jewish] children were put in cars . . . they took [them] to the crematorium." This led many mothers to think that all the children would suffer the same fate, and some women went mad with grief as the loaded trucks drove off. Even babies were taken away, and during the first night, many of the separated children, sure they were about to be shot or burned, cried until daybreak.

The Russian children were not killed at this point but were taken off to the new camps. The majority ended up at Lodz-Konstantynow, where they would join the Lidice children, a few Rhineland Bastards, and other "useful" children from all over the Reich. At Lodz, following Himmler's directives, blonds were separated from dark-haired children. Blood continued to be taken. The few "Germanizables" were given better treatment. The camp had both German and Russian directors, the latter being quite humane at times. There was a little more food and clean uniforms were issued, but discipline was military and everyone had to work making straw shoes, sewing buttons on uniforms, and doing other tasks involving military equipment. Quotas were established and failure to fulfill them caused meals to be withheld. Four- and five-year-olds, some so young they did not even know their last names or where they were from, polished floors, carried small objects around, and worked in the kitchen. For the privileged there was even some fun and "education." Classes in German were given so that the children would understand orders; there were some sports and even the odd *gemütlich* songfest, all aimed at preparing a new generation of obedient and docile slave labor. For the "dark" un-Germanizables there was only misery, as one boy, twelve when he entered the camp, recalled:

> We swelled everywhere because of undernourishment, which also affected the nerves, on top of which there was the cold, the blows, and the exhausting labor. Many went out of their mind. . . . The children were given blankets that were as thin as spider's webs and the temperature fell to minus twenty degrees in winter. During the night they froze. Next morning we had to use picks to cut the stiff bodies away from the plank beds. . . . We flung them into a mass grave . . . sometimes they were not quite dead. . . . On an average 120 of the 3–4,000 children died every day.[141]

The camp at Lodz held only a fraction of the Soviet young people conscripted. Tens of thousands more were taken from all along the long front from the Baltic to the Black Sea and sent to work camps in the smallest corners of Germany. The journeys to the camps were hardly ever direct, but were often made up of exhausting and picaresque wanderings. Nikolai Dorozhinski, fourteen, began his odyssey to a concrete factory near Erfurt in Germany with a trek through Moldavia, Romania, and Bessarabia. On the way he escaped once and was taken in by a Jewish tailor and his family who were in hiding. Recaptured by the Romanian police, he and the tailor's son were handed over to the Gestapo and transferred to a satellite camp of the Mauthausen concentration camp, near Vienna. Nikolai told the Nazis that the Jewish boy was his brother, thereby saving his life. From Vienna Nikolai was finally sent to Erfurt. At the concrete factory he was the youngest of 150 *Ostarbeiter*, who would remain there until the war ended.[142]

The Erfurt camp was quite civilized compared to Dachau, where twelve-year-old Ivan Stepanov was part of a detail that had the job of collecting the bodies of those who had died of typhus. The children, chosen for this duty because they were thought to be less susceptible to the disease, had to remove the bodies and bedding from the bunks, stack them on a cart, and take the gruesome cargo to the crematorium. The camp authorities were appreciative: on the days the Russian children had such duty they were given a nice dessert in the evening.[143]

The Nazis never gave up their enslavement operations. Even in mid-June 1944, Army Group Center, still clinging to a salient centered on Minsk in Belorussia, announced that it "had the intention to apprehend 40,000 to 50,000 youths at the ages of ten to fourteen" in its area of control, because the youths, who had lost their parents to labor conscription, were causing "considerable inconvenience" in the battle zones. Later in the long memo announcing this *Heu-Aktion*, or Operation Hay, it becomes clear that there are other issues. The children must not be allowed to fall into the hands of the Soviets, as that would "amount to reinforcing the enemy's potential war strength." The operation also must be "strongly fortified by propaganda under the slogan 'Care of the Reich for White-Ruthenian Children,'" a process already begun by the youth organization set up for them, which had by now sent more than 28,000 teenagers to the Reich factories and military service in the SS and other formations.[144] Alfred Rosenberg of the Ostministerium, clearly worried by now about his postwar fate, raised objections to the last-ditch project: the operation, especially where children under fifteen were concerned, not only would have "unfavorable political consequences" but also would be seen as "child abduction." These quibbles were dismissed by the SS, which now admitted that the operation was also aimed at "the reduction of [the enemy's] biological potentialities as viewed from the perspective of the future," ideas that had been "voiced not only by the Reichsführer SS, but also by the Führer."[145]

12. Seek and Hide: Hidden Children

On July 26, 1942, the Jewish Council in the Netherlands, like its counterparts in the East, was informed by the director of the Office for Jewish Emigration in Amsterdam that all Jews between the ages of sixteen and forty would be taken to "labor camps" in "Germany." The council was responsible for notifying the deportees and processing the complex paperwork. They could not know that these deportations were only one part of the massive "resettlement" operations initiated for all of Europe at the infamous Wannsee Conference in Berlin in January 1942, where plans were made for the "Final Solution of the Jewish Question," or that between January and June, in a hasty building effort, four new extermination camps had been constructed in Poland at Birkenau, Belzec, Sobibor, and Treblinka to bolster the inadequate killing capacities of those already functioning at Chelmno and Auschwitz. Coordination of the transport of groups from so many different countries was crucial and dependent on very specific logistics, most important of which, here as in the East, was the availability of trains.

The allocation of vast transportation facilities to this racial cleansing when Germany was struggling in its war with the Soviet Union is truly remarkable. Nazi race officials knew that the trains would not be available for long. To make sure they would be full, agencies responsible for Jewish affairs in each area would be responsible for producing fixed quotas of human beings at the precise moment the trains were ready to leave.[1] Woe betide the Nazi official who failed in his quotas. Adolf Eichmann, in charge of the whole Western operation, is said to have personally telephoned the officer in charge of the French deportations in a rage when one train was canceled because it could not be filled, fuming that he had lost prestige vis-à-vis the Reich Transportation Ministry.[2]

As we have seen, the deportation of Jews from the West had begun somewhat chaotically in Vienna in 1939 and had had to be delayed. But by the fall of 1941 things were more organized, and much more territory, far from prying eyes, was available for the disposition of those transported. In October, while tens of thousands were still simply being shot in the USSR, massive deportations began from such major Reich cities as Frankfurt and

Vienna. As the new and theoretically more efficient killing centers came on line one by one in March and April 1942, these transports increased, while tens of thousands more would begin to be taken from the Polish ghettos. With this amount of traffic, it was little wonder that the rail line leading to Sobibor soon needed major repairs, forcing temporary closure of its facilities. Undeterred, the Nazis rerouted their cargoes to the other camps, and by late July 1942, the trains would also begin to roll from Western Europe.

Things did not go smoothly at first in Holland. The Jewish Council there reported that it could only come up with 350 or so deportees a day. By now it was clear that conditions in the so-called labor camps were brutal and many Jews did not respond to the summons to present themselves to the authorities. Thousands more negotiated temporary exemptions as essential workers or war veterans, while others, like Anne Frank and her family, went into hiding. To fill his quotas, therefore, SS Lieutenant Colonel F. H. Aus der Fünten, Eichmann's deputy in Holland, had to take Jews from their residences or from the streets. The process was facilitated by the fact that the Jews had been concentrated in Amsterdam and by the requirement, finally instituted on May 2, 1942, that all Jews over the age of six in Holland wear a yellow star. Family members were gathered from wherever they might be; once the parents were in hand, their children were even collected from their classrooms. The first big roundup, or *razzia*, took place on July 14. By the end of July some 6,000 people had been sent to the former refugee camp at Westerbork, now transformed into a transit camp to the "East." By the end of November 1942 it would be a staggering 36,000, which would mount to 103,000 by 1944.[3] To even out the flow, another holding area was established in the Hollandsche Schouwburg, a theater in Amsterdam where those to be deported stayed for hours, days, or weeks to await their turn to be funneled into the deadly pipeline.

There was only one sure method of exemption for full Jews in Holland, and it would not come into force until May 1943. The estimated 8,000 Jews in mixed marriages could, by agreeing to "voluntary" sterilization, avoid deportation and remove their stars, recover their assets, and be eligible for certain jobs. "Voluntary" meant choosing between "going to Poland" or undergoing surgery, which, cynically, would be performed by Nazi surgeons at the Jewish hospital in Amsterdam. This was necessary, as the Nazis knew full well that such procedures would cause an uproar at the regular hospitals. But as news of this measure inevitably leaked out, there was an uproar anyway. Only days after the sterilizations were instituted, the major religious denominations sent Nazi commissioner Seyss-Inquart a joint letter telling him he would be called to account before God, and that "sterilization means bodily and psychological mutilation . . . as well as a violation of both God's commandments and human law. It is the final consequence of an anti-Christian and nation-destroying racial doctrine." Seyss-Inquart replied that the sterilizations were voluntary and told the churches to talk to the SS. There is some evidence that the ruling was too much even for some Nazis. The German doctors assigned to sterilization duty soon resigned, and the SS doctor charged with deciding who should be sterilized seems to have certified that surgery was unnecessary due to impotence in an unusually high percentage of cases. But most of those given this awful choice simply did not respond to the offer.[4]

The very public spectacle of the arrests and deportations was a Guernica-like revelation to many in Amsterdam. Within days, groups began to form with the aim of hiding Jews, and in particular Jewish children.[5] Some had their work literally thrust upon them. Desperate parents who had been summoned often had little time to prepare, and gave their children to trusted friends or even to not-so-well-known neighbors. The generosity of these families was extraordinary, as was the constant danger they faced. One household even took a three-year-old deaf child, luckily blond and blue-eyed, and made sure he went to a special school.[6] Another woman, Cor Bastiaanse, who suddenly found her living room full of children sleeping all over the place, recruited student friends to help her find places for them to stay. One student left four children at a friend's mother's house. She in turn asked her son to find them homes.

From this small beginning came the Utrechtse Kindercomité, mostly run by students, which worked closely with another group of their peers in Amsterdam. Both were based on former student organizations. Other networks, some associated with the Dutch Reformed Church, also relied heavily on young people. Working with children appealed to many of the students: it was nonviolent and (they wrongly assumed) safer: the Nazis, they reasoned, would not blame them so much if they hid children.[7] But harboring Jews of whatever age, the Germans would soon make clear, could cost you your life. Despite this, hundreds of adults and children were hidden until the liberation.

The most important thing was to get the children out of Amsterdam. Nowhere were they more concentrated than at the converted Hollandsche Schouwburg.[8] Indeed, conditions were so crowded there that in October 1942, Jewish Council officials easily persuaded the Nazi authorities, in the interests of hygiene, to allow children up to thirteen to be taken across the street to a crèche. When parents were scheduled for deportation, the children would be brought back to them. The crèche would soon become the most important escape route in Holland for Jewish children. If, after agonizing considerations, parents agreed, their children were spirited away by the student organizations. Officials of the Jewish Council and, it is thought, some Germans with a conscience then altered the records in several places so that the number of family members leaving for deportation would match those that had been arrested. When there was no time to alter the records, parents of very small children were given wrapped-up dolls or pillows to carry onto the trains.[9]

The real children, depending on their size, were taken out of the crèche in backpacks, laundry baskets, and garbage cans. Babies were given pacifiers and buried under heaps of old clothes and trash. Matters were greatly aided by the fact that there was a teacher training school next door to the crèche, with a connecting garden. To relieve crowding, the Nazis accepted the kind offer of the training school principal to let some of the crèche children take naps in a spare classroom. With the full knowledge of all the students and faculty, operatives used the school to save hundreds of older children: their stars were removed, their clothes were changed, and they simply walked out with their "relations."

The Nazis, always terrified of disease, were also persuaded that the children would be healthier if they took walks. During these excursions children would disappear around corners or through doorways into the arms of waiting *Kinderwerkers*. The little ones were, of course, counted before they left, and their caretakers resorted to all sorts of subterfuges to make the numbers come out right, including fomenting general chaos at the front door, during which an extra child would be slipped into the crowd, or handing children out of the windows of the crèche to join the diminished returning group.[10] Given the extraordinarily fast pace of the deportations, speed was of the essence, but the number of children removed each day could not be noticeable or the whole network would collapse. Particularly attractive children were at a disadvantage: one of the German guards took a shine to a tiny orphaned boy and even brought him a big teddy bear. This made it impossible for him to be rescued, and the child, like many other orphans, was used to bring one day's quota up to the required level and deported in April 1943.[11] When word came that orphaned children were to be chosen, the crèche workers, to whom the idea of a small child facing deportation without parents to comfort him was unbearable, did what they could to protect them. Some were hidden in attics. Older ones were even sent out to wander the streets for a time, a

marginally lesser danger. But in the end a certain number always had
to go:

> In the mirror of my memory I see a line of children crossing the street,
> out of the crèche—into the Schouwburg. Backpacks on. Those were
> children with no parents. They had to go when there were not enough
> adults for a transport. Aus der Fünten came himself to choose the chil-
> dren. I could not do anything about it. . . . I let the children cross, I did
> not hold them back. What do you think keeps me awake at night? Not
> the children I found after the war in Limburg, but the children that I let
> cross the street.[12]

Little did the crèche worker know: one report notes that the biggest
transport to leave the Dutch staging camp at Westerbork consisted of
3,017 unaccompanied children and their escort. Its destination was the
extermination camp at Sobibor.[13] In the end only 600 children could be
rescued from the crèche out of the estimated 5,000 to 6,000 who passed
through, but hundreds of others would be collected from individual families and taken to safety.

For the students the hardest part of the process was picking up children
from their homes:

> I have the most terrible memories of it. Actually I believe that I only
> now realize how awful it was. That you walked in. Just to an address.
> And everything was ready. Packed up. A bundle and a small child or
> sometimes two children. And you left with them. You got their papers
> and then you went down the stairs. And they didn't know your name,
> they didn't know where you were going, they knew you would have no
> contact with them. . . . Sometimes you were impatient that they were
> taking so long because you had to go to another address.[14]

Another student *Kinderwerker* agreed, noting later that it was just as
well that none of them had had children yet, otherwise these partings
would have been unbearable.[15] Their impatience was not insensitivity:
more than once the students arrived at the appointed address only to find
that they were too late and that the whole family had already been
arrested.

The trips, usually by train, to take these strange, fugitive children to
shelter, though less emotional, were no less nerve-racking. The best couriers were young girls, less likely to be questioned by the Germans than
military-age boys. Most of them knew next to nothing about children,
especially small ones: "There I sat with such a baby. A child three weeks

old. With a measly cotton suit on. Terrible, so shabby. Oh, and that child looked so bluish and sick . . . that I was mortally afraid each time I looked to see if it was still alive or not. I had no experience whatsoever with little children."[16]

Traveling with very Jewish-looking children added to the tension. Some were said to be from Indonesia, then a Dutch colony. But much depended on the tacit cooperation of fellow travelers and above all on the railroad personnel, who must have recognized the students who made repeated journeys on the same routes, always with different children. The latter, if old enough, had almost always been well instructed by their parents and behaved remarkably well. Toddlers could be a problem: talkative ones were apt to say that Mommy had gone away, sing Jewish songs, or refuse nonkosher food. But even very small children, somehow aware of the danger, could behave with remarkable restraint. In July 1943, at the height of the deportations, Mien Bouwman had to take fourteen-month-old David from Amsterdam to the north of Holland:

> He was not toilet-trained. . . . He was a circumcised boy, so that was not so great. At that time you didn't have plastic pants and so forth. If a child peed, everything got wet. I didn't want to have to change that child's pants. From Amersfoort to Zwolle an NSB [Dutch Nazi] woman sat across from me. That kid didn't look at all Jewish. He was blond and you didn't notice right away. That woman said: "Cute child." . . . I had my story ready of course: he was my nephew and I was taking him to relations in Groningen. He was from Rotterdam. The story was good, but the crazy thing was that I thought: "Either you get off the train or I do." Somewhere in your heart you are so terribly angry. Because I thought: "Rotten woman. Here you say how cute this child is. And if I gave you your way, you would kill him."

Not only did brave David not wet his pants on the train; he waited until he was safely inside the farmhouse that was to be his refuge.[17]

Moving children one by one was the least conspicuous method, but as the numbers of Jews left in Holland diminished, the Nazis decided to close the crèche and ship off all its remaining inhabitants. Typically, they picked one of the most sacred Jewish feast days, Rosh Hashanah, the New Year, for this action. This led the students to take chances. Three young men brazenly took a group of fourteen children out of the crèche and on by train to the south of Holland. The headmaster of the neighboring teaching school chose twelve others from the hundred or so remaining: "That was the hardest day of my life. You know you can't take them all. You know for sure that the ones you do not take are condemned to death. I took twelve. Later you ask yourself: 'Why not thirteen.' "

The agony was not all on the side of the rescuers. Fifteen more children were hidden in the offices of the Dutch Jewish Council. One of them, thirteen at the time, remembers:

> Our biggest problem was to keep the little ones quiet. We pre-chewed cookies for them. While we were there people came to look at us, students who were not strangers to us because we had seen them at the crèche. They took us away one by one. I was the last to leave. Because I was so old I was hard to place. . . . I had to go to the Central Station and buy a ticket to Limburg. In Venray a lady with a blue skirt and a yellow purse walked by. That was the signal for me to get out of the train.[18]

The rest of the children of the crèche were deported a few days later in buses, which for four hours shuttled between the converted theater and the waiting trains.

Once the children were rescued, the problem was what to do with them. Their numbers grew so rapidly that taking them to friends and relatives soon did not suffice. The difficulties were enormous. The children needed the national identification cards that were the norm in European countries, and had to be registered in their place of residence. They also needed ration cards for food. Reasons for their presence in a family had to be convincing. If they were to be new brothers and sisters, age and appearance had to be taken into consideration.

It was hard at first to persuade people in the countryside that there was an urgent problem. The Nazi-controlled press did not, of course, publicize the deportations, and in remote farm villages most inhabitants had never met a Jew and knew nothing of their situation. The caretaker networks expanded at first with agonizing slowness. All sorts of subterfuges were used to explain the presence of the children. "Foundlings" were left on prearranged doorsteps and were then registered as such with the authorities. The Nazis soon caught on. In January 1943 they declared that in the future all foundlings would be assumed to be Jewish.[19] Many children were said to be refugees from bombed-out Rotterdam. Brave female *Kinderwerkers* told neighbors that they had borne an illegitimate child, not at all acceptable at that time. And in an act of remarkable love a man with a Jewish wife, whose newborn child had died at home, called the *Kinderwerkers* to say that they would take one of the threatened children. In the week it took to find a suitable baby, the mother, making crying sounds, pretended for the sake of the neighbors that her own infant was

*Two sons of the Bogaard family with Jewish girls they hid on their farm in the Netherlands.
Three members of the family were caught by the SS and died in concentration camps.*

still alive. The courier who brought the new child took the dead one away and buried it deep in his own mother's garden.[20]

Efforts were made to send fairer children to the northern provinces and darker ones to the south of Holland, where blending with Southern European cultures was marginally greater. Children were carefully distributed so that no area would be saturated. A complex support operation, involving local church and government officials, produced false identification and ration cards and, with the connivance of "good" teachers, even allowed some of the children to go to school. By late 1943 so many Jews had been deported that the flow of children slowed down, but the couriers still had to visit the caretaker families to deliver clothes, money, and up-to-date ration cards, for the Nazis, well aware that thousands of Jews and Dutch resisters were in hiding, frequently changed the format and number of documents needed, in order to flush them out. These efforts were foiled by the complicity of many a local bureaucrat.

Extraordinary patience and kindness on the part of caretakers was needed to help the small refugees, usually terrified and sometimes defiant, assume whole new identities. Although this was successful in most cases, not all the families could deal with the children they were given, nor could some of the children manage the needed transformations that required them to respond to different names, forget their relations, traditions, and former homes, and eat strange food. The less adaptable the child, the more remote his refuge. Denunciations were a constant threat, and there were cases of abuse and exploitation. This meant that the student networks had to be ready to move children at a moment's notice. Indeed, some were moved many times and often a group house, which was the most dangerous situation, was the only solution.

The Nazis never let up in their pursuit of hidden Jews or their caretakers. Many of the networks were betrayed, and the Jews involved were sent to Auschwitz and Bergen-Belsen. Their Dutch protectors went to prisons and camps in Holland; if they were lucky enough to be released, they went underground themselves.

After D-Day, in June 1944, the buildup of German forces in Holland made hiding people ever more difficult, as troops were billeted in farmhouses or came to requisition food. By now the Nazis were looking for downed pilots, forced labor evaders, and Resistance workers as well as for Jews. Houses were raided on the slightest pretext. Ingenious hiding places abounded, and the hidden children became adept at all sorts of dissimulation and evasion. But their experiences were often terrible. One girl, hidden between the springs and mattress of a bed, survived even though German soldiers repeatedly stabbed the mattress with bayonets.[21] Other children took to sleeping in the woods, from where many witnessed the arrests of their couriers and caretakers. The safe houses became fewer and often had to be shared with escaping pilots and a variety of other fugitives. By early September 1944, the Allies were so close that thousands of Dutch Nazis fled to the Reich, but liberation would not come for eight more months. During that time, while starvation reigned, hundreds more Resistance workers were arrested and hiding places revealed. In the end, the student networks alone, with the help of an estimated 3,300 to 4,400 households, saved some 1,000 children (and many more would survive in random situations), but most of the Kinderwerkers, to this day, are profoundly distressed that they could not do more.

Once the deportations began, underground efforts to save Jewish families and children went on in every occupied country, their methodologies adapting as necessary to their particular variety of German occupation government and their geographical peculiarities. In Denmark, a German shipping official, Georg Duckwitz, informed Danish politicians of SS plans to arrest all 8,000 Jews in the country in one massive operation. So fast did the news spread and so universal was the willingness of Danes to take Jews in that only 284 prisoners were arrested to fill the two large ships that the SS had commandeered to transport their victims to Poland. A fleet of small fishing boats, with the blatant collusion of many regular German military units, moved most of the rest to Sweden, which in an unprecedented move had publicly broadcast its willingness to receive the Danish Jews.[22]

The situation in France was more complex. The country was unique among the conquered nations in having an unoccupied zone run by the autonomous government in Vichy, which still had certain powers in the German-controlled Occupied Zone. This was convenient for the Germans, who lacked sufficient manpower to replace the French agencies, among them the police. The Vichy regime, deluding itself that it was maintaining control in its country and assuring future influence for itself in Germany's New Order in Europe, cooperated in major fashion with the Germans and had even beaten them to the punch when it came to restrictive legislation. This was not difficult, for, as previously indicated, the ideology of Pétain's National Revolution was remarkably compatible with that of the Nazis in many areas. Within weeks of the French surrender, prohibitions on anti-Semitic articles in the press had been rescinded. On October 3, 1940, a Vichy *Statut des juifs*, echoing the anti-Jewish laws of the Reich, relegated all Jews in France, native or foreign, to second-class status. The next day, another law authorized local officials to intern foreign Jews at will or to require those who could support themselves outside the internment camps to live in specified localities under police supervision. The German authorities, meanwhile, to the distress of the French, were concentrating on pushing as many Jews as possible into unoccupied Vichy and establishing their own racial agencies in Paris. Of particular interest to the Nazis was a central Jewish organization of the type already extant in the Reich and Holland, which they would be able to use to enforce ordinances, produce a census of Jews, promote emigration, and exploit Jewish assets.

Anxious to retain control of these matters in both their zone and the German-controlled areas, the Vichy government, in March 1941, hastily formed its own Jewish agency, the Commissariat-General for Jewish Affairs, which constantly issued new regulations. This was fine with the Germans, who could now leave the blame and bureaucratic aspects of administering anti-Jewish programs to the French. Soon the anti-Jewish laws were so complicated that Vichy had to publish a special guidebook for lower-level officials.[23] But the French were far too lenient for the Nazis. Despite more and more stringent residence rules and the ferocious

Aryanization of Jewish businesses, the Pétain government continued to exempt war veterans, long-established Jewish families, relations of Vichy higher-ups, and celebrities of various kinds from the harsher regulations. Jewish youths were soon banished from the Chantiers de la Jeunesse, but younger children would attend French schools throughout the war and the universities were still allowed to allot 3 percent of their classes to Jews. In addition, the byzantine French bureaucracy, much of which had survived the invasion, slowed the emigration process, even for those who could obtain visas, to a crawl.[24]

Impatient with all this, in June 1941 the Nazis required a new census of Jews in Vichy France, and by November had forced all Jewish organizations to unite in the Union Générale des Israélites de France (UGIF). In December all personal documents of Jews had to be stamped with a "J." On the fourteenth of that month, the Germans announced, among other things, that deportations of "criminal Judeo-Bolshevik elements" would soon begin and decreed that the sheltering of wanted Jews was a felony. Vichy protests of these tough measures were of no avail. In March 1942 the first group of more than 1,000 Jews was sent from the internment camp at Drancy, just outside Paris, to Auschwitz, and the pressure continued to mount. On June 7, 1942, all Jews in the Occupied Zone were required to wear yellow stars, one of the few measures steadfastly rejected by the Vichy government and never instituted in their zone. Two weeks later 5,000 more were deported. It was only the beginning: at a meeting in Berlin on June 11, Himmler had ordered that 100,000 Jews be sent east "for labor service" from both zones of France. The process would be supervised by a new official from Himmler's command, Higher SS and Police Leader Carl Albrecht Oberg, who had had plenty of experience in Poland, and who would not be restrained by the scruples of the regular Army. On June 27 a German emissary duly informed Vichy Prime Minister Pierre Laval that he would be required to provide 50,000 Jews for deportation effective immediately.[25]

This was not quite what Vichy had in mind for French Jews, but it was the perfect opportunity for them to rid themselves of the foreign and stateless refugees who filled the terrible internment camps and were scattered about the countryside. Those who lived in supervised residence areas could be sent to camps at any time by order of the departmental prefects and, eventually, the supply could be sustained by further limiting the emigration of foreign Jews. "Foreign" was defined as anyone who had come to France after January 1, 1935, even if they had been naturalized. Later this would be rolled back to 1933, but Nazi efforts to push the limit to 1927 were refused by Pétain himself.[26] The Germans, interested mainly in filling their trains, and intending to deport all the French Jews in the fullness of time, agreed to begin with the foreigners, who would be supplied by the French authorities.

In France, as everywhere, the pace of deportation, once under way, would be staggering. In an operation unbelievably named Spring Wind (*Vent printanier*), 28,000 Jews were arrested in the Paris region on July 16 and 17. Instead of a theater, the French operation would once again make use of the Vélodrome d'Hiver stadium as a staging area. The arrests were not random. Lists had been prepared using the meticulously maintained census and residence records of the Paris police. Children could not be left behind. In the end about 13,000 Jews were detained in this sweep, of whom 7,000, including 4,000 children, were jammed into the stadium, where, once again, no sanitation, food, water, or bedding of any kind were provided during the week they were held there. The Germans were not pleased at the 15,000-person shortfall, due in large part to leaked warnings and deliberate inefficiencies on the part of the French police, who had done the rounding up.

From the Vél d'Hiv the Jews were taken to various internment camps and finally to Drancy, which, like Westerbork in Holland, would now change from a refugee facility to the main deportation camp in the north of France. There French administrators, until they were replaced by Germans in July 1943, decided who would go on the trains. The more "French" you were, the better the chance for delay in departure. Among children, preference was given those with French nationality whose parents were both still at liberty; but infants and toddlers who were with their mothers were not in this lucky group, nor were children under sixteen with only one free parent or those between sixteen and twenty whose parents had been deported or soon would be. If children were in the camp hospital when the rest of the family went, it was too bad, and they were left behind for the time being.[27]

The situation of unaccompanied children at Drancy, often so small that they did not know their own names, was dreadful beyond belief:

> The children [ages two to twelve] got out of the buses and the older ones immediately took the tiny ones by the hand and did not let go during the short trip to the dormitories. . . . The children were in bare rooms in groups of one hundred. Buckets for toilet purposes were placed on the landings, because many of them could not walk down the long . . . stairways to the toilets. The little ones, unable to go alone, would wait agonizingly for help from female volunteers or another

child. This was the time of the cabbage soup at Drancy . . . it was hardly suited for children's digestion. Very quickly all the children suffered from acute diarrhea. They soiled their clothing . . . with no soap, dirty underclothing was rinsed in cold water, and the child, almost naked, waited for his underclothes to dry. . . . Every night one heard the perpetual crying of desperate children . . . and from time to time the distraught calling out and the wailing of children who had lost all control.[28]

The Germans, desirous of having able-bodied workers constitute 90 percent of the early transports, were at first not enthusiastic about taking children along, and indeed soon began dumping them in Vichy. But after repeated requests from Laval, who also did not wish to be burdened with their care, and whose minions found the young useful for filling their quotas for the relentlessly appearing freight cars, the issue went to Eichmann himself, who finally agreed to their inclusion. Soon carloads made up entirely of children would leave Drancy.[29] The scenes at their departures made clear why the Nazis had not wanted to deal with the process: "The day of the deportations the children were awakened at 5:00 a.m. sometimes a whole dormitory of 100, seemingly overcome by uncontrollable panic and dread, no longer heard the soothing words of the grownups . . . then gendarmes were called to carry down the children who were screaming in terror."[30]

Once this first wave from the Occupied Zone was on its way, deportations began in Vichy. The Nazi quota fillers had high hopes for this area, having mistakenly assumed that there were 40,000 foreign Jews in the internment camps alone. Clearly expecting to net French Jews as well as foreign ones, the Nazis set a quota of 32,000 from Vichy France to be delivered by September. Deportations from the internment camps began in the second week of August, and a general roundup was to take place from August 26 to August 28. The difference was that parents were at first allowed to leave their children behind if they wished.[31]

The agencies that had been involved with the physical well-being of children in the camps now turned to rescue. This was nothing new, especially for operatives of the French rescue organization, OSE, who had been moving families and children illegally from the Occupied Zone to Vichy for many months. But now time was short and the Nazis' appetite more voracious. The formal OSE office in Paris was closed and replaced with a "social club" in an obscure location where children could be left by their parents and taken to refuge with gentile families. This office operated throughout the war, at great peril to its workers, and is said to have saved some 700 children.[32]

In Vichy news of the deportations led to frantic efforts to extract children from the camps. The methodology of the French sometimes aided this effort. When a transport was to take place, all the apparently "deportable" Jews in a camp, plus those collected from the countryside, would be herded into a sorting pen. French officials would then decide, case by case, who might be exempt. All sorts of excuses, from being a war veteran to baptismal certificates, were brought forth; lives could depend on some tiny element of documentation. The child welfare workers, of various religions and nationalities, used every conceivable argument and deception, and were constantly helped by sympathetic officials. They pretended to be Swiss Red Cross workers, falsified passes, and wore down the deporting committees with endless arguments. Success in exempting the children was not the occasion for joy; the parents' decision to part with a child was no easier here than anywhere else:

> No one slept the night before the children were to be moved out of the camp, now almost entirely occupied by men and women whose fate was sealed. Those hours will remain an ineffaceable memory. Some groups, both Christian and Jewish, spent the night in prayer. Some parents passed hours writing out final admonitions for their children: many wrote wills, disposing of property they had left in Germany. . . . The terrible morning came, with the military trucks drawn up before the office. Families clung to each other—many cried out in wild affliction and others stood dry-eyed and tense as children were loaded into the trucks. We would never forget the moment when the vehicles rolled out of the camp, with parents trying in one last gaze to fix an image to last for eternity.[33]

As it became clear that this quasi-legal method of rescue was too slow, the agencies took to adventuresome and dangerous methods not usually associated with Quakers, the YMCA, or men of the cloth. A group of teenaged boys was hidden behind the water tank on the roof of a camp for four days and fed by the camp cook until they managed to escape.[34] At the Rivesaltes camp, a delivery man built a special compartment in his truck, in which he removed two or three small children on each trip. A group of young Protestants arrived with vans at the gates of a prison where forty children were being held for deportation and, using forged papers ordering the children moved to another holding area, loaded them up and simply drove away.[35] In another extraordinary operation, twelve teams of rescuers, including priests in their cassocks, cut the wire fences and main power cable at the transit camp at Vénissieux, crept into the barracks, and in the pitch darkness tried to persuade the doomed families inside to part with their children, some very small. The anguish of having to make such a decision in these chaotic conditions is unimaginable, but one by one, a hundred children were carried beyond the barrier and spirited off to two German military buses that had been purloined for the occasion. Both of these groups were first taken to convents and from there were scattered to farms and Catholic boarding schools. Some very young children taken from Vénissieux, who did not know their own names, were never identified; their parents, as far as is known, did not survive.[36]

News of the roundups and deportations soon spread abroad, doing little for Nazi public relations. Parisians, who had paid scant attention to the legal and economic exclusion of the Jews, were outraged by their public humiliation and the imposition of the yellow stars. Once again, the centrally located train stations were scenes of horror as human beings were jammed into filthy freight cars. A gendarme in charge of a train with 960 "passengers" reported as follows:

> The special train of September 1 carried a mixed group of men, women, children, old people, sick and disabled who were left to their fates from the time of departure. . . . The mass of people was crowded together on straw soaked with urine. Desperate women could find no place to satisfy their natural needs in privacy. Those who fainted from the heat and stench could not be helped. The spectacle of this train made a strong and unfavorable impression on the non-Jewish French populations who saw it, especially in the stations.[37]

Many churchmen protested, including the French Protestant leader Marc Boegner, and Catholic Archbishop Saliège of Toulouse, never a Vichy supporter, issued a passionate pastoral letter:

> Both rights and duties are part of human nature. . . . They were sent by God. They can be violated. But no mortal sin can suppress them. The treatment of children, women, fathers and mothers like a base herd of cattle, the separation of members of a family from one another and their deportation to unknown destinations are sad spectacles. . . . Why does the right of asylum of the church no longer exist? Why are we defeated. . . . In our own diocese . . . scenes of horror have taken place. Jews are men and women. . . . They too are members of the human

race. They are our brothers like so many others. A Christian cannot forget that.[38]

Detailed news of the scenes of deportation was immediately flashed abroad by the international welfare agencies working in France and by diplomatic representatives of the nations accredited to the Vichy government. Even German officials in France fussed to Laval that the public separations of children and parents were bad PR. The uproar was double-edged: those objecting to the separation of families on humanitarian grounds led Laval to be ever more adamant that children should be sent to the "new settlements for Jews in the East" along with their parents, a stance that would help doom the first serious gesture by the United States to take in endangered Jewish children.

The precedent of exemptions to normal visa processing set for the British children in 1940 was now put to good use by the American State Department.[39] Available quota numbers plus the ability to issue special visitor's visas made it possible for the State Department to approve 1,000 visas for children in mid-September without approaching Congress. The number was increased to 4,000 in October. Mexico, Ecuador, Uruguay, the Dominican Republic, and Switzerland agreed to take several thousand more.[40] The problem now lay with exit visas from France. The Vichy government, under pressure from the Germans, who did not want a propaganda extravaganza to surround the arrival of the children in America, insisted that the United States promise that there would be no publicity. This was actually fine with the State Department, which did not want to give Congress any excuse for new hearings. Alas, confidentiality foundered on the eternal problem of funding. The secret was revealed when the news that some $900,000 had been raised to save the first 1,000 children appeared in the *New York Times* on October 15.[41] In the end Laval agreed to let 500 leave, but he continued to add ludicrous and time-consuming regulations. Undaunted, aid workers fought to deal with the red tape, and managed to charter a ship and to get an escort team of social workers and medical personnel under way from New York to Lisbon by November 7, so that all would be ready when the visas were issued. They need not have bothered. The next day, U.S. forces landed in North Africa and Pétain broke off relations. He need not have bothered either: on November 11, rubbing in his reversal of the Allied victory in World War I, Hitler took over all of Vichy France except for a small strip on the Mediterranean coast.

With the Germans in full control, French child-saving operations went further and further underground and became more perilous. The group homes had been convenient targets for arrests from the beginning, but at first only children over sixteen were usually removed. With the arrival of the Germans, these homes were "blocked" and all movement of children forbidden. In late January 1943, 800 children from the homes were deported. The welfare groups now began to move children out into the countryside. A number were taken to the part of France occupied by Italy, where the racial laws were not strictly enforced. This was a good stopping-off point for illegal entry into Switzerland, but was taken over by the Germans when the Mussolini government fell. In response, the OSE and its partners set up a complex rescue network in the south of France. Divided into four carefully compartmentalized zones, it came to be known as the Garel Network after the Resistance fighter who was in charge. The methods were much the same as those used in Holland: names were changed, children were sent to places where no one knew them, and they were supported by constantly traveling workers who supplied ration cards, clothes, and emergency transfers.[42]

Operatives of every denomination arranged foster homes; there was no dearth of offers to hide children. It soon became clear which departmental prefects were less inclined to enforce the anti-Jewish laws, and more children were sent in their direction. According to the organizations there were, eventually, some 6,000 unaccompanied children hidden in France. This number does not include those who were placed without reference to the organizations, which were surely many more.

The success of the sheltering of children required a high level of deception by all concerned. In many cases virtually all the inhabitants of a town united to hide the fugitives, nowhere more so than in the famous Huguenot village of Le Chambon sur Lignon, tucked away in the mountains of the Massif Central, southwest of Lyon. The Huguenots had themselves suffered terrible persecutions in the past, and quiet defiance came easily to them. It is estimated that the 3,000 residents of the village and its surrounding farms, using Boy Scouts, housewives, and dogs in their warning system, saved at least 5,000 fugitives. Funding for the hundreds of children lodged in "farm schools," boarding houses, and the residences of the Cévenol boarding school was secretly funneled in by a plethora of international agencies. A benefactor, unknown to this day, regularly left blank official ID cards, which could be filled in to fit each new arrival, on a table at the entrance of the house of Huguenot pastor André Trocmé. The Chambonnais reveled in their ability to frustrate the Vichy police, who, at the height of the roundups, arrived in the town with several buses and considerable manpower to take away the Jews they knew must be there. After three weeks of fruitless effort, during which the electricity mysteriously failed and Boy Scout activity strangely increased, the gendarmes withdrew with only one prisoner. The searchers did not give up, however. A year later, despite all the precautions, one of the residence houses at Le Chambon was taken by surprise. The children were lined up against the walls and interrogated, one by one. The Protestant head of the house and all but one Spanish refugee boy, who had saved a German soldier from drowning a few weeks before, were deported.[43]

The foster home system was augmented by a remarkable underground railway network that took children into Spain and Switzerland. The Swiss government, when asked by Nîmes Committee officials, who had set up offices in Geneva after the German takeover of Vichy, to take in some of the children who were eligible for American visas, never replied formally to the request, but the estimated 1,600 children who managed the harrowing trip across the border were well taken care of if they could get there. One route led through the small town of Annemasse, on the Swiss border, where local officials and partisans tried to provide warnings of Nazi patrols. Groups of twenty-five or so children would be taken to a small playing field, bordered by forest, where they would play soccer and other outdoor games. At dusk, they would melt into the woods with their guides and head for the barbed-wire fences at the frontier. They did not always make it. One report notes, with incredible understatement, that "there was a tragic mishap when the Nazis put their dogs on a small group of children being helped through the barbed wire on the Swiss frontier, and the whole group perished," adding that the nearby grave of their "courageous young French woman guide" was found after the war.[44]

But the protectors in hundreds of locations could not compete with the deadly zeal of the Nazi racial agents and their frequently criminal informers, who never gave up searching for "deportables." As late as April 1944, the SS in France ordered its operatives to step up arrests of Jews, regardless of nationality.[45] "In order to save work and petrol," operatives were exhorted to greater efficiency. All members of extended families were to be collected at one time. If "not all members of the Jewish family are found in the apartment, it should be occupied until the missing Jew returns." Offspring who had been sent to children's homes were included. To avoid unpleasant scenes, "when children are taken from these homes, it is advisable to do this, if feasible, in the presence of one Jewish parent." In addition to these delicate measures, bonuses for informers ("not too

high, nevertheless . . . high enough to give sufficient encouragement")
were increased and the pretense of cooperation with the increasingly
reluctant French police and the regular German forces was dropped in
favor of the vicious and pro-Nazi paramilitary Milice.[46] On the Thursday
of Easter Week 1944, a holiday, one of the few remaining OSE group
homes, hidden in the tiny farm town of Izieu, was raided while the children were at breakfast. It is thought that they were betrayed by a local
farmer. The forty-four children, aged four to seventeen, unable to initiate
their carefully rehearsed escape plans, were "thrown like packing cases"
into trucks along with seven of their caretakers. Within ten days, with
great efficiency, thirty-four had been processed through Drancy, transported to Poland, and killed in the gas chambers.[47]

This little group had been sitting ducks; for individual Jews and their
children trying to live in the vast spaces of rural France, survival was often
a matter of luck. Fifteen-year-old Stanley Hoffmann and his mother, worn
down by fear, left Nice in late 1943 for the village of Lamalou, in the
Hérault, three months after Stanley's best friend had been arrested on his
way home from school. Provided with false identity papers by Stanley's
history teacher, they traveled to Lamalou in a blacked-out train, hoping for
peace and quiet. To their surprise they found that the village was being
used as a training camp for 1,000 teenaged Wehrmacht draftees. Despite
this, the Hoffmanns were taken in by the villagers, whose older children
were, by now, also threatened by Nazi forced-labor roundups. It soon
appeared that the mostly sixteen-year-old German soldiers had no interest
at all in Jews, and Lamalou, where the SS seems not to have had serious
influence, turned out to be quite safe.[48]

Little Isaac Levendel, aged seven, was not so lucky. His mother had
continued to run her tiny shop in the town of Le Pontet, near Avignon,
until the combination of Allied bombings, growing hostility to her in the
town, and a new registration of Jews in May 1944 finally persuaded her to
leave. On June 4, traveling by bus and donkey cart, the two joined another
Jewish family on a cherry farm deep in the country. The next day Mme
Levendel, rejecting the advice of her friends, decided she must return to
Le Pontet to get some things from her store. She did not come back. Frantic, Isaac and one of the daughters of the other family also went back to Le
Pontet to try to find out what had happened:

> I ran into the store. . . . Now, the shelves and the cash drawer were
> menacingly empty. In the half-light, I could see that everything was
> gone. Claire found me in the kitchen staring at a dried and charred

omelet inside the open door of the cold kitchen stove. Obviously, my mother did not get to start her meal. I do not remember how I had gotten to the kitchen . . . I just recall my loneliness in front of the dried omelet. . . . Our stove had been full of life before . . . there my mother used to read me stories before going to bed . . . there I learned to forget my fear of lightning in the safety of her arms. . . . Now the stove stood dead, and the kitchen was empty.[49]

Isaac, crushed by his loss, was taken to a large and cozy farm family who accepted him with no prior notice and no discussion. This was brave: their neighbor, accused of being in the Resistance, had recently been tortured by having both legs cut off with an electric saw before he was shot and his farm set on fire. Isaac survived the war, but Mme Levendel, who had been arrested by two French agents, was deported and did not return.

The rounding-up process continued all over France, as it did everywhere, until the very last moments of the Nazi occupation. Despite the Allied landings in Normandy on June 6, 1944, the Vichy regime was still urging the completion of a new census of Jews on July 4. By the end of the war the number removed from France would reach some 75,000, which was approximately 25 percent of the total, but far below Nazi expectations.

Once the clearing of the ghettos began, and even before that time, children were, of course, also hidden in Poland. But in this realm of total German domination, where the gentile population was, for the most part, just as expendable as the Jews, there was little safety anywhere. There were other complications, principal among them the fact that Jews and gentiles in the region essentially lived in separate societies, each with its own rigid religious beliefs and strong customs. So self-contained was most of the Jewish community in Poland that an estimated 85 percent did not speak Polish but communicated in Hebrew and Yiddish. Nor had there been much love lost between the two communities over the years, and anti-Semitism, pumped up before the war by the Polish government in its unsuccessful efforts to align itself with Germany, was strong. Most "Poles" and "Jews" (so denominated even though all were Polish citizens), interdependent when it came to commerce, lived separately at the personal level. To this mix the Germans had added a new power class in their promotions of the *Volksdeutsche*, some of whom were eager to out-German the Germans in anti-Semitism, while the Russians had exacerbated ancient ethnic rivalries in their zone before losing it to the Nazis. In

A group of children from the Lodz Ghetto boarding a deportation train.

this cauldron, for every ethnic group survival was all, and for many this was based on the utterly misguided policy of pleasing the new masters and praying that they would go away soon. Jewish leaders hoping to satisfy the voracious monster had advised their brethren to go to the ghettos, work hard, and cooperate. Thousands of Poles, trying to avoid deportation, pretended to be *Volksdeutsche*, and many others, hoping to save themselves, collaborated in the worst atrocities of the Nazis. But the vast majority of both Poles and Jews tried to keep low profiles and obey just enough to avoid trouble.

From the beginning, however, there were also people who helped others without thought of ethnic origin. At the time of the invasion, no one in Poland could possibly have imagined what the Nazis' plans really were, but even early on conditions were so bad for Jews that officials in the Polish Welfare Administration in Warsaw had set up a secret help network that specialized in false documents and other assistance and had managed to make contact with Jewish organizations inside the ghettos. As the Nazis' intent became clearer and evidence of extermination grew, and as the numbers of those seeking hiding places as whole families or desirous of sending away their children burgeoned, other help organizations came into being, many of which eventually amalgamated into the Council for Aid to Jews, known as Zegota. This group was sanctioned by the Polish government in exile and received small amounts of funding from it via the underground. Zegota, which was similar in many ways to the organizations in France, took hundreds of children out of the Warsaw Ghetto through secret tunnels and by other means placed them in families and convents, and underwrote their care. Zegota operatives moved children to new locations when exposure threatened and dealt with their documentation. As had also been true in Holland, midwives working for Zegota delivered babies for women in hiding and tried to place them in foster families. This was of vital importance: a crying infant in a walled-up bunker beneath a house, which might hold a number of people, would betray them all, and such babies, in acts of surpassing tragedy, were often killed by their own parents.

The basic problems of identity change, feeding, concealment, and the risk of betrayal, present in the West, were all intensified in Poland. The punishment for sheltering Jews, promulgated on October 15, 1941, was death, as was the penalty for leaving the ghettos without permission. These penalties were carried out without even the pretense of a trial or hearing wherever fugitives were found. Dr. Klukowski reported as follows in his diary:

> March 22 [1943]: At the hospital I admitted a villager from Gruska Zaporska. He had been hiding six Jews from Radecznica in his barn, giving them not only shelter but food for several weeks. When the Germans began searching his farm he attempted to escape and was wounded. He died a few hours after his admission to the hospital. The Germans ordered that he be buried in the cemetery as a bandit, which means without a casket in an unmarked grave. The next day this man's wife, his eight-year-old son, and his three-year-old daughter were executed, along with the six Jews.[50]

For Jews from smaller towns who either never went to a ghetto or who escaped from one, hiding with farmers in the country was frequently the only option. Not all hosts supplied food. Older children, often disguised as peasant women, would creep out to nearby villages to buy or steal what they could. But once they were suspected, they had to disappear altogether and became totally dependent on outside help. As their situations deteriorated some families left caches of valuables with Polish friends or acquaintances. Sometimes these trustees sold things off slowly and, if they knew where the owners were, got cash to them. Other fugitives risked all to go back to retrieve money or jewelry, which not infrequently had disappeared. Many of the host families simply threw the hidden families out or denounced them when there was no more money or when buying extra food aroused suspicion. Much depended on luck.

Marianna Adameczek was nine when, wounded in the arm, she fled from the site where most of her family and many others were being shot. She managed to reach a prearranged hiding place her father had set up with Polish friends. With another girl, she would spend the next two years in a "specially prepared hole dug in the barn." There she was cold, in pain until her wound healed, and miserable at having to be silent at all times (a need for almost every hidden child), but she at least had company and kind caretakers.[51] Hiding was different for Leszek Allerhand, who spent his days completely alone inside a large tomb in a cemetery while his mother searched for food. Later he was put in a closed-up apartment and "forbidden to walk, move, use gas, light, toilet, or the bathroom." He was told to sleep on the floor and stay away from the windows. As he put it:

> I was to be lifeless. And thus I barely lived. . . . Every couple of days, in the morning, I would find food and a note from Mother. Weeks passed. Not a living soul around. I talked to myself. I dreamed about having a look at the street. I read . . . old newspapers, calendars. Near a window stood a wardrobe. I discovered that when I got on top of it and covered myself with a blanket, I could observe the street unnoticed. I lay on my wardrobe, the sun shone, it was warm. I looked out and dreamed.[52]

Leszek was lucky to be outside the wardrobe. Hundreds of other children were condemned to hours and days of darkness and forced silence inside these often huge pieces of furniture in which false backs and other compartments could be constructed. They too lived in a world of dreams alternating with terror when the rooms outside were searched by police, a frequent happening in Poland where fleeing forced labor conscripts and partisans were just as numerous as Jews. Some children stayed so long in these and other cubbyholes of infinite variety that they could not walk or talk when they emerged. Leszek was also lucky to be warm, but this would not last, for like most such hidden children, he and his mother would move again and again, from haystacks to flophouses to a space beneath the bed of a kindhearted *Volksdeutsche* prostitute who entertained German soldiers over their heads. Along the way they were taunted, blackmailed, and denounced a number of times by Poles who saw that they were Jews, and unexpectedly helped or released an equal number of times by other Poles, including a policeman. This we know because they survived. Those who did not find people with consciences cannot tell their stories, but they were many.

Thousands of children, once they had escaped or had found a way out of the ghettos, were entirely on their own. Friends to whom they had been sent would panic during roundups and turn them out on the street, where they would be swept up in the deportations. Almost none stayed in one place for long. Jerzy Frydman, about eight years old, was separated from his mother in the Warsaw Ghetto and "could not find her anymore." He joined a group of children playing near the ghetto gate who "would rush the gate like a swarm of locusts and try to get over to the other side," a maneuver that was not successful. Jerzy finally managed to get out by burying himself in a load of garbage. The driver of the cart, perfectly aware that he was there, let him off in the woods near Blonie, a few miles west of Warsaw. Jerzy, who spoke no Polish, survived for a time by begging. One man fed him and then locked him in a closet, intending to denounce him and collect the bounty paid for each Jewish child turned in; but Jerzy got away and continued to prowl the outskirts of villages. One night, amazingly, he encountered his father, also in hiding, who, before vanishing once more, told the boy to learn to pray in Polish. His father was shot a few days later. The child's terrible wanderings and adventures continued in a cycle of betrayals, imprisonments, and threats of execution interspersed with odd jobs given to him by relatively more humane Nazi operatives. At one such workplace he fell into a farm machine and lost an arm. His employers arranged medical care, but Jerzy did not trust them or the hospital staff and he escaped once again. Hiding was now far more difficult for the one-armed child, and wherever he was spotted, a hunt was organized to capture him. Still there were people who gave him refuge. One "splendid" woman in a "tiny village" hid him under her floor until the village was totally burned by the Germans, whereupon she sent him away, saying, "Go away and don't come back to me, because I do not have any strength left." The boy spent the last winter of the war roaming the forest and making forays into villages for scraps of food. Sometimes he would hide in a cellar at night, which is where he was found when the Red Army arrived in early 1945.[53]

Not all the children who escaped were condemned to constant wandering. Many stayed with families who not only cared for them but, with tremendous dedication, taught them Polish and the art of dissimulation, which in Poland required total familiarity with the rituals of the Catholic Church. Much has been made of the forced conversions of hidden Jewish children, but while the teaching of Catholic ritual may have been roughly imposed at times, it is unquestionable that ignorance of Catholic customs in Poland was a dead giveaway that could doom both the fugitive and his protectors. The ability to conform was particularly vital in convents and Catholic orphanages, which took in an estimated 1,200 Jewish children.

The various orders of nuns that existed all over Poland before the war were in many cases fugitives themselves.[54] All but a couple of orders founded in Germany had been expelled, along with their needy charges, to the General Gouvernement, where they set up in temporary quarters and tried to continue their traditions of child care. Among the prewar orphans were a number of Jewish children, whom the Germans ordered to be sent to the ghettos, a policy approved by the Jewish Councils. This trend was soon reversed. As the clearing of the ghettos began, more and more "foundlings" were left on convent doorsteps. Sometimes they were retrieved by parents who had found refuges "on the Aryan side," but many would stay in the convents for the duration. Poles who found children wandering on the streets directed them to the convents. One nun saw a four-year-old girl, who had found her way out of the ghetto through the sewers of Warsaw, struggling to climb out of a manhole, and took her to a convent in a neighboring town.[55]

Zegota also took children to the Catholic institutions and supplied them with false documents, but space was always limited by the fact that the Jewish children could not be in the majority, as the convents and homes were often inspected by Nazis. During these incursions children fled to prearranged hiding places. If the raid was sudden, the nuns had to think fast. In one convent two little girls were put inside long dresses hanging in a wardrobe and by a miracle escaped being slashed by the searchers' bayonets. Another survived at the bottom of a large basket of eggs that the beautiful nun in charge flirtatiously persuaded the Germans not to confiscate.[56]

Transfers were extrememly dangerous, especially in groups, and very Jewish-looking children who had to be moved might have their faces bandaged or their hair dyed, while those who spoke no Polish pretended to be deaf-mutes. Such measures did not make trips any easier:

> We had to wait all night for our train. The waiting room was so crowded that the children had to stand. One German was decent and made room for the children to lie down. Then the Jewish children knelt down and started to pray aloud: "Our Father which art in heaven" which they did with a Jewish accent, to which the people, frightened, said that they were Jewish. The children must have heard these words, for they stopped praying and put their heads to sleep. But the fear did not pass, for it happened that a Jewish child cried out something in Yiddish while asleep. To save the situation, I had to wake him up. I was so worried the entire time. I was constantly on the lookout for Germans who might seize the suspicious children.[57]

This group was headed for a large orphanage at Turkowice, which would shelter about thirty-two Jewish children among its population of around 250. Life in such places was particularly hard for circumcised Jewish boys, who, in addition to everything else that had to be learned, always had to undress, urinate, and bathe where no one could see them, and often lived in constant loneliness and fear of discovery. Bathing was at a minimum, however, in impoverished Turkowice, which crawled with vermin. Late in the war the orphanage would also be threatened by Ukrainian partisans, who were anti-Polish as well as anti-Semitic. The nuns made plans to evacuate all 250 children to the forest, but before they could do so one sister and eight young boys were murdered when they went out to buy supplies.[58]

Within the institutions a "don't ask, don't tell" policy often reigned, although it was usually clear to the adults, at least, just who everyone really was. In these situations Jewish children who spoke Polish and were from more assimilated families naturally fared best. Here too the hidden children often gave themselves away by their accents or by being too Catholic: "Jewish children stood out by a mile. When they started eating they crossed themselves three times. 'Do not cross yourself so often or else people will think that you are Jews,' I explained . . . but that didn't help much."[59] The Jewish children had to receive the same religious instruction as their Catholic peers in these institutions. The teaching, depending on the forcefulness with which it was delivered, was an experience that could be devastating when there was talk of Jewish guilt for the death of Christ, and of the sacrilege associated with the taking of Communion by the unbaptized. Many of the hidden children remember to this day the humiliation they felt.

But to others the convents and orphanages were refuges where they found overwhelming relief from fear and unquestioning love. Rachela G., five when the war began, was blond and blue-eyed, and safer than most with the Polish farm family to whom she had been sent. But as the roundups intensified the farmers became more and more frightened, as did Rachela, who witnessed

> Jewish children running away to hide someplace. Just like animals being chased by dogs. These children were refused entry into homes; they ran through the fields, the Germans shooting after them. I had been ordered not to admit my Jewish heritage, not to say a word—so I was just in a stupor. . . . In a panic the people with whom I was staying decided I had to be sent to a convent. . . . First they took me to . . . where my mother and sister were hiding. . . . My mother decided

to commit suicide with the help of the farmer. Suicide by drowning. Together with my little sister. She was three years old then. I was left by the river and told to wait. . . . Finally the farmer came back and said that everything was over. . . . I was taken to Trzesowka. The convent was visible from a distance. . . . The farmer left me in the field and said: "Go there; they will take you in."

Rachela was, indeed, taken in, and once there was made to feel safe, surely not easy after what she had just experienced. She soon made friends; the nuns were kind and the religious instruction low-key. Rachela, like many others who were taken into convents in every country, found the ritual beautiful and comforting. After the war, still afraid of anti-Semitism and "not wanting to return to something that had been so tragic for me," she would become a Catholic.[60]

All the efforts of the Dutch students, the Polish nuns, and rescuers of every variety in every occupied country to protect Jewish children could, in the end, save only a tiny percentage of the estimated 1.5 million who were being swept away to fates as yet not clearly understood in the human blitzkrieg so carefully organized by the Nazis. The rescuers should not have felt guilty for not having been able to do more, for by the end of 1942, many had themselves become the targets of Nazi manhunts.

13. Arbeit Macht Frei: Forced Labor

Nineteen forty-two was a busy year in the Nazi bureaucracies. To the Jewish deportations, the ethnic rearrangements and labor round-ups in the East, and the pressures of fighting an extended war was now added a vast program of labor conscription in the Western occupied lands. Labor chief Fritz Sauckel's insatiable need for workers, unfulfilled by the enslaved millions of the East, would now require major forced recruitment in the West. This would involve groups previously not considered liable for such duty and be the catalyst for major resistance.

A quota of 129,000 workers was demanded from Holland for the period from April through November 1942.[1] At the deadline the roster was 24,000 short, which caused Sauckel to cast his gaze on university students, up to now exempt. On December 2, he ordered education authorities to produce, within two weeks, 6,000 to 8,000 of them, which was approximately half the entire student population. The Dutch secretary general of education in the Seyss-Inquart administration managed to postpone this action until after the Christmas holiday and to obtain assurance that the students, if taken, would serve only one year in "suitable," high-grade jobs.

Sauckel relented, but stated that if the requested numbers were not forthcoming, all Dutch students would be rounded up and sent to Germany. The rectors of the universities, sworn to secrecy, were informed of the situation and commanded to produce lists of names immediately. Fearing that the students, once in the Reich, would end up fighting on the Eastern Front, the rectors leaked the news. To prevent any *razzias* (roundups) of the kind being visited on the Jews, the Free University of Amsterdam began its Christmas vacation six days early. In a fiery speech to the students before they dispersed, one of the professors exhorted them:

> Never give an inch to the enemy. Know that nobleness has obligations, and raise high the nobility of your Dutchness. . . . No matter what the enemy asks, or how he flatters . . . or how secretaries-general, professors of different universities, and men of influence confer and intrigue, we know only one answer: that answer is never![2]

Illegal Dutch Scouts soon to be rounded up for forced labor in Germany.

The call to resistance was taken up by the underground Council of Nine, which represented the banished student organizations of the major universities. The council immediately circulated a pamphlet declaring that they "would never be slaves." Two more universities closed early. At the University of Utrecht members of the Kindercomité broke into the registrar's office and burned registration records. Spontaneous strikes took place at three more universities. Afraid that the unrest would spread, the Germans withdrew the quota demand for the time being. On December 16, Christmas vacation began. But in the university offices the compiling of conscription lists secretly went forward.

The winter term began nervously; there was sporadic unrest. In early February Resistance operatives attacked two high Dutch Nazi officials. One of them, before he died, identified his assassins as "students." In reprisal, 600 students were rounded up and sent to the concentration camp at Vught, where they were told that those who behaved well and agreed to sign a loyalty oath to the Nazi government could be released. SS authorities, casting about for other ways to bring in students, now decreed that 5,000 young men, aged eighteen to twenty-five, the sons of "plutocrats," who they assumed would be enrolled in higher education, were to be arrested and sent to hard labor in Germany. Lists of boys in this odd category had to be produced within twenty-four hours by the mayors of selected towns, many of whom stayed up all night to comply. On the morning of February 9, 1943, the first roundups began. They were not a success. Not only were many of the addresses inaccurate, resulting in the arrest of a number of Dutch Nazi youths, but for once the SS had slept too late, and most of those targeted, who were not students at all, had left for work. The raiders, desperate to fill the required quota, began to pick up distinctly nonplutocratic boys at random on the streets. Schools and all sorts of businesses and buildings were surrounded, and young men who seemed to fit the profile were dragged out. As word of the *razzia* was telephoned all over the country, thousands of boys took cover, and in the end only 1,200 were captured.[3] Himmler was so furious at this debacle that he ordered his minions to arrest all the sons of "plutocrats" in the country, plus their fathers. The hapless mayors who had provided incorrect data were to be sent to work in coal mines.[4]

Reichskommissar Seyss-Inquart, still trying to preserve his dream of converting the Dutch elite into National Socialists, refused to implement this drastic proposal, and instead ordained that all students sign a loyalty oath immediately and do one year of labor service in Germany after their graduation.[5] The students were given one month to comply.

It was not clear what the best strategy would be. Refusal to sign, some reasoned, would result in being sent to forced labor anyway, which would only strengthen Germany. Compliance was a gamble, as it was possible that the war might end before the students would be inducted. The university authorities, fearful of being imprisoned for "sabotage," a favorite Nazi euphemism, printed up the oaths and distributed them to the students by mail. But resistance had taken hold. In BBC messages beamed from London by the Dutch government in exile came encouragement to refuse. The secret student organizations were tougher, declaring that any student who signed the loyalty oath was "a deserter, who, now that the need of the Dutch people is greater even than it was in 1940, withdraws from the front we are forming."[6] In the end, only 3,000 of 14,000 eligible students signed.

This was not acceptable to the Nazis. On May 5, 1943, all male students who had not signed were ordered to report to processing centers the next day and to bring with them two suitcases containing "weekday and Sunday" clothes and blankets. There was no time for coordinated resistance. Nevertheless, only 3,800 students appeared, and of these only 2,900 would go to Germany. Despite their desperate need for manpower and the elaborate coercive measures, the Germans even now did not lower their physical or ideological standards for these workers, who, because they came from a "Nordic" nation, would be in close contact with German nationals. Some 900 of those who reported were rejected because they had Indonesian blood or physical defects or were theology students. Later, with equally dismal results, 2,000 girls were also called up to do social service in Holland.[7]

In October 1943, the Dutch universities were ordered to reopen, but few students were now inclined to enroll. To all intents and purposes higher education no longer existed in the Netherlands except in clandestine gatherings, and thousands of students would join the hidden Jewish children in strange exiles.[8]

The students who had reported were sent to a camp at Ommen, in central Holland near the German border, where a tent city had been prepared for them. From here they went on to a staging area near Berlin. The 800 medical students among them were scattered to relatively good jobs in small hospitals, the idea being not to have too many in one place. Students from other disciplines did not fare so well. For them it would be the factory, and their living conditions, in the usual lice-ridden barracks, were hardly elitist. Food, supposed to be better than that of the Poles and Russians, was by now remarkably similar, as the designated supplies were frequently sold off on the black market by corrupt camp administrators. Room and board were deducted from the students' tiny salaries, and what little was left they spent on food in the towns. Their eighty- or ninety-hour workweeks were so long that time for study, which they had been promised, was nonexistent. A significant number were sent off to punishment camps, and none were treated in any way as fellow members of the Master Race; even the dreadful Bulgarian cigarettes they were given were labeled "For Foreigners." Indeed, authorities in Holland were informed that the student-workers were not behaving as young members of the Master Race should, but had made themselves unpopular and even hated by "singing the 'Internationale' with French and Russian workers [and] English songs on the streetcars, and by going out with Polish girls."[9]

The forced recruiting in Holland was only a small part of Sauckel's Western manpower hunt. Even in perfectly Nordic Norway universal labor conscription was ordered in 1943 for boys and girls twelve and over. The younger ones were supposed to help in civil defense. Those over fifteen would be put to work. After Oslo University students protested against this measure, their main auditorium burned down under suspicious circumstances; the fire was blamed on Communist agitation in the student body. Roundups followed, and eventually 12,000 students were sent to a camp in the far north of the country and from there, in December 1943, to Germany. Here too a loyalty oath was the ticket to release, but few signed. Six hundred fifty of the students were sent to a special camp where an unsuccessful effort was made to train them for the SS, after which they too went to the factories.[10]

A much more tempting source of labor for the Nazis was the youth of France, which not only was much more numerous, but also was racially less desirable and therefore more exploitable. But restraint had to be shown toward the French, who must be kept pacified as long as the war in the East continued. In September 1941, there were already well over a million French POWs and some 50,000 volunteer workers in Germany.[11] Many more were employed by the German occupation agencies in France. But by 1942 the number of new French volunteers had fallen off just as much as that of the Poles, and few of those recruited early on, who found working in Germany very unpleasant indeed, were willing to renew their contracts.

In May, therefore, Sauckel demanded that France supply 350,000 workers by June 30. Pierre Laval, as he had done in the case of the deportation of Jews, wanted to keep control of recruiting in French hands while satisfying the German request. By early June he had succeeded in making a deal that would allow the repatriation of one French POW for each three skilled French workers, an arrangement known as the *Relève*. To promote enrollment for work in Germany, Vichy launched a huge propaganda campaign. This program had little effect; by the end of August the response was so inadequate that Sauckel ordered forced conscription. Laval again preempted the Nazi action by passing a French law requiring all men eighteen to fifty and single women twenty-one to thirty-five to register. This effort was, if anything, even less successful. Laval's own Cabinet objected to the "Polonization" of France.[12] Young men disappeared in droves, and some local officials openly advised others not to register. The police, already overextended and unhappy enforcing the anti-Jewish measures, were often reluctant to engage in the pursuit of French young people. There were strikes and demonstrations and murmurings against "mobilization for slavery." Upon the German occupation of Vichy France in November 1942, this would all change. Roundups at gunpoint became common in Paris, and there were tough reprisals: the ailing seventy-year-old father and seventeen-year-old brother of one boy who refused to register were sent to Dachau.[13] These measures were quite effective: by the end of December 240,000 workers had gone to Germany.

But Sauckel and his Führer, who reportedly had suggested that one to

two million Frenchmen should be conscripted for service in the rear areas
of the Eastern Front, wanted more.[14] In January 1943, Sauckel demanded
another 250,000 by March. Laval, desperate to fill the quota, on February
16 ordered the creation of the Service de Travail Obligatoire (STO), which
basically revived the French draft, but this time to provide manpower for
the enemy. Service was for two years and exemptions were given only to
essential agricultural workers and those holding jobs "useful to the needs
of the country." Needless to say, the exemptions did not include full-time
students or the young people who had so far been protected by participation in the Chantiers de la Jeunesse and the Compagnons de France.

Not everyone thought this drastic order was bad. The Vichy press
touted the "healthy European experiences" in store for the young, who,
they gushed, might even be allowed to take their bicycles with them. General de la Porte du Theil of the Chantiers, in a speech considered scandalous by most, told his boys that they should obey because "it is necessary
above all to avoid falling under the yoke of Bolshevism." Some zealous
officials felt that a little forced labor would do wonders for France's "deca-
dent" youth; the *préfet* of Rouen was especially pleased to be able to send
all of the long-haired, hip *zazous* of the city to Germany. Others were not
so eager, and even Laval is said to have encouraged some of his underlings
to "drown" the process in "administrative magma."[15]

Resistance to the STO became quite creative. One intrepid bureaucrat,
Jean Isméolari, a former labor inspector, set up an entirely fake "Commission of Appeal" for those seeking exemptions from the STO that issued
release documents on an impressive letterhead covered with seals,
stamps, and illegible signatures. This one-man agency, which was not suspected by either the Germans or Vichy, is said to have exempted thousands from forced labor.[16] The Vichy Secretary of the Navy redistributed
two classes of cadets from the Naval Academy at Toulon to technical training programs whose work was "important to the nation," and young communications "cadets" were hired by the post office.[17] In a more brazen
effort, one Chantiers de la Jeunesse leader took six truckloads of boys to a
transit camp to be registered. As they entered, they stood up in the trucks,
singing loudly. The boys were duly processed and had their documents
properly stamped. The trucks then departed, apparently empty. No one
noticed that they in fact contained 240 boys, lying on top of one another
and covered with old bags and blankets.[18]

The universities and high schools, whose students had heretofore been
exempted from labor call-ups, a fact that had led to a marked increase in
enrollment, also went into action. Ironically, the only ones exempted from

the beginning were the few remaining Jewish students, who were, how-ever, expected to register for agricultural work in France. The Vichy gov-ernment managed to have the tour of duty in Germany for the 32,000 targeted students reduced to one year, after which they would have to do another year of community service in France. In addition, a complex structure of deferments was concocted by the universities, and many fac-ulties cheated by hiring extra teaching assistants, falsifying records, and turning a blind eye to ID cards that were not quite in order. The French Resistance emulated their Dutch colleagues by stealing the registration files of the Sorbonne. The passive attitude of many students had been blown away long since by the excesses of German anti-Jewish measures. The June 1942 requirement that Jews wear stars was a major catalyst; few have forgotten the impact of the first day on which these badges were dis-played. Some teachers told their students to come to school wearing simi-lar badges. In Bordeaux, as in many other places, a whole class of girls came to school wearing stars in order to be like their one Jewish classmate. University students did likewise, and when questioned, said that the let-ters JUIF on their stars stood for *Jeunesse Universitaire Intellectuelle Française*.[19] The Nazis were not amused: non-Jews wearing stars could be sent off to Dachau.[20]

The apparent coddling of students by the Vichy government, which reduced the number eligible for induction in the STO to 15,000, plus the large number who simply did not register, was unacceptable to the Ger-mans, and led to all sorts of harassment. Required physicals for STO service were scheduled in the middle of medical school exams in Clermont-Ferrand. In Montpellier, Germans rounded up students as they emerged from their finals, lest they escape. In the end, it is thought that only some 6,000 university students actually went to Germany. Many more would be sent to German projects within France. But the fear of arrest and deportation soon led to a 26 percent decrease in university enrollment.[21]

All this resistance took much time and effort for small results; it was also dangerous. There was no way to compete with the combined power of the Nazis and the collaborationist police organizations, to whom human rights were meaningless, and there was no letup in the pressure. Both the Jewish deportations and the forced labor actions showed how well the Nazis had learned the efficacy of fast and ruthless activity. As the demand for bodies increased, victims were grabbed in the Métro, cafés, or even brothels. University classrooms could be a trap, and whole Chantier encampments were shipped directly to Germany with no time to say good-bye to families or pack belongings. In one three-day period in May 1943, 5,200 young men were taken straight from a Chantier to the huge I. G. Farben plant next to the Auschwitz death camp; 16,372 would leave France by August. There was seemingly no end to it. In May and again in August, Sauckel would ask for a total of 720,000 more bodies. The age limit was lowered to seventeen, which made high school pupils eligible.[22]

By the spring of 1944 even France's very proper *Grandes Écoles,* traditional training grounds for the nation's government, scientific, and business elites, were resorting to distinctly illegal measures to save their endangered students. Othar Zaldastani, second in his class at the engineering school of Ponts et Chausées and the son of Georgian exiles who had fled to France in the 1920s, was doubly vulnerable because he held a Nansen passport and was therefore considered stateless. After the Allied landing in Normandy, the director of the school urged Zaldastani to leave Paris. To protect him, the director arranged for him to work at a Ponts et Chausées office in the small town of Besançon, in the east of France, until Paris should be liberated. This was definitely a "nationally essential" job, as the Germans depended on the French to keep the roads and bridges open for their armies. By August 1944, the Vichy government had fallen and there was no restraint on the Germans. Zaldastani's colleagues advised him to flee to Switzerland. He did not make it. Picked up by a German patrol, he too would be taken to Germany and fed into the STO program with other French students.[23]

For all those considering going into hiding, even within France, the prospects were bleak. Without the proper STO stamp on one's work card, one could not get ration coupons, pick up letters at the post office, be employed, or withdraw funds from a bank. Families were endangered and a fugitive was dependent on those willing to protect him. Refuge with French underground organizations was one option, but in 1943 these groups were still not widespread and were specific in their politics, and most young people had no safe way to contact them.

Little effort was made to charm the new French employees of the Reich once their journeys began. Depersonalization began right away. At their assigned transit centers, which were usually surrounded by armed French guards and barbed wire, they were given uniforms in the traditional *bleu de travail* of the French laborer unless they were already wearing the uniforms of the Chantiers or Compagnons de France. Food and bedding were previews of the turnip soup and dirty straw mattresses to come. The conscripts were given aptitude tests and "contracts," which no one bothered to sign. Transport, luxurious compared to that of the Jews being deported, was in decrepit and often unheated passenger cars that left from platforms cordoned off by police and off limits to families. If there had been any illusions about their real situation, these were swept away at the German frontier, where loudspeakers proclaimed that they were now in Reich territory and that protests and patriotic demonstrations, frequent during the voyage, would no longer be tolerated. In some places Hitler Youth boys threw rocks at their trains. Guards with dogs patrolled the stations, luggage was searched, and much was confiscated.

Eventually the young workers were taken to triage camps, where laborers of all nationalities, but not the Jews, were massed together in extreme and chaotic squalor. Here small children begged for cigarettes, and young girls from the East offered themselves for a piece of bread or a cupful of the soup that the French, still sufficiently well fed, would reject. Othar Zaldastani, puzzled by the strange behavior of several boys in the mess hall of the triage camp at Offenbach, later learned that they had been buried up to their necks for days as punishment for some infraction and had lost their reason.[24] Most shocking to the new arrivals were "flocks of starved beings in rags" followed by screaming guards. A Nazi official organizing the French assured them that they were not the same as these "Russian dogs."[25] Indeed, before their eyes, one of the Russians was shot for accepting food from a Frenchman.

In these Dantesque enclosures the unskilled foreign workers were looked over by labor officials, chosen, and redistributed to their new workplaces, usually without any reference to their "aptitudes." Not all the billets were civilian. To their dismay, many were sent to serve with the Nazi Todt Organization, which at this time was entirely dedicated to building military projects, and even to support units for the Waffen-SS and the Wehrmacht. In these units they were made to wear German uniforms and were supposed to act in a military fashion, which as a form of resistance they generally refused to do.

Lodgings in the 22,000 labor camps in Germany ranged from the back rooms of small businesses through converted hotels, tent cities, and converted passenger ships to the vast barracks cities of the Krupp organization, which held some 50,000 workers. Bed linens and heating were rare, and sanitation often appalling. One camp of 600 workers near Vienna had a single outdoor faucet, which froze in the winter; another, at Friedrichshafen, provided only six toilets for 900 men.[26]

The French, as members of Group C (non-Germanic allies), did have some important privileges. They did not have to wear badges, and on their days off they could go into nearby towns and attend movies, concerts, and even the opera if they could find a ticket. One group, instead of going on home leave, even managed a ski trip. As we have seen, the French soup was thicker than that of the Poles and *Ostarbeiter*. Theoretically entitled to the same amount of food as German workers, the Western laborers were given ration coupons that they could spend on the German economy. But it soon became clear that their choice was limited to particular items, and that many shops and restaurants were closed to them. Their reception by the German public was mixed. Those working on farms generally were accepted and well treated, but the industrial workers in towns, often not very presentable due to the limited laundry and bathing facilities in their barracks, did not fare so well, and contempt for them was frequent. One German, complimented by a forced laborer on his knowledge of French, replied, "Masters, of course, must learn the language of their slaves." There were other problems for the students: the Germans soon began to renege on their one-year service limit, and leaves became less and less possible. In addition, since they were, in theory, volunteers, they did not get any help from the Red Cross and other organizations as the POWs did, but could receive packages from home. This was nice when the packages arrived, but many families in France could not afford to send off their own rationed food, and the bundles that got through had often been looted en route. But any little thing was gold for the workers, whose relations managed to hide forbidden items such as medicine, perfume, cosmetics, and even small bottles of wine inside jars of jam or bags of beans, all of which could be bartered in the flourishing black markets of the labor camps.

The Nazis allowed the Vichy government to send a series of entertainers and lecturers for the edification of the workers, but these, which included Vichy officials and even a French SS officer, were scorned for the exercises in propaganda they obviously were. Courses and exams were offered so that students could continue their education as promised, but they were of low intellectual content, and the long work hours and crowded living conditions were not conducive to study. Various attempts to initiate sports programs failed, largely due to the exhaustion and malnutrition of the participants. Despite all, the French students and older workers still managed to put on plays and theatricals (one production of *The Barber of Seville* had fifty-eight performances), and derived considerable pleasure from thinking up innumerable go-slow types of resistance.

Overt resistance could mean death.[27] The French and Dutch student workers, despite their elevated status, in fact had no more rights under German law than did those from the East. In the world of punishment the SS reigned supreme. The slightest infraction, such as writing graffiti, giving food to an *Ostarbeiter,* writing "Long live escape" in a letter home, failing to doff one's cap, taking an unauthorized trip, or any perceived act of sabotage, could become grounds for imprisonment in the special punishment camps, where national status no longer mattered. The installations had a variety of names, ranging from Education Camp to Punishment Camp, but there was little difference in their programs. Here the workers were starved and subjected to all the refinements of SS sadism. One young Frenchman remembered his horror at his first sight of his fellow inmates, who were

> completely naked, these people, with skeletal thighs, covered with their own excrement . . . truly like animals. They were brought a pot of soup—they threw themselves at it and fought over it. . . . In the same camp at Dusseldorf, which held some 3,000 men, they had at least 100 dogs . . . they put us in a little warehouse with a door at each end. When it was time to go out they opened both doors: the dogs came in one end—there was panic and pushing to get out the other. People trampled those who fell . . . there were always deaths.[28]

Work in these establishments was in fact punishment. At Nuremberg barefoot prisoners shoveled gravel until they dropped of exhaustion. Those who collapsed were apt to be shot. Young men were sent to clear land mines, and stood for hours in the snow for roll calls. The guards around them amused themselves by having them jog and do push-ups just after the minuscule bread rations had been distributed, so that the food became coated with mud. Inmates were whipped, and forced to beat other prisoners to death. Medical care, as in all such camps, was minimal; the death rate from shootings, beatings, diseases such as typhus and dysentery, and of course malnutrition, was enormous. Five hundred of the 800 Frenchmen incarcerated at the Grossbeeren camp succumbed. Those who survived these camps were often in such bad condition that they died soon after their release back into the labor force.

If forced labor was a trap of varying levels of cruelty for non-Jewish young people of every occupied nation, to be avoided by any means possible, for Jewish youth it offered the only small possibility of survival. In Germany, the Nuremberg Laws and subsequent decrees, which excluded Jewish students from mainstream training and education and destroyed their families' economic resources, drove many of them into blue-collar jobs at an early age. By May 1940 registration for forced labor had been made obligatory for all German Jews eighteen and over, and by early 1941 some 20 percent of them had been called up.[29] In the following months call-ups increased and the minimum age continued to fall; by the spring of 1941, Jewish fourteen-year-olds were common in the workplace.[30]

The usual protections provided to child laborers were not granted to Jews, and apprentice training programs for skilled labor were closed to them. The young workers routinely labored long hours and were given the most dangerous, repellent, and unhealthy jobs. As the relentless drafting of German men into the armed forces continued, the number of Jews and foreign laborers working in the Reich soared. By the late summer of 1942, at the huge Zeiss-Ikon plant in Dresden, only 500 free German workers were left out of an original 7,000. Here, Jewish girls of fifteen and sixteen, in the so-called kindergarten, worked day and night shifts amounting to twenty-four hours out of forty-eight.[31] These extreme conditions, combined with the reduced food and clothing rations allowed to Jews, especially those sent to camps in the country or to factories where lodging and sanitation were, as usual, minimal, led to rapid declines in health.

Legitimate businesses were not the only ones using Jewish labor. The SS Inspectorate of Concentration Camps also used inmate labor to build and expand its camps, which were conveniently sited near granite quarries and other such projects, and to work in SS-run companies such as the German Earth and Stoneworks Co., Ltd., established in 1938. The work, at first mostly punitive, by the mid-1930s had become more profit-oriented, and in the spring of 1939 the SS formalized its industrial wing by establishing an SS Economic and Administrative Office.

Deportations of Jews from the expanded Reich to Russian and Polish ghettos had started in October 1941. In the summer of 1942, when the mass deportations from the Western occupied countries began, the extermination camps at Belzec, Sobibor, and Treblinka being fully operative, the often life-saving stopovers in the ghettos became logistically unnecessary, and the transports went directly to the death camps. By early October 1942, even Jews already in concentration camps in Germany were sent to the East.[32] In Berlin, where most of the remaining German Jews were by this time, those working in war industries, particularly in munitions factories, were exempted from the first transports, but in early 1943, under pressure to make the capital as well as the concentration camps *judenrein* (free of Jews), SS units raided the weapons factories and seized thousands of Jewish workers. They did not get them all: Goebbels fumed that "shortsighted industrialists" had warned 4,000 in time, who were now "wandering about Berlin . . . and are naturally quite a public danger," and ordered that they be hunted down immediately.[33]

In Poland, random groups of Jews aged fourteen to sixty had also been set to work by the Wehrmacht immediately after the German invasion in 1939. The labor consisted at first of clearing rubble, breaking stones in quarries, and other heavy construction work on fortifications, drainage projects, and roads. The Luftwaffe dragooned hundreds more for airfield construction. On some sites run by German industries, relatively good wages were paid at first for the grueling twelve- and even eighteen-hour shifts.[34] Later the Jewish Councils would continue to supply workers on demand.

The SS also expanded its forced labor to Poland, and by early 1940 had a network of some 400 Forced Labor Camps for Jews (ZALs). Among the duties of these inmates, like those from Germany, were the construction of the extermination camps and the ongoing expansion of Auschwitz. Eventually, the major concentration camps, such as Auschwitz and Majdanek, would have their own in-house labor sections, and sub-camps would be specially set up for private firms such as I. G. Farben. In these units, the Jewish laborers, if they could survive the often horrendous conditions, were protected from extermination for varying lengths of time. Thousands of boys and girls were selected for forced labor in the ZALs in the weeks before the dissolution of the ghettos and during the roundups as the deportation trains were being loaded.

In smaller Polish towns Jews were sometimes warned ahead of time of the coming departures, but nothing could prepare them for the chaotic inhumanity of the process. Infants were often shot on the spot as houses were cleared. Once assembled, typically in the town square, triage was brutal. The old and sick were thrown bodily into waiting trucks, which took them to the cattle cars. The same was done to children and toddlers, whose parents, if they were fit enough to work, were frequently commanded to leave their babies behind. Many mothers and fathers refused this order, thereby unknowingly condemning themselves to death.

The chaos of these horrific scenes was deceptive: the usefulness of each group had been carefully calculated beforehand. Older girls and boys were separated from their families, forced forty or fifty at a time into trucks, and, with no time for farewells, driven directly to work camps. The larger ghettos were also not cleared all at once, but in multiple raids that left useful industries intact, a strategy that inspired some ghetto councils to certify children as young as ten as bona fide workers in order to save them.

Further triage took place upon arrival at the concentration camps. The terrible selection process of the deportees arriving at Auschwitz-Birkenau from Poland and other European countries, in which lives were lost and saved by the merest chance, has been immortalized in myriad histories, books, and films. Here Anne Frank was selected to work, thereby gaining a few more months of life, as was Elie Wiesel, who survived. Both of them were in their teens. For small children there was no hope. With a very few exceptions, such as twins or others who seemed useful in some way to the medical researchers, they were trucked or marched directly to the gas chambers, sometimes with a relative, but often enough, it would appear, without any familiar adult to comfort them. The SS had learned a lot from the slaughters in Russia. Considerable efforts were made to prevent panic, which might lead to the situation getting out of control, and to reassure the doomed as they awaited their turn in the gas chamber. A photograph survives of mothers and children sitting calmly in a little grove of trees at Auschwitz, waiting for their "showers."

For those who went to the four extermination camps at Chelmno, Belzec, Sobibor, and Treblinka there was no selection. Here even greater efforts of deception had been made. At Sobibor, newcomers saw only a few barracks and some fences covered with pine branches behind which were trees.[35] Treblinka was much more elaborate: there they arrived at a cheerily painted train station complete with a fake clock, timetables on the walls, carefully tended flower plots, and inviting benches.[36]

It is clear from the accounts of contemporary observers, however, that the passengers on the trains knew something terrible awaited them. Zygmunt Klukowski, the Polish town doctor of Szczebrzeszyn, which lay on the rail line to Belzec, noted on April 8, 1942:

> We know for sure that every day two trains, consisting of twenty cars each, come to Belzec. . . . On the way . . . the Jews experience many terrible things. They are aware of what will happen to them. Some try to fight back. At the railroad station in Szczebrzeszyn a young woman gave away a gold ring in exchange for a glass of water for her dying child. In Lublin people witnessed small children being thrown through the windows of speeding trains.[37]

Treatment of the 5,000 or more people who arrived at the death camps in each transport depended on their country of origin. Eastern Europeans were greeted by guards with whips and screaming SS soldiers, while those from Western Europe, which included whole carloads of unaccompanied children, were more often met by polite guards and "medical staff" ready

Unaware of their fate, Jewish women and children too young for work calmly await the deadly showers of Auschwitz.

to "help" those who had become sick on the journey. This must have been quite a large number, if conditions on the trains, observed by many along their slow routes, are any indicator. Hubert Pfloch, a young Austrian draftee whose train to the Eastern Front was just behind a transport, watched as it was loaded and made its way to Treblinka on August 21, 1942:

> I saw a loading platform with a huge crowd of people—I estimated about 7,000 men, women and children. All of them were squatting or lying on the ground and whenever anyone tried to get up, the guards began to shoot. . . . And then, when they are being loaded into cattle cars, we become witnesses of the most ghastly scenes. . . . The guards . . . cram 180 people into each car, parents into one, children into another, they didn't care how they separated families. They scream at them, shoot and hit them. . . . When some of them manage to climb out through the ventilating holes, they are shot . . . a massacre that made us sick to our souls, a blood bath such as I never dreamed of. A mother jumps down with her baby and calmly looks into a pointing gun barrel—a moment later we hear the guard who shot them boast . . . that he managed to "do them both with one shot through both their heads." . . . Eventually our train followed the other train and we continued to see corpses on both sides of the track—children and others. When we reach Treblinka station the train is next to us again—there is

such an awful smell of decomposing corpses in the station, some of us vomit.[38]

At the camp platform the trains were unloaded five cars at a time, and the victims, separated by sex, were sent in to undress for their "bath." Once naked, they were marched and—as the realization of some horror about to overtake them grew—driven, down a long, curved corridor between two greenery-covered fences, toward the gas chambers. So great were the numbers that hundreds had to await their turn to enter, sometimes in cold so severe that children's feet froze to the ground. Very occasionally, boys and girls were extracted from the mass to serve as "work Jews," or as cooks and orderlies for the camp officers. Most of these were murdered later, but a few would survive to describe the unimaginable.[39]

The volume of killings was so massive that the gas chambers, as well as the train tracks, often had to be closed down for repairs and expansions. Nor were the various methods of corpse disposal up to the task, a situation that led to the piling up of bodies and temporary, improvised killing methods. It was during such a breakdown that one of the few eyewitnesses to the satanic scenes at the extermination camps, the young Polish Resistance courier Jan Karski, managed to get into Belzec disguised as a guard. His words, which he would carry out to the Allies in the autumn of 1942, need no elaboration:

> As we approached to within a few hundred yards of the camp the shouts, cries and shots cut off further conversation. . . . We passed through a small grove of decrepit looking trees and emerged directly in front of the loud, sobbing, reeking camp of death. It was on a large, flat plain and occupied about a square mile . . . surrounded on all sides by a formidable barbed wire fence. . . . The camp itself contained a few small sheds or barracks. The rest of the area was completely covered by a dense, pulsating, throbbing, noisy human mass. Starved, stinking, gesticulating, insane human beings in constant agitated motion. Through them . . . walked the German police and the militia men. They walked in silence, their faces bored and indifferent. . . . A small child, clad in a few rags was lying on the ground. He was all alone and crouched quivering on the ground, staring up with the frightened eyes of a rabbit. No one paid any attention to him. . . . There was no organization of any kind. None of them could possibly help or share with each other. . . . They had become, at this stage, completely dehumanized. The chaos, the squalor, the hideousness of it all was simply indescribable. There was a suffocating stench of sweat, filth, decay, damp straw and

excrement.... Finally I noticed a change in the motion of the guards ... they walked less and they all seemed to be glancing in the same direction—at the passage to the [train] track.... The whole system had been worked out with crude effectiveness. The outlet of the passage was blocked off by two cars of the freight train ... so that any attempt ... to escape ... would have been completely impossible.... A volley of shots from the rear sent the whole mass surging forward madly.... Impelled and controlled by this ring of fire, they filled the two cars quickly.... Alternately swinging and firing with their rifles, the policemen were forcing still more people into the cars which were already over-full.... The floors of the car had been covered with ... quicklime.... Here the lime served a double purpose.... The moist flesh coming in contact with the lime is rapidly dehydrated and burned. The occupants of the cars would be literally burned to death before long ... the lime would prevent decomposing bodies from spreading disease. It was efficient and inexpensive.... It took three hours to fill up the entire train by repetitions of this procedure. It was twilight when the forty-six cars were packed.... From one end to the other, the train with its quivering cargo of flesh, seemed to throb, vibrate, rock and jump ... moan and sob, wail and howl. Then these ... ceased.... The train would travel about eighty miles and finally come to a halt in an empty ... field. Then nothing at all would happen. The train would stand stock-still, patiently waiting while death penetrated into every corner of its interior. This would take from two to four days.[40]

Conditions in the labor camps for Jews selected for forced labor were extremely varied, and assignments were a matter of luck. Some workers might find themselves in small, private factories where food, bedding, and general treatment were very good.[41] Others were simply graced with good luck, as was eleven-year-old Arek Hersh. In 1940 Arek was deported as a quota substitute for his father to a particularly brutal camp at Otoczno on the Warsaw-Berlin train line, where track was repaired. Water was hauled to the camp in a long tank pulled by roped-together teenagers. One of the guards, who apparently felt sorry for the small boy, released him from the harness and let him walk beside the contraption. The camp commandant also took a shine to Arek and used him as an orderly for a time before sending him back to the ghetto, but not before Arek had accidentally witnessed a group of his friends being loaded by force into some "strange-looking lorries" that were supposed to be taking the laborers "home," but that in fact were mobile gas chambers. When the ghetto was liquidated in 1942, Arek, still too small to work, was accidentally put in a group going to the workshops of the Lodz Ghetto instead of to Chelmno, where the rest of his family perished. Sent to Auschwitz from Lodz, he once again managed to switch from the line of the condemned to that of those going to work, and ultimately survived the war.[42]

Arek and those in the nice factories were fortunate indeed. For most, the labor camps were a nightmare from the beginning. The sufferings of the inmates who had preceded them were often all too clear At Jedlinsk, where thousands of Russian POWs had died of starvation, Sam Dresner was shown floorboards that the dying soldiers had gnawed in their desperate hunger. At the huge and notorious camp at Skarzysko-Kamienna, fifteen-year-old Chaim Olmer, who arrived at night, was greeted by a surreal scene that was "like something out of hell. Yellow people, dressed in paper sacks, shuffled along as if in a dream." Near his hut, "the smell was unbearable. By the washroom was a big wooden crate. The dead bodies were put into it and it was emptied when it was full."[43] The inmates were yellow from working with picrine, a chemical that worked its way into the skin and lungs and usually caused death within three months.

There was no peace in these camps. The heavy work was designed to kill. Inmates were regularly shot and hanged. Those who got too thin and weak on the pathetic rations were selected once again and sent to the death camps. Typhus swept the barracks. Transfers from one camp to another were arbitrary and frequent, but sometimes a new place provided more humane conditions, especially if the supervisor was of the type immortalized by Oskar Schindler.

Lowest of the low though they were, the Jewish young people occasionally found others to pity. The labor camp at Czestochowianka was near another, which held 10,000 Russian prisoners of war who suddenly disappeared. The puzzled Jewish prisoners were told by local Poles that the Russians had deliberately been fed cabbage soup infested with green caterpillars. In two weeks all but twenty-four of them, who had purposely been given uncontaminated food, had died of dysentery. The survivors, after burying their comrades, were also killed. No wonder the spoons used to stir Russian soup were kept separate.[44]

By June 1943, with the Soviets retaking large areas of the Ukraine and the extermination camps being closed down, an estimated 120,000 Polish Jews still survived in the ZALs of the General Gouvernement. Their chances of survival might have seemed to have improved, but in November, 43,000 of these laborers would be slaughtered without warning in a five-day orgy cynically named Operation Harvest Festival. The purge put a large dent even in the production schedules of the SS's own war industries and dismayed other officials and factory owners, whose productivity was constantly being reduced both by the German draft and by the wanton killing or starvation of assigned workers.[45]

Continuing pressure from industry did lead to a slight amelioration in the treatment of the workers and, as the war ground on, the use of concentration camp labor of all origins in the armaments industry continued to grow, rising eventually to some 500,000 inmates, of whom at least 25 percent were Jews. This policy was enthusiastically, if schizophrenically, backed by Himmler, whose agencies simultaneously continued to exterminate thousands in the by now hugely expanded facilities at Auschwitz and in hundreds of other camps. In an even greater reversal of Nazi policy, the greatest number of Jewish forced laborers, all considered expendable, would be put to work on a vast network of secret underground factories within the virtually *judenrein* Reich itself. The majority would come from Hungary, whose Vichy-like government had protected its own Jews until early 1944.

The inefficiency of the selection process for these slave laborers was, in general, a shock to industrialists more interested in production than extermination. On several occasions armaments czar Albert Speer and others complained that most of the "workers" sent to them were old people and children. One vast underground plant at Landsberg, in Bavaria, received a transport of middle-class Hungarian Jews and their families. After a time, the SS sent a unit from Dachau to surround the camp and truck the children away to an unknown destination. The project engineer, who protested this action, was also horrified to see that "almost half the people" on a train bringing more workers were dead; he later asked Speer "how the people in Berlin thought we could work with these half dead people, many of them women and almost-children."[46]

Survival for these workers, many very young, was a true miracle. So ghastly were the conditions in the underground world that even Speer, during an inspection of the notorious Camp Dora in the Harz Mountains, where the V-2 rockets were to be produced, was badly shaken at the sight of "dead men" and "those still alive" who "were skeletons."[47] Indeed, Speer and his staff were so upset that the official record of their trip pathetically made note of a rather different sort of forced journey: "This tremendous mission drew on the leaders' last reserves of strength. Some of the men were so affected that they had to be forcibly sent off on vacations to restore their nerves."[48]

Despite all the segregation of sexes and nationalities and the ferocious propaganda forbidding fraternization and its more advanced aspects, including sexual intercourse, which for many categories of workers could bring a death sentence, foreign laborers of all nations found Germans and one another, made love, and produced babies. More babies came into the Reich in utero on the terrible transport trains. This natural process was a major headache for the labor procurers and even more so for the racial agencies assigned to protect the purity of German blood. A pregnant woman's productivity was naturally lower, and after giving birth, in those days, she was not considered fit to return to the workplace for several weeks. In the early days of the importation of Eastern workers, pregnant women were simply sent home, but it soon became clear that getting pregnant was a good way to escape forced labor, and this practice was stopped.

From the beginning, the slightest contact between male forced laborers, no matter what their origin, and German women was strictly forbidden.[49] As we have seen, Polish boys who became involved with German girls were executed, unless they were found to be of high racial value. Making contact with French and Dutch workers was much easier, as these were sometimes allowed out of their camps. But, despite repeated efforts of the race agencies to do so, the death sentence was not imposed on the Western workers, as such drastic action would not only violate the Geneva Convention, but would also surely be reported at home and might encourage even greater resistance than was already going on. Punishment of the Western men therefore usually consisted of prison sentences of a year or two.

German girls, who to the outrage of the Nazi authorities seem to have been quite attracted to "foreigners" and little concerned with racial issues, did not have a good time of it either if a relationship was discovered. Even a small act of kindness, such as giving a worker on a town construction project a cup of tea or a piece of bread, could bring down a Gestapo investigation upon the donor. These inquiries were often initiated by anonymous letters from informants with some nasty imagined reason to seek revenge on the victim. Punishments, imposed after interrogations in which questions of the most personal nature were asked, ranged from head shaving or some other form of public humiliation to jail sentences of varying lengths.

To drive the point home in some jurisdictions, Polish and Eastern workers involved in such cases were executed in public.

Out in the countryside, where foreign farmworkers often became part of the family, and the *droit du seigneur* was tempting, things were harder. To combat fraternization there, farmers had, early on, been given leaflets exhorting them:

> Maintain the purity of German blood! That applies to both men and women! Just as it is considered the greatest disgrace to become involved with a Jew, any German engaging in intimate relations with a Polish male or female is guilty of sinful behavior. Despise the bestial urges of this race! Be racially conscious and protect your children. Otherwise you will forfeit your greatest asset: your honor.[50]

None of this seems to have been effective: by early 1941 fraternization incidents were increasing, leading the authorities to push the factories to construct more brothels, at least for the Western workers. These facilities were given special allocations of bedding by the rationing agencies, and large numbers of foreign ladies were recruited to occupy them. Eastern workers did not have brothels per se. Men and women were supposed to be recruited "in equal numbers," after which nature could, apparently, take its course. Despite these regulations, the SD estimated that by January 1942 there were nearly 20,000 illegitimate German–foreign labor babies, a number that did not include those born within the labor community itself. Clearly, more drastic measures were needed.[51]

The Nazi policy of promoting abortion for those of "bad" blood in Poland was soon extended to the USSR, where Himmler not only encouraged but ordered abortions for "non-German" women impregnated by members of the police or SS, "unless that woman is of good stock." But even in this world of *Untermenschen,* abortion was not something that could be openly acknowledged as policy. The order was to be kept secret from Russian doctors, who were to be told that the procedures were being done randomly, "for reasons of social distress."[52]

Introduction of abortion, illegal in Germany, into the Reich itself was much trickier. It was one thing to perform the procedure on criminals and mental incompetents, but quite another to do so on perfectly normal young forced laborers who often worked side by side with Germans. In addition, the race authorities, terrified of losing any drops of German blood, were now faced with a whole new set of duties: each case would have to be investigated to determine the racial worth of the unborn child.

Nevertheless, a decree announcing that "in the case of Eastern female workers, pregnancy may be interrupted if the pregnant woman so desires" was issued by the Reich Health Leader on March 11, 1943, and sent to all race and police agencies in June. The decree, which was "not suitable for passing on to the district and local police authorities," suspended "criminal prosecution of abortion" for these cases. There were caveats: the "interruption" could only take place after an expert opinion was given by the "locally competent medical office," and if it was determined by SS investigators that the probable father was not a "German or a member of an ethnically related (Germanic) race."[53]

A bit later, another directive, which certainly might encourage "volunteering" for abortion, was issued, confirming the policy that pregnant female workers were not to be sent home anymore. Orders for their treatment and that of their offspring were appended. They were not kind. Women would go back to work as soon as possible. Births would take place in camp infirmaries and not in a German hospital, unless the woman was useful as "examination material for the training of students or midwives," and then only when "separation from pregnant Germans could be guaranteed." Once born, the babies would be taken from their mothers and put into "special" nurseries "of the simplest kind" (*Auslaender-Kinder Pflegestaetten*). Exceptions to this rule were "children of foreigners who partly are of a similar race and bearers of German blood," that is, Danes, Norwegians, and other "Nordic" peoples, who would still be taken from their mothers, but were to be raised as German children. Determining who belonged in which category of course meant more racial examining, for which another lengthy set of rules was enclosed. A few special mothers would be granted entrance to a Lebensborn home. But most of the babies lucky enough to be chosen would be taken by the Nazi Welfare Agency to "special children's homes for foreigners' children of good racial stock" (*Kinderheim für Auslaenderkinder*) or sent to private families.[54]

The subtle difference in the titles of the two children's institutions was undoubtedly no more accidental than the monumental difference in the treatment of the tiny children. Conditions in one home for "bad" children in Austria horrified even an SS inspector, Major General Hilgenfeldt, who wrote to Himmler that he had found "all of the babies . . . undernourished," and noted that if they continued to receive the officially mandated rations, they would "perish . . . in a few months." The general reported that he had ordered the rations increased until Himmler's opinion on the matter had been obtained. His own feelings, expressed in the careful language required to dispel any impression of disagreement with Nazi leaders, are clear:

> Partially the opinion exists that the children of the Eastern workers should die, partially there is an opinion that they should be raised. Since a clear-cut decision had not been achieved as yet and as I was told "one had to save face towards the Eastern workers," the babies are given insufficient nourishment which will cause their death within a few months. . . . I consider the manner in which this matter is treated at present as impossible. There exists only one way or the other. Either one does not wish that these children remain alive—then one should not let them starve to death slowly and take away so many liters of milk from the general food supply; there are means by which this can be accomplished without torture or pain. Or one intends to raise these children in order to utilize them later on as labor. In this case they must be fed in such a manner that they will be usable as workers.[55]

The General was not the only one who was disturbed. Health officials in the south of Germany reported that "a minority of reactionary Catholic physicians" and "even physicians whose political orientation is positive" had objected to the abortion policy for *Ostarbeiter* and Polish women. Indeed, one of the "politically sound" doctors had said that "in accord with medical and especially with German ethics . . . a pregnant woman is inviolable." Nurses in the Seekreis, the district around Lake Constance, who "belong to religious societies" had "sternly" refused to collaborate. Many other health professionals had "argued that the abortion decree was not in accordance with the moral obligation of a physician to preserve life" and that "a discriminatory evaluation of fellow nationals and of foreign nationals should not be permitted . . . in the field of medicine." Some doctors, clearly aware that the war was not going so well, said that they would not obey the decree for fear that they later would be "executed" for performing abortions. There were also fears that "encouragement would be given to the prevailing tendency to approve of abortions"; this would have "a damaging effect upon the morals of German women and girls, which through the exigencies of war have to a great extent become unstable."[56]

Hard-core Nazis were disgusted with such "ridiculous prejudices originating in the time of liberalism," and determined to continue their battle to protect the Volk from contamination. To get around the German doctors, orders were issued that abortions for *Ostarbeiter* and Poles were to be carried out if possible "by Russian doctors in the huts of the Eastern workers" right at the factories.[57] To improve efficiency further, nurseries were also set up by industrial firms to care for the babies delivered "in the huts." From reports on the conditions in one such nursery run by the Krupp firm at Voerde, near Essen, it is clear that Himmler had not decided in favor of making much of an effort to nurture Eastern babies.

A Krupp employee testified after the war that the children in the nursery were "undernourished. There was no child at all whose arms or hands were thicker than my thumb." The babies, up to two years old, lay naked on straw mattresses covered with rubber sheets. *Ostarbeiter* nurses caring for the children told him that they had very little to eat and that "fifty or sixty died every day, and as many were born every day, because there was a constant influx of eastern female workers with children."[58]

This was probably an exaggeration, and was vehemently denied by other Krupp workers, though one of them, Hans Kupke, did admit that the deaths were due to "a measure of mal-administration" for which, of course, he personally could not accept any responsibility, blaming these events on the chief camp physician.[59] Moreover, the camp was swept at one point by a diphtheria epidemic, which may have produced a temporary increase in mortality. But Krupp's own records showed that 88 children died in the 120-bed nursery between August 1944 and March 1945, some 23 of them from malnutrition and many others of "general weakness"—a staggering death rate for any institution theoretically dedicated to child care.[60]

The abortion and child care policies were much harder to enforce out in the countryside, where tens of thousands of *Ostarbeiter* were at work and where an estimated 80 percent of the illegitimate births were occurring. For the Slavic workers there could, technically, be no legitimate births, as they were not allowed to marry one another, much less a German. The racial authorities were appalled to find that German farm wives were taking care of alien babies along with their own while the mothers worked in the fields. This was very bad, as "even the German farm wife and the members of her family and the farm easily fall into a relationship of psychological attachment with the infant of alien blood." In Hannover, where some 1,500 "children of alien stock" were born in 1943, it was observed that a "very perilous infiltration problem" had developed, as "the bigger children played on the farms with the German children and the latter began already to include words in the foreign language in their speech."

In such remote areas it was difficult to set up special nurseries for the alien children, but the racial authorities insisted that the effort be made.

In the community of Echemin, in Hannover, all that could be managed was a day-care center set up in a "shed used before as a garage for farm machinery and fertilizer," measuring twenty by five meters. This edifice was fixed up in no time with the support of many Nazi agencies and local citizens. It boasted a kitchen, a dayroom, two dormitories, and a bedroom "for the alien nurse." No mention is made of bathrooms, perhaps an oversight in the report, or perhaps not. A bombed-out German family was brought in to supervise, "living near the care center." The parents were permitted to visit "twice a month for two fixed hours on Sundays."[61]

Faced with an ever-increasing number of babies, some fanatic racial operatives lobbied for extreme prevention tactics even as the war was drawing to a close. It is clear that opinion was not unanimous. In May 1944, a long, vividly written memo lambasted weak-willed officials who advised letting alien children stay with their mothers until they were five years old and required farmers to sign a document saying that they would care for babies born to their workers. Instead the memo advocated "ruthless but skillful propaganda" about alien children who were "produced on the soil of the German people" that would inform the parents that they should expect "immediate separation between parents and children, eventually complete estrangement. . . . It must be constantly on the mind of the female farm worker of alien blood that to give birth to a child in Germany would mean to lose it at the same time." In order to "round out the propaganda in a practical way, contraceptives should be quietly distributed (with the Reich bearing the cost)," as "there is no harm in leaving a valve open to the natural desires of the persons of alien blood."

For the babies that arrived despite all these dire precautions, due to the "primitive sensuality and fertility of the farm workers of alien race," a chain of rural homes like that in Echemin was to be established. Expenses for child care in these homes would be deducted in advance from the workers' pathetic wages. After the war, children and parents, not necessarily together, should be returned to their "countries of origin," a job that would soon fall not to the Nazis, but to the Allies.[62]

14. Total War

On February 18, 1943, Joseph Goebbels, speaking to some 14,000 top Nazi Party members assembled in the vast Sportpalast in Berlin, announced a new policy of "total war" for the German people. Despite the fact that virtually all of Europe was now enmeshed in the Nazi web, he did not have much choice. The preceding months had marked a distinct decline in German fortunes. In January alone the siege of Leningrad had been broken; Stalingrad had fallen; the British had brazenly bombed Berlin in broad daylight during the annual celebrations of Hitler's accession to power; and Jews in the Warsaw Ghetto, led by a twenty-four-year-old commander, had dropped their passive stance and killed Nazi officers attempting to deport the remaining inhabitants, an act of resistance that would soon burgeon into the first major overt armed challenge to Nazi power by civilians in the occupied nations.

Goebbels's speech was supposed to rally the German people's fighting spirit by generating fear that the Russians and the Allies would exterminate them if the Reich was defeated. This was facilitated by the Allies, who, at the Casablanca Conference in mid-January, had demanded unconditional surrender by Germany and ordered a huge combined bombing offensive to encourage the Nazis to comply. Goebbels also wished to unite public opinion behind new economic policies that would put all industry on a war footing and would require, among other things, obligatory registration for labor by all German women between the ages of seventeen and fifty, a measure unthinkable a year before. Also among the other things, undoubtedly inspired by the combined bombing offensive, was an order that antiaircraft batteries would now be manned by Hitler Youth and Bund Deutscher Mädel girls aged fifteen and sixteen, an order that included its auxiliaries, such as the Flieger HJ, whose members were as young as thirteen. Another as yet unpublished directive, on February 16, had initiated negotiations between the Reich Youth Directorate and the Waffen-SS with the aim of forming an entire combat division of boys aged seventeen and eighteen. It was no coincidence that 1943, following the HJ tradition of naming years after the most important goal to be achieved, was dubbed "The Year of War Service of German Youth."[1]

Hamburg after Allied bombing.

As the end drew nigh, no Nazi youth organization was left out. The Labor Service (RAD) camps became tough basic training operations where sixteen-year-olds were taught "how to storm make-believe enemy trenches with drawn bayonets and how to fire bazookas at haystacks."[2] One month after arriving for labor duty in 1944, William Kern, sixteen, and his unit were given a few rifles and sent off in a French cattle car to a village in Lorraine twenty miles behind the front lines. There they were lodged on straw mattresses in an old French barracks. Their job, along with other units "working on this fortification as far as the eye could see," was to dig, by hand, enormous antitank trenches for the Westwall defenses. Before they started on the trenches, the boys were ordered to dig foxholes for themselves. They would need them: Allied planes regularly strafed the vast construction site as the terrified boys lay facedown in the often water-filled foxholes. Labor duty had none of the glamorous aura of the Army and was generally detested. Kern, the only university-bound student in his unit, was hazed relentlessly by his squad leader; his only available revenge was to use the leader's toothbrush to clean the toilets when he was assigned to punitive latrine duty.[3]

Farther along the line, the Westwall workers were even younger. Proud Hitler Youth member Alfons Heck, swept away by the exhilaration of Nuremberg five years before and still an enthusiast, found himself, at fifteen, armed with a pistol and in command of an HJ unit of more than 100 boys. This group not only dug trenches, but also manned an antiaircraft gun. Heck's naive enthusiasm was dampened only slightly by the presence of a disillusioned veteran of the Eastern Front, assigned to coordinate Westwall construction operations after he had lost an arm in battle.

The HJ unit was housed in a requisitioned convent and its neighboring school. Meals were prepared by a large contingent of BDM and RAD girls. There was plenty of flirtation, and relations with the townspeople, after a rocky start, were not bad, as the presence of the HJ guaranteed a good food supply. The teenagers relaxed in the evenings by singing their hypnotic songs. Within a few months, Heck had been put in command of 2,800 boys and 80 girls. His dedication to his work was only increased by meeting Speer and Hitler during a visit they made to the Westwall project just before the Battle of the Bulge. There were few attacks in Heck's area, and before the Allies reached the Westwall his unit was withdrawn and he returned to his family's farm in the Rhineland, just inside the Luxembourg border. The reality of war would not come to him until Christmas Eve 1944, when the farm was bombed by Allied planes. His family was unharmed, but the buildings and animals were blown to bits. The physical damage left him cold, but when his grandmother, weeping in the ruins of her life's work, cursed him for his mindless loyalty to Hitler, he was moved. Still, his only tears came for the death of his dog, and the whole experience fueled a fierce desire for revenge. Heck resumed his HJ duties, and, along with many of his comrades, reported with enthusiasm for induction into the Luftwaffe, as ordered, on his seventeenth birthday.[4]

Germany's own did not suffice to construct the by now hopeless defenses against the Allied armies on both its eastern and western frontiers. In the summer and fall of 1944 in Poland and the eastern Reich, all men up to the age of sixty-five who were not in military service were required by the Nazi Party leadership to report for three- or four-week stints of trench digging. In November, some 50,000 men and boys were rounded up in Rotterdam and taken to work sites by barge and train, or on foot. Seventy thousand more would follow by December and be maintained in the usual miserable conditions.[5]

By this time huge numbers of the young forced laborers already in the Reich had also been moved into war production and to the vast construction sites on the borders. For this group there were no barracks, good food, or songfests. At one site near Nordhaven, on the Dutch border, Polish boys, among them Julian Nowak and his compatriots originally sent to the jute factory in Bremen, were housed in a barbed-wire enclosure guarded by uniformed SS. Reveille was at 4:30 a.m. From their unheated barracks they marched for half an hour to a train of cattle cars for a one-and-a-half-hour ride to a station near the project that was reached by another hour-long walk. Here, working alongside Dutch concentration camp inmates, the boys were set to work digging antitank trenches. In the Northern European winter the work was wet and heavy. Those at the bottom of the pit stood knee-deep in freezing water. Many Dutch prisoners were shot by the SS for perceived disobedience. The Polish boys, being "workers" and not "prisoners," escaped this extreme fate, though they were beaten with gun butts if, for example, their shovels were not full enough. One had to request permission to use the field latrines. A specific amount of time, from one to five minutes, was stipulated; if a boy lingered too long, the SS set their dogs on him:

> The SS man shouted the time twice, then he let the dog loose. The Pole tried to run away, but the dog caught up with him, attacked him and knocked him down. The SS man came over himself and calmly looked to see how the boy on the ground had been bitten. Only then did he call the dog off before giving the worker a few kicks with the comment that next time he would not call the dog back.[6]

Work went on until dark, when the whole three-hour march-train-march process was reversed. Back at their barracks, after a minimal meal, the boys, some by now in their fifth year of captivity, fell into their bunks still wearing their frozen, wet clothes, which never dried. But now, at least, there was a little hope. They too saw the planes:

> English planes flew low over our column. They were so low that we could see the faces of the pilots in the cockpits. We jumped up onto the earthworks we had just built and waved to them. They didn't shoot. Our guards had, according to regulations, thrown themselves on the ground. We knew that the liberation was close.[7]

They were too optimistic. In the remaining months of the war, their lives were ever more expendable. The arms factories, with their huge complements of forced labor, were prime targets for Allied bombing attacks. The young conscripted workers were not allowed into the underground bomb shelters provided for Germans, but had to find their own refuges in the surrounding ruins. Soon the raids were so frequent that work was virtually impossible. Julian and his friends were now assigned to digging rubble out of the Atlas factory on the outskirts of Bremen, one of the most heavily bombed cities in Germany. In the dark and smoke of the attacks, the boys clung to one another and, if they survived, only with difficulty found their way back to their filthy barracks. But despite all, they were called out to work day after day to the very end of the war, a phenomenon that occurred all across the Reich and allowed the Nazis to maintain production at an amazing level despite the total devastation raining upon them.

By the time of Goebbels's speech, the war was indeed "total": there were few people on earth, including small children, who were unaffected by the conflicts generated by Hitler and his Axis. Thousands of British and Dutch children were interned in squalid Far Eastern camps by the Japanese.[8] Even for children in America, who would never experience the hunger or the grim dangers of a war zone, the war was all-pervasive. Most fathers were away in the armed forces, no one knew exactly where, for months and years on end. When and if they came home, it was only for a day or so, looking strange in uniforms from which might issue the subtle aroma of the fuels that propelled submarines and bombers. Mothers left the house in overalls or were, mysteriously, picked up by police cars at night to be taken to their jobs at air-raid warning centers. Windows were covered with big black shades. Small children brought dimes to school to buy American flag stamps, which they messily glued into little squares in a special booklet that when full earned them a war bond. Christmas trees, bereft of tinsel, were decorated with American flags instead. Small boys who saw flashes off the Florida coast were told that ships were being blown up by torpedoes. No one could go for a drive because gas was rationed, and at least one little girl would not understand until much later why her grandmother had told her to name the yellow calico dachshund brought by Santa "Hitler—because it is a yellow dog."

Life was harsher in America for those of Axis origins. Not surprisingly, thousands of nationals and illegal aliens from these nations had been detained at the outbreak of hostilities in 1941. And, as is well known, some 78,000 Japanese-Americans, despite being citizens, were interned in dreary, wind-blown camps in Montana, Texas, California, and elsewhere. Less well known is the fact that many of these camps also contained whole families of German and Italian permanent residents of the United States who had not bothered to become citizens. Nearly 600,000 foreign-born Italians, required to register under the Alien Registration Act of 1940, were ordered to move away from the coasts, restricted in employment, and subjected to curfews that caused many who worked in the fishing and restaurant industries to lose their jobs. The panicky precautions did not create goodwill: travel restrictions prevented Joe DiMaggio's father from visiting his famous son, and a woman named Rosina Trovato was forcibly moved out of her house in Monterey on the day she was notified that her son, serving in the U.S. Navy, had died at Pearl Harbor.[9] The Italian program was soon discontinued as unworkable and impolitic, but the Japanese families remained incarcerated until the end of the war, even though many of their menfolk fought heroically in the U.S. armed forces.

Those of German origin, whether citizens or not, were, due to sheer numbers, a more complicated problem.[10] The anti-German passions of World War I had not been forgotten, and Nazi intentions were more and more suspect. During the 1930s Hitler's minions had not been the only ones making lists noting the inclinations of German-Americans: the FBI, under the direction of J. Edgar Hoover, was just as interested and had secretly created a Custodial Detention Index, which listed possible subversives and classified them according to potential degree of threat.[11] As had been the case in Britain, refugees from Nazism were included. Roundups of people on these lists began within days of Pearl Harbor and Hitler's declaration of war. There was little observance of their rights. Suspects were arrested at dawn, their houses were ransacked, and they were taken off to detention with no time to pack or make financial arrangements. A few were bona fide spies and serious Nazi activists, but most, though they may have been admirers of the Führer, were not. As had been the case with the Italians, the idea of restricting the activities of millions of German-Americans along the coasts was soon dropped, and by war's end, of the hundreds of thousands detained and investigated, just over 10,000 Germans, all noncitizens, were actually interned, and of these only a handful could be considered serious threats. For children, the experiences of arrest and confinement, even if temporary, were traumatic. Teenagers were humiliated while traveling to jails and camps by being handcuffed to police escorts who would accompany them even to the bathroom. One eleven-year-old girl was mortified when two large armed guards were assigned to take her to the doctor in San Antonio, causing quite a sensation on the streets.[12]

When families were split up, some youngsters were sent to state-run children's homes for a time. Others did not even get this sort of attention:

ten-year-old Alfred Plaschke and his little brother, both born in America and therefore citizens, were left alone when both their father and mother were arrested. Not knowing what else to do, they simply went to the local jail where their parents were being held and lived there with them for some months. The Plaschke brothers played "all spring in the fenced-in yard between the jail and the fire station" until the whole family was sent to an internment camp in the Seagoville prison, near Dallas.[13] After a time, more than 6,000 German, Japanese, and Italian internees rounded up by South and Central American nations were sent to the forty-plus U.S. camps, among them eighty-one German Jewish families who had to be rescued by help organizations.[14] Though armed guards were always visible and there were frequent roll calls, life in the camps was not too bad for young children: food was plentiful, and there were schools and entertainment. For their parents, whose careers were ended and houses lost, the incarceration could be devastating. Repatriation was possible: to the dismay of their children, many of whom eventually returned to America, nearly 4,500 of the German internees, far fewer than Hitler and Göring had hoped, asked for repatriation to the Reich during the war and were sent back on Swedish vessels in exchange for Allied and neutral nationals.

By 1944, another sort of internment camp had been set up in the United States. This was Fort Ontario in Oswego, New York, a small town on Lake Ontario, north of Syracuse. To this remote spot some 950 refugees, 90 percent of them Jews, had been brought from Europe in August of that year.[15] With the exception of the few hundred children who had come to the United States earlier, in fits and starts, the families at Oswego were the only tangible human result of all the commissions, lobbying, and hearings that had tried to find a way for the U.S. government to offer refuge to those uprooted by the Nazis. While refusal to change immigration laws for people who were merely threatened with expulsion from their homelands was marginally understandable, refusal to save people threatened with brutal death was not. But, despite the evidence of the exterminations communicated to the Allies by multiple sources, rescue continued to founder on the eternal problem of where to resettle those who might escape.

In April 1943, Gerhard Riegner, the World Jewish Congress representative in Switzerland, proposed a plan to facilitate the transmission of funds from American Jewish organizations to those caring for the hidden children of France and also to groups trying to transfer Romanian Jewish children out of camps in the Romanian-Soviet border regions known as

Transnistria to Palestine. To the plan for the children was later added the possibility that Romania would release their parents too, in all about 70,000 people.[16] The proposal, which would not cost the U.S. government anything, did, however, have to be approved by the Treasury and State departments, as it involved the transfer of funds from the United States to an enemy power. In addition, it was clear that most of the 70,000 would head for Palestine in violation of British efforts to limit Jewish immigration to that area. The idea was enthusiastically supported by Treasury Secretary Henry Morgenthau and approved by President Roosevelt. But nativist elements in the State Department, and more importantly, the British, disagreed. The bickering continued for months; but by now the feeling that something must be done was mounting in many areas of public opinion. On November 9, 1943, a resolution recommending the creation of an immediate plan to rescue "the surviving Jewish people of Europe from extinction at the hands of Nazi Germany" was introduced in the Congress.[17] Although support for the measure in the press and elsewhere was strong, its passage was far from automatic, as the usual opponents had lost none of their resolve. Breckinridge Long, a frequent nemesis of immigration at the State Department, in secret testimony that caused an uproar when it was leaked, gave negative and misleading statistics on the number of refugees who had already been given visas. Even more astonishing was the continued opposition of Zionist leaders and congressmen, who argued against the measure because it did not specify the immediate opening of Palestine to all Jewish refugees. Once again, the Congress would take no action: Roosevelt, at the urging of Morgenthau, preempted what was shaping up to be a nasty floor debate, especially undesirable in an election year, with an executive order on January 22, 1944, establishing the War Refugee Board, which would deal with the whole issue.

This small, minimally funded agency was headed by John Pehle, a determined and very humane former Treasury official. During its short existence, the WRB is thought to have saved more than 250,000 people by supporting the secret direct negotiations carried on by operatives such as Raoul Wallenberg and Ira Hirschmann with the now wavering Axis partners of Germany, as well as with the neutral nations, and even, at one point, with Himmler himself. Through these negotiations thousands would find protection and support in France, Sweden, Switzerland, and Spain. Far larger numbers would be saved by persuading Romania simply to move the Jews in Transnistria out of their foul transit camps and away from the path of the retreating Germans, and Bulgaria to rescind its anti-Jewish laws. Wallenberg, working in Budapest in the midst of the Nazi deportations, would manage against all odds to save 120,000.

But fewer than a thousand of those rescued would be admitted to Camp Oswego in the United States under WRB auspices, and then only due to an executive order signed by Roosevelt, which, to keep Congress happy, promised that their stay would only be temporary. From the beginning, the gloomy and remote camp was not a fun place to be. The internees were carefully supervised; the only ones allowed out for more than six hours at a time were the 180 children, who went to the local schools. This measure meant that no one could look for a job or go anywhere. The seventeen different nationalities represented did not get along and did not want to do the menial work needed for the running of the camp. Those who had relatives in the United States could not fathom why they could not go and live with them. It was not until a few days before Christmas 1945 that Harry S. Truman, who had become President upon FDR's death in April, realized, for reasons that will later become clear, that repatriation was not possible and allowed the Oswego internees to leave the camp and remain in the United States as legal immigrants.

In the occupied nations of Western Europe, existence, even for those living at home, and particularly in towns and cities, had been utterly transformed by the end of 1943. Deception and secrecy pervaded everything. To protect their valuables from German requisitioning raids, families buried silver in their gardens, created secret compartments in attics, and hid radios in cellars. Relatives and friends fleeing from various kinds of pursuit were routinely hidden behind false walls. Children knew all these things and became used to strange noises in the night, but knew better than to tell anyone. Without telephones or radios, which were illegal, most news was circulated by word of mouth and underground newspapers. To this furtive mix was added simple fear. Fathers and brothers could be arrested without warning, taken from their homes, and tortured to reveal Resistance connections or be held for months as hostages, who were regularly executed in reprisal for hostile acts by the population.

As time passed and war production eliminated consumer goods, the problems became more physical.[18] Shoes disappeared. Parents remade their own clothes for their growing children; by 1944, many a mother had only one dress to her name. Diminishing fuel supplies forced families to huddle in one room of a house, often on an upper floor, which was marginally warmer, and no amount of money could buy municipal utilities such as natural gas, water, or electricity, which were frequently cut off altogether. Hot baths were rare, and all sorts of tiny stoves, which could cook a pot of food and simultaneously provide warmth, were constructed. Slowly but relentlessly, urban parks and streets were denuded of trees, which were followed by wooden furniture, picture frames, doorjambs, and parquet floors. To ignite these often beloved objects, libraries and magazine collections were shredded for kindling. Sporadic raids by German troops took away blankets, sewing machines, pots and pans. As food supplies and consumer goods vanished, so did shops and the jobs and salaries that went with them.

What was not burned in the stoves was bartered for food from farmers and black marketeers who often visited their clients in the dark of night. By 1943, most small children had never seen a banana or an orange. Since men and boys were in constant danger of being picked up by patrols, the hunter-gatherer role now fell to women and children. Procuring even authorized items with ration stamps required hours of standing in line. Girls and younger boys performed this endless duty and also trekked out of the cities to forage for fuel and beg farmers for milk and bread. They had plenty of time: the combination of no heat, little food, and the need for boths boys over twelve and male teachers to hide led to the closure of schools in many areas. In Holland, some teachers would write assignments on the blackboard every Monday and students would come in to copy them and go home to study. But cold, dark, smoky rooms and the constant hunt for food were not conducive to homework, and health was so endangered by malnutrition that children who would not normally be at risk suffered from fatigue and died of diphtheria, scarlet fever, and other childhood ills.

Nor was there entertainment outside the home for the average person. After D-Day, ever stricter curfews made going out at night in the pitch-dark cities impossible and most restaurants, theaters, and movie houses were closed or limited to collaborators, German officials, and the nouveaux riches of the black market economy. Few could offer anyone else much of a meal at home, and most outdoor activities were too exhausting for those who seldom saw meat and lived on bread and, if they were lucky, things like boxes of dried peas they had had the foresight to procure early in the war. By September 1944, with Allied forces well into France and Italy, relief was tantalizingly near for the rest of Europe. But the Nazis would not give up easily. By this time, for many, only the churches remained as gathering places. On Christmas Eve 1944, as Allied forces struggled not far away in the Battle of the Bulge, the Germans lifted the curfew in Holland for midnight services. Fourteen-year-old Cornelia Fuykschot and her friends crossed the blacked-out town of Utrecht to the only church allowed to turn on its interior lights. After months of living in darkness, what the girl found inside the huge neo-rococo Catholic basilica was almost overwhelming:

> As we approached the church, the streets seemed to be alive with dark figures, all moving in the same direction. . . . Only a little door inside the big doors could allow the celebrants in, otherwise too much light would escape through the portal to the outside. . . . White was the ceiling and white were the walls . . . white above all that mass of people that covered not only the seats but also all the floor space . . . white lined with gold which only intensified the brightness. . . . The eye could only move up, up to all this white, heavenly light following all the roses and garlands and angels which seemed to produce the jubilant music with their golden trumpets that in fact came from an organ we could not see. What else could the pastor preach about but the light that had come into the darkness and conquered it? How well we understood what that meant.[19]

The Nazis, who, for entirely different reasons, were equally enamored of the light-and-darkness analogy, understood also, which was why the curfew was only lifted for one night.

　　In the early summer of 1943, the war in many areas of Western Europe would cease to be limited to physical and spiritual deprivations and the disappearances of friends and family, and instead became violent. On June 10, Allied forces landed in Sicily and began their slow and terrible progress up through Italy, a campaign that, due to the ferocious defense of the Germans, would last until the end of the war in 1945 and have brutal effects on the civilian population. The bombing of England by the Germans, which had continued only sporadically after the Battle of Britain, was now revived and, in 1944, was augmented by Hitler's terrifying "secret weapons," the V-1 and V-2 rockets, some 3,000 of which fell on London alone. It was also in 1943 that the destruction of war, to a degree never before seen, began to fall upon Germany itself, from many thousands of Allied bombers whose actions would eventually kill some 650,000 civilians, giving credence in the minds of many to Goebbels's warnings that the Allies were bent on extermination.

The 100,000 Hitler Youth recruited to man the antiaircraft emplacements were badly needed. Eighteen thousand boys and girls were brought in from the Baltics, Belorussia, and the Ukraine to increase their number.[20] An estimated two million people would be involved in antiaircraft defense by 1944. The flak guns were a major deterrent to the bombers until they were overwhelmed by the technological advances and the sheer production capacity of the Allies. At the beginning, the bombing raids were exciting for German kids; like those in Spain, they collected and traded shrapnel splinters. To some, being in the raids gave them "the feeling that we were like the soldiers fighting at the front." Teenaged girls in Leipzig hoped the raids would last all night so that school would be closed the next day. Children everywhere patrolled the rooftops and learned how to pick up and throw off unexploded incendiary bombs: "The bombs were soon our favorite toys. We threw them down from walls . . . we wanted to be just like grown-ups putting out fires and recovering the injured. That was our everyday play."[21]

Boys sent to the flak emplacements were also excited to "be soldiers." The tracking of the aircraft and the guns themselves were endlessly fascinating. Usually the boys were assigned with schoolmates; for a time, efforts were made to have teachers go to the gun positions to give them lessons. Most emplacements had one adult gunner, two fifteen- or sixteen-year-old assistants, and a varying number of younger boys and girls who manned the searchlights, passed ammunition, and acted as messengers. It was all great fun playing in the piles of equipment and even, at one post, in a stack of stored coffins. The children were supposed to be assigned to batteries near home, but as the bombing increased they were often transferred to the Ruhr and other major target areas. The fun wore off fast, but the children's indoctrination, bolstered by the horrors they witnessed all around them and their natural desire to defend home and family, only led to greater determination. In a Berlin suburb, BDM leader Melita Maschmann, back from her duty in Poland,

> saw a row of dead anti-aircraft auxiliaries lying side by side. . . . The . . . base where these schoolboys were serving had received several direct hits: I went into a barrack room where the survivors were gathered. They sat on the floor along one wall, and the white faces they turned toward me were distorted with fear. Many of them were weeping. . . . In another room lay the wounded. One of them, a boy with a soft, round childish face, held himself rigid when the officer . . . asked him if he was in pain. "Yes, but it doesn't matter. Germany must triumph."[22]

The horrors became more and more extreme. Some 700,000 Hitler Youth were used in Fire Defense Squads and more as helpers in airraid shelters, which had become quite sophisticated in design, ranging from complex tubelike bunkers in Hamburg to the enormous flak towers of Berlin, which held several thousand persons along with tons of art objects and boasted sophisticated medical facilities. In Hamburg, thirteen-year-old Hitler Youth Uwe Köster opened and closed shelter doors, brought milk for children, handed out sedatives to nervous adults, and pumped air into the bunkers. He was not supposed to stay inside the shelter. Wearing a gas mask, a helmet, and his uniform, he was required to continue working and to carry messages from place to place even during the worst part of a raid. On July 24, 1943, and during the ten days that followed, Hamburg was subjected to six major air attacks by some 2,600 Allied bombers. Dropping the tinsel forbidden on American Christmas trees over the city to deceive radar, the planes poured an estimated 1.5 million incendiary bombs into densely inhabited areas. The biggest raid, on July 27, created a firestorm with temperatures nearing 1,000 degrees Celsius and winds reaching 150 miles per hour.[23]

> You could hear them getting closer and closer all the time. By the sound of it huge bomber formations were circling over Hamburg, flying in from all directions. The entire sky was lit with hundreds of flares, . . . which glistened brightly as they slowly made their way to the ground. Amid this, the roaring and rumbling, the whizzing and whistling of the falling bombs passing through the air seemed never to end. I ran out of my shelter and headed home. The city was an inferno because of the unbearable heat . . . getting to the river and swimming was the only [route]. . . . Up above the sky had turned a deep red. . . . People were running crazily back and forth . . . slapping themselves with towels . . . some were already lying totally still on the street.[24]

German records estimated that, in all, 41,800 people died instantly in these raids and that 37,800 more were injured, of whom many probably died subsequently.[25] Uwe Köster was in the midst of it. He could not get to his post at first, and when he did, his duties were grim indeed:

> My mother, my sister and I went down the stairs but could get no further . . . we huddled in a small corner for the entire attack, two hours, standing up. We couldn't go into the street. . . . It was literally hailing fire bombs, incendiaries with phosphorus canisters. . . . Afterwards we were called in to clear the streets. We cleared out the corpses, sometimes the burned bodies of people in cellars. . . . We stacked the bodies

in 30 to 35 layers on top of each other. We stacked them all, and if you went by two or three days later you could only go with cellophane over your eyes because everything was smoky. The air was absolutely still. We didn't have any sun at all for three or four days; it was completely dark out. . . . The corpses were beyond identification. We would dig entire families out of their basements . . . they were completely mummified, burned and melted together by the heat.[26]

Hamburg was only the beginning. A few months later the Associated Press reported from Sweden that "haggard, red eyed arrivals from Berlin, many of whom still were wearing clothes singed as they walked through streets walled by fire," were describing "almost unbelievable destruction wrought by . . . intensive RAF assaults," destruction that included the Sportpalast, the site from which Goebbels had made his total war announcement. The witnesses said that "much of the city simply no longer exists." Local firefighters had been "unable to cope" with the fires and "trucks crowded with firemen from neighboring cities were seen entering Berlin."[27]

For nearly two more years similar scenes would take place, most terribly in Dresden, until the majority of Germany's cities had become deserts of rubble and hundreds of thousands of people had succumbed to the horrible types of death that the Nazis had so wantonly visited upon their victims:

We had hardly been in Cologne for two weeks. On September 27, 1944, I wanted to take my two small children, who were three and six . . . to the insurance company in the city to apply for the orphan's pension, since my husband had been killed at the front. . . . A kindergarten teacher who knew me and the children, saw us and said "Don't take the children into the city. There could be another air raid; they're safer here." I gave in and traveled to the city alone. . . . The air raid warning sounded while I was sitting in a streetcar. . . . All I could think about was my children. As soon as the all clear sounded I ran frantically back to . . . look for them. . . . I saw other children but I couldn't find my own two. . . . Later that afternoon I heard that a whole group of people had been buried in a house . . . including children from the kindergarten. . . . My two children were pulled out dead. You could hardly see any injuries on them . . . I was in a state of total shock . . . I wanted to scream "You Nazis, you murderers!" A neighbor, who had only been released from a concentration camp a few days before grabbed my arm and pulled me aside. He said, "Do you want to get yourself arrested too?"[28]

The fear of arrest for any protest was very real. By 1942 many German university students had, in the course of their Labor Service duties and draft obligations, seen the terrible things happening on the Eastern Front and much more, and they were determined to resist in some way. Among these were a small group of Munich university students known as the White Rose.[29] The members of this little ring printed up leaflets and managed to distribute them by mail across the south of Germany. But their passion overcame their caution when two of the principals, Hans and Sophie Scholl, decided to scatter leaflets from a balcony in the atrium of the University of Munich on February 18, 1943. Retribution was swift. By 5:00 p.m. on February 22, Hans, Sophie, and another colleague had been executed by guillotine after a brief show trial. Their work was carried on after their deaths by a few others, among them Hans Leipelt, who was a *Mischlinge* of the first degree—that is, he had two Jewish grandparents but was not a practicing Jew. Leipelt had been allowed to serve in the Wehrmacht early in the war, but by the fall of 1940 he had been given a "dishonorable" discharge and been publicly stripped of his insignia and decorations, which included the Iron Cross. A year later he was dismissed from the university; in 1942, his Jewish grandmother was sent to Theresienstadt, where she perished. He and other students at the University of Hamburg who were associated with this "flash quickly extinguished by the ubiquitous Gestapo and general fear" would also be systematically killed.[30]

On July 20, 1944, there would be a far bigger flash. On that day Colonel Claus Schenck Graf von Stauffenberg, part of an extensive plot, planted a bomb in the conference room where Hitler was being briefed on the Eastern Front situation. The Führer survived, but the conspirators did not. More than 5,000 people were arrested and some 200 were executed in short order. The retribution did not end with those directly involved, but was extended even to their grandchildren. The Gestapo was very thorough about tracking down these small relatives. The widow of Claus von Stauffenberg was arrested and sent with her six-month-old baby to a hospital in Potsdam. Her other children, aged four, six, eight, and ten, as well as two cousins, seven and five, were taken away to a Nazi Welfare Agency children's home at Bad Sachsa in the Harz Mountains. The grandchildren of Ulrich Goerdeler, another conspirator, nine months and three years old, went there too, along with several others.[31]

Some were harder to find. Twenty-five-year-old Fey von Hassell, daughter of the conspirator Ulrich von Hassell, the former German ambassador to Italy, had married an Italian.[32] In July 1944, she was living in her husband's villa near Venice with her two sons, Corrado and Roberto, aged four and two. Here she was arrested in August, briefly taken to an Italian jail, and then allowed to go home under house arrest. This was not too bad, but in late September she was informed that she and her children were to be taken to Germany and had twenty-four hours to prepare. Distraught family retainers stayed up all night knitting sweaters for the children, and the local cobbler made them shoes. To this day, Corrado remembers the arrival of the big black car that picked them up at 4:00 a.m., as "it was the first time I had ever been out after dark."[33] All three were taken first to a prison in Innsbruck and later to a hotel. The following day Fey was told that she had to go to the prison for questioning, and that the boys were to be sent, "temporarily," to "a good children's home." Corrado, immediately afraid, "kept asking" if his mother was going away, but she was powerless:

> Two SS "nurses" arrived, both large blond women without the slightest hint of gentleness. They inquired about the children's habits but made no effort to be friendly with them. With the calmness that comes from icy fear, I put on their little coats and told Corradino as calmly as I could, "Mama will follow you very soon, but first you will go for a nice walk." Robertino thought this was a wonderful idea and confidently took the nurse's hand. But Corradino suddenly gave way to wild panic, flinging himself backward and howling crazily. He tried desperately to escape from the SS woman . . . tearing at the hand she had clamped around his little wrist. . . . I had to stand there like a statue, listening to Corradino's wails growing fainter and fainter as he and Robertino were pulled down the stairs.[34]

The two tiny blond boys were taken to a children's home outside Innsbruck, their names were changed to Vorhof, and they vanished into Himmler's reservoir of "good blood" along with the other small children related to the conspirators. Their parents and older family members, all from highly distinguished German families, were rounded up and until the end of the war would be moved from one prison to another, along with other VIP prisoners such as Léon Blum, the former Premier of France. The prisons ranged from very nice hotels to Buchenwald, Stutthof, and Dachau. Treatment of this "privileged" group, though harsh, was, for motives known only to the SS (who perhaps hoped to use them as barter for Germans held by the Allies), marginally better than that of other concentration camp inmates. For the prisoners themselves who survived

typhus, hunger, and cold, as for so many other inmates, the worst torture
was not knowing the fate of their children.

Undeterred by the many indicators that victory was no longer
possible, in June 1943 the Nazi leadership had given orders to proceed
with the organization of an SS–Hitler Youth combat division. Boys of seventeen and eighteen were to be recruited from a variety of sources,
including the special War Preparation Camps (WEL). These camps were
by now a major source of supply to the SS, which could not take boys
through the regular draft. The WEL camps included within them youths
from all the Nordic occupied countries, as well as *Volksdeutsche* from the
East. Kept carefully segregated according to ethnic origin, they were
trained by hardened SS veterans with little empathy for teenagers,[35] who,
as had been the case in the KLV evacuation camps, were left to run their
own societies and correct one another. Brutality and all kinds of abuse
were frequent. In one camp, boys who broke the unwritten rules had their
heads shaved and a description of the offense painted on their bare scalps.
When there were suicides, the leadership, apparently unconcerned, left
the burial of the victims to their peers.[36]

Officers and NCOs for the Hitler Youth division would be provided
from former HJ leaders in the Wehrmacht and remnants of the tough SS
Leibstandarte Adolf Hitler division, which had been decimated in the
USSR. Training was to take place in occupied Belgium, where, by August,
10,000 boys had been assembled, many of them well below the stipulated
age and most unclear about what their future duties would be. There was
a battalion of Dutch recruits who thought they were headed for the Eastern Front. Boys who had signed up for the aviation and naval programs of
the Hitler Youth now suddenly found themselves in what was to be a
Waffen-SS Panzer division. It was not very spiffy at first: there were not
enough uniforms or weapons, much less tanks. But the officers, who introduced less-Prussian training methods and encouraged informality, were
effective. The boys got superior food plus extra candy instead of the normal ration of cigarettes, which, to their chagrin, they were deemed too
young to smoke. It was all very folksy and much like a big school outing:
company commanders were even encouraged to keep in touch with the
families of the teenaged recruits. By the spring of 1944, the division, now
formally called the 12th SS Panzer Division Hitlerjugend, was performing
impressively in maneuvers. Hitler had high hopes for the young soldiers.
In July 1943, Himmler had told the Führer that the average age of two

*Wounded and decorated young Germans attend a ceremony
honoring fallen colleagues.*

other SS divisions, including officers, was eighteen. Hitler thought this
was fine, noting approvingly that battle reports showed that "the youngsters who come from the HJ are fanatical fighters . . . some only sixteen
years old fight more fanatically than their older comrades."[37] The boys
would not let Hitler down. Sent into battle the morning after D-Day, they
would continue to perform well through the long summer of 1944. Amazing the Allied commanders with their ferocity and refusal to surrender,
they fought all across Normandy, where, under the grim black gravestones
of the German military cemeteries, most of the original 10,000 boys now
lie. In September, when the division retreated into Germany, its roster had
been reduced to a reported 600.[38]

In October 1944, Hitler created a home guard known as the Volkssturm.[39] All men aged sixteen to sixty were required to register, but as
Germany was engulfed, the lower age limit dropped dramatically. Some
recruits were so young when called up that their mothers had to take them

to the barracks. A boy of eight who had destroyed an American tank with a Panzerfaust (the German version of the bazooka) was found in an Allied POW enclosure after the war. Much of this "third wave" of the Volkssturm was created by simply mobilizing existing Land Service and Hitler Youth formations, which, of course, had long since been working on military projects. Among them were some 180 boys who were involved in the defense of the bridge at Remagen. Flak helper Heinz Schwartz, sixteen, who lived in a nearby village, was stationed at the eastern end. For days he had been watching exhausted Wehrmacht troops retreating across the span. On March 7, 1945, when American troops appeared on the far bank, he and other teenagers were ordered to destroy their ammunition and leave. Soon the bridge came under fire, and Heinz, wanting to see it blow up, hid in a railroad tunnel to await the big moment. But the bridge was not destroyed, and the young warrior barely managed to get out of the tunnel and "run home to my mother as fast as I could" before the Americans arrived.[40]

The use of these children was promoted enthusiastically by the Reich Youth Directorate. Some officials envisioned groups of young boys who would carry on a sort of guerrilla warfare against the invading troops, much like the groups set up by the Soviets in Leningrad. Others went further. Thirty-two-year-old Artur Axmann, head of the Youth Directorate, was eager to get the boys into full-fledged combat, and even set up a special youth sniper training course. Elaborate mobilization plans, never initiated, were drawn up for the Bavarian HJ/BDM. But in March 1945, the HJ was instructed to begin training 4,200 boys for antitank units, many of which, after extremely minimal instruction, were attached to combat units on the Eastern Front, by now within the borders of Germany.

It was in Berlin that the German youths would see the most action. An estimated 5,000 boys and girls under sixteen would take part in the final battles in the ruins of Berlin, despite strong protests by regular Wehrmacht commanders who repeatedly ordered the HJ to be withdrawn. Only 500 are thought to have survived. During the battle they fought, helped wounded civilians and soldiers, and worked until they literally dropped. Fear and "defeatism" among this group was often punished just as brutally by the SS as it was among older soldiers, whose bodies hung all over Berlin labeled "traitor" or "coward." One thirteen-year-old Jungvolk member, whose formation was converted wholesale into a combat unit, later reported that "when we wanted to . . . go home we were stopped and had to join the escape across the canal. . . . My *Jungzugführer*, who refused, was strung up on the nearest tree by a few SS men. . . . But then he was already fifteen years old."[41]

Although the rate of desertion was high, it was fear of such a fate and of capture by the "subhuman" Bolsheviks that kept most of the young defenders fighting. Some loved the glory of blowing up a tank and, dressed in motley uniforms and helmets that were far too big, fought with valor. But the total inadequacy of their training led to high casualties and made clear the hopelessness of their situation. Many officers, appalled at the slaughter, dismissed the boys and sent them home. Oblivious to it all, Hitler, in his last appearance outside his bunker, awarded medals to a pathetic troop of these children, patting them on the cheek in a grandfatherly way as he did so, certainly not a normal gesture when the medals were for adults.

Near the end, a unit of Hitler Youth boys was given a final duty: after the last concert of the Berlin Philharmonic on April 12, 1945, an all-German program that ended with the music from the final scene of *Götterdämmerung*, in which "Valhalla is seen in the distance in flames—final illumination of that twilight of the Gods which is now to darken into eternal night,"[42] the uniformed children are said to have stood at the exits holding baskets of cyanide capsules for those of the Party faithful who now contemplated suicide.[43]

If the change in Germany's fortunes had led to unprecedented combat experiences for many of its young people, in the occupied lands the turn of the tide had encouraged ever greater involvement in Resistance activities. This had occurred both because the hope of liberation now seemed more real and because Nazi reprisals had become progressively more brutal, pushing many who had previously been passive to action fueled by hatred, revenge, and despair.

Resistance is made to order for teenagers, secrecy and defiance of authority being so natural to them and the excitement of clandestine activity so appealing. In every occupied area the young itched to be part of the action and free of parental restraint. The eleven-year-old son of Dr. Klukowski, our observer of Polish occupation life, had run away to join the partisans twice by May 1942. He was sent home on both occasions. By October of the following year attitudes had changed so much that his father allowed the boy to be sworn in as a member of the Home Army. It was an emotional moment:

Today my twelve-year-old son Tadeuz was sworn in as a member of the
Home Army. . . . This was my attempt to start him in conspiracy work,
in the type of work permitted at his young age. During the entire ceremony, which took place in my private office, I was present. But at one
moment when I looked into the face of my boy, I felt so moved that to
avoid crying I left the room.[44]

Not everyone felt this way. One mother went right into a partisan camp
to retrieve her two teenaged daughters; another, who had pursued her
sixteen-year-old son and taken away his shoes to keep him from joining up,
was forced at rifle point by the boy's platoon commander to return the
shoes and let her son be a partisan.[45] Before 1942, there had been even
greater adult objection to active resistance within the ghettos, where the
Judenrats and conservative elements were convinced that cooperation
with the Nazis and the sacrifice of a few would save the majority, and
where activities for the young were channeled into clandestine education
and preparation for new lives in Palestine and other future destinations of
refuge.

In the early days of the war few young people were accepted by the
underground organizations, who feared teenaged carelessness would lead
to exposure. But by 1943, a growing number of organizations all over
Europe, deeply involved in publishing illegal newspapers, rescuing
downed pilots, sheltering the hunted, and fomenting unrest with minor
sabotage and nuisance activities had found that young people were
extremely useful. Small newsboys in Warsaw tucked illegal pages into the
authorized Nazi newspapers sold on the streets. These were usually boycotted by the Poles unless the vendors shouted, "Today you have extraordinary news," which indicated that there was a "special" supplement.[46]
Children, already adept at stealing food, acted as couriers and copyboys
for the clandestine press, feeding information received on hidden radios
to underground writers. One group of boys pulled down the swastika flying over the Parthenon in Athens; another, in Warsaw, known as the "Little
Wolves," specialized in anti-Nazi graffiti, puncturing tires, and putting up
satirical posters referring to Nazi decrees. After an order in late 1942 requisitioning furs from the Polish population for German forces on the Eastern Front, the city was covered with images showing "a gaunt, glaring
German soldier . . . swathed in a very feminine mink coat with a silver fox
muff protecting his hands," captioned, "Now that I am so warm, dying for
our Führer will be a pleasure."[47]

Girls were especially useful as messengers and for making deliveries of small arms and components of such items as illicit radios.[48] The work, often involving long treks by foot or bicycle in all kinds of weather, during which constant vigilance was essential, was, after a time, exhausting. One young Polish girl, for whom the adventure had worn off after three years on the job, admitted that she kept "dreaming of just one thing. I wish the war were over and that I might have a job where I could stay just where I am, in one spot all the time and have people come to me. I would like to be the matron in a ladies rest room, I really mean it."[49]

Punishment for those who were caught was brutal and age was no mitigating factor. Girls and boys alike were subjected to unspeakable tortures in the cellars and attics of Gestapo buildings in order to extract the names of their colleagues. If they survived, the young resisters were sent to concentration camps. In the West, for girls, this usually meant Ravensbrück, where they were fed into the slave labor force or used for medical experiments, including injections of gangrene-producing matter and sterilization by X-ray.[50] The sterilization program at Ravensbrück was a major operation by 1943. Established in 1941 with Himmler's blessing, it had been accorded ever-increasing amounts of equipment and numbers of subjects by the Reichsführer SS, who in July 1942 had ordered the researchers to find out "how long it would take to sterilize one thousand Jewesses." By June 1943, the methods were so developed that the chief researcher, a Professor Clauberg, could report to Himmler that with the proper equipment and the right number of trained assistants he could sterilize "several hundred or even a thousand a day." The new X-ray methodology, he was pleased to note, would also be very practical for "our normal eugenic sterilizations," as it could replace surgery. The "training" would continue into 1945 on whoever came to hand, including non-Jewish teenage "terrorist" Resistance workers and little Gypsy girls as young as eight, at least one of whom died after four days of agony during which an incision in her abdomen was kept open so that the experimenters could view the effects of the radiation on her uterus.[51]

By 1943 not everyone still had relatives to try to stop them from dangerous resistance work. Thousands of teenagers, left alone when whole villages were destroyed and their families were murdered, no longer had anyone to restrain them or give them refuge. Nowhere was this truer than in the Eastern ghettos after the initial massive deportations, which had targeted the very young and the old, eliminating both parents and small siblings of those young people reprieved by their ability to work. It was among this group that active Jewish resistance would be born. Organizing had begun in Vilna in January 1942, in the face of violent protest from many conservative ghetto residents. As the deportations and executions grew, some spontaneous responses occurred. In September, in the Ukrainian town of Tuczyn, young residents openly urged their elders not to go to the assigned assembly area and persuaded them to start fires and destroy their houses and possessions. In the resulting massive conflagration and chaos 2,000 Jews were able to escape into the forests. Taking to the woods was no guarantee of escape: most of the young people from the Kovno Ghetto in Lithuania who tried to join the partisans perished of wounds, exposure, or after being betrayed.[52]

More serious organization took place in October in the Warsaw Ghetto, from which tens of thousands had already been deported. With much negotiation Jewish Zionists, Communists, and other factions united to form the Jewish Combat Organization, which soon became the dominant power in the ghetto, where somewhere between 40,000 and 70,000 people still remained.[53] By January 1943, some twenty-two small combat units, whose members were aged eighteen to twenty-five, had been formed and hundreds of secret tunnels and bunkers had been built. An attempt by the Germans to organize further deportations in late January was met with gunfire. Surprised, the Nazis, who had suffered a few casualties, withdrew. On April 19 they returned in strength. The Combat Organization's heroic but hopeless defense is now legend.[54] The Nazis, even during this battle, which lasted until May 16, still managed to load and dispatch their death trains. But things had changed: in the summer and fall of 1943 more revolts, equally doomed, would take place right in the extermination camps of Treblinka and Sobibor, and in other ghettos.

There was nothing altruistic about the leaders and supporters of the Resistance movements. Alliances between underground groups were temporary and aimed at getting rid of the Germans. But for all of them the question of postwar control was paramount. While young people sought out the partisans to get revenge on the Germans, find romantic adventure, or obtain security and food, most of those controlling the groups had more specific agendas, which were supported by domestic factions or governments in exile. Added to these were gangs of bandits seeking booty and tribal hegemonies of various kinds. Nowhere would the cynical manipulation of partisans be more manifest than in a second uprising in Warsaw, this time of the Polish population. The underground Home Army, supported by the Polish government in exile in London, had been waiting for years for the perfect moment to rise up against the Nazis. In late July 1944, with the Red Army nearing Warsaw, and encouraged by Radio

Moscow, they felt the time had come, and set 5:00 p.m. on August 1 as their D-Day.

Full of excitement, the younger members of the Resistance comported themselves with dangerous defiance during the hours leading up to the rebellion, which, when it came, surprised the Germans despite much leaked information. Their response was brutal. Two of the Nazis' most experienced antipartisan operatives, Oskar Dirlewanger and Mieczyslaw Kaminski, whose units, consisting largely of convicts and mercenaries, we have already seen in action in the USSR, were sent to Warsaw. Within days, using the techniques that had been perfected in destroying the Warsaw Ghetto, the Nazis shot thousands of Poles in mass executions, without mercy for children, pregnant women, or the elderly. Whole blocks were looted and burned, and the streets and courtyards piled with bodies. The uprising was large, involving at least 25,000 armed Poles, who fought with desperation, but it could not succeed without help from outside. The hope of help from the Red Army and Polish units fighting with it was not fulfilled. Nor would Stalin permit British and American bombers to use his air bases so that they could attack German units moving toward Warsaw, which limited the help the Western Allies could provide to a few airdrops of supplies. By allowing the non-Communist Home Army to fight things out with the Nazis, Stalin knew he could kill two birds with one stone, and he did. Against all odds the Poles continued to fight until October 5. By then much of Warsaw had been destroyed and a reported 200,000 fighters and civilians had been killed. Most of the remaining population was then deported to concentration camps, and the city remained a virtual ghost town.[55]

Out in the countryside, the problems presented by partisan activity were even more difficult, because of their sheer unpredictability. In many a village, be it in Poland, the Ukraine, or the Balkans, there was little choice between the violence and atrocities of the Germans and those of the partisans, both of whom demanded compliance at the point of a gun. More often than not, villages were subjected to reprisals from both sides. This was particularly true in Greece. Like Spain before it, Greece would be consumed by a multifaceted civil war within the world war in which "rightists" and various adventurers would join the Germans to suppress the "Andartes," a miscellaneous amalgamation of groups, aided at times by the British, that eventually evolved into the Communist-dominated ELAS

(Greek People's Liberation Army). The Greek "right" and "left," supported
in quite a different order by the Cold War powers, would continue their
vicious conflict for four long years after the end of World War II.[56]

By the fall of 1943 the main lines of this terror war had been drawn.
The Italians had withdrawn, leaving the suppression of the Greek Resistance to the Germans, and Allied aid had begun to flow to the insurgents,
who were organizing rapidly. Young people were very much in demand.
Here too the Germans attempted to carry out labor roundups. Teenagers
of all classes escaped from the cities to find the Resistance units, spurred
on by the lack of jobs and the closure of schools and universities. In the
countryside, partisan chieftains of various persuasions would appear in villages flaunting guns and wearing dramatic, if somewhat thrown together,
uniforms featuring capes, crossed bandoliers, and other accoutrements.
There would be hilarious propaganda skits and dancing in the town
square. The leftist ELAS organized a youth wing and even a branch for
small boys, known as the "Little Eagles." The allure was powerful, especially to young village children heretofore kept under very tight parental
supervision:

> These ELAS convocations loom large in my earliest memories. . . . To a
> small boy they seemed marvelously exciting and entertaining. . . . I
> remember the serpentine line of uniformed men . . . dancing the slow
> steps of the *tsamiko* or performing acrobatic leaps and somersaults to
> the lively rhythm of the dance of the eagles. When the guerillas raised
> their voices in the songs of ELAS, even the smallest children would join
> in, and I'd hear the sweet sopranos of the unseen village girls, peering
> from behind shutters, as they sang.[57]

But for most, no such colorful persuasion was necessary. Costas
Gkioulekas was fifteen when he began doing minor jobs for the partisans
in Macedonia. He and his friends distributed leaflets, listened to the BBC,
and sometimes got to carry guns. Their activity ceased to be a game when
the Germans killed the parents of one of his best friends. Later, more than
300 were murdered in his own parents' hometown, including children
three and four years old. One acquaintance was shot as she ran away from
soldiers trying to rape her, and others died in burning warehouses.[58] For
those who remained reluctant to help the partisans after such events, pressure to join was applied with threats of retribution to families. The families, which soon consisted mostly of women, children, and the old, were in
a no-win situation. If they had a relative in a leftist partisan force, they
were subject to reprisal by the Nazis and their Greek collaborators; if their

young did not join the partisans, the whole family was suspected of being pro-German, and was equally at risk.

By the end of 1943, "antibandit" warfare in Greece, and every other theater, had become a major part of Goebbels's "anti-Bolshevist" total war. The Nazis did not leave the disciplining of the Greeks just to the Wehrmacht, but brought in elements of the Einsatzgruppen and other SS formations that had gained so much experience in the USSR. Here too, Hitler authorized "any measures without restriction even against women and children if these are necessary for success."[59] The Nazis were aided in their work by their Italian and Bulgarian allies and by the murderous competition between the various partisan groups. So-called Security Battalions mustered by the anti-Communist Greek puppet government aided the Germans too, as did a number of independent bandits and collaborators who had no compunctions about killing their countrymen or sharing in the spoils of the deportation of the Greek Jews.

The increasingly tragic situation of the Greek population in the regions where the activities of these myriad forces were greatest was observed in detail by courageous Red Cross operatives, who, having dealt with the famine in Athens, continued to try to deliver food and medicine to the neediest in the face of terror, counterterror, and the arbitrary prohibitions of the Nazis. As early as January 1943, the Red Cross had pointed out that the restriction of distribution points by the occupation powers and limitations on the amount of food each person could obtain on each visit, especially in the northern mountains, where travel even on foot was extremely difficult in winter, would "condemn a whole population to death by starvation." In August, two Red Cross officials from the Thessalonika office, M. Wenger and Mme Haidis, reported on a four-day tour of the region around Kastoria in the northwest corner of Greece (western Macedonia). The team had seen twelve towns and villages. In Lechovo, the first stop, Germans and Greek auxiliaries had given the townspeople so little warning to leave their houses before a raid that they did not have time to put their children's shoes on. All the cattle had been driven into the houses, which were then burned. Nothing was left—"not even a tea cup." Those who had returned were living on some Red Cross food and the produce of their gardens, and many children were already ill. In Vogatzikou the Italians had "burned every house in which no men were present," leaving the women and children homeless. And around the bigger town of Kozani, thirteen small villages had been totally destroyed, leaving 24,500 refugees without anything at all. In many places the Italian or Bulgarian soldiers present refused the Red Cross entry or interfered with their delivery of food, even to invalids and children.[60] In Epiros, added terror was provided by Turco-Albanian bands that preyed on Christians and stole their cattle and food.[61]

By December, the bishop of Grevina, pleading for food and fearing that 60,000 would die, wrote in outrage that in more than thirty burned-out villages in his diocese the inhabitants remained "in the open air at such a time of year, deprived of shelter and clothes, starving and prey to malaria, infectious diseases, such as diphtheria, typhus. . . . There are more dead every day, especially among the children; mothers dig holes with their own hands in order to bury not one, but often two or more of their children." Furthermore, he wrote, when seventy-two women from a village that had been burned four times had arrived in Kozani, after walking for two days on snowy paths through steep mountains, they were refused all help, as the Germans, obedient to Goebbels's total war policy, had forbidden any aid to such supposed "Bolsheviks." The bishop had intervened and obtained bread and money for them, but the women had not been allowed to buy anything with the funds, not even medicine and blankets for their babies, and left Kozani in the greatest despair.[62]

With the growing presence of SS units and their collaborators in 1944 came an increase in reprisals in every occupied country. These units, whose officers were radicalized beyond all help and who now, after the news of D-Day, felt the fear of inevitable defeat, often viewed the entire population as the enemy. On June 11, a Waffen-SS battalion commanded by Fritz Lautenbach, a young graduate of the SS Leibstandarte Division, whose troops included a large number of very young and inexperienced *Volksdeutsche,* passed through the Greek town of Distomo,[63] about fifteen miles east of the tourist mecca at Delphi. The inhabitants were not unduly frightened. Distomo was not a center of resistance, and relations with the Germans had been good. Just outside the village, however, the SS troops were attacked by partisans. After this skirmish the Germans returned to Distomo and spent the next three hours killing the population with unparalleled viciousness. Pregnant women were eviscerated with bayonets and their intestines wrapped around their necks. People were decapitated and children's heads crushed. Houses were burned with all the occupants inside. Women and little girls were raped, then executed. All the beasts of burden were killed too. It was estimated that 50 to 60 percent of the approximately 350 dead were children.

Aleco Zaoussis, a young medical student working with the Red Cross, and his colleagues, who arrived on the scene from Athens soon after the massacre, were overwhelmed by what they saw and by the stench of unburied bodies and dead animals, whose bloated shapes lay scattered

*A Greek widow and her children who survived the Nazi
destruction of Distomo.*

everywhere. Bloodied and stunned children were found hiding under
bushes and in the rocky landscape all around the village. One little boy had
survived by lying down between the bodies of his parents and splashing
himself with blood, so that the SS men sent to finish off the wounded
would think he was dead. A little girl in one of the three truckloads of surviving children taken to Athens by the Red Cross "became mad with fear"
on the way. On the lists of the orphaned and homeless children evacuated
the oldest age recorded is thirteen.[64] The atrocities were thought to be
excessive even by the German command, and there was an inquiry, but
the attack was ultimately declared to have been a "military necessity."[65]

It was not a good week for children, or indeed their parents, anywhere.
On June 13 the first V-1 rocket landed on London. The day before Lieutenant Lautenbach had attacked Distomo, a fellow SS division, Das Reich,
which also had a large complement of young *Volksdeutsche* draftees, some
of them Alsatians, had inflicted similar atrocities on the French town of
Oradour-sur-Glane, near Limoges.[66] If the soldiers had any doubts about
what was taking place, their officers, also veterans of the East, did not.
Oradour too was suspected of being a center of resistance, which it

appears not to have been. Here the massacre was a bit more organized. The SS troops came into town after lunch on a busy Saturday, sealed off all access roads, and ordered everyone to assemble in the town square. All the men were then put in barns and garages while the women and children were locked up in the church. Six hundred forty-two people, unable to escape from the church and the barns, among them 205 children, including babies and toddlers, were sprayed with machine gun fire. They were then covered with phosphorous and other materials and set ablaze; many were burned alive. Some of the children had come into Oradour from outlying villages to go to school. Their mothers, who had gone to look for them when they did not come home on time, would also die in the church. Anyone still moving in the town after these events was hunted down and shot, and the rest of the houses were set on fire. Two days later, the Nazis came back and tried to cover up the magnitude of their crimes by burying the half-burned bodies in shallow graves or hiding them under debris.[67] These almost simultaneous atrocities at Oradour and Distomo were apparently not directly coordinated, but were separate manifestations of the relentless total war against partisan resistance mandated by the SS high command in the now dwindling reaches of Hitler's Reich.

Distomo was far from being the last doomed village in Greece. The gruesome reprisals continued on into September, until life for many was unbearable. M. Wenger of the Red Cross, returning from inspecting particularly terrible attacks at Gianitsa, came face-to-face with a crowd of fleeing inhabitants in a scene that was being repeated all over Europe:

> A poignant drama is taking place all along the road. Women, children, starving, perishing of cold, having spent every night outside, without anything to eat except a few grains of corn picked up in the fields. They come toward us in tears, asking us not for food, but to put an end to their agony, because they feel pursued like dogs and don't know where to find refuge.[68]

By the fall of 1944 there were an estimated one million homeless people in Greece, of whom a large percentage were children. Desperate mothers had sent boys and girls off to other villages and even to Athens and other cities to fend for themselves. There they formed street gangs that foraged for food and slept in whatever shelter they could find, from abandoned boats to caves. Little groups of siblings in which a ten- or twelve-year-old had become the head of the family haunted the soup kitchens. Orphanages, holding the victims of towns like Distomo, were jammed. These waifs were not of racial interest to the Germans, but they were of interest to the Communists in the ELAS, who kept careful track of all the children in the areas they controlled. After the defeat of the Germans, during the continuing Greek Civil War, more than 28,000 children were first taken to homes and camps in Albania and then sent on to the USSR and its satellite countries. They were not necessarily orphans, but had been sent away for temporary "protection" by their parents at the urging of the ELAS leaders, who thereby kept their hold on the families.[69] The Communists were not the only ones indulging in these good works. The "right" would also rescue tens of thousands of children from the civil war zones under a program set up by the Greek Queen Fredericka, with the aim of taking them "before the Communists do." Indoctrination was heavy on both sides and competition fierce in this *Paidomazoma,* or expatriation of the young. The Communists' removal of the children was condemned by the United Nations, and according to some sources they were badly treated behind the Iron Curtain. There is, however, some evidence that, like the Spanish Civil War children, many in fact were treated well and were carefully educated in Greek, and that some were reunited with their families, who had followed them into exile.[70] But for all of them, whether fate had deposited them left or right, as well as for millions of others in Europe, the forlorn dream of a return to lives gone forever would never vanish.

The despair of the hunted Greek women and children would soon be a common phenomenon in the frontier areas of the New Reich, long since breached by the Allied armies. Flight and evacuation had been taking place on every front, but nowhere would it be more traumatic than in the vanishing Eastern *Lebensraum.* The liberation of the Western nations would cause thousands to flee their homes during battle, and require major efforts by the Americans and British to supply food and shelter and to sort out displaced persons of myriad nations. In the East, the situation was quite different. The millions of ethnic Germans resident there knew that they could expect little good from either the Red Army or the local populations. Revenge would be harsh, and the prospect of life in the Stalinist state was frightening. The numbers involved were vast. In addition to the various forms of Germans who had been resettled or were permanent residents, there were now hundreds of thousands of temporary residents who had been evacuated from bombing targets in Germany, or who were working in the Nazi administrations. Then there were all the slaves, incarcerated in the world of labor and concentration camps, who could not be left behind to bear witness to Nazi excess or as possible man-power for the enemy, but must be taken back into the Reich to keep its sputtering industries going.

But the possibility of defeat was inadmissible to Nazi thought and, by extension, to the officials who would be responsible for the massive evacu-ations. The evidence that the war was lost was, however, inescapable. The hapless settlers from Hegewald and other such colonies in Russia had long since been retreating back to Poland. Throughout the spring of 1944, resi-dents of East Prussia had watched, and given aid to, colorful processions of ethnic Germans from Belorussia, Lithuania, and the Ukraine who were moving west, mostly in horse-drawn carts loaded with blankets and little children. This had inspired many to prepare their own contingency plans. But it was necessary to be discreet. One landowner who had secretly ordered her workers to prepare wagons for their future, but inevitable, flight was denounced and warned by a Party official that if she "continued in defeatist preparations for flight [she] could expect harsh punishment."[71] The official did not know it, but at that very moment Himmler himself was frantically ordering arrangements to be made in Austria and Bavaria for the reception of 240,000 ethnic Germans from Romania and other areas in southeastern Europe, many of whom were already en route by trek and train. Their withdrawal had been necessitated by Romania's change of allegiance: its troops were now fighting on the side of the Soviets. SS underlings indicated that room would soon be needed for at least 200,000 more refugees and ordered, even at this late date, that the usual "filtering" agencies be set up at the reception points lest certain "non-Germans" try to get into the Reich.[72]

The Balkan refugees were far away from the Germans in occupied Poland and East Prussia, but the real situation in those areas became clear in July 1944, when the German commandant of Warsaw ordered all Ger-man women, children, and low-level service personnel working for the occupation authorities to leave immediately, and news came that the Red Army had taken Lublin. Another wave of 600,000 refugees was generated in October as the Russians moved into the Baltic states. These people were sent to East Prussia and, as there was not enough space for them there, on to central Germany. During the subsequent lull in the Soviet advance, little more of a practical nature was done. Local officials tried to organize, but even when the Red Army began to move again in January 1945, most of the Nazi officials were not authorized to evacuate their pop-ulations until the enemy was within hours of overrunning them.

The numbers needing to move were a staggering 4.5 million. Trains were, as always, at a premium and, unbelievably, priority on many of them was given to the concentration camp inmates and slave laborers who were being removed for further exploitation in the Reich. And the trains were often a mixed blessing. Once on them one was a virtual prisoner, frozen and often with no hope of food. A Swiss journalist observed, "The only people beyond the reach of help are those mothers whose children have died on the long journey in unheated coaches or in compartments with broken windows." For people who waited too long to take a train, the evacuations would be on foot or in peasant carts drawn by oxen, horses, and even cows. With only a few hours' notice in most cases, the treks, largely made up of women, children, and the elderly, took to roads covered with deep snow and ice, into the coldest winter weather in memory. In many villages there was no official evacuation notice or any transportation. The luckiest people attached themselves to retreating Army units if they could. The roads became so completely jammed that there was often no movement at all. Some people simply went back home, but most, terrified of the Russians, went on and on, for weeks and months, stopping when they could in barns, abandoned farms, or any kind of shelter, where, from time to time, the authorities did manage to provide some hot food. The Swiss journalist found a column that was fourteen miles long:

> Two thousand horses, stumbling from exhaustion, pulled 1,000 vehicles carrying 20,000 people, all old men, women, girls, and children without a single middle-aged man or adolescent among them. These have stayed behind as members of the *Volksturm*. . . . The women's faces are wrapped up against the cold, which at times reaches four degrees below zero. . . . The journey . . . has impaired the health of many thousands, mostly children and babies. Their limbs froze from exposure. . . . For days they went without hot food or milk. . . . Many a child had to pay with its life.[73]

Crossroads where lines of refugees had to merge were chaotic. At these intersections there were rules: priority was given in the traffic jams to the treks of prisoners on their "death marches" from the concentration camps. There had been plenty of planning for them. At Auschwitz, exterminations of the "useless" had been stepped up in the few weeks before the camp was evacuated. Fifteen thousand Polish, Russian, and Czech prisoners had been shipped out to slave labor camps in the Reich to prevent any pro-Soviet uprisings. Thousands of others, like Anne Frank, were sent west too. Tons of packed-up clothes taken from the dead went with the prisoners, along with several dismantled barracks that were to be reassembled in the Reich. Before they left, inmates in several camps had been kept busy attempting to obliterate mass graves and get rid of the tons of ashes from the crematoria. Between January 17 and 21, the final evacuation of 56,000 prisoners would leave Auschwitz and its subcamps. The columns moved out on foot with the aim of reaching railheads to the west from which trains would take them to camps in the Reich such as Buchenwald and Belsen. Those who could not keep up were shot. It is thought that between 9,000 and 15,000 prisoners from Auschwitz alone perished during these treks, which left thousands of bodies lying along the roads. Many more would die in the open freight cars in which they continued their journey.[74] Fey von Hassell, a political prisoner, was lucky to be in one of the few covered, though unheated, cars on the train moving the inmates of the Stutthof concentration camp from Poland back to the Reich. Drifts of snow constantly stopped forward progress. From her window she could watch

> never-ending columns of refugees escaping from the advancing Russian armies . . . most were just wrapped in woolen clothing, salvaged at the last moment. Many who had been too weak to go on had collapsed and lay dead or dying beside the corpses of horses and mules . . . some . . . were children who had lost their families and were just blindly following others. At one point, one of our SS guards picked up a little boy who lay unmoving in the snow. . . . At first I thought he must be dead, but after a vigorous massage by the guard he regained consciousness and was given some food. Shortly afterward he was handed down to the care of a group of retreating soldiers.[75]

But he was not allowed on the train, which went on with its load of slaves, who when they died of cold were thrown out beside the tracks.

Meanwhile, hundreds of German refugees had been encircled in the area between Königsberg and Danzig by the Red Army. For them, the only escape was on foot across a frozen inlet of the Baltic to one of the ships sent to rescue wounded troops and anyone else who could get aboard. Crossing the ice was a nightmare. Lore Ehrich and her two exhausted little boys, who had been traveling for days and were suffering from the dysentery known as "the highway illness," had managed to get on a farm cart for the trip:

> During the very first half hour the colt, which was going at the side of the cart, broke his legs and had to be left behind. A short time afterwards one of the two strong horses pulling the cart fell into a hole in the

ice and was with great difficulty liberated with an axe. The farmer trembled from head to foot, because he was afraid that also this animal might break its legs, for one horse alone would not have been able to do the hard work. . . . We were compelled to remain for hours at the same spot. Everyone who tried to overtake the others was greeted with the most violent words. . . . Occasionally the way was . . . indicated by torches. Then one could see the endless rows of the treks. . . . I felt it was like an enormously long funeral procession, and slowly and relentlessly the cold kept creeping up on us.[76]

Once across the ice, the refugees had to get to the ships. This last piece of road was sometimes the breaking point: "On the way we witnessed shocking scenes. Demented mothers threw their children into the sea, people hanged themselves; others fell upon dead horses, cut flesh out of them and fried the pieces over open fires; women gave birth to children in carts."[77]

Lore Ehrich made it to a ship that took her to Denmark. Not all were so lucky. Among the vessels was, ironically, the *Graf Steuben*, which had, five years before, brought so many thousands of Baltic Germans to their new "homeland." This time Stalin was not as cooperative. The *Steuben*, loaded with refugees, would be sunk by a Russian submarine only days after the huge liner *Wilhelm Gustloff* had suffered the same fate, with the loss of more than 5,000 lives, and in the end some 18,000 people would die on this route. One man, traveling with his daughter and two grandchildren, was thrown into the icy Baltic when his ship was hit. He was rescued by a German minesweeper and was amazed to find his two-and-a-half-year-old grandson on board. Sailors told him that they had found the child "sitting astride a short beam holding on with his two little hands and crying bitterly." The boy's mother, who had perhaps managed to put him on the beam before she died, and his other grandchild had drowned along with some 850 others.[78] Despite these horrific events, many thousands were rescued by a huge variety of vessels from this German Dunkirk before it was taken by the Soviets.

The treks, willing and unwilling, of some eleven million Germans back to the shattered Reich, during which an estimated one million people died, would continue from all the areas conquered by the Germans long after the official end of the war in Europe on May 8. Now it was up to the Allies to deal with the gigantic masses of humanity so brutally rearranged by the Nazis, a task fraught with complexities not covered by the joyous words "liberation" and "peace."

PART V Aftermath

Official definitions are scrupulously colorless and one may well fail to guess the misery masked by such terms as "displaced person" . . . . or—supreme understatement to cover total bereavement and desolation—"unaccompanied child."

DOROTHY MACARDLE, *Children of Europe*

15. Liberation and Repatriation

By the time the frozen millions from the East had begun trek-king toward the supposed safety of the Nazi homeland, the armies of the Western Allies were fast approaching its frontiers. Behind them lay enor-mous tracts of liberated territory, each with humanitarian needs of the most challenging nature, most particularly when it came to children. The Allies had recognized early on that the problem of caring for the civilian populations in war zones would be extremely difficult. In August 1940, during the Battle of Britain, Winston Churchill had promised relief to the people of occupied Europe, come the day of Nazi defeat:

> We shall do our best to encourage the building up of reserves of food all over the world, so that there will always be held up before the eyes of the peoples of Europe, including—I say it deliberately—the German and Austrian peoples, the certainty that the shattering of the Nazi power will bring to them all immediate food, freedom and peace.[1]

This highly optimistic promise was not mere rhetoric. In 1941, a num-ber of agencies were duly established to plan for postwar needs, and by the fall of that year one of them, the Middle East Relief and Refugee Administration, had organized a string of camps in North Africa and the Middle East for Polish and Greek refugees who had fled or been evacu-ated to that region. In 1942, President Roosevelt created his own agency, the Office of Foreign Relief and Rehabilitation Operations (OFRRO), under Herbert Lehman, the former governor of New York. UNRRA, the United Nations Relief and Rehabilitation Administration, which would later absorb the others, finally got around to producing its charter, approved with the ostensible support of forty-four nations, in November 1943.

These impressive-sounding groups had the best of intentions. The problem, already encountered in Greece and the USSR, was the control and delivery of goods and services. Lehman vaguely explained to Congress that in the early stages relief would have to be "distributed by local civilian personnel," perhaps the Red Cross. The Army knew better. In the initial "chaotic stages," as they had already learned the hard way in North Africa, only the military could supply the security, transport, and organization needed "to do the job on the ground."[2] UNRRA, therefore, would not only be subordinate to the British and American army commands in liberated areas; it also could be asked to wait for up to sixty days after the front had moved on to begin operations, and it would not be allowed to give aid to citizens of "enemy countries," including Italy and Germany. In addition, UNRRA was expected to defer to the governments of the liberated countries and their agencies, coordinate itself with long-established entities such as the Friends and the Red Crosses, and all the while satisfy Congress, on which it depended in great measure for funds. Needless to say, the rosy idea of a noble international aid organization was soon consumed in turf wars of myriad variety. The USSR quickly dropped out. Thus, as was true of every other agency involved in normalizing liberated Europe, the genuinely vital work achieved by UNRRA, and the successor organizations into which it morphed with accompanying acronymic variations, was the result of the extraordinary individual initiatives of the field operatives, military and civilian, of many nationalities, who would save innumerable lives.

The complexity of the problems to come was illustrated in microcosm in the North African refugee camps. As we have seen, the German attack on the USSR had led to the release of hundreds of thousands of Poles from captivity. Many of the men had joined Polish Army units that were formed in the USSR, where they languished in terrible conditions before being evacuated to Iran and British jurisdiction. Those not in the Polish Army—overwhelmingly, of course, women and children, the latter estimated at 60 percent of the total[3]—were scattered in the areas bordering Iran, most notably Tashkent, where the Russians had made no preparations for them and where Polish aid groups tried to help them. Plenty of food and supplies were stockpiled for the Poles in Iran, but transporting the materials into the USSR proved difficult. Meanwhile, the Soviet government had arbitrarily declared the refugees citizens of the USSR, thereby making emigration dependent on Russian permission. Hundreds of children were sent to Soviet orphanages, where they were "Russified" and subjected to harsh punishments,[4] and it was only with the greatest difficulty that the USSR was persuaded to release some 20,000 children, many of whom were placed in schools across the Middle East. Thousands of other Polish children, some with their mothers, were scattered in the British colonies in Africa, in Palestine, Iran, and in refugee camps in Egypt.

To these Poles, 30 percent of whom are thought to have been Jewish, were soon added relays of Greek and Yugoslav refugees from the Balkan conflicts to a total of about 80,000 persons, who were sent to camps not only in North Africa and the Middle East, but also in Cyprus, Mexico, New Zealand, Kenya, and India. The camps were generally set up on national lines, and within them political opposites were, when possible, kept apart. There were numerous special installations for children suffering from malnutrition and tuberculosis or for teenaged boys receiving vocational and pre-military training. Amenities and staff were few. In February 1944, an observer visiting the huge camp of El Shatt in the desert near the town of Suez, where 20,000 Yugoslavs would eventually be lodged, found it primitive indeed. Located in a dusty, windblown site, which seemed to be de rigueur for such camps, the evacuees lived twelve to twenty in army tents without beds or "other furniture, even the most primitive," and sheets and blankets were "scarce." The visitor felt that the food, supplied by the British, was "inadequate for people who were for a long time undernourished to the point of starvation." The meal he saw consisted of a bowl of soup with rice, a slice of bread, a small square of cheese, and an orange. Despite this, the children looked healthy, a fact he attributed to sacrifices by the adults, who did not look so well. Discipline, controlled by a Yugoslav committee, was good, and everything was immaculate.[5] Things were still pretty basic three months later, when nurse Margaret Arnstein came to inspect:

> In camps we have none of the conveniences. You run miles for water and when you get there, there is no hot water. . . . We had very little equipment. . . . We had only two cups for the whole Children's Ward of 50 patients . . . and it meant we had to run back and forth washing these cups, which was perhaps only a gesture in view of the fact that we had no hot water. We did not have sufficient linen or diapers. . . . One had to go outdoors from the children's ward in order to get to the kitchen . . . and when wind and sand were blowing, this was not like strolling along a green lawn.

Other camps she visited in the region were little better. At Khataba, forty miles northwest of Cairo, there was a measles epidemic and "an enormous amount of broncho-pneumonia." At Nuseirat, near Gaza in Palestine, where 9,000 Greeks lived in tent barracks in an old Army camp, there was measles too, and only two nurses. Miss Arnstein noted that the overworked nurses everywhere were quite crabby, and that although the "refugees *are* in good condition for *refugees*," one saw "*much, much* more infant and child diarrhea . . . broncho-pneumonia, malnutrition of the serious nature among the babies than one sees in the worst sections at home." The nurses would not get any rest soon. In the Yugoslav camps, refugees were arriving in groups of 3,000 to 5,000 at a time. During one such avalanche Miss Arnstein helped a doctor and a Quaker "ambulance boy" give 1,200 inoculations for typhus in one morning: "You can well imagine that doing it at this speed, our technique was non-existent, but I am glad to say that apparently there were no abscesses or infections."[6] The camps did gradually improve. A later UNRRA publication reported that El Shatt had set up schools, language classes, play centers, an "excellent" hospital, and all sorts of cottage industries. It also boasted a choir and a newspaper. The writer noted that the refugees had been very inventive; they had "produced implements and tools and other useful assets to the camp, out of scrap and materials rescued from salvage,"[7] not a description implying that living conditions had risen anywhere near a normal level of existence.

By the time Nurse Arnstein was giving her assembly-line injections, the Allied armies in Italy, which they had invaded in June 1943, nearly a year before, were deeply mired in refugee matters. Since Italy was an enemy nation, agencies like UNRRA were at first not supposed to work there, but the Italians' surrender in September and the subsequent occupation of the country by the Germans had changed its status. By 1944, the magnitude of the refugee and displaced person problem was so great that the Allied military was desperate for civilian help. Things had not gone as expected in Italy, as the amount of food and medical help available was far below expectations, based as they were on the propagandistic and essentially false statistics put out for years by the Fascist government. The Allies had stockpiled supplies but had assumed that the liberated areas would be self-sufficient within about six weeks. They had not counted on the disintegration of the Italian infrastructure that was taking place; they were also forced to admit that they had "not fully realized at the beginning the importance transportation played in the economic life of a country and the vital need for its speedy rehabilitation." By November 1943, the danger of starvation in Sicily had become so great that officers feared civil unrest and even "the total failure of the occupation" of the island. The Allied commander, General Dwight D. Eisenhower, in a cable demanding more supplies, declared that food requisitions were not "based on humanitarian or any other factor but that of military necessity." In December 1943, sufficient food was brought in to avert disaster in Sicily, but now the mainland of Italy and the winter lay before the Allied planners.[8]

Minturno, Italy: refugee children receive food from British soldiers until they can reach safe areas in the rear.

They had been unrealistic about food and transportation, and, apparently not having absorbed the lessons of the massive exodi that had followed the Spanish Civil War or the German blitzkrieg, they were even less prepared to take care of huge, mobile masses of people uprooted by the fighting. The first weeks of progress of the Allied armies up the coasts of the boot of Italy had produced only a few needy refugees, but by late November the British Eighth Army was dealing with 7,000 people, and the number would burgeon from then on, due in great part to the scorched-earth policy of the slowly retreating Germans and their deliberate expulsion of civilians into the Allied line of advance. Improvisation by desperate civil affairs officers was the order of the day:

> Friday, 10 December at 0930 hours, an A.A. ammo transport column brought in 160 refugees. Investigation showed that they were picked up at some road corner. . . . The sergeant in charge could not say who gave them to him or where they came from.
>
> I collected them. They were in the most pitiful state, all ages from six months to 79 years, two pregnant women, one third without any shoes, etc. I found only twelve kili of bread in the communal bakery; luckily I scrounged 28 more. . . . They were all at the point of starvation. . . .
>
> It is impossible to receive refugees here. No room, no staff to handle

them, no accommodations of any kind. There is also no food. Bread cannot be had constantly on hand to face eventual influx of refugees.[9]

Refugees such as these were sent back from the front lines in Army trucks returning from supply deliveries. The people were deposited near railheads; when trains became available, they would be taken farther south. While they waited, some were given shelter in old freight cars. One report stated that "sanitation" had been provided (one wonders just how), and that "it has been our hope to get some arrangements for warming up food or producing a stove to warm them up," adding that "weather conditions are becoming progressively more severe." In the meantime, "we give them Army rations."[10]

As the flow of refugees increased, efforts were made to billet them in towns farther away from the fighting. There was much buck passing over who was to care for the wanderers. The consensus was that the Italians should provide services and the Allies supplies. This did not work very well: a helpful reporter from the *Chicago Daily News* wrote to headquarters to tell them that people were being given flour, but had "no means at all of baking bread."[11] One group was put in the local prison for a time, another in a cinema. As one officer described the predicament, "People don't like refugees and it is difficult to billet them."[12] By December it had become clear, once again, that the only solution was to set up a series of camps. By now the American Red Cross had sent two field representatives to help, and the Italian Red Cross in Naples was showing signs of revival. Their first project was to create a small hostel in Naples, which was certainly a major exercise in improvisation.

The hostel was to be housed in a half-destroyed school building in one of the less savory parts of the city. The damaged half could be walled off, and there was a good kitchen and seemingly sufficient bathroom facilities. The Red Cross representatives got a few dollars to buy cleaning materials. The work was not easy, as "the refugees had arrived without notice" and no cleaning could be done in advance. Electricity and plumbing were not wonderful either. The intrepid Red Cross man again went forth and found an engineer who put "the lights in the toilets and on the first floor in temporary working condition." The rest of the lights and the toilets, however, "have been so demolished or robbed of wire and pipes that the amount of repair needed is extensive." The engineer, like all of his kind, promised to come back sometime and fix things. Meanwhile, the Red Cross bought candles and "loaned their flashlights the first night." Thereafter, the refugees "were fed and got to bed before dark." What constituted "bed"

was minimal indeed. At first it was on the floor, but straw was "finally" procured. Food involved a great deal of scrounging and was augmented at
one point by "a generous gift from the Negro soldiers (US Army) who
drove the trucks of refugees . . . to Naples: they pooled together $10 and
bought two big gunny sacks of oranges for the refugees, saying, 'I guess we
got it pretty good in the States.' " The oranges came in handy, as "no wood
had been procured" for cooking and there was no kitchen equipment.
Once again everyone rose to the occasion:

> The soldiers made primitive fireplaces with stacks of tiles found in the
> courtyard. . . . The FRs [Red Cross field representatives] got 5 G.I. cans
> and 7 pails from the Salvage Depot . . . to cook the food in. A can
> opener, spoon, and ax were borrowed from the portiere, and a soldier
> whittled out a wooden spoon with a handle 2 feet long for stirring the
> soup. . . . The FRs discovered about 300 china cups in one of the store-
> rooms, and these were washed . . . by the soldiers and used with pieces
> of biscuit serving as spoons.

Soldiers dished out the soup to groups of twenty-five refugees at a time:

> That first night was really a show—the dark courtyard lit only by the
> fires and the lights of our command car, the FRs handing out food, the
> patient dazed grateful peasants grasping food and babies in both hands,
> the soldiers catching the spirit and carrying cups of soup to the steps for
> overburdened mothers.[13]

This touching and rather theatrical scene was fine for the 225 refugees
involved, but obviously would not do for the far greater masses certain to
need help as the Allies began their major drive toward Rome. In early January 1944, the Army, estimating that it would have to deal with at least
50,000 people in January and February and 200,000 by "midsummer,"
finally set up a special Refugee Branch to handle such matters. These estimates were considered low by one officer, who calculated that more than a
million people, at least 30 percent of them under the age of fourteen,
could be defined as refugees in the areas already liberated, where they
were living nomadic existences in the country or crowding into the cities.
Planning and the search for suitable sites for big camps went forward at a
snail's pace, despite reports of the ever-worsening conditions of the
refugees. The little hostel in Naples, meanwhile, had doubled its population but not its equipment. Cooking continued to be done in the courtyard, there was no hot water, and sleeping facilities still consisted only of

straw and a few blankets. The overwhelmed "sanitary facilities" were now filthy beyond belief, as all the plumbing was stopped up and sewage was seeping into the food storage areas, a condition the sanitation officer inspecting the premises superciliously attributed not only to the massive overcrowding and lack of maintenance, but also to "the personal habits of the refugees—most of them *contadini* . . . accustomed to only the most primitive ways of living"; though he did have to admit that the "rooms where the refugees sleep are clean."[14]

At the end of February, considerable space would be provided by the opening of a large staging camp at Aversa and of others at Vairano, Bari, Foggia, Capua, and Naples, plus a string of forward camps nearer the battle lines. From these the refugees were gradually sent farther south. It was none too soon. By this time Allied landing craft, instead of trucks, were evacuating 10,000 more civilians from the embattled Anzio beachhead back to Naples. Landing craft have few amenities, and the bad weather, which required some to stand off the port for hours, was not good for the stomach. Seasickness was just the beginning. On Easter Monday, Anthony Saverese, an eighteen-year-old pharmacist's mate from Brooklyn, was called upon to deliver a baby at sea. Having little experience of obstetrics, he consulted the Navy medical manual, which, of course, was not helpful. But the young sailor, luckily fluent in Italian, "using common sense" and with the help of other Italian ladies on board, boiled water and delivered the baby with no problem. The grateful mother named it George Raymond in honor of the two crewmen who contributed the most to a collection taken up for the infant.[15]

This event turned out well, but lack of planning at the arrival end forced long delays in the unloading of the ships and hours without food and water. Some of the boat commanders simply dumped their miserable cargoes on the dock. As one outraged officer noted, with a certain amount of understatement, "elderly and infirm refugees and children simply cannot stand the buffeting of journeys involving perhaps 36 to 48 hours at sea and 24 hours in a railway box wagon," adding that due to lack of foresight "many thousands of battle zone refugees have been handled under conditions little better than conditions under which cattle are handled in peace time in the United States and Britain."[16]

But being handled like cattle was preferable to the fate of certain others. By the time the Allied armies were within reach of Rome, the officers dealing with refugees were beginning to find evidence of Nazi total war much like that in Greece and France. At a small field hospital in the transit camp at Campobasso, northeast of Naples, medical officers were called upon to treat numerous "refugees . . . who escape through the enemy lines and were injured by the enemy deliberately, and not accidental battle casualties." The stories, new to these officers, are all too familiar. Villages had been burned down; people had been shot indiscriminately. The victims were not just peasants this time, but included educated people and a great many children who had fled from larger towns and cities as far away as Venice. Their experiences were of unbelievable horror:

> Case II. Was in labour with her fifth child when Germans arrived and told her husband to evacuate the house. Husband shot dead. She herself was thrown out of the house and the house burnt down with two children . . . the baby was eight days old when she arrived at the camp. Birth in woods beside the ruins of the house.
>
> Case III. . . . awaiting birth of twins . . . house burnt down, and her husband killed. Babies five days old on arrival. Birth in a field.
>
> Case VI. Five girls . . . crossing the Sangro River towards the British lines. Two . . . shot dead. Three wounded. . . .
>
> Case X. Three children, all under the age of ten. Father and mother killed by German soldiers and their home destroyed. They were picked up by British soldiers, suffering from starvation and exposure. . . .
>
> . . . only one person was treated by the German Medical Corps. None of the others had had treatment until they had passed through the British lines. The Germans appeared to have removed Italian medical stores from the shops and the hospitals.[17]

Not surprisingly, considering such incidents, the Allied armies were collecting more and more orphans. They did not feel that these should be sent along on the trains to the transit camps, but instead that they should be put into the many local children's institutions that still managed to function. Help from such groups and any others who could get themselves together was vital: as the field officers had predicted, by the end of May 1944, with Rome and its millions of citizens just ahead of them, the American Fifth Army was feeding 200,000 people in its area, while the British Eighth Army reported that its main camps had already processed some 45,000 refugees.[18]

The Germans were not the only ones creating orphans and uprooting children. The Allies had been bombing the ports and industrial cities of northern Italy for months, and thousands of children had been sent south to rural areas for safety. British and American planes had also attacked smaller towns and villages along the way. In Grosseto, just in from the coast south of Livorno, bombers reportedly strafed holiday crowds cele-

brating at a carnival, perhaps thinking that the tents containing a merry-
go-round and other entertainments were an enemy encampment.[19] After
the surrender of the Italian government, partisan activity increased in the
German-occupied part of the country, and the woods were full of Allied
prisoners of war, released by the Italians but relentlessly hunted by the
Germans, and young Italian boys trying to escape the German draft and
forced labor roundups, all of them armed to the teeth. Such things made
life in the countryside no less dangerous at times than it was in the
bombed cities, though the food supplies were generally better.

Children were sheltered everywhere. Hospitals, convents, and palazzos
were full of them. Iris Origo, an Anglo-American married to an Italian
aristocrat, first took in twenty-three children in January 1943. They would
stay on her farm at Val d'Orcia, in Tuscany, for nearly two years as the
Allies approached, passed through, and only months later liberated their
hometowns to the north. During that time a dizzying series of German
units came and went; their men ranged from hard-bitten veterans, who
looted with abandon, to convinced Nazis to kindly inductees. The Origos
were lucky not to have to deal with any SS units. Most of the Germans
they encountered were sympathetic to small children, their brutality
in this region being directed more at young partisans and those trying
to escape conscription. Along with the Germans, a constant stream of
refugees passed through, all needing food and clothing. Everyone in the
towns did what they could for these wanderers, making children's clothes
from curtains and diapers from sheets, but supplies were finite.

By mid-June 1944, Val d'Orcia was literally on the front lines. After
sheltering for nearly a week in the cellars of their house with some sixty
people, among them a number of infants, including one of their own, and
all the refugee children, the Origos were told by a German officer that
they must leave immediately:

> The babies were howling, and with Donata in my arms, I couldn't
> help . . . much, but we managed to pack a basket with the babies' food,
> and the pram with some of their clothes. . . . Each of the children car-
> ried his own coat and jersey. The grown-ups each carried a baby, or a
> sack of bread. And so in a long straggling line . . . half walking, half run-
> ning, we started off. . . . We had been warned to stick to the middle of
> the road, to avoid mines, and to keep spread out, so as not to attract the
> attention of Allied planes. German soldiers, working at mine-laying,
> looked up in astonishment as we passed. *"Du lieber Gott!* What are
> those children still doing here?" And all the time the shells were
> falling . . . and the planes flew overhead. . . . When we came out into

the open cornland . . . shells were bursting with a terrific din. The children were afraid to go on, but on we must. Some more planes came over, and we lay down for cover in . . . tall corn. I remember thinking at that moment, with [my daughter] lying beside me and two other children clutching at my skirts: "This can't be real—this isn't really happening."

After four hours the exhausted group had to rest just short of their objective, the town of Montepulciano. They began to doubt if they would really be able to find shelter there, but townspeople who had seen the line of fleeing children from the ramparts came out to meet them: "Never was there a more touching welcome. Many of them were partisans; others were refugees themselves. . . . They shouldered the children . . . and in a triumphant procession . . . we climbed up the village street."

Liberation would not come for another week, during which bombing and artillery fire continued and food ran low, but for this lucky group, only one of thousands caught up in the fighting, the worst was over.[20]

For millions of others in the rest of Italy and Europe the long process of liberation had just begun. The great invasion in Normandy was launched on D-Day, June 6, 1944 and a few weeks later Allied forces would land in the south of France. Planning for these events had gone on for more than a year in Washington and London, where many lessons had by now been learned about the handling of civilian populations and refugees. A uniform policy was developed for the countries of the European Theater that aimed at maximum use of the structures of the indigenous governments and their "loyal" bureaucrats. Cadres of liaison officers were prepared from the exiled governments of each country, and civil affairs agreements were made in advance. This was not achieved without considerable fussing, especially in the case of France, where it was not clear exactly who the recognized authority would be. The Civil Affairs Division for the European Theater was increased to 6,000 officers and men, who were divided into detachments of about forty each. These would be placed in towns as they were taken and would remain there as the various combat units moved on, thereby providing continuity. Huge stockpiles were built up of what were now known to be the most needed items—food, medical and sanitary supplies, soap, clothing, and shoes. Everyone was warned that the liberated must be informed right away that the fact of liberation did not mean an instant end to the hardships of wartime life. The planners, undoubtedly thinking of Rome, where the Vatican had been feeding 400,000 people in soup kitchens by the time the city was liberated, were particularly worried about Paris, whose huge population they expected to find covered with lice and in a state of starvation. There were many unknowns, above all whether the brutal scorching by retreating Nazis, seen in the USSR and parts of Italy, would also be inflicted on the rest of Europe.[21]

The first three months after D-Day went quite smoothly for Civil Affairs officers, if not for the inhabitants of the battle zones, who would lose many relatives to the fighting and to the continuing sporadic atrocities of withdrawing SS troops. One Allied officer had

> brought a 12-year-old girl to the hospital who with four women had been deliberately machine-gunned by the SS when in a slit trench. This officer said at one village he met a man, wounded in the hand . . . who told him [that] while [he was] burying his wife and daughter, killed during the fighting, German SS stood about laughing and making apparently ribald remarks and looting what remained of his possessions.[22]

But no significant scorching had taken place, and despite the total destruction of many towns, the battles had left large sectors of the French countryside untouched and some shelter and food supplies had been preserved. French welfare agencies, both public and private, having by now been through many a refugee crisis, functioned well where they could get access. It soon became clear that the greatest problem, once again, would be transportation and controlling the movements of populations who had been forced to evacuate by the Germans or had fled from the battle zones. No good way was found to stop the estimated 250,000 people who, by the end of July, were hitching rides in Army trucks and swarming along the main roads in their efforts to get home or find help of various kinds. To keep them from clogging roads needed for military operations, therefore, selected roads were designated "Route Autorisée aux Civils" and primitive feeding stations were set up along the way.

It rained and rained. Home, when one finally got there, might have been destroyed or looted, or occupied by Allied soldiers. Babies who had lacked milk and warm clothing for many days were dangerously weak, and many children had been wounded:

> Visited by man from La Haye du Puits. He had come to Cherbourg to leave sick child at Hôpital Pasteur. The vehicle on which he was traveling had overturned just outside Cherbourg. . . . He was very anxious to

return to La Haye because he had left behind 3 other children—his wife had been killed in the recent bombardment.... I had him returned under MP supervision.[23]

Other children had been separated from their families, who were desperately looking for them. Some were lodged for the time being in foster homes. Here too improvised children's homes sprang up everywhere. The Marquis de Balleroy took seventy infants into his château near Bayeux when their previous abode was destroyed.[24] A prescient Allied officer felt that the "chief enemy of civilian morale was anxiety concerning missing relatives," and that a central information pool, which could later become the basis for a "wide-world" scheme to be carried out "some day" by UNRRA, should be set up to help "avoid the troubles caused by half-demented parents wandering about illegally in the battle areas."[25] For all these things, more help was needed. In late August, fifty American Red Cross workers with thirty-five motor vehicles and "six combination Weapons Carriers and Trailer Kitchens" were permitted to leave the United States for France, rather an improvement on the team of two first sent to Italy.[26]

Although the French were willing to work for the welfare of their own citizens, they were less enthusiastic about foreign displaced persons. Little planning had been done for this group, which had apparently not been expected in France. Civil Affairs detachments did not know exactly what to do with the 4,300 people of various nationalities found in two internment camps at Clermont and Vittel, and were surprised to find 842 Russian POWs abandoned in one of the installations of the former Maginot Line, of whom 217 had "active pulmonary TB," and 370 others were suffering from other illnesses, wounds, or malnourishment. Another detachment was even more puzzled when two young girls emerged from a bunker along with a squad of German soldiers. It seemed that they were Eastern workers sent to clear rubble. The embarrassed American officer interrogating them told American correspondent William Shirer, "This one isn't in the books.... It doesn't say here what to do with dames you capture. But damned if I'll put them back with the Krauts."[27]

As the Allies moved east they had also begun to find more obvious groups of forced laborers left behind by the Nazis. In Normandy most of these had been assigned to the military construction crews of the Todt Organization, which had been working on the coastal defenses, and were treated as German prisoners of war, but in the eastern areas of France and Belgium that had been annexed to the Reich, a different sort of worker began to be seen. At Mézières approximately 10,000 Polish laborers, "mostly women and children," were found on a huge "Vichy/German" collective farm.[28] Another report noted in October that an "exceptionally large percentage" of the displaced persons in its area were Russian, and in November and December 1944, some 40,000 "Russian and Polish displaced persons were moved back from the Moselle industrial areas." They were not what the Allies would normally consider workers. One camp of 3,500 Russians set up in a French Army barracks had "family units, composed of man and wife and children." This group was generally healthy, but that was thought to be because "the ill and weak had mostly died in Germany at earlier date," a suspicion substantiated by the fact that only thirty of these people were less than two years old and fewer than fifty of them were over forty.[29] The officers dealing with these groups, puzzled by their bizarre composition, did not know it at the time, but they had found the tip of an iceberg.

Once out of the Normandy beachhead region, there had been no stopping the Allied forces. Paris, not at all lice-ridden but low on food, was liberated with wild rejoicing on August 25. By November, the Allies had swept up to the Westwall defenses of Germany and even across them in a few places. Belgium and a third of Holland had fallen before the momentum was stopped by supply problems and the ferocious German defense of its own frontiers. The Allies had expected Holland to be surrendered in its entirety, and many had thought the Germans themselves would surrender before their borders were crossed. But Hitler, ever more remote from reality, did not consider himself finished yet, and in a final major offensive would confront Allied forces in southeast Belgium in the Battle of the Bulge. The attack would bring combat conditions mixed with the hardships of extreme winter weather to the area, where Civil Affairs detachments were forced in some places to take up combat positions on the front lines while they struggled to evacuate and feed the inhabitants. German losses were vast, but Hitler did gain an estimated six-week delay of the final Allied offensive on his western frontier, which would enable him to resist within the Reich until May 1945. The six weeks would not change the ultimate outcome but would be fatal for the millions still surviving in precarious conditions under Nazi rule, nowhere more so than in the Netherlands, which would remain under siege until the final German surrender, and where drastic disruption of the food supply system would now bring a "Hunger Winter" to the Dutch.[30]

Food reserves in Holland were already dangerously low by November 1944. They were further depleted by a defiant strike by Dutch railway workers and by restrictions on maritime operations ordered in retaliation by the Nazis, plus their stepped-up requisitions for the homeland, deprived now of a great percentage of its own food sources. In January, the familiar pattern of starvation began. Soup kitchens with ever-diminishing supplies were opened in the Dutch cities, but in some places they could, from the beginning, provide children with only one meal a week. Black market prices soared as rationed goods became scarcer. Whole families began to live on half a loaf of bread a day. By the end of January, many were not getting more than 500 calories a day, and cases of hunger edema and related problems increased. In some towns special starvation hospitals were installed in schools and other vacant buildings. Members of the Resistance helped set these up and smuggled in what food they could procure.[31] There were not enough coffins for the dead, and many families were so unable to cope with funeral arrangements that 3,000 bodies had to be stored temporarily in one of Amsterdam's great churches. In the food lines, children, more agile than their elders, would run over and lick the sidewalk if anything dripped from the huge vats of soup, and later would hang suspended on the edges of the empty containers to clean off any remaining morsel. Bakery deliveries, such as they were, required police escorts to distribution points. For mothers whose husbands had been conscripted for labor service, the stress of the struggle to find food and live without electricity or fuel was crushing:

> I stayed behind with six children . . . we go to bed early, and don't undress as I already have traded many blankets for food. I hope that my children will sleep through this night and will not wake up crying from hunger . . . tomorrow I will chop up the linen chest, because, otherwise, I don't know how I can dry the baby's diapers. . . . My oldest wakes up and says he cannot sleep because he is so hungry . . . groping in the dark I look in the kitchen where I know there is still a cabbage stalk and give it to him . . . I am near despair and think that it cannot be possible that I will see my children die of hunger before my eyes. I have to figure out . . . what else I can trade or steal to keep the seven of us alive another day . . . my children are skeletons.[32]

The despair was largely that of middle- and working-class city dwellers. The rich could find things on the black market, and farmers had far greater resources. The farmers were soon besieged by desperate food seekers. In the terrible cold, often so weak that they could hardly carry a bundle, thousands of people went out into the countryside on bicycles and on foot, some with money and others without. In general, the farmers did what they could, but there were many cases of war profiteering. The Nazis did not help: even this fellow Nordic population was forbidden to bring certain "black market" foods, obtained at terrible cost, into the cities. The foragers were often searched and their pathetic take confiscated.

City governments made great efforts to give children a little extra sustenance, but it soon became clear that the only way to save many of them would be by sending them to foster families in the farming districts in the north and east of the country, where food was still relatively plentiful. Parents, churches, and finally, after desperate pleas from Dutch Nazi officials, even the German occupation government ran evacuation programs.[33] Some parents simply put nametags on their children and sent them out of the city with instructions to knock on doors, but more than 50,000 youngsters would be officially evacuated in moving vans, garbage trucks, barges, and on foot:

> None of us was used to walking like this. Everyone had foot problems. There were children whose socks were soaked with blood, but they had to go on. I had never realized that children would be so brave. . . . We walked for hours and hours in the rain. Many of the children had no coats . . . and shivered from the cold. It was still raw in the early days of March and we got little food. There were places where they took care of us . . . but there were also places where we sat in the cold for hours in wet clothes until we got a bowl of soup.[34]

As had been true for the British children, and for the hidden Jewish children the evacuees now sometimes encountered, the adjustment to a new family that had not always chosen one willingly was not easy; but the presence of food overcame most inhibitions: "My foster parents came to get me and when I went into the kitchen I couldn't believe what I saw . . . sausages and bacon hanging up over the fireplace! My mouth watered. . . . They fed me bacon until I was sick."[35]

To the astonishment of health workers, some of these children gained ten or twenty pounds in a month. Later, packages of food would come in from Sweden, Denmark, and Switzerland. These shipments had been requested in early October 1944 by the Dutch government in exile, but were not approved for months by the Nazis, and more red tape would delay their distribution until February 1945. None of this food would, however, go to the tens of thousands of Dutchmen aged sixteen to forty-six who had been conscripted to dig border defenses. Allied nutrition experts investigating the Dutch famine immediately after liberation, unaware that what they were seeing was not unusual in the Reich, found only two groups of "severely malnourished patients" in the east of Holland where, unlike the west, there had been adequate food supplies. One group was in an insane asylum, the other was made up of the forced laborers:

> The men who had survived their experience . . . had been distributed in hospitals. . . . They were in surprisingly bad condition . . . when one considers that they . . . were in the Todt camps for only a period of three to four months. Questioning . . . revealed that it was maltreatment, poor living conditions and disease rather than uncomplicated lack of food, that were responsible for their condition. They had been billeted during the exceptionally severe winter in sheds with roofs but no walls and most of them suffered frostbite. There had been no sanitary facilities and diarrhea had become an almost universal complaint . . . the Germans had refused to provide any food to those who could not work. . . . Even after four weeks of hospital, these men showed evidence of severe cachexia [malnutrition]. . . . Average weight of 106 of these men ranging in age from 16–46 . . . was 54.5 kg [120 pounds].[36]

In April, General Eisenhower warned General Blaskowitz, the Wehrmacht commander for the Netherlands, that he and each member of his command would be regarded "as violators of the laws of war who must face the certain consequences of their acts" if they did not allow airdrops of food for the Dutch population. The drops were arranged, as were future shipments by land and sea, after a few unpleasant face-to-face meetings between high-ranking German and Allied officials.[37] The "disgruntled and unhappy" Germans agreed not to target the food planes and to help distribute the food. Leaflets were scattered to alert everyone, and the airdrop took place on April 29, just a week before the end of the war but too late for some 20,000 Dutch citizens, many of whom were children:

> A soft droning could be heard from far off. The droning swelled. The people on the rooftops shouted and pointed at the sky. There they were—scores, perhaps hundreds of heavy four-engined bombers thundered low over the city. The roar of the engines was deafening. The people in the streets and on the roofs shrieked, screamed, shouted, howled, cheered. Tears rolled down thin cheeks. Never have I seen so many adults crying at one time. Strangers fell into each other's arms. People waved red-white-blue flags. Everyone was mad with happiness. The children didn't understand what was going on. First they looked

with amazement at the planes and the crazed grown-ups, but then, infected by the crowd, they began to sing and dance.[38]

While the Allies were progressing toward the Reich frontiers, the Red Army had continued its own liberating advance across hundreds of miles in the East, regions in which there had been no lack of scorching. The Soviet troops had been greeted, mile after mile, with evidence of the horrors visited on their countrymen: they saw the burned villages, heard of the forced abductions of thousands, and found hideous piles and pits full of the decomposing bodies of prisoners of war, Jews, and other civilians. By D-Day they were approaching Poland, and on July 23 would take Lublin and along with it the Majdanek concentration camp. This was the first of the camps to be liberated in which there had been killing on an industrial scale. Many of its structures had survived total destruction due to procrastination by the SS, which had, however, already moved all but about 2,000 of the still living inmates back into the Reich, among them the Russian "partisan children," who were taken to Lodz-Konstantynow. Treblinka, Sobibor, and Belzec, the extermination camps farther east, had been shut down in good time by the Nazis in the fall of 1943, their installations demolished and the terrain replanted with trees or disguised as farmland. The Red Army had swept past them unaware, and Majdanek, where 360,000 Jews, Russians, and Poles had died, was a revelation. The Russians, no amateurs at concentration camps, were appalled at what they found, and required their soldiers to take guided tours of the killing apparatus.

London *Times* correspondent Alexander Werth was one of the first to see the gas chambers and skeleton-strewn crematoria. That was just the beginning. There were huge piles of shoes, and a five-story "department store" filled with the possessions of the dead, all carefully sorted out and ready for mail orders from the Reich: "It was like being in a Woolworth store: here were piled up hundreds of safety razors, and shaving brushes, and thousands of pen-knives and pencils. In the next room were . . . children's toys: teddy-bears, and celluloid dolls and tin automobiles by the hundred, and simple jigsaw puzzles, and an American-made Mickey Mouse."[39] At one end of the camp were huge piles of human ashes, "among them masses of small human bones . . . even a small femur, which can only have been that of a child." Just beyond were fields where acres of luxuriant cabbages, fed by this rich fertilizer, had been planted. Huge trenches in another area contained the bodies that the crematoria, even at their full capacity of 2,000 a day, had not been able to consume in time.[40]

The Western press, which found the first stories from Majdanek literally unbelievable, did not report them for several weeks. Articles in *Pravda* describing the camp were not immediately picked up, and Werth's dispatch to the BBC was not used, as editors in London considered it a "Russian propaganda stunt." The *New York Herald Tribune* also declined to run the story early on, commenting: "Maybe we should wait for further corroboration of the horror story that comes from Lublin. Even on top of all we have been taught of the maniacal Nazi ruthlessness, this example sounds inconceivable."[41]

But it was not inconceivable. Six long months later, Russian forces reached the Lodz-Konstantynow camp for "Eastern children," where hundreds of small figures were found huddled in the cellars of nearby houses, or in whatever shelter they could find, waiting for the battle to pass. One prisoner rescued that day still remembers that the Red Army soldiers wept when they saw the emaciated children, many of whom, as would be the norm for such camp inmates, were in such bad condition that they could not be moved for over a month.[42] In Auschwitz, which the Red Army reached on January 27, 1945, they would find 7,000 starving prisoners, including more than 600 children under seventeen, many of them Mengele's twins. In all these camps the Soviets, aided by the Polish Red Cross, rushed in field hospitals and whatever medical personnel they could spare. The challenge was tremendous, and the ailments they encountered were new to most of the health workers. At Auschwitz alone nearly 5,000 of the inmates, including 200 children, needed immediate, full-time hospital care. Most were stricken with "starvation diarrhea," which had covered the floors of their barracks with layers of excrement so deep that it "first had to be scraped off with shovels" before the floors could be washed. It was difficult in the terrible winter weather to keep the barracks warm and, as had been true in North Africa, hot water and stoves were minimal. The patients could at first tolerate only one tablespoon of potato soup three times a day, a ration that had to be increased very gradually. The children who had been used for experiments were terrified of any medical procedures, such as injections, and, of course, by the suggestion of a bath. Forty percent of them had tuberculosis, and all were eleven to thirty-seven pounds underweight, even though most, being late deportees, had been in Auschwitz less than six months.[43]

During the last months of their rule, as we have seen, the Nazi racial agencies did not flag in their duties, even in areas imminently in danger of Allied conquest. Jews were deported from Rome, Hungary, and Paris until the last moment, and the last transport from the main Dutch transit camp at Westerbork would not leave until September 13, 1944. This one did not go to Poland but to Bergen-Belsen, which was within the borders of Germany, and which was also one of the main destinations for the concentration camp inmates being marched back from the battle zones. The Nazis were not concerned only with these thousands of alien blood. Their institutions and hospitals within the Reich continued their experiments and purification operations, including the starving of unworthy German children. But by March 1945, the directors of the myriad types of homes and camps housing children of "good blood" that were scattered all over the empire were being ordered not only to take their precious charges to safety, but also to disguise any Nazi affiliations. The leaders of a KLV camp for young German bombing evacuees were exhorted by the local Hitler Youth administration as follows:

> The enemy threatens your camp. I am compelled by the present situation of the war to put the destiny of the children entrusted to your care into your hands and to leave all responsibility to you. In this hour of need use all your willpower. The most difficult task of your life is imminent. The existence of our nation through our German children is decidedly in your hands! The youth of Germany has got to exist! The time will come that they will erect the banner and will avenge our dead comrades!

The camp leaders were then ordered to "keep quiet . . . give clear commands," suppress "personal sorrows," and think only of the children. Under the heading "In Case of Invasion," they were told to pack carefully and move away from the enemy. Precise lists of clothes and food to be taken along were supplied. If there were not enough backpacks, they should make some "from blankets or BDM skirts (well camouflaged)." The route should be carefully planned to go from one KLV camp to another, and if there were no trucks they should march "during the night." Before leaving, they must burn all documents including the instruction memo, "which may give the enemy information about KLV." If the "threat" was imminent, the actions to be taken depended on who the enemy was. If it was the "English-Americans," the children were to be kept in the camp, but certain preparations were to be made: all Nazi decorations, such as pictures and banners, were to be taken down, uniform badges and camp shields removed, and the installation referred to only as a "residential school." If it was the Russians, the motto was "No child in the hands of the barbarous Soviets," and flight was recommended, with the helpful note that "All difficulties can be conquered with improvisation."[44] The evacuation order for children was an offshoot of a much more dramatic series of directives by Hitler, issued in late March and April, which called for total evacuation of the population from the areas about to be overrun by the Western Allies plus destruction of all industry, communications, and transportation networks. These measures, opposed even by Hitler's inner circle, were never carried out,[45] but the children were moved away from harm.

Just what that meant can be illustrated by the odyssey of a group of very small *Reichsdeutsche* children from an NSV home in Pardubice, near Prague, who made it back as far as Wels, in Austria, just short of the German frontier. The home had started as a day-care center. As the fronts closed in, it began to take in foundlings and German refugee children unable to continue their flight. Some of these were found at railroad stations, or simply wandering along the roads. As the end of the war approached, parents had been asked to come for their children, but a measles epidemic in the home prevented the release of a large number. On May 8, 1945, with the war in fact over, the NSV nurses felt they could wait no longer and, with twenty-three infants and toddlers, most still suffering from measles, they fled by train toward Germany. It took them seventeen days, during which time their food was stolen and they had little water, to go the 185 miles to Wels. Meanwhile, they had acquired three more foundlings, but had lost all the identifying documents for their charges. Two children died on arrival in Wels. The others were simply handed over to families willing to care for them or were put in whatever homes or hospitals were still operating in the vicinity. The nurses, undoubtedly feeling that they had fulfilled their duty, then fled on.[46] Similar chaotic scenes were taking place all over Germany, even among Himmler's special children from the Lebensborn homes.

During the summer of 1944, as the Allies advanced, small groups of Lebensborn babies in Norway, France, and Belgium, along with a few mothers, were brought back to the Reich. By February 1945, the last group departed Poland. In Germany itself, the hapless children and all expectant mothers, in accordance with the instructions on avoiding threats, were shuffled from home to home. As the end neared, some 300 newborns and toddlers, plus Lebensborn's chief doctors and staff, had been squeezed into the headquarters home, Hochland, at Steinhöring, near Munich.[47] Travel had not been luxurious for this elite group either: a French prisoner from Dachau working on a labor gang was shocked to find that some of the blanket-wrapped packages he was loading onto one of the Lebensborn trucks along with sacks of food were actually babies.[48] And not all had been moved. In the Hohehorst home, near Bremen, where much packing and burning of documents had been witnessed, more than fifty children and mothers were in residence when the British arrived. They were still being cared for by a few nurses, who had with fore-sight traded in their brown Nazi garb for brand-new Red Cross uni-forms.[49] At Steinhöring, most of the Lebensborn workers did not wait for the arrival of the Allies. Following the evacuation directive rather less than to the letter, they too spent days burning documents in bonfires and pack-ing up food and valuables, after which they left, but without the children. Only Dr. Ebner, chief racial analyst for Lebensborn, and a few nurses stayed behind and continued to deliver and care for the babies until the Americans arrived.[50]

Some of the homes in which the children of the Eastern workers were kept were also moved back in fits and starts from the combat areas, and their groups too were randomly added to and dispersed. There was no support for such babies from local German authorities. Most of the infants in the group escorted by Eugenia Wolokushina, a twenty-one-year-old Soviet *Ostarbeiterin*, were near death when the Americans arrived in the Austrian town of Mauerkirchen, as the local mayor had refused to provide any food for the *Untermenschen*. Quite by chance, Eugenia saw a car with a Red Cross on it. She flagged it down and, speaking in German, somehow communicated the plight of the children to an American officer. Food was brought in for them, and later they were moved to an UNRRA home. Dutiful Eugenia stayed there with the babies for two more years, until, unclaimed by any parent, they were all repatriated to the USSR.[51]

From the beginning, British and American officials had known that their job within Germany would be gigantic, and that there would be millions of forced laborers and POWs needing care. This did not include the further millions of German and *Volksdeutsche* refugees who would be fleeing the battle zones. Plans were accordingly made to help each affected country set up efficient units to control and expedite repatriation of its citizens. It was also recognized that some of the displaced persons, or DPs as they came to be called, would not want to go home. These, the Allies theorized, would be resettled by the so far ineffectual Intergovern-mental Committee on Refugees, just where not being stipulated. Mean-while, governments were supposed to work with one another, through

American soldiers struggle to feed a swarm of refugees, Germany, 1945.

UNRRA if necessary, and be fair to displaced citizens other than their own nationals, treating and feeding them, without racial, religious, or political discrimination, "as equals."

In the early planning for medical care, the prevalence of malnutrition as well as tuberculosis, malaria, typhus, and other infectious diseases was correctly foreseen but the Western Allies wrongly assumed, in December 1944, before the liberation of any of the concentration and slave labor camps, that "the majority of the displaced nationals of the United Nations in Germany . . . will be able bodied men, who have been used in Germany as workers and who are likely, for that reason, to have been subject to some medical supervision, and to have been fairly well fed." And they even more naively assumed that the Germans would continue to feed forced laborers and POWs until the surrender, as "everything possible will be done to impress on the enemy their strict accountability in this respect." One planning document also predicted that after their long servitude the DPs would be "tractable, grateful, and powerless."[52] But even before the Allied entry into Germany, Civil Affairs officers in contact with the DPs had become aware of what they termed their "liberation complex," produced by "revenge, hunger and exultation, which three qualities combined to make displaced persons, when newly liberated, a problem as to behavior and conduct" that could "assume critical proportions at times."[53] They had also become aware that the French aid agencies, though well organized, could not possibly handle the huge projected numbers of DPs that would head home, and liaison teams were sent to help them.

The French authorities had set up twenty-one reception centers, five supply depots, and four rail transit centers along its borders with Germany and Belgium, designed to deal with 40,000 people a day. They would need all the help they could get. What started as a trickle was a deluge by March 1945. In April alone, 262,197 persons returned; by V-E Day, May 8, the total would be 500,000, and by June 30, 1.2 million. Hundreds of thousands more returned from Germany to Belgium and Holland, or were moved through France to Greece and Italy. A U.S. Army summary of these events, dated June 30, proudly reported:

> They came by plane, by train, by truck convoy, on bicycles and on foot, carrying . . . their poor pitiful possessions. . . . At the border control stations each . . . was registered, photographed, screened for security, bathed, X-rayed, disinfected, given ration cards, identity papers and money for immediate need; if ragged he was clothed, if sick he was hospitalized. The border control stations, working around the clock, cleared a repatriate . . . and started him toward home within hours.[54]

The report also noted in passing that "the Russians were moved eastward to the border of the Russian-American zone of occupation" and were turned over to representatives of their countries. That had not been a small operation either: the total Russian repatriation count was believed to be over five million individuals.

The optimistic U.S. Army report, written in France, had also made reference to a new category of DP that it called "problem nationals":

> In the very large family of displaced persons there are those members who require special care. These are the non-repatriables, who for political or other reasons, must be maintained until decisions are reached between governments as to their ultimate disposition. The Poles, the nationals of the Baltic States, the Jugoslavs and the Spaniards will remain the wards of the Army until such time as they can either be repatriated to their countries of origin or turned over to the governments of the countries in which they are located.

Maintaining the "non-repatriables" had almost immediately become a challenge. The Allied armies, which needed enormous maintenance themselves, were still fighting hard on all fronts. They did not cross the Rhine into the heart of Germany until March 22, 1945, and still faced some six weeks of battle. The care of the millions of mobile DPs who were heading home was already a twenty-four-hour-a-day operation, and their numbers continued to increase. To avoid excessive clogging of roads and trains, the authorities detained many thousands in transit centers and sent them back to their home countries in stages. This process sometimes required a long stay, and after a time it became clear that a large number of the refugees did not want to move on. In the transit camps little attention could be paid at first to the segregation of disparate groups, nor was there time to make more than minimal improvements to the accommodations that were set up in whatever edifices were still standing in the rubble of cities, or in castles, barns, and warehouses in the hinterlands. Despite the gradual arrival of UNRRA teams to help the military, there were never enough workers. Inspectors found unofficial encampments of DPs in every conceivable place. Many DPs, exhorted to do so by Allied leaflets and radio broadcasts, had deserted their jobs before the liberation and taken to the countryside, where they preyed on farms and villages in their search for food.

To these relatively healthy wanderers would soon be added a quite different sort of problem national. In the beginning of April, Allied forces reached and liberated the first major concentration and labor camps in Germany. These had been swollen enormously beyond their normal overcrowding by the continuing evacuation of outlying camps of all types, as the SS attempted to cover up atrocities and to salvage workers. The first death marches from Auschwitz and other camps in the East had been only a tiny part of the massive relocations of prisoners of all ages that had ended in the center of Germany. On the way, tens of thousands had died, but so vast were the numbers of inmates that many more thousands would still be found at Belsen, Buchenwald, Ravensbrück, and Dachau, to name only the best-known camps; and there were scores of others, large and small, with every variety of prisoner.[55] Now it was the turn of the Western Allies to see what had been described and rumored, but had to date been beyond their imagination. This time there was no question about the press running the stories. After Eisenhower saw the horrors of the rather small camp at Ohrdruf, near Weimar, which he visited with Generals George Patton and Omar Bradley, he sent photographers in to record the terrible scene, so that no one could ever say it was a propaganda stunt. Later he

*A horrified German boy, along with the rest of the residents of his town,
is required by U.S. soldiers to view Nazi atrocity victims.*

wrote that he had "never at any other time experienced an equal sense of
shock."[56]

But even then it was hard to believe that each camp was not some sort
of aberration. *Life* photographer Margaret Bourke-White said:

> If we had encountered just one camp run by a maniac, we would have
> considered it merely the work of madness. But at a certain stage in the
> advance of our armies we began meeting these camps everywhere;
> along the Western front all *Life*'s photographers simultaneously began
> to run into them. . . . It was the wide prevalence of the system that testi-
> fied to its vicious purpose.[57]

Bourke-White would have been even more shocked had she known that
nearly two weeks after the discovery of Ohrdruf, the SS, still trying to
cover up the extent of their guilt, would hang fifty more of their prisoners
in an empty school in Hamburg: twenty-two Jewish children, aged four to
twelve, who had been used for medical experiments at the Neuengamme
camp; the inmate doctors and nurses who had cared for them; and twenty-
four Russian prisoners of war who had had the misfortune to share the
same hospital ward and become witnesses to the SS crimes.[58]

Eisenhower, like the Russian commanders, ordered his troops to view the carnage at Ohrdruf. He did not forget the Germans. The people, some with their children, of this and many other towns were required to file through the camp and were conscripted to help bury the piles of bodies. In Leipzig, the mayor was ordered to provide caskets for the remains of seventy-five inmates of a small camp at Leipzig-Mochau, where an international group of slave laborers had been locked in their barracks and burned alive, while those who managed to escape, according to one witness, were shot by Hitler Youth firing from tanks.[59] The dead were given a full-fledged funeral and burial in Leipzig's most beautiful cemetery. All city officials were required to attend the ceremony, which was conducted by Army chaplains both Christian and Jewish. Nine hundred other Germans came voluntarily and placed flowers on the graves.[60] The mayor of the town near Ohrdruf didn't do so well. After his tour, he and his wife committed suicide. Eisenhower, when told, said, "Maybe there is hope after all."[61] *Pravda* did not fail to report the liberation of the camps, but could not let the British and Americans upstage them. Buchenwald, they declared, was "Majdenek, but in miniature. Our Allies had not seen what we had. Now that they too have seen, now that they share what we know, they will understand us better."[62]

Military and aid authorities were less concerned about publicity than about how to cope with the massive needs of the concentration camp inmates and still keep up with the DP migrations and the war. Belsen's 40,000 inmates and Buchenwald's 20,000 were liberated within days of each other in the second week of April. Among them were some 1,500 children under the age of sixteen, as well as many older teenagers who had entered the camp system several years before and had recently been transferred to Belsen; one of the latter was Anne Frank, who died before the camp was liberated. Belsen was unusual because it was actually surrendered by Wehrmacht troops, who, on April 12, proposed a three-day truce to the British so that they could take it over and thereby "prevent an epidemic." The first British officers arrived in Belsen late on April 15, far too late for any prevention: typhus had been raging for weeks. Overwhelmed by what they found, the small unit nevertheless managed to bring in water and food the same evening. Within days, relays of British medical teams both military and private, plus ninety-six medical students, were rushed in. This was not easy, as the truce had expired and the camp was surrounded by fighting. Richard Dimbleby of the BBC was one of the first to see it. Like everyone else, he was not prepared: "I think one of the most awful things about it was the suddenness. No one had told us this was a concentration camp—we understood it was some sort of refugee center where there was an epidemic."[63]

The first indicator for most was the smell, which was noticeable four miles away and even to RAF pilots overhead. In a large clearing flanked by forested areas were a hundred or so decrepit wooden huts surrounded by barbed wire. In the huts, designed for about 50 people and now holding 600, and in mud-floored, flimsy tents among the trees, the 40,000 prisoners had been jammed

> in the most awful state of emaciation and neglect and suffering from practically every known disease . . . dying in thousands daily. . . . Ten thousand unburied dead, some of whom had been decomposing for three weeks, lay in gruesome piles. . . . The huts were so crowded that the inmates were often unable to lie down. . . . Countless numbers were without even this shelter. Masses of dead remained where they fell, or were pushed under the floorboards to make room for the living, who were beyond caring.

Dimbleby was appalled to see people falling over before his eyes, and frightened by a woman with "fingers . . . like old brown pencils, her face a stretched parchment" who clutched at his ankle just before she died and whose age was estimated to be twenty by the doctor escorting him.[64]

Here too the starvation dysentery seen at Auschwitz had affected everyone, creating unbelievable squalor: "Those lying in the lower bunks had no protection from the excreta dripping from above. On the floors the excrement was six inches deep, mixed with rubbish and rags. The walls were heavily contaminated also." Muriel Knox Doherty, an Australian nurse brought in to run the Belsen hospital, wrote this description in a letter home, adding that her readers might think it was "sordid and unnecessary" to do so, but insisting that they read on: "The world should know what suffering and degradation this New Order in Europe brought to millions, lest it be quickly forgotten and rise again in another guise." It appeared that the inmates had not had any food or water for seven days, and precious little before that. The Nazis had also deliberately destroyed the water system before they left, as well as most of the camp records, which made it impossible to identify the dead. There was no shortage of food or medical help in the vicinity. The countryside was full of cattle, and about a mile from the huts was the main part of Belsen, a luxuriously appointed and highly manicured German military base with storerooms bursting with supplies, a huge state-of-the-art military hospital, and all sorts of amenities, including an officers club with chandeliers, a theater, and a swimming pool.[65]

In all such camps there was little the rescuers could do at first but give emergency first aid to those who seemed most likely to survive, or in this case, to those closest to the doors of the huts, as it was nearly impossible to reach those farther in without stepping on people. Assembly-line methods for bathing, delousing, and examining the inmates were instituted. The posh German base was turned over to the victims and the "Horror Camp," once emptied, was burned with much celebrating on May 21. By then the British had buried 23,000 bodies. Very small children were given high priority in the rescue process. There were 500 at Belsen, where a special hospital, which had to be extended into tents, was set up for them. British soldiers made wooden cribs for the littlest ones. Malnourished and riddled with tuberculosis and typhus, the children died in droves. Among them were tiny ones with Auschwitz tattoos, Gypsies, and a boy of undetermined origin with "two tiny sisters" whom he guarded carefully. Most of the children were thought to be orphans, but in many cases this could not be verified.[66]

Buchenwald, where conditions were much like those at Belsen, was an all-male camp that held nearly 1,000 boys. Some of the young ones had worked in the factories, but many more had been hidden within the camp for months by older inmates. The Americans forced German workers and Hitler Youth to clean out and refurbish several buildings, but it took aid workers some doing to gain the liberated boys' trust:

> At first it was hard to persuade the youngsters to move from their hideouts and the buildings were unnaturally quiet for some days after they moved in. They refused to play outdoors and showed little elation over such things as the chocolate ration which the field reps managed to collect from the soldiers in nearby camps. Their new clothing which field rep had made in clothing factories he started made a great impression upon them. The smart little suits and caps which replaced the prison stripes worked a miracle. Two weeks after they had moved to their new home, outdoor games were going on full tilt in front of their buildings and you could hardly hear yourself think in their halls.[67]

While the neediest children of the concentration camps were being cared for in situ, thousands more, of all varieties, had been arriving at the DP transit camps. Some came with families, relatives, or adults with whom they had formed bonds; others were alone. The often huge camps, some with more than 10,000 inhabitants, were not ideal environments for children. Groups came and went unceasingly. Much depended on the organizing abilities of the DPs themselves, and conditions varied wildly. The best camps had strong DP committees that directed work programs, organized cooking, and created a disciplined social structure. In some, all nationalities got along well; others were completely polarized. Much depended as well on the Army or UNRRA officials who were technically in charge. They too varied enormously. Communication was not always easy, given the range of nationalities both of the DPs and of the UNRRA workers, who often could not understand either their charges or the Allied officers, who were reassigned with dizzying frequency. Corruption and human weaknesses in the administrators and the DPs caused problems, as did the general lack of experience in social work and the baffling complexities of Army organization. UNRRA ran a short training course for its workers, which all agreed was not useful. In addition, UNRRA appointees were transferred to hot spots with glacial bureaucratic slowness, and such details as pay were not well organized.

But no one could really have been trained for the situation in immediate postwar Germany, where the provision of first aid was soon skewed by the ancient hatreds and new political problems of the displaced and by the essentially uncontrolled movements of nearly twelve million people. A letter from Richard Winslow, director of an UNRRA team that was sent in to run a group of camps of very mixed nationalities, shows this all too clearly:

> Our immediate superior authorities are a Displaced Persons Detachment . . . they all seem to have been part of fighting units . . . and were not trained or in any other way previously experienced in any comparable work. They were merely "detached" from their usual duties in order to perform this "necessary evil" function. All nice . . . most terribly weary and fed up with war, "furriners" and chaos. DPs are more often viewed as a terrible nuisance and constant mass irritant rather than as ex-slaves, PWs and political prisoners. They are most often handled as crudely as their erstwhile masters; e.g., they are kept within a compound almost as if in a concentration camp. It is said (probably, truly, often) that if allowed out they will loot, forage and even kill.

The personnel of the camp he describes as a combination of "hangers-on, intruders, intermediaries, and mostly women from a French military liaison team," noting that "anyone who can find what the spheres of authority,

responsibility and sources of information etc. between all the parties operating here are will surely deserve a special medal."

The living conditions of his UNRRA Team 143 were not much better
than those of the DPs. One had to build a wood fire to get a hot bath, and
on many days there was no water at all. Days were spent trying to find
medical supplies, DDT, space for latrines and garbage disposal, soap,
mops, toilet paper, clothes, needles and thread. The food supply, "our
hardest daily problem . . . is a maze of red tape, endless waiting and moving from office to office." These procurements were made more difficult
by an early UNRRA policy that cars would not really be necessary, and by
the lack of good telephone service. Winslow's description of a few days'
activity paints a scene seemingly beyond solution and a direct result of
Hitler's mad demographics:

> Tues AM huge thefts are discovered on the part of a certain DP doctor
> and nurse . . . scandal and chaos. In the midst of this mess in comes a
> Capt. from another Corps area where he has for 3 days been holding
> about 1500 DPs of many nationalities in barns and fields far from any
> inhabited centers. He wants to dump them on our already overcrowded
> camp of 2500. No one knows who to phone for other solutions . . . but I
> win and block the dump on us. At mid-afternoon 1000 French DPs and
> PWs come thru town on train . . . and drop off 350 strongly nationalistic
> Slovakian ex-student revolutionaries . . . who are not too crazy about
> USSR, but the only place with space to feed and house them is our
> Russian Camp. . . . Next afternoon suddenly appear 5 truckloads of
> people, all good Soviets except one truckload which is solid with émi-
> grés of intelligentsia in Revolution and who weep and quake at prospect
> of even one night in USSR camp, but there's no other place. . . . As
> expected half of them . . . slip out and cross 2 rivers past MPs somehow
> and are at our other camp in the morning. . . . Next AM, after sending
> convoy of 800 Russians home, we find that during the night the Russian
> Camp also took in 65 men, women and babies who were dumped there
> by two weary GIs who said they had orders to drop Russian speak-
> ing peoples there. But . . . we find them to be Ukrainians, to be sure,
> but of German descent a couple of centuries back and still feel Ger-
> man, speak German and want to live in Germany. They were evacuated
> from Ukraine by Nazis . . . we were so relieved not to find any
> lynched . . . stopped at Burgomeister's and told him to cart 'em away
> fast. . . . On top of this we found 30 Poles from the Ukraine dumped by
> ignorance in the Russian camp too; so we haul them away. . . . Today
> suddenly at 11 AM come orders to move all the Yugoslavs and all of the
> Italians (500 each) from Maierhof camp to the Russian camp on hopes

Reds can be sent home tomorrow . . . and Yugos and Itals will have new
camps of their own. In meantime we hear several hundred more Russians are expected so I force a postponement of moving the Italians for
24 hours. (Imagine mixing those two anyhow; battle of Trieste may be
settled in our backyard.) Meanwhile we press to ship most or all of
remaining Reds home; tonight we get 30 trucks to do it with tomorrow
AM, plus Slovaks, and at that moment in come 5 more new loads of
Russians! Oh well! It's mad, it's disorganized, it's crude, cruel . . . and
much else, but people *are* moving from dawn to dusk every day.[68]

But Winslow also thought it "thrilling" to see "35 trucks loaded with
ragged but gay people, 700 of 'em, pull out singing and cheering, a flag on
each truck and a huge picture of Stalin on some" to begin what everyone,
at that early stage, assumed would be a happy homecoming.

Not all the camps were as transient as this one. In some that had been
set up early in the spring of 1945, where the inhabitants now awaited processing, things had gotten quite homey. DPs had established rudimentary
day-care centers and schools, and families had made some effort to wall
off tiny areas for themselves in the barracks. Cottage industries, especially
sewing and shoemaking, were common. And as time had gone on the DPs
had begun to sort themselves into national and political groups, a process
of necessity condoned by the Army. Some of the larger camps were in fact
small towns. One of the largest was at Wildflecken ("Wild Place"), a huge
and heavily camouflaged former SS base set in an isolated region about
fifty miles north of Würzburg.[69] Indeed, it was so secret that it did not
appear on any map, and the polyglot team of eighteen UNRRA workers
sent to run it had a great deal of trouble finding it. They had expected a
camp of 2,000. Clerical error had misinformed them: its population was
actually 20,000 Poles and more were expected. The camp had twelve
kitchens, which baked nine tons of bread a day, and five hospitals where
babies were being born in impressive numbers. Before he left, the Army
major who was handing over the camp informed the horrified new director that all the rations and the wood for heating would have to be trucked
in "before the snows fell" and the roads iced over, which would cut the
camp off from the outer world.

To headquarters personnel and planning staffs, DPs were essentially
objects requiring specialized handling for quick repatriation, known only
as numbers and statistics. A large body of rules was promulgated to deal
with them. To the aid workers in the camps, the DPs soon became human
beings with an infinite variety of problems and desires for which there

were no generic solutions, and they constantly found themselves questioning the regulations. For example, the DPs were not allowed to leave their camps without permission. What to do when a small Polish Boy Scout, who had followed leads from camp to camp all over Germany to find his mother and sister, whom he had managed to have transferred to Wildflecken, now wanted permission to go forth again to get his father, who had been seen in the ruins of Munich?[70] It was even harder to deal with demanding DPs who wandered and lived outside the camps, but who were eligible for the same rations and services as the rest. Black market dealings were rampant, and gangs of inmates took everything not well secured. There were frequent forays into the hated German communities for livestock, which was slaughtered and hidden in remarkably clever ways, and the crime rate was high. In Bremen, 23 murders, 677 robberies, 319 burglaries, and 753 thefts were attributed in the first year of occupation to DPs "over fourteen years of age," some of whom operated in armed gangs.[71] In response, the Army carried out frequent raids in the camps, sometimes unwisely with the help of the German police, to search for contraband and thieves, operations that did nothing to improve community relations.

In the first year of occupation 100,000 Poles would arrive at and be repatriated from Wildflecken alone, in back-to-back trainloads of 1,000 at a time. In one two-month period, 10,000 would come and go. The trains were made up of the same weary cattle cars used by the Nazis, with not many more amenities than they had ever had. On them dysentery was rife, people died, and babies were born. The trains were endlessly delayed and ran out of food and diapers. The American escort officers were frequently undone by the nightmarish scenes. But the DPs, ecstatic to be free, adorned the squalid cars with fresh branches and flowers to celebrate their liberation. The repatriation trains, still made up of cattle cars, but with a luxurious limit of twenty-five passengers per car and wood stoves and piles of food in each, were even more festively decorated with greenery and national flags, and were often sent off with music from DP bands. The camp officials were less festive. The pace of work was relentless. Every new load, which could arrive without warning day or night, brought new diseases and challenges to the very limited accommodation space. Food and fuel procurement here, as everywhere, was unbelievably difficult, and items requisitioned from the Army either never came or were inadequate.

At Wildflecken and many other camps, the food crisis was relieved for a time by the distribution of hundreds of thousands of Red Cross packages intended for Allied POWs, who had not materialized. These packages, containing cigarettes, cocoa, Spam, and tuna fish, items not seen in Europe for six years, or even, under rationing, in the United States, were worth their weight in gold on the black market and posed an overwhelming temptation to all involved in their distribution. The Army was well aware of this, and the packages were accompanied by a directive from Eisenhower himself on their handling. The idea was to empty the boxes into the general food stores and use the contents gradually. The DPs, who had had nothing but gray soup for years, did not agree, and at Wildflecken began to demonstrate in favor of an immediate distribution of one box per person. It was clear that this excited group could not be trusted to open the packages and store their contents. Kathryn Hulme, the UNRRA worker in charge of the boxes, decided to give the job to the camp's children, who, all felt, could be controlled. Hulme and her coworkers, forgetting that most of the children had not seen a shop for years, thought it would be a game "sort of like playing store" for them. In a huge warehouse, they set up a long table low enough for the children to work on:

> We saw them marching up the hill toward us, fifty little boys and girls two abreast and in close formation, swinging their arms and singing lustily. . . . Once inside the cavernous warehouse we lined [them] up beside the long table that held twenty-five food items spaced at intervals on both sides . . . which had to be sorted out and put in the . . . stalls at the rear where horses used to be. When the chewing gum, the chocolate and the tins of jam were held up before those fifty pairs of child eyes, I thought for one wild moment that I was going to sob. The . . . eyes regarded unwaveringly, as in a trance, a raspberry jam label depicting a solid mass of red berries dripping with sugary highlights . . . a packaged bar wrapped in chocolate-colored paper scored off in small squares like the chocolate inside. . . . You knew that these things must have torn at the vitals of the children though not one of them gave any outward sign.

Once the processing began, the children worked "with furious concentration, not at all like shop keepers." Silent at first, they soon began to talk and joke, calling one another by the name of whichever product they were sorting, such as "Miss Tea-Bags" or "Mr. Tuna." Hulme was fascinated by the children's efficiency, noting that even the littlest ones "knew what to do without asking questions." Why this was so was soon revealed to her:

> I stood beside the lad in charge of cigarettes . . . watching how he patted the packs in edgewise until he came to the end of the box. I waited

for the next cigarettes to come down the table to see what he would do. He took the next seven packages and laid them in flat for the final layer, bringing it exactly flush with the top of the box.

"*Schön!*" I said, admiring his ingenuity.

He looked up and grinned with professional pride. The one tooth missing in front gave his face the classical look of the rugged small boy the world over.

"*Wie in der Fabrik,*" he said, patting his perfect packing with one stubby hand.

As in the factory! For an instant I did not take it in. It was as if Huckleberry Finn had spoken out of character. He brushed back a shock of sun-bleached hair and held up his fingers fanned out to five.

"*Fünf Jahre,*" he said, nodding like an old man.

That was the explanation for the children's dexterity and knowingness with small objects. The Germans had used their fast fingers in factories and war plants, had trained them to handle small parts with speed and precision.[72]

The international welfare community had responded quickly to the plight of the children found in the concentration camps. All were agreed that they should be taken elsewhere as soon as possible, for conditions in the camps were still grim, with reminders of atrocities everywhere, and the adults surrounding the children were "disturbed, depleted in energy, slow in responses and mentally unstable." Within a month of the liberation of the major camps, the French government offered to take groups of "unaccompanied" Allied, stateless, or German Jewish children up to sixteen years of age for temporary stays. By June 5, some 540 Jewish children from Buchenwald and Belsen, now in quite good health, had been chosen and processed and were on their way to France. Switzerland, Denmark, and England would soon offer to take more, and Sweden sent a hospital ship that took a large number of ailing children from Belsen back for treatment. Choosing which children should go was not always easy. The upper age limit was frequently waived or deliberately disguised for humanitarian reasons. A seventeen-year-old boy who "headed a family of six brothers and sisters" was admitted with the rest. In many cases it was not known if the parents had survived, and Allied workers in Germany were reluctant to release children to anyone before every effort had been made to find their families, but the dire conditions in many of the camps, and in Germany itself, led them to make many exceptions to this policy.[73] For those not sent abroad, UNRRA had, by early July, set up a special camp for children of "all nations" aged from one week to eighteen years at Kloster-Indersdorf, near Munich, and there would soon be seventeen more.[74]

It was not easy to procure suitable premises for the children, because most buildings in good shape had already been taken over by the military. Nor was it easy to dislodge Nazis, especially if, as had been the case of the euthanasia operations in Kaufbeuren where Richard Jenne lay dying, the buildings were considered to be "hospitals." UNRRA personnel trying to set up a children's home at Aglasterhausen, twenty miles east of Heidelberg, had to fight for two months to dislodge such an institution from the buildings they wanted. This "hospital" had been used as a collecting point for mentally defective children, who were then sent on to a killing center. When the building was requisitioned, there were still thirty-seven employees and sixty-seven patients in residence. The Germans had been ordered to leave immediately and were told to arrange other accommodations for their patients. But when the UNRRA team arrived one evening, they found all the patients and most of the staff, who had hoped to sidetrack the requisition, still there. Taken by surprise, the Germans immediately began to remove all the furniture and fittings from the building, "looking like a stream of ants, carrying stoves and couches . . . etc. into the nearby village." The UNRRA team soon put a stop to this, but were forced to share the premises with the Nazis for six more weeks while the latter petitioned Army authorities for permission to remain. During this time the German staff either denied knowledge of or deplored the euthanasia operations, though the head doctor, "a kindly looking" man who was an ordained minister of the Evangelical Church, at one point slipped up and proudly said that *he* had made the selections "because he was qualified to do so," and another staff member joked "with a wink and a laugh" that the selected children had been taken to *"Ewigheim bei Brandenburg"*—"eternal home" in the killing center near Brandenburg. The Nazi staff had also failed to follow the Führer's directives on burning the records of the institution; the files made quite clear that many of the children sent away had been the offspring of anti-Nazis or concentration camp inmates. The children themselves, though "forlorn and ragged," did not seem unintelligent and were sent elsewhere for evaluation. The UNRRA team revealed all their findings to the Army War Crimes investigators, who did not immediately follow up on the information, as, at this early date, "crimes against the German population were not of concern."[75]

In the reams of military working documents and reports in the archives resulting from the early processing of DPs, the statistical tables always refer to nationalities and not to ethnicities or political groupings. After a time a new category enters the endless lists, that of "stateless persons." Sometimes other euphemisms are used. But this category of problem nationals was not national at all; instead it referred to Jews, a designation that was at first unacceptable in U.S. Army parlance. Needless to say, these first victims of the Nazi racial laws were not eager to stay in Germany. Nor did Jews from the East, where anti-Semitism in certain places was as strong as ever, wish to return to regions that only held terrible memories, where their communities had been destroyed and they would have to continue to live in fear. It also soon became clear that they generally preferred to be housed together in all-Jewish DP camps. These gradually began to evolve as the non-Jews of the various nationalities were also separated into their own camps. Conditions in the Jewish camps were no better or worse than those of the others; but even more than their gentile counterparts, the Jewish DPs had a liberation complex that was not amenable to discipline or denial and in a number of cases would lead to confrontations with Germans and the Allied military.

On June 22, 1945, President Harry Truman, under pressure from numerous groups Jewish and otherwise, directed Earl G. Harrison, dean of the University of Pennsylvania law school, to investigate the situation of the Jews in the DP camps. Escorted by the European director of the American Jewish Joint Distribution Committee and accompanied by representatives of the War Refugee Board and the Intergovernmental Committee on Refugees, of which he was also a member, Harrison, like everyone who saw such a camp, was shocked at the conditions in which the DPs were living, and deplored the fact that they were in settlements surrounded by barbed wire and guarded by MPs, which he too thought were remarkably similar to the former concentration camps. He was also critical of the lack of food, heating, clothes, and rehabilitation programs. Harrison felt that the Jews, "the first and worst victims of Nazism," should be given special status within the DP category as "persecutees," and that help for them should be expedited. This was, of course, desirable; but with an extraordinary lack of recognition of the magnitude of the job of repatriation and feeding of millions that was taking place all over Europe, as well as of the round-the-clock efforts by hundreds of welfare workers that had gone on for months in the concentration camps themselves, Harrison declared that the Jews, "beyond knowing that they are no longer in danger of the gas chambers, torture and other forms of violent death . . . see, and

there is—little change." The knowledge that they no longer faced extermination would in itself seem to have been quite a big change, but Harrison
reiterated further on in his report that "aside from having brought relief
from the fear of extermination, hospitalization for the serious starvation
cases and some general improvement in conditions . . . relatively little
beyond the planning stage has been done during the period of mass repatriation, to meet the special needs of the formerly persecuted groups." He
concluded with amazing unfairness, "We appear to be treating the Jews as
the Nazis treated them, except that we do not exterminate them."[76]

This accusation was disputed by Eisenhower in a letter to Truman,[77]
and by a civilian team dispatched to check on Harrison's findings by Assistant Secretary of War John J. McCloy, who termed Harrison's accusation
"fantastic." The team found none of the camps "scandalous or anywhere
near so," and reported "unexpectedly sound morale, adequately nourished
appearance and low sick rate in spite of cold and lack of fuel with Trojan
efforts to achieve cleanliness."[78] The issue was not, of course, the improvement of the bad living conditions, which had already been suggested in an
earlier report covering all DPs by Sir George Reid, the former director of
the welfare division of UNRRA. Harrison was principally interested in
promoting the quick resettlement of Jews who, with good reason, did not
wish to be repatriated to their countries of origin, and who now faced the
exact same problems of refuge they had faced before the war, which neither the War Refugee Board nor the Intergovernmental Committee had
been able to solve. For this longtime issue, Mr. Harrison, a former commissioner of the Immigration Service, now had a perfect solution that
would enable almost everyone to keep their immigration walls intact: he
suggested that 100,000 Jews be immediately evacuated from Germany
and, as was clearly the preference of most, allowed to "find peace and
quiet in Palestine." He did recommend that the United States admit Jews
who had relatives living there, but only "under existing immigration laws"
and in "reasonable numbers."[79]

Harrison's suggestions were, of course, nothing new. Increased Jewish
immigration to Palestine was a long-cherished objective of the Zionists.
The immediate difference now was that the United States wished to be rid
of the DP problem in Germany as soon as possible, and that the idea of
"peace and quiet" and a safe haven in Palestine, which had sustained the
Jews who had managed to survive, had, with the revelation of the Holocaust, reached a high level of intense emotion and become an unstoppable
force. These factors, and various others, would result, after much maneuvering and conflict, in the founding of the state of Israel in 1948.[80] The

more immediate results of Harrison's report and its subsequent publicity were frequent inspection visits by high-ranking officers (including Eisenhower and General Walter Bedell Smith) to the Jewish camps, the appointment of Judge Simon Rifkind as special adviser on Jewish problems to Eisenhower's staff, an increase of rations for Jews over those of other DPs, and the provision of other amenities. In September 1945, regulations restricting the activities of the remaining DPs were also eased, causing much trepidation to all involved in running the camps, who correctly feared an upsurge in illegal activity.

Those concerned with child welfare, especially for "unaccompanied children," would soon have to deal in a serious way with the movement toward Palestine, but it was only one of many problems. The Allied social workers running children's homes and camps did not at first have sufficient staff or facilities for the separation of their charges into national or ethnic groups, as well as gender and age cohorts. The situation was made even more challenging by the fact that Jewish children and Eastern children—who had undergone intensive Germanization and had been indoctrinated to hate Jews—often arrived at the same time. Before the Germanized children could be repatriated, their identities and nationalities had to be elucidated, which was especially difficult with smaller children who had no memory of home. Once identified, they had to be "de-Germanized," often an agonizing process. They had all been deeply affected by their experiences in the Nazi world:

> This . . . has been proven by the emotional outbursts and conflicts of children brought to our Center for care, the most notable examples being the Polish and Jugoslav groups who renounced their country, language and culture, and vehemently declared they were Germans. Russian and Ukrainian children and many others while not reaching this stage of Germanization have been completely poisoned against their own countries, and while not wishing to remain in Germany will not countenance return to the land of their birth. Children from labor gangs were usually ready and anxious to go home. Jewish children hate the Germans wholeheartedly, and their aim is to leave Germany for a free life in Palestine, America or other parts of the world.[81]

But before dealing with nationality problems, the welfare workers were more concerned with physical ones. Malnourishment was common. They saw rickets, boils, ringworm, tuberculosis, bad teeth, and many other ailments. There were children "with large heads and small bodies who appear at least five years younger than the average for their chronological age." Many cringed from any touch and had scars "which tell the story of cruel treatment," while others were afflicted with tics, fainting spells, excessive sweating under stress, bed-wetting, and amnesia. Some could not give consistent accounts of their experiences. Little ones rocked back and forth continuously or suffered from chronic hunger that made them scream constantly for food. Almost all were completely indifferent to the dead and were particularly good at dissimulating, the talent by which they had survived. Ages were altered to fit whatever end they had in mind. The children lied, cheated, stole food and hid it in their clothing as they had done in the camps, and were suspicious of everything and everyone. When reprimanded for such acts, they sometimes went on hunger strikes or ran away. But at the same time they deeply craved affection and formed emotional relationships and group bonds that made them resistant to repatriation or individual placement in families. For most, food and humane treatment worked miracles on health and behavior within weeks.[82]

It was far more difficult to overcome indoctrination, and the process was not helped by pressure from the representatives of national groups for whom possession of the children soon became an obsessive battlefield. The UNRRA child welfare workers, who in the main dreamt of international harmony in their camps and homes, where the children would be prepared physically and mentally by teachers from the various countries for voluntary repatriation or congenial resettlement elsewhere, were constantly undermined in their efforts by powerful political and religious interests, which included Communists, royalists, the Catholic Church, and the Zionists. Moreover, the repatriation officers of each country had specific criteria for who would or would not be taken back or released for resettlement. The USSR wanted immediate and compulsory return of all children and refused to supply any teachers or social workers for the UNRRA camps. The borders of a number of countries had changed with the end of hostilities: parts of Poland and the Baltic countries were now de facto parts of the USSR, anathema to many children from those regions who remembered family deportations with horror or who had heard nothing but anti-Soviet propaganda for years. The Poles in Warsaw were determined to recover all the children kidnapped by the Nazis but were reluctant to accept Polish *Volksdeutsche* children trying to get back to their families. The émigré Poles, who had managed to return from Soviet exile and had fought alongside the Allies, were equally eager to recover Polish children for themselves, and to prevent their return to what was clearly becoming a Soviet-dominated area. Similarly, Yugoslav children were sought by both the exiled royalists and the new Communist regime headed by Marshal Josip Broz Tito. The Norwegians and Belgians did not, at first, want their war babies back, whereas underpopulated France not only welcomed these, but often spirited children in its zone out of Germany without knowing exactly who they were or informing the military authorities or UNRRA, who were trying to reunite families.

The U.S. Army did not particularly care what became of the 600,000 or so DPs left over after the initial massive returns in the spring and summer of 1945, as long as they left Germany, and it used every sort of inducement short of force to encourage them to go home. Repatriating the DPs took on even more urgency when the Allied leaders decided at Potsdam, in late July, to allow Poland, Czechoslovakia, and Hungary to expel an estimated 6.5 million *Volksdeutsche,* all of whom would have to be absorbed into the already struggling German economy, starting in January 1946.[83] To expedite the process, reluctant Poles were offered such incentives as several months of food rations if they would return to Poland. When the State Department, prodded by Truman, announced in late December 1945 that, for humanitarian reasons, it would set up consulates in or near DP camps to issue visas to those eligible under the American quotas, the Army reacted with dismay: "Expect announcement will abruptly halt present repatriation movements. . . . If [DPs] learn of prospects for going to US, it is strongly believed that they will not accept repatriation."[84]

But it was already too late for such considerations. There had been early suspicions that many Soviet nationals were being executed as soon as they were out of sight of the American or British units that had escorted them to the borders of the Soviet zones of occupation in Austria and Germany. This had been confirmed in June 1945, during the repatriation of more than 20,000 Cossacks from the British Zone of Austria. These soldiers, many of whom were accompanied by their families, had fought with the Germans in an effort to rid Russia of Stalin. The Western Allies, wanting to assure the return of their own POWs from Soviet-held areas, had agreed at the Yalta summit conference to repatriate the Cossacks and all other Soviet nationals. When the fact that they were being sent back was revealed to the Cossacks, there was mass hysteria and active resistance to what was a virtual death sentence. One mother threw her two babies into a raging river and then jumped in herself. A Cossack father killed his whole family before committing suicide. The scenes during the loading and unloading of the repatriation trains were so horrific that some of the tough British combat troops involved were reduced to tears. This incident was not the only one. Similar scenes took place during the processing of Soviet POWs for repatriation from camps where they had been held in

the United States and Great Britain.[85] These events led officers of both
nations to devise means to circumvent the Yalta agreements by tacitly
obstructing the access of Soviet liaison officers to POWs and DPs. All sorts
of red tape was put into place. A top secret British memo in early 1946
stated that

> forcible repatriation will NOT be carried out and the Russian LO's [liai-
> son officers] will NOT be so informed, or allowed to deduce from
> actions taken that there has been a change in repatriation policy. . . .
> Should the LO enquire what action has been taken in this matter, a
> non-committal answer should be given to the effect that the matter is in
> hand, and that while pressure of work or . . . commitments have pre-
> cluded any action to date, it is hoped to deal with it in the near future.[86]

Similar measures were taken by the Americans. This left a body of Russian
nationals who would never go back but instead would become part of the
"hard-core un-repatriables," a group that would have to be gradually
absorbed by other nations.

It had also become clear that hundreds of Poles, many of them the
young people who had left on the flower-bedecked trains, were unhappy
with conditions in Poland and were secretly returning to the camps in
Germany. They were not alone. Large numbers of Eastern Jews who had
never been in Germany before had also begun to "infiltrate" the American
Zone. What began as a stream of 300 or 400 a day in November 1945
would rise to over 1,000 by December. More came into the U.S. sector of
Berlin. The influx was not surprising. Polish-Jewish relations were still terrible and had included murders and pogroms. Things were so unsettled
that some Polish families who had hidden Jewish children felt compelled
to continue to do so in order to protect both the children and themselves.[87] Word of the good treatment that could be expected in the U.S.
Zone had spread, and much publicity had been given to an idea proposed
by Jewish Affairs Adviser Rifkind to create a temporary refuge under
Army protection in Germany for "the remnants" of Eastern Jewry. More
diplomatic than Harrison, Rifkind declared in a later report that the Army
had breathed the spirit of life into the "small heap of dry bones" to which
the Jews of Europe had been reduced. Now, he said, the Army had "in its
keeping not a group of discrete individuals but a 'people,'" and that "destiny has called upon the military forces to preserve that people and to
channel its migration."[88]

UNRRA and other organizations, responding in part to the publicity
surrounding Harrison's accusations, were doing their best to "channel"

migration out of Germany, especially for "un-repatriable" and "unaccom-panied" children. In the late summer of 1945, Britain had offered to take 1,000 and France a second group of 500. It was clear that most of these DPs would be Jewish. The groups in Britain organizing the transfer fully intended that the children, once rehabilitated, would go on to Palestine or other destinations, such as Australia.[89] The transfers, sponsored by organi-zations such as the British Jewish Refugee Committee and the Union of Orthodox Rabbis of the United States and Canada, aided by the Quakers and others, were elaborately planned to provide good accommodation, Jewish group leaders, kosher food, and religious instruction in the receiv-ing countries. When the possibility of going to England was announced at Belsen, hundreds of "precocious and bitter" teenagers whose "only thought was to get out of Germany" mobbed the registration office, fre-quently lying about their ages, as anyone over sixteen would be rejected.[90]

No one in the aid community was prepared for the virulent reaction against these transfers from an entity called the Central Committee of Liberated Jews in Bavaria. In a dramatic resolution passed on October 14, 1945, they declared that "the Remnant of Israel (Sharith-Ha-Platah)" was not willing to remain in "strange countries" any longer:

> The last station of our suffering way is behind the gates of concentra-tion camps and behind the iron doors of crematories and gas-chambers. We shall wait here with embittered endurance until the gates of our old-new homeland will open wide to let emigrate the remainder of European Jewry, for only there can we find a permanent home for us and for the coming generations and only in that atmosphere could the still wide and bloody wounds be healed.
>
> We declare that we will not allow ourselves to be pushed from one country to another and that we have decided to remain in the camps of Germany until the conscience of the world will at last open the gates of EREZ ISRAEL.[91]

The situation was so tense that the authorities had to conceal the names of the children cleared to go to Britain. On the day of departure, a passion-ate confrontation in the registration office between the Jewish committee in Bavaria and the Jewish agencies in England was only resolved when the military commander intervened and ordered the children to board the waiting trucks. This first transfer did take place, but on November 4 the Bavarian committee, declaring that it had no confidence in the British as they were using force against Jews in Palestine, demanded that no more children go to England or anywhere but Palestine. Two days later committee agents broke into UNRRA offices and destroyed the dossiers of the children who had been chosen to leave for England. When UNRRA officials told the committee chairman that the children had gone very willingly, he retorted that they had done so because they were from a camp "where they had been isolated and inaccessible to the influence of the Jewish leaders within the camp," a situation that had now been "remedied" by sending "an educator" to that location.[92] Meanwhile, a delegation of children had appeared at the central UNRRA headquarters for Germany with a petition demanding that they be permitted to migrate to England and stating that they were prepared to fight those in the camp who opposed their movement.[93] The dismayed UNRRA staff now appealed to Judge Rifkind to reason with the Jewish committee so that the "opportunity for living a normal life in England while resettlement plans are being worked out" would not be denied to the children.[94] Rifkind, clearly distressed, spoke to future Israeli Prime Minister David Ben-Gurion at the Jewish Agency for Palestine in London, saying that the camps should not become an "open battle ground" and that the transfers should either be allowed to proceed or be abandoned. Ben-Gurion promised to send someone to "appraise" the situation.[95] In the end, all the children already scheduled to leave for England were allowed to go, but in late November UNRRA was advised that no more unaccompanied children were "to be sent out of the US Zone of Germany for temporary or permanent care in other countries" until further notice, unless they had relatives in the other country.[96] This was unfortunate, as, unbeknownst to the American authorities, many thousands more were about to arrive in their zone.

When the flood of Jewish child "infiltrees" began, the UNRRA organizers had no warning at all that any were coming, much less how many there were or where they had come from. It was not unusual to find a large number of children in a camp in the morning who had not been there the night before. Although there had been sporadic appearances of groups of unaccompanied children ever since the end of the war, the first major "infiltration" took place on December 16, 1945. A train had arrived in Munich bearing 360 unaccompanied children from Budapest. Refugee authorities received a series of anonymous calls with conflicting information and could not find the children, 120 of whom, escorted by a Hungarian doctor, suddenly appeared at an overflowing DP transient center set up in the Deutsches Museum. The boys and girls, forty-eight of them between two and ten, "dazed and fatigued beyond speech" but still proclaiming that they were "on their way to Palestine," were processed and "settled on army cots hurriedly thrown up in a large corridor." After a few days they were taken to one of the adult Jewish camps. Within the next four weeks there were six other surprise arrivals totaling about 600 children, some as young as six, and usually escorted by young adults. It was not clear how many, if any, were orphans, as in the early batches at least 20 percent referred to living parents.[97] By January 7, 1946, UNRRA had managed to open a special camp for infiltree children at Strüth, near Ansbach, and there would soon be more. These camps would not be run according to UNRRA's usual methods, as it quickly became clear that the groups coming in were not random, but were controlled by young leaders of varying philosophies who planned to keep the children together in separate kibbutz settlements when they arrived in Palestine. The Army ordered that the infiltrees be kept separate from the "regular" DPs "pending firm policy" regarding them, but unlike the British they did not refuse them entry into the U.S. Zone.[98]

The overwhelming majority of infiltree children were from families that had fled to or lived in eastern Poland and then been sent to Siberia or other remote locations in the USSR. Large numbers also came from Hungary, where conditions even after liberation were horrendous. One group of Polish and Czech orphans had been gathered together in Budapest before the German occupation in 1943 by a doctor who had escaped from the camps. They had pretended to be a Christian children's home, but no one was deceived, and the house was raided by the Nazis. Some of the orphans escaped and regrouped elsewhere. More children, some as young as six months, were brought in from cellars, woods, and caves to another house disguised as belonging to the International Red Cross. After the Russians came, some of the children found their parents and others were sent to Palestine. The remainder, left with few resources, had nearly starved during the winter of 1945, and many had died: every morning those who were bedridden were shaken to see if they were still alive, and often they were not.[99]

Smaller numbers of the infiltrees were children who had been hidden in Poland, lived with partisans, or had survived the camps. They had been gathered up by Zionist and other organizations both during and after the war. After the fall of Germany, representatives of these organizations met repatriation trains coming into Poland from Russia and scooped up children who were alone or persuaded arriving parents to release them. Other workers scoured the towns and villages looking for hidden children. All agree that some foster parents were paid when the children were given over to the organizers. Whether the money is characterized as a demand by the foster parents before they would release the child, or as a "reward" encouraging them to do so, depends on the point of view of the reporter.[100] But it is clear that those who came for the children were viewed with suspicion by those who had hidden them. The decision to hand over a child was often an agonizing one for the caretaker, particularly if the so-called relative claiming the child had no proof whatsoever of any connection, or if the child was frightened and reluctant to leave. In some cases, particularly where adolescents were concerned, the children absolutely refused to leave their protectors. Even if the retriever was a parent, many visits might be necessary to re-create the relationship and to persuade the child to depart from the place where he felt safe. There were many who did remain in Poland and managed to live quite well, either as Jews or as converts to Catholicism, though many of the former later emigrated to Israel.[101] Among these was Jerzy Frydman, the boy whose wanderings had begun when he was eight, and who had lost his arm. He was not found by the Jewish searchers until 1948, and the wild, illiterate child was only persuaded with great difficulty to leave the primitive farm where he was working. But kindness prevailed at the children's home to which he was taken; the staff soon found traces of the boy's family, and his long-delayed education progressed quickly. Jerzy became a mathematician and worked for some years in Lodz before emigrating to Israel, where he married and had two children.[102]

The aim of the gathering-up exercise in Poland was to get the children to the U.S. Zone of Germany or other starting points, from which, it was felt, they would have the best chance of emigration to Palestine. Families were persuaded not only that unaccompanied children were more apt to be allowed to emigrate than whole families, but also that having a child go ahead and be accepted would facilitate entry for its relations. The UNRRA people dealing with this flood of arrivals realized very soon that the infiltration was not spontaneous. Camp director Helen Matouskova observed, "Emissaries from here are traveling openly to Poland, Hungary and Romania and organize whole trainloads . . . the whole issue is a definitely political one, with the aim to break through in the Palestine question." But all were aware that it was "impolitic" to mention this fact.[103]

Meanwhile, the waves of children kept coming in, requiring the establishment of ten more camps and the hiring of Yiddish-speaking staff that included representatives of the Jewish Agency for Palestine. A special transit center was opened at Rosenheim, where the always unheralded groups could be registered and directed to the proper permanent camps, which after a time were made up exclusively of one kibbutz denomination or another. For the camp directors, generally trained child welfare workers, these camps were unlike anything in their experience. Most of the small refugees refused to have anything to do with the UNRRA teams, whose authority was widely ignored, and the social workers had trouble establishing any rapport with individual boys and girls. The children in the kibbutz groups were cared for and controlled entirely by their leaders (*madrichim*), who were often only sixteen or seventeen themselves. Two weeks after it opened, Rosenheim had nine different kibbutz groups. They ate, played, and spent their free time totally separated from one another, and resented the appearance of new groups in the camp. They wanted their own kitchens, and actively proselytized one another's members. Clothes in each group were owned in common and carefully parceled out to whoever needed them most. At all-camp activities organized by UNRRA, such as concerts and theatricals, where attendance was required, it was noticed that the "spark was missing" and that communal facilities such as playrooms were completely ignored. This exclusivity, plus the constant appearance and disappearance of groups, also made camp schools difficult to organize. All aspects of group life were decided in discussions within the subdivisions of each kibbutz, with the result, one UNRRA worker felt, that "frequently the time for action is long past while the pros and cons are still being discussed." But she did admire the feeling of a "happy, well united family" engendered by the evenings of singing and dancing the children put on. Most UNRRA workers were upset by the political orientation of the kibbutz groups. One wrote that this was "contrary to the elementary principles of democratic education," noting that it was "very disturbing to see that children actually are considered as part of the political group already at age of 4–6."[104]

The kibbutzim often went further than separating themselves within the camps. One group of eighty simply picked up and left Rosenheim for another camp, which had no facilities for them. Orders to return were resisted at first, but after a time forty of the children and all the *madrichim* went back by train. The other forty boys adamantly refused to board trucks sent for them, saying that "the Army would not force them to go since the American Army was not the Gestapo." That was true, but the thirteen MPs called in to deal with the situation knew obstreperous kids when they saw them and simply picked them up and put them in the trucks. Once under way, the officer in charge reported that "instead of crying, they began to laugh and sing."[105]

The fact that an estimated 70 percent of the infiltree children had one or both parents alive but were not with them violated the principles of many UNRRA workers, who were above all dedicated to reuniting families. The aid workers spent much effort compiling lists of children that could be matched with the inquiries of parents searching for family members. They also felt very strongly that the children should be informed of other living relatives who might be found and have a say in their own placement: some children had said, for instance, that they did not want to go to Palestine and be farmers but preferred to be jewelers or dentists "in the USA." Children were sometimes released by the kibbutz groups to join their families, but this was not easy to achieve. Five boys who wished to return to their parents in Poland were not permitted to do so until they circumvented their leader and went to UNRRA representatives with their request. The *madrichim* apparently were afraid that letting the five go would start a trend. Three other children who found relatives in the United States, and applied for emigration, asked to be sent to another camp as soon as this became known, as they knew that the fact that they no longer planned to go to Palestine would make life "less pleasant in the same surroundings."[106] There was also controversy about letting youngsters leave the children's centers to join relatives in the big DP camps. An entity called the Jewish Child Care Committee argued that they would be living "in slum conditions," and further urged that parents be allowed to send their offspring from the camps to the children's centers, which under Army and UNRRA rules were only for "unaccompanied children."[107]

Faced with such determination, most UNRRA workers soon gave up trying to deal with intra-Jewish relations and concentrated on facilitating resettlement, if not always to Palestine, noting in one report that "the answer to the Jewish problem is emigration, not case work, not make work projects, but emigration from the lands of blood and infamy . . . they deserve a chance to build a new life."[108] By late 1946, greater efforts were made to coordinate activities with the Jewish organizations, and as time wore on and it became clear that departure to Palestine was not imminent, all sorts of educational and athletic programs did flourish. But the focus of the kibbutzim on the Promised Land and the building of a Jewish national state, to them the only answer to anti-Semitism, was never lost.

In April 1946, a large group of children and adults with legal entry certificates was finally sent to Palestine via Marseilles. UNRRA workers escorted the children on the train from Germany, a journey that, like most such trips, suffered from lack of planning. The children, who had started in high spirits, cheering and singing and defiantly flying flags at every station in Germany, became more and more exhausted and subdued. The train was cold and food service on board difficult, as it was impossible to get from one car to another. At Marseilles, where no advance preparations had been made, the children, along with a large number of adults, were required to spend four days in an inadequate camp with the familiar lack of sanitation and cooking facilities. The UNRRA workers, by now quite attached to their nervous charges, were worried that most of the children would be "placed in the hold" of the ship, where no mattresses were in evidence. These were "to be provided" and placed on long tables, but an hour and a half before departure none had arrived, nor was there any evidence of meals being prepared. The children complained of "being herded like cattle" onto the boat, and the UNRRA observers felt that little concern was shown for them "individually rather than collectively." This they attributed to excitement and to the fact that for the young representatives of the Jewish agencies "the movement of the group was the thing that mattered most. Inconveniences . . . had to be taken in stride . . . in the endeavor to attain their goal. To be able to send close to 900 persons from a land of persecution to a land of promise, that was a feat to accomplish and this the JAFP [Jewish Agency for Palestine] has accomplished against all odds." And indeed, as the ship sailed, the children "in quest of a new life" swarmed onto the decks. Cheering and singing, tentative at first, soon "mounted the wave of enthusiasm emanating from those who made their departure possible."[109]

On April 13, just before this voyage, the Anglo-American Committee of Inquiry on Jewish Problems in London had recommended that 100,000 refugees be admitted to Palestine immediately. This stimulated thousands more infiltrees to pour into Germany, among them many more groups of children. Once again their leaders viewed the UNRRA camps merely as way stations where they would be given food and shelter. These basics were harder and harder to provide as Europe's food supply system struggled to revive. In August, the Army had to resort to setting up tent cities holding 5,000 each to shelter the infiltrees, who were coming in at a rate of 1,000 a day. An estimated 13,878 children, 2,500 of them verified as "unaccompanied," came into the U.S. Zone between June and November 1946, bringing the total under UNRRA care to about 26,500.[110] Unknown thousands were not included in this official total. According to one camp director, "There is little we can do to control or even keep track of their movements. I am convinced that we cannot stop this exodus from Europe, nor delay it, and there is little sense trying too hard to manage these people who have only one goal in mind and who recognize no law or rules but their own."[111]

Nothing exemplified this passion more than the voyages undertaken by illegal and often fatal means. These were countered with growing ferocity by the British, who were trying to enforce Jewish immigration quotas into the Palestinian Mandate, which would be their responsibility until 1948. In the most famous of these interdictions, the British Navy, in July 1947, would forcibly turn back 4,700 people without visas who had sailed from France on a rickety American passenger boat that had seen better days as a Chesapeake Bay steamer. Bought in the United States by the Haganah, the Palestine-based Jewish underground army, it had been renamed the *Exodus 1947*. Defying warnings to turn back, the *Exodus* was rammed and boarded at sea. After a fight in which several people died, the vessel was towed into Haifa. The voyagers were searched, disarmed, deloused, and immediately transferred to three British transports that sailed back to France. There they refused to disembark. Trying to force them off, the British kept them jammed on the stifling ships for over a month, but only a few gave in. Finally, the vessels were sent to Hamburg, where the defiant travelers, among them hundreds of children, were, once again, put into a camp.[112] The gates of violence-torn Palestine would not open until May 1948, after which some 650,000 Jews from Europe, North Africa, and the Middle East would emigrate to the newly founded state of Israel,[113] where, sad to say, they would not soon find the "peace and quiet" they had sought for so long.

The Zionists were not the only ones who complicated the running of the camps. Passions ran just as high among Poles, Yugoslavs, and Russians. The Iron Curtain was falling fast, and the Great Powers had shifted frontiers about in complex wheelings and dealings that affected the nationalities of millions of people. American and British pressure for repatriation was countered in the camps by representatives of governments in exile whose supporters would be in dire peril under the new Communist regimes that had taken over their countries. The Polish government in London was aided in its efforts to keep people away from the Warsaw government by several hundred thousand members of the Polish armed forces who had fought with the Allies, and who had not returned home. According to a British report, 75 percent of the 20,000 Yugoslavs in DP camps in Germany would "like to repatriate, but are prevented from doing so by terroristic and anti-repatriation activities of the other 25 percent." The situation was so tense that Yugoslav repatriation officers could only

A repatriation convoy leaving for Poland.

enter the camps accompanied by armed British MPs.[114] Adults, of course, could make up their own minds, but the unaccompanied children were, once again, up for grabs, and the child welfare workers, who were required to adhere to the Allies' recognition of the Communist-dominated governments of both Poland and Yugoslavia, would again be caught in the middle.

From the beginning there had been difficulties with groups of Polish boys arriving from the concentration camps. A group of fifty-five, sent to Auschwitz with their families after the Warsaw insurrection, had been separated from them and moved to the Mauthausen camp. There, they were secretly organized into a Polish Boy Scout troop by a man rightly worried about their moral decline in the camp atmosphere. After liberation they had stayed together with this leader, who was trying to educate them to be honest, helpful, and above all, proudly Polish and anti-Communist, teaching them such slogans as "Poland, freed from Swastika, has been captured by the Sickle and Hammer! Dachau and Buchenwald have been replaced by the ice of Siberia!"[115] In these educational efforts he seems to have succeeded, and in so doing to have attracted the attention of the émigré Poles, who wished to move the boys from the UNRRA camp in Germany where they had settled, and where their leader had become one of the staff, to another camp in Italy controlled by the émigré Polish Red Cross. The Warsaw Poles were not in favor of this unless it could be shown that the boys were "Polish Catholic children who no longer have any ties in

Poland but have relatives in other countries." UNRRA also required that the status of the parents or relatives be determined. Meanwhile, the boys were to remain at the special UNRRA Polish children's camp that had been installed in a castle at Regendorf. The decision did not please the Scout leader, clearly not of the Warsaw persuasion, who was soon dismissed by UNRRA. Before he left, he gave a dramatic farewell speech to the children, "whereupon all [of them] disappeared from the center." It seemed that they had been collected in trucks, taken elsewhere, and been billeted with émigré Polish families.[116] These boys were retrieved, once again with help from the Army, but that was not the end of the issue.

A schism also developed among the Polish Red Cross workers helping UNRRA in Austria. Here, the so-called Second Polish Corps Red Cross, mostly very anti-Communist Poles, deserted to set up their own camps and took with them most of the records relating to unaccompanied children. The dissident actions were tolerated at first by UNRRA and the Army, as the Second Corps homes and camps were extremely well supplied with food and better able to take care of the children. Their supplies were more plentiful because they were being subsidized by the Vatican, Polish exile groups in the United States and Britain, the Swiss, and other charities, as well as by rations donated by Second Polish Corps soldiers. Everything went swimmingly for a time, but when it became known that all the Polish children, like the Jewish ones, must be centrally registered with UNRRA so that they could be repatriated if their parents were found in Poland, the Second Corps people also began to hide children in houses outside the camps. This group of Poles also avoided sending names to the various tracing services run by civilian and military agencies.[117] UNRRA was never able to compile proper lists, and after a time it was clear that here too groups of children were clandestinely being brought out of Poland and taken from other UNRRA camps to Italy and France without checking their origins. These hasty transfers led to mistakes: six of the children in one batch were from a German family who had appealed to UNRRA in desperation for the return of their offspring. Protests from UNRRA and the U.S. Army over the Polish actions sank into red tape and obfuscations of all kinds, as the Second Corps contingent had plenty of sympathy in the Western world. At one point they did repatriate twenty-two youngsters who had parents in Poland through UNRRA, but thousands of Polish children who had been scattered all over the world during the war were never reported to the international agencies. Many would be kept away forever from their now Communist-run homeland, and their parents would never see them again.[118]

The conflicting interests of "blood," religion, and politics were even more complex in the case of Yugoslav children. In March 1946, a group of girls and boys, aged six to seventeen, were brought by U.S. Army trucks to the center at Kloster Indersdorf. They were escorted by a deacon of the Innere Mission, a charity run by the German Lutheran Church. The deacon, who had made several attempts to escape from the transport with the children, claimed that they were all orphans or that their "parents could not care for them," and that the parents had not been real Yugoslavs but German Lutherans whose ancestors had been driven out of Germany into Slovenia 170 years ago. The Wehrmacht had evacuated the children to Germany in October 1944, where they had been ever since. The children themselves seemed terrified and only with difficulty were they persuaded to put down their luggage. It soon became clear that they were also very hungry, as the deacon had ordered them to throw away the chocolate and food provided by American soldiers. A meal was prepared, but the children refused to eat it until the deacon said a prayer and gave them permission. After dinner they prayed again and sang hymns. It was not until they were taken to have baths that, in the opinion of the UNRRA workers, they talked and laughed like normal children. The next day, after much discussion, the deacon was told that he must leave the children at Indersdorf. Upon hearing this news, the children became very emotional and the deacon "stood as if in a trance with both arms raised and eyes turned to heaven. He made no effort to part with the children, who clung to him wailing and moaning hysterically. It was with the greatest difficulty that we separated the children from him." After he left, "it required hours to get the children calmed down. Through the help of the other children in the Center, they finally accepted their stay here, and by evening settled down more or less." Soon after the deacon left, a delegation from the office of the bishop in Munich in charge of the Innere Mission was sent to claim the children, maintaining that they were German because

1. Their names are German. 2. Their ancestors and relatives were German. 3. Their religion was Lutheran. 4. They are German-speaking. 5. They were brought up in an Institution and are not interested in Yugoslavia.

UNRRA and the Army, which by now had encountered similar groups (including one in which several teachers had been arrested as members of the SS and their replacements pressured by other "older colleagues" to continue the "teaching program of the past six years"), refused to release the children pending further investigation.[119]

The Catholic Church was no less determined than the Protestants to "save" Yugoslav children. At about the same time as the deacon was being escorted away from Indersdorf, representatives of the Austrian branch of UNRRA became aware of a group of forty-nine boys who were living in a resort hotel at Ramsau-bei-Schladming. They came from a Catholic school in Zagreb that had been under Nazi supervision and had been evacuated in response to Himmler's orders in November 1944. The boys were well taken care of by three nuns. British occupation authorities had duly inspected the setup, sent in some clothes and food, and, so far, left it undisturbed. The nuns had told the inspectors that all the parents of the children "were peaceful Croatian farmer families of Catholic religion" who had not been involved in politics, but had, nevertheless, been killed by Communist partisans. Sister Anka, in charge of the group, also declared that the boys had no other relatives whatsoever who could care for them, that they were "in God's hands," and that she was "awaiting orders from Rome as to their disposition." But the Yugoslav repatriation authorities, when asked, indicated that they would like to have the children back, and the UNRRA and Army child welfare workers now had to decide the children's fate.

Conversations with the children, aged ten to fourteen, soon revealed discrepancies in Sister Anka's statements. The boys, interviewed in her presence, had clearly been told what to say. Very few reported that they had seen their parents killed, and many revealed that they had brothers and sisters. There was no evidence of any postwar effort to find the families. Sister Anka said she was afraid of what would happen to the children if they went home, a valid reaction given the combined partisan activity and civil war that had riven Yugoslavia, as it had Greece. UNRRA therefore instituted a search for relatives and requested assurances from the authorities that children without families would be well taken care of if they returned. By October fourteen families had been found, and UNRRA inspectors, who had gone to Yugoslavia to check services for orphans, had determined these to be adequate. It was therefore decided to repatriate the Ramsau children who had families and to remove the rest to an UNRRA home while investigations continued.

When an UNRRA commission, accompanied by Yugoslav government representatives, arrived at Ramsau to arrange these transfers, they found Father Kelava, a Franciscan priest who had come from Rome, waiting for them. Most of the children, when interviewed anew, said, in remarkably similar statements, that they wanted to go to Rome and become priests.

Father Kelava said that the boys were part of a group of ninety-six children who were to go to Rome for training as missionaries. The Pope himself, he said, was interested in the children, who were "happy and enthusiastic at the thought of becoming priests." He also said that the boys had been "handed over to us" by the parents, whose existence was now suddenly recognized. To this he added that requests from these same parents that the boys come back were probably not voluntary: "Taking into consideration the present government in Jugoslavia . . . who will dare to say no?" In his opinion, it was the church's "moral" and "humane" right to take the children to Italy. The boys, he declared, were so afraid of being sent to Yugoslavia that "if they knew that they might have to leave Ramsau, tomorrow morning all the children would have disappeared."

This remark was a red flag for the UNRRA officers, who decided to take the children to their own facility immediately and requested transportation for the following morning. During the night, Sister Anka and Father Kelava helped the children pack their rucksacks, and as the trucks approached at dawn the next day, the boys could be seen running away into the woods. Police were called and the frontier patrolled. It took two days to reassemble the children, who came back in bedraggled ones and twos and were immediately driven off in UNRRA vehicles. Here too there were dramas:

> At one point Father Kelava came downstairs in tears and the two maids were screaming and crying, saying that Sister Anka was dying. Father Kelava also told some children just about to leave . . . that Sister Anka was dying, thereby upsetting them. On the other hand, when separated . . . the children laughed and played, and particularly had a very good time in the jeep.

Later investigations found the parents of all but four of the children. At the UNRRA home the children were "reoriented," now with the help of the Yugoslav Red Cross, approved by the Tito government, who were somewhat hypocritically "astonished by the extent to which political and religious dogma in opposition to repatriation had been impressed on the minds of young children." Sister Anka, having recovered miraculously, continued to write to the boys, and it was suspected that she had enlisted staff members at the UNRRA home to encourage them to run away, which, indeed, two attempted to do. The first group of boys was sent back home in January 1947. They were still so afraid that they entrusted items like watches to their UNRRA escort, being convinced that such things would be stolen from them by the Communists at the border. Instead, they were greeted with great celebration and fanfare. At the station in Zagreb were bands, flags, rows of children singing songs, and relays of local school groups and teachers who chatted with them. There was food in abundance, and everyone got new pants and shoes.

As soon as the children were settled in a home in Zagreb, Syma Klok, the UNRRA escort, went to find some of the families who had not yet been notified of the group's arrival:

> I went to visit the mother of the K. child. This child had been told that his mother had been killed by Partisans; she was alive and well. She was a poor peasant woman, and chickens were running in and out of the house, but it was very clean. When I went in the eldest daughter, aged about 14 or 15 years, was doing her lessons, and the two other boys were sitting reading. I asked her whether she had another son and whether she knew where he was; she said that she had no idea. . . . When I told her that the child was well and would be brought back to her she fainted and there was a scene I shall never forget.

Another parent heard of his daughter's arrival on the radio and came the same day to see her, and a boy who said he "had no one" was amazed when his sister appeared. Before she left, Miss Klok asked the boys if they wished to return to the UNRRA home with her. All declined, and one small boy apologized for having run away, "and thanked me for fetching him back and for bringing him home . . . he said he would never forget it." The repatriation was not 100 percent successful, however. Two of the boys were lured away by Sister Anka and did not return to Yugoslavia for some time. Father Kelava is reported to have found at least fifty-seven other boys to take to Rome, with written permission this time from their sometimes illiterate parents.[120]

The Russian problem was different. Although the British and Americans opposed the forcible repatriation of adults, child welfare workers felt that unaccompanied Soviet children should go home, if their nationalities could be verified by such documents as birth certificates, naturally not always obtainable. Limitations imposed by the Western Allies on the activities of Soviet repatriation officers in their zones made this process even more difficult, but a number of groups were taken back under UNRRA escort. Persuading the Russians to release children held in their own zone who had parents in the West was harder.

At the end of the war a group of White Russian émigré children, who had been evacuated by the Germans from Belgrade, had ended up in the Soviet Zone. Their parents knew where they were. One enterprising mother had simply gone to the home where they were lodged and managed to come away with eight of them. An officer there had told her to take as many as she liked, but that if they were not retrieved soon they would be taken to the USSR. Five other mothers then went to the school, and after a certain amount of drama they were also given their children. The rest went off to Russia in February 1946. Senior UNRRA officials pursued the case, suggesting diplomatically that the Russians had perhaps not been aware that the children in fact had living parents. In June, the Soviets agreed to meet with a group of parents, in the presence of American officials, to see if their claims to the children were valid. It was rather an extraordinary encounter between White and Red Russians:

> At first the parents were a little nervous, but as time went on they seemed more at ease and in fact there was apparently some amusing conversation. The hearing was extremely well . . . conducted according to the White Russian. . . . He mentioned that some of the remarks and comments made by both parents and officers were highly amusing and witty. . . . Hardly had the last parent left the room than a very spirited discussion started—democracy versus communism, with the White Russian staff member holding his own. The young American officer listened rather tensely, but informed me that both sides were exceedingly well informed and that the discussion was an interesting one. He did not participate.

A few weeks later, the children were brought back to Germany. The Soviets were happy to return them to their parents, but wanted the parents to come to the home where the children were lodged, as they wanted them "really to understand that the children have had good care." But the émigrés were afraid to go to the Russian Zone, so the children, who "sang Russian songs quite lustily most of the time" on the train, were instead brought to the DP camp where their parents were living and handed over in a little ceremony "carried out with dignity and restraint." Each family was called in turn and requested to "sign a paper stating that they had received their children and that they were in good condition. Each parent was asked to write a statement of appreciation on the back of the form." Only one refused. The UNRRA observers, who had expected all sorts of propaganda and unpleasantness, reported with some amazement that the Soviet officers "were sympathetic and courteous" with their former countrymen.[121]

The struggles over the groups of children scattered and moving around in the chaos of Germany were intense, but both there and in the less damaged West when the controversy involved individual children who had been placed in foster families, no matter what the reason, things became much more complicated. The problem was how to define the "best interests" of the child. Here too politics and religion would play a major part, but just as important at times were the bonds that had developed between the child and the foster family. Nowhere would this issue be more openly debated than in the Netherlands when it came time to decide the fate of the Jewish children who had been hidden there.

As soon as the southern part of Holland had been liberated, committees with both Jewish and gentile members were formed to take over responsibility for hidden children. These early groups were more concerned with food and education than religion, and in the unsettled conditions still prevailing they made no effort to move the children.[122] By early 1945, funding was coming in to the committees from the American Jewish Joint Distribution Committee and the Intergovernmental Committee on Refugees. Everyone gave high priority to the registration of the hidden children. The Dutch Resistance, concerned lest the children vanish in the chaos of combat, had distributed a pamphlet in September 1944, when the German surrender seemed imminent, asking foster parents not to relinquish their charges to anyone, even parents, without informing the Resistance. Later, Gesina van der Molen, a formidable leader of the Resistance[123] who had been a member of a child rescue network, went further. She conveyed to the Dutch government in exile a proposal for the establishment of a nonsectarian Custody Commission for War Foster Children (OPK), which would take over all responsibility for children whose parents did not claim them within a month of the end of the war. If the parents appeared later, the OPK would decide if they were still fit to care for the children, and if not, or if the parents had died, who was. In its discussions on the creation of the OPK, the Resistance committee, which included a number of Jews, had leaned toward leaving children in foster homes if they were happy there. It is not clear how much, if anything, religion had to do with the proposal, but it is certain that the Resistance felt that "Dutchness" was important and that they wished to replace the "dual-fated community" of the Nazi years by a "general merging together."[124] It is also clear that many of the prospective Jewish members of OPK no longer liked the idea of reestablishing a central Jewish Council, the institution that had been so well exploited by the Nazis. OPK was duly authorized and would begin operations immediately after the German surrender in May 1945. Their jurisdiction extended beyond the hidden children to include all kinds of war orphans.

There were other Jewish groups, however, that did not like the sound of OPK's principles, and were suspicious of Miss van der Molen, who was a member of the Dutch Reformed Church, not famous for its tolerance. Above all, she was known to regard Dutch children as just that and not particularly as Jews or Christians, and to be associated with Jews who favored assimilation. Those Jews who favored a more independent stance now set up their own commission, and Abraham de Jong, who was Orthodox and Zionist, founded yet another. The fragmented situation was not improved by a letter sent to the patriotic Miss van der Molen by Chief Rabbi Herzog of Palestine in which he thanked the Dutch people for having rescued Jewish children, but declared that

> all Jewish children . . . now that the Nazi scourge has been definitely removed, should with the least possible delay be handed over to their community to be placed in Jewish institutions under proper religious communal management. . . . Public Jewish bodies will assume responsibility for the maintenance of those institutions. Our ultimate goal is to bring these children to the Holy Land . . . meanwhile they will stay in your hospitable country under specific Jewish care.[125]

Despite the admonitions of the Resistance, hundreds of foster parents had, without informing the OPK, and often with great emotion, immediately handed over the children they had hidden when their parents reappeared. Four thousand more children were registered with the organization, and about half of these were also quickly returned to their families. In the next four years, more than 1,300 custody cases relating to the remainder would be considered by the OPK. The Dutch Jews, who were in the minority on the commission, were not all as enthusiastic as Rabbi Herzog about sending the children to Palestine, but did feel that the probable wishes of the deceased parents regarding the upbringing of the children should be considered. This was not a problem when the parents were known to have been observant. The children were then placed in Jewish families or, since there were not enough of these, in Jewish orphanages. Decisions were more difficult for the offspring of assimilated families.

Some Jewish members of the committee were outraged when gentiles attempted to decide if a child was really Jewish. They felt that non-Jews did not understand "the social and cultural aspects of Jewish identity," and they insisted that all the children were still Jewish (an attitude considered "racist" by the gentiles). Furthermore, the Jewish members felt that OPK's policies violated the Dutch tradition of self-determination within any given religion.[126]

Others joined the controversy: a psychologist wrote articles stating that the children would be traumatized by being removed from their foster homes, and Rabbi Herzog, not giving up, wrote the Dutch Prime Minister requesting that the children "be restored forthwith to their rightful guardian—the Jewish Community."[127] He also invited Miss van der Molen and a companion to visit Palestine. The two ladies were very favorably impressed with all the schools and child care facilities they saw, agreeing that Palestine was a good place for children to go. Gesina Van der Molen, educated as a lawyer, did not, however, approve of the idea of a purely Jewish state, and wrote to the Dutch Foreign Minister that she was afraid that Jews who had converted to Christianity were "oppressed" there.[128] Meanwhile, the pro-Zionist Jewish committees in Holland had enlisted the soldiers of the Jewish Brigade (a unit that had served with the British and sported spiffy uniforms with a Star of David emblem) to visit the children in Holland and to send them letters describing how happy the boys and girls in Palestine were and inviting the Dutch children to come and help "build up our beloved motherland."[129] Relations on the OPK deteriorated steadily; the Jewish members were, for example, not informed of court hearings on the placement of the children, some of whom were given to gentile families without counterarguments. In July 1946, most of them resigned. This contretemps was patched up, and the work went on with better cooperation. An estimated 75 percent of the boys and girls ended up in Jewish households or orphanages.

It is hard to say exactly how much these controversies affected the children's placement. The piles of case histories that survive show many different situations and sensible efforts to resolve them humanely. Some do contain accusations by relatives that foster parents had attempted to convert children permanently to Christianity, against their desires. There are numerous recommendations to remove children from these and other foster families for all sorts of reasons. In some cases, Jewish relatives abroad requested that a child be sent to them, which was done. Some older children asked to go to the Jewish children's homes and found tremendous solace in their atmosphere, but would still visit their foster parents for weekends or outings. Others ended up in the homes when life with the Jewish families in which they had been placed was unhappy. One boy could not bear the sadness of living with a couple who had lost all their own children in the camps, and another was thrown out by his aunt and uncle when he wanted to visit his Protestant wartime protectors, who had allegedly had "Christian influence" on him.[130]

The cases are often complex. In June 1946, the aunt and uncle of Sally and Lieslotte D., aged nine and six, went to court to get custody of the girls. Their parents had perished at the hands of the Nazis, and they had been living with Christian foster parents, who, everyone agreed, were wonderful. Indeed, two other uncles and two second cousins "declared themselves emphatically in favor of the continuation of the residence of the said infants" with the foster family. The judge, clearly agonizing over the religious aspect, noted that both the parents and grandparents of the children had been Communists, and that probably "education . . . in any outspoken Jewish religious sense was not intended," adding with some feeling, "For my part, I have only to look into and after the interest of the infants and I cannot consider it my task to make a stand for the Jewish community of blood and/or race as such." Since the foster mother had promised not to baptize the children and to leave them free to "determine their religious conception of life for themselves," the judge ordered that they stay with her.[131]

The situation of nine-year-old Max G. was sadder. His foster mother admitted that Max had been homesick for a month when he arrived and that she had spanked him with the rug-beater when he misbehaved. She also said that she wasn't really very fond of Jews and admitted that she liked her own children better. The OPK interviewer noted that the house was unwelcoming and messy. But the family situation of Max's uncle Lion W., who was petitioning for custody, was not ideal either. Lion, who had spent time in the camps in Poland along with his father, had a new wife who seemed fond of Max, but was very busy with her new baby. The grandfather, Simon W., "a somewhat brutal, aggressive figure," lived in the same house along with his mistress-cousin, who was an Auschwitz survivor and "somewhat unbalanced." In this situation, the OPK worker felt that the best place for "attractive," "bright" Max would be the Jewish orphanage.[132]

Despite all the fussing, there were only a few open rebellions against the OPK decisions, the most famous being the widely publicized and much appealed case of nine-year-old Anneke Beekman, the child of Orthodox Jews, who had been left in the care of five Catholic spinsters.[133] The girl disappeared when it was decided that she was to go to a Jewish family. The sisters, despite several stints in jail, refused to give her up. The Dutch authorities tried for years to find Anneke, but she did not surface until after her twenty-first birthday in 1961, having lived under a false name in France with one of the ladies. Her reappearance was a national sensation. She was interviewed on television, and at a press conference she was peppered with tough questions about the Holocaust and asked why she did not feel Jewish. Anneke seemed unable to answer most of the inquiries and denied that she had been abducted. After this unsettling experience, she went back to the five sisters' house, where she lived quietly until 1965, when she married a Frenchman and left Holland.[134]

The question of the "best interests" of the child arose in a different form in Germany. Although the child welfare workers had encountered numerous groups of "Germanized" children, they did not for many months fully understand the Nazi programs behind the children's transformation. They had quickly become aware of the fact that unaccompanied children of "United Nations" nationalities were to be found not only in the DP camps, but also in the German community. The workers also knew about the Nazi policy of separating Eastern workers from their offspring and had wrongly assumed that most of the children living in German households and institutions were in that category. In the late summer of 1945, therefore, a directive was sent to Civil Affairs units requesting that they require German burgomasters to list all foreign children in their towns. In the frenetic activity of the early days of occupation, this census was not promulgated or followed up with efficiency, and results were meager. And, although lost children were registered in a centralized tracing bureau set up for all refugees, there was as yet no special clearing file for children.

By the late fall, UNRRA workers sent out to find and register adult DPs living on their own on the German economy had found more than 1,000 children they were sure were foreign in German institutions in the eastern part of the U.S. Zone. In the British Zone a Polish group reported that a group of children who might be Polish were living on one of the Frisian islands in the North Sea near Bremerhaven. The children had apparently been seen by "people in UNRRA uniforms" in the summer of 1945, but no record of this visit had reached headquarters. It was not until December 1946 that the thirty-one children, aged eight to fourteen, and the two nuns caring for them were found. They had been evacuated to the island by the

Nazis from an institution where they were forbidden to speak Polish, which by now they had mostly forgotten. Since the local authorities thought they were German, they had not received the extra food given to DPs, and were seriously malnourished.[135] UNRRA was convinced that there were many more cases like this one, and that the children, if not discovered, would soon disappear forever into the German population. But, required to deal with the care and repatriation of the children already in the camps and later with the infiltrees, they did not have sufficient resources to begin a thorough search. They knew little enough about most of the children they did bring in, as the Germans had done a good job of destroying records and, as one UNRAA worker noted, "amnesia seemed to be a prevalent malady in Germany." Thus the Lebensborn children who had been brought together by the Nazis at Steinhöring were found and taken to the UNRRA children's center at Kloster-Indersdorf with no indication of who they were.[136]

As the camps and homes for unaccompanied children started to stabilize and the boys and girls became less fearful, the welfare workers began to hear disturbing stories about their "schools" and experiences. During these conversations, it became clear that there were other children not only in institutions, but also on farms and in families all over Germany, and indeed, numerous Yugoslav boys had been found working on farms in Bavaria in October 1945.[137] Soon the names and true character of Nazi organizations began to surface. The NSV was prominent among them. One boy told an UNRRA team, "If your father was German and your mother was Polish the NSV took you away from them and made you speak only German." Another, from Serbia, described being taken away to a home in Katowice, in Poland, where there were about 200 children, all of whom spoke Polish. The whole group was constantly urged to speak only German, and "when I spoke Serbian they boxed my ears." This story was confirmed by a Polish nun who had accompanied some of the children when they were moved to Germany from Silesia. A thirteen-year-old Polish girl described medical experiments performed on her and her friends at a special hospital for "backward" children, at Loeben (Lubliniece), and said that the children who could not endure the treatment were sent "to a special house" where they all died and were buried in mass graves in the woods. Another nun, "though apparently reluctant to acknowledge German misdoings," verified these facts and admitted that her order was required to "Germanize all foreign children" in its children's home; the order had also been instructed that "all the children whose parents were not Germans have to be sent to Loeben," where they were given "injections and pills, after which the children became mad or they were gone."[138]

All these indicators led the UNRRA workers to press for more resources to find children in the German communities. It was clear that a very systematic search was needed. In January 1946, German officials were once again ordered to report the names of all foreigners, and notices and advertisements were put in publications and on the radio. But the still unsettled condition of the entire population—millions of people trying to get home, and groups of children and their caretakers wandering from institution to institution in a desperate search for shelter—made anything systematic nearly impossible.

The terse information on a series of case history forms filled in for children found during 1946 shows just how difficult any sort of identification could be, especially when it came to babies. Two-month-old Stefan P. had been "found beside a dead woman who was killed by artillery fire" near Nuremberg in April 1945, and taken in by a German woman. The burgomaster's office had collected documents indicating that the child was the son of a Yugoslav worker who was thought to be the dead woman. Doubts were cast upon this analysis by the fact that a package of documents referring to a French worker had been found in a suitcase of baby clothes lying next to the child. The Frenchwoman, who had allegedly also had a baby in Germany and shared a room with the Yugoslav, had been repatriated. When she was found in Paris she denied, unconvincingly, that she had ever had a child. The German woman wanted to keep the boy, and the Yugoslavs wanted him back. Gathering of statements from France and Yugoslavia took months; the case was still not resolved by January 1947. In Czechoslovakia, American soldiers found an infant lying between his parents, who had been shot, but the GIs did not bring in any identifying information with the baby. Two-year-olds Barbara and Klaus, origins totally unknown, had been found at the Ratibor railroad station on the Polish-Czech border, moved five times, and deposited at a children's home in Germany, where workers said that little Klaus "did not call for his mother, neither did he cry."[139] It was thought that many of these babies were the illegitimate offspring of Eastern workers who had been forced to give them away and now no longer wanted them, either because they could not support them or because they were ashamed to take them home.

By the early spring of 1946, more information about Lebensborn's relation to the Germanization program began to be known. A Frankfurt city councillor said he had heard rumors that vital statistics had been falsified. The French National Tracing Bureau added numerous details, including the fact that children they were finding in their zone had been taken away from their parents and reported as orphans. The Polish Red Cross delegate for Austria found one of the Lebensborn Germanization schools. A secretary who had worked there said that children had been sent to foster homes from the institution; she even had a list of names with destinations, but it was so full of errors that the UNRRA workers felt sure they were not unintentional.[140] They also found incriminating RKFDV documents, as did the officers sifting through the tons of records gathered for the Nuremberg trials, which had begun in November 1945. It appeared that the Nazi records destroyers had not been perfect. Polish investigators, who had begun making lists of their missing children in August 1945, found NSV file cards and dossiers on 8,500 children in Lodz and Katowice. Dr. Roman Hrabar, the Plenipotentiary for the Vindication of Polish Children, raised the estimate of the missing to 200,000. More documents were discovered in Czechoslovakia, including falsified birth certificates and evidence that three truckloads of children from Lidice had been sent from their transit camp in Lodz to the Chelmno extermination camp.[141] As usual, the USSR did not provide any estimates of how many of the tens of thousands of its young people taken away by the Nazis had failed to return, but was always eager to have Soviet children repatriated. Even without the Soviet statistics, however, the abundance of evidence and the dogged persistence of the child welfare workers eventually persuaded upper echelons in both the British and American zones to authorize special Child Search teams to scour the German countryside.

The teams were far better at conducting searches than individuals were, especially in German institutions that did not want to release the children. By the time a single investigator had interviewed two or three children in such places, the rest would have been prepared by their peers or the staff to produce doctored stories aimed at preventing identification. A team, on the other hand, could do many simultaneous interviews in numerous languages. Operating as a team also provided "balance when missionary zeal went too far," for, as time went on, the welfare workers had become more and more outraged at the Nazi methods and obsessed with saving every possible child. Their determination did not diminish when they were confronted with children who, under the baleful eye of German staff, blurted out obviously memorized answers, even before a question had been asked: "I am German, I am not Czech. I speak only German. My parents spoke only German . . ."; after which they "ceased breathlessly, looking for reassurance at the nun nearby." One sister was heard to tell a child to "remember what answers you are to give."

The interviewers soon learned ways to get around these preparations. Smaller children would often sing along with a casually hummed song, or finish a prayer in their original language. Everything depended on how one asked a question. A sudden provocation might lead the child to cry out in his native tongue. Indirection also worked well. John Troniak, director of the first Child Search team in Germany, and himself a refugee, was a master of this technique:

> We have to let the child forget about the drastic subject and let him tell what we want to know in another way. If necessary, we do not spare compliments. . . . "I like your German. I have never heard children who speak so nicely as you do. . . . How long . . . have you been speaking this language?" "Four years, since I came to the children's home"—is the answer. "All right, but you are nine years old now, what language did you speak before?" A little hesitation, then: "Polish." "Did you speak only Polish at home, or did you speak with your parents German too?" "No, never, I spoke Polish only." "You say your parents spoke Polish. Were they Poles or Germans?" "They were Polish." . . . "Are you sure?" "Yes, I am." "If both your parents were Polish, do you think you are German?" "I don't know. I have forgotten my Polish, but I think if I learn it again, I can become Polish too."[142]

By the summer of 1946, Dr. Raphael Lemkin, an adviser to the Judge Advocate General's Office of the U.S. War Department who had coined the term "genocide," was interested enough in the issue of Germanization to request a report from UNRRA on its findings about children for use as evidence in the second round of war crimes trials, being prepared even as the trials of the major war criminals proceeded. The information would become part of the documentation used to qualify the Germanization programs as war crimes, which were prosecuted in Case VIII, the Greifelt or RuSHA Case, which would begin on October 10, 1947. The UNRRA data would be added to the vast amounts collected by Dr. Hrabar, in charge of the Polish search programs, and to the evidence found in other nations. Together, the fragments would give a devastating picture of this aspect of the Nazi racial programs. The War Crimes office also provided information, as it came in, to the Child Search workers, and was certainly instrumental in promoting continued funding for their efforts, which were constantly threatened with cuts in budget and personnel by the Military Government.

The trial was a revelation to the Child Search workers and to many others. As the testimony unrolled, their suspicions and exhausting work seemed justified. Eileen Davidson, chief of the Child Search and Tracing Division of UNRRA, and her colleagues could not believe what they were hearing:

> One German foster father on the stand said he still had in his home a German boy of 14 from Lebensborn. When the Defense finished and the Prosecution staff took over, the man was asked if he intended to adopt the child. He said no, they had taken an older child to help them really. (!) Had they sent him to school? No. Why not? Well, he could not speak German! What did he speak? Polish!!! What did they know of his parents? Nothing. Where did he come from? They did not know.
>
> So finally the Prosecution said, "Looking back now, does it not seem to you a matter of the gravest injustice that a human being could be taken with so few particulars known about him and placed in your home to receive whatever care—good or bad—you happened to give him?" The foster father said, "Well, when I came to think about it, it does seem unfair."!!!

There followed testimony about ten more "German" children, all of whom were listed in the Child Search tracing files and were being sought by relatives. Davidson wrote that they had "pieced together a fascinating but devilish story." She had several times "longed to give . . . up and run away from all this sordidness forever, but, in my mind's eye, I have a mental picture of a group of distraught women from whom SS Troops are wrenching their children . . . and now, I feel that we who were so long in coming to the rescue have a small, very, very small opportunity of undoing what was done."[143]

On November 10, 1947, Dr. Klukowski (the observer and diarist from the Zamosc region), who was testifying at the trial, and Dr. Hrabar brought three repatriated children to Child Search headquarters. Four days before, the children themselves had stood before the court and charged five officials of Lebensborn and RuSHA, the SS racial agency, with crimes against humanity, crimes against children, and against their families. Dr. Hrabar noted that the children's parents had been afraid to let them come back to Germany. Now, in person, Alina Antczak and the others told their stories. A Polish social worker from Lodz indicated that 15,000 to 20,000 children were missing from that city alone. So far, only

about 1,300 had been reunited with their families. She was sure more had
been repatriated, but as their names had often been changed when they
were very young, there was no way of knowing who they really were.[144]

The war crimes trials changed some minds: after hearing the cynical
plans Lebensborn had made for its war babies, Norway reversed its former
decision and asked that they be returned. The Child Search teams were
now even more determined to continue their work, but their very existence was threatened: UNRRA would cease to exist in 1947. Its functions
would be transferred first to the Preparatory Commission for the International Refugee Organization (PCIRO) and eventually, in 1948, to the
International Refugee Organization (IRO) itself. This organization, based
in Geneva, was not enthusiastic about Child Search, in large part because
the countries that had lost the most children were all in Eastern Europe,
and not members of the IRO. Their officials put forth the now familiar
argument that it was wrong to "disrupt" the children who had been in German homes for several years "another time" and to "disturb the security
the new family has given them." But the Child Search workers had seen
enough families up close to convince them that the security was often
ephemeral:

> We are finding many instances in which the family tosses over the child
> the moment life becomes complicated for them, older boys and girls
> used for farm and household labor who have never been sent to school
> in Germany, children who are reminded daily that they must never
> reveal their non-German origin, children keenly aware of the fact that
> they had other homes and other families.[145]

There were plenty of case histories to back up these remarks. The Child
Search workers continued to find neglected babies left behind by Soviet
forced laborers, and preteens who had been used as virtual household
slaves. Some families were financially pressed by having to care for their
foster children (though the German Youth Department, which had replaced its Nazi predecessors, did give them small subsidies) and wanted to
be rid of them. It was clear that many Germans knew that these conditions
needed remedying; the youth authorities were often the ones who
reported the cases to the search teams. One farm wife wanted to send a
thirteen-year-old Polish girl back to her mother, but was afraid to do so
because her husband wanted the child to stay and work. A Norwegian tod-
dler who was left alone for days on end with a "big dog" and the twelve-
year-old daughter of the foster parents, who "often beat and teased him,"

was reported to UNRRA by German neighbors. A Polish couple who had been slave laborers and had been forced to leave their son with a mentally unbalanced German woman could not take him home because the woman "had absconded with him." In this case too, the neighbors reported terrible conditions in the home: "child mostly all day with 4–8 dogs in a small room. This child is bitten often and sometimes cries over one hour . . . the neighbors cannot help because the woman locks the door when going out." Then, there was nine-year-old Lucie, a Lebensborn child born in Poland,

> reported to IRO by the German foster father. He obtained the girl through the Lebensborn. He stated that when he and his first wife divorced, the latter told the child that she was Polish and was not theirs. The second wife did not want to keep the child since they now have three children of their own. The foster father asked IRO to relieve him of the child. He said he had not been able to manage her since she learnt the truth about herself.[146]

Not all the situations were so nasty. There were numerous German families who came forward voluntarily and returned their well-cared-for charges, and there were places where the children were happy and deeply loved. But their future was not secure. German laws forbidding the adoption of foreign children, the lack of such documents as birth certificates, and other nationality questions made the rights of the foster children in Germany problematical. Nevertheless, some families went to great lengths to keep the children by hiding them from the Child Search teams or by simply refusing to hand them over.

Lack of personnel, especially in Austria, often required individual UNRRA workers to be searchers. Such forays were not for the faint-hearted, especially as cars were hard to come by, information was often vague, and the postwar population nomadic. After tracking down lists of possible households with foreign children in Vienna for days, one worker said she felt more like a postman and that her specialty had become "stairs and door bells." Even more fortitude and sleuthing were needed in the country. Here transportation was sometimes bizarre: one searcher was so determined to reach a certain town that she rode up a mountain in a coffin-shaped cargo box on a ski lift. Workers haunted pubs and marketplaces, and questioned village priests and burgomasters:

> In one small village, having gone by car as far as possible, I then walked across meadows, crossed a brook, climbed a stile and eventually braving my way through a flock of geese, found myself at the Burgomeister's

house. His office, a complete contrast to the rural isolation of the cottage, struck me most forcibly. The Burgomeister was amazed to think I had troubled to come there. He laid down his Tyrolean pipe and exclaimed . . . to his daughter, "This lady had come all the way from London to see us."

That was just the beginning of the adventure. Once armed with locations, the searchers had to go to the houses. Although most were decent enough, there were exceptions:

> It was getting dark, I had left the car by the road-side and walked through snow for half-an-hour when I located the house I had been looking for. As I pushed open the door and found myself in a dark porch, I felt a little boy and asked him where his mother was. He opened the next door and what I saw was a filthy kitchen, black ceiling and walls, dirty pots and pans hanging on the wall and a large untidy old woman stirring a pot. She did not seem to understand me and looked at me vacantly, so I asked the boy to find his father. . . . In the meantime a tall youth, an idiot, came in and stared at me. I must confess that I did not enjoy this very much at the time (all this was happening in a barely lit room and I never did feel happy in the dark). At last the foster father appeared. He was carrying two bottles and his eyes were bloodshot. . . . He explained how he came to have the child. The mother had given it to him whilst she was working on a farm and later when she had come back for him the foster parents had refused to give him back. What he must have told the poor woman I leave to the imagination, but she never dared return. . . . Had I had a children's home anywhere, I would have broken all the rules and taken the child away. As it was, I had to wait until morning.[147]

The legal division of the Military Government was reluctant to authorize the Child Search workers to enter such homes and forcibly remove children, and never issued clear directives on this delicate subject. The uncertainly often led to delays and disputes in court over "the best interests of the child" and made the process longer and more agonizing.[148] Indeed, many of the searchers themselves dreaded the terrible scenes the separations created, and had very mixed feelings about the justice of their actions. The distinguished historian Gitta Sereny worked in Germany on one of these teams. In an article written fifty-three years later, she described her visit to a German farm family that had been given Polish twins four years previously by Lebensborn. The blond boy and girl, now six, were particularly dear to this family, as one of their own children, also a twin, had died very young. The farmer and his family believed that the twins, who were healthy and happy in the big farmhouse, were "German orphans from the Eastern territories." But photographs of the children at the time of their arrival in Germany were identified by their parents, who were alive and well near Lodz. This proof overrode all other factors, and the twins were taken from the farm to an UNRRA center. Sereny did not perform this dreadful task, but a few months later, she visited the center and recognized the children, who had no memory of Poland or their parents and were clearly miserable and disturbed. They recognized her too. It was a devastating encounter:

> The two children's appearance—their faces were sallow and there were shadows under their eyes—and Johann's reaction to me and Marie's awful apathy shook me to the core. Marie was scrunched up in a chair, her eyes closed . . . her thumb in her mouth, but Johann raced up as soon as he saw me, and shouted hoarsely, "*Du! Du! Du!*" (You! You! You!), and hit out at me with feet and fists.[149]

Later, Sereny escorted a trainload of children back to Poland to be reunited with their parents, and what she saw there made her feel better:

> Just as I can't forget the pain of the German foster parents when they had to see the children leave, I will never, as long as I live, forget the welcome they received in Poland, never forget the faces of the parents, grandparents, uncles, aunts, brothers and sisters. The miracle of recognition of a long lost child by those who love them is awesome to behold.[150]

Other Child Search workers agreed with this aspect of the process: one man could not forget the face of a Pole who for months had met every train of repatriates, asking for his granddaughter.[151]

The decision to leave Germany was harder for older children in middle-class families who were given a say in their fate. They had often been required to be members of the Hitler Youth or Bund Deutscher Mädel, eventually had full social lives at German schools, and considered themselves completely German. The discovery of their origin, or that parents long thought dead were still alive, brought forth mixed emotions. One girl wrote to her birth mother in Poland that she was very happy and lacked for nothing with her foster parents: "We have a lovely house with a garden, also a car in which my father always takes me riding. . . . Next year I shall learn to drive." She was glad to hear from her mother and to know that she was alive, but said that she did not wish to go back to Poland, noting that "at this age [fifteen] I should already know whom to be thankful to and where I can have a good life. My parents will be pleased if you will visit me someday." It is clear that the girl did not know of the Nazi plans for those of "good blood." Her letter reveals considerable inner struggle. With some resentment she continues, "Dear mother, I am thinking, why did you put me in an orphanage when I was little? Why do you ask about me now," but then says that she would like to "hear something about [my father] some-day." And she not only sent her mother a picture of herself with her new family, but asked for one in return. The emotional pressure on her, and a remarkable lack of comprehension on the part of her German family, are illustrated by a note from the foster mother to the birth mother: "I should like to write you a short note. I love your child so much, that I am not able to be without her. Today [she] has been saying to me, Mother do not cry, I shall stay with you. My good lady, leave the child with me." This girl appar-ently did not go back; the dossier contains a series of ever more frantic let-ters from her mother, but no replies.[152] But there were others who, after early denial and hesitations, did return, and there were even cases in which parents, foster parents, and children ended up visiting back and forth and became friends.

Both the Child Search program and ongoing repatriation, valiantly pro-moted at the United Nations by former UNRRA team director Richard Winslow, who enlisted Eleanor Roosevelt on his side, would struggle on under the aegis of various agencies, fighting all the while against funding cuts and, as seems inescapable, subject to changing political winds. The Soviet attempt to prevent Allied access to Berlin in 1948 offered dramatic evidence that Communism would prevail in the East, and occupation offi-cials, who had to approve all repatriation requests, were less and less inclined to send children to Communist countries, even if there was proof that they had parents there. In 1951, an Allied judge rejected the custody request of a Yugoslav mother who had survived Auschwitz. Although he was sure that she would be able to give her ten-year-old son, who had been taken by Lebensborn, a satisfactory home, he felt that the Germans who had taken care of the boy for eight years deserved to keep him. When welfare workers argued that the family had been Nazis, the judge declared dismissively that they had now been "de-Nazified."[153] This anti-repatriation trend was exploited both by émigré organizations and by Ger-man foster parents determined not to lose their children, and eventually led to the easing of restrictions on resettling children in Western nations, including the United States.

The Child Search programs of the IRO were ended in August 1950, and its files and a small staff were transferred to the International Tracing Service at Arolsen in Germany. In his final report on Child Search, IRO chief Herbert Meyer indicated that there were 13,517 unfinished investigations of children who had been adopted by Germans or who were still in foster care or in German institutions. There was no doubt in his mind that most of these cases, if left to the German authorities, would not be resolved in favor of foreign parents seeking their children, and that the result would be that these and perhaps thousands of other children "would remain in Germany and for their whole lives be ignorant of their identity and background."[154]

The unaccompanied children were only a small part of the larger DP problem, which had not vanished by 1948 as the Allies had hoped. The opening of Palestine was a great help, but this still left an estimated 750,000 DPs, mostly from Eastern Europe, also generally viewed as undesirable in the West, who were unlikely to be repatriated. Among them were many families with children. With glacial slowness, small groups suitable for specific tasks were admitted to Allied nations. In the fall of 1946, Britain, which had already allowed more than 100,000 Polish Army veterans to stay, began to recruit young Baltic girls for hospital work and later expanded this campaign to include other nationalities who would be employed as nursing aides and domestic workers. The program was so successful that in 1948 79,000 more DPs were admitted as "European Voluntary Workers." Belgium, Holland, and France took tens of thousands of men to work in their coal mines and other industries. Australia at first agreed to accept a small group of workers without families, but was careful to choose only blue-eyed blonds. The early arrivals were so acceptable that 180,000, hair color unknown, eventually followed. Canada too, surprised to find it had a labor shortage, eased its normal immigration requirements and allowed in DPs who had close relatives there. By the end of 1951, Canada had taken more than 150,000. Others went to South America. In all, more than fifty countries had, by 1951, sent representatives to Germany to screen and process suitable immigrants.[155]

The United States was for a long time an exception to these special admissions. Forty thousand DPs, mostly Jewish, could and did come in under the quotas, but it was not until June 1948, after the usual anti-immigration battles in Congress, that a bill allowing entry for 200,000 DPs was passed. Public pressure was strong. Earl Harrison, who had so vehemently criticized the conditions in the Jewish DP camps, now lobbied just as dramatically and successfully for the dissolution of all such camps. Noting that the United States had created "an arsenal of democracy" and "produced the atom bomb" in a "brief period of time," he challenged Congress to drop its "moral lethargy" and take care of the DPs or risk being "accused of callousness just as the Nazis have been accused of cruelty."[156] The bill that passed was still very limited: preference was given to individuals whose nations had been "annexed by a foreign power," such as the largely Nordic and non-Catholic Balts, whose countries were now controlled by the USSR. It did not include Poles, as Poland was technically independent, and of course it excluded Russians. The bill also required that 30 percent of those admitted should have "agricultural experience," and that the DP must have arrived in Germany before December 22, 1945—which eliminated most Jewish and Polish infiltrees. The law was amended in 1950 to cancel these discriminatory clauses and to allow in 200,000 more DPs, including *Volksdeutsche* expelled from the countries bordering Germany, as well as Greeks, Italians, and Yugoslavs.[157] More than 2,000 unaccompanied children came to the United States under the auspices of the Committee for the Care of European Children and were resettled by a plethora of organizations; several thousand more went to other countries.

The vetting for resettlement could be cruel, and for many DPs was remarkably similar to that of the Nazis. Families had to appear before endless screeners and committees and deal with miles of documentation. Those who were ill or disabled were not acceptable, which sometimes led to tragedy: one blind father committed suicide so his daughters could be admitted to the United States. There were, of course, humanitarian programs: among others, Sweden took a large group of tuberculosis patients, Belgium admitted some of the elderly, and the United States a few of the handicapped.[158] But these programs were far from enough. An unaccompanied child who was handicapped or sick could be refused resettlement to a foster home in another country. If the child had a family, the suggested solutions were harsh: they could stay in Germany permanently with the child; postpone emigration until the child could be rehabilitated; or emigrate without the child, which "sometimes involves placing him permanently in an institution under the custody of IRO." These remedies, as one welfare worker aptly wrote, were "complicated by reality factors," not least among which were the shortage of acceptable institutions and the fact that IRO was about to be terminated. One Lithuanian family was rejected because one of their four children seemed to be retarded.

Their argument that they could care for the child was of no avail and, in despair, they returned to their DP camp. A sympathetic doctor there thought the boy might have a thyroid problem. After five months of treatment, the child had improved so much that the family was accepted for resettlement.

As of January 10, 1950, IRO could identify at least 200 disabled children, many whom could not be rehabilitated, and felt that there would probably be many more as increased numbers of families were screened for emigration. Physical handicaps were not at issue, as these were readily identifiable, but it was often not clear to social workers if the children who seemed to have mental problems were really permanently disabled or only deeply affected by their living conditions, as was the case of eight-year-old Konstanty:

> He does indeed make a rather slow, awkward retarded impression; could not (or would not) at first even sign his name . . . and even when he did block lettered it laboriously and had to be helped. . . . Mentally deficient? Emotionally blocked? In need of glasses? Of physical attention? Never given adequate schooling? Who can say? But I did learn that when he was presented . . . at the Consulate, it was just after a move to another Children's Center and in company with a bright child who happened never to have been in anything but a private family, so that the contrast between the two was painful. Also Konstanty's little suit . . . was much too small for him, hunching his shoulders together, causing his arms to dangle unnaturally at his sides, thus contributing to the impression of awkwardness and dullness.

Konstanty, an orphan, was finally allowed to be resettled, partly because welfare workers who cared about him noticed that after he had spent two weeks with an Army family that had volunteered to provide DP children with short vacations he seemed transformed into "another boy—beaming, full of talk, almost lively." But there were many who were not so lucky. For them, by early 1950, the IRO had arranged to set up one rehabilitation center for the less extreme cases and, for the rest, admission to a huge 1,200-bed institution near Darmstadt run by the Germans, not a cheery prospect.[159] As one disapproving medical officer put it, these children were now "condemned to an institutional life, a terrible enough fate in any community, but in their case to be aggravated by the withdrawal of our protection and the replacement of that protection by a control from the very race who persecuted them and broke their lives."[160]

And there were always more needing a place to go. In July 1951, *New*

York Herald Tribune reporter Sonia Tomara and a friend visited the IRO Children's Village at Bad Aibling, south of Munich. The facility, soon to be closed, still had 309 young inmates of more than seventeen nationalities, all with heartrending histories. Some were about to be sent to America, others were still in various states of legal limbo. Just before leaving, the visitors were taken to see the nursery for small children:

> A little wide-eyed mite rushed to my friend, who loves children, buried her nose in her skirts and cried: "Mama, mama, don't go away, stay with me." . . . Was this a mere childish instinct, a memory of the mother, or a deep longing for a mother? My friend was moved to tears. But it was too late, we had an appointment in Munich, and had to leave without further inquiries.[161]

Responsibility for sad little children such as this one, who might still not be resettled by the end of the Allied occupation, or who were discovered later, was gradually transferred to child welfare authorities in Germany or wherever else they found themselves.

The International Tracing Service still exists at Arolsen in Germany, and now has a Web site. At the end of the Cold War, it was overwhelmed with nearly 200,000 inquiries a year from families suddenly able to communicate again from Eastern Europe. The records and services of the ITS, now placed under the International Red Cross and funded in great part by Germany, are constantly used, and every year help reunite family members for whom the longing for completeness has never vanished.

16. The Defeated

Among the parents desperately seeking their children were those who had been imprisoned by Hitler after the assassination attempt of July 20, 1944. Being German, they were not eligible to use the resources of UNRRA. Fey von Hassell had returned to Italy after her liberation, but could not get permission from the U.S. Army to go to Germany to look for her children, Corrado and Roberto, who had been taken from her almost a year before. The search was, therefore, undertaken by Fey's mother, the widow of executed conspirator Ulrich von Hassell. In the months following the surrender, travel in Germany was nearly impossible: permits from the Military Government were needed to go anywhere, and the devastated transportation system was overwhelmed with refugees. But this family was lucky. A car that had been confiscated from them was found in Munich and returned. Even better, the American Military Governor of Bavaria not only received Mrs. von Hassell, but gave her a travel permit.

The search was long and full of false leads, and each foray required new travel documents. When she returned to the Military Governor for the fourth time, seeking permission to go to Innsbruck, where the children had first been processed by the Nazis, the American officer, who by now had heard too many terrible stories, was pessimistic. He said that Innsbruck was in the French Zone of Austria and that she would have to "deal with the French . . . if you think it's still worth it." Mrs. von Hassell was not to be denied. Taking a chance, she went to a DP office, where an inexperienced young soldier, not too clear about the regulations for Germans, wrote her a travel pass to Austria.

In Innsbruck, a fortuitous encounter with the former janitor of the hotel where Corrado and Roberto had been housed finally gave her the name of the Nazi children's home. The director, who was quite friendly, immediately recognized photographs of the boys. She reported that they had hated to be separated and that Corrado had protected his little brother and helped him dress in the morning. When the boys were brought to her, Mrs. von Hassell instantly recognized Corrado, but she was not sure about Roberto, who had been a baby when she last saw him.

Not wanting to take the wrong child, she tried speaking to him in Italian, which he clearly did not understand. She was wondering what to do next when Roberto suddenly pointed "his little finger at a tiny white spot on a photograph I was still holding on my lap" and said just one word, "Mirko!" The child had recognized the little white pony kept at his house in Italy, and there could now be no doubt of who he was.

The boys had been found just in time: arrangements had already been made for them to be adopted by farmers in the vicinity. The director, apologizing for having "done so much wrong by these children," gave them a sack of warm clothes "to help them through the winter." As they left, Roberto seemed to hesitate, but Corrado, pulling him along, said, "We're going home now. . . . Don't you understand? We're really going home."[1]

These boys, privileged both by birth and by the Resistance activities of their late grandfather, would find home much as it always had been. They were fortunate that their grandmother lived in an area that had undergone no major bombing or battles. For millions of Germany's children, however, life after the surrender would be grim indeed. Some, the final sacrificial victims of the Nazis, would not live to see it. Down in the bunker where their adored Führer had already taken his own life, Propaganda Minister Joseph Goebbels and his wife administered morphine injections followed by poison to their six children, aged four to twelve. Allied troops found the offices of the Leipzig City Hall filled with the neatly arranged dead families of the mayor and a number of other city officials, one family to a room.[2] Other Nazi parents, having dutifully produced multiple progeny for the Fatherland, had not waited for their leaders' example. On April 16, American Military Government officials received this notice from the chief doctor of the small town of Hummelshain, near Erfurt:

> I found . . . in the buildings of the school in Hummelshain, that the whole family P. and the nurse, Miss Lieslotte S., were dead. I believe that it was their free will to die. They are:

> Mr. Karl P., born 31/7/86
> Mrs. Anna P., born 12/9/11
> Child Dietrich P., born 18/12/34
> Child Ingrid P., born 26/6/36
> Child Heinrich Bernhard P., born 6/7/37

Child Rüdiger P., born 18/9/38
Child Siegrun P., born 24/3/41
Child Karl Heinz., born 3/3/43
Miss Lieselotte S., born 16/8/26[3]

Americans who came upon such scenes had considerable doubt about the "free will" aspect, especially when it came to children. Some parents were apparently driven to ultimate despair by Goebbels's last-ditch propaganda broadcasts, which informed the German people that Allied soldiers were bent on extermination, a policy hard-core Nazis certainly understood. *Life* photographer Margaret Bourke-White found this tragedy in Schweinfurt:

> The young wife of this house, hearing that her soldier husband had been killed . . . just the day before, gave poison to her two little children and, after arranging their small bodies in the dismal front parlor, went down to the coal cellar and shot herself. Making myself photograph those tiny pathetic bodies, victims of forces which should be utterly remote from the life of a child, was one of the most difficult jobs I have ever had.[4]

Goebbels's warnings were not entirely mistaken. The millions of ethnic Germans who had survived their flight before the Red Army in early 1945 were, despite their dreadful voyages, far better off than their compatriots who faced the Red Army in the border areas between Poland and Germany or in what would later become the Soviet Zone of the shattered Reich. In these regions the combined effects of the atrocities committed in the Soviet Union, the publicity given to the liberation of Majdanek and other camps, and the constant propaganda emanating from Moscow, which was intended to fuel a final supreme effort by the exhausted Soviet troops, fostered a vicious desire for revenge:

> Germany is a witch. . . . The Germans have no souls. . . . Not only divisions and armies are advancing on Berlin. All the trenches, graves and ravines filled with the corpses of the innocents are advancing on Berlin, all the cabbages of Majdanek. . . . The boots and shoes and the babies' slippers of those murdered and gassed at Majdanek are marching on Berlin. The dead are knocking on the doors . . . of Unter den Linden and all the other cursed streets of that cursed city. . . . We shall put up gallows in Berlin. . . . An icy wind is sweeping along the streets of Berlin. But it is not the icy wind, it is terror that is driving the Germans

and their females to the west. . . . We shall forget nothing. . . . Germany,
you can now whirl round in circles, and burn, and howl in your deathly
agony; the hour of revenge has struck![5]

Rage was exacerbated by jealousy of the material comforts of the Germans that the Russian soldiers saw everywhere, and by amazement that people who lived so well would feel the need to attack the USSR. Red Army men looted, burned houses and factories, and were apt to shoot anyone they thought was a Nazi. They drank cellars dry and, particularly when drunk, they raped, sometimes in whole platoons, German women and girls as young as ten. Deaths were not uncommon after these sessions, and it is not surprising that, as the news spread of their possible fate, many Germans in the East also preferred to die by their own hand. In one village a whole BDM unit reportedly perished in a group wrist slashing, and an estimated 1,000 people committed suicide in the Pomeranian town of Stolp (population 50,000) as the Red Army approached.[6] Some Soviet officers on the scene were appalled at the behavior of the troops. Among them was Aleksandr Solzhenitsyn, who wrote a poem of outrage after seeing the body of a small girl killed in a gang rape.[7]

As time went on there was increasing realization in the upper echelons of the Soviet government that excessive destruction of property was not to the advantage of the USSR and that total alienation of the German populace would only make them resist more. These realities led to immediate reduction in the torching of factories and houses; but, despite the efforts of some commanders to stop them, the attacks on women and the looting of private property continued unabated for many months. Ethnic Germans who remained in Poland and the areas of Germany that would be annexed to it became the new *Untermenschen* overnight, despised and preyed upon by both Poles and Russians. It was now their turn to be thrown out of their houses, be deported to Siberia, see their families rent asunder, live in forced labor camps, and have their children given to Poles in foster care. The looting and rapine would continue in what would be the future Soviet Zone of occupation, most notably in Berlin, until early June 1945, when a zone-wide military government was established and Soviet policy turned to the creation of a pacified German Communist state.

The soldiers of the Western Allies, whose anti-German feelings were also very strong, were generally less extreme. They too looted houses and drank up liquor supplies, but their dislike of the Germans was usually less personal, and they were not yet fully aware of the extent of the Nazi atrocities. The problem of rape, though certainly present, was frequently resolved by more or less willing arrangements that often involved food or other amenities. Unlike the Soviets, the American and British commands insisted on complete separation of their troops from the Germans, who were to be treated with the contempt and coldness befitting their guilt. Fraternization was strictly forbidden and German families were evicted when their houses were taken over for billets.

The nonfraternization policies were doomed from the beginning. American detachments that established the first small footholds in Germany in late 1944 were often greeted as liberators by the populace, who plied them with food, drink, and other comforts. Many an officer found dining with the local gentry in their schlosses quite appealing. Civil Affairs units taking control of villages in the Rhineland, after establishing their authority and appointing non-Nazi mayors, treated the rest of the citizenry in much the same way as they had the French, and often found the Germans more cooperative. The object of their exercise, before the surrender, was the usual one of preventing starvation, disease, and unrest in what was still a combat zone. In the early days, the Americans, who had also heard their share of propaganda, were amazed at the docility of the German population, which seemed more sullen and frightened than defiant, and by the peaceful normalcy of those towns and villages that had escaped destruction. Easygoing local commanders frequently allowed Germans to continue to inhabit rooms in their requisitioned houses. This folksy feeling would dissipate considerably after the Battle of the Bulge, and as the evidence of Nazi atrocities became known. It was hard for the Allies to understand the strange emotional detachment of many individual Germans from the actions of the Nazis. William Shirer, revisiting Berlin in the fall of 1945, observed:

> What the German people regret, you soon find, is not that they made this war, but that they lost it. If only Hitler had listened to his generals during the Russian campaign; if only he hadn't declared war on the United States; if only the whole world hadn't ganged up on poor Germany, they whimper, Germany would have won and been spared the present sufferings. . . . There is no sense of guilt or even remorse. . . . They are sorry only for themselves; not at all for those they murdered and tortured and tried to wipe off this earth.[8]

One upper-class German woman, who had been allowed to stay in her house by two soldiers billeted there, reacted as follows to the American

GIs' passionate feelings at the revelations of the death camps. It was not an unusual response:

> They were very nice and we understood each other well. I spoke good English and they gave us a lot of things for the children. . . . Then one day, one of them came with a copy of *Stars and Stripes* . . . and was beside himself. His face was chalk white and he said . . . "Look at this. Look at this." . . . The Americans had discovered and entered the concentration camps. . . . They were so completely beside themselves with horror, that well, the whole mood was ruined. . . . They became very circumspect. . . . That it was grisly and how could such a thing be possible and whether we had known anything about it. We said as for known, one heard something and guessed and so. There had been rumors. But one never knew anything definitely. It was also too dangerous. One could not ask. . . . Well, I already knew it. I knew such places existed, where they first did euthanasia. . . . They did away with it later, because the people began to rebel. Then they built the camps. One knew of Dachau. . . . And one knew that in Poland were camps. But how it all was and who. . . . Of course we were horrified. . . . If you asked, you'd simply be taken away. . . . [The Americans] were really beside themselves with horror. Because they could not comprehend it. They were from some American . . . God knows where, Middle West or somewhere. Never heard of such a thing in all their lives. . . . And then were confronted with such atrocities. . . . Of course it made me feel awful. . . . But what could you say? We were Germans. And this happened in our . . . not in our country because all the extermination camps were in Poland.[9]

In both East and West it was the children who, in the first days of the invasion, fared best at the hands of the Allied conquerors. American GIs threw bread, packages of cheese and crackers, chocolates, and cigarettes to them from their advancing tanks. The ban on American fraternization with German children, nowhere observed by the soldiers, was, of necessity, lifted at General Eisenhower's suggestion on June 11.[10] The Russians had a soft spot for children too. Even the most horrific accounts of Red Army actions are interrupted by reports of extraordinary kindnesses toward young people. To the surprise of many Hitler Youth boys, the enemy, when first encountered, did not treat them as Goebbels's propaganda had led them to expect. Allied troops in general felt pity for the malnourished youngsters in man-sized uniforms and huge helmets, who often burst into tears when faced with capture and death. Sixteen-year-old Lothar Loewe, fighting in Berlin, was amazed when Russian soldiers, after, predictably, taking his ring and watch, "pressed two packs of cigarettes" into his hand and then took him to a Red Army field hospital, where his wounds were treated and he was fed. For Loewe, "the image of the Soviet sub-humans I had carried with me" collapsed:

> The average Russian sympathized with young boys like us, and there were quite a few of us in this campaign. . . . I had neither mess kit nor a spoon. I had nothing. And it was this Bolshevik, this person I'd always believed to be a monster, who lent me, the Nordic German, his mess kit and spoon to eat with. I had seen many Soviet POWs . . . I had seen how they were treated . . . they were made to look like the sub-humans we imagined them to be. The idea that a German soldier would give a Russian prisoner his mess kit to eat from was unimaginable to me. And the fact that this Soviet gave me his, voluntarily, happily, because he felt sorry for me, shook my foundations of my image of them. That's when I told myself that maybe the Soviets were much different from what they told us to believe.[11]

American troops, perhaps unaware that eighty or ninety HJ boys had been killed, and many more wounded, fighting against them in Nuremberg, cut off the bottoms of the oversized uniform pants the young boys were wearing and laughingly told them, "Go home to your mother."[12] Other Allied units, moving along at great speed during the combat phase, simply put the HJ boys to work. Walker Hancock, assigned to protect the cathedral at Aachen from the artillery fire still being exchanged by the armies, tracked down the HJ group that had been doing fire duty on the ancient building's roof, and ordered them back to their posts, but this time in civilian clothes. The frightened boys, who had clearly thought they were being arrested, were instead given passes and a month's supply of food by the U.S. Army, and proudly obeyed.[13]

As they moved into the fallen Reich, members of all the Allied armies collected young "mascots" without much thought about the children's origins. American GIs, violating all regulations, successfully smuggled a nine-year-old Italian boy back to Boston, where his adoption became a cause célèbre. Other boys attached themselves to the troops in Germany, who not only dressed them in miniature uniforms, sometimes complete with sidearms, but also provided them with PX cards and plied them with cigarettes, food, and candy. The soldiers encouraged the children to pretend that they were Americans and built up their hopes of "going home" to the United States by teaching them English and coaching them on Americanisms. These deceptions were easily revealed, and the sudden demobiliza-

*Hitler Youth soldiers taken prisoner
by the U.S. Army.*

tions of their mentors left many of the mascots abandoned and defiant.
For these "invariably . . . interesting and attractive" boys, who were "usually precocious, pathetically self-sufficient, bold, aggressive, and demanding, as they had been thoroughly spoiled by their units," a special school
was eventually established under the auspices of the YMCA in order to
"de-mascot" them.[14]

The treatment of German child soldiers was not always so gentle. The
revelation of the truth about Hitler and the regime to which they had
dedicated their lives was especially devastating to those members of the
HJ and BDM who had taken their indoctrination to heart. In Munich,
American forces captured a group of boys aged ten to fourteen who had
been ordered to defend a barricade across the Maximilian Bridge. When
American tanks came into view, the boys had been too scared to fire and
had been captured. The next day the terrified young prisoners were taken
to Dachau. There they were marched through a silent mass of staring
inmates to a train standing on a siding within the camp: "An American
soldier . . . ordered us to open one of the freight carriages . . . the first
thing that fell out was the skeleton of a woman. After that nothing more
fell out, for the dead bodies were standing so close to one another, like

sardines, that one supported the other." After this the boys were shown the crematorium, which was scattered with half-burned bodies. That night they could not sleep: "The impact of what we had seen was too great to be immediately digested," one of the boys later said. "I could not help but cry."[15]

Fear led many higher-level HJ members who were not captured in battle to go underground. Alfons Heck, seventeen, smitten, as we have seen, since the age of ten with adoration of Hitler, after having graduated to the Luftwaffe from Westwall construction, was suddenly returned home in March 1945 and made HJ Bannführer of his region, a job that theoretically gave him command over 6,000 girls and boys. His "troops" were largely imaginary, but Heck was ordered to deploy those he could find against American forces penetrating the Rhineland. In this command capacity, he was involved in several skirmishes and placed fellow HJ boys as young as fourteen in bunkers where, aiding the regular forces, they were to slow down American tank units with Panzerfausts. After a few weeks, he was recalled to the Luftwaffe and, hoping for flight duty, eagerly volunteered to fight to the last. His wiser commander, knowing that western Germany was about to be overrun by the Americans, assigned Heck to a useless mission that included a mandatory "furlough" in his hometown, which, as the commander had known it would be, was taken the day after the boy arrived there.

Like millions of his compatriots, Heck burned his HJ uniform, buried the Luftwaffe one, and stayed out of sight. After a time, fearful of what he might face, he finally ventured out of the house. The Americans in the town, thinking him a farm boy, paid no attention to him at all until he answered a question in English. This caused the astonished HJ leader to be appointed interpreter for the town commander. His equally surprised fellow citizens did not give him away. When the fact that he was a member of the Luftwaffe was discovered by the Americans, who still had no inkling of his HJ connection, Heck was told to give himself up as a POW. But the next town commander also found the boy's language skills useful, and sent him to work in a field hospital. The Americans did not start serious de-Nazification until after the surrender, and even then, those over eighteen were investigated first. Heck was finally denounced by someone in his town and was arrested when the French took over the area in the summer of 1945. They were not so forgiving. The former HJ leader was told that he would be executed and was put in solitary confinement. The sentence was not carried out, but a military court did sentence him to two years restriction to the town, six months expulsion from school, and a month of hard

and nasty labor, which included exhuming and reburying the bodies of
French POWs killed in an air raid. Heck and other HJ members were, like
most Germans, forced to watch films of the liberation of the death camps
that, still unable to feel anything beyond anger at their own defeat and
betrayal by their leaders, they refused for a long time to believe were
authentic.[16]

Older members of the HJ and BDM leadership were detained if they
were identified, but this also did not happen immediately. BDM leader
Melita Maschmann, who had been so active in Poland, now well into her
twenties, fled into the Austrian mountains with a group of SS officers. She
had nowhere else to go: her parents had been killed in a bombing raid. In
this redoubt the renegades lived miserably in a hut, drank a lot, wallowed
in self-pity, and tried to maintain the Nazi structure of their lives. They
also discussed joining possible resistance operations linked to the so-called
Werewolf units, which Himmler had set up in late 1944. The Allies were
greatly worried by German radio propaganda about the Werewolves. A
few such units, made up of teenaged operatives, were indeed mobilized
and trained by the SS. The largest, Battle Group Harz, made up of 600 HJ
members, including some NAPOLA students, was decimated early on by
American forces. Two survivors, aged sixteen and seventeen, who managed to hide out until June 1945, were caught and executed as spies.
There were sporadic murders and sabotage efforts by a few fanatic Werewolves, but after the death of Hitler they found little support from their
countrymen, and soon disappeared.[17] Maschmann came down from the
mountains when Allied patrols began to round up her fellow renegades.
She wandered around southern Germany until July 1945, when she was
caught and put in a prison for high-ranking Nazi women.[18]

The Allies were not quite sure what to do with the families of the Nazi
leaders. Few had followed Goebbels's example when it came to their offspring. Speer had moved his wife and six children up to the Baltic coast,
hoping, successfully, that they would fall into the hands of the British.
Göring's wife and daughter were arrested with him in Austria and sent at
first to live in a cottage on one of his many estates. Himmler's wife and
defiant daughter, arrested in Italy, would spend many months in detention. Some of the children were alone at the end. Martin Bormann's eldest
son, also named Martin, a fifteen-year-old student at the elite Nazi school
that before the war had sponsored the exchanges with American prep
schools, was moved to the Tyrol with a number of other students. There,
Nazi party officials gave him money and false documents and sent him off

on his own. He was taken in by a farmer who did not know who he was. Later, during the Nuremberg trials, most of the wives of the leaders were detained and interrogated. Arrangements for their children were haphazard. Edda Göring, aged seven, was first placed in an orphanage and then sent to join her mother in prison. Bormann's wife, who had fled with her other eight children, was less fortunate: the children were left behind when she was arrested, and it was only with help from a prison chaplain that she managed to send word to a former housekeeper, who went to care for them. Mrs. Bormann never saw them again. She died in prison, after which the children were placed in foster families. Martin Jr., still in hiding on the farm, learned of this, and later of his father's death sentence in absentia, from the newspapers. Once his identity was revealed, the boy was also interrogated by the Allies, but he could not provide them with any information about his father, who had disappeared at the fall of Berlin. After his release, young Bormann was accepted at a seminary and became a priest. By late 1946, most of the families had been freed and could go home, if they still had one. Some were allowed to live in small houses on their former properties while Allied officers were billeted in the main dwellings. Others would find more anonymous quarters. The children, who knew little of their fathers' activities, would eventually go on to school and to varied futures, but would never be free of the world's terrible curiosity.[19]

Young people under eighteen who were in mainstream German combat units were treated as regular prisoners of war. Like the Germans before them, the British and Americans were not prepared for the huge number of POWs they had to care for while the war still went on. The German prisoners were herded into enclosures that each held tens of thousands of men. On the way they were fed very little, if anything. In the big "cages" there was no shelter, and the prisoners, often lacking coats or blankets, were sometimes so crowded that they could hardly lie down, which was not desirable anyway in what was usually mud. These enclosures were little better than those set up by the Nazis, the difference being that the German POWs were generally moved on to better facilities after a fairly short time. As one progressed up the ladder of camps, rations improved very gradually, but weakness, and especially exposure, caused thousands of deaths. Large contingents of POWs were sent to France as forced labor and housed in compounds where the camp guards were mostly liberated Eastern European forced laborers who took considerable sadistic pleasure in making life as miserable as possible for their former captors. But the treatment they received in France, though frequently brutal, was fine indeed compared to that in the USSR, from which many thousands never returned.

The British maintained a number of German military units intact as "Disarmed German Troops" under strictly supervised German command. These groups also were short on food, and the ravenous young soldiers, who were not kept in enclosures, soon resorted to stealing from local farmers and other illegal foraging. Incessant drills were held for a time in an effort to maintain discipline. Former Jungvolk leader Jürgen Herbst, conscripted into the Wehrmacht at the very end of hostilities, thought his captured unit was being prepared for a possible defense of the British Zone from the Russians, but the military exercises soon evolved into hard labor restoring Germany's devastated infrastructure. None of the POWs were allowed to send or receive letters or even to inform their families that they were alive, but in the West their incarceration was short-lived, and most of those who were not known to have been in Nazi formations such as the SS would be released by the late fall of 1945.[20]

Once the basic elements of control were in place in Germany, the Allies turned to plans for its future. In the months preceding the surrender, the Allied governments had tried without much success to agree on precisely what would be done with the conquered Reich. Arguments raged over which of its parts would be controlled by each of the victors, and over the issue of reparations. But there was general agreement that Hitler's empire should be dismembered, disarmed, de-Nazified, and have its economic power severely curtailed. Henry Morgenthau, President Roosevelt's Secretary of the Treasury, had early on proposed a draconian plan, remarkably similar to that proposed by the Nazis for Eastern Europe, which would reduce Germany to a totally agrarian economy and allow conscription of its workers by Allied nations. By the time of the Yalta Conference, in February 1945, these ideas, which were not considered advisable by others in the Roosevelt administration, had been modified, but the main American directive for the arriving Military Government, approved on May 11, 1945, still declared that Germany would "not be occupied for the purpose of liberation, but as a defeated enemy nation," and that it should be brought home to the Germans that they "cannot escape responsibility for what they have brought upon themselves."[21]

In practical terms, as far as daily life was concerned, the directive meant that the mass of Germans now had to face many of the same problems their government had imposed on the nations it had conquered. The directive declared that no action would be taken to "support living conditions in Germany . . . on a higher level than those existing in any one of the neighboring United Nations." For the time being, the German population was to be allowed fuel and food rations sufficient only to prevent "starvation or widespread disease or such civil unrest as would endanger the occupying forces." That food was to come from Germany's own economy, and any "surpluses" could be used by the Allies to feed themselves or the DPs and POWs.[22] Viable dwellings and public buildings could be requisitioned at a few hours' notice by the Allied military governments. Once again, families being evicted from their houses were watched carefully lest they remove beds and other necessities of life. Where the evicted went was their problem. There were, at first, no camps of any kind for these new refugees, who generally crammed themselves in with relatives and friends. And, once again, the incoming tenants could be faced with awful human problems. Ruth Anderson, posted to Berlin to work for the Allied Control Authority, was placed in a house with no hot water or window glass, but with the services of an ancient maid who had worked there for years. The owners had been killed by the Russians and were buried in the garden. To Miss Anderson fell the terrible duty of informing the couple's son, a returning POW who appeared at the door, that his parents were dead. To make things worse, she then had to tell him that he could not stay in his dead parents' requisitioned house.[23]

More precise policy for Germany was to be defined at the final summit meeting of the Great Powers scheduled for July 1945 in Potsdam. There, the policy of total suppression of German industry was modified to allow the development of a more balanced economy and the production of consumer goods. The Western Allies, at this stage, advocated a single economy for all of Germany. That would never come to pass, due to the Soviets' refusal to participate. For the same reason, the Allied Control Council, set up to run Germany as a whole, never had any real power, and each Allied nation essentially ran its zone as it pleased. This would immediately create enormous problems, especially when it came to interzonal distribution of food and fuel. The problems would be exacerbated a hundredfold by another Potsdam decision, which authorized the expulsion back to Germany proper of all the ethnic Germans still living in Poland, Czechoslovakia, and Hungary, including the millions recently moved into those areas by the Nazi racial agencies.

The expulsion idea seemed a fine one to all of Germany's recent victims. Czechoslovakia and Poland had been planning revenge for the Nazi

takeover of their territory and the expulsion of their people throughout
the war. Brutal uprooting and detention of ethnic Germans, using all the
methods perfected by the Nazis short of gassing and cremation, began as
soon as German power was overturned, sometimes in incidents so violent
that Allied troops were forced to intervene. As usual, tens of thousands of
children and other innocents were swept up in the murderous process.[24]
The Allied leaders, after much debate, supported the expulsion policy for
reasons of their own. The Soviet Union simply wanted the Germans out of
its newly extended sphere of influence, and some British and American
diplomats thought that the removal of German minorities from the
nations bordering the former Reich would promote future stability, particularly in the large chunk of eastern Germany being ceded to Poland. Winston Churchill had opposed both the cession of German territory to
Poland and the expulsion of the inhabitants, and correctly foresaw that the
influx of millions more refugees into Germany would be disastrous, but he
was voted out of office in the middle of the conference and his views did
not prevail.[25] Both Truman and Churchill had flown over Germany and
toured Berlin. The devastation they had seen shocked them, though not
enough, apparently, to cause Truman to think twice a few days later, when
he would authorize the use of the atomic bomb on Japan. Though they too
believed that the Germans "had brought this on themselves," the difficulty
of life in such a wasteland was obvious. The resettlement policy was,
nonetheless, easily approved as Article XIII of the Potsdam Agreement,
which specified that the transfers should be "effected in an orderly and
humane manner." It also decreed that the incoming Germans should not
all be sent to one place, but that there should be "equitable distribution of
these Germans among the several zones of occupation" in order to lessen
the burden of their assimilation.[26]

The transfers were no small undertaking: 6.5 million people were to be
moved and would now join the 4 to 5 million who had started back months
before and were far from settled. Allied personnel were unnerved by the
ubiquitous, pitiful groups: "To be compelled daily to see people struggling
from place to place under back-breaking loads is awful. Many families can
move only at night in the unlit, cluttered streets. I have heard such expeditions—the creaking carts, the grunting exclamations of the mother, the
frightened outcries of the small children, the heavy breathing of the
grandparents as they try to help."[27]

All of the expellees would, in theory, be taken care of by the "old" Germans, who had not, however, been consulted about the whole idea, and
whose food situation had deteriorated steadily since the surrender. A spe-

cial Combined Repatriation Executive, quite separate from the simultaneous DP and infiltree operations, was set up in October 1945 to organize the German transfers. The new agency decided that from December 1, 1945, to July 31, 1946, 28,000 people a day should be moved into Germany. This theoretical schedule proved to be impossible in reality, and the first transfers, like the grim unofficial trainloads full of half-clothed and dying Germans that had been arriving for months, were certainly not "orderly and humane." An UNRRA worker reported: "Someone had put some German children on an unheated train and sent them to Germany from Austria. Two children died of the cold. Others were found to have their legs frozen. General Truscott is very upset, as indeed is everyone. . . . Surely such things should not happen."[28]

It was not surprising that they did. Those loading the trains in the expelling countries had no sympathy for Germans, and Allied coordinators were exhausted after months of fourteen-hour days, working on the logistics of the successive waves of vast human transfers. Enforcing the transportation regulations was challenging to one's humanity. One Allied train commander had to order a boxcar holding thirty-five women and children, which had been procured and somehow illegally attached to his train by a German refugee and a German Red Cross nurse, to be detached and left on a siding. It seemed cruel, but as Ruth Anderson put it, "You can't have little groups of people everywhere trying to get home, hitching their freezing box cars to Allied trains." Later she described her fellow workers in the office that arranged the eternal trains as having

> frequent blind spots about the problems of individuals or groups of individuals—it means one's back turned on the grittiness of life in the . . . camps—often no food—no clothing—no petrol—it means an attitude that says sure move 'em, and by God it moves 'em and dumps them out in some God-forsaken spot and heaves the sigh of relief for the job well done. It means . . . a group of people who are tired and depressed and satiated and want to go home. I'm talking about the US Army now—who see things here for what they are—who can't cope with it—who haven't much confidence in those who are coping.[29]

But those who were coping were aware enough of the terrible conditions on the trains and at the arrival points to delay the expellee program until after the worst of the winter was over. To the problem of cold was added a shortage of trains, which were also busy carrying DPs and POWs back and forth, so that large numbers of expellees were not moved until March 1946. By the summer, 10,000 people a day were being transferred into the U.S. Zone, which would receive 1.5 million expellees by October. The process was temporarily halted at that time, as there were some 100,000 refugees stuck in transit camps for whom no lodgings could be found in German communities.[30] The British reported 1.2 million new arrivals in their zone by the end of August 1946, not including those who had come by "illegal movement." Because able-bodied men tended to be kept back for forced labor, 80 percent of the expellees were women, children, and old people, who were "undernourished" and arrived in "an exhausted condition." Poorly clothed and with few possessions, the old were incapable of "any form of heavy work" and the women who could work "are accompanied by young children."[31] The Soviets too would receive 2.4 million in their zone by the spring of 1947. In addition to the expellees authorized by Potsdam, tens of thousands of POWs and "obnoxious" Germans were being returned to the homeland from nations around the world, 17,000 of the latter from the Netherlands alone,[32] and all of them would have to be fed and housed.

The idea was that the new arrivals would be spread out so as not to form "ghettos" or minority enclaves of any kind. A British publication said that it "was to be hoped that a future central Government in Germany would make sure that those expatriated should remain where they are now: in the heart of Germany, scattered among the original inhabitants where there is a hope that within the lifetime of one, two or, at the most three generations they will be absorbed by the people and only faint memories of their origin remain."[33] Responsibility for settling the new arrivals was given to local German authorities. Hitler's desire to bring together all those of Germanic blood had finally been achieved, but, alas, without the necessary *Lebensraum*.

Processing the new Germans was much the same as it had been in the Nazi empire. In five huge and horribly crowded centers, the hapless families were once more paraded past officials who gave them physical examinations, delousing, new documents, and various classifications. From there they were sent to subcamps across Germany, where they would await lodging, usually with indigenous families. The only trouble was that their fellow Germans were not in the least pleased to have whole families thrust into their communities, much less into their households. U.S. Military Government reports alluded diplomatically to "discord" and "initial lack of mutual understanding." A German cardinal was blunter, noting in August 1946 that "there was scarcely a German family living alone; of course they quarrel, and homes are disrupted"; and the *New York Times* reported that police had to be called at times to "stimulate the hospitality of reluctant householders."[34] In many communities, the expellees were treated like vagrants, and to be called *Evakuierte* was not a compliment. In one town the "old" residents put up this sign, not exactly welcoming, at the railroad station where the expellees arrived: WHEN THE RESETTLERS CAME AND THE BARK BEETLES MOVED IN, THAT WAS THE END OF PEACE AND QUIET. The old residents were not joking:

> When my parents arrived, the rain was coming down in torrents and people wouldn't let them in. They just left them standing outside. . . . The sacks they brought along were completely wet. Until my sister went for help to the district council . . . then someone came to help them. He got them inside by force. Then the electricity was turned off, they had a type of fuse for this purpose . . . and we had to pay five marks for electricity. It was not a good relationship we had then.[35]

For the exhausted incoming Germans, the shock of reality, in what years of propaganda had implied was the Nordic Valhalla, was devastating. Nazi propaganda radio had never revealed the true extent of the bombing damage to Berlin and other major cities, nor the near-total destruction of industry and food production. There were numerous incidents of Sudeten farmers attempting to return to their lands, and even rustling incidents in which they tried to round up their former herds and drive them back into Germany.[36] But for most, there was no alternative to the forced migration.

In September 1946, a Dr. Neckar, President of the Düsseldorf District, wrote to the British Military Government that the "absorbtive capacity" of his area was "exhausted." Many people had therefore "been conveyed to cellars and bunkers." He had done a lot of calculations and could report that certain communities were 112.47 percent, 116.93 percent, and 118.53 percent above their 1939 populations, while 45 percent of the housing was destroyed (2 percent) or partially damaged (43 percent). Furthermore, he complained, "the precipitated and . . . often compulsory conveys to private lodgings are spoiling the relations between the population and the refugees in the very beginning already" and had not only caused "increased listlessness" and "decreased will to deliver goods" on the part of the farmers but had led to multiple thefts. Dr. Neckar, still writing in a rather predefeat, dictatorial style, requested that the British "see to it" that no more refugees be sent, "as the people can no longer be sheltered in a way worthy of human beings," and he added that it was "fully beyond discussion" that the living space allotted to each person be limited to four square meters, "for it is unworthy of human beings to be folded like that. If this would be carried through not only every domestic life would be eradicated but also the men themselves would be completely worn down physically and psychically." All of which, of course, was true, as so many millions of victims of the Nazis already knew.[37]

Space was not the worst problem, however. In the chaos of the postwar months, most people's lives were dominated by the procurement of food. By the summer of 1945, whatever reserves of food individual Germans had been able to salt away were much reduced or gone, especially in urban areas. Given the destruction of transportation capacity and the fact that crops had not been planted during the combat phase, plus the disappearance of foreign forced labor and every form of normal commerce, Germans had little improvement in view. At the beginning, the American Military Government was not prepared to provide food to Germans except in "acute emergencies," even if they were children.[38]

Ten-year-old Wolfgang Samuel, who had fled with his mother and grandmother ahead of the Red Army, was lucky, as they had found a Wehrmacht supply wagon full of food, pulled by two big horses, for their journey. Just east of Lübeck they ran into the Americans, who directed them to a farm that was serving as a holding camp for a motley assortment of groups, including a captured SS detachment, Polish DPs, and Italian POWs. The Nazi prisoners and non-German groups were fed by the Allies and gradually taken off to other camps or released. After that, American soldiers still were present outside the gates of the farm, but they did not distribute any food or water to the German refugees, and there was nothing for sale anywhere. The local people, once again, were not helpful even to these refugees who only needed food, ignoring them "as if we didn't exist":

> They, too, were Germans, but to them we were nothing. We were like foul air—an invisible, stinking presence. They milked their cows, but gave us no milk even when we begged for it. They had potatoes, carrots and beets for themselves and the animals, but they shared none with us.[39]

Wolfgang and his mother survived on their supply wagon stores and shared what they could. Eventually they managed to make friends with a

*A GI applies bug spray around garbage cans marked to inform
the hungry German population of their contents.*

nearby farmer, who took care of their hungry horses and invited them to
eat with him. Soon there was an outbreak of cholera in the camp, and children began to die. The Americans and British still did nothing. In July, the
Americans left the town, which was to be taken over by the Russians. Most
of the refugees immediately followed, but Wolfgang and his mother did
not go far enough and were caught in the Soviet Zone. In the following
months, they continued to be treated like pariahs by the local Germans
and terrorized by the Russians; Frau Samuel almost died of cholera.
Defeated, the family returned to the East German town from which their
flight had begun months before. They would finally escape to the British
Zone, on foot, and in a blizzard, in late December 1946.[40] There they
would be less afraid, but no better fed.

As had been the case in Athens and the Netherlands, the lack of
rationed food led to an explosion of the black market, which, even though
it was strictly prohibited by the Allied authorities, was heavily exploited by
members of the occupation forces, and was universally acknowledged as
having kept millions of Germans alive. By October 1945, the food ration
for Germans was 1,300 calories a day, about one-third the normal GI
ration of 3,600, and well below that of the DPs. Allied military authorities
knew that even this low standard was often not met, and that it would be
difficult to maintain through the winter. In August, a young aide visiting

Berlin with a group of congressmen who were looking at DP camps had been surprised to see that the Germans looked worse than the DPs, whom he had found pathetic enough:

> I studied the passing Germans on the street. . . . Two days in Berlin failed to produce over one fat or well-fed native. The children and women have skinny legs and hollow cheeks. Their eyes are dark and sunken. Their hair lacks any luster. . . . I am not soft and I still have deep resentment toward Germans as a whole, but when you see these stalking Zombies, gray with the pallor of the starved, yet clean and washed as always, you must submerge your hatred and accept the fact that fellow humans, right or wrong, are suffering. You must accept, too, that long before the coming winter has passed many of these humans will have died of hunger, starvation and cold . . . for no German will get any coal this winter.[41]

The Western Allies had not been unprepared for hunger in Germany. They had arrived with 600,000 tons of grain, which was divided among the Western zones. But in their prewar planning they had not counted on the enormous influxes of refugees or the fact that no food would come from the Soviet Zone, which had huge agricultural areas. Requests for more aid from the United States and Britain in November 1945 were not fruitful; food production in all war zones had been disrupted, and even the United States was feeling the pinch. To conserve both food and fuel, the American Military Government set up community kitchens for Germans, who were still required to use ration coupons and pay for their meals. More than 4.5 million such meals were served each month in Bavaria alone.[42] Army messes went so far as to mark their garbage cans "edible" or "nonedible," and leftovers were distributed daily to institutions. In December, a few private relief agencies were authorized to send supplies to particularly stricken areas. Sometimes it was easier to move the hungry to the food: in the appropriately named Operation Stork, the British evacuated 20,000 babies from Berlin to the Western zones.[43]

In February 1946, an Allied official in Berlin confided "in a whisper" to a colleague he met in a bar that he "was supposed to be in charge of rationing, and there wasn't anything to ration."[44] In March, General Lucius Clay, the American Military Governor, emphasizing that the "suffering was real" and that incoming stocks were nearly depleted, once again appealed for food shipments. A commission led by former President Herbert Hoover, who, at Truman's request, had gone to Europe to look into the food situation, agreed that the situation in Germany was grim. By now, the Americans, not as immune as the Nazis to massive death tolls, were beginning to waver on the economic punishment of Germany. In both April and May 1946, Clay was forced to reduce the minimum ration and dig into the Army's own supplies to sustain even the new calorie low. Assistant Secretary of War McCloy had already said that industry must be restored, "unless we are to establish permanent soup kitchen feeding." He and many others felt that Germany could not be kept in "medieval isolation," and that unless normal commerce was restored there would be "collapse and progressive physical and social deterioration of the people in an area whose influence is such that it will set the level of European living so low that we also will be demoralized by it."[45] All agreed that lack of food might cause unrest and require "a larger army of occupation for a longer period of time,"[46] not a popular idea back in the United States. Germans had been heard to say that they had been better fed under the Nazis, and no one wanted a repeat of the post–World War I conditions, which might lead to the rise of another Hitler or, more importantly in 1946, to empowerment of the Communists.

Hoover, meanwhile, had some success. Both Britain, which had very severe rationing itself, and the United States delved into their national reserves in the first half of 1946 and allocated grain for Europe, most of which would go to Germany.[47] Publicity generated by Hoover's activities and by numerous congressional junkets also stimulated the traditional aid agencies in the United States, which were already involved in relief efforts in the rest of Europe. The ban on such private relief was lifted and the groups were allowed to combine into the Council of Relief Agencies Licensed to Operate in Germany, or CRALOG, which would send its first shipment of clothes, food, and medical supplies to Bremen in April 1946. The agency, which was made up of fifteen disparate organizations such as the American Friends Service Committee, the International Rescue and Relief Committee, labor unions, all sorts of church groups, and the Russian Children's Welfare Society, would soon be joined by other aid co-ops, including the International Red Cross, representing non-American groups, and later by CARE (Cooperative for American Remittances to Europe), which would be permitted to send its soon-to-be-famous packages to Germans starting in June 1946.[48]

All these efforts were a good beginning, but still not enough. An investigation in Mannheim revealed that 60 percent of individuals who received physical examinations showed signs of rickets. Just how dire the need had become, particularly where children were concerned, was made clear in

England by a series of passionate articles, letters, and photographs published by an unlikely source. Victor Gollancz, an English Jew, visited the British Zone in late October 1946. He was appalled by the physical condition of the children he saw. He also found the often luxurious lifestyle of some of the officers of the Allied armies to be an unattractive contrast to the abject situation of the Germans. Taken around the most devastated areas of a number of cities by Salvation Army and Red Cross workers, Gollancz described dreadful conditions. Thousands lived in damp and moldy basements with virtually no sanitation. He saw numerous cases of hunger edema, tuberculosis, and malnutrition. In the awful cellars he visited, people were jammed together in far less than the four square meters that had been declared inadequate in Düsseldorf:

> We went down two long flights of stairs to an awful couple of rooms below. There was, of course, no natural light, and no ventilation of any kind. The place, which had recently been flooded for four weeks, was inhabited by two women and five children belonging to two different families. Every inch of room was crammed with furniture and beds in double tiers. The lavatory was a pail. I ventured into a wet, disused room with a curtain over the entrance; the stench was so frightful that I had to suck lozenges all the way back. One of the women was pregnant. A child, whose face was covered with sores, played with my torch and called me "uncle"; he wouldn't let me go. We visited cellar after cellar of this type; some of them were wonderfully clean, and on occasion decorated with home-made silhouette pictures, photographs and the like. Crucifixes were frequent. The worst place, I think, was a cellar of two rooms divided by a long wet passage without light of any kind. A mother lived in one room, her daughter with several children in the other. They were cheerful. Down below, somewhere else, was an injured woman, who couldn't move from her bed except with the aid of two sticks; she smiled at first, but presently began to sob, and kept repeating "*Alles verloren.*" . . . All of them were grateful, terribly grateful, when they were given something.[49]

Nowhere was there enough food or any other basic necessity. Over and over again, Gollancz met mothers who had returned home empty-handed after hours of standing in line for bread. Items such as shoes, diapers, and baby clothes were simply not obtainable. There were clothes held in stock by UNRRA and sent in by American relief agencies, but the Germans, and especially the refugees, got last choice after DPs and certain essential workers such as miners. A British welfare officer, imploring his headquarters for clothes, wrote in November 1946, "My argument is that the DP is now fairly well clothed and the need of the definitely unclothed refugee child is much greater."[50]

The winter of 1946–47 was far worse than the one before. Food allocations were minimal for all of Europe, and Allied Military Government officials, whose own rations were also limited, were constantly confronted with desperately hungry Germans:

> While I stood with my rations in my arms, a woman with a little boy came up and asked me for food . . . one does what one can, but it's impossible to take on the whole German people. We are permitted $40 apiece at the Commissary and the prices have jumped up so high . . . that buying quite modestly . . . I have already exceeded our $80 limit for March . . . and we must eat on $65 next month in consequence. All of this doesn't leave too much extra to give largesse.[51]

In May 1947, Churchill described starving Europe as "a rubble heap, a charnel house, a breeding ground of pestilence and hate." American Secretary of State George Marshall had also been appalled at the conditions he had seen. Amid rising fears of the total collapse of Western Europe, Truman and Marshall initiated planning for the massive aid program that would come to be called the Marshall Plan.[52] While their discussions were progressing, Hoover persuaded Congress to allow the Army to set up a child-feeding program in the German schools. The program, which used 40,000 tons of Army rations and other food, made possible a tiny daily 350-calorie lunch for some 3.5 million German children in the combined British and American zones. Military Governor Clay thought this program had "saved the health of German youth." The food ration would improve with terrible slowness from then on: the magic number of 2,000 calories, considered the minimum sufficient for maintenance, would not be reached until the summer of 1948.[53]

The collapse of the Nazi regime and its highly regimented school and youth activities had left German children in a state of limbo. There were no more HJ and BDM meetings and duties, and the total immersion in the final defense of the homeland, which had occupied everyone at the end, was over. In its place was unaccustomed leisure time. The disillusionment and letdown were especially hard for teenagers. The uniforms, the parades, the mass intoxication, and the excitement that living in extreme danger with one's peers can give were all gone. There were few older people to talk to about what had happened. Parents and relatives retreated into protective silences and concentrated on the basics of living. In the cities, supervision was minimal in the many single-parent households (if a cellar under a bombed house can be so described), usually run by mal-nourished women working at whatever job they could find as they waited for husbands to return from POW camps or other incarcerations. There were hundreds of thousands of homeless and orphaned children in the ruins and the countryside. Nine hundred young "vagrants" were picked up in Munich in April 1945 alone. The Bavarian Red Cross listed 11,000 in its region and set up shelters for them. The director of one such home said that the boys he encountered, in the seventeen- to twenty-one-year-old range, were "completely cold and blasé, entirely calculating in what they do. They have lost every feeling of relationship with their homeland and home, with parents and relatives, even with their mothers. Memories mean nothing to them. Their only interests are food, sleep, money and girls."[54]

The British Red Cross found 2,000 highly indoctrinated, uniformed KLV boys and girls, evacuated from bombing zones by the German gov-ernment, who had been marooned in homes in Austria. Thirteen hundred were sent home; the rest were collected in a school run by the Quakers to await processing. The mood was not cheery. The young people, aged ten to eighteen, were all too aware of Germany's defeat and felt hopeless about the future. Some had been away from home for three years. They disliked the British and were contemptuous of the obsequiousness toward the Allies so common among their elders. The wise Quakers decided to combine fun and work and avoid all ideology. The children chopped wood, set up a theater, and decorated rooms. There was a Christmas pageant, presents came from England, and British soldiers handed out food. And gradually, "these boys and girls realized that outside the Nazi world there was another and a wider one in which it was pleasant to live."[55]

By 1945 the Save the Children Fund in Aachen was running a recep-tion center for more than 20,000 children, many of whom had been left alone when their parents were sent to jail. Gang life had great appeal to those young people whose lives no longer had any structure. Most chil-dren involved in acts of petty theft were looking for food either to eat or to sell on the black market. Some were sent on bartering expeditions by their families. One gang near Aachen specialized in smuggling food in from Belgium, an enterprise that required frequent illegal crossings of the fron-tier. The border guards, perfectly aware of what was going on, did not arrest very many. Some of the foraging was less innocent: a group of enterprising boys of about thirteen learned how to control railway signals so that they could stop and loot trains.[56]

There was more defiance in the Soviet Zone, where small gangs of fifteen- to seventeen-year-old former HJ and BDM members spent a lot of time painting anti-Soviet graffiti and making rude remarks during the propagandistic newsreels shown at the movies. They sang Nazi songs, interrupted speeches at meetings held by the Free German Youth, the new Soviet-approved youth organization, and were generally obnoxious. There were a few cases of groups of boys beating up Red Army soldiers. The Soviet NKVD was not amused. Hundreds were arrested on the grounds that they were part of the Werewolf organization. This was probably not the case, but the punishment was severe. The teenagers were taken off to places unknown, without any legal procedures, and were not allowed to communicate with their parents. It is not clear if most went to the USSR or to the camps at Buchenwald and Sachsenhausen, among others, which the Russians had recycled and found quite handy as an addition to the Gulag. A number were released after a time, but most would remain in detention until 1948, when a general amnesty and end to de-Nazification was declared in the Soviet Zone.[57]

It was clear to all the Allies that the revival and de-Nazification of the school system was essential for the rehabilitation of German youth. Each of the four Allied nations would attempt to guide German policy for the new schools after its own fashion, particularly by setting up teacher training programs and later encouraging exchange programs abroad. But in the chaos of defeated Germany any major transformations were pushed aside for years by basic issues. In all zones new textbooks, cleansed of Nazi propaganda, and de-Nazified teachers were a primary requirement. The first new school in Western-occupied Germany, for 1,000 children in grades one through four, opened on June 4, 1945, in Aachen, which had been taken by the Allies the previous October. The local Military Government detachment had managed to have 40,000 textbooks printed in London, found a half-Jewish school superintendent, and recruited twenty-six middle-aged, non-Nazi former housewives as teachers.[58] This sort of efficiency would be hard to duplicate on a larger scale, when millions of students were involved. School buildings were virtually nonexistent. In Cologne, 92 percent of them had been destroyed, and in many places any intact structures were being used for military purposes or had become DP housing. There was a huge shortage of paper for new textbooks. Both Soviet and American education officers reverted for a time to Weimar-period texts, even though they were full of militarism and negative allusions to Allied policy after World War I. Sometimes they were forced to simply tear acceptable pages out of the Nazi books and glue them together.[59]

Despite these difficulties, elementary schools were opened in all zones by the early fall of 1945. De-Nazified teachers were few, and vetting in the face of such great need was not always careful. Many teachers had to be brought back from the ranks of the retired and were challenged by enormous classes of as many as seventy-five streetwise children. The lack of classroom space required children in most areas to go to school in shifts. In the bombed-out areas of Hamburg, Victor Gollancz found a school for 800 pupils set up in a dank and windowless air-raid bunker. Everywhere, the schools lacked adequate sanitation and even lightbulbs. Concentration was not easy: there was no heat, and the hungry children had few warm clothes. Shoes were even scarcer. In some families, one pair of shoes was shared by several children, who took turns going to school.

Secondary schools and universities began to open by December 1945. For thousands who had not been to school for two years, high school was a matter of making up what they had missed and escaping into such non-combative subjects as music and poetry. In the university towns, food shortages and the lack of decent lodging dampened college life. De-Nazification of faculty was uneven at best: newspaper stories reported eugenics professors teaching much as before, and there was considerable dissembling by university administrations. The presence in the student body of many recently demobilized soldiers, angry at their nation's defeat, worried the Allied authorities. At a speech to the students of Erlangen, in February 1946, the famed pastor Martin Niemoller, speaking on collective responsibility for war guilt, was drowned out by the young men shuffling their boots on the floor.[60] The students were not pro-Nazi so much as irritated that their war service was not appreciated. But in general, they were simply glad to be free and avoided anything political or ideological in favor of the pure pragmatism of training themselves for individual survival. The collective life of Nazism, with its insistence on the sacrifice of self to one leader and his ideas, was over. The doctrine of glorious devotion to nation and race had disappeared in the terrible deaths of millions, and each of Germany's children would now have to find his own way to the future.

They would not have much help from their parents or their schools when it came to understanding and coming to terms with the Nazi era, and would live for a long time in a world of silence and veiled denial that would not begin to reveal the inner secrets of the Reich for many years.

In every zone, it was also evident that, in addition to school, some sort of controlled extracurricular youth activity was vital. Nonfraternization rules made this difficult to organize at first, as did the ban on participation by most HJ and former Wehrmacht members, especially as leaders or counselors. Catholic and Evangelical groups, which many suspected had continued to function underground all along, revived quickly. There were also socialist and Communist organizations and various other groups run by sports and labor organizations. The Soviets allowed the Free German Youth and unsuccessfully tried to promote local branches of their own Pioneers. The British, in particular, felt that a diversity of organizations and mutual tolerance were vital. All the organizations had to be registered in the British Zone; those that seemed too authoritarian, such as the Scouts and the Bündische Jugend, which wanted to have uniforms and "tests of courage" reminiscent of the past, were carefully watched.[61]

The American Military Government allowed many of the same organizations and set up a Youth Office, which was run by Germans. This agency often put children to work clearing public areas of war debris or helping craftsmen to restore schools. In Offenbach and Munich, children volunteered to collect medicinal plants for pharmacies and pick off potato bugs in the fields.[62] Alongside this official entity, local Army units, ignoring the nonfraternization rules, early on organized many kinds of informal programs for the children they found around them. GIs bulldozed rubble to make playgrounds, transformed ruins into weatherproof clubhouses, and gave Christmas parties featuring chocolate and toys. It soon became clear to the Military Government that such interaction, discouraged at first, was a good thing, and once the nonfraternization rules were abandoned, the Army efforts were greatly expanded and formalized in the German Youth Activities program. The GIs liked working with kids: "It keeps your mind off sex and desertion," one said. Soon the Germans were initiated into the mysteries of softball and American football, and there was even a Theater Athletic School in Stuttgart that trained coaches and put on tournaments.[63] Adults were sometimes resentful and suspicious of GYA activities, which they felt competed with German organizations. For their children, the food and clothes distributed by the GYA were probably more of an attraction than crafts or baseball. Nevertheless, there were many genuine gestures of appreciation on the part of the young people. In Darmstadt, 9,000 ten- to fourteen-year-olds made thousands of toys as Christmas presents for the children of the U.S. soldiers.[64] The Americans had their motives too: they wanted to get the gangs off the streets and prevent any revival of Hitler Youth activities. Things were improved by an amnesty in the Western zones for HJ and Wehrmacht members born after January 1, 1919, which the Americans passed in August 1946 and the British in May 1947, thereby ending the exclusion of many young people from numerous educational and vocational programs.

If there was a single thing that changed the feelings of German children toward the British and the Americans it was perhaps the Berlin Airlift, the extraordinary operation to keep the people of West Berlin alive when the Soviets tried to block access to the city by the Western Allies. For almost a year, day and night, the RAF and the U.S. Air Force flew in coal, food, and other necessities. All over western Germany, children watched the planes being loaded, and cheered as they took off. In Berlin, the constant sound of the engines became a comfort instead of a signal of imminent destruction. Fifty-four airmen were killed in the effort, and life in the dark, unheated city was harsh indeed. But all concerned were determined to succeed, and an extraordinary team spirit soon developed. Children collected aircraft numbers and everyone knew which flying or tonnage record had been broken on a certain day. Boys and girls took presents to the airfields for the pilots and clamored to be taken to see the British Sunderland flying boats landing on the Schwanenwerder, part of the huge lake also known as the Wannsee, in the western part of Berlin.[65]

Gail Halvorson, an American pilot, touched by his encounter with a group of hungry children, told them to wait at the end of the runway that evening. The next time he brought his plane in for a landing, the crew tossed out candy bars on parachutes that the men had made out of handkerchiefs. Soon everyone was doing it, using old shirts and whatever other materials came to hand. German Youth Activities members were recruited to make more parachutes and funding for the project, called Operation Little Vittles, was provided by the Air Force. CARE dropped twenty-five Schmoos, the little creature from the comic strip *L'il Abner* that loved people so much that it would turn itself into the object of their desire, usually a ham or other food item. This time the Schmoo, when taken to a CARE office, would turn into ten pounds of lard, an incredible treasure in starved Berlin.[66]

The Schmoos were topped at Christmas by the far more dramatic arrival of Clarence the camel. Before his trip to Berlin, Clarence was sent

Clarence the Camel.

around the American Zone to encourage people to give contributions for the airlift. He did pretty well, collecting some 5,000 pounds of candy and tons of toys, but before he was able to fly to Berlin with his takings, he was injured by a kick from a nasty Army mule. A replacement Clarence, in fact a lady camel, was rushed in. His, or her, arrival (not by parachute) made a lasting impression on the children who swarmed to the airport to greet him.[67]

The Russians backed down in the spring of 1949. A fifteen-year-old Berlin girl wrote that the pilots' sacrifices in the airlift "remind us that in this world there are higher things than national egoism—namely humanity and the existence of all peoples in human dignity."[68] Humanity, as always, had shown itself in the individual actions of the blockade, which were contained within a larger and more pragmatic context. By the time the last plane landed, the Cold War was a fact and the Marshall Plan, or European Recovery Program, approved only weeks before the start of the blockade, was well under way. General Marshall had described the objectives of the plan, which have lost none of their validity:

> Our policy is directed not against any country or doctrine, but against hunger, poverty, desperation and chaos. Its purpose should be the revival of a working economy in the world so as to permit the emer-

gence of political and social conditions in which free institutions can
exist.[69]

The Soviet Union had been invited to join Europe and take part in the
program, but Stalin refused, thereby making Hitler's dream of uniting the
Western Allies and Germany against the East come true, though not quite
as the Nazi leader had imagined.

17. No Place Like Home

During all the months and years of their travails, the young people swept up in the Nazi whirlwind, if they were old enough, preserved an inner vision and memory of home. Returning there was their hope and aim. Home had not always been idyllic. Many of the displaced children came from the poorest levels of their society and many had been in orphanages in their own country. But home means many things. It is language, a familiar street, a certain light, the sounds of known birds, accustomed food, friends and relatives. It is, above all, the fact of belonging. In times of hardship, a virtual walk in the mind's eye through beloved places, lingering over every remembered detail, can, for a few moments, transport one out of present horror and into the happier past. Few would find home and its inhabitants unchanged by the war when they finally returned. And for millions, home would have to be re-created in a new land, among strangers.

For older children, the instinct to return to their own was very strong, and in unstoppable bands they walked, hitchhiked, and used any possible means to get home. They crammed themselves into the coal bins and every other space on trains that were so crowded that one Polish boy strapped himself to a brake handle with his belt to keep from being pushed off.

Some of the travels were full of adventure, especially for Soviet citizens, who, before the final surrender of Germany, had to travel in the war zones if they were going east. Vladimir Kuts, a forced laborer, now seventeen, who had been liberated from his kindly farmer by the Americans, was enlisted by them because of his language abilities and familiarity with the terrain. They gave him a uniform and trained him to drive and shoot. He accompanied them in their victorious sweep to Munich in April 1945. The war was still on, but Vladimir was determined to head home, and his GI friends found a confiscated German Mercedes for him. To protect him from air strikes they painted the roof bright orange. Exhilarated by his freedom, Kuts said, "I didn't drive, I flew." At one point he was surrounded by a retreating SS unit, but he was able to rush on unnoticed. The trip did not last long. Ordered to stop by an American MP, the young

A Russian family comes home to devastation.

Russian put on the brakes, which did not work, and ran into a line of parked U.S. Army Studebakers. Arrest followed. But this American unit also found the boy useful, and took him along as they advanced toward the agreed demarcation line between American and Soviet forces. Once the two armies met, Kuts, under pressure because he was the son of a Gulag prisoner, was recruited by the NKVD, to whom he provided information about his former hosts. When his NKVD mentor found that the boy was under eighteen, he sent him home and advised him never to mention his service with the Americans. (This promise Kuts, like many others, would keep for more than forty years, until the dissolution of the Soviet Union.) Home was not as he remembered it. Vladimir found his mother there, but the house had been destroyed and his older sister killed in a battle near Moscow. His father was still in Siberia. There was little food, and the youth fell ill. His euphoria gone, he even contemplated suicide. Eventually, once again with help from his NKVD connections, he was able to get an internal passport, and went to Siberia to join his father, who had by now been liberated. There Kuts became an engineer, married, and stayed for twenty-seven years.[1]

This pattern was not unusual. Returning DPs and POWs who did not pass NKVD scrutiny, or who refused to cooperate with the Soviet authorities, were executed or sent into the Gulag. Many of those who were allowed to go home would be forever suspect and unable to advance in their careers. Their status would also prevent them, until very recently, from claiming the disability payments and compensation that was given to other veterans and victims.

Younger children did not usually have these political issues, but their homecoming could be equally difficult. Nikolai Mahutov, eight, liberated with the rest of his partisan band at the Polish border, got home in the fall of 1944 with the help of the Russian Red Cross. He too found little to eat. He was so hungry one day that he ate dried clover from a bale of hay, and then "fell down . . . and had sweet dreams." He thinks that the clover acted like a drug and that he "slept for three days." People told him later that he "looked so happy and pink-cheeked lying there that they didn't wake him up."[2] The dreams were not so sweet for others. Whole families of siblings, their parents dead and their towns destroyed, were sent directly to orphanages. Others went to these institutions on their own initiative after they had gone home only to find that everyone in their family had perished. Little is known about the Soviet orphanages, but life in comparable places in Poland in 1946 was harsh:

> There is a great deal of malnutrition, which might be termed "slow starvation." The problems of children confronting the Ministry are overwhelming. Staffs are hastily recruited; professional social helpers and doctors are very scarce. They expect to care for 80,000 children in institutions and 240,000 in foster homes. The hazards in this large placing job are obvious. It is . . . assumed that 2,400,000 children need supplementary feeding. Conditions of large families living in bombed cities such as Warsaw are hazardous. Those living in the bombed, totally destroyed areas of the old battlefields are really worse off. God knows how this country will pull out of the morass, but they go ahead very bravely.[3]

Elena Putilina, by now eleven, and her little brother, who had been liberated from the Lodz-Konstantynow camp for Eastern children, were treated for malnutrition and then taken to a children's home in the Soviet Union. There, social workers tried to weave their memories and the names they remembered into addresses. Their mother was finally located, but could not come to them for over a year because she was ill. In the meantime, people tried to adopt Elena, but she refused to leave her brother. Their mother did finally arrive, unannounced, one day at dinnertime:

> Suddenly there appeared an old woman, as I remember, a frail old woman, and she said . . . "Are there children in this house called Lena

and Petja" . . . The girls asked, who are you, how do you know
them . . . and she said, "But they are my little children." They pointed
at me—"Lena, that is your mother." "You have grown," she said, and
held me. When my little brother came he said, "That is not my
mother . . . my mother was young, not gray haired." My mother
wept . . . but as always, we embraced her.

From the children's home, Elena, Petja, and their mother made their way
back to Vitebsk and then to their village. Petja was excited and impatient,
but reality was a shock:

When we came to the village there were no houses . . . all was burned.
We asked if we had a house . . . she said yes . . . but all was burned
except chimneys. . . . Then we saw a hump . . . it was a mud hut where
our mother lived, with a little window, some pine branches, some
planks on the wall, planks to sleep on. Nothing was left.

Elena later managed to get herself admitted to a boarding school in
Vitebsk. Her father, one brother, and a sister had all perished. Petja stayed
home, and still lives in the village with his children. There were hundreds
such villages where mud huts were the norm, and where there were no
horses, so women had to pull the farm carts. The reigning hunger did not
just affect humans: in one town, children going to school were terrorized
by a pack of starving German shepherds left behind by Nazi forces.[4]

The arrival back to desolation was not limited to the USSR. Similar
scenes greeted those returning to Yugoslavia, Greece, Poland, and many
other places. Stefanie Burger-Kelih, now nineteen, had been in the so-
called Youth Protection Camp at Uckermarck, a subsidiary of Ravensbrück, where, in addition to being used as forced labor, the young inmates
were used in "biological" juvenile delinquency experiments developed by
the same Dr. Ritter who had "analyzed" the Gypsies. She did not get home
to Slovenia until September 8, 1945, after traveling for months in trucks
and trains. She covered the last few miles on foot:

I knew where I was when I came to the place where my sister had
lived. . . . I went across the fields to my sister's and thought, if I find a
four-leaf clover, then my parents are alive. I found everyone there
except my father. . . . We had no furniture . . . nothing since our house
was so remote. . . . The Germans . . . had used our furniture to build
fires. And later the Partisans warmed themselves the same way. There
was no more china, the neighbors gave us some. I don't know where the
livestock went, the sheep and the rest. I think the neighbors took them.

They gave us some back. . . . We found a table in a partisan bunker. . . . I was home. What could one do? Almost no clothes, no money, nothing. I worked. My father did not come home. We lost our fields. We rented the farmhouse.[5]

The disillusionment of return was devastating for middle-class Jewish children too. Marian Helft and her family, hidden by friends in the Hungarian and Slovakian borderlands, had escaped deportation under harrowing circumstances. Liberated by the Russians, they decided to go home to Budapest, even though their house had been destroyed by bombs. Marian, eleven, sustained by the "brilliant image" of that city as she remembered it and as her parents had spoken of it, was excited at the prospect. The trip back was far from luxurious. They went by horse cart, in an open and freezing freight car in which they had to lie on artillery shells, and then in the locomotive of another train, which was so hot that they could not touch the walls or sit down. They arrived in a bad, dirty neighborhood of Budapest in the very early morning. It was hardly brilliant. The first thing Marian saw in the dusty gloom was a "woman with a shaved head pushing a cart loaded with her belongings," a vision she has never forgotten. After a long walk, they arrived at her grandparents' apartment, which consisted of three small rooms. Marian sat down and cried. When the family asked why she was crying, she said it was because her feet hurt, but it was really because her dream of coming home to "something brilliant" had been dashed.[6]

Marian's family was lucky to have the three rooms. Many other Jewish survivors found their houses destroyed or occupied by strangers. In most areas, in the first postwar years there was no way of evicting such squatters, and the former owners were forced to seek shelter elsewhere. The furnishings of the houses had also migrated. It was not unusual for the neighbors to serve the returnees tea from cups that they recognized as their own. Friends to whom valuables had been entrusted suddenly developed amnesia about such arrangements, especially if the claimant was very young. In Poland and other Eastern European countries, returning Jews were often greeted not with sympathy, but with surprise that they were still alive. This atmosphere made clear that it would be better to leave, but many, full of hope, were determined to await the possible return of parents and children to what had been home before departing once again. More often than not, the wait was futile.

Wherever they were, Jewish children who had been hidden on the Continent or taken to England on the Kindertransports waited with trepi-

dation for news of their parents. By 1943, most of the Kindertransport
children had stopped receiving mail from their parents. After the war, letters from remote relatives, messages from strangers, and official notifica-
tions little by little made clear to many that they had become orphans. The
fact of their parents' death, in a place and manner unknown, was hard to
absorb. Some children did not want to know the details. "I have never
been able to face with equanimity photographs, newsreels, etc., of concentration camps for fear of discovering my mother's fate," one said.[7] Others did not want to admit the truth to themselves. Isaac Levendel, the little
boy who had been hidden with French farmers, did not ask about his
mother: "I was afraid of the answer I might get, and since I did not want
anyone to destroy my fantasies, silence was the best way to hold on to my
dreams." Although he could acknowledge that she had "disappeared," it
was not until he overheard his father and the woman who would become
his new wife discussing how to obtain a death certificate for his mother
that "my mother and her death were explicitly connected. . . . My blood
froze in my veins, and I wanted to shout that this was a lie and drown out
their voices. . . . Instead, I lowered my head and concealed my emotions. I
retreated into the silence I had imposed upon myself since my mother's
departure."[8]

For children who had spent five or more happy years with foster parents, the news of their parents' fate led to mixed emotions. One nine-year-
old, told with trepidation by her foster mother that her parents and all her
relations, whom she hardly remembered, had perished, said, "Oh, now I
can stay with you." Her astounded foster mother wrote, "The tragedy was
that she heard the news with relief." But it was not quite so simple. For
some days afterward, she found the little girl crying at night. When she
asked why, the child said: "I don't want you to die."[9]

Older children were sometimes so upset at the thought of leaving their
foster families that their surviving parents did not insist. When parents
and children did meet again, relationships could be difficult. The children
who had been in England for years no longer felt Austrian, German, or
Czech; many had forgotten their original language. Mothers and foster
mothers were mutually jealous, and the children often felt guilty when
they were unable to love both equally. Young exiles who were at university,
or were beginning careers, sometimes resented having to drop everything
and deal with relations who turned up in desperate shape after their
wartime experiences. For parents who found the docile little children they
remembered transformed into streetwise teenagers, the relationships

could be hard to revive. Sad to say, in many cases, after five or six years of war and separation, the bonds were too frayed, and the families never lived together again, but contented themselves with visits, as if they were remote cousins.

The evacuated Jewish children would go in many directions and settle in many countries, but they do have some things in common. They, like most refugees and transients, feel that they do not "belong" where they have settled, but for them there is an added element:

> For a long time I did not concern myself with being a refugee. I assumed that this was something I would grow out of.... Instead, I have been liberated only from the fear of the past.... This is the most difficult thing I ever had to face: that my Jewish childhood in Nazi Germany and my orphan exile ... must remain a part of my life always: it will never be as if it had not happened, I shall never be "just like everybody else."[10]

Most of the small British evacuees started home in 1944. One nurse who had taken care of a whole houseful of toddlers in the countryside proudly noted that they were going home to London toilet trained and with greatly improved table manners.[11] The "Bundles from Britain" who had been sent to the United States gradually went home too. The teenagers among them, by now deeply involved in the life of American high schools, often wished they could stay. For all, the longed-for return was bittersweet: "I had two sets of parents.... I had a past that was hardly known to my American family and rapidly accumulating experience ... in Ohio that would never be totally conveyable to my parents in England."[12]

Eleven-year-old Anthony Bailey and a number of other boys went home in October on an escort aircraft carrier loaded with replacement aircraft. For security reasons their departure and arrival dates were kept secret. The trip was exciting, as the crew made the lads part of their routines and kept them busy. They sat in the planes, were shown how the guns worked, and played endless games of British Monopoly. There was a frightening torpedo alert. Despite the secrecy, Bailey's mother was on the dock when the ship arrived at Glasgow. As would all too often be the case, he did not recognize her:

> I shook hands with the officers and went down a gangplank to a dockside building where a small wavy-haired woman hugged me—her action convincing me, after a few moments reflection, that she must be

more than the friend of the family or aunt I first took her for. In the crowded overnight train going south to England, I slept against my mother's shoulder.[13]

The phenomenon of detachment affected children from every country, and the impetus did not always come from the child. Parents' lives also had changed and made family relations difficult. One English girl returned home from America, where she had been sent at age two, to a mother and stepfather she had forgotten, as well as two new siblings. Before he was killed on D-Day, her own father had remarried and had two sons, whom she would not meet until 1999. Her mother and stepfather eventually emigrated to South Africa. The little girl did not go with them, but went back to her American foster mother, a generous lady who loved the English girl as her own and gave her every advantage. She also sent financial help to her family, whose farm in South Africa did not thrive. The child did see her relations from time to time, but she stayed in the United States. There she lives happily, but does admit, with a certain sadness, that she sometimes thinks of herself as having been "bought."[14]

The problems of families were hard, but the fact that they existed, even in another place, was better than the awful loneliness of having no one. A host of children's homes, orphanages, and agencies would care for those who had no parents, but no organization can replace family, no matter how dysfunctional. The most loving social workers or directors of children's homes are not parents, but employees, and they retire and change jobs. If their charges had become fond of them, such changes, devastating enough when there was some hope that parents would return, were far worse once that hope was gone. Children under the care of the most conscientious organizations tended to be moved from one place to another like so many sacks of potatoes. They were thought of in categories such as age group, religion, nationality, or gender rather than as individuals. From time to time, relatives or old family friends might appear and the child would be "taken out" for meals or other entertainments. But as one girl in France, who had by 1946 been in three foster families and six institutions, said of her parents' friends, who, with the best intentions, had helped her in various ways, "Not one person ever asked me if I would like to live with them. I felt like a leper."[15]

Institutional care was also finite. In many places, orphans were expected to start working at age fourteen. By eighteen, an orphan was considered an adult capable of taking care of himself and any stipend going to foster parents or institutions for his care ended. Only a lucky few would manage to get scholarships and other perks of higher education, much less find a family to live with. The Kindertransport children in England were the first to experience this enforced independence. They worked in every kind of menial job, which a plethora of agencies helped them to find, often sending out little résumés, such as the following, supplied to a potential sponsor in New York by the Children's Marrainage Scheme in London, of which Mrs. Lionel Rothschild was president:

> PAULETTE S.
> Born 30.1.33 in Paris of French nationality.
> Both parents died in deportation, Paulette and her brother were hidden in the country.
> The girl is apprenticed to a dressmaker.
> Paulette is always happy and gay and full of life and fun.[16]

The practical option of food and lodging led one girl in England to take a job as a chambermaid in a boardinghouse. Another managed to get into a residential nursing school that combined training and paid employment. Some had no idea how to budget their tiny salaries. One sixteen-year-old boy, out on his own for the first time, lived on cornflakes for months. For young refugees who were not provided rooms by their employers, finding a place to live was daunting:

> I found landladies always extremely suspicious that a girl of sixteen— I looked younger—should want to rent a room. I was invariably asked why I wasn't living with my parents—a question I could not answer without bursting into tears. . . . One of them turned me away saying she did not want someone with foreign habits in the house. To this day, I don't know what she meant.[17]

Above all, such young people, with only organizations and committees of strangers to talk to for advice and comfort, were terribly isolated, especially when it came to holidays and social life, and would have to build their own family-like structures, bit by bit. Walter Nowak, a Polish forced laborer who emigrated to the United States, later said:

> Since this country give us home and take us in, the orphans we were, we very grateful. You sweat, you work, your time didn't go for nothing. What else can we say? We are just happy. The other thing is almost behind us. But I tell you we still carry deep scars. We never, never could

hear from the family and what happened to them. They don't know what happened to us. You just live to survive. We can't dwell and live backwards.[18]

The children of collaborators suffered from a different kind of loneliness. Their parents' politics had made them outcasts and sometimes de facto orphans in their own land. In the first days after liberation, such boys and girls, even very young ones, were treated with hostility and contempt. Many had to be taken out of school. In a phenomenon common to all of Europe, girls who had gone out with German soldiers had their heads shaved and, surrounded by mocking crowds, were marched through the streets. In Holland an estimated 150,000 people were arrested as collaborators, not always with good reason. Most were subjected to mob humiliation and some were beaten, but this sort of scene was repellent to most citizens and was soon prohibited by the authorities. If both parents were detained, their children twelve and over were taken with them to the detention camps. Some 20,000 younger children were sent to children's homes or foster families where they were not always well treated. In the camps, some members of the Dutch Nazi Party (NSB) also had their heads shaved and painted with orange stripes. NSB members who had fled to Germany were returned with their families and incarcerated with the others in the camps, including Westerbork, the notorious deportation camp, where surviving Jews made the collaborators follow the same brutal routines that they had been forced to endure.[19]

It was in these enclosures that many of the children first learned the dreadful details of the activities of their parents and their German colleagues. One group of teenagers was taken to see the exhumed bodies of Dutch hostages the Germans had executed, and shown atrocity pictures from the liberated concentration camps. The stigma of their parents' actions would stay with many of these children for the rest of their lives:

> I felt guilty about everything that my parents, the NSB, the Nazis, that Hitler, had done. Precisely because you had heard so much about it, because your parents respected the movement so much and now everyone was tearing it all down, as their child you felt all dirty and you couldn't do anything about it. I had no parents I could be proud of. That feeling of guilt and shame stayed for a long time. I was angry that their choice poisoned my youth, and even a big part of my life.[20]

Reentry was not easy for anyone who had been exiled or evacuated. Provincialism had not been erased by the world war. Everyone at home

*In Germany, months after the formal surrender, relatives
mourn a child killed by an unexploded grenade.*

tended to be focused on his own experiences and recovery. Young children coming back to the Netherlands from the Japanese internment camps in Indonesia were mocked at school because of the ill-fitting and often exotic clothes supplied to them by the rescue agencies. None of the returnees to any country knew any of the local war jargon, or what had happened there under the Nazis while they had been gone. They were often way behind in their studies and had to be placed in classes with younger schoolmates. Attempts by older boys and girls to find sympathetic listeners who might reassure them were met by counterstories from those who considered their own experiences just as bad, which they often were. The enormous publicity surrounding the liberation of the concentration camps and the vast number of horror stories everyone heard soon led older people to talk of other things, an avoidance increased by an ingrained wariness of confiding in others and by the unwillingness of many victims to relive their recent pain. Above all, sheer survival in the ruins of Europe, or trying to escape it, took every ounce of energy. Almost all memoirs and oral histories of the period, which would come forth in floods twenty-five and more years after the war, refer to this strange silence, especially between generations, which would not be broken for many years.

·   ·   ·

And so the war ended, piecemeal, receding like a putrid tide leaving behind every kind of human desolation and detritus. It would be a long time before Europe ceased to be somber and gray, and before warmth and food were taken for granted. Traces remain even seventy years later. Spanish Refugee Aid still cares for a small group of elderly Civil War exiles who live in France. Poles, Balts, Russians, Jews, and small remnants of every other uprooted people are scattered around the world. All have made their way in some manner, some very well, but they remain people apart.

One might have thought that the events of the Nazi era and the forty million dead would open every eye to the evils of intolerance and extremism and would cause people to fall into each other's arms in common sorrow, but they did not. Even as World War II ended, new conflicts began, and others have succeeded them without cease, bringing horror and corruption, which "stream like blood out of our televisions," to millions of children.[21] In the face of the power of induced collective suppression and violence, the actions of rational and humane individuals, who are present everywhere, and who, in the cruel Nazi world, saved those they could, still remain the best hope for mankind.

Notes

ABBREVIATIONS

DGFP	*Documents on German Foreign Policy, 1918–1945*
FRUS	*Foreign Relations of the United States*
IMT	*International Military Tribunal*
IWM	Imperial War Museum, London
LC/MS	Library of Congress, Manuscript Division
NA	National Archives, College Park, Maryland
NIOD (formerly RIOD)	Nederlands Instituut voor Oorlogsdocumentatie, Amsterdam
PRO	Public Record Office, Kew, Great Britain
RG	Record Group (in National Archives)
TWC	*Trials of War Criminals*
UNA	United Nations Archives, New York
UNRRA	United Nations Relief and Rehabilitation Administration

PROLOGUE

1. NA RG 338/54, ETO/USFET, Detachment F1F3, report, "Asylum at Kaufbeuren, Swabia," 5 July 1945; NA RG 238, Nuremberg Doc. 1696-PS; Ernst Klee, *Euthanasie im NS-Staat* (Frankfurt, 1983), pp. 452–54.
2. Alan Bullock, *Hitler and Stalin: Parallel Lives* (New York, 1993), pp. 983, 805.
3. Hermann Rauschning, *Hitler Speaks* (London, 1939), pp. 113, 229–30, as cited in Richard Pipes, *Russia Under the Bolshevik Regime* (New York, 1993), p. 280.
4. Adolf Hitler, *Mein Kampf,* ed. D. C. Watt (London, 1974), p. 367.
5. Ibid., p. 368.

CHAPTER 1. APPLIED EUGENICS

1. Daniel J. Kevles, *In the Name of Eugenics* (Cambridge, MA, 1995), pp. 96–97.
2. Hitler, *Mein Kampf,* p. 400.
3. For a complete history of this undertaking and its fate, see the study by Nancy L. Gallagher, *Breeding Better Vermonters: The Eugenics Project in the Green Mountain State* (Hanover, NH, 1999).
4. Ibid., pp. 122–24; Appendix C, p. 185, gives the full text of the law.
5. Kevles, *In the Name of Eugenics,* p. 115.
6. This account is based on ibid., pp. 110–11; quote on p. 111.
7. Stephen Jay Gould, *The Mismeasure of Man* (New York, 1981), pp. 335–36. See also Kevles, *In the Name of Eugenics,* p. 329, n. 48.
8. Gould, *The Mismeasure of Man,* pp. 172, 233.
9. *Washington Post,* 29 September 2003.
10. Kevles, *In the Name of Eugenics,* pp. 112, 116.
11. Ibid., p. 120.

12. Hitler, *Mein Kampf*, p. 368.

13. See, for example, Gunnar Broberg and Nils Roll-Hansen, *Eugenics and the Welfare State* (Ann Arbor, MI, 1996).

14. Michael Burleigh, *Death and Deliverance: Euthanasia in Germany, 1900–1945* (Cambridge, UK, 1994), p. 42; William Shirer, *The Rise and Fall of the Third Reich* (New York, 1960), pp. 234–35.

15. Gregor Ziemer, *Education for Death: The Making of the Nazi* (Oxford, 1941), p. 27.

16. For the best summary of this process, see Henry Friedlander, *The Origins of Nazi Genocide: From Euthanasia to the Final Solution* (Chapel Hill, NC, 1995), Chapter 2.

17. For a summary of this issue, see Lisa Pine, *Nazi Family Policy, 1933–1945* (New York, 1997), Chapter 4.

18. NA RG 59, LM 193/16/440–47, 862. 12/26, W. W. Adams, 23 November 1935.

19. Gisela Bock, "Racism and Sexism in Nazi Germany," in *When Biology Became Destiny*, ed. Renate Bridenthal, Atina Grossmann, and Marion Kaplan (New York, 1984), pp. 271–96.

20. Cited in Stefan Kühl, *The Nazi Connection: Eugenics, American Racism, and German National Socialism* (Oxford, 1994), pp. 87–88.

21. For a detailed account of the controversy on which the following is based, see Keith L. Nelson, "The 'Black Horror' on the Rhine: Race as a Factor in Post–World War I Diplomacy," *Journal of Modern History* 42 (December 1970), pp. 606–27.

22. Cited in Robert C. Reinders, "Racialism on the Left: E. D. Morel and the 'Black Horror on the Rhine,' " *International Review of Social History* 13 (1968), p. 1.

23. *Christian Science Monitor*, 28 October 1920, cited in Nelson, "The 'Black Horror' on the Rhine," p. 618.

24. Nelson, "The 'Black Horror' on the Rhine," p. 621.

25. Reiner Pommerin, *Sterilisierung der Rhinelandbastarde: Das Schicksal einer farbigen deutschen Minderheit, 1918–1937* (Düsseldorf, 1979), pp. 24–27.

26. Hitler, *Mein Kampf*, p. 295.

27. Nelson, "The 'Black Horror' on the Rhine," p. 626.

28. Melita Maschmann, *Account Rendered: A Dossier on My Former Self* (London, 1965), p. 13.

29. The following account is taken from Pommerin, *Sterilisierung der Rhinelandbastarde*.

30. Ibid., p. 47.

31. Ibid., p. 84.

32. Burleigh, *Death and Deliverance*, p. 58.

33. Ludwig Eiber, *"Ich wuste, es wird schlimm." Die verfolgung der Sinti und Roma in München, 1933–1945* (Munich, 1993), pp. 16–18.

34. Ibid., p. 45.

35. On Ritter, see Wim Willems, *In Search of the True Gypsy* (London, 1997), Chapter 5.

36. Cited in Isabel Fonseca, *Bury Me Standing* (New York, 1996), p. 258.

37. Willems, *In Search of the True Gypsy*, pp. 255–56.

38. Sybil Milton, "Nazi Policies Toward Roma and Sinti, 1933–1945," *Journal of the Gypsy Lore Society* 5, 2:1 (1992), p. 6; Guenter Lewy, *The Nazi Persecution of the Gypsies* (Oxford, 2000), pp. 52–55.

39. Willems, *In Search of the True Gypsy*, p. 259.

40. Eiber, *"Ich wuste, es wird schlimm,"* p. 58.

41. Interrogation transcript of Franz August Wirbel, Landeskriminalamt, Baden-Württemberg, 8/26/1982, in Sybil Milton and Henry Friedlander, *Archives of the Holocaust* (New York, 1993), Vol. 22, Doc. 110, pp. 261–71.

42. Lewy, *The Nazi Persecution of the Gypsies,* pp. 68–70.

43. Conti to Central Office, Kripo, 1/24/40, in Milton, "Nazi Policies Toward Roma and Sinti," p. 15, n. 33.

44. Lewy, *The Nazi Persecution of the Gypsies,* pp. 70–81.

45. Ibid., pp. 135–43, 193.

46. Ibid., pp. 146–47.

47. Helena Kubica, "Children and Youths at KL Auschwitz," in *Auschwitz: Nazi Death Camp,* ed. Franciszek Piper and Teresa Swiebocka (Oswiecim, 1996), p. 129.

48. Elzbieta Piekut-Warszawa, in Irena Strzelecka, "Experiments," in Piper and Swiebocka, eds., *Auschwitz: Nazi Death Camp,* pp. 94–97.

49. Ibid., pp. 103–5.

50. *Ambassador Dodd's Diary, 1933–1938,* ed. William E. Dodd, Jr., and Martha Dodd, (New York, 1941), entries for 16 August and 1 September 1933.

51. For the best description of this process from the personal point of view, see Victor Klemperer, *I Will Bear Witness: A Diary of the Nazi Years, 1933–1945,* 2 vols. (New York, 1998, 1999).

52. Malcolm Muggeridge, in *Fortnightly Review,* 1 May 1933, in Robert Conquest, *The Harvest of Sorrow: Soviet Collectivization and the Terror-Famine* (New York, 1986), p. 260.

53. F. Belov, *The History of a Soviet Collective Farm* (New York, 1955), pp. 12–13, in Dana G. Dalrymple, "The Soviet Famine of 1932–1934," *Soviet Studies* 15:3 (1964), p. 261.

54. Harry Lang, *New York Evening Journal,* 15 April 1935, in Dalrymple, "The Soviet Famine," p. 262.

55. Conquest, *The Harvest of Sorrow,* p. 284.

56. *New York Evening Journal,* 16 April 1935, in Conquest, *The Harvest of Sorrow,* p. 287.

57. Conquest, *The Harvest of Sorrow,* p. 286.

58. Ibid., p. 291.

59. Ibid., p. 298.

60. Lev Kopelev, *The Education of a True Believer* (New York, 1977), pp. 11–12, 235, cited ibid., pp. 232–33.

61. Conquest, *The Harvest of Sorrow,* p. 297.

62. Ibid., pp. 294–95; *New York Times,* 22 August 1933, p. 1; Ewald Ammende, *Human Life in Russia* (London, 1936), pp. 102–3 (citing Reuters, 21 May 1934) and 236–37.

63. Arch Getty and Oleg Naumov, eds., *The Road to Terror: Stalin and the Self-Destruction of the Bolsheviks, 1932–1939* (Yale 1999), pp. 468–79 and Docs. 168–70.

64. Ibid., pp. 486–87.

65. *New York Times,* 7 September 1933, p. 64.

66. NA RG 59, LM 193/21/060, 862.4016/496 Messersmith to State, 25 March 1933.

67. Ibid.

68. J. Noakes and G. Pridham, eds., *Nazism, 1919–1945: A History in Documents and Eyewitness Accounts,* 2 vols. (New York, 1990), Vol. 1, Doc. 394, p. 524.

69. NA RG 59, LM 193/21/199–202, editorial from *Der Angriff,* Berlin, 28 March 1933.

70. NA RG 59, LM 193/21/180, 862.4016/568, Messersmith to State, 31 March 1933.

71. The literature on the anti-Jewish measures in Germany is vast. For a clear summary, see Raul Hilberg, *The Destruction of the European Jews* (New York, 1985), Chapters 2 and 3.

72. Ibid., p. 38.

CHAPTER 2. PURGING THE UNFIT

1. NA RG 238, Nuremberg Doc. NO-665.
2. Burleigh, *Death and Deliverance*, p. 18.
3. For detailed and fascinating discussions of this debate, see ibid.; Friedlander, *The Origins of Nazi Genocide;* and Klee, *Euthanasie im NS-Staat.*
4. Klee, *Euthanasie im NS-Staat,* pp. 31–32.
5. Burleigh, *Death and Deliverance,* p. 97; see also p. 315, n. 11.
6. Ibid., p. 97, and p. 315, n. 12.
7. NA RG 59 LM 193/16, 862.1232/3, 9 July 1934, "Cremation Law of 15 May 1934."
8. Noakes and Pridham, eds., *Nazism,* Vol. 2, Doc. 720, p. 1003.
9. Klee, *Euthanasie im NS-Staat,* pp. 76–77.
10. Götz Aly et al., *Cleansing the Fatherland: Nazi Medicine and Racial Hygiene* (Baltimore, 1994), pp. 29–30.
11. Burleigh, *Death and Deliverance,* p. 99.
12. Christian Pross and Götz Aly, eds., *Der Wert des Menschen. Medezin in Deutschland, 1918–1945* (Berlin, 1989), Plate 78.
13. NA RG 238, Nuremberg Doc. NO-1313, 20 August 1940.
14. Noakes and Pridham, eds., *Nazism,* Vol. 2, Doc. 740, p. 1021; Friedlander, *The Origins of Nazi Genocide,* p. 67.
15. Aly et al., *Cleansing the Fatherland,* pp. 48–49.
16. Full text in Klee, *Euthanasie im NS-Staat,* pp. 303–4.
17. NA RG 338/334/54, ETO/USFET/ECAD/MISC DETS/Detachment F1F3, "Asylum at Kaufbeuren."
18. Burleigh, *Death and Deliverance,* pp. 105–7.
19. Friedlander, *The Origins of Nazi Genocide,* p. 166.
20. Linda Orth, *Die Transport Kinder aus Bonn* (Cologne, 1989) pp. 45–48.
21. Friedlander, *The Origins of Nazi Genocide,* p. 168.
22. Klee, *Euthanasie im NS-Staat,* p. 429.
23. Ibid., p. 310.
24. NA RG 59, LM 193/57/819, 862.143/12.
25. NA RG 59, LM 193/57/806, enclosure to 862.1241/15, 13 March 1941.
26. NA RG 238, Nuremberg Doc. NO-836, Attorney General of Stuttgart to RJM, 12 October 1940.
27. NA RG 238, Nuremberg Doc. NO-629PS, 8 July 1940.
28. NA RG 238, Nuremberg Doc. NO-829, Chief Prosecutor of Stuttgart to Reich Minister of Justice, 1 August 1940.
29. Burleigh, *Death and Deliverance,* pp. 169–71.
30. NA RG 238, Nuremberg Doc. NO-832, 24 July 1940.
31. NA RG 238, Nuremberg Doc. NO-002, 25 November 1940.
32. NA RG 238, Nuremberg Doc. NO-018, 19 December 1940.
33. Burleigh, *Death and Deliverance,* p. 167.
34. NA RG 59, LM 193/57, 862.12/33, 2 February 1941, Enclosure 2 to Report 380, U.S. Consulate Stuttgart.
35. Noakes and Pridham, eds., *Nazism,* Vol. 2, Doc. 757, p. 1035.
36. Ibid., Doc. 758, p. 1036.
37. Burleigh, *Death and Deliverance,* p. 180; Noakes and Pridham, eds., *Nazism,* Vol. 2, Doc. 761, p. 1040.
38. NA RG 238, Nuremberg Doc. NO-896, Schellmann affidavit.
39. Aly et al., *Cleansing the Fatherland,* p. 221, Wentzler to Blankenburg BAP KdF #242.
40. Ibid., pp. 216–19.

41. Burleigh, *Death and Deliverance*, pp. 117–18, 265.
42. Aly et al., *Cleansing the Fatherland*, p. 224; Nuremberg Doc. L 170, n. 169.
43. Klee, *Euthanasie im NS-Staat*, p. 300.
44. Testimony of H. Bunke, in Aly et al., *Cleansing the Fatherland*, pp. 225–26.

CHAPTER 3. INCREASING THE MASTER RACE

1. For excellent discussions of Nazi family policy, see Jill Stephenson, *Women in Nazi Society* (New York, 1975), and Pine, *Nazi Family Policy.*
2. Willems, *In Search of the True Gypsy*, pp. 259–60.
3. NA RG 238/M894/16, Doc. NO-5351, Affidavit von Schlippenbach, 6 October 1947, and Doc. NO-5351c, Higher SS Leader for Bohemia and Moravia to S., 19 January 1944.
4. Stephenson, *Women in Nazi Society*, p. 47.
5. Bock, "Racism and Sexism in Nazi Germany," p. 276.
6. Pine, *Nazi Family Policy*, pp. 19–20.
7. Stephenson, *Women in Nazi Society*, p. 42.
8. Gitta Sereny, *Albert Speer: His Battle with Truth* (New York, 1996), p. 110.
9. Pine, *Nazi Family Policy*, pp. 26–28, 34, 38.
10. Ibid., pp. 72–87.
11. Ziemer, *Education for Death*, pp. 34–35.
12. Ibid., pp. 35–43.
13. Pine, *Nazi Family Policy*, p. 31.
14. Ziemer, *Education for Death*, pp. 47–51.
15. Stephenson, *Women in Nazi Society*, pp. 48–51.
16. Ibid., pp. 63–65, and Pine, *Nazi Family Policy*, pp. 42–44.
17. Noakes and Pridham, eds., *Nazism*, Vol. 1, Doc. 363, p. 493.
18. NA RG 238/M894/14, Nuremberg Doc. NO-3325, "Instructional Pamphlet #3 of the SS Health Office," 31 May 1937.
19. Larry V. Thompson, "*Lebensborn* and the Eugenics Policy of the *Reichsführer SS*," *Central European History* 4 (1971), p. 71, n. 41.
20. Ibid., pp. 61–62.
21. Ibid., pp. 64–65.
22. Georg Lilienthal, *Der "Lebensborn e.V." Ein instrument nationalsozialistischer Rassenpolitik* (Stuttgart, 1985), pp. 42–43. This is the definitive work on Lebensborn.
23. Nuremberg Doc. NO-3325, p. 2.
24. Lilienthal, *Der "Lebensborn e.V.,"* pp. 85–86.
25. Ibid., p. 94.
26. Ibid., p. 63, and Dorothee Schmitz-Köster, "*Deutsche Mutter, Bist du Bereit . . .*" *Alltag im Lebensborn* (Berlin, 1997), p. 98.
27. Lilienthal, *Der "Lebensborn e.V.,"* pp. 63–64 and n. 54.
28. Schmitz-Köster, "*Deutsche Mutter,*" pp. 147–48.
29. Lilienthal, *Der "Lebensborn e.V.,"* p. 68.
30. Ibid., p. 77.
31. Ibid., pp. 98–99.
32. Ibid., pp. 96–97, and Schmitz-Köster, "*Deutsche Mutter,*" pp. 107–9.
33. Lilienthal, *Der "Lebensborn e.V.,"* pp. 242–44.
34. Stephenson, *Women in Nazi Society*, pp. 67–68.
35. NA RG 238, Nuremberg Doc. NO-2825-PS, "SS Soldatenfreund 1943," pp. 31–33.
36. *Die Schwarze Korps*, 24 July 1941, in NA RG 59, LM193/57/ 799, U.S. Consul General, Zurich, to State, 22 September 1941.

37. Ibid., p. 2.
38. Oron J. Hale, "Adolf Hitler and the Post-War German Birthrate: An Unpublished Memorandum," *Journal of Central European Affairs* 17:2 (July 1957), pp. 166–73.

CHAPTER 4. EDUCATION FOR THE NEW WORLD ORDER

1. Hitler, *Mein Kampf,* pp. 370–74.
2. NA RG 59 LM 193/25, R. Geist memo, "The Aryan Law in Germany Regulating the Number of Students," 25 April 1933.
3. Richard Grunberger, *A Social History of the Third Reich* (New York, 1979), p. 561.
4. NA RG 59 LM193/58, "Statement of Archbishops and Bishops of Germany Gathered at the Tomb of St. Boniface," 26 June 1941, and sermon of Bishop Galen at Overwater Church, Münster, 30 July 1941.
5. NA RG 59 LM193/58, 862.404/320, Tittmann to SecState, 16 October 1941.
6. NA RG 59 LM193/58, 862.404/323, Morris to SecState, 3 November 1941.
7. NA RG 59 LM193/58, 862.404/318, Stewart to SecState, 15 October, 1941.
8. Bernt Engelmann, *In Hitler's Germany* (New York, 1986), pp. 3–6.
9. Noakes and Pridham, eds., *Nazism,* Vol. 1, pp. 430–32.
10. Helga Bergas, Leo Baeck Institute, New York, cited in Marion Kaplan, *Beyond Destiny and Despair: Jewish Life in Nazi Germany* (New York, 1998), p. 25.
11. E. C. Helmreich, "Jewish Education in the Third Reich," *Journal of Central European Affairs* 15:2 (July 1955), p. 136.
12. NA RG 59 LM193/25, GRC862.42/77, Geist to SecState, 12 January 1934, p. 4.
13. Jurgen Herbst, *Requiem for a German Past* (Madison, WI, 1999), p. 57.
14. NA RG 59 LM193/25, 862.42/73, G. C. Dominian to SecState, 27 November 1933.
15. NA RG 59 LM193/25, 862.42/77, Geist to State, 12 January 1934.
16. NA RG 59 LM193/25, 862.42/95, Dodd to State, 21 November 1934, p. 2.
17. Ibid., p. 4.
18. Herbst, *Requiem for a German Past,* p. 58.
19. NA RG 59 LM193/25, 862.42/77, Dodd to State, 12 January 1934.
20. Franz Braun and A. Hillen Ziegfeld, *Geopolitischer Atlas zur Deutschen Geschichte* (Dresden, 1934).
21. NA RG 59 LM193/12, 862.014/61, U.S. Consul, Stuttgart, to SecState, 25 September 1933.
22. Ziemer, *Education for Death,* p. 69.
23. See, on this subject, Philip Dray, *At the Hands of Persons Unknown: The Lynching of Black America* (New York, 2002), p. 338, and, for example, *New York Times,* 19 October 1933, "Mob of 2000 Hangs Negro in Maryland," p. 1.
24. Maschmann, *Account Rendered,* p. 66.
25. Erika Mann, *School for Barbarians* (New York, 1938), pp. 66–68.
26. From Richard Alshuer, *Sprachkundische Kleinarbeit in Neuen Geiste* (Leipzig), quoted ibid., p. 70.
27. Mann, *School for Barbarians,* p. 57.
28. H. W. Koch, *The Hitler Youth: Origins and Development, 1922–45* (New York, 1996), pp. 140–41.
29. Stephenson, *Women in Nazi Society,* Chapter 6, pp. 116–28.
30. NA RG 59 LM193/25, 862.42/102, Leverich report, 28 March 1935.
31. Lewy, *The Nazi Persecution of the Gypsies,* pp. 89–90.
32. Dorothea Schosser in Johannes Steinhoff et al., eds., *Voices from the Third Reich: An Oral History* (New York, 1994), p. 45.

33. Hans A. Schmitt, *Quakers and Nazis: Inner Light in Outer Darkness* (Columbia, MO, 1997), pp. 41–42.

34. Marianne Regensburger in Steinhoff et al., eds., *Voices from the Third Reich,* pp. 59–61.

35. Gideon Behrendt in Bertha Leverton and Shmuel Lowensohn, eds., *I Came Alone: The Stories of the Kindertransports* (Lewes, UK, 1996), p. 30.

36. Frau Verena Groth in Alison Owings, *Frauen: German Women Recall the Third Reich* (New Brunswick, NJ, 1995), p. 106.

37. Kaplan, *Beyond Destiny and Despair,* p. 108.

38. Ernest Heppner, *Shanghai Refuge: A Memoir of the World War II Jewish Ghetto* (Lincoln, NE, 1995), p. 13.

39. Klaus Scheurenberg in Steinhoff et al., eds., *Voices from the Third Reich,* p. 54.

40. Kaplan, *Beyond Destiny and Despair,* p. 96.

41. H. P. Herz in Steinhoff et al., eds., *Voices from the Third Reich,* p. 48.

42. Marta Appel in Mark M. Anderson, ed., *Hitler's Exiles: Personal Stories of the Flight from Nazi Germany to America* (New York, 1998), pp. 49–50.

43. Ibid., p. 58.

44. This discussion is based on Peter Kramp and Gerhard Benl, *Vererbungslehre, Rassenkunde und Rassenhygiene: Lehrbuch für die Oberstufe Höherer Lehranstalten,* 2 vols. (Leipzig, 1936), and Otto Steche, *Leitfaden der Rassenkunde und Vererbungslehre der Erbgesundheitspflege und Familienkunde für die Mittelstufe* (Leipzig, 1934).

45. Steche, *Leitfaden,* p. 40.

46. For numerous case histories, see Kaplan, *Beyond Destiny and Despair,* pp. 98–99.

47. Peter Gay, *My German Question: Growing Up in Nazi Berlin* (New Haven, CT, 1998), pp. 94–95.

48. Marta Appel in Anderson, *Hitler's Exiles,* p. 52.

49. Frau Verena Groth in Owings, *Frauen,* pp. 111–12.

50. Kaplan, *Beyond Destiny and Despair,* pp. 103–4.

51. Kenneth Carey in Leverton and Lowensohn, *I Came Alone,* pp. 52–53.

52. NA RG 59 LM193/25, 862.42/112, Dodd to SecState, 16 September 1935.

53. Helmreich, "Jewish Education in the Third Reich," p. 144.

54. NA RG 59 LM193/25, 862.42/76, Dodd to SecState, 10 July 1934.

55. Geoffrey J. Giles, *Students and National Socialism in Germany* (Princeton, NJ, 1985), pp. 108–9.

56. Klemperer, *I Will Bear Witness,* Vol. 1, p. 212, 11 February 1937.

57. Ibid., pp. 15, 174.

58. Ibid., pp. 30–31.

59. *Ambassador Dodd's Diary,* pp. 219–20, 250.

60. Rhoda Sutherland, Lady Margaret Hall, Oxford, conversation with author, 1963.

61. Giles, *Students and National Socialism in Germany,* p. 251.

62. *Morning Post,* 30 July 1935, in Grunberger, *A Social History of the Third Reich,* p. 393.

63. Giles, *Students and National Socialism in Germany,* p. 252.

64. Ibid., pp. 4–6.

65. Ibid., pp. 253–54.

66. Grunberger, *A Social History of the Third Reich,* p. 402.

67. R. G. S. Weber, *The German Student Corps in the Third Reich* (London, 1986), p. 150.

68. Giles, *Students and National Socialism in Germany,* pp. 139–43.

69. Ulrich von Hassell, *Journal d'un conjuré, 1938–44* (Paris, 1996), p. 62.

70. Ibid., pp. 258–60.
71. Weber, *The German Student Corps in the Third Reich,* pp. 129–30.
72. NA RG 59 LM193/25/862.42/108GDG, Dodd to SecState, 8 July 1935.
73. Giles, *Students and National Socialism in Germany,* p. 139.
74. Ibid., pp. 174, 219, 248–49.
75. Weber, *The German Student Corps in the Third Reich,* p. 166.

CHAPTER 5. HITLER'S CHILDREN

1. Noakes and Pridham, eds., *Nazism,* Vol. 1, Reichenberg, 4 December 1938, No. 297, p. 417.
2. *New York Times,* 21 August 1933.
3. Gay, *My German Question,* p. 55.
4. Heppner, *Shanghai Refuge,* pp. 8–10.
5. Koch, *The Hitler Youth,* p. 96, n. 90.
6. Gerhard Rempel, *Hitler's Children: The Hitler Youth and the SS* (Chapel Hill, NC, 1989), p. 10.
7. Koch, *The Hitler Youth,* p. 113.
8. Maschmann, *Account Rendered,* p. 11.
9. *Völkischer Beobachter,* 1 August 1934, in NA RG 59 LM193/25, 862.42/87, "Education of Nazis," Dodd to SecState, 14 August 1934.
10. Herbst, *Requiem for a German Past,* p. 91; Maschmann, *Account Rendered,* p. 18.
11. Ziemer, *Education for Death,* p. 96.
12. Noakes and Pridham, eds., *Nazism,* Vol. 1, p. 422.
13. Ibid., pp. 55–59; Rempel, *Hitler's Children,* p. 177; Koch, *The Hitler Youth,* pp. 112–13.
14. Hans J. Massaquoi, *Destined to Witness: Growing Up Black in Nazi Germany* (New York, 1999), pp. 97–103.
15. Herbst, *Requiem for a German Past,* pp. 23–25.
16. Erna Tietz, in Owings, *Frauen,* p. 267.
17. Albert Bastian, in Steinhoff et al., eds., *Voices from the Third Reich,* p. 14.
18. Maschmann, *Account Rendered,* pp. 44–45, 35.
19. Peter Kurth, *American Cassandra: The Life of Dorothy Thompson* (Boston, 1990), pp. 200–201.
20. Alfons Heck, *A Child of Hitler: Germany in the Days When God Wore a Swastika* (Frederick, CO, 1985), pp. 19–26.
21. William Shirer, *Berlin Diary* (New York, 1941), entries for September 9–14, 1938.
22. William H. Kern, "The Second World War, 1939–1945: Growing Up in Wartime Germany," unpublished ms., p. 2.
23. Koch, *The Hitler Youth,* p. 229.
24. Noakes and Pridham, eds., *Nazism,* Vol. 1, Doc. 310, p. 430.
25. Rempel, *Hitler's Children,* pp. 31–32.
26. Hans Holtzrager, *Die Wehrertüchtigungslager der Hitler-Jugend, 1942–1945, Ein Dokumentarbericht* (Ippesheim, 1991), pp. 17–21.
27. For a vivid description of an Aviation unit, see Heck, *A Child of Hitler,* pp. 57–85.
28. Koch, *The Hitler Youth,* p. 104.
29. Herman Rosenau, in Steinhoff et al., eds., *Voices from the Third Reich,* pp. 301–5.
30. Rempel, *Hitler's Children,* pp. 180–81.
31. NA RG 59/LM193/25/739/862.42/82, White to SecState, 7 April 1934.
32. On the relationship of the Land Service to the SS, see Rempel, *Hitler's Children,* Chapter 5.

33. Maschmann, *Account Rendered,* p. 33.
34. Ibid., pp. 32–35.
35. Noakes and Pridham, eds., *Nazism,* Vol. 1, Doc. 241, p. 354.
36. Ibid., Doc. 243, pp. 355–56, SOPADE Berichte, 1938, pp. 480–81.
37. On dissent and the SRD, see Rempel, *Hitler's Children,* Chapter 3; Koch, *The Hitler Youth,* Chapter 10.
38. Rempel, *Hitler's Children,* p. 58.
39. Koch, *The Hitler Youth,* p. 219.
40. NA RG 59 LM193/57/703 #2115, A. Kirk, 20 March 1944.
41. Massaquoi, *Destined to Witness,* p. 160.
42. Ibid., p. 162.
43. Rempel, *Hitler's Children,* p. 104.
44. Herbst, *Requiem for a German Past,* pp. 75–76.
45. Noakes and Pridham, eds., *Nazism,* Vol. 1, Docs. 299 and 300, pp. 419–20.
46. Rempel, *Hitler's Children,* p. 71.
47. Karma Rauhut, in Owings, *Frauen,* pp. 347–57.
48. Rempel, *Hitler's Children,* pp. 97–100.
49. Ibid., pp. 74–75.
50. Herbst, *Requiem for a German Past,* p. 64.
51. Koch, *The Hitler Youth,* p. 103.
52. NA RG 260/185, Nuremberg Doc. 136-PS.
53. Koch, *The Hitler Youth,* pp. 199–203.
54. Ibid., p. 201.
55. Ibid., pp. 196–99.
56. NA RG 238 M894/14, Doc. NO-3736, Heissmeyer to Brandt, 21 September 1944.
57. Koch, *The Hitler Youth,* p. 181.
58. Ibid., p. 185.
59. P. Petersen, in Steinhoff et al., eds., *Voices from the Third Reich,* p. 8.
60. Hans Bieber, in *NSD Oberschule Starnbergersee, 1937–38* (Munich, 1938), p. 26. The yearbook was kindly provided to me by Dr. Walter Filley.
61. Interview with Walter Filley; yearbook, pp. 15–17.
62. Conversation with Frank Lee, March 2002.
63. Filley interview.
64. Gene Keith, in *The Choate News,* June 4, 1938, p. 1.
65. Theo Loch, in Steinhoff et al., eds., *Voices from the Third Reich,* p. 11.
66. *The Choate News,* May 14, 1938, p. 2.
67. Ibid., and Filley interview.
68. Jost Hermand, *A Hitler Youth in Poland: The Nazis' Program for Evacuating Children During World War II* (Evanston, IL, 1997), pp. xxiv–xxvi; see also Koch, *The Hitler Youth,* pp. 195, 241.
69. Hermand, *A Hitler Youth in Poland,* p. 49.
70. Ibid., p. 50.
71. Ibid., pp. 53–56.
72. Ibid., pp. 68–73.
73. Ibid., p. 88.

CHAPTER 6. THE FLOODGATES CLOSE

1. Sergei Hackel, *Pearl of Great Price: The Life of Mother Maria Skobtsova, 1891–1945* (New York, 1981), p. 1.

2. Schmitt, *Quakers and Nazis,* pp. 13–17. These programs were taken over by the German government in 1924. Help to Austria continued until 1933.

3. T. H. Watkins, *The Hungry Years: A Narrative History of the Great Depression in America* (New York, 1999), pp. 157–58.

4. Ibid., pp. 54–55, 58, 71.

5. George Orwell, *The Road to Wigan Pier* (New York, 1958), p. 63.

6. Watkins, *The Hungry Years,* pp. 398–401.

7. Georges Mauco, *Les Étrangers en France* (1932), pp. 558, 560, cited in Weber, *The German Student Corps,* pp. 90–91n.

8. A. J. Sherman, *Island Refuge: Britain and Refugees from the Third Reich, 1933–1939* (Ilford, UK, 1994), Appendix 2.

9. For exhaustive analyses of American immigration policy, see David S. Wyman, *Paper Walls: America and the Refugee Crisis, 1938–1941* (Amherst, MA, 1968), and Richard Breitman and Alan M. Kraut, *American Refugee Policy and European Jewry, 1933–1945* (Bloomington, IN, 1987). W. D. Rubenstein's *The Myth of Rescue* (London, 1997) contains interesting statistics and gives a different point of view.

10. Michael R. Marrus and Robert O. Paxton, *Vichy France and the Jews* (Stanford, CA, 1995), p. 36.

11. Sherman, *Island Refuge,* pp. 47–48.

12. Anderson, *Hitler's Exiles,* p. 136.

13. Marta Appel, cited ibid., p. 148.

14. Sherman, *Island Refuge,* pp. 39–40.

15. *Ambassador Dodd's Diary,* entries for 18 October 1933, 9 August and 1 November 1934, pp. 50–51, 145–46, 183–84.

16. Ibid., 7 February 1933, pp. 78–79.

17. Judith Tydor Baumel, *Unfufilled Promise: Rescue and Settlement of Jewish Refugee Children in the United States, 1934–35* (Juneau, AK, 1990), pp. 16–19.

18. Breitman and Kraut, *American Refugee Policy,* pp. 24–25.

19. Braumel, *Unfulfilled Promise,* p. 19.

20. Sherman, *Island Refuge,* p. 52.

21. Ibid., p. 60.

22. Claude G. Bowers, *My Mission to Spain: Watching the Rehearsal for World War II* (New York, 1954), p. 284.

23. Dorothy Legarreta, *The Guernica Generation: Basque Refugee Children of the Spanish Civil War* (Reno, NV, 1984), pp. 34–36.

24. Ibid., pp. 20–22.

25. NA RG 59 LM074/5 AFSC, bulletin of Committee on Spain, 28 June 1937.

26. NA RG 59 LM074/5, bulletin of Spanish Relief Conditions, Committee on Spain, AFSC, Vol. 1, No. 4, 5 August 1937.

27. Legarreta, *The Guernica Generation,* pp. 35–36.

28. Ibid., pp. 30, 25.

29. Bowers, *My Mission to Spain,* p. 343.

30. Statement by Father A. Onaindia, ibid., p. 345.

31. Bowers, *My Mission to Spain,* p. 344.

32. Ronald Fraser, *Blood of Spain: An Oral History of the Spanish Civil War* (New York, 1979), p. 442.

33. *FRUS* 1937, Vol. 1, p. 546, Bowers to SecState, 2 September 1937.

34. Fraser, *Blood of Spain,* p. 167.

35. Ibid., pp. 156–57.

36. Ibid., pp. 455, 152, 477–48.

37. Legarreta, *The Guernica Generation,* pp. 38–39.

38. *FRUS* 1937, Vol. 1, p. 525, Chapman to State, 9 July 1937.

39. "Annual Report of the Secretary of Labor, 1939," in Rubenstein, *The Myth of Rescue,* p. 99.

40. *FRUS* 1937, Vol. 1, pp. 498–547. For pro/con correspondence of organizations, NA RG 59 LM074/3/729–70.

41. *FRUS,* 1938, Vol. 1, Efforts for the Relief of Spanish Refugees, pp. 364–83.

42. Ibid., and NA RG 59 LM074/3/729–70.

43. This and following descriptions in Legarreta, *The Guernica Generation,* pp. 103–6.

44. Ibid., pp. 162–64.

45. Fraser, *Blood of Spain,* pp. 433–37.

46. Stéphane Courtois et al., eds., *The Black Book of Communism: Crimes, Terror, Repression* (Cambridge, MA, 1999), p. 350.

47. Legarreta, *The Guernica Generation,* p. 145.

48. Ibid., Chapter 3.

49. NA RG 59 LM074/4/881, 852.48/415, Paris, Wilson to SecState, 14 March 1939. Enclosure I, Noel H. Field, "Confidential Report on Conditions in Spanish Refugee Camps in Southern France," 4 March 1939, p. 2.

50. Ibid., pp. 2–3.

51. Ibid., p. 7.

52. NA RG 59 LM074/5 ONI 854.48, Attaché's report, "Visit to Spanish Refugee Camp at 'Guers,' Basse-Pyrenees," 19 July 1939.

53. NA RG 59 LM074/5/181, International Commission for the Assistance of Spanish Child Refugees, report, 10 July 1939.

54. G. E. R. Gedye, *Fallen Bastions: The Central European Tragedy* (London, 1939), pp. 295–96.

55. Milton and Friedlander, eds., *Archives of the Holocaust,* Vol. 2, AFSC Philadelphia, Part 1, 1932–39, doc 117, p. 344, Florence Barrow to Clarence Pickett, 19 May 1938.

56. Gedye, *Fallen Bastions,* p. 349.

57. Breitman and Kraut, *American Refugee Policy,* p. 58.

58. *FRUS* 1938, Vol. 1, p. 740.

59. Marrus and Paxton, *Vichy France and the Jews,* pp. 60–62.

60. *FRUS* 1938, Vol. 1, p. 742, Gunther to SecState, 13 April 1938.

61. *FRUS* 1938, Vol. 1, p. 743, Welles to Gunther, 21 April 1938.

62. L. de Jong, *Het Koninkrijk der Nederlanden in de Tweede Wereld Oorlog,* 14 vols. (The Hague, 1974), Vol. 1, pp. 462, 479, 488.

63. Sherman, *Island Refuge,* pp. 98–99; PRO FO 371/21634, C3588/1667/62, 21 April 1938.

64. PRO FO372/3284 51593 T 7056, "Visas for Holders of German or Austrian Passports Entering the United Kingdom. General Principles," 27 May 1938.

65. PRO FO 372/3284 51593 T10774, Gaines to Hutcheson, 9 August 1938.

66. De Jong, *Het Koninkrijk,* Vol. 1, pp. 472–73.

67. Ibid., p. 143.

68. See, on this subject, Sherman, *Island Refuge,* pp. 139, 221.

69. NA RG 59 LM193/58, 862.4016/1800, Biddle to SecState, 29 October 1938.

70. *FRUS* 1938, Vol. 1, pp. 778–80, Biddle to State, 30 August 1938.

71. *FRUS,* 1938, Vol. 1, pp. 835–36, Memo, Pierrepont Moffet, 19 November 1938.

72. Sherman, *Island Refuge,* p. 164.

73. NARA RG 59, LM193/58, Cables 862.4016/2078,2093,2129, Winship, Biddle, Warsaw, to SecState, 25, 27 January, 27 February 1939.

74. Milton and Friedlander, eds., *Archives of the Holocaust,* Vol. 2, Doc. 215, p. 618, "Perry Report of Trip to Poland, July 20–27, 1939."

75. NA RG 239/66, Nuremberg Doc. 2237-PS.

76. NA RG 59 LM193/58, Honaker to Messersmith, 862.4016/2002 15/11/38, and Honaker to Wilson, 800/840.1, "Anti-Semitic Persecution in the Stuttgart Consular District," No. 307, 11 December 1938.

77. De Jong, *Het Koninkrijk,* Vol. 1, p. 485.

78. *FRUS,* 1938, Vol. 1, pp. 847–49, Waller to State, 1 December 1938.

79. See note 76.

80. Heppner, *Shanghai Refuge,* p. 45.

81. Truus Wijsmuller-Meijer, *Geen Tijd voor Tranen* (Amsterdam, undated), pp. 120–25.

82. Sherman, *Island Refuge,* pp. 232–37.

83. George Rublee, "Reminiscences," unpublished ms. of interviews by the Oral History Research Office, Columbia University, p. 298. Kindly provided by George Rublee II.

84. Wyman, *Paper Walls,* p. 55. For a full discussion of the Intergovernmental Committee, see Chapter 2.

Chapter 7. Saving the Children

1. Wijsmuller-Meijer, *Geen Tijd voor Tranen,* p. 48.

2. For a complete account of the activities of this organization, see Amy Zahl Gottlieb, *Men of Vision: Anglo-Jewry's Aid to Victims of the Nazi Regime, 1933–1945* (London, 1998).

3. Ibid., pp. 99–100.

4. Ibid., pp. 66–72.

5. Sara Kadosh, director, AJDC Archives, USHMM Symposium, 3 April 2003.

6. IWM, Dept. of Documents, MISC 53/818, Papers of Margareta Burkill, "The Refugee Children's Movement Ltd., 1938–1948," p. 3.

7. De Jong, *Het Koninkrijk,* Vol. 1, p. 488.

8. Wijsmuller-Meijer, *Geen Tijd voor Tranen,* pp. 70–75.

9. De Jong, *Het Koninkrijk,* Vol. 1, p. 489.

10. Wijsmuller-Meijer, *Geen Tijd voor Tranen,* p. 105.

11. Ibid., p. 106.

12. De Jong, *Het Koninkrijk,* Vol. 3, p. 412.

13. Karen Gershon, ed., *We Came as Children: A Collective Autobiography* (London, 1966), p. 22.

14. Ibid., pp. 22–25.

15. Wyman, *Paper Walls,* p. 76.

16. Papers of Robert F. Wagner, Georgetown University, Washington, DC, Alien Files 1938, 1939, Boxes 636–47.

17. Wyman, *Paper Walls,* p. 78.

18. This account is summarized from Wyman's detailed analysis, ibid., pp. 75–98.

19. Leverton and Lowensohn, *I Came Alone,* p. 30.

20. Ibid., p. 91, account of Charles Feld.

21. Gershon, *We Came as Children,* p. 26.

22. Ibid., p. 27.

23. Ibid., p. 30.

24. Ibid., p. 28.

25. Ibid., passim.

26. Wijsmuller-Meijer, *Geen Tijd voor Tranen,* pp. 87–88.

27. Gershon, *We Came as Children,* p. 64; Gottlieb, *Men of Vision,* pp. 117–19, 123–25.

28. Sherman, *Island Refuge,* p. 258.

29. For a touching account of such a home, see Ian Buruma, "Churchill's Cigar," *Granta* 65 (Spring 1999), pp. 327–43; kindly pointed out to me by Paul Kramer.

30. Ruth E. Wolman, *Crossing Over: An Oral History of Refugees from Hitler's Reich* (New York, 1996), pp. 8–11.

31. Speech by Lord Attenborough, June 15, 1999, at the sixtieth anniversary of the Kindertransports, London.

32. Gershon, *We Came as Children,* p. 49.

33. Interview, Egon Guttmann, Washington, DC.

34. Gershon, *We Came as Children,* p. 52.

35. De Jong, *Het Koninkrijk,* Vol. 2, pp. 114–17, 373–75.

36. This and subsequent events from Henri Amouroux, *La Grande Histoire des Français sous l'occupation.* Vol. 1, *Le people du désastre, 1939–1940* (Paris, 1976), Chapter titled "Le Moral des Civils."

37. Travis L. Crosby, *The Impact of Civilian Evacuation in the Second World War* (London, 1986), Chapter 2.

38. Edward R. Murrow, *This Is London* (New York, 1941), entries for 28 and 31 August, and 4 September 1939.

39. Susan Isaacs, ed., *The Cambridge Evacuation Survey: A Wartime Study in Social Welfare and Education* (London, 1941), pp. 34–35.

40. IWM, Dept. of Documents, 91/5/1, Papers of Terence Nunn, pp. 41–44.

41. IWM, Dept. of Documents, 92/9/1, Papers of Mrs. M. D. Brand, p. 2.

42. Isaacs, *The Cambridge Evacuation Survey,* p. 40.

43. For an excellent discussion of this and other problems, see Ruth Inglis, *The Children's War: Evacuation, 1939–1945* (London, 1989).

44. Gottlieb, *Men of Vision,* pp. 167–71; Sherman, *Island Refuge,* p. 256.

45. Gershon, *We Came as Children,* p. 91.

46. Ibid., pp. 92–96.

47. Interviews, Walter Fletcher and Fred Hochberg, Kindertransport Reunion, 1999.

48. Shirer, *The Rise and Fall of the Third Reich,* p. 723.

49. Shirer, *Berlin Diary,* May 20, 1940.

50. De Jong, *Het Koninkrijk,* Vol. 3, pp. 98–100.

51. Jacques De Launay, *La Belgique à l'heure allemande* (Brussels, undated), p. 44.

52. Amouroux, *La Grand Histoire,* Vol. 1, p. 379.

53. Ibid., p. 389.

54. Donald A. Lowrie, *The Hunted Children* (New York, 1963), pp. 29–30.

55. Amouroux, Vol. 1, p. 394.

56. Ibid., p. 400.

57. Lowrie, *The Hunted Children,* p. 28.

58. Joël Mettay, *L'Archipel du Mépris: Histoire du camps de Rivesaltes de 1939 à nos jours* (Canet, 2001), pp. 14–15.

59. Marrus and Paxton, *Vichy France and the Jews,* p. 65.

60. Ibid., pp. 165–66.

61. See Lowrie, *The Hunted Children,* Chapter 8.

62. Wyman, *Paper Walls,* p. 129.

63. Ibid., p. 134.

64. Mettay, *L'Archipel du Mépris,* pp. 45–49.

65. Ibid., p. 130.
66. Ibid., pp. 64–67.
67. Lowrie, *The Hunted Children,* pp. 122–23, 144.
68. Inglis, *The Children's War,* p. 82.
69. Ibid., p. 83.
70. Ibid., p. 85.
71. Wyman, *Paper Walls,* p. 117.
72. Ibid., pp. 98–101.
73. Ibid., p. 133.
74. Inglis, *The Children's War,* pp. 105–9.
75. Wyman, *Paper Walls,* p. 119.
76. Ibid., pp. 120–21.
77. Ibid., pp. 124–25.
78. Vera Brittain, cited in Inglis, *The Children's War,* p. 113.
79. IWM, Dept. of Documents, 88/26/1, Papers of M. A. Walford, p. 4.
80. IWM, Dept. of Documents, 91/37/1, Papers of Mrs. A. W. Winter, pp. 12–14.
81. IWM, Dept. of Documents, 97/3/1, Papers of Cadet Officer D. Haffner, "The Torpedoing of the SS *City of Benares,*" unpaginated.
82. IWM, Dept. of Documents, 91/37/1, Papers of Miss B. Walder, letter to Miss Simonis, 1 October 1940.
83. IWM, Dept. of Documents, 97/3/1, Haffner, "The Torpedoing of the SS *City of Benares.*"
84. PRO MT9/3461/51557, clipping, *Montreal Gazette,* 23 September 1940.
85. For a charming account of the experiences of a Seavac, see Anthony Bailey, *America Lost and Found: An English Boy's Adventure in the New World* (New York, 1980).

Chapter 8. Good Blood

1. NA RG 59 LM 193/12/333-336, 344, Dodd cables, 7/17/33, 7/21/33, and 8/15/33.
2. Otto Schaefer, *Sinn und Wesen des VDA,* Frankfurt, 1933, p. 21, as cited in Alton Frye, *Nazi Germany and the American Hemisphere, 1933–1941* (New Haven, CT, 1967), p. 17.
3. *DGFP,* Series C, Vol. 2, Doc. 140. 12/14/33, pp. 255–59.
4. LC/MS, Captured German Records, DAI, Reel 290.
5. Ibid., Reel 443.
6. Ibid., Reel 290, Correspondence German Consulate, Chicago, 9/27/37, 11/8/37.
7. NA RG 59 LM 193/12/274, Scanlan memo, 8/18/38, 862.012/122.
8. LC/MS, Captured German Records, DAI, Reel 292.
9. Ibid., Reel 443, VDA Rundschreiben Nr. 6-Karteikarten, 7/11/38, to DAI.
10. Ibid., Reel 292.
11. Ibid., Reel 474, Kloss to Stahmer (VoMi), 2/15/38.
12. Ibid., Reel 474, unidentified clipping.
13. Dray, *At The Hands of Persons Unknown,* p. 497, n. 339.
14. See Frye, *Nazi Germany and the American Hemisphere,* Chapter 6, pp. 82–91.
15. *DGFP,* Series D, Vol. 4, Docs. 500–502, 11/8–15/38.
16. Ibid., Docs. 509, 510, and 513, 12/16–19/38.
17. NA RG 238 M894/16, Doc. NO-5630, Himmler memo to Bormann, 4/23/42.
18. Frye, *Nazi Germany and the American Hemisphere,* pp. 65–79.

19. LC/MS, Captured German Records, DAI, Reel 474, "Politisches Bericht uber das Mandatsgebiet Neuguinea," 9/22/36.

20. See Robert L. Koehl, *RKFDV: German Resettlement Policy and Population Policy, 1939–1945: A History of the Reich Commission for the Strengthening of Germandom* (Cambridge, MA, 1957), pp. 40–41. This is the definitive study on the RKFDV.

21. *DGFP,* Series D, Vol. 8, Doc. 153, p. 162, Weizsacker to Ribbentrop, 9/28/39.

22. *DGFP,* Series D, Vol. 8, Doc. 176, p. 188, "Memo of a Conversation Between the Führer and Count Ciano," 10/2/39.

23. Nuremberg Doc. NO-3075, "Decree by the Führer and Reich Chancellor for the Consolidation of German Folkdom, 10/7/39, cited in Koehl, *RKFDV,* p. 247.

24. Berlin Document Center, *The Holdings of the Berlin Document Center: A Guide to the Collections* (Berlin, 1994), pp. 12, 37, and n. 50.

25. Dietrich A. Loeber, *Diktierte Option: Die Umsiedlung der Deutsch-Balten aus Estland und Lettland, 1939–1941* (Neumünster, 1972), Doc. 109, p. 136, German Legation in Reval to Foreign Ministry, 10/15/39.

26. *DGFP,* Series D, Vol. 8, p. 227, Hitler's speech to the Reichstag, 10/6/39.

27. NA RG 59 T1243/40, 760i.62/37, Wiley (Riga) to SecState, 10/8/39.

28. NA RG 59 T1243/40, 760i.62/35, Leonard (Tallinn) to SecState, 10/8/39.

29. *DGFP,* Series D, Vol. 8, Doc. 239, p. 266, 10/11/39.

30. NA RG 59 T1243/40, 760i.62/46, Steinhardt (Moscow) to SecState, 10/14/39.

31. *Times* (London), 10 October 1939.

32. See Loeber, *Diktierte Option,* Docs. 310–15, pp. 635–62.

33. Ibid., Doc. 39, p. 163, *Rigasche Rundschau,* 10/9/39.

34. Ibid., Doc. 142, p. 185, *Revalsche Zeitung,* 10/11/39.

35. Ibid., Doc. 321, p. 672, Arvid von Nottbeck, *Baltische Briefe,* 1963, No. 11, p. 4.

36. Ibid., Doc. 153, p. 207, 10/10/39, and Doc. 154, p. 208, 10/15/39.

37. Ibid., Doc. 132, p. 167, "Frau Kurtson will nicht," *Rigasche Rundschau,* 11/9/39.

38. Ibid., Doc. 156, pp. 210–11, November 1939.

39. Joseph B. Schechtman, *European Population Transfers, 1939–1945* (New York, 1946), p. 103.

40. *Rigasche Rundschau,* 12/9/39, cited ibid., p. 98.

41. Schechtman, *European Population Transfers,* p. 105.

42. Olrik Breckoff, "Zwischenspiel an der Warthe-und was daraus wurde," in *Jahrbuch des Baltischen Deutschtums, 1994,* p. 142.

43. Berndt von Staden, "Erinnerungen an die Umsiedlung" in *Jahrbuch des Baltischen Deutschtums, 1994,* p. 62.

44. A. Meyer-Landruth, in Steinhoff et al., eds., *Voices from the Third Reich,* p. 103.

45. Karen Grunerwald, "Ich werde Landfrau in Kalisch," *Jahrbuch des Baltischen Deutschtums, 1994,* pp. 101–2.

46. Ibid., p. 102.

47. Berlin Document Center, *Holdings,* pp. 43–44.

48. Koehl, *RKFDV,* pp. 106–7.

49. Breckoff, "Zwischenspiel," pp. 144–45.

50. N. N. Metz, "Heim ins Reich," in *Jahrbuch des Baltischen Deutschtums, 1994,* pp. 131–33.

51. A. Meyer-Landruth, in Steinhoff et al., eds., *Voices of the Third Reich,* p. 103.

52. NA RG 238, Nuremberg Doc. No. 2916-PS.

53. Maschmann, *Account Rendered,* pp. 63–75.

54. LC/MS, Captured German Records, Reel 490, "Der BDM-Osteinsatz hilft Heimat schaffen."

55. NA RG 242 T81/277; Frames 397640-962 contain a series of required diaries and reports on their Eastern Duty experiences, which are excerpted here.

56. Maschmann, *Account Rendered,* pp. 126–27.

57. Ibid., pp. 93–97.

58. Ibid., pp. 115–17.

59. Ibid., pp. 81–83.

60. NA RG 242 T81/277/397 958.

61. Hermand, *A Hitler Youth in Poland,* p. 82.

62. Milton and Friedlander, eds., *Archives of the Holocaust,* Vol. 11, BDC, Part 1, Doc. 150, p. 276.

63. NA RG 242 T81/277, L. Hintz diary, summer 1940.

64. Maschmann, *Account Rendered,* pp. 119–22.

65. NA RG 242 T81/277, "Generalbericht vom studentenischen Osteinsatz, 1940–1941," Josef N. report, pp. 124–27, 397, 813–16.

66. Herbst, *Requiem for a German Past,* Chapter 6.

67. Maschmann, *Account Rendered,* pp. 130–31.

68. LC/MS, Captured German Records, Reel 490, "BDM-Osteinsatz," p. 17.

69. Rempel, *Hitler's Children,* pp. 155–56.

CHAPTER 9. BAD BLOOD

1. *DGFP,* Series D, Vol. 7, Doc. 193.

2. NA RG 59 M982 740.00116/74, Biddle to SecState, 9/19/39.

3. Sevek Finkelstein and Ben Helfgott, in Martin Gilbert, *The Boys: Triumph over Adversity* (London, 1996), pp. 52–54.

4. On the Einsatzgruppen in Poland, see Richard Breitman, *The Architect of Genocide: Himmler and the Final Solution* (New York, 1991), pp. 66–71, and Ian Kershaw, *Hitler, 1936–1945: Nemesis* (New York, 2000), pp. 240–48.

5. Polish Ministry of Information, *Black Book of Poland,* p. 134, cited in Richard Lukas, *Forgotten Holocaust: The Poles Under German Occupation, 1939–1944* (Lexington, KY, 1986), p. 3.

6. Noakes and Pridham, eds., *Nazism,* Vol. 2, Doc. 654, pp. 937–38.

7. Hilberg, *The Destruction of the European Jews,* p. 75.

8. For a detailed discussion of the Nisko operation, see Jonny Moser, "Nisko: The First Experiment in Deportation," *Simon Wiesenthal Center Annual* 2 (1985), pp. 1–30.

9. *New York Times,* 20 November 1939, p. 6, col. 3.

10. Ibid., 17 November 1939, p. 7, col. 2.

11. Noakes and Pridham, eds., *Nazism,* Vol. 2, p. 1054.

12. NA RG 238, Nuremberg Doc. 2233-PS, undated excerpts from Frank diaries, 10/25–12/15/39.

13. Noakes and Pridham, eds., *Nazism,* Vol. 2, Docs. 776 and 777, pp. 1057–58.

14. Ibid., Doc. 655, pp. 938–40.

15. For a detailed discussion of the JDC and other agencies, see Yehuda Bauer, *American Jewry and the Holocaust: The American Jewish Joint Distribution Committee, 1939–1945* (Detroit, 1981), Chapters 3 and 13.

16. Ibid., p. 90.

17. Leon Harari, "Die Kinderrepublik des Janusz Korczak. Erinnerungen," in *Die*

Verfolgung von Kindern und Jugendlichen, Dachauer Hefte No. 9, Dachau, November 1993.

18. For the life of children at Theresienstadt, see Marie Krísková et al., eds., *We Are Children Just the Same: Vedem, the Secret Magazine by the Boys of Terezin* (Philadelphia, 1995), and Deborah Dwork, *Children with a Star: Jewish Youth in Nazi Europe* (New Haven, CT, 1991), Chapter 4.

19. Niklas Frank, *In the Shadow of the Reich* (New York, 1991), pp. 136–37, 151–53.

20. Bauer, *American Jewry and the Holocaust,* pp. 98–99.

21. For a complete discussion of the role of the War Refugee Board, see David Wyman, *The Abandonment of the Jews: America and the Holocaust, 1941–1945* (New York, 1998), pp. 280–84.

22. Abraham Lewin and Emmanuel Ringelbaum, quoted in Dwork, *Children with a Star,* p. 200.

23. Sabina Wylot, in Wiktoria Sliwowska, ed., *The Last Eyewitnesses: Children of the Holocaust Speak* (Evanston, IL, 1998), pp. 144–45.

24. Dwork, *Children with a Star,* pp. 202–3.

25. Zygmunt Klukowski, *Diary from the Years of Occupation, 1939–44* (Chicago, 1993), entry for 23 July 1940, p. 103.

26. *IMT,* Nuremberg Doc. 2916-PS.

27. Klukowski, *Diary from the Years of Occupation,* pp. 120–21.

28. Ibid., pp. 132–33.

29. Kyril Sosnowski, *The Tragedy of Children Under Nazi Rule* (New York, 1983), Chapter 5.

30. NA RG 242 T81/277, Generalbericht vom studentischen Osteinsatz, 1940–41, pp. 201–2.

31. NA RG 238 M894/16, Doc. NO-3089, Conti to Himmler, 3/9/42 and Himmler to Conti, 3/21/42.

32. NA RG 238 M894/15, Doc. NO-1125, "Re Handling of Subsistence Claims of Illegitimate Polish Children Against Their Polish Fathers," Conference at Reich Ministry of Justice, 3/10/43.

33. Noakes and Pridham, eds., *Nazism,* Vol. 2, p. 979, Doc. 691.

34. Ibid., p. 933, Doc. 651.

35. NA RG 238 M894/14, Doc. NO-4616, Reichsführer SS to Delegate of the RKFDV, Kattowitz, 10/23/40.

36. NA RG 238 M894/14, Doc. NO-3732, W. Gross, NSDAP, Treatise on the Treatment of Poles and Jews, 11/25/39.

37. NA RG 238 M894/14, Doc. NO-1880, "Reflections on the Treatment of Peoples of Alien Races in the East," 5/15/40.

38. Noakes and Pridham, eds., *Nazism,* Vol. 2, Doc. 652, pp. 934–35.

39. NA RG 238 M894/15, Doc. NO-1615, Greifelt memo—Regulation 67/I.

40. NA RG 238 M894/15, Doc. NO-5268, Wawelska interrogation.

41. NA RG 238 M894/15, Doc. NO-5251, Suliscz affidavit.

42. NA RG 238 M894/15, Doc. NO-5256, Dzieginska affidavit.

43. NA RG 238 M894/15, Docs. NO-4899–4903, Bukowiecka correspondence.

44. NA RG 238 M894/15, Doc. NO-4945, 11/30/44 and 12/23/44.

45. NA RG 238 M894/15, Docs. NO-5252–5253, Schwakopf and Hammer affidavits.

46. NA RG 238 M894/14, Doc. NO-1669.

47. NA RG 238 M894/15, Doc. NO-5268, Wawelska affidavit.

48. NA RG 238 M894/15, Doc. NO-4822, Heinze-Wisswede affidavit, p. 5.

49. NA RG 238 M894/15, Doc. NO-1616, Regulation 67/I, p. 9.

50. NA RG 238 M894/15, Doc. NO-2793, Bader memo, 12/10/42.

51. NA RG 238 M894/16, Doc. NO-5131, Antczak affidavit.

52. NA RG 238 M894/15, Doc. NO-5229, Hauser affidavit.

53. NA RG 238 M894/15, Doc. NO-4822, Heinze-Wisswede affidavit.

54. NA RG 238 M894/15, Doc. NO-4950.

55. NA RG 238 M894/16, Doc. NO-1387, Ebner to Solmann, 8/25/41, "Report of My Visit to the Orphans from the Banate."

56. NA RG 238 M894/15, Doc. NO-4821, Heinze affidavit.

57. NA RG 238 M894/15, Doc. NO-2870, Bauke to Ebner, 11/5/43; Ebner to Legal Office, 11/16/43.

58. NA RG 238 M894/15, Doc. NO-5251, Sulisz affidavit.

59. NA RG 238 M894/16, Doc. NO-5131, Antczak affidavit.

60. NA RG 238 M894/15, Doc. NO-4821, Heinze affidavit.

61. NA RG 238 M894/16, Doc. NO-3463, Vaclar Hanf, p. 1.

62. Ibid., pp. 2–3.

63. UNA-NY, PAG 4/4.2/81, Cornelia D. Heise, ed., 1 February 1948. UNRRA "History of Child Welfare," Exhibit 5, Fischer to Lodz Office, 12 June 1942.

64. *New York Times,* 11–13 June 1942.

65. Edna St. Vincent Millay, *The Murder of Lidice* (New York, 1942), Verse 18, p. 25.

66. NA RG238 M894/15, Doc. NO-435, illegible to Brandt, 13 June 1944; Sosnowski, *The Tragedy of Children Under Nazi Rule,* Annex 54. Data from V. Konopka, *Zde stavaly Lidice* (Prague, 1959).

67. NA RG 238 M894/16, Docs. NO-5470 and NO-5471, Hronik and Kohlicek affidavits.

68. NA RG 238 M894/15, Doc. NO-4173, 6/21/43, and Doc. NO-2218, 5/20/44.

69. NA RG 238 M894/14, Doc. NO-2481, Greifelt to Himmler, 8/2/41.

70. NA RG 238 M894/14, Doc. NO-3938, Himmler Ordinance No. 51, 10/1/41.

71. NA RG 238 M894/14, Doc. NO-2267, Creutz to Himmler, 2/20/42.

72. NA RG 238 M894/15, Doc. NO-5269, Pieskarska interrogation.

73. NA RG 238 M894/14, Doc. NO-2760, Brandt to Baron Oeynhausen, 11/9/44.

74. NA RG 238 M894/14, Doc. NO-2762, Oeynhausen to Brandt, 11/20/44.

75. Ulrich Herbert, *Hitler's Foreign Workers: Enforced Foreign Labor in Germany Under the Third Reich* (Cambridge, UK, 1997), pp. 28–29.

76. Ibid., pp. 61–64.

77. Ibid., pp. 71–79.

78. Klukowski, *Diary from the Years of Occupation,* 19 May 1940, pp. 86–87.

79. Herbert, *Hitler's Foreign Workers,* p. 85.

80. Christoph U. Schmink-Gustavus, *Hungern für Hitler: Erinnerungen polnischer Zwangsarbeiter im Deutschen Reich, 1940–1945,* (Hamburg, 1984) "Julian Nowak. Von Lager zu Lager," pp. 32–68.

81. Ibid., p. 26.

82. Ibid., pp. 45–49.

83. Ibid., pp. 23–24.

84. Celina Drozdek, "Dorn Meiner Jugend. Erinnerungen an die Zwangsarbeit in der Bremer Jutespinnerei, 1940–1942," in Schmink-Gustavus, *Hungern für Hitler,* pp. 181–214.

85. Herbert, *Hitler's Foreign Workers,* p. 203.

86. Henryk Grygiel, "Hungern für Hitler. Erinnerungen an die Zwangsarbeit bei Focke-Wulf," in Schmink-Gustavus, *Hungern für Hitler,* pp. 138–39.

87. Courtois et al., eds., *The Black Book of Communism*, pp. 366–67.

88. Irena G. Gross and Jan T. Gross, *War Through Children's Eyes* (Stanford, CA, 1981), Introduction.

89. N. S. Lebedeva, "The Deportation of the Polish Population to the USSR, 1939–41," in Alfred J. Rieber, ed., *Forced Migration in Central and Eastern Europe, 1939–1950* (London, 2000), p. 30.

90. Gross and Gross, *War Through Children's Eyes*, p. 21.

91. Ibid., pp. 24–27.

92. Lebedeva, "The Deportation of the Polish Population," pp. 31–33.

93. Gross and Gross, *War Through Children's Eyes*, Doc. 68, p. 156.

94. Lebedeva, "The Deportation of the Polish Population," pp. 33–34.

95. Gross and Gross, *War Through Children's Eyes*, Doc. 44, p. 104.

96. Ibid., Doc. 110, p. 207.

97. Ibid., Doc. 110, p. 207; Doc. 91, p. 172; Doc. 43, p. 101.

98. Ibid., Doc. 23, pp. 78–79.

99. Lebedeva, "The Deportation of the Polish Population," p. 42.

100. Janka Goldberger, *Stalin's Little Guest* (Chatham, UK, 1988), pp. 18–19.

101. Gross and Gross, *War Through Children's Eyes*, Doc. 1, pp. 46–48.

102. Goldberger, *Stalin's Little Guest*, Chapter 4.

103. Lebedeva, "The Deportation of the Polish Population," p. 35.

104. Harold Olin, *An Oral History*, Heartland Historical Research Service, 2000, pp. 19–21.

105. Gross and Gross, *War Through Children's Eyes*, p. 66.

106. Olin, *An Oral History*, p. 28.

107. Gross and Gross, *War Through Children's Eyes*, Doc. 8, p. 54.

108. Olin, *An Oral History*, p. 28.

109. Gross and Gross, *War Through Children's Eyes*, Doc. 57, p. 123.

110. Irena Wasilewska, "Note Concerning Children Deported into the USSR," Hoover Institution, PAC, File 266, cited ibid., p. xxiv.

111. Goldberger, *Stalin's Little Guest*, Chapter 24.

CHAPTER 10. GERMANIZING THE WEST

1. Lilienthal, *Der "Lebensborn e.V.,"* p. 167.

2. Breitman, *The Architect of Genocide*, p. 117.

3. NA RG 242 T580/325; correspondence of Centrale Dienst voor Sibbekunde, The Hague.

4. Rempel, *Hitler's Children*, p. 189.

5. De Jong, *Het Koninkrijk*, Vol. 5a, pp. 245–46.

6. Ibid., p. 245.

7. Werner Warmbrunn, *The German Occupation of Belgium, 1940–1944*, American University Studies, Series 9, History, Vol. 122 (1993), p. 187.

8. NA RG 238 M894/16, Docs. NO-4836/4837, 17 and 22 May 1940.

9. Lilienthal, *Der "Lebensborn e.V.,"* p. 176, n. 39.

10. Marc Hillel and Clarissa Henry, *Of Pure Blood* (New York, 1977), p. 128, and Lilienthal, *Der "Lebensborn e.V.,"* pp. 176–81.

11. Schmitz-Köster, *"Deutsche Mutter,"* pp. 202–3.

12. Lilienthal, *Der "Lebensborn e.V.,"* pp. 182–83.

13. Schmitz-Köster, *"Deutsche Mutter,"* p. 202.

14. NA RG 238 M894/16, Doc. NO-4973, Adolf Froehl affidavit.

15. NIOD 108S19, Seyss-Inquart to Directors of NSV and Lebenborn, 10/9/43.

16. Lilienthal, *Der "Lebensborn e.V.,"* pp. 169–70. Hitler's statement of June 27, 1941, is also cited there.

17. NA RG 242 T580/325, Channel Islands correspondence, various agencies; Lilienthal, *Der "Lebensborn e.V.,"* pp. 201–2.

18. W. D. Halls, *The Youth of Vichy France* (Oxford, 1981), p. 232.

19. Eberhard Jäckel, *Frankreich in Hitlers Europa: Die deutsche Frankreichpolitik im 2. Weltkrieg* (Stuttgart, 1966), pp. 228–31.

20. NA RG 239 M894/14, Doc. NO-3600, monthly report, 11/1–12/1/43, RuS-Leader France.

21. Lothar Kettenacker, *Nationalsozialistische Volktumspolitik im Elsass* (Stuttgart, 1973), p. 194.

22. NA RG 239 M894/14, Doc. NO-3508, "Registration and Naturalization of Persons of German Stock in Northern France," 3/25/43.

23. NA RG 238, Nuremberg Doc. NO-1416.

24. NA RG 238 M894/14, Doc. NO-2478, "Final Report on the Registration of People of German Stock in Northern France," undated SS Secret File, No. 17/12.

25. On the conquest of Norway, see Shirer, *The Rise and Fall of the Third Reich,* pp. 700–712, and Richard Petrow, *The Bitter Years: The Invasion and Occupation of Denmark and Norway* (New York, 1979), Chapter 8.

26. Dorothy Macardle, *Children of Europe* (London, 1949), p. 122.

27. Ibid., p. 123.

28. A. M. Hansen, *Children in Norway Today—How Have the Times Affected Their Minds?*, report to the Commission of Ministers of Education, London, January 1945, cited ibid., pp. 125–26.

29. Petrow, *The Bitter Years,* pp. 111–13; Macardle, *Children of Europe,* p. 132.

30. Macardle, *Children of Europe,* p. 129.

31. De Jong, *Het Koninkrijk,* Vol. 5a, pp. 248–49.

32. NIOD CNO 114K / 76, School inspectors Comello and Brons, 5/14/40.

33. David Barnouw, *Van Nivo tot Reichschule* (The Hague, 1981), p. 100.

34. De Jong, *Het Koninkrijk,* Vol. 4b, p. 627.

35. Cornelia Fuykschot, *Hunger in Holland: Life During the Nazi Occupation* (Amherst, MA, 1995), pp. 24–26, 48, 50.

36. NIOD CNO 114K/76, correspondence, Department van Opvoeding, Wetenschap en Kulturbescherming, and Inspecteur van het Lager Onderwijs in de Inspectie Breda, March–July 1942.

37. J. C. H. Pater, *Het Schoolverzet* (The Hague, 1969); summary in English, pp. 495–501.

38. NIOD CNO 114K/76, Inspecteur Heerlen to Secretaris General-Apeldoorn, 7/9/43.

39. De Jong, *Het Koninkrijk,* Vol. 5a, p. 526.

40. Melissa Müller, *Anne Frank: The Biography* (New York, 1998), pp. 124, 127.

41. De Jong, *Het Koninkrijk,* Vol. 5a, p. 528.

42. Bert Jan Flim, *Omdat hun hart sprak: Geschidenis rande Georganiseerde Hulp aan Joodse Kinderen in Nederland, 1942–1945* (Kampen, 1996), pp. 20–21.

43. NIOD CNO 114f/76, Inspecteur Leiden, August 1943; de Jong, *Het Koninkrijk,* Vol. 5a, p. 530.

44. Interview, Mance Post, Amsterdam, July 1999.

45. De Jong, *Het Koninkrijk,* Vol. 5a, pp. 248–49.

46. Wilhelm Kemper, 2/12/42, cited in Barnouw, *Van Nivo tot Reichschule,* pp. 26–27.

47. This account is taken from Barnouw, *Van Nivo tot Reichschule,* Chapter 3, pp. 29–48.

48. Ibid., Chapter 4.

49. See ibid., Part 2, "Nederlandse meisjes in Duitse vakantiekampen, zomer 1940," and Barnouw, "De Nationale Jeugdstorm," in J. Zwaan, ed., *De Zwarte Kameraden: Een geïllustreerde geschiedenis van de NSB* (Weesp, 1984).

50. Halls, *The Youth of Vichy France,* pp. 215, 169.

51. Robert O. Paxton, *Vichy France: Old Guard and New Order, 1940–1944* (New York, 1982), pp. 148–53.

52. Peyrade, 1 January 1941, quoted in Halls, *The Youth of Vichy France,* p. 163.

53. Halls, *The Youth of Vichy France,* pp. 214–15.

54. Ibid., p. 224. For an excellent summary of German plans for France, see ibid., Chapter 9, and Paxton, *Vichy France,* pp. 357–74.

55. Halls, *The Youth of Vichy France,* p. 201.

56. Ibid., p. 295.

57. Paxton, *Vichy France,* p. 164, and Halls, *The Youth of Vichy France,* p. 303.

58. Raymond Josse, "La naissance de la résistance étudiante à Paris et la manifestation du 11 novembre 1940," *Revue d' histoire de la deuxième guerre mondiale* 47 (July 1962), p. 1.

59. Macardle, *Children of Europe,* pp. 121–22.

60. Josse, "La naissance," pp. 9–11.

61. Ibid., pp. 18–23.

62. Ibid., p. 24.

63. De Jong, *Het Koninkrijk,* Vol. 6b, pp. 547–55.

Chapter 11. Nightmares in Utopia: Russia and Greece

1. Shirer, *The Rise and Fall of the Third Reich,* p. 796.

2. Kershaw, *Hitler,* p. 353; Breitman, *The Architect of Genocide,* p. 147.

3. Kershaw, *Hitler,* p. 957, n. 6.

4. Shirer, *The Rise and Fall of the Third Reich,* p. 830.

5. Ibid., p. 854.

6. Ibid., pp. 830–31.

7. See Omer Bartov, *The Eastern Front, 1941–45: German Troops and the Barbarisation of Warfare* (Oxford, 1985), Chapter 3.

8. NA RG 238, Nuremberg Doc. NO-1805, *Der Untermensch,* Nordland Verlag, undated.

9. NA RG 238, Nuremberg Doc. NO-4274, 11 July 1941.

10. Hilberg, *The Destruction of the European Jews,* p. 104.

11. Bullock, *Hitler and Stalin,* pp. 720–22.

12. Alexander Werth, *Russia at War, 1941–1945* (New York, 1984), pp. 162–64.

13. NKVD Order No. 270, 16 August 1941; see also Bullock, *Hitler and Stalin,* p. 723, and Gerald Reitlinger, *The House Built on Sand: The Conflicts of German Policy in Russia, 1939–1945* (New York, 1960), p. 103.

14. Werth, *Russia at War,* pp. 216–18.

15. Cynthia Simmons and Nina Perlina, *Writing the Seige of Leningrad: Women's Diaries, Memoirs, and Documentary Prose* (Pittsburgh, 2002), p. xiii.

16. Harrison E. Salisbury, *The 900 Days: The Siege of Leningrad* (New York, 1985), pp. 105, 143, 205–6.

17. Interview Elena Bovisovna Delone, Moscow, 2000.

18. Salisbury, *The 900 Days,* pp. 168–69.

19. Ibid., p. 305, statement of A. Veresov.

20. Salisbury, *The 900 Days,* pp. 247, 327, 337.

21. Werth, *Russia at War*, pp. 239–40.

22. *IMT*, Vol. 37, p. 672. Stahlecker Doc. 180-L, cited in Breitman, *The Architect of Genocide*, pp. 171–72.

23. Hilberg, *The Destruction of the European Jews*, pp. 116–18.

24. Nuremberg Doc. PS-2992, here as cited in Noakes and Pridham, eds., *Nazism*, Vol. 2, Doc. 823, pp. 1100–1101.

25. These figures taken largely from Reitlinger, *The House Built on Sand*, Chapter 3.

26. Ibid., p. 100. See also *FRUS*, 1941, Vol. I, pp. 1005–1018, for American efforts to persuade the Russians to adhere to the conventions.

27. Reitlinger, *The House Built on Sand*, p. 118.

28. See, for example, Antony Beevor, *Stalingrad: The Fateful Siege, 1942–1943* (New York, 1999), Chapter 24.

29. Ernst Kern, *War Diary, 1941–45: A Report* (New York, 1993), pp. 19–20.

30. I. Fleischhauer and B. Pinkus, edited by E. R. Frankel, *The Soviet Germans Past and Present* (London, 1986), pp. 90–91.

31. Ibid., pp. 89–91, statement of Evegeniia Evelson.

32. Ibid., pp. 78–91, and Robert Conquest, *The Nation Killers: The Soviet Deportation of Nationalities* (London, 1970), pp. 64–66.

33. Fleischhauer et al., *The Soviet Germans Past and Present*, p. 78; Conquest, *The Nation Killers*, pp. 107–9.

34. Hilberg, *The Destruction of the European Jews*, p. 136.

35. Kern, *War Diary*, Chapter 1.

36. Bartov, *The Eastern Front*, pp. 125–28.

37. Werth, *Russia at War*, Chapter 4.

38. NA RG 59 T1250/20, 861.48/2540, letter dated 4 October 1941, US legation, Bern, 21 November 1941.

39. NA RG 59 T1250/20, 861.48/2488, Dienst aus Deutschland, US embassy, Berlin, 3 September 1941.

40. Bartov, *The Eastern Front*, p. 112.

41. Kern, *War Diary*, pp. 22–23.

42. Olga Berggolts, cited in Salisbury, *The 900 Days*, p. 339.

43. Salisbury, *The 900 Days*, pp. 372–73.

44. Yulia Aronova Mendeleva, "Excerpt from *The Defense of Leningrad*," in Simmons and Perlina, *Writing the Siege of Leningrad*, pp. 156–62.

45. Simmons and Perlina, *Writing the Seige of Leningrad*, p. xvii.

46. Salisbury, *The 900 Days*, p. 415.

47. Ibid., p. 380.

48. Ibid., p. 386.

49. Ibid., p. 416.

50. Interview, Mikhail Ostrovsky, Moscow, 2000.

51. Salisbury, *The 900 Days*, pp. 490–91, statements of Dr. Milova and A. N. Mironova.

52. Salisbury, *The 900 Days*, pp. 484, 513–18.

53. NA RG 59 T1250/23, 861.5018/53, 2 April 1942.

54. Kershaw, *Hitler*, pp. 360–69.

55. Interview A. Lykiardopoulos, Athens, July 1998.

56. Interview A. Lagoudaki, Arlington, Virginia, 1997.

57. PRO FO 371/32460, S. Petropoulos, Banque Agricole de Grece, Note 11/17/41.

58. Mark Mazower, *Inside Hitler's Greece: The Experience of Occupation, 1941–1944* (New Haven, CT, 1993), Chapter 3.

59. Two major Red Cross reports analyze the situation in Greece in 1941–42: PRO 371/32460/W3831, "Rapport sur la situation en Grece," Alexander Junod, 31 January 1942; and PRO 371/36485/51572, "Exposition of the Food Situation in Greece," A. Tsaousopoulos, 12 November 1942. Here, Tsaousopoulos, p. 2.

60. PRO FO 371/33175/51557, British Legation Berne, No. 13/10/42, 14 January 1942, and No. 13/84/42, 21 March 1942.

61. Noakes and Pridham, eds., *Nazism*, Vol. 2, Doc. 634, pp. 901–2.

62. PRO FO 371/33175/51557, Smyrna report No. 877, 26 December 1941; A. C. Simonds, GSI GHQ, MEF to N. R. Crockatt, War Office, 30 January 1942.

63. *FRUS*, 1942, Vol. 2, p. 726, Greek Minister to SecState, 24 December 1941.

64. PRO 371/32460/W 3831, Junod report, p. 10.

65. PRO 371/36485/51572, Tsaousopoulos report, p. 10.

66. Ibid., p. 14.

67. N. Deas Archive, Benaki Museum, Athens, 262/3/3-3a, 7/23/42.

68. Mazower, *Inside Hitler's Greece*, p. 46.

69. *FRUS*, 1942, Vol. 2, pp. 749–50.

70. *FRUS*, 1941, Vol. 2, p. 89ff., "Concern of the United States over Franco-German Collaboration and the Matter of Furnishing Food and Medical Relief to Unoccupied France."

71. Ibid., p. 190; SecState to Winant, 21 August 1941.

72. Shirer, *The Rise and Fall of the Third Reich*, pp. 666–68, 915; see also p. 1170, n. 16.

73. *New York Times*, 23 June 1941.

74. Doris Kearns Goodwin, *No Ordinary Time: Franklin and Eleanor Roosevelt: The Home Front in World War II* (New York, 1995), p. 236.

75. Ibid., pp. 255–56.

76. For extensive correspondence on aid to the USSR, see NA RG 59/T1250, Reels 20, 21.

77. NA RG 59/T1250/20, 861.48/2492, 11 September 1941.

78. NA RG 59/T1250/20, 861,48/2744, J. E. Hoover to A. Berle, 13 January 1943.

79. NA RG 59/T1250/20, 861.48/2505, 22 October 1941.

80. NA RG 59/T1250/20, 861.48/2519A, 2525-27, 5–17 November 1941.

81. NA RG 59/T1250/20, 861.48/2556 and passim, T1250/23 861.5018/48, 53.

82. NA RG 59/T1250/20, 861.48/2619, 13 November 1942; 2632 February 42; 2715 21, August 1943.

83. NA RG 59/T1250/21, 861.48/2719, 3 September 1943.

84. Interview, Klose family, Moscow, 2000.

85. NA RG 59/T1250/21, 861.48/Rci/43-12.21, 21 December 1943.

86. *FRUS*, 1942 Vol. 2, p. 724, SecState to Winant, 3 December 1941.

87. PRO FO 371/32460/51593 W 3329, and various others.

88. PRO FO 371/36485/51572 W64, 30 December 1942.

89. Mazower, *Inside Hitler's Greece*, pp. 47–48; Wyman, *The Abandonment of the Jews*, p. 281.

90. N. Deas Archive, Benaki Museum, Athens, 262/3/12.

91. For detailed histories of the German occupation policy in the USSR, see Alexander Dallin, *German Rule in Russia, 1941–1945* (London, 1957), and Reitlinger, *The House Built on Sand.*

92. Steinhoff et al., eds., *Voices from the Third Reich*, pp. 136–37.

93. NA RG 238 M894/16 Doc. NO-5223.

94. Dallin, *German Rule in Russia*, p. 284.

95. Ibid., p. 285.
96. NA RG 238 M894/16, "Report of Activities," 19 July 1942, Doc. NO-3727.
97. NA RG 242 T81/277/398071, *Frankfurter Zeitung*, 8/14/42.
98. NA RG 242 T580, Reichskommissar für die Festigung deutschen Volkstums. Reels 745 and 746 contain day-to-day working documents for the establishment and administration of the Hegewald settlement. This account draws from hundreds of them; therefore, only long citations will be noted.
99. NA RG 242 T580/745, memo, "Waldgut Zman," 9/12/42.
100. NA RG 242 T580/745, 10/8/45.
101. NA RG 242 T580/745, "Unterlagen des Sonderstabes für den Bericht des Gebiethauptmanns Hegewald an Reichsführer SS," 11/20/42, p. 2.
102. Koehl, *RKFDV,* pp. 152–53.
103. NA RG 242 T 580/751, Hauptabteilung I Dr.St/Em, Memo, "Planung im Generalgouvernement-Distrikt Lublin," 7/22/42.
104. Breitman, *The Architect of Genocide,* p. 185.
105. Klukowski, *Diary from the Years of Occupation,* summer and fall 1942, quotation, October 27, p. 222.
106. Ibid., 14 November 1942, p. 224.
107. "Arbeitsanweisung für das Polensammellager Zamosc," 10/31/42, SLG Polen BD 339 s.214–17; in Milton and Friedlander, eds., *Archives of the Holocaust,* Vol. 22, Doc. 57, p. 135.
108. NA RG 238 M894/15, Josef Rembacz testimony, Doc. NO-5266; Zwirner affidavit.
109. Lukas, *The Forgotten Holocaust,* p. 22.
110. Kubica, "Children and Youths at KL Auschwitz," pp. 131–32.
111. Lukas, *The Forgotten Holocaust,* p. 23.
112. Hilberg, *The Destruction of the European Jews,* p. 217.
113. Koehl, *RKFDV,* pp. 154–60.
114. Klukowski, *Diary from the Years of Occupation,* 8 December 1942, p. 231.
115. NA RG 242 T580/745, Sonderstab Henschel, "Unterlagen des Sonderstabes für den Bericht des Gebiethauptmanns Hegewald and Reichsführer-SS," 11/20/42.
116. NA RG 242 T580/745, Sonderstab Henschel, "Merkblatt für die Durchführung der Volksweinachtsfeiern in den Dörfen des Gebietes Hegewald," undated.
117. Werth, *Russia at War,* p. 897.
118. NA RG 238 M894/16, Docs. NO-1257, Pohl Report, 6 February 1943; NO-606, Himmler to Pohl, Acktun to Brandt, 27 November 1942.
119. NA RG 242 T580/745, "Wohnungsverhältnisse der im Herbst 1942 umgesiedelten Ukrainer aus dem Gebiet Hegewald," 9 May 1943.
120. NA RG 242 T580/745, NSDAP Landesleitung Ukraine to Henschel, 7/17/43.
121. NA RG 242 T580/745, Tölke, Office of Reichstudentenführer, Einsatzleitung Ost to Leiterin der Landfrauenschule, Wittigen b. Gnesen, 6/29/43.
122. NA RG 242 T580/745 "Aktenvermerk. Betr.: Landfrauenschule Wittingen," 8/16/43.
123. D. Czech, H. Kubica, and F. Piper, in Piper and Swiebocka, eds., *Auschwitz,* pp. 31, 134, 165–66.
124. This account of the policies of deployment of Soviet POWs and civilians is taken largely from Herbert, *Hitler's Foreign Workers,* Chapter 6.
125. *IMT,* Nuremberg Docs. 1193-PS and 1206-PS, Vol. 27, pp. 56ff. and 65–66, as cited ibid., p. 149.
126. Herbert, *Hitler's Foreign Workers,* pp. 156–57.
127. Ibid., p. 161.
128. Cited ibid., p. 175, Doc. 081-PS, *IMT,* Vol. 25, pp. 164–65.

129. NA RG 242 T454/3, "Programm sur Verkündung des Weissruthenischen Jugendwerkes," 22 June 1943.

130. Memorial, Moscow, Dossier No. 345504.

131. Interview, Vladimir Kuts, Moscow, 2000.

132. Memorial, Dossier No. 215662.

133. Interview, Aldona Valinskaya, Moscow, 2000.

134. Reitlinger, *The House Built on Sand*, p. 235; Werth, *Russia at War*, p. 724.

135. NA RG 238 M894/16, Doc. NO-2513, "Summary of Hitherto Existing Decrees and Suggestions with Regard to Placing of Children of Partisans," 13 July 1943.

136. Himmler Order, 10 July 1943, attached to Doc. NI-10040, Krauch to Himmler, 27 July 1943, *IMT*, Vol. 8, pp. 532–34.

137. Lukas, *The Forgotten Holocaust*, pp. 198–99.

138. Interview, Olga K. Pavlovskaia, Moscow, 2000.

139. Interview, Nikolai A. Mahutov, Moscow, 2000.

140. The accounts of the Vitebsk families are from *"Dann kam die deutsche Macht," Weissrussische Kinderhäftlinge in deutschen Konzentrationslagern, 1941–1945, Eine Dokumentation* (Cologne, 1999).

141. Jan Wosczyk, in Hillel and Henry, *Of Pure Blood*, pp. 173–74.

142. Interview, Nikolai N. Dorozhinski, Moscow, 2000.

143. *"Dann kam die deutsche Macht,"* pp. 101–3.

144. Reitlinger, *The House Built on Sand*, p. 281.

145. NA RG 238/M894/16, Doc. 031-PS, "Re: Evacuation of Youths from the Territory of Army Group Center (Heu-Aktion)," 12 June 1944.

CHAPTER 12. SEEK AND HIDE: HIDDEN CHILDREN

1. See Hilberg, *The Destruction of the European Jews*, pp. 170–74, for a brief analysis of this process.

2. Marrus and Paxton, *Vichy France and the Jews*, p. 246.

3. Flim, *Omdat hun hart sprak*, pp. 19, 24–26.

4. See de Jong, *Het Koninkrijk*, Vol. 7a, pp. 274–85.

5. My principal source for the activities of the Dutch *Kinderwerkers* is Flim, *Omdat hun hart sprak*. For an excellent account in English, see Dwork, *Children with a Star*, Chapter 2. See also de Jong, *Het Koninkrijk*, passim.

6. Interview, Mance Post, Amsterdam, 2000.

7. Flim, *Omdat hun Hart Sprak*, pp. 38–40.

8. Ibid., Chapter 4.

9. Ibid., p. 139.

10. Ibid., pp. 151–52.

11. Ibid., p. 138.

12. Virrie Cohen, quoted ibid., p. 164.

13. Gerhard Hirschfeld, "Niederlande," in Wolfgang Benz, ed., *Dimension des Volkermörds* (Oldenbourg, 1991), p. 163; Flim, *Omdat hun hart sprak*, p. 469, n. 140.

14. Hetty Voute, in Flim, *Omdat hun hart sprak*, p. 84.

15. Piet Meerburg, in Dwork, *Children with a Star*, pp. 51–52.

16. Jooske de Neve, in Flim, *Omdat hun hart sprak*, p. 99.

17. Mien Bouwman, ibid., p. 244.

18. Flim, *Omdat hun hart sprak*, pp. 156–57.

19. Ibid., pp. 74–75.

20. Rut Matthijsen, ibid., p. 92.

21. André Stein, *Hidden Children: Forgotten Survivors of the Holocaust* (New York, 1994), pp. 86–87.

22. Petrow, *The Bitter Years,* Chapter 15.

23. Marrus and Paxton, *Vichy France and the Jews,* p. 148.

24. Ibid., pp. 161–64.

25. Ibid., pp. 226–28.

26. Ibid., pp. 323–26.

27. Ibid., pp. 254–55.

28. Georges Wellers, *de Drancy à Auschwitz* (Paris, 1946), pp. 56–57, cited in Marrus and Paxton, *Vichy France and the Jews,* p. 264.

29. Marrus and Paxton, *Vichy France and the Jews,* pp. 263–65.

30. Cited in Robert Aron, *Histoire de Vichy, 1940–1944* (Paris, 1954), pp. 465–66.

31. Ibid., pp. 256–57, and Mettay, *L'Archipel du Mépris,* pp. 68–69.

32. Serge Klarsfeld, *The Children of Izieu: A Human Tragedy* (New York, 1985), p. 22.

33. Lowrie, *The Hunted Children,* p. 217.

34. Klarsfeld, *The Children of Izieu,* p. 24.

35. Lowrie, *The Hunted Children,* p. 239.

36. Ibid., pp. 229–35.

37. Aron, *Histoire de Vichy,* p. 466.

38. Philip Hallie, *Lest Innocent Blood Be Shed: The Story of the Village of Le Chambon and How Goodness Happened There* (New York, 1994), p. 187.

39. Wyman, *Paper Walls,* p. 133.

40. Lowrie, *The Hunted Children,* p. 220.

41. Ibid., p. 223.

42. Klarsfeld, *The Children of Izieu,* p. 25–26; Dwork, *Children with a Star,* pp. 59–62.

43. Hallie, *Lest Innocent Blood Be Shed,* passim.

44. Lowrie, *The Hunted Children,* p. 240.

45. NA RG 238, Nuremberg Doc. NO-1411, Knochen IV B 4, "Memorandum Concerning the Increase of the Number of Jews to Be Arrested Within the Province of the Befehlshaber der Sicherheitspolizei in France," 14 April 1944.

46. Marrus and Paxton, *Vichy France and the Jews,* pp. 334–35.

47. Klarsfeld, *The Children of Izieu,* pp. 31–35.

48. Stanley Hoffmann, "Etre ou ne pas être Français (I)," *Commentaire,* Tiré-à-part, Numero 70/Eté 1995, pp. 317–18; kindly provided to me by Dr. Charles G. Cogan.

49. Isaac Levendel, *Not the Germans Alone: A Son's Search for the Truth of Vichy* (Evanston, IL, 1999), pp. 100–101.

50. Klukowski, *Diary from the Years of Occupation,* p. 247.

51. Sliwowska, *The Last Eyewitnesses,* pp. 3–4.

52. Ibid., pp. 153–63.

53. Ibid., pp. 48–52.

54. For an account of the activities of Polish nuns, see Ewa Kurek, *Your Life Is Worth Mine: How Polish Nuns Saved Hundreds of Jewish Children in German Occupied Poland, 1939–1945* (New York, 1997).

55. Sliwowska, *The Last Eyewitnesses,* p. 280.

56. Kurek, *Your Life Is Worth Mine,* p. 66.

57. Ibid., p. 60.

58. Sliwowska, *The Last Eyewitnesses,* p. 114, and account of Michal Glowinski, pp. 56–68.

59. Kurek, *Your Life Is Worth Mine,* p. 60.

60. Ibid., pp. 166–69, account of Sister Roberta Sutkowska, and pp. 185–88, account of Rachela G.

CHAPTER 13. ARBEIT MACHT FREI: FORCED LABOR

1. This account comes from de Jong, *Het Koninkrijk,* Vol. 6b, pp. 547–98.
2. Ibid., p. 573.
3. Ibid., p. 597.
4. Ibid., p. 706, n. 1.
5. Ibid., pp. 704–28.
6. Ibid., p. 711.
7. Ibid., Vol. 7a, pp. 543–45.
8. For extensive documentation of this issue, see NIOD Archive 216, "Collectie Nederlandse Overheidsinstellingen (CNO) (1939) 1940–1945," Section 107. NIOD finding aid No. 61 contains excellent abstracts of the documents.
9. De Jong, *Het Koninkrijk,* Vol. 7a, p. 560.
10. Macardle, *Children of Europe,* pp. 133–34.
11. Herbert, *Hitler's Foreign Workers,* pp. 95–98.
12. Aron, *Histoire de Vichy,* p. 492.
13. Jacques Evrard, *La déportation des travailleurs français dans le IIIe Reich* (Paris, 1972), p. 80.
14. Ibid., p. 71.
15. Ibid., pp. 76–77, 91–92, 86; Aron, *Histoire de Vichy,* p. 576.
16. Evrard, *La déportation des travailleurs français,* pp. 128–42.
17. Aron, *Histoire de Vichy,* p. 576.
18. Evrard, *La déportation des travailleurs français,* pp. 92–93.
19. Claude Singer, *Vichy, l'université et les juifs* (Paris, 1992), pp. 193–97.
20. *New York Times,* 27 June 1942.
21. Halls, *The Youth of Vichy France,* pp. 379–90.
22. Evrard, *La déportation des travailleurs français,* p. 93; Halls, *The Youth of Vichy France,* p. 389.
23. Interview, Othar Zaldastani.
24. Ibid.
25. Evrard, *La déportation des travailleurs français,* pp. 173–74.
26. Ibid., pp. 200–201.
27. See, on this subject, Herbert, *Hitler's Foreign Workers,* pp. 313–40, and Evrard, *La déportation des travailleurs français,* Chapter 4.
28. Evrard, *La déportation des travailleurs français,* pp. 371–73.
29. Kaplan, *Beyond Dignity and Despair,* pp. 174–75.
30. Anderson, *Hitler's Exiles,* pp. 118–19.
31. Klemperer, *I Will Bear Witness,* pp. 47, 141.
32. Donald Bloxham, "Jewish Slave Labour and Its Relationship to the 'Final Solution,' " in *Remembering for the Future: The Holocaust in an Age of Genocide,* ed. John Roth and Elizabeth Maxwell (London, 2001), p. 170.
33. Hilberg, *The Destruction of the European Jews,* pp. 181–82.
34. Gilbert, *The Boys,* p. 70.
35. Gitta Sereny, *Into That Darkness: An Examination of Conscience* (New York, 1983), p. 115.
36. Ibid., p. 219.
37. Klukowski, *Diary from the Years of Occupation,* p. 191.

38. Sereny, *Into That Darkness,* pp. 158–59.
39. Ibid.
40. Jan Karski, *Story of a Secret State* (Boston, 1944), pp. 344–50.
41. Gerda Weissmann Klein, *All but My Life* (New York, 1995).
42. Gilbert, *The Boys,* various references to Arek Hersh.
43. Gilbert, *The Boys,* pp. 135, 139.
44. Ibid., pp. 157–59.
45. Bloxham, "Jewish Slave Labour," pp. 166–69.
46. Sereny, *Albert Speer,* pp. 413, 479–81.
47. Ibid., pp. 404–5.
48. Albert Speer, *Inside the Third Reich* (New York, 1970), p. 371.
49. For extensive discussion of this issue, see Herbert, *Hitler's Foreign Workers,* pp. 124–36.
50. NSDAP leaflet, "Wie verhalten wir uns gegenüber den Polen?" 8 March 1940, cited ibid., p. 77.
51. Herbert, *Hitler's Foreign Workers,* pp. 124–33, 269.
52. NA RG 238 M894/16 Doc. NO-1622, 26 March 1943.
53. NA RG 238 M894/16 Doc. NO-3520, 9 June 1943.
54. NA RG 238 M894/16 Docs. NO-1383 and 4141, 27 July 1943.
55. NA RG 238 M894/16 Doc. NO-4665, Hilgenfeldt to Himmler, 11 August 1943.
56. NA RG 238 M894/16 Doc. 1753-PS, SD Sector Bayreuth, 25 October 1943
57. NA RG 238 M894/16 Doc. L-8 SD, Subdistrict Koblenz, 18 February 1944.
58. *TWC,* No. 10, Nuernberg, October 1946–April 1949, Washington, 1950, Vol. 9. "Extracts from Testimony of Prosecution Witness Ernst Wirtz," pp. 1112–19.
59. Ibid., p. 1120.
60. Ibid., p. 1111.
61. NA RG 238 M894/16 Doc. NO-5312, Gau-East Hannover, "Community Work," 24 March 1944.
62. NA RG 238 M894/16 Doc. NO-5311, "Immediate Reich Measures to Decrease the Dangers from Infiltration in View of the Numerous Births of Alien Race in Rural Areas," 13 May 1944.

CHAPTER 14. TOTAL WAR

1. Koch, *The Hitler Youth,* pp. 239–43.
2. Herbst, *Requiem for a German Past,* p. 174.
3. Kern, *War Diary,* pp. 10–20.
4. Heck, *The Burden of Hitler's Legacy,* passim.
5. B. A. Sijes, *De Arbeitsinzet: De gedwongen arbeit van Nederlanders in Duitsland, 1940–1945* (The Hague, 1990), pp. 689–91.
6. J. Nowak, in Schmik-Gustavus, *Hungern für Hitler,* p. 55.
7. Ibid., pp. 59–60.
8. The history of these children is beyond the scope of this book. For a vivid memoir of a child's experience in such a camp, see Ernest Hillen, *The Way of a Boy: A Memoir of Java* (New York, 1995).
9. *New York Times,* 11 August 1997, p. A10.
10. See, on this subject, Arnold Krammer, *Undue Process: The Untold Story of America's German Alien Internees* (New York, 1997).
11. Ibid., pp. 10–11.
12. Ibid., p. 116.

13. Ibid., p. 38.

14. Ibid., pp. 98–99.

15. For the full story of the Oswego camp, see Wyman, *The Abandonment of the Jews,* pp. 268–76. Wyman's book is also my principal source for the following account of the establishment and activities of the War Refugee Board.

16. Ibid., pp. 178–80.

17. Ibid., p. 193.

18. For an excellent account of the occupation of the Netherlands from a child's point of view, see Fuykschot, *Hunger in Holland,* from which many of these examples are taken. I am also indebted to Helen Walker and many others for their reminiscences.

19. Ibid., pp. 112–13.

20. Robin Lumsden, *Himmler's Black Order* (Gloucestershire, UK, 1997), p. 133.

21. Steinhoff et al., eds., *Voices from the Third Reich,* p. 217.

22. Maschmann, *Account Rendered,* p. 157.

23. Robert Goralski, *World War II Almanac, 1931–1945* (New York, 1981), p. 273.

24. Erich Andres, in Steinhoff et al., eds., *Voices from the Third Reich,* p. 205.

25. Goralski, *World War II Almanac,* pp. 273–75.

26. Steinhoff et al., eds., *Voices from the Third Reich,* pp. 210–12.

27. Edwin Shanke, Associated Press, 25 November 1943.

28. Käthe Schlechter-Bonnesen, in Steinhoff et al., eds., *Voices from the Third Reich,* p. 462.

29. Catalog, "The White Rose Exhibition on the Resistance by Students Against Hitler, Munich 1942/43," White Rose Foundation, Munich, 1991.

30. Peter Hoffmann, *The History of the German Resistance, 1933–1945* (Cambridge, MA, 1979), p. 278.

31. NA RG 331/54/2814, dossier on the search for the "July 20" children.

32. Fey von Hassell, *Hostage of the Third Reich: The Story of My Imprisonment and Rescue from the SS* (New York, 1989).

33. Interview, Corrado Pirzio-Biroli, Washington, DC.

34. Von Hassell, *Hostage of the Third Reich,* p. 116.

35. Rempel, *Hitler's Children,* p. 189.

36. Irene Vrijenhoek, *Oorlogskinderen in Nederland tijdens de Duitse bezetting* (Amsterdam, 1994), p. 56.

37. "Mittagslage vom 26 July 1943," from *Hitler's Lagebesprechungen,* cited in George H. Stein, *The Waffen SS: Hitler's Elite Guard at War, 1939–1945* (Ithaca, NY, 1966), pp. 207–8.

38. Koch, *The Hitler Youth,* pp. 243–47.

39. Rempel, *Hitler's Children,* pp. 235–44.

40. Steinhoff et al., eds., *Voices from the Third Reich,* p. 410.

41. Koch, *The Hitler Youth,* p. 250.

42. Percy A. Scholes, *The Oxford Companion to Music* (Oxford, 1956), p. 887.

43. Sereny, *Albert Speer,* p. 507.

44. Klukowski, *Diary from the Years of Occupation,* 27 October 1943, p. 286.

45. Ibid., 19 June 1943 and 3 May 1944, pp. 262 and 323.

46. Karski, *Story of a Secret State,* pp. 270–71.

47. Ibid., p. 301.

48. For a description of such activities, see Mark Bles, *Child at War: The True Story of Hortense Daman* (London, 1992).

49. Karski, *Story of a Secret State,* p. 285.

50.   Bles, *Child at War,* Chapter 10.

51.   Genevieve De Gaulle, "La condition des enfants au camp de Ravensbrück," *Revue d'histoire de le deuxième guerre mondiale* 45 (January 1962), annex and pp. 80–81.

52.   Lucy S. Davidowicz, *The War Against the Jews, 1933–1945* (New York, 1981), p. 449.

53.   Hilberg, *The Destruction of the European Jews,* p. 207.

54.   Davidowicz, *The War Against the Jews,* Chapter 15; Hilberg, *The Destruction of the European Jews,* pp. 199–210.

55.   Lukas, *The Forgotten Holocaust,* Chapter 7; Courtois et al., eds., *The Black Book of Communism,* pp. 372–74.

56.   See Mazower, *Inside Hitler's Greece,* for a definitive analysis of this complex history.

57.   Nicholas Gage, *Eleni: A Savage War, a Mother's Love, and a Son's Revenge: A Personal Story* (New York, 1983), p. 83.

58.   Interview, Costas Gkioulekas, Athens, 1998.

59.   Keitel order of 16 November 1942, cited in Mazower, *Inside Hitler's Greece,* p. 152.

60.   Deas Archive, Benaki Museum, No. 262/4, Note pour Mr. le President, 14 January 1943; No. 262/5, "Extraits d'un rapport sur le voyage d'inspection du 17–20 Aout 1943 de M. Wenger accompagné de Mme Hiadis."

61.   Deas Archive No. 262/4, telegramme P. L. Christodimos, 25 October 1943; M. Bickel and M. Helger, "Rapport comparatif de la situation en Epire d'une part et celle de la region d'Aegion, Patras et Kalavryta en Peloponese de l'autre," November 1943.

62.   Deas Archive No. 262/5, Metropolitan Theoclitus of Grevina to Minister of National Planning, 30 December 1943.

63.   Mazower, *Inside Hitler's Greece,* p. 212.

64.   Interview, Aleco Zaoussis, Athens, 1998; Deas Archive No. 262/6—Sheets 200–210 and 223 contains numerous documents on Distomo; Macardle, *Children of Europe,* p. 86.

65.   Mazower, *Inside Hitler's Greece,* pp. 212–14.

66.   Sarah Farmer, *Martyred Village: Commemorating the 1944 Massacre at Oradour-sur-Glane* (Berkeley, CA, 1999), p. 136.

67.   For a good description of these events, see ibid., pp. 20–28.

68.   Deas Archive, No. 262/5, E. Wenger, "Rapport sur nos voyages en province du 15 au 21 Septembre 1944," p. 5.

69.   S. Courtois and Jean-Louis Panné, "The Comintern in Action," in Courtois et al., eds., *The Black Book of Communism,* pp. 330–31.

70.   Interviews, C. Stamatopoulos and C. Gkioulekas, Athens, 1998.

71.   Countess Marion Dönhoff, *Before the Storm: Memories of My Youth in Old Prussia* (New York, 1990), pp. 177–78.

72.   NA RG 331/57/2936, "Evacuation of Civilians from South East Europe into the Reich. Position at End October 1944," SHAEF G-2 GBI/OI/Docs/R1258, 13 March 1945.

73.   NA RG 331/57/2912/1 SHAEF G-5/DP/2711/5, "Analysis of Evacuation of Refugees and Displaced Persons in Germany," 10 February 1945, pp. 2–3.

74.   Andrzej Strzelecki, "Evacuation, Liquidation and Liberation of the Camp," in Piper and Swiebocka, eds., *Auschwitz,* pp. 264–89.

75.   Von Hassell, *Hostage of the Third Reich,* p. 157.

76.   Theodore Schieder, ed., *Documents on the Expulsion of the Germans from Eastern-Central Europe.* Vol. 1: *The Expulsion of the German Population from the Territories East of the Oder-Neisse Line* (Bonn, undated), Doc. No. 23, p. 140.

77.   Ibid., Doc. No. 20, p. 135.

78.   Ibid., Doc. No. 33, pp. 144–45, 41.

CHAPTER 15. LIBERATION AND REPATRIATION

1. National Planning Association Planning Pamphlets Nos. 30–31, *UNRRA: Gateway to Recovery*, February 1944, p. 9.
2. Harry L. Coles and Albert K. Weinberg, *Civil Affairs: Soldiers Become Governors*. United States Army in World War II: Special Studies (Washington, DC, 1964), pp. 52–54.
3. NA RG 59 T1250/20, "For Norman Davis from Bullitt," 22 January 1942.
4. Gross and Gross, *War Through Children's Eyes*, pp. xxiv–xxvi, 241–42.
5. NA RG 331/3136/579-98, OSS "Egypt–Yugoslavia–Internal Conditions at Yugoslav Evacuees Camp at Suez (MERRA)," 26 February 1944.
6. UNA PAG 4/4.1/9, "Excerpts from Miss Margaret Arnstein's Letter of May 19, 1944."
7. UNRRA, European Regional Office, DP Division No. 4, *People Displaced: UNRRA Part in Their Repatriation*, 2nd ed., rev., December 1944, p. 58.
8. Coles and Weinberg, *Civil Affairs*, pp. 306–16.
9. Ibid., p. 329, penciled memo, Seguin, CAO, San Salvo, Chieti Province, 12 December 1943.
10. NA RG 331/3113, AMG 15th Army Group to Hume, AMG/66/86, 25 November 1943.
11. NA RG 331/3113 4673, William H. Stoneman to Colonel Warren, 21 December 1943.
12. NA RG 331/3113, AMG CAO Northern Division to SCAO, HQ, Naples, 12 December 1943.
13. NA RG 331/3113, Civilian War Relief, Field Report for 10–31 December, Silber and Boie, ARC, 5 January 1944.
14. NA RG 331/3313, E. A. Turner, "Sanitary Report on Refugees Camps at Piccolo Cottolengo and Piazetta Forcella," 27 February 1944.
15. NA RG 331/3113/4243, *Stars and Stripes*, 4 March 1944.
16. NA RG 331/3113 4644-46, "Refugee Operations—Western Italy," 10 March 1944.
17. NA RG 331/3113 4475-74, "Report by Captain Outred Namo and Medical Staff of No. I Refugee Center," March? 1944.
18. Coles and Weinberg, *Civil Affairs*, p. 332.
19. Iris Origo, *War in Val d'Orcia: A Diary* (London, 1984), pp. 28–29.
20. Ibid., pp. 217–21.
21. Coles and Weinberg, *Civil Affairs*, Chapter 22.
22. NA RG 331/53/2749/1, E. G. de Pury, "Recce Report on Bayeux," 4 July 1944.
23. NA RG 331/52, Daily Report, W. C. Henderson, Det. A1A1, 16 July 1944.
24. NA RG 331/53/2748/8 G-5, DP Branch, Schottland, "Trip to Normandy," 12 August 1944, p. 3.
25. NA RG 331/52, 1st ECAR Regiment, Detachment A1A1, "Report on Cherbourg, 27 June–11 August 1944," 16 August 1944.
26. NA RG 331/54/2821/2, ARC, "Report of Operations as of October 31, 1944."
27. William Shirer, *End of a Berlin Diary* (New York, 1947), p. 16.
28. NA RG 331/53, Detachment B1D1, Bradshaw Report, 18 September 1944.
29. NA RG 331/53/2748/9, P. Wood, "Report on Visit to DP Assembly Center Chalons sur Marne," 10 December 1944.
30. See, on this subject, de Jong, *Het Koninkrijk*, Vol. 10b, Part 1, pp. 160–279; Vrijenhoek, *Oorlogskinderen in Nederland*, Chapter 4.
31. General State Printing Office, The Hague, *Malnutrition and Starvation in Western Netherlands, September 1944–July 1945* (The Hague, 1948).
32. Diary of M. Klee-Ripson, cited in de Jong, *Het Koninkrijk*, Vol. 10b, Part 1, p. 206.
33. NIOD CNO 188F/126, Binnenl. Zaken Gem. Utrecht, Nov 1941/Mei 1945, passim.

34. De Jong, *Het Koninkrijk,* Vol. 10b, Part 1, p. 256.

35. Vrijenhoek, *Oorlogskinderen in Nederland,* p. 96.

36. General State Printing Office, The Hague, *Malnutrition and Starvation in Western Netherlands,* pp. 45–46.

37. Coles and Weinberg, *Civil Affairs,* pp. 830–32, passim; General State Printing Office, The Hague, *Malnutrition and Starvation in Western Netherlands,* p. 44.

38. Vrijenhoek, *Oorlogskinderen in Nederland,* p. 101.

39. Werth, *Russia at War,* p. 897.

40. Ibid., pp. 892–93.

41. Ibid., p. 898.

42. Elena Putilina, pp. 43–51, in Projektgruppe Belarus im Jugendclub Courage Koln e. V., *"Dann kam die deutsche Macht." Weissrussische Kinderhäftlinge in deutschen Konzentrationslagern, 1941–1945. Eine Dokumentation* (Cologne, 1999).

43. Piper and Swiebocka, *Auschwitz,* pp. 281–86, 139.

44. UNA PAG 4/4.2/81, UNRRA History of Child Welfare, Cornelia D. Heise, ed., 1 February 1948, Exhibit 7, Fortner to Camp Leaders, 21 April 1945.

45. See, for example, Speer, *Inside the Third Reich,* Chapter 30.

46. UNA PAG 4/4.2:24 S-0524-008, UNRRA Historian Subject File 1944–1947, Austria, Child Welfare in DP Program, No. 20, enclosure 5, W. van Dop, "Searching for Unaccompanied Non-Austrian Children in Upper Austria," 22 November 1946.

47. Lilienthal, *"Lebensborn e.V.,"* pp. 235–36.

48. Hillel and Henry, *Of Pure Blood,* pp. 207–8.

49. Schmitz-Köster, *"Deutsche Mutter,"* p. 206.

50. Hillel and Henry, *Of Pure Blood,* pp. 210–13.

51. UNA PAG 4/4.2:24 S-0-524-0048, Austria Child Welfare enclosure 7, Miller to Starov, 23 January 1947.

52. UNRRA Handbook, *People Displaced,* DP Division No. 4, 2nd ed., December 1944, p. 3 and passim.

53. Coles and Weinberg, *Civil Affairs,* p. 858.

54. Ibid., Stearns, G5 ETOUSA, report, 30 June 1945, pp. 858–59.

55. NA RG 331/57/2912/1 SHAEF G5/DP, Report No. 30, 30 April 1945.

56. Dwight D. Eisenhower, *Crusade in Europe* (New York, 1948), p. 409.

57. Margaret Bourke-White, *"Dear Fatherland Rest Quietly": A Report on the Collapse of Hitler's "Thousand Years"* (New York, 1946), p. 76.

58. Sereny, *Albert Speer,* p. 515.

59. Bourke-White, *"Dear Fatherland Rest Quietly,"* p. 79.

60. Earl F. Ziemke, *The U.S. Army in the Occupation of Germany, 1944–1946,* Army Historical Series (Washington, DC, 1975), p. 245.

61. David Eisenhower, *Eisenhower at War, 1943–1945* (New York, 1987), p. 765.

62. Ibid., p. 766.

63. Muriel Knox Doherty, *Letters from Belsen, 1945: An Australian Nurse's Experiences with the Survivors of War* (Sydney, 2000), p. 169.

64. Ibid., pp. 42, 169.

65. Ibid., pp. 43, 36–37.

66. Ibid., pp. 72–73.

67. NA RG 331/54 2821/2 50 174, ARC-CRW reports, 7 June 1945.

68. Papers of Richard S. Winslow, Winslow letters, 11 and 15 June 1945.

69. All descriptions of Wildflecken are taken from Kathryn Hulme's extraordinary book *The Wild Place* (Boston, 1953).

70. Ibid., p. 15.

71. Ziemke, *The U.S. Army in the Occupation of Germany,* p. 358.

72. Hulme, *The Wild Place,* pp. 60–66.

73. NA RG 331/54/2814 contains numerous documents on these transfers, especially from Buchenwald.

74. UNA PAG 4/4.2/81, UNRRA History of Child Welfare, pp. 3, 86.

75. UNRRA History of Child Welfare, Exhibit 31, Rachel Greene, "Report on Aglasterhausen Children's Center," 5 May 1947.

76. The full text of Harrison's preliminary report was published in the *New York Times* on 30 September 1945.

77. UNA PAG 4/4.1/8, Eisenhower to President, 8 October 1945.

78. NA RG 200/10, Clay Papers, NX-55599 USFET Main 20/11, McCloy to Acheson, Eisenhower et al., 10 October 1945.

79. UNA PAG 4/4.1/8, Sir George Reid, "Report on an Enquiry into the Provisions Made for Displaced Persons in Germany," 24 May 1945.

80. See, for example, David McCullough, *Truman* (New York, 1992), pp. 595–620.

81. UNA PAG 4/4.2/81, UNRRA History of Child Welfare, p. 82.

82. Ibid., passim.

83. Joseph B. Schechtman, "Resettlement of Transferred Volksdeutsche in Germany," *Journal of Central European Affairs,* 7:3 (October 1947), pp. 262–63.

84. McNarney to WARCOS, 25 December 1945, cited in Ziemke, *The U.S. Army in the Occupation of Germany,* p. 418.

85. On this subject, see Nicholas Bethell, *The Last Secret* (New York, 1974).

86. PRO FO 1013/2109 51593, Russian Repatriation, 53/DP/100 (3), Hilden, 6 March 1946.

87. Winslow Papers. Memo, Samuel Margoshes to Gerald Keith, "The Jews in Poland," 12 February 1946.

88. Winslow Papers, War Department Press Release, 6 April 1946, Report by Judge Simon H. Rifkind.

89. UNA S-0437-0016/2, UNRRA Germany Mission, Subject files of the Department of Field Operations in the U.S. Zone, "DP Children—Movement of Children to England," 11/1/45–11/30/46, Rhatigan memo, 8/26/45.

90. UNA S-0524-0106, UNRRA—Historian Subject Files, 1944–1947; PAG-4/4.2/82, Dorothy Pearse, "Historical Documentation of Child Welfare Services in British Zone, German Operations," DP BR No. 21, undated.

91. Winslow Papers, UNRRA memo to G. K. Richman, "Meeting with Central Committee of Liberated Jews in Bavaria," E. M. Davidson, 10 November 1945.

92. Ibid.

93. UNA S-0437-0015 No. 11, Rifkind to Guyler, 14 November 1945.

94. UNA S-0437-0016/1, Guyler to Rifkind, 7 November 1945.

95. UNA S-0437-0015 No. 11, Rifkind to Guyler, 14 November 1945.

96. UNA S-0437-0016/1, Schottland to Director UNRRA, U.S. Zone.

97. Winslow Papers, Davidson to Winslow, 16 December 1945.

98. Winslow Papers, Cable USFET MAIN 091445A, Ref No. S-34347, 9 December 1945.

99. UNA S-0437-0013, Subject files, Field Operation in the U.S. Zone. DP—Children Center—Strüth. Jewish Area Team 1041, Ansbach. "Operation of the Project," January 1946.

100. UNRRA History of Child Welfare, Exhibit 25, "Rosenheim Children's Transient Center," UNRRA Area Team 1069.

101. See Kurek, *Your Life Is Worth Mine,* Appendix 5; Sliwowska, *The Last Eyewitnesses,* which contains more than sixty histories of Jewish children who remained in Poland.

102. Sliwowska, *The Last Eyewitnesses,* pp. 51–52.

103. Winslow Papers, letters from E. Davidson, H. Matouskova, 6 and 7 January 1946.

104. UNA S-0437-0015/15, UNRRA Germany Mission, Field Ops—U.S. Zone, 1945–48, DPs—Children—Jewish Infiltree Children, 22/2/46–22/5/47, 29 November 1946, "Report on Illegal Movement of Jewish Children from Rosenheim to Lindenfels" and "Segregation of Jewish Unaccompanied Children in Accordance with Their Political Affiliation," 5 November 1946.

105. "Report on Illegal Movement of Jewish Children from Rosenheim to Lindenfels."

106. UNRRA History of Child Welfare, Exhibit 25, pp. 6–7, 8, 10.

107. UNA S-0437-0015/6, UNRRA Germany Mission, Field Ops—U.S. Zone, 1945–8, DPs—Children, Ruth Cohen to Child Care Committee, Jewish Children, 22 February 1947, and UNA S-0437-0015/7, "Minutes of Jewish Child Care Committee Meeting," 13 March 1947.

108. UNA S-0437-0015 Field Ops—U.S. Zone, DPs—Children—Children's Centers— Strüth Jewish Area Team 1041 Ansbach, "Operation of the Project," p. 58.

109. UNRRA History of Child Welfare, Exhibit 37, L. Pinsky and M. J. Matthews, "Children's Transport to Palestine," 25 April 1946.

110. UNA S-0437-0015/11, DPs—Children—Jewish Children—Infiltrees, 11/4/46–2/10/47, "Draft Report on Infiltree Children," C. D. Heise, undated.

111. Winslow Papers, Dorothy Johnson to Winslow, 4 August 1946.

112. There are many accounts of this incident. See, for example, Douglas Botting, *The Aftermath: Europe* (New York, 1983), pp. 100–111.

113. Marc Wyman, *DP: Europe's Displaced Persons, 1945–1951* (Philadelphia, 1989), p. 192.

114. PRO FO 1013/2108 51583, Review of PW and DP work up to December 1947, 11 June 1948.

115. UNA S-0437-0016/9, UNRRA Germany Mission, Field Ops—U.S. Zone, DPs Children—Nationality Policy—General, 2/12/46–1/28/47, "Formula of the Boy Scouts Detachment," March 1946.

116. UNA S-0437-0016/9, UNRRA Germany Mission, Field Ops—U.S. Zone, DPs Children—Nationality Policy—General, 2/12/46–1/28/47, "Disappearance of 74 Polish Children from Children's Centre in Regendorf," L. Pinsky, undated.

117. UNA S-0437-0013, UNRRA Germany Mission, Field Ops—U.S. Zone, DPs— Children—Child Search and Tracing, 2/1/46–6/30/47, "Monthly Report—Child Welfare U.S. Zone—February 1946," Heise.

118. UNRRA History of Child Welfare, Exhibit 33, S-0437-0017/14, DP—Plans for Unaccompanied Children, 11/1/45–12/28/45, Morgan to Heise, 18 December 1945; UNA S-0524-0048 PAG-4/4.2: 24, UNRRA Historian Subject Files, 1944–1947, Austria Child Welfare, DP Program. No. 20, report by Anita Brownlee; Winslow Papers, Davidson to Winslow, 21 December 1945.

119. UNRRA History of Child Welfare, Exhibit 14, UNRRA Team 182, "Yugoslav Children Admitted to DP Children's Center, March 28, 1946," Henshaw, 10 April 1946; UNA S-0437-0013/11, "Unaccompanied Children—XII Corps. American Friends Report," L. Pinsky, 27 October 1945.

120. UNA S-0524-0048 PAG-4/4.2:24, UNRRA Historian Subject Files, 1944–1947. Austria Child Welfare. DP Program No. 20. Report by Anita Brownlee. "Jugoslav Children and Rome," pp. 18–30.

121. Ibid., pp. 7–12 and enclosures 24–30, "White Russian Children and the USSR."

122. Chaya Brasz, *Removing the Yellow Badge: The Struggle for a Jewish Community in the Postwar Netherlands, 1944–1955* (Jerusalem, 1995), pp. 46–47.

123. Elma Verhey, *Om het Joodse Kind* (Amsterdam, 1991), Chapter 2.

124. Brasz, *Removing the Yellow Badge*, p. 67.

125. NIOD 197K/6/4a, Herzog to van der Molen/OPK, 3 February 1946.

126. Brasz, *Removing the Yellow Badge*, pp. 74–85.

127. NIOD 197K/4a, Herzog to Prime Minister, 12 July 1946.

128. Van der Molen Archive, Historische Documentatiecentrum voor het Nederlands Protestantisme, Vrije Universiteit Amsterdam (HDNP), 30 July 1946, cited in Verhey, *Om het Joodse Kind,* pp. 133–34.

129. Verhey, *Om het Joodse Kind,* pp. 128–29; Brasz, *Removing the Yellow Badge,* p. 69.

130. NIOD 197k/6/4a, passim.

131. NIOD 197k/6d, County Court of Rotterdam, 3 June 1946.

132. NIOD 197k/2/2c, Excerpt from OPK report on Max G., undated.

133. NIOD 197K/6d, "The Case of the Dutch-Jewish War Orphans, Pereira and Spier," May 1954.

134. NIOD 197K/6/6b, various press clippings re A. Beekman.

135. UNA PAG-4/4.2:82 S0524-0106 UNRRA Historian Subject Files 1944–47, DP-BR-21, Dorothy Pearse, Historical Documentation of Child Welfare Services in British Zone, German Ops, undated, pp. 34–35.

136. UNRRA History of Child Welfare, p. 43.

137. Winslow Papers, John Troniak, UNRRA Team 1048, Regensburg, "The Beginning of Child Search," 12 April 1947, p. 3.

138. UNRRA History of Child Welfare, testimony of Sister Reinelis, 9 April 1946, Exhibit 43, p. 14.

139. UNRRA History of Child Welfare, Exhibits 52–54.

140. UNA S-0524-0048, UNRRA Historian, Austria-Child Welfare in DP Program No. 20, Wilhelmina van Dop, "Report: SS Lebensborn Activities in Upper Austria. Children's Home Alpenland, Oberweiss," 11 March 1947.

141. UNRRA History of Child Welfare, p. 46.

142. Winslow Papers, UNRRA Team 566, "Our Work—Our Task," Interviewing of Unaccompanied Children, S. Butrym, April 1946.

143. Winslow Papers, Eileen Davidson to Winslow, 22 January 1948.

144. Winslow Papers, Minutes of Staff Meeting, 10 November 1947, PCIRO HQ, Ludwigsburg.

145. Winslow Papers, Cornelia Heise to Winslow, 6 December 1947.

146. Winslow Papers, Eileen Davidson, "Removal from German Families of Allied Children. Reasons Why This Is to the Best Interest of the Child," 21 January 1948.

147. UNA S-0524-0048, Austria No. 20, "Child Searching in the French Zone," H. Weitz, 1 April 1947.

148. UNRRA History of Child Welfare, pp. 51–56. Also, on this complex issue, see UNA S-0524-0018, UNRRA Historian Subject File, 1944–1947, Germany (CHQ), Eileen Blackey, "UNRRA Closure Report on United Nations' Unaccompanied Children in Germany," June 1947, Sections 3 and 4.

149. Gitta Sereny, "Stolen Children," *Talk Magazine,* November 1999, p. 221.

150. Sereny, *Albert Speer,* p. 215.

151. UNA S-0524-0048, Austria No. 20, "Report on Repatriation Train to Poland," 20 March 1947, Martin Sherry.

152. Winslow Papers, International Tracing Service—Child Search Branch, "Correspondence Between a Polish Mother and Her Daughter, 1941–48," 9 November 1948.

153. Winslow Papers, Case of Iwan P., HICOG Court Session, Marburg, 6 June 1951,

unidentified clipping enclosed in letter from J. Troniak to Winslow, 29 June 1951.

154. Winslow Papers, ITS Child Search Branch, Herbert H. Meyer, "History of the Search for Unaccompanied Children," 11 September 1950.

155. PRO FO 1013/2108/ 51593, BAOR S. Ault "Review of PW and DP Work up to December 1947," 11 June 1948; also, Wyman, *DP,* pp. 188–95.

156. E. G. Harrison, "The Crime of Our Century," *The Displaced Persons Digest* (Winter 1947–48), pp. 3–4.

157. Wyman, *DP,* pp. 194–95; McCullough, *Truman,* p. 651.

158. Wyman, *DP,* p. 203.

159. Winslow Papers, Marie B. Wills, "Survey of Mentally and Physically Handicapped Children and Rehabilitation Program," Child Care Section, Zone HQ, 10 January 1950.

160. Winslow Papers, L. Findlay to Philip Ryan, Chief of Operations, IRO, U.S. Zone, 23 January 1950.

161. S. Tomara, "Village of Displaced Children," *New York Herald Tribune,* 5 July 1951.

Chapter 16. The Defeated

1. Von Hassell, *Hostage of the Third Reich,* Chapter 16; conversations with Corrado and Cecile Pirzio Biroli.

2. Bourke-White, *"Dear Fatherland Rest Quietly,"* pp. 49–50.

3. NA RG 260 ETO/USFET, 54 9th Mil. Gov. Gatling, transmittal of death certificate, 18 April 1945.

4. Bourke-White, *"Dear Fatherland Rest Quietly,"* p. 45.

5. Ilya Ehrenburg articles cited in Werth, *Russia at War,* p. 965.

6. Wolfgang Samuel, *German Boy: A Refugee's Story* (Jackson, MS, 2000), p. 175; Scheider, *Documents on the Expulsion,* No. 208, p. 227.

7. Aleksandr Solzhenitsyn, *Prussian Nights,* trans. Robert Conquest (New York, 1977), p. 7, cited in Norman M. Naimark, *The Russians in Germany: A History of the Soviet Zone of Occupation, 1945–1949* (Cambridge, MA, 1997), p. 73.

8. Shirer, *End of a Berlin Diary,* pp. 131, 146.

9. Owings, *Frauen,* p. 131.

10. Ziemke, *The U.S. Army in the Occupation of Germany,* p. 323.

11. Steinhoff et al., eds., *Voices from the Third Reich,* pp. 473–74.

12. Holtztrager, *Die Wehrertüchtigungslager der Hitler-Jugend,* pp. 101–2.

13. Walker Hancock, "Experiences of a Monuments Officer in Germany," *College Art Journal* 5:4 (May 1946), pp. 274–76.

14. *Boston Herald,* 16 July 1945; *UNRRA History of Child Welfare,* pp. 57–59.

15. Koch, *The Hitler Youth,* p. 250.

16. See Heck, *A Child of Hitler,* Chapter 11.

17. Rempel, *Hitler's Children,* pp. 244–49.

18. Maschmann, *Account Rendered,* Chapters 15 and 16.

19. There are several studies of the children of the Nazi leaders. See, for example, Dan Bar-On, *Legacy of Silence: Encounters with Children of the Third Reich* (Cambridge, MA, 1991); Stephan Lebert and Norbert Lebert, *My Father's Keeper: Children of the Nazi Leaders—An Intimate History of Damage and Denial* (New York, 2001).

20. Herbst, *Requiem for a German Past,* Chapter 14; Kern, *War Diary,* pp. 43–52.

21. For full text of this directive, usually referred to as "JCS 1067," despite many permutations, see 90th Congress, 1st Session, Committee on the Judiciary, United

States Senate, Subcommittee to Investigate the Administration of the Internal Security Act and Other Internal Security Laws, 20 Nov. 1967; Morgenthau diary, Vol. 2, pp. 1287–1303.

22. Ibid., pp. 1294–95.

23. Interview, Ruth Anderson Katz, Washington, DC., 2000–2001.

24. A. F. Noskova, "Migration of the Germans After the Second World War: Political and Psychological Aspects," and S. Schraut, "Make the Germans Do It: The Refugee Problem in the American Zone of Post-War Germany," in Rieber, ed., *Forced Migration in Central and Eastern Europe.*

25. Winston S. Churchill, *The Second World War.* Vol. 6: *Triumph and Tragedy* (Boston, 1953), pp. 647–48.

26. Schechtman, "Resettlement of Transferred Volksdeutsche in Germany," p. 262.

27. T. J. Kent, "Report on Berlin, 1945," reprint from *Journal of American Institute of Planners,* Winter 1946; collection of Ruth Anderson Katz.

28. Winslow Papers, Eileen Davidson to Richard Winslow, 16 December 1945.

29. Ruth Anderson Katz, "Letter to My Family," Berlin, 20 October 1945, and "Berlin, 1946," collection of author.

30. Schechtman, "Resettlement of Transferred Volksdeutsche in Germany," pp. 265–66.

31. PRO FO 1013/2103 51593, HQ Military Gov. Land North Rhine/Westphalia, PWDP Branch, Monthly Report ending 30 September 1946, Appendix O.

32. PRO FO 1013/2092 51593, CRX Report, 11 September 1946.

33. Schechtman, "Resettlement of Transferred Volksdeutsche in Germany," p. 267, n. 13; *Central European Observer* (London), 3 April 1947.

34. Schechtman, "Resettlement of Transferred Volksdeutsche in Germany," p. 270.

35. Susanne Spülbeck, "Ethnography of an Encounter: Reactions to Refugees in Post-War Germany and Russian Migrants after Re-Unification—Context Analogies and Changes," in Rieber, *Forced Migration,* pp. 177–78.

36. Ibid., p. 271.

37. PRO FO 1013/2103 51593, Der Regierungs-Präsident to Mil. Gov. Regierungsbezirk, Düsseldorf, 9 September 1946.

38. Ziemke, *The U.S. Army in the Occupation of Germany,* p. 195.

39. Samuel, *German Boy,* p. 135.

40. Ibid., passim.

41. UNA S-0524-0001 PAG-4/4.0: 1 UNRRA Historian Subject Files, 1944–1947, "Excerpts from Richard Brown's Diary of Trip with Congressmen, 21 Aug.–22 Sept., 1945."

42. Ziemke, *The U.S. Army in the Occupation of Germany,* p. 410.

43. Ken Walsh, "The Revival of Youth Work," in *The British in Germany: Educational Reconstruction After 1945,* ed. Arthur Hearnden (London, 1978).

44. R. A. Katz, letter home, February 1946, collection of author.

45. NA RG 200, Clay Papers, Box 10, NX 55599, McCloy to various, 10 October 1945.

46. Ziemke, *The U.S. Army in the Occupation of Germany,* pp. 436–37.

47. PRO FO 1013/2108 51593, Political Background Guidance No. 3, Appendix A to HQ/092324/Sec. P, 3 June 1946.

48. Lucius Clay, *Decision in Germany* (New York, 1950), pp. 276–77.

49. Victor Gollancz, *In Darkest Germany* (New York, 1947), p. 120.

50. PRO FO 1013/2103 51593, "Notes on Conference with Major General E. on 20 November 1946," No. 38, p. 2.

51. R. A. Katz, letter, "Winter of '46–'47," collection of author.

52. McCullough, *Truman,* pp. 561–62.

53. Clay, *Decision in Germany*, pp. 268–70.
54. Ziemke, *The U.S. Army in the Occupation of Germany*, p. 438.
55. Macardle, *Children of Europe*, p. 210.
56. Ibid., pp. 288–89.
57. Naimark, *The Russians in Germany*, pp. 382–85, 390–97.
58. Ziemke, *The U.S. Army in the Occupation of Germany*, p. 277.
59. Naimark, *The Russians in Germany*, p. 453.
60. *New York Times*, 18 February 1946.
61. Walsh, "The Revival of Youth Work," pp. 225–26.
62. OMGUS Military Government Weekly Information Bulletin, No. 16, 10 November 1945, p. 19.
63. Franklin M. Davis, Jr., *Come as a Conqueror: The United States Army's Occupation of Germany, 1945–49* (New York, 1967), p. 224.
64. Ibid., p. 229.
65. W. Phillips Davison, *The Berlin Blockade: A Study in Cold War Politics* (Princeton, NJ, 1958), p. 361.
66. Ann Tusa and John Tusa, *The Berlin Blockade* (London, 1989), pp. 343–44.
67. Ibid., pp. 344–45.
68. Ibid., p. 331.
69. McCullough, *Truman*, p. 563.

CHAPTER 17. NO PLACE LIKE HOME

1. Interview, Vladimir Kuts, Moscow, 2000.
2. Interview, Nikolai Mahutov, Moscow, 2000.
3. UNA S-0437-0016 #9 UNRRA Germany Mission, UNRRA Mission to Poland: Warsaw, M. Lay to C. Heise, 29 April 1946.
4. Projektgruppe Belarus im Jugendclub Courage Köln e. V., *"Dann kam die deutsche Macht,"* pp. 43–51, 60.
5. Katja Limbacher, Maike Merten, and Bettina Pfefferle, eds., *Das Mädchenkonzentrationslager Uckermark* (Münster, 2000), "Wenn ich das gewust hätte, ware ich auch in den Wald gegangen," interview with S. Burger-Kelih, September 1999, pp. 153–54.
6. Interview, Marian Helft, Washington, DC, 1996.
7. Gershon, *We Came as Children*, p. 113.
8. Levendel, *Not the Germans Alone*, pp. 130, 169.
9. Gershon, *We Came as Children*, pp. 113–14.
10. Ibid., p. 159.
11. IWM, Dept. of Documents, 96/26/1, Papers of Mrs. D. Pool, p. 6.
12. Bailey, *America Lost and Found*, p. 127.
13. Ibid., p. 147.
14. Interview and correspondence, JCW, 1999.
15. Stein, *Hidden Children*, p. 194.
16. Kindly provided to me by Fern Schad.
17. Gershon, *We Came as Children*, p. 103.
18. Studs Terkel, *"The Good War": An Oral History of World War Two* (New York, 1985), p. 431.
19. De Jong, *Het Koninkrijk*, Vol. 10b, Part 2, p. 1154.
20. Vrijenhoek, *Oorlogskinderen in Nederland*, p. 60, translation LHN.
21. Interview, Mance Post, Amsterdam, July 1999.

Bibliography

SECONDARY SOURCES

Books and Articles

Allen, William S. *The Nazi Seizure of Power: The Experience of a Single German Town, 1930–1935.* Chicago, 1965.

Aly, Götz, Peter Chroust, and Christian Pross. *Cleansing the Fatherland: Nazi Medicine and Racial Hygiene.* Baltimore, 1994.

Ammende, Ewald. *Human Life in Russia.* London, 1936.

Amouroux, Henri. *La Grande Histoire des Français sous l'occupation.* 10 vols. Paris, 1976–93.

Anderson, Mark M., ed. *Hitler's Exiles: Personal Stories of the Flight from Nazi Germany to America.* New York, 1998.

Aron, Robert. *Histoire de Vichy, 1940–1944.* Paris, 1954.

Bailey, Anthony. *America Lost and Found: An English Boy's Adventure in the New World.* New York, 1980.

Barnouw, David. *Van Nivo tot Reichschule.* The Hague, 1981.

Bar-On, Dan. *Legacy of Silence: Encounters with Children of the Third Reich.* Cambridge, MA, 1991.

Bartov, Omer. *The Eastern Front, 1941–45: German Troops and the Barbarisation of Warfare.* Oxford, 1985.

Bauer, Yehuda. *American Jewry and the Holocaust: The American Jewish Joint Distribution Committee, 1939–1945.* Detroit, 1981.

Baumel, Judith Tydor. *Unfulfilled Promise: Rescue and Settlement of Jewish Refugee Children in the United States, 1934–35.* Juneau, AK, 1990.

Beevor, Antony. *Stalingrad: The Fateful Siege, 1942–1943.* New York, 1999.

Belov, F. *The History of a Soviet Collective Farm.* New York, 1955.

Benz, Wolfgang. *Dimension des Volkermörds.* Oldenbourg, 1991.

Bethell, Nicholas. *The Last Secret.* New York, 1974.

Blend, Martha. *A Child Alone.* London, 1995.

Bles, Mark. *Child at War: The True Story of Hortense Daman.* London, 1992.

Bloxham, Donald. "Jewish Slave Labor and Its Relationship to the 'Final Solution.'" In *Remembering for the Future: The Holocaust in an Age of Genocide,* ed. John Roth and Elizabeth Maxwell. London, 2001.

Bock, Gisela. "Racism and Sexism in Nazi Germany." In *When Biology Became Destiny,* ed. Renate Bridenthal, Atina Grossmann, and Marion Kaplan. New York, 1984.

Borkin, Joseph. *The Crime and Punishment of I. G. Farben.* New York, 1978.

Botting, Douglas. *The Aftermath: Europe.* New York, 1983.

———. *In the Ruins of the Reich.* London, 1986.

Bourke-White, Margaret. *"Dear Fatherland Rest Quietly": A Report on the Collapse of Hitler's "Thousand Years."* New York, 1946.

Bowers, Claude G. *My Mission to Spain: Watching the Rehearsal for World War II.* New York, 1954.

Brasz, Chaya. *Removing the Yellow Badge: The Struggle for a Jewish Community in the Postwar Netherlands, 1944–1955.* Jerusalem, 1995.

Braun, Franz, and A. Hillen Ziegfeld. *Geopolitischer Atlas zur Deutschen Geschichte.* Dresden, 1934.

Breckoff, Olrick. "Zwischenspiel an der Warthe-und was daraus wurde." *Jahrbuch des Baltischen Deutschtums, 1994.*

Breitman, Richard. *The Architect of Genocide: Himmler and the Final Solution.* New York, 1991.

Breitman, Richard, and Alan M. Kraut. *American Refugee Policy and European Jewry, 1933–1945.* Bloomington, IN, 1987.

Broberg, Gunnar, and Nils Roll-Hansen. *Eugenics and the Welfare State.* Ann Arbor, MI, 1996.

Bullock, Alan. *Hitler and Stalin: Parallel Lives.* New York, 1993.

Burleigh, Michael. *Death and Deliverance: Euthanasia in Germany, 1900–1945.* Cambridge, UK, 1994.

Buruma, Ian. "Churchill's Cigar." *Granta* 65 (Spring 1999).

Churchill, Winston S. *The Second World War.* 6 vols. Boston, 1948–53.

Clay, Catrine, and Michael Leapman. *Master Race: The Lebensborn Experiment in Nazi Germany.* London, 1995.

Clay, Lucius D. *Decision in Germany.* New York, 1950.

Coles, Harry L., and Albert K. Weinberg. *Civil Affairs: Soldiers Become Governors.* United States Army in World War II: Special Studies. Washington, DC, 1964.

Conquest, Robert. *The Harvest of Sorrow: Soviet Collectivization and the Terror-Famine.* New York, 1986.

———. *The Nation Killers: The Soviet Deportation of Nationalities.* London, 1970.

Conway, John. *Nazi Persecution of the Churches, 1933–1945.* London, 1968.

Courtois, Stéphane, et al., eds. *The Black Book of Communism: Crimes, Terror, Repression.* Cambridge, MA, 1999.

Crosby, Travis L. *The Impact of Civilian Evacuation in the Second World War.* London, 1986.

Dachauer Hefte No. 9. *Die Verfolgung von Kindern und Jugendlichen.* Brussels, 1993.

Dallin, Alexander. *German Rule in Russia, 1941–1945.* London, 1957.

Dalrymple, Dana G. "The Soviet Famine of 1932–1934." *Soviet Studies* 15:3 (1964).

Davidowicz, Lucy S. *The War Against the Jews, 1933–1945.* New York, 1981.

Davis, Franklin M., Jr. *Come as a Conqueror: The United States Army's Occupation of Germany, 1945–49.* New York, 1967.

Davison, W. Phillips, *The Berlin Blockade: A Study in Cold War Politics.* Princeton, NJ, 1958.

De Gaulle, Genevieve. "La condition des enfants au camp de Ravensbrück." *Revue d'histoire de la deuxième guerre mondiale* 45 (January 1962).

De Jong, L. *Het Koninkrijk der Nederlanden in de Tweede Wereld Oorlog.* 14 vols. The Hague, 1974.

De Launay, Jacques. *La Belgique à l'heure allemande.* Brussels, undated.

Dodd, William E., Jr., and Martha Dodd, eds. *Ambassador Dodd's Diary, 1933–1938.* New York, 1941.

Doherty, Muriel Knox. *Letters from Belsen, 1945: An Australian Nurse's Experiences with the Survivors of War.* Sydney, 2000.

Dönhoff, Countess Marion. *Before the Storm: Memories of My Youth in Old Prussia.* New York, 1990.

Dray, Philip. *At the Hands of Persons Unknown: The Lynching of Black America.* New York, 2002.

Dwork, Deborah. *Children with a Star: Jewish Youth in Nazi Europe.* New Haven, CT, 1991.

Eiber, Ludwig. *"Ich wuste, es wird schlimm."* *Die verfolgung der Sinti und Roma in München, 1933–1945.* Munich, 1993.

Eisenhower, David. *Eisenhower at War, 1943–1945.* New York, 1987.

Eisenhower, Dwight D. *Crusade in Europe.* New York, 1948.

Engelmann, Bernt. *In Hitler's Germany.* New York, 1986.

Evrard, Jacques. *La déportation des travailleurs français dans le IIIe Reich.* Paris, 1972.

Farmer, Sarah. *Martyred Village: Commemorating the 1944 Massacre at Oradour-sur-Glane.* Berkeley, CA, 1999.

Fleischauer, I., and B. Pinkus, edited by B. R. Frankel. *The Soviet Germans Past and Present.* London, 1986.

Flim, Bert Jan. *Omdat hun hart sprak: Geschiedenis van de Georganiseerde Hulp aan Joodse Kinderen in Nederland, 1942–1945.* Kampen, 1996.

Fodor, Denis J. *The Neutrals.* New York, 1982.

Fonseca, Isabel. *Bury Me Standing.* New York, 1996.

Frank, Niklas. *In the Shadow of the Reich.* New York, 1991.

Fraser, Ronald. *Blood of Spain: An Oral History of the Spanish Civil War.* New York, 1979.

Friedlander, Henry. *The Origins of Nazi Genocide: From Euthanasia to the Final Solution.* Chapel Hill, NC, 1995.

Frye, Alton. *Nazi Germany and the American Hemisphere, 1933–1941.* New Haven, CT, 1967.

Fuykschot, Cornelia. *Hunger in Holland: Life During the Nazi Occupation.* Amherst, MA, 1995.

Gage, Nicholas. *Eleni: A Savage War, a Mother's Love, and a Son's Revenge: A Personal Story.* New York, 1983.

Gallagher, Nancy L. *Breeding Better Vermonters: The Eugenics Project in the Green Mountain State.* Hanover, NH, 1999.

Gay, Peter. *My German Question: Growing Up in Nazi Berlin.* New Haven, CT, 1998.

Gedye, G. E. R. *Fallen Bastions: The Central European Tragedy.* London, 1939.

General State Printing Office. *Malnutrition and Starvation in Western Netherlands, September 1944–July 1945.* The Hague, 1948.

Gershon, Karen, ed. *We Came as Children: A Collective Autobiography.* London, 1966.

Getty, Arch, and Oleg Naumov, eds. *The Road to Terror: Stalin and the Self-Destruction of the Bolsheviks, 1932–1939.* New Haven, CT, 1999.

Gilbert, Martin. *The Boys: Triumph over Adversity.* London, 1996.

Giles, Geoffrey J. *Students and National Socialism in Germany.* Princeton, NJ, 1985.

Gissing, Vera. *Pearls of Childhood.* London, 1994.

Goldberger, Janka. *Stalin's Little Guest.* Chatham, UK, 1988.

Gollancz, Victor. *In Darkest Germany.* New York, 1947.

Goodwin, Doris Kearns. *No Ordinary Time: Franklin and Eleanor Roosevelt: The Home Front in World War II.* New York, 1995.

Goralski, Robert. *World War II Almanac, 1931–1945.* New York, 1981.

Gottlieb, Amy Zahl. *Men of Vision: Anglo-Jewry's Aid to Victims of the Nazi Regime, 1933–1945.* London, 1998.

Gould, Stephen Jay. *The Mismeasure of Man.* New York, 1981.

Gross, Irena G., and Jan T. Gross. *War Through Children's Eyes.* Stanford, CA, 1981.

Gross, Jan Tomasz. *Neighbors: The Destruction of the Jewish Community in Jedwabne, Poland.* Princeton, NJ, 2001.

Grunberger, Richard. *A Social History of the Third Reich.* New York, 1979.

Grunerwald, Karen. *"Ich werde Landfrau in Kalisch."* *Jahrbuch des Baltischen Deutschtums,* 1994.

Hackel, Sergei. *Pearl of Great Price: The Life of Mother Maria Skobtsova, 1891–1945.* New York, 1981.

Hale, Oron J. "Adolf Hitler and the Post-War German Birthrate: An Unpublished Memorandum." *Journal of Central European Affairs* 17:2 (July 1957).

Hallie, Philip. *Lest Innocent Blood Be Shed: The Story of the Village of Le Chambon and How Goodness Happened There.* New York, 1994.

Halls, W. D. *The Youth of Vichy France.* Oxford, 1981.

Hancock, Walker, "Experiences of a Monuments Officer in Germany." *College Art Journal* 5:4 (May 1946).

Hassell, Fey von. *Hostage of the Third Reich: The Story of My Imprisonment and Rescue from the SS.* New York, 1989.

Hassell, Ulrich von. *Journal d'un conjuré, 1938–44.* Paris, 1996.

Hearnden, Arthur, ed. *The British in Germany: Educational Reconstruction After 1945.* London, 1978.

Heck, Alfons. *A Child of Hitler: Germany in the Days When God Wore a Swastika.* Frederick, CO, 1985.

Helmreich, E. C. "Jewish Education in the Third Reich." *Journal of Central European Affairs* 15:2 (July 1955).

Heppner, Ernest. *Shanghai Refuge: A Memoir of the World War II Jewish Ghetto.* Lincoln, NE, 1995.

Herbert, Ulrich. *Hitler's Foreign Workers: Enforced Foreign Labor in Germany Under the Third Reich.* Cambridge, UK, 1997.

Herbst, Jurgen. *Requiem for a German Past.* Madison, WI, 1999.

Hermand, Jost. *A Hitler Youth in Poland: The Nazis' Program for Evacuating Children During World War II.* Evanston, IL, 1997.

Hilberg, Raul. *The Destruction of the European Jews.* New York, 1985.

Hillel, Marc, and Clarissa Henry. *Of Pure Blood.* New York, 1977.

Hillen, Ernest. *The Way of a Boy: A Memoir of Java.* London, 1995.

Hitler, Adolf. *Mein Kampf.* Ed. D. C. Watt. London, 1974.

Hoffmann, Peter. *The History of the German Resistance, 1933–1945.* Cambridge, MA, 1979.

Hoffmann, Stanley. "Etre ou ne pas être Français (I)." *Commentaire,* Tiré-à-part, Numero 70/ Été 1995.

Holtztrager, Hans. *Die Wehrertüchtigungslager der Hitler-Jugend, 1942–1945. Ein Dokumentarbericht.* Ippesheim, 1991.

Hulme, Kathryn. *The Wild Place.* Boston, 1953.

Inglis, Ruth. *The Children's War: Evacuation, 1939–1945.* London, 1989.

Isaacs, Susan, ed. *The Cambridge Evacuation Survey: A Wartime Study in Social Welfare and Education.* London, 1941.

Jäckel, Eberhard. *Frankreich in Hitlers Europa: Die deutsche Frankreichpolitik im 2. Weltkrieg.* Stuttgart, 1966.

Josse, Raymond. "La naissance de la résistance étudiante à Paris et la manifestation du 11 novembre 1940." *Revue d'histoire de la deuxième guerre mondiale* 47 (July 1962).

Kaplan, Marion A. *Beyond Destiny and Despair: Jewish Life in Nazi Germany.* New York, 1998.

Karski, Jan. *Story of a Secret State.* Boston, 1944.

Keegan, John, ed. *The Times Atlas of the Second World War.* New York, 1989.

Kern, Ernst. *War Diary, 1941–45: A Report.* New York, 1993.

Kershaw, Ian. *Hitler, 1936–1945: Nemesis.* New York, 2000.

Kettenacker, Lothar. *Nationalsozialistische Volktumspolitik im Elsass.* Stuttgart, 1973.

Kevles, Daniel J. *In the Name of Eugenics.* Cambridge, MA, 1995.

Kintner, Earl W. *The Hadamar Trial.* London, 1949.

Klarsfeld, Serge. *The Children of Izieu: A Human Tragedy.* New York, 1985.

Klee, Ernst. *Euthanasie im NS-Staat.* Frankfurt, 1983.

Klein, Gerda Weissmann. *All but My Life.* New York, 1995.

Klemperer, Victor. *I Will Bear Witness: A Diary of the Nazi Years, 1933–1945.* 2 vols. New York, 1998, 1999.

Klukowski, Zygmunt. *Diary from the Years of Occupation, 1939–44.* Chicago, 1993.

Koch, H. W. *The Hitler Youth: Origins and Development, 1922–45.* New York, 1996.

Koehl, Robert L. "The Deutsche Volksliste in Poland, 1939–40." *Journal of Central European Affairs* 15 (1956).

———. *RKFDV: German Resettlement and Population Policy, 1939–1945: A History of the Reich Commission for the Strengthening of Germandom.* Cambridge, MA, 1957.

Konopka, V. *Zde Stavaly Lidice.* Prague, 1959.

Krammer, Arnold. *Undue Process: The Untold Story of America's German Alien Internees.* New York, 1997.

Kramp, Peter, and Gerhard Benl. *Vererbungslehre, Rassenkunde und Rassenhygiene: Lehrbuch für die Oberstufe Höherer Lehranstalten.* 2 vols. Leipzig, 1936.

Krízková, Marie, Kurt Kotouc, and Zdenek Ornest, eds. *We Are Children Just the Same: Vedem, the Secret Magazine by the Boys of Terezin.* Philadelphia, 1995.

Kubica, Helena. "Children and Youths at KL Auschwitz." In *Auschwitz: Nazi Death Camp,* ed. Franciszek Piper and Teresa Swiebocka. Oswiecim, 1996.

Kühl, Stefan. *The Nazi Connection: Eugenics, American Racism, and German National Socialism.* Oxford, 1994.

Kurek, Ewa. *Your Life Is Worth Mine: How Polish Nuns Saved Hundreds of Jewish Children in German Occupied Poland, 1939–1945.* New York, 1997.

Kurth, Peter. *American Cassandra: The Life of Dorothy Thompson.* Boston, 1990.

Lebert, Stephan, and Norbert Lebert. *My Father's Keeper: Children of the Nazi Leaders— An Intimate History of Damage and Denial.* New York, 2001.

Legarreta, Dorothy. *The Guernica Generation: Basque Refugee Children of the Spanish Civil War.* Reno, NV, 1984.

Levendel, Isaac. *Not the Germans Alone: A Son's Search for the Truth of Vichy.* Evanston, IL, 1999.

Leverton, Bertha, and Shmuel Lowensohn, eds. *I Came Alone: The Stories of the Kindertransports.* Lewes, UK, 1996.

Lewy, Guenter. *The Nazi Persecution of the Gypsies.* Oxford, 2000.

Lilienthal, Georg. *Der "Lebensborn e.V." Ein instrument nationalsozialistischer Rassenpolitik.* Stuttgart, 1985.

Limbacher, Katja, Maike Merten, and Bettina Pfefferle, eds. *Das Mädchenkonzentrationslager Uckermark.* Münster, 2000.

Loeber, Dietrich A. *Diktierte Option: Die Umsiedlung der Deutsch-Balten aus Estland und Lettland, 1939–1941.* Neumünster, 1972.

Lowrie, Donald A. *The Hunted Children.* New York, 1963.

Lukas, Richard C. *The Forgotten Holocaust: The Poles Under German Occupation, 1939–1944.* Lexington, KY, 1986.

Lumsden, Robin. *Himmler's Black Order.* Gloucestershire, UK, 1997.

Macardle, Dorothy. *Children of Europe.* London, 1949.

Mann, Erika, *School for Barbarians.* New York, 1938.

Marrus, Michael R., and Robert O. Paxton. *Vichy France and the Jews.* Stanford, CA, 1995.

Maschmann, Melita. *Account Rendered: A Dossier on My Former Self.* London, 1965.

Massaquoi, Hans J. *Destined to Witness: Growing Up Black in Nazi Germany.* New York, 1999.

Mazower, Mark. *Inside Hitler's Greece: The Experience of Occupation, 1941–1944.* New Haven, CT, 1993.

McCullough, David. *Truman.* New York, 1992.

Mettay, Joël. *L'Archipel du Mépris: Histoire du camps de Rivesaltes de 1939 à nos jours.* Canet, 2001.

Metz, N. N. "Heim ins Reich." *Jahrbuch des Baltischen Deutschtums, 1994.*

Millay, Edna St. Vincent. *The Murder of Lidice.* New York, 1942.

Milton, Sybil. "Nazi Policies Toward Roma and Sinti, 1933–1945." *Journal of the Gypsy Lore Society* 5, 2:1 (1992).

Milton, Sybil, and Henry Friedlander, eds. *Archives of the Holocaust.* New York, 1993.

Moser, Jonny. "Nisko: The First Experiment in Deportation." *Simon Wiesenthal Center Annual* 2 (1985).

Mosse, George L. *Nazi Culture: A Documentary History.* New York, 1981.

Müller, Melissa. *Anne Frank: The Biography.* New York, 1998.

Murrow, Edward R. *This Is London.* New York, 1941.

Naimark, Norman M. *The Russians in Germany: A History of the Soviet Zone of Occupation, 1945–1949.* Cambridge, MA, 1997.

Nelson, Keith L. "The 'Black Horror' on the Rhine: Race as a Factor in Post–World War I Diplomacy." *Journal of Modern History* 42 (December 1970).

Noakes, J., and G. Pridham, eds. *Nazism, 1919–1945: A History in Documents and Eyewitness Accounts.* 2 vols. New York, 1990.

Olin, Harold. *An Oral History.* Heartland Historical Research Service, 2000.

Origo, Iris. *War in Val d'Orcia: A Diary.* London, 1984.

Orth, Linda. *Die Transport Kinder aus Bonn.* Cologne, 1989.

Orwell, George. *The Road to Wigan Pier.* New York, 1958.

Owings, Alison. *Frauen: German Women Recall the Third Reich.* New Brunswick, NJ, 1995.

Pater, J. C. H. *Het Schoolverzet.* The Hague, 1969.

Paxton, Robert O. *Vichy France: Old Guard and New Order, 1940–1944.* New York, 1982.

Petrow, Richard. *The Bitter Years: The Invasion and Occupation of Denmark and Norway.* New York, 1979.

Pine, Lisa. *Nazi Family Policy, 1933–1945.* New York, 1997.

Piper, Franciszek, and Teresa Swiebocka, eds. *Auschwitz: Nazi Death Camp.* Oswiecim, 1996.

Pipes, Richard. *Russia Under the Bolshevik Regime.* New York, 1993.

Pommerin, Reiner. *Sterilisierung der Rheinlandbastarde: Das Schicksal einer farbigen deutschen Minderheit, 1918–37.* Düsseldorf, 1979.

Projektgruppe Belarus im Jugendclub Courage Koln e.V. *"Dann kam die deutsche Macht." Weisrussische Kinderhäftlinge in deutschen Konzentrationslagern, 1941–1945. Eine Dokumentation.* Cologne, 1999.

Rauschning, Hermann. *Hitler Speaks.* London, 1939.

Reinders, Robert C. "Racialism on the Left: E. D. Morel and the 'Black Horror on the Rhine.' " *International Review of Social History* 13 (1968).

Reitlinger, Gerald. *The House Built on Sand: The Conflicts of German Policy in Russia, 1939–1945.* New York, 1960.

Rempel, Gerhard. *Hitler's Children: The Hitler Youth and the SS.* Chapel Hill, NC, 1989.

Rieber, Alfred J., ed. *Forced Migration in Central and Eastern Europe, 1939–1950.* London, 2000.

Ritter, Ernst. *Das Deutsche Ausland Institut in Stuttgart, 1917–1945.* Wiesbaden, 1976.

Rubenstein, W. D. *The Myth of Rescue.* London, 1997.

Salisbury, Harrison E. *The 900 Days: The Siege of Leningrad.* New York, 1985.

Samuel, Wolfgang. *German Boy: A Refugee's Story.* Jackson, MS, 2000.

Schechtman, Joseph P. *European Population Transfers, 1939–1945.* New York, 1946.

———. "Resettlement of Transferred Volksdeutsche in Germany." *Journal of Central European Affairs* 7:3 (October 1947).

Scheider, Theodore, ed. *Documents on the Expulsion of the Germans from Eastern-Central Europe.* Bonn, undated.

Schmink-Gustavus, Christoph U. *Hungern für Hitler: Erinnerungen polnischer Zwangsarbeitter im Deutschen Reich, 1940–1945.* Hamburg, 1984.

Schmitt, Hans A. *Quakers and Nazis: Inner Light in Outer Darkness.* Columbia, MO, 1997.

Schmitz-Köster, Dorothee. *"Deutsche Mutter, Bist du Bereit . . ." Alltag im Lebensborn.* Berlin, 1997.

Sereny, Gitta. *Albert Speer: His Battle with Truth.* New York, 1996.

———. *Into That Darkness: An Examination of Conscience.* New York, 1983.

———. "Stolen Children." *Talk Magazine.* November 1999.

Sherman, A. J. *Island Refuge: Britain and Refugees from the Third Reich, 1933–1939.* Ilford, UK, 1994.

Shirer, William. *Berlin Dairy.* New York, 1941.

———. *End of a Berlin Dairy.* New York, 1947.

———. *The Rise and Fall of the Third Reich.* New York, 1960.

Sijes, B. A. *De Arbeitsinzet. De gedwongen arbeit van Nederlanders in Duitsland, 1940–1945.* The Hague, 1990.

Simmons, Cynthia, and Nina Perlina. *Writing the Seige of Leningrad: Women's Diaries, Memoirs, and Documentary Prose.* Pittsburgh, 2002.

Singer, Claude. *Vichy, l'université et les juifs.* Paris, 1992.

Sliwowska, Wiktoria. *The Last Eyewitnesses: Children of the Holocaust Speak.* Evanston, IL, 1998.

Smith, Arthur L. *Deutschtum of Nazi Germany.* The Hague, 1965.

Sosnowski, Kyril. *The Tragedy of Children Under Nazi Rule.* New York, 1983.

Speer, Albert. *Inside the Third Reich.* New York, 1970.

Staden, Berndt von. "Erinnerungen an die Umsiedlung." *Jahrbuch des Baltischen Deutschtums, 1994.*

Steche, Otto. *Leitfaden der Rassenkunde und Vererbungslehre der Erbgesundheitspflege und Familienkunde für die Mittelstufe.* Leipzig, 1934.

Stein, André. *Hidden Children: Forgotten Survivors of the Holocaust.* New York, 1994.

Stein, George H. *The Waffen SS: Hitler's Elite Guard at War, 1939–1945.* Ithaca, NY, 1966.

Steinhoff, Johannes, Peter Pechel, and Dennis Showalter, eds. *Voices from the Third Reich: An Oral History.* New York, 1984.

Stephenson, Jill. *Women in Nazi Society.* New York, 1975.

Stojka, Karl. "A Childhood in Birkenau." U.S. Holocaust Memorial Museum catalog. Washington, DC, 1992.

Terkel, Studs. *"The Good War": An Oral History of World War Two.* New York, 1985.

———. *Hard Times: An Oral History of the Great Depression.* New York, 1986.

Thompson, Dorothy. *Refugees: Anarchy or Organization?* New York, 1938.

Thompson, Larry V. "*Lebensborn* and the Eugenics Policy of the *Reichsführer* SS." *Central European History* 4 (1971), pp. 54–77.

Thurner, Erika. *National Socialism and Gypsies in Austria.* Tuscaloosa, AL, 1998.

Totten, Samuel, William S. Parsons, and Israel Charny, eds. *Century of Genocide: Eyewitness Accounts and Critical Views.* New York, 1997.

Tusa, Ann, and John Tusa. *The Berlin Blockade.* London, 1989.

United States Holocaust Memorial Museum. *Hidden History of the Kovno Ghetto.* Washington, DC, 1997.

Verhey, Elma, *Om Het Joodse Kind.* Amsterdam, 1991.

Vrijenhoek, Irene. *Oorlogskinderen in Nederland tijdens de Duitse bezetting.* Amsterdam, 1994.

Warmbrunn, Werner. *The German Occupation of Belgium, 1940–1944.* American University Studies, Series 9, History, Vol. 122, 1993.

Watkins, T. H. *The Hungry Years: A Narrative History of the Great Depression in America.* New York, 1999.

Weber, R. G. S. *The German Student Corps in the Third Reich.* London, 1986.

Werth, Alexander. *Russia at War, 1941–1945.* New York, 1984.

Whitehead, Dorit Bader. *The Uprooted: A Hitler Legacy.* New York, 1993.

White Rose Foundation, Munich. "The White Rose Exhibition on the Resistance by Students Against Hitler, Munich 1942/43." Exhibition catalog. 1991.

Wijsmuller-Meijer, Truus. *Geen Tijd voor Tranen.* Amsterdam, undated.

Willems, Wim. *In Search of the True Gypsy.* London, 1997.

Wolman, Ruth E. *Crossing Over: An Oral History of Refugees from Hitler's Reich.* New York, 1996.

Wyman, David S. *The Abandonment of the Jews: America and the Holocaust, 1941–1945.* New York, 1998.

————. *Paper Walls: America and the Refugee Crisis, 1938–1941.* Amherst, MA, 1968.

Wyman, Marc. *DP: Europe's Displaced Persons, 1945–1951.* Philadelphia, 1989.

Ziemer, Gregor. *Education for Death: The Making of the Nazi.* Oxford, 1941.

Ziemke, Earl F. *The U.S. Army in the Occupation of Germany, 1944–1946.* Army Historical Series. Washington, DC, 1975.

Zwaan, J., ed. *De Zwarte Kameraden: Een geïllustreerde geschiedenis van de NSB.* Weesp, 1984.

Published Collections of Documents

Documents on German Foreign Policy, 1918–1945. Washington, DC, 1954.

Foreign Relations of the United States. Washington, DC. Annual.

International Military Tribunal: The Trial of the Major War Criminals Before the International Military Tribunal. Nuremberg, 1947–1949. 42 volumes.

Trials of War Criminals Before the Nuernberg Military Tribunals, October 1946–April 1949. Washington, DC, 1952. 12 volumes.

Unpublished Sources
Public Collections

Great Britain
Imperial War Museum, London
    Department of Documents
Public Record Office, Kew

Greece
Benaki Museum, Deas Archive

Netherlands
Nederlands Instituut voor Oorlogsdocumentatie, Amsterdam

Russian Federation
Memorial, Moscow

United States
Georgetown University, Washington, DC
    Papers of Robert F. Wagner
Library of Congress, Washington, DC, Manuscript Division
    Captured German Records
National Archives, College Park, MD
    Record Groups:
        59 General Records of the Department of State
        84 Records of the Foreign Posts of the Department of State
        200 National Archives Gift Collection
        238 Collection of World War II War Crimes Records
        242 Collection of Seized Enemy Records
        260 Records of U.S. Occupation Headquarters, World War II
        330 Records of the Office of the Secretary of Defense
        331 Records of the Allied Operational and Occupation Headquarters, World War II
        338 Records of United States Army Commands
United Nations Archives, New York
    United Nations Relief and Rehabilitation Administration (UNRRA) Records
United States Holocaust Memorial Museum Archives, Washington, DC
Yale University Library, New Haven, CT
    Fortunoff Video Archive for Holocaust Testimonies

Private Collections
Ruth Anderson Katz; William H. Kern; George Rublee II; Richard Winslow

Interviews and Conversations
Sheppie Abramowitz; Elna Barros; Stuart Blue; Joanna Breyer; Ella Burling; Henry Cohen;
    Doda de Wolf; Marion di Sidi; Nikolai Dorozhinsky; Maria Fafalios-Dragonas; Walter
    Filley; Walter Fletcher; Nada Geroulanos; Costas Gkioulekas; Maria Gryziecka-
    Goldberger; Egon Guttmann; Marian Helft; Fred Hochberg; Ruth Anderson Katz; Edith
    Kaye; Klose Family; Philippe and Olivier Kraemer; Vladimir Kuts; Nikos Kyriazides;
    Athena Lagoudaki; Sperry Lea; Frank Lee; Janina Goldberger Lunzer; Anthony Lykiar-
    dopoulos; Nikolai Mahutov; Gudrun McCann; Dr. Mikhail Ostrovsky; Dr. Franciszek
    Piper; Corrado and Cecile Pirzio-Biroli; Mance Post; George Rublee II; Trina Sobotka;
    Sigrid Spalding; Costas Stamatopoulos; Rhoda Sutherland; Veronica Tate; Aldona Volyn-
    skaya; Helen Walker; Joanna Wilmerding; Richard Winslow; Othar Zaldastani; Dr.
    Alexander Zaoussis; Jerri Zbiral; Yelena B. Zhemkova

Providers of Miscellaneous Information and Documentation
Gerald Aalders, NIOD; Anne and Stelios Atlamazoglou; Alfred Bader; David Barnouw,
    NIOD; Jill Brett, Library of Congress; Preston Brown; Joan Challinor; Margaret Childers,
    Spanish Refugee Aid; Charles Cogan; Charles Cutter, Brandeis University; Elena
    Borisovna Delone; Karina Dmitrieva; Judy Donald, Choate–Rosemary Hall; Malgosia

Drozdz; Monica Dugot; Robin and David Evans; Stuart Feldman; Bea Green; Richard Griffin; Rita Henninger; Lord Janner; Robert Keller; Erasmus Kloman; Brennan Klose; Paul Kramer; Natalia Kulkova; Amy Landreth; Jane Loeffler; Jarek Mansfelt, Auschwitz guide; Gundega Michele, Riga; Clover Nicholas; Phyllis Nudelman; Nikita Okhotin; Jonathan Petropoulos; Pavel Polian; Arlene Rodman; Phyllis Ruffer; Fern Schad; Jane Siena; Elizabeth Simpson; Natalie Spingarn; Zbigniew Suszczynski; Anna Swinbourne; Kirby Talley; Shaw Thacher; Rosie Thompson; Elma Verhey; Natalia Vogiekoff-Brogan; Diana Walker; Robert Whistler; Rebecca White

Photo Credits

Bildarchiv Pruessischer Kulturbesitz, Berlin: 105, 148

Bundesarchiv, Koblenz: 64

Imperial War Museum, London: 176

Mein Erstes Buch (Dortmund, 1935): 78

National Archives, College Park, MD: 2, 130, 203, 405, 445, 463, 466, 524, 535, 545, 548, 557

Nederlands Instituut voor Orlogsdocumentatie: 281, 359, 380

Panstwowe Muzeum w.Oswiecim: 259

Voula Pappaioannou, Benaki Museum, Athens: 319, 431, 439

Suddeutsche Verlag Bilderdienst: 9, 193, 421

John Topham: 127

United States Holocaust Memorial Museum: 12, 39, 98, 243, 297, 300, 372

Wiener Library, London: 87

Richard Winslow: 491

Yad Vashem: 393

Collection of the author: 216

Permissions Acknowledgments

Grateful acknowledgment is made to the following for permission to reprint previously published material:

Houghton Mifflin Company: Excerpt from *Story of a Secret State* by Jan Karski. Copyright © 1944, and renewed 1972 by Jan Karski. All rights reserved. Reprinted by permission of Houghton Mifflin Company.

Northwestern University Press: Excerpts from *The Last Eyewitnesses* by Wiktoria Sliwowska. Reprinted by permission of Northwestern University Press.

Rutgers University Press: Excerpts from *Frauen* by Alison Owings. Copyright © 1993 by Alison Owings. Reprinted by permission of Rutgers University Press.

The University of Wisconsin Press: Excerpts from *Requiem for a German Past* by Jurgen Herbst. Copyright © 1999. Reprinted by permission of The University of Wisconsin Press.

Index

Page numbers in *italics* refer to illustrations.

A Note About the Author

LYNN H. NICHOLAS was born in New London, Connecticut, and educated in the United States, England, and Spain. She is the author of *The Rape of Europa: The Fate of Europe's Treasures in the Third Reich and the Second World War,* a winner of the National Book Critics Circle Award. The publication of *The Rape of Europa* inspired an international debate and a movement to locate and repatriate works of art and other property that were confiscated and stolen by governments and individuals before and during World War II. Ms. Nicholas has become widely known across the United States as a lecturer, panelist, and expert witness on this subject. She was awarded the Légion d'Honneur by France and the Amicus Poloniae by Poland.

A Note on the Type

This book was set in Caledonia, a typeface designed by W. A. Dwiggins (1880–1956). It belongs to the family of printing types called "modern face" by printers—a term used to mark the change in style of the type letters that occurred around 1800. Caledonia borders on the general design of Scotch Roman, but it is more freely drawn than that letter. This version of Caledonia was adapted by David Berlow in 1979.

Composed by North Market Street Graphics,
Lancaster, Pennsylvania
Printed and bound by Berryville Graphics,
Berryville, Virginia
Maps by George Colbert
Designed by Anthea Lingeman